T0134687

Lecture Notes in Computer Science 13382

More information about this series at https://link.springer.com/bookseries/558

Osvaldo Gervasi · Beniamino Murgante ·
Sanjay Misra · Ana Maria A. C. Rocha ·
Chiara Garau (Eds.)

Computational Science and Its Applications – ICCSA 2022 Workshops

Malaga, Spain, July 4–7, 2022
Proceedings, Part VI

 Springer

Editors
Osvaldo Gervasi (iD)
University of Perugia
Perugia, Italy

Sanjay Misra (iD)
Østfold University College
Halden, Norway

Chiara Garau (iD)
University of Cagliari
Cagliari, Italy

Beniamino Murgante (iD)
University of Basilicata
Potenza, Potenza, Italy

Ana Maria A. C. Rocha (iD)
University of Minho
Braga, Portugal

ISSN 0302-9743   ISSN 1611-3349 (electronic)
Lecture Notes in Computer Science
ISBN 978-3-031-10591-3   ISBN 978-3-031-10592-0 (eBook)
https://doi.org/10.1007/978-3-031-10592-0

This Springer imprint is published by the registered company Springer Nature Switzerland AG
The registered company address is: Gewerbestrasse 11, 6330 Cham, Switzerland

Preface

These six volumes (LNCS 13377–13382) consist of the peer-reviewed papers from the workshops at the 22nd International Conference on Computational Science and Its Applications (ICCSA 2022), which took place during July 4–7, 2022. The peer-reviewed papers of the main conference tracks are published in a separate set consisting of two volumes (LNCS 13375–13376).

This year, we again decided to organize a hybrid conference, with some of the delegates attending in person and others taking part online. Despite the enormous benefits achieved by the intensive vaccination campaigns in many countries, at the crucial moment of organizing the event, there was no certainty about the evolution of COVID-19. Fortunately, more and more researchers were able to attend the event in person, foreshadowing a slow but gradual exit from the pandemic and the limitations that have weighed so heavily on the lives of all citizens over the past three years.

ICCSA 2022 was another successful event in the International Conference on Computational Science and Its Applications (ICCSA) series. Last year, the conference was held as a hybrid event in Cagliari, Italy, and in 2020 it was organized as virtual event, whilst earlier editions took place in Saint Petersburg, Russia (2019), Melbourne, Australia (2018), Trieste, Italy (2017), Beijing, China (2016), Banff, Canada (2015), Guimaraes, Portugal (2014), Ho Chi Minh City, Vietnam (2013), Salvador, Brazil (2012), Santander, Spain (2011), Fukuoka, Japan (2010), Suwon, South Korea (2009), Perugia, Italy (2008), Kuala Lumpur, Malaysia (2007), Glasgow, UK (2006), Singapore (2005), Assisi, Italy (2004), Montreal, Canada (2003), and (as ICCS) Amsterdam, The Netherlands (2002) and San Francisco, USA (2001).

Computational science is the main pillar of most of the present research, and industrial and commercial applications, and plays a unique role in exploiting ICT innovative technologies. The ICCSA conference series provides a venue to researchers and industry practitioners to discuss new ideas, to share complex problems and their solutions, and to shape new trends in computational science.

Apart from the 52 workshops, ICCSA 2022 also included six main tracks on topics ranging from computational science technologies and application in many fields to specific areas of computational sciences, such as software engineering, security, machine learning and artificial intelligence, and blockchain technologies. For the 52 workshops we have accepted 285 papers. For the main conference tracks we accepted 57 papers and 24 short papers out of 279 submissions (an acceptance rate of 29%). We would like to express our appreciation to the Workshops chairs and co-chairs for their hard work and dedication.

The success of the ICCSA conference series in general, and of ICCSA 2022 in particular, vitally depends on the support of many people: authors, presenters, partic008ipants, keynote speakers, workshop chairs, session chairs, organizing committee members, student volunteers, Program Committee members, advisory committee members, international liaison chairs, reviewers, and others in various roles. We take this opportunity to wholehartedly thank them all.

We also wish to thank our publisher, Springer, for their acceptance to publish the proceedings, for sponsoring some of the best papers awards, and for their kind assistance and cooperation during the editing process.

We cordially invite you to visit the ICCSA website https://iccsa.org where you can find all the relevant information about this interesting and exciting event.

July 2022

Osvaldo Gervasi
Beniamino Murgante
Sanjay Misra

Welcome Message from Organizers

The ICCSA 2021 conference in the Mediterranean city of Cagliari provided us with inspiration to offer the ICCSA 2022 conference in the Mediterranean city of Málaga, Spain. The additional considerations due to the COVID-19 pandemic, which necessitated a hybrid conference, also stimulated the idea to use the School of Informatics of the University of Málaga. It has an open structure where we could take lunch and coffee outdoors and the lecture halls have open windows on two sides providing optimal conditions for meeting more safely.

The school is connected to the center of the old town via a metro system, for which we offered cards to the participants. This provided the opportunity to stay in lodgings in the old town close to the beach because, at the end of the day, that is the place to be to exchange ideas with your fellow scientists. The social program allowed us to enjoy the history of Malaga from its founding by the Phoenicians...

In order to provoke as much scientific interaction as possible we organized online sessions that could easily be followed by all participants from their own devices. We tried to ensure that participants from Asia could participate in morning sessions and those from the Americas in evening sessions. On-site sessions could be followed and debated on-site and discussed online using a chat system. To realize this, we relied on the developed technological infrastructure based on open source software, with the addition of streaming channels on YouTube. The implementation of the software infrastructure and the technical coordination of the volunteers were carried out by Damiano Perri and Marco Simonetti. Nine student volunteers from the universities of Málaga, Minho, Almeria, and Helsinki provided technical support and ensured smooth interaction during the conference.

A big thank you goes to all of the participants willing to exchange their ideas during their daytime. Participants of ICCSA 2022 came from 58 countries scattered over many time zones of the globe. Very interesting keynote talks were provided by well-known international scientists who provided us with more ideas to reflect upon, and we are grateful for their insights.

Eligius M. T. Hendrix

Organization

ICCSA 2022 was organized by the University of Malaga (Spain), the University of Perugia (Italy), the University of Cagliari (Italy), the University of Basilicata (Italy), Monash University (Australia), Kyushu Sangyo University (Japan), and the University of Minho, (Portugal).

Honorary General Chairs

Norio Shiratori	Chuo University, Japan
Kenneth C. J. Tan	Sardina Systems, UK

General Chairs

Osvaldo Gervasi	University of Perugia, Italy
Eligius Hendrix	University of Malaga, Italy
Bernady O. Apduhan	Kyushu Sangyo University, Japan

Program Committee Chairs

Beniamino Murgante	University of Basilicata, Italy
Inmaculada Garcia Fernandez	University of Malaga, Spain
Ana Maria A. C. Rocha	University of Minho, Portugal
David Taniar	Monash University, Australia

International Advisory Committee

Jemal Abawajy	Deakin University, Australia
Dharma P. Agarwal	University of Cincinnati, USA
Rajkumar Buyya	Melbourne University, Australia
Claudia Bauzer Medeiros	University of Campinas, Brazil
Manfred M. Fisher	Vienna University of Economics and Business, Austria
Marina L. Gavrilova	University of Calgary, Canada
Sumi Helal	University of Florida, USA, and University of Lancaster, UK
Yee Leung	Chinese University of Hong Kong, China

International Liaison Chairs

Ivan Blečić	University of Cagliari, Italy
Giuseppe Borruso	University of Trieste, Italy

Elise De Donker	Western Michigan University, USA
Maria Irene Falcão	University of Minho, Portugal
Robert C. H. Hsu	Chung Hua University, Taiwan
Tai-Hoon Kim	Beijing Jiaotong University, China
Vladimir Korkhov	St Petersburg University, Russia
Sanjay Misra	Østfold University College, Norway
Takashi Naka	Kyushu Sangyo University, Japan
Rafael D. C. Santos	National Institute for Space Research, Brazil
Maribel Yasmina Santos	University of Minho, Portugal
Elena Stankova	St Petersburg University, Russia

Workshop and Session Organizing Chairs

Beniamino Murgante	University of Basilicata, Italy
Chiara Garau	University of Cagliari, Italy
Sanjay Misra	Ostfold University College, Norway

Award Chair

Wenny Rahayu	La Trobe University, Australia

Publicity Committee Chairs

Elmer Dadios	De La Salle University, Philippines
Nataliia Kulabukhova	St Petersburg University, Russia
Daisuke Takahashi	Tsukuba University, Japan
Shangwang Wang	Beijing University of Posts and Telecommunications, China

Local Arrangement Chairs

Eligius Hendrix	University of Malaga, Spain
Inmaculada Garcia Fernandez	University of Malaga, Spain
Salvador Merino Cordoba	University of Malaga, Spain
Pablo Guerrero-García	University of Malaga, Spain

Technology Chairs

Damiano Perri	University of Florence, Italy
Marco Simonetti	University of Florence, Italy

Program Committee

Vera Afreixo	University of Aveiro, Portugal
Filipe Alvelos	University of Minho, Portugal

Hartmut Asche	Hasso-Plattner-Institut für Digital Engineering gGmbH, Germany
Ginevra Balletto	University of Cagliari, Italy
Michela Bertolotto	University College Dublin, Ireland
Sandro Bimonte	TSCF, INRAE, France
Rod Blais	University of Calgary, Canada
Ivan Blečić	University of Sassari, Italy
Giuseppe Borruso	University of Trieste, Italy
Ana Cristina Braga	University of Minho, Portugal
Massimo Cafaro	University of Salento, Italy
Yves Caniou	ENS Lyon, France
Ermanno Cardelli	University of Perugia, Italy
José A. Cardoso e Cunha	Universidade Nova de Lisboa, Portugal
Rui Cardoso	University of Beira Interior, Portugal
Leocadio G. Casado	University of Almeria, Spain
Carlo Cattani	University of Salerno, Italy
Mete Celik	Erciyes University, Turkey
Maria Cerreta	University of Naples Federico II, Italy
Hyunseung Choo	Sungkyunkwan University, South Korea
Rachel Chieng-Sing Lee	Sunway University, Malaysia
Min Young Chung	Sungkyunkwan University, South Korea
Florbela Maria da Cruz Domingues Correia	Polytechnic Institute of Viana do Castelo, Portugal
Gilberto Corso Pereira	Federal University of Bahia, Brazil
Alessandro Costantini	INFN, Italy
Carla Dal Sasso Freitas	Universidade Federal do Rio Grande do Sul, Brazil
Pradesh Debba	Council for Scientific and Industrial Research (CSIR), South Africa
Hendrik Decker	Instituto Tecnológico de Informática, Spain
Robertas Damaševičius	Kaunas University of Technology, Lithuania
Frank Devai	London South Bank University, UK
Rodolphe Devillers	Memorial University of Newfoundland, Canada
Joana Matos Dias	University of Coimbra, Portugal
Paolino Di Felice	University of L'Aquila, Italy
Prabu Dorairaj	NetApp, India/USA
M. Noelia Faginas Lago	University of Perugia, Italy
M. Irene Falcao	University of Minho, Portugal
Florbela P. Fernandes	Polytechnic Institute of Bragança, Portugal
Jose-Jesus Fernandez	National Centre for Biotechnology, Spain
Paula Odete Fernandes	Polytechnic Institute of Bragança, Portugal
Adelaide de Fátima Baptista Valente Freitas	University of Aveiro, Portugal
Manuel Carlos Figueiredo	University of Minho, Portugal
Maria Celia Furtado Rocha	Federal University of Bahia, Brazil
Chiara Garau	University of Cagliari, Italy
Paulino Jose Garcia Nieto	University of Oviedo, Spain

Raffaele Garrisi	Polizia di Stato, Italy
Jerome Gensel	LSR-IMAG, France
Maria Giaoutzi	National Technical University of Athens, Greece
Arminda Manuela Andrade Pereira Gonçalves	University of Minho, Portugal
Andrzej M. Goscinski	Deakin University, Australia
Sevin Gümgüm	Izmir University of Economics, Turkey
Alex Hagen-Zanker	University of Cambridge, UK
Shanmugasundaram Hariharan	B.S. Abdur Rahman Crescent Institute of Science and Technology, India
Eligius M. T. Hendrix	University of Malaga, Spain and Wageningen University, The Netherlands
Hisamoto Hiyoshi	Gunma University, Japan
Mustafa Inceoglu	Ege University, Turkey
Peter Jimack	University of Leeds, UK
Qun Jin	Waseda University, Japan
Yeliz Karaca	UMass Chan Medical School, USA
Farid Karimipour	Vienna University of Technology, Austria
Baris Kazar	Oracle Corp., USA
Maulana Adhinugraha Kiki	Telkom University, Indonesia
DongSeong Kim	University of Canterbury, New Zealand
Taihoon Kim	Hannam University, South Korea
Ivana Kolingerova	University of West Bohemia, Czech Republic
Nataliia Kulabukhova	St. Petersburg University, Russia
Vladimir Korkhov	St. Petersburg University, Russia
Rosa Lasaponara	National Research Council, Italy
Maurizio Lazzari	National Research Council, Italy
Cheng Siong Lee	Monash University, Australia
Sangyoun Lee	Yonsei University, South Korea
Jongchan Lee	Kunsan National University, South Korea
Chendong Li	University of Connecticut, USA
Gang Li	Deakin University, Australia
Fang (Cherry) Liu	Ames Laboratory, USA
Xin Liu	University of Calgary, Canada
Andrea Lombardi	University of Perugia, Italy
Savino Longo	University of Bari, Italy
Tinghuai Ma	Nanjing University of Information Science and Technology, China
Ernesto Marcheggiani	Katholieke Universiteit Leuven, Belgium
Antonino Marvuglia	Public Research Centre Henri Tudor, Luxembourg
Nicola Masini	National Research Council, Italy
Ilaria Matteucci	National Research Council, Italy
Nirvana Meratnia	University of Twente, The Netherlands
Fernando Miranda	University of Minho, Portugal
Giuseppe Modica	University of Reggio Calabria, Italy
Josè Luis Montaña	University of Cantabria, Spain

Zequn Wang	Intelligent Automation Inc, USA
Robert Weibel	University of Zurich, Switzerland
Frank Westad	Norwegian University of Science and Technology, Norway
Roland Wismüller	Universität Siegen, Germany
Mudasser Wyne	National University, USA
Chung-Huang Yang	National Kaohsiung Normal University, Taiwan
Xin-She Yang	National Physical Laboratory, UK
Salim Zabir	France Telecom Japan Co., Japan
Haifeng Zhao	University of California, Davis, USA
Fabiana Zollo	Ca' Foscari University of Venice, Italy
Albert Y. Zomaya	University of Sydney, Australia

Workshop Organizers

International Workshop on Advances in Artificial Intelligence Learning Technologies: Blended Learning, STEM, Computational Thinking and Coding (AAILT 2022)

Alfredo Milani	University of Perugia, Italy
Valentina Franzoni	University of Perugia, Italy
Osvaldo Gervasi	University of Perugia, Italy

International Workshop on Advancements in Applied Machine-Learning and Data Analytics (AAMDA 2022)

Alessandro Costantini	INFN, Italy
Davide Salomoni	INFN, Italy
Doina Cristina Duma	INFN, Italy
Daniele Cesini	INFN, Italy

International Workshop on Advances in Information Systems and Technologies for Emergency Management, Risk Assessment and Mitigation Based on the Resilience (ASTER 2022)

Maurizio Pollino	ENEA, Italy
Marco Vona	University of Basilicata, Italy
Sonia Giovinazzi	ENEA, Italy
Benedetto Manganelli	University of Basilicata, Italy
Beniamino Murgante	University of Basilicata, Italy

International Workshop on Advances in Web Based Learning (AWBL 2022)

Birol Ciloglugil   Ege University, Turkey
Mustafa Inceoglu   Ege University, Turkey

International Workshop on Blockchain and Distributed Ledgers: Technologies and Applications (BDLTA 2022)

Vladimir Korkhov   St Petersburg State University, Russia
Elena Stankova   St Petersburg State University, Russia
Nataliia Kulabukhova   St Petersburg State University, Russia

International Workshop on Bio and Neuro Inspired Computing and Applications (BIONCA 2022)

Nadia Nedjah   State University of Rio De Janeiro, Brazil
Luiza De Macedo Mourelle   State University of Rio De Janeiro, Brazil

International Workshop on Configurational Analysis For Cities (CA CITIES 2022)

Claudia Yamu   Oslo Metropolitan University, Norway
Valerio Cutini   Università di Pisa, Italy
Beniamino Murgante   University of Basilicata, Italy
Chiara Garau   Dicaar, University of Cagliari, Italy

International Workshop on Computational and Applied Mathematics (CAM 2022)

Maria Irene Falcão   University of Minho, Portugal
Fernando Miranda   University of Minho, Portugal

International Workshop on Computational and Applied Statistics (CAS 2022)

Ana Cristina Braga   University of Minho, Portugal

International Workshop on Computational Mathematics, Statistics and Information Management (CMSIM 2022)

Maria Filomena Teodoro   University of Lisbon and Portuguese Naval Academy,
                               Portugal

International Workshop on Computational Optimization and Applications (COA 2022)

Ana Maria A. C. Rocha   University of Minho, Portugal
Humberto Rocha   University of Coimbra, Portugal

International Workshop on Computational Astrochemistry (CompAstro 2022)

Marzio Rosi   University of Perugia, Italy
Nadia Balucani   University of Perugia, Italy
Cecilia Ceccarelli   Université Grenoble Alpes, France
Stefano Falcinelli   University of Perugia, Italy

International Workshop on Computational Methods for Porous Geomaterials (CompPor 2022)

Vadim Lisitsa   Sobolev Institute of Mathematics, Russia
Evgeniy Romenski   Sobolev Institute of Mathematics, Russia

International Workshop on Computational Approaches for Smart, Conscious Cities (CASCC 2022)

Andreas Fricke   University of Potsdam, Germany
Juergen Doellner   University of Potsdam, Germany
Salvador Merino   University of Malaga, Spain
Jürgen Bund   Graphics Vision AI Association, Germany/Portugal
Markus Jobst   Federal Office of Metrology and Surveying, Austria
Francisco Guzman   University of Malaga, Spain

International Workshop on Computational Science and HPC (CSHPC 2022)

Elise De Doncker   Western Michigan University, USA
Fukuko Yuasa   High Energy Accelerator Research Organization
                               (KEK), Japan
Hideo Matsufuru   High Energy Accelerator Research Organization
                               (KEK), Japan

International Workshop on Cities, Technologies and Planning (CTP 2022)

Giuseppe Borruso   University of Trieste, Italy
Malgorzata Hanzl   Lodz University of Technology, Poland
Beniamino Murgante   University of Basilicata, Italy

Anastasia Stratigea   National Technical University of Athens, Grece
Ginevra Balletto   University of Cagliari, Italy
Ljiljana Zivkovic   Republic Geodetic Authority, Serbia

International Workshop on Digital Sustainability and Circular Economy (DiSCE 2022)

Giuseppe Borruso   University of Trieste, Italy
Stefano Epifani   Digital Sustainability Institute, Italy
Ginevra Balletto   University of Cagliari, Italy
Luigi Mundula   University of Cagliari, Italy
Alessandra Milesi   University of Cagliari, Italy
Mara Ladu   University of Cagliari, Italy
Stefano De Nicolai   University of Pavia, Italy
Tu Anh Trinh   University of Economics Ho Chi Minh City, Vietnam

International Workshop on Econometrics and Multidimensional Evaluation in Urban Environment (EMEUE 2022)

Carmelo Maria Torre   Polytechnic University of Bari, Italy
Maria Cerreta   University of Naples Federico II, Italy
Pierluigi Morano   Polytechnic University of Bari, Italy
Giuliano Poli   University of Naples Federico II, Italy
Marco Locurcio   Polytechnic University of Bari, Italy
Francesco Tajani   Sapienza University of Rome, Italy

International Workshop on Ethical AI Applications for a Human-Centered Cyber Society (EthicAI 2022)

Valentina Franzoni   University of Perugia, Italy
Alfredo Milani   University of Perugia, Italy

International Workshop on Future Computing System Technologies and Applications (FiSTA 2022)

Bernady Apduhan   Kyushu Sangyo University, Japan
Rafael Santos   INPE, Brazil

International Workshop on Geodesign in Decision Making: Meta Planning and Collaborative Design for Sustainable and Inclusive Development (GDM 2022)

Francesco Scorza   University of Basilicata, Italy
Michele Campagna   University of Cagliari, Italy
Ana Clara Mourão Moura   Federal University of Minas Gerais, Brazil

International Workshop on Geomatics in Agriculture and Forestry: New Advances and Perspectives (GeoForAgr 2022)

Maurizio Pollino	ENEA, Italy
Giuseppe Modica	University of Reggio Calabria, Italy
Marco Vizzari	University of Perugia, Italy

International Workshop on Geographical Analysis, Urban Modeling, Spatial Statistics (Geog-An-Mod 2022)

Giuseppe Borruso	University of Trieste, Italy
Beniamino Murgante	University of Basilicata, Italy
Harmut Asche	Hasso-Plattner-Institut für Digital Engineering gGmbH, Germany

International Workshop on Geomatics for Resource Monitoring and Management (GRMM 2022)

Alessandra Capolupo	Polytechnic of Bari, Italy
Eufemia Tarantino	Polytechnic of Bari, Italy
Enrico Borgogno Mondino	University of Turin, Italy

International Workshop on Information and Knowledge in the Internet of Things (IKIT 2022)

Teresa Guarda	State University of Santa Elena Peninsula, Ecuador
Filipe Portela	University of Minho, Portugal
Maria Fernanda Augusto	Bitrum Research Center, Spain

13th International Symposium on Software Quality (ISSQ 2022)

Sanjay Misra	Østfold University College, Norway

International Workshop on Machine Learning for Space and Earth Observation Data (MALSEOD 2022)

Rafael Santos	INPE, Brazil
Karine Reis Ferreira Gomes	INPE, Brazil

International Workshop on Building Multi-dimensional Models for Assessing Complex Environmental Systems (MES 2022)

Vanessa Assumma	Politecnico di Torino, Italy
Caterina Caprioli	Politecnico di Torino, Italy
Giulia Datola	Politecnico di Torino, Italy

Federico Dell'Anna   Politecnico di Torino, Italy
Marta Dell'Ovo   Politecnico di Milano, Italy

International Workshop on Models and Indicators for Assessing and Measuring the Urban Settlement Development in the View of ZERO Net Land Take by 2050 (MOVEto0 2022)

Lucia Saganeiti   University of L'Aquila, Italy
Lorena Fiorini   University of L'aquila, Italy
Angela Pilogallo   University of Basilicata, Italy
Alessandro Marucci   University of L'Aquila, Italy
Francesco Zullo   University of L'Aquila, Italy

International Workshop on Modelling Post-Covid Cities (MPCC 2022)

Beniamino Murgante   University of Basilicata, Italy
Ginevra Balletto   University of Cagliari, Italy
Giuseppe Borruso   University of Trieste, Italy
Marco Dettori   Università degli Studi di Sassari, Italy
Lucia Saganeiti   University of L'Aquila, Italy

International Workshop on Ecosystem Services: Nature's Contribution to People in Practice. Assessment Frameworks, Models, Mapping, and Implications (NC2P 2022)

Francesco Scorza   University of Basilicata, Italy
Sabrina Lai   University of Cagliari, Italy
Silvia Ronchi   University of Cagliari, Italy
Dani Broitman   Israel Institute of Technology, Israel
Ana Clara Mourão Moura   Federal University of Minas Gerais, Brazil
Corrado Zoppi   University of Cagliari, Italy

International Workshop on New Mobility Choices for Sustainable and Alternative Scenarios (NEWMOB 2022)

Tiziana Campisi   University of Enna Kore, Italy
Socrates Basbas   Aristotle University of Thessaloniki, Greece
Aleksandra Deluka T.   University of Rijeka, Croatia
Alexandros Nikitas   University of Huddersfield, UK
Ioannis Politis   Aristotle University of Thessaloniki, Greece
Georgios Georgiadis   Aristotle University of Thessaloniki, Greece
Irena Ištoka Otković   University of Osijek, Croatia
Sanja Surdonja   University of Rijeka, Croatia

International Workshop on Privacy in the Cloud/Edge/IoT World (PCEIoT 2022)

Michele Mastroianni	University of Campania Luigi Vanvitelli, Italy
Lelio Campanile	University of Campania Luigi Vanvitelli, Italy
Mauro Iacono	University of Campania Luigi Vanvitelli, Italy

International Workshop on Psycho-Social Analysis of Sustainable Mobility in the Pre- and Post-Pandemic Phase (PSYCHE 2022)

Tiziana Campisi	University of Enna Kore, Italy
Socrates Basbas	Aristotle University of Thessaloniki, Greece
Dilum Dissanayake	Newcastle University, UK
Nurten Akgün Tanbay	Bursa Technical University, Turkey
Elena Cocuzza	University of Catania, Italy
Nazam Ali	University of Management and Technology, Pakistan
Vincenza Torrisi	University of Catania, Italy

International Workshop on Processes, Methods and Tools Towards Resilient Cities and Cultural Heritage Prone to SOD and ROD Disasters (RES 2022)

Elena Cantatore	Polytechnic University of Bari, Italy
Alberico Sonnessa	Polytechnic University of Bari, Italy
Dario Esposito	Polytechnic University of Bari, Italy

International Workshop on Scientific Computing Infrastructure (SCI 2022)

Elena Stankova	St Petersburg University, Russia
Vladimir Korkhov	St Petersburg University, Russia

International Workshop on Socio-Economic and Environmental Models for Land Use Management (SEMLUM 2022)

Debora Anelli	Polytechnic University of Bari, Italy
Pierluigi Morano	Polytechnic University of Bari, Italy
Francesco Tajani	Sapienza University of Rome, Italy
Marco Locurcio	Polytechnic University of Bari, Italy
Paola Amoruso	LUM University, Italy

14th International Symposium on Software Engineering Processes and Applications (SEPA 2022)

Sanjay Misra	Østfold University College, Norway

International Workshop on Ports of the Future – Smartness and Sustainability (SmartPorts 2022)

Giuseppe Borruso	University of Trieste, Italy
Gianfranco Fancello	University of Cagliari, Italy
Ginevra Balletto	University of Cagliari, Italy
Patrizia Serra	University of Cagliari, Italy
Maria del Mar Munoz Leonisio	University of Cadiz, Spain
Marco Mazzarino	University of Venice, Italy
Marcello Tadini	Università del Piemonte Orientale, Italy

International Workshop on Smart Tourism (SmartTourism 2022)

Giuseppe Borruso	University of Trieste, Italy
Silvia Battino	University of Sassari, Italy
Ainhoa Amaro Garcia	Universidad de Alcalà and Universidad de Las Palmas, Spain
Maria del Mar Munoz Leonisio	University of Cadiz, Spain
Carlo Donato	University of Sassari, Italy
Francesca Krasna	University of Trieste, Italy
Ginevra Balletto	University of Cagliari, Italy

International Workshop on Sustainability Performance Assessment: Models, Approaches and Applications Toward Interdisciplinary and Integrated Solutions (SPA 2022)

Francesco Scorza	University of Basilicata, Italy
Sabrina Lai	University of Cagliari, Italy
Jolanta Dvarioniene	Kaunas University of Technology, Lithuania
Iole Cerminara	University of Basilicata, Italy
Georgia Pozoukidou	Aristotle University of Thessaloniki, Greece
Valentin Grecu	Lucian Blaga University of Sibiu, Romania
Corrado Zoppi	University of Cagliari, Italy

International Workshop on Specifics of Smart Cities Development in Europe (SPEED 2022)

Chiara Garau	University of Cagliari, Italy
Katarína Vitálišová	Matej Bel University, Slovakia
Paolo Nesi	University of Florence, Italy
Anna Vanova	Matej Bel University, Slovakia
Kamila Borsekova	Matej Bel University, Slovakia
Paola Zamperlin	University of Pisa, Italy

Federico Cugurullo   Trinity College Dublin, Ireland
Gerardo Carpentieri   University of Naples Federico II, Italy

International Workshop on Smart and Sustainable Island Communities (SSIC 2022)

Chiara Garau   University of Cagliari, Italy
Anastasia Stratigea   National Technical University of Athens, Greece
Paola Zamperlin   University of Pisa, Italy
Francesco Scorza   University of Basilicata, Italy

International Workshop on Theoretical and Computational Chemistry and Its Applications (TCCMA 2022)

Noelia Faginas-Lago   University of Perugia, Italy
Andrea Lombardi   University of Perugia, Italy

International Workshop on Transport Infrastructures for Smart Cities (TISC 2022)

Francesca Maltinti   University of Cagliari, Italy
Mauro Coni   University of Cagliari, Italy
Francesco Pinna   University of Cagliari, Italy
Chiara Garau   University of Cagliari, Italy
Nicoletta Rassu   Univesity of Cagliari, Italy
James Rombi   University of Cagliari, Italy
Benedetto Barabino   University of Brescia, Italy

14th International Workshop on Tools and Techniques in Software Development Process (TTSDP 2022)

Sanjay Misra   Østfold University College, Norway

International Workshop on Urban Form Studies (UForm 2022)

Malgorzata Hanzl   Lodz University of Technology, Poland
Beniamino Murgante   University of Basilicata, Italy
Alessandro Camiz   Özyeğin University, Turkey
Tomasz Bradecki   Silesian University of Technology, Poland

International Workshop on Urban Regeneration: Innovative Tools and Evaluation Model (URITEM 2022)

Fabrizio Battisti   University of Florence, Italy
Laura Ricci   Sapienza University of Rome, Italy
Orazio Campo   Sapienza University of Rome, Italy

International Workshop on Urban Space Accessibility and Mobilities (USAM 2022)

Chiara Garau	University of Cagliari, Italy
Matteo Ignaccolo	University of Catania, Italy
Enrica Papa	University of Westminster, UK
Francesco Pinna	University of Cagliari, Italy
Silvia Rossetti	University of Parma, Italy
Wendy Tan	Wageningen University and Research, The Netherlands
Michela Tiboni	University of Brescia, Italy
Vincenza Torrisi	University of Catania, Italy

International Workshop on Virtual Reality and Augmented Reality and Applications (VRA 2022)

Osvaldo Gervasi	University of Perugia, Italy
Damiano Perri	University of Florence, Italy
Marco Simonetti	University of Florence, Italy
Sergio Tasso	University of Perugia, Italy

International Workshop on Advanced and Computational Methods for Earth Science Applications (WACM4ES 2022)

Luca Piroddi	University of Cagliari, Italy
Sebastiano Damico	University of Malta, Malta

International Workshop on Advanced Mathematics and Computing Methods in Complex Computational Systems (WAMCM 2022)

Yeliz Karaca	UMass Chan Medical School, USA
Dumitru Baleanu	Cankaya University, Turkey
Osvaldo Gervasi	University of Perugia, Italy
Yudong Zhang	University of Leicester, UK
Majaz Moonis	UMass Chan Medical School, USA

Additional Reviewers

Akshat Agrawal	Amity University, Haryana, India
Waseem Ahmad	National Institute of Technology Karnataka, India
Vladimir Alarcon	Universidad Diego Portales, Chile
Oylum Alatlı	Ege University, Turkey
Raffaele Albano	University of Basilicata, Italy
Abraham Alfa	FUT Minna, Nigeria
Diego Altafini	Università di Pisa, Italy
Filipe Alvelos	Universidade do Minho, Portugal

Marina Alexandra Pedro Andrade	ISCTE-IUL, Portugal
Debora Anelli	Polytechnic University of Bari, Italy
Gennaro Angiello	AlmavivA de Belgique, Belgium
Alfonso Annunziata	Università di Cagliari, Italy
Bernady Apduhan	Kyushu Sangyo University, Japan
Daniela Ascenzi	Università degli Studi di Trento, Italy
Burak Galip Aslan	Izmir Insitute of Technology, Turkey
Vanessa Assumma	Politecnico di Torino, Italy
Daniel Atzberger	Hasso-Plattner-Institute für Digital Engineering gGmbH, Germany
Dominique Aury	École Polytechnique Fédérale de Lausanne, Switzerland
Joseph Awotumde	University of Alcala, Spain
Birim Balci	Celal Bayar University, Turkey
Juliana Balera	INPE, Brazil
Ginevra Balletto	University of Cagliari, Italy
Benedetto Barabino	University of Brescia, Italy
Kaushik Barik	University of Alcala, Spain
Carlo Barletta	Politecnico di Bari, Italy
Socrates Basbas	Aristotle University of Thessaloniki, Greece
Rosaria Battarra	ISMed-CNR, Italy
Silvia Battino	University of Sassari, Italy
Chiara Bedan	University of Trieste, Italy
Ranjan Kumar Behera	National Institute of Technology Rourkela, India
Gulmira Bekmanova	L.N. Gumilyov Eurasian National University, Kazakhstan
Mario Bentivenga	University of Basilicata, Italy
Asrat Mulatu Beyene	Addis Ababa Science and Technology University, Ethiopia
Tiziana Binda	Politecnico di Torino, Italy
Giulio Biondi	University of Firenze, Italy
Alexander Bogdanov	St Petersburg University, Russia
Costanza Borghesi	University of Perugia, Italy
Giuseppe Borruso	University of Trieste, Italy
Marilisa Botte	University of Naples Federico II, Italy
Tomasz Bradecki	Silesian University of Technology, Poland
Ana Cristina Braga	University of Minho, Portugal
Luca Braidotti	University of Trieste, Italy
Bazon Brock	University of Wuppertal, Germany
Dani Broitman	Israel Institute of Technology, Israel
Maria Antonia Brovelli	Politecnico di Milano, Italy
Jorge Buele	Universidad Tecnológica Indoamérica, Ecuador
Isabel Cacao	University of Aveiro, Portugal
Federica Cadamuro Morgante	Politecnico di Milano, Italy

Rogerio Calazan	IEAPM, Brazil
Michele Campagna	University of Cagliari, Italy
Lelio Campanile	Università degli Studi della Campania Luigi Vanvitelli, Italy
Tiziana Campisi	University of Enna Kore, Italy
Antonino Canale	University of Enna Kore, Italy
Elena Cantatore	Polytechnic University of Bari, Italy
Patrizia Capizzi	Univerity of Palermo, Italy
Alessandra Capolupo	Polytechnic University of Bari, Italy
Giacomo Caporusso	Politecnico di Bari, Italy
Caterina Caprioli	Politecnico di Torino, Italy
Gerardo Carpentieri	University of Naples Federico II, Italy
Martina Carra	University of Brescia, Italy
Pedro Carrasqueira	INESC Coimbra, Portugal
Barbara Caselli	Università degli Studi di Parma, Italy
Cecilia Castro	University of Minho, Portugal
Giulio Cavana	Politecnico di Torino, Italy
Iole Cerminara	University of Basilicata, Italy
Maria Cerreta	University of Naples Federico II, Italy
Daniele Cesini	INFN, Italy
Jabed Chowdhury	La Trobe University, Australia
Birol Ciloglugil	Ege University, Turkey
Elena Cocuzza	Univesity of Catania, Italy
Emanuele Colica	University of Malta, Malta
Mauro Coni	University of Cagliari, Italy
Elisete Correia	Universidade de Trás-os-Montes e Alto Douro, Portugal
Florbela Correia	Polytechnic Institute of Viana do Castelo, Portugal
Paulo Cortez	University of Minho, Portugal
Lino Costa	Universidade do Minho, Portugal
Alessandro Costantini	INFN, Italy
Marilena Cozzolino	Università del Molise, Italy
Alfredo Cuzzocrea	University of Calabria, Italy
Sebastiano D'amico	University of Malta, Malta
Gianni D'Angelo	University of Salerno, Italy
Tijana Dabovic	University of Belgrade, Serbia
Hiroshi Daisaka	Hitotsubashi University, Japan
Giulia Datola	Politecnico di Torino, Italy
Regina De Almeida	University of Trás-os-Montes and Alto Douro, Portugal
Maria Stella De Biase	Università della Campania Luigi Vanvitelli, Italy
Elise De Doncker	Western Michigan University, USA
Itamir De Morais Barroca Filho	Federal University of Rio Grande do Norte, Brazil
Samuele De Petris	University of Turin, Italy
Alan De Sá	Marinha do Brasil, Brazil
Alexander Degtyarev	St Petersburg University, Russia

Federico Dell'Anna	Politecnico di Torino, Italy
Marta Dell'Ovo	Politecnico di Milano, Italy
Ahu Dereli Dursun	Istanbul Commerce University, Turkey
Giulia Desogus	University of Cagliari, Italy
Piero Di Bonito	Università degli Studi della Campania, Italia
Paolino Di Felice	University of L'Aquila, Italy
Felicia Di Liddo	Polytechnic University of Bari, Italy
Isabel Dimas	University of Coimbra, Portugal
Doina Cristina Duma	INFN, Italy
Aziz Dursun	Virginia Tech University, USA
Jaroslav Dvořak	Klaipėda University, Lithuania
Dario Esposito	Polytechnic University of Bari, Italy
M. Noelia Faginas-Lago	University of Perugia, Italy
Stefano Falcinelli	University of Perugia, Italy
Falcone Giacomo	University of Reggio Calabria, Italy
Maria Irene Falcão	University of Minho, Portugal
Stefano Federico	CNR-ISAC, Italy
Marcin Feltynowski	University of Lodz, Poland
António Fernandes	Instituto Politécnico de Bragança, Portugal
Florbela Fernandes	Instituto Politecnico de Braganca, Portugal
Paula Odete Fernandes	Instituto Politécnico de Bragança, Portugal
Luis Fernandez-Sanz	University of Alcala, Spain
Luís Ferrás	University of Minho, Portugal
Ângela Ferreira	Instituto Politécnico de Bragança, Portugal
Lorena Fiorini	University of L'Aquila, Italy
Hector Florez	Universidad Distrital Francisco Jose de Caldas, Colombia
Stefano Franco	LUISS Guido Carli, Italy
Valentina Franzoni	Perugia University, Italy
Adelaide Freitas	University of Aveiro, Portugal
Andreas Fricke	Hasso Plattner Institute, Germany
Junpei Fujimoto	KEK, Japan
Federica Gaglione	Università del Sannio, Italy
Andrea Gallo	Università degli Studi di Trieste, Italy
Luciano Galone	University of Malta, Malta
Adam Galuszka	Silesian University of Technology, Poland
Chiara Garau	University of Cagliari, Italy
Ernesto Garcia Para	Universidad del País Vasco, Spain
Aniket A. Gaurav	Østfold University College, Norway
Marina Gavrilova	University of Calgary, Canada
Osvaldo Gervasi	University of Perugia, Italy
Andrea Ghirardi	Università di Brescia, Italy
Andrea Gioia	Politecnico di Bari, Italy
Giacomo Giorgi	Università degli Studi di Perugia, Italy
Stanislav Glubokovskikh	Lawrence Berkeley National Laboratory, USA
A. Manuela Gonçalves	University of Minho, Portugal

Leocadio González Casado	University of Almería, Spain
Angela Gorgoglione	Universidad de la República Uruguay, Uruguay
Yusuke Gotoh	Okayama University, Japan
Daniele Granata	Università degli Studi della Campania, Italy
Christian Grévisse	University of Luxembourg, Luxembourg
Silvana Grillo	University of Cagliari, Italy
Teresa Guarda	State University of Santa Elena Peninsula, Ecuador
Carmen Guida	Università degli Studi di Napoli Federico II, Italy
Kemal Güven Gülen	Namık Kemal University, Turkey
Ipek Guler	Leuven Biostatistics and Statistical Bioinformatics Centre, Belgium
Sevin Gumgum	Izmir University of Economics, Turkey
Martina Halásková	VSB Technical University in Ostrava, Czech Republic
Peter Hegedus	University of Szeged, Hungary
Eligius M. T. Hendrix	Universidad de Málaga, Spain
Mauro Iacono	Università degli Studi della Campania, Italy
Oleg Iakushkin	St Petersburg University, Russia
Matteo Ignaccolo	University of Catania, Italy
Mustafa Inceoglu	Ege University, Turkey
Markus Jobst	Federal Office of Metrology and Surveying, Austria
Issaku Kanamori	RIKEN Center for Computational Science, Japan
Yeliz Karaca	UMass Chan Medical School, USA
Aarti Karande	Sardar Patel Institute of Technology, India
András Kicsi	University of Szeged, Hungary
Vladimir Korkhov	St Petersburg University, Russia
Nataliia Kulabukhova	St Petersburg University, Russia
Claudio Ladisa	Politecnico di Bari, Italy
Mara Ladu	University of Cagliari, Italy
Sabrina Lai	University of Cagliari, Italy
Mark Lajko	University of Szeged, Hungary
Giuseppe Francesco Cesare Lama	University of Napoli Federico II, Italy
Vincenzo Laporta	CNR, Italy
Margherita Lasorella	Politecnico di Bari, Italy
Francesca Leccis	Università di Cagliari, Italy
Federica Leone	University of Cagliari, Italy
Chien-sing Lee	Sunway University, Malaysia
Marco Locurcio	Polytechnic University of Bari, Italy
Francesco Loddo	Henge S.r.l., Italy
Andrea Lombardi	Università di Perugia, Italy
Isabel Lopes	Instituto Politécnico de Bragança, Portugal
Fernando Lopez Gayarre	University of Oviedo, Spain
Vanda Lourenço	Universidade Nova de Lisboa, Portugal
Jing Ma	Luleå University of Technology, Sweden
Helmuth Malonek	University of Aveiro, Portugal
Francesca Maltinti	University of Cagliari, Italy

Benedetto Manganelli	Università degli Studi della Basilicata, Italy
Krassimir Markov	Institute of Electric Engineering and Informatics, Bulgaria
Alessandro Marucci	University of L'Aquila, Italy
Alessandra Mascitelli	Italian Civil Protection Department and ISAC-CNR, Italy
Michele Mastroianni	University of Campania Luigi Vanvitelli, Italy
Hideo Matsufuru	High Energy Accelerator Research Organization (KEK), Japan
Chiara Mazzarella	University of Naples Federico II, Italy
Marco Mazzarino	University of Venice, Italy
Paolo Mengoni	University of Florence, Italy
Alfredo Milani	University of Perugia, Italy
Fernando Miranda	Universidade do Minho, Portugal
Augusto Montisci	Università degli Studi di Cagliari, Italy
Ricardo Moura	New University of Lisbon, Portugal
Ana Clara Mourao Moura	Federal University of Minas Gerais, Brazil
Maria Mourao	Polytechnic Institute of Viana do Castelo, Portugal
Eugenio Muccio	University of Naples Federico II, Italy
Beniamino Murgante	University of Basilicata, Italy
Giuseppe Musolino	University of Reggio Calabria, Italy
Stefano Naitza	Università di Cagliari, Italy
Naohito Nakasato	University of Aizu, Japan
Roberto Nardone	University of Reggio Calabria, Italy
Nadia Nedjah	State University of Rio de Janeiro, Brazil
Juraj Nemec	Masaryk University in Brno, Czech Republic
Keigo Nitadori	RIKEN R-CCS, Japan
Roseline Ogundokun	Kaunas University of Technology, Lithuania
Francisco Henrique De Oliveira	Santa Catarina State University, Brazil
Irene Oliveira	Univesidade Trás-os-Montes e Alto Douro, Portugal
Samson Oruma	Østfold University College, Norway
Antonio Pala	University of Cagliari, Italy
Simona Panaro	University of Porstmouth, UK
Dimos Pantazis	University of West Attica, Greece
Giovanni Paragliola	ICAR-CNR, Italy
Eric Pardede	La Trobe University, Australia
Marco Parriani	University of Perugia, Italy
Paola Perchinunno	Uniersity of Bari, Italy
Ana Pereira	Polytechnic Institute of Bragança, Portugal
Damiano Perri	University of Perugia, Italy
Marco Petrelli	Roma Tre University, Italy
Camilla Pezzica	University of Pisa, Italy
Angela Pilogallo	University of Basilicata, Italy
Francesco Pinna	University of Cagliari, Italy
Telmo Pinto	University of Coimbra, Portugal

Fernando Pirani	University of Perugia, Italy
Luca Piroddi	University of Cagliari, Italy
Bojana Pjanović	University of Belgrade, Serbia
Giuliano Poli	University of Naples Federico II, Italy
Maurizio Pollino	ENEA, Italy
Salvatore Praticò	University of Reggio Calabria, Italy
Zbigniew Przygodzki	University of Lodz, Poland
Carlotta Quagliolo	Politecnico di Torino, Italy
Raffaele Garrisi	Polizia Postale e delle Comunicazioni, Italy
Mariapia Raimondo	Università della Campania Luigi Vanvitelli, Italy
Deep Raj	IIIT Naya Raipur, India
Buna Ramos	Universidade Lusíada Norte, Portugal
Nicoletta Rassu	Univesity of Cagliari, Italy
Michela Ravanelli	Sapienza Università di Roma, Italy
Roberta Ravanelli	Sapienza Università di Roma, Italy
Pier Francesco Recchi	University of Naples Federico II, Italy
Stefania Regalbuto	University of Naples Federico II, Italy
Marco Reis	University of Coimbra, Portugal
Maria Reitano	University of Naples Federico II, Italy
Anatoly Resnyansky	Defence Science and Technology Group, Australia
Jerzy Respondek	Silesian University of Technology, Poland
Isabel Ribeiro	Instituto Politécnico Bragança, Portugal
Albert Rimola	Universitat Autònoma de Barcelona, Spain
Corrado Rindone	University of Reggio Calabria, Italy
Ana Maria A. C. Rocha	University of Minho, Portugal
Humberto Rocha	University of Coimbra, Portugal
Maria Clara Rocha	Instituto Politécnico de Coimbra, Portugal
James Rombi	University of Cagliari, Italy
Elisabetta Ronchieri	INFN, Italy
Marzio Rosi	University of Perugia, Italy
Silvia Rossetti	Università degli Studi di Parma, Italy
Marco Rossitti	Politecnico di Milano, Italy
Mária Rostašová	Universtiy of Žilina, Slovakia
Lucia Saganeiti	University of L'Aquila, Italy
Giovanni Salzillo	Università degli Studi della Campania, Italy
Valentina Santarsiero	University of Basilicata, Italy
Luigi Santopietro	University of Basilicata, Italy
Stefania Santoro	Politecnico di Bari, Italy
Rafael Santos	INPE, Brazil
Valentino Santucci	Università per Stranieri di Perugia, Italy
Mirko Saponaro	Polytechnic University of Bari, Italy
Filippo Sarvia	University of Turin, Italy
Andrea Scianna	ICAR-CNR, Italy
Francesco Scorza	University of Basilicata, Italy
Ester Scotto Di Perta	University of Naples Federico II, Italy
Ricardo Severino	University of Minho, Portugal

Jie Shen	University of Michigan, USA
Luneque Silva Junior	Universidade Federal do ABC, Brazil
Carina Silva	Instituto Politécnico de Lisboa, Portugal
Joao Carlos Silva	Polytechnic Institute of Cavado and Ave, Portugal
Ilya Silvestrov	Saudi Aramco, Saudi Arabia
Marco Simonetti	University of Florence, Italy
Maria Joana Soares	University of Minho, Portugal
Michel Soares	Federal University of Sergipe, Brazil
Alberico Sonnessa	Politecnico di Bari, Italy
Lisete Sousa	University of Lisbon, Portugal
Elena Stankova	St Petersburg University, Russia
Jan Stejskal	University of Pardubice, Czech Republic
Silvia Stranieri	University of Naples Federico II, Italy
Anastasia Stratigea	National Technical University of Athens, Greece
Yue Sun	European XFEL GmbH, Germany
Anthony Suppa	Politecnico di Torino, Italy
Kirill Sviatov	Ulyanovsk State Technical University, Russia
David Taniar	Monash University, Australia
Rodrigo Tapia-McClung	Centro de Investigación en Ciencias de Información Geoespacial, Mexico
Eufemia Tarantino	Politecnico di Bari, Italy
Sergio Tasso	University of Perugia, Italy
Vladimir Tcheverda	Institute of Petroleum Geology and Geophysics, SB RAS, Russia
Ana Paula Teixeira	Universidade de Trás-os-Montes e Alto Douro, Portugal
Tengku Adil Tengku Izhar	Universiti Teknologi MARA, Malaysia
Maria Filomena Teodoro	University of Lisbon and Portuguese Naval Academy, Portugal
Yiota Theodora	National Technical University of Athens, Greece
Graça Tomaz	Instituto Politécnico da Guarda, Portugal
Gokchan Tonbul	Atilim University, Turkey
Rosa Claudia Torcasio	CNR-ISAC, Italy
Carmelo Maria Torre	Polytechnic University of Bari, Italy
Vincenza Torrisi	University of Catania, Italy
Vincenzo Totaro	Politecnico di Bari, Italy
Pham Trung	HCMUT, Vietnam
Po-yu Tsai	National Chung Hsing University, Taiwan
Dimitrios Tsoukalas	Centre of Research and Technology Hellas, Greece
Toshihiro Uchibayashi	Kyushu University, Japan
Takahiro Ueda	Seikei University, Japan
Piero Ugliengo	Università degli Studi di Torino, Italy
Gianmarco Vanuzzo	University of Perugia, Italy
Clara Vaz	Instituto Politécnico de Bragança, Portugal
Laura Verde	University of Campania Luigi Vanvitelli, Italy
Katarína Vitálišová	Matej Bel University, Slovakia

Daniel Mark Vitiello	University of Cagliari, Italy
Marco Vizzari	University of Perugia, Italy
Alexander Vodyaho	St. Petersburg State Electrotechnical University "LETI", Russia
Agustinus Borgy Waluyo	Monash University, Australia
Chao Wang	USTC, China
Marcin Wozniak	Silesian University of Technology, Poland
Jitao Yang	Beijing Language and Culture University, China
Fenghui Yao	Tennessee State University, USA
Fukuko Yuasa	KEK, Japan
Paola Zamperlin	University of Pisa, Italy
Michal Žemlička	Charles University, Czech Republic
Nataly Zhukova	ITMO University, Russia
Alcinia Zita Sampaio	University of Lisbon, Portugal
Ljiljana Zivkovic	Republic Geodetic Authority, Serbia
Floriana Zucaro	University of Naples Federico II, Italy
Marco Zucca	Politecnico di Milano, Italy
Camila Zyngier	Ibmec, Belo Horizonte, Brazil

Sponsoring Organizations

ICCSA 2022 would not have been possible without tremendous support of many organizations and institutions, for which all organizers and participants of ICCSA 2022 express their sincere gratitude:

Springer International Publishing AG, Germany (https://www.springer.com)

Computers Open Access Journal (https://www.mdpi.com/journal/computers)

Computation Open Access Journal (https://www.mdpi.com/journal/computation)

University of Malaga, Spain (https://www.uma.es/)

University of Perugia, Italy
(https://www.unipg.it)

University of Basilicata, Italy
(http://www.unibas.it)

Monash University, Australia
(https://www.monash.edu/)

Kyushu Sangyo University, Japan
(https://www.kyusan-u.ac.jp/)

University of Minho, Portugal
(https://www.uminho.pt/)

Universidade do Minho
Escola de Engenharia

Contents – Part VI

International Workshop on Sustainability Performance Assessment: Models, Approaches and Applications Toward Interdisciplinary and Integrated Solutions (SPA 2022)

Road Infrastructure as a Guarantee of Social Inclusion:
The Case of Tourists' satisfaction in the South of Italy 3
    Nicola Montesano, Giuseppina Anatriello, Elisabetta Cicchiello,
    and Francesca Pagliara

Challenges in the Implementation of the 2030 Agenda at the Local Scale.
The Case Study of the Municipal Masterplan of Cagliari 19
    Maddalena Floris and Francesca Leccis

Implementing Solutions for SECAP Transport Sector Towards Climate
Neutrality. 31
    Luigi Santopietro and Francesco Scorza

Tourism and Abandoned Inland Areas Development Demand:
A Critical Appraisal 40
    Rachele Gatto, Luigi Santopietro, and Francesco Scorza

Roghudi: Developing Knowledge of the Places in an Abandoned Inland
Municipality. 48
    Rachele Gatto, Luigi Santopietro, and Francesco Scorza

A First Financial Assessment of SEAP Public Energy Interventions
Performance Through Municipal Budget 54
    Luigi Santopietro, Silvia Solimene, Ferdinando Di Carlo,
    Manuela Lucchese, Francesco Scorza, and Beniamino Murgante

International Workshop on Specifics of Smart Cities Development in Europe (SPEED 2022)

A Preliminary Survey on Smart Specialization Platforms: Evaluation of
European Best Practices. 67
    Simone Chiordi, Giulia Desogus, Chiara Garau, Paolo Nesi,
    and Paola Zamperlin

Industry 4.0 Technologies and Italian Urban System: Between Smart
Development and Increasing Inequalities 85
    Michela Lazzeroni and Paola Zamperlin

Measuring Urban Competitiveness Through the Lens of Sustainability:
An Application at the Urban Districts Level in the City of Naples (Italy). . . .   93
  Sabrina Sgambati, Gerardo Carpentieri, and Carmela Gargiulo

Lack of Correlation Between Land Use and Pollutant Emissions: The Case
of Pavia Province   109
  Roberto De Lotto, Marilisa Moretti, Elisabetta M. Venco,
  Riccardo Bellati, and Melissa Monastra

Smart Solution for a Smart City: Using Open Source Maps in Municipal
Waste Management   125
  Ingrid Majerova, Radim Dolak, and Martin Murys

Smart Interventions for Smart Cities: Using Behavioral Economy in
Increasing Revenue from Local Fees and Why It Might Sometimes Fail   141
  Nikoleta Jakuš Muthová, Mária Murray Svidroňová,
  and Katarína Vitálišová

A Traffic Model with Junction Constraints for Smart Cities Development . . .   157
  Sabrina Francesca Pellegrino

Searching for Heterogeneous Geolocated Services via API Federation   173
  Ala Arman, Pierfrancesco Bellini, and Paolo Nesi

Communication as a Part of Smart Governance in Local Municipalities   191
  Katarína Vitálišová, Kamila Borseková, Anna Vaňová, Darina Rojíková,
  and Peter Laco

The Market Concentration as the Public Services Contracting Out
Efficiency Factor at the Local Government Level: The Case of Slovakia   204
  Beáta Mikušová Meričková, Daniela Mališová, and Kristína Murínová

The Value Chains in Smart Regions – The Role of ICT Through
the Eyes of Consumers   219
  Lenka Veselovská, Mária Pomffyová, and Mária Sirotiaková

**International Workshop on Theoretical and Computational Chemistry
and Its Applications (TCCMA 2022)**

A Theoretical Study on *trans*-Resveratrol - Cu(I) Complex.   237
  Concetta Caglioti, Antonella De Luca, Chiara Pennetta,
  Lorenzo Monarca, Francesco Ragonese, Paola Sabbatini,
  Maria Noelia Faginas Lago, Andrea Lombardi, Federico Palazzetti,
  and Bernard Fioretti

Theoretical Study of the Reaction $O(^3P)$ + 1,2-Butadiene.   249
  Gianmarco Vanuzzo, Andrea Giustini, Marzio Rosi,
  Piergiorgio Casavecchia, and Nadia Balucani

The Assembly of a Computing Platform for Studying Protein Inhibitors
Against COVID-19 Replication.   264
    Leonardo Pacifici, Ribi Akbar, Andrea Lombardi, Giuseppe Vitillaro,
    and Maria Noelia Faginas Lago

Confinement of CO_2 Inside (20,0) Single-Walled Carbon Nanotubes.   275
    Noelia Faginas-Lago, Andrea Lombardi, Yusuf Bramastya Apriliyanto,
    and Leonardo Pacifici

Structural Basis of the Biomolecular Action of Paddlewheel-
and N-Heterocyclic-Carbene-Based Antitumor Metallodrugs:
A Computational Perspective   290
    Iogann Tolbatov and Alessandro Marrone

Quantum Confinement Effects in Materials for Daytime Radiative Cooling:
An *Ab-initio* Investigation   305
    Costanza Borghesi, Claudia Fabiani, Anna Laura Pisello,
    and Giacomo Giorgi

Coding Cross Sections of an Electron Charge Transfer Process.   319
    Emília Valença Ferreira de Aragão, Luca Mancini, Xiao He,
    Noelia Faginas-Lago, Marzio Rosi, Daniela Ascenzi,
    and Fernando Pirani

Simulation of CO_2 Sorption from the Gas Stream by the Grain
of Soda-Lime Sorbent   334
    Vadim Lisitsa, Tatyana Khachkova, Yaroslav Bazaikin,
    and Vladimir Derevschikov

Protein Networks by Invariant Shape Coordinates and Deformation
Indexes   348
    Lombardi Andrea, Noelia Faginas-Lago, and Leonardo Pacifici

International Workshop on Urban Form Studies (UForm 2022)

Modernist Housing Estates – Examining the Conditions of Redevelopment
of Outdoor Space. The Case Study from Łódź, Bałuty.   363
    Małgorzata Hanzl

**International Workshop on Urban Regeneration: Innovative Tools
and Evaluation Model (URITEM 2022)**

On the Phenomenon of Depopulation of Inland Areas   381
    Federica Russo, Alessandra Marra, Roberto Gerundo,
    and Antonio Nesticò

International Workshop on Urban Space Accessibility and Mobilities (USAM 2022)

A Smart Approach for Integrated Land-Use and Transport Planning—An Application to the Naples Metro Station Areas 395
Carmen Guida, Gerardo Carpentieri, and John Zacharias

Developing Cities for Citizens: Supporting Gender Equity for Successful and Sustainable Urban Mobility 410
Tiziana Campisi, Georgios Georgiadis, and Socrates Basbas

Sustainable Mobility and Accessibility to Essential Services. An Assessment of the San Benedetto Neighbourhood in Cagliari (Italy) 423
Gloria Pellicelli, Barbara Caselli, Chiara Garau, Vincenza Torrisi, and Silvia Rossetti

Health and Mobility in the Post-pandemic Scenario. An Analysis of the Adaptation of Sustainable Urban Mobility Plans in Key Contexts of Italy . . . 439
Alfonso Annunziata, Giulia Desogus, Francesca Mighela, and Chiara Garau

International Workshop on Virtual Reality and Augmented Reality and Applications (VRA 2022)

A Multi-agent Body Tracking Application Framework Applied to Physical and Neurofunctional Rehabilitation 459
Felipe Reis Valente, Marcelo de Paiva Guimarães, Elder José Reioli Cirilo, and Diego Roberto Colombo Dias

A Mobile App to Help People Affected by Visual Snow 473
Damiano Perri, Marco Simonetti, Osvaldo Gervasi, and Natale Amato

Strategies for the Digitalization of Cultural Heritage 486
Osvaldo Gervasi, Damiano Perri, Marco Simonetti, and Sergio Tasso

International Workshop on Workshop on Advanced and Computational Methods for Earth Science Applications (WACM4ES 2022)

UAV Photogrammetry for Volume Calculations. A Case Study of an Open Sand Quarry 505
Giuessppina Vacca

The *Pulcinella* Diagnostic Project: Introduction to the Study of the
Performances of Close-Range Diagnostics Targeted to a Wooden Physical
Twin of a Carnival Historical Mask. 519
    Luca Piroddi, Ilaria Catapano, Emanuele Colica, Sebastiano D'Amico,
    Luciano Galone, Gianfranco Gargiulo, and Stefano Sfarra

Joint Use of GPR Surveys, Terrestrial and Aerial Photogrammetry for the
Study of the Portico of the Cathedral of S. Pietro (Isernia, Italy). 534
    Marilena Cozzolino, Vincenzo Gentile, Paolo Mauriello, and Enza Zullo

Integrated Methodologies for the Survey and the Documentation of Two
Byzantine Churches at the UNESCO Archaeological Site of Umm ar-Rasas
(Jordan). 547
    Andrea Angelini, Marilena Cozzolino, Roberto Gabrielli,
    Pasquale Galatà, Vincenzo Gentile, and Paolo Mauriello

Diffraction Imaging After Diffraction Separation in Data Domain 560
    M. Protasov

An Integrated and Cooperative Approach Between Regional and Local
Public Authorities to Sustainable Development: City Logistics Projects
in Calabria. 572
    Francesco Russo, Giuseppe Iiritano, Giovanna Petrungaro,
    and Maria Rosaria Trecozzi

Geotechnologies for Geological Mapping at the State of Tocantins/Brazil. . . . 585
    Pedro Benedito Casagrande, Diego Guilherme da Costa Gomes,
    Jonas de Oliveira Laranjeira, and Ítalo Sousa de Sena

**International Workshop on Workshop on Advanced Mathematics
and Computing Methods in Complex Computational Systems
(WAMCM 2022)**

An Example of Use of Variational Methods in Quantum
Machine Learning. 597
    Marco Simonetti, Damiano Perri, and Osvaldo Gervasi

**International Workshop on Transport Infrastructures for Smart
Cities (TISC 2022)**

Sardinia Granite Scraps Application in Road Pavement Layers 613
    J. Rombi, F. Maltinti, and M. Coni

Sidewalk Cafe: Analysis of Safe Solutions for Customers 624
    Francesca Maltinti, Nicoletta Rassu, Alessandro Plaisant,
    and Francesco Pinna

Performance Evaluation of in Situ Application of Anhydrous Calcium
Sulphate in Pavement Layers   640
   J. Rombi, M. Olianas, M. Salis, A. Serpi, and M. Coni

Safety Oriented Road Asset Management Methodology for Urban Areas   650
   Mauro D'Apuzzo, Azzurra Evangelisti, Giuseppe Cappelli,
   and Vittorio Nicolosi

Deflection and Friction Performance of Waste-Wooden Block Pavements . . .   663
   Mauro Coni, Giovanna Concu, Carla Carcangiu,
   tand Francesca Maltinti

Author Index   679

International Workshop on Sustainability Performance Assessment: Models, Approaches and Applications Toward Interdisciplinary and Integrated Solutions (SPA 2022)

Road Infrastructure as a Guarantee of Social Inclusion: The Case of Tourists' satisfaction in the South of Italy

Nicola Montesano[1], Giuseppina Anatriello[1], Elisabetta Cicchiello[1], and Francesca Pagliara[2(✉)]

[1] ANAS S.p.A, Rome, Italy
{n.montesano,g.anatriello,e.cicchiello}@stradeanas.it
[2] Department of Civil, Architectural and Environmental Engineering, University of Naples Federico II, Naples, Italy
fpagliara@unina.it

Abstract. This paper discusses the concept of social inclusion as it relates to transport, and how it is currently embedded within the Italian roads transport planning.

Transportation systems may not always be inclusive both from a geographical point of view as well as from an economic point of view. However roads bypass this issue since they are always accessible in time and space.

Through the support of a questionnaire submitted to tourists visiting the most popular tourist destinations in Campania region, in the south of Italy, it was possible to analyze their satisfaction with respect to the roads travelled during their journeys. Tourists were interviewed along some of the main roads managed by ANAS S.p.A. (Azienda Nazionale Autonoma delle Strade, National Autonomous Company of Roads), i.e. the Italian company managing road infrastructures.

The analysis revealed a difference between tourists with a low and those with a medium–high income. They perceived a different level of satisfaction with respect to road management and traffic management.

Keywords: Social inclusion · Transportation systems · Roads · South of Italy

1 Introduction

The origin of the concept of social exclusion can be traced back to France, where the term was used to define the rupture of the relationship between the individual and the society due to the failure of societal institutions to integrate individuals [1].

Today the question of inequality related to transport systems is becoming an issue that governments, at the different territorial scales, should face to find solutions to restrict the consequences. In 2015 the OECD (Centre for Opportunity and Equality) platform was developed with the aim of fostering policies on trends, causes and consequences of inequalities [2].

According to Keynon et al. (2003) [3] by social exclusion it is meant "the unique interplay of a number of factors, whose consequences is the denial of access to the opportunity to participate in the social, and political life of the community, resulting not only in diminished material and non-material quality of life, but also in tempered life chances, choices and reduced citizenship".

Church et al. (2000) [4] introduced seven factors limiting the mobility of socially excluded users and they are physical exclusion, i.e. physical barriers, such as lack of disabled facilities or timetable information, limiting accessibility to transport services; geographical exclusion which prevents people from accessing transport services, especially those living in rural or peripheral urban areas; exclusion from facilities, which concerns the low accessibility connected with facilities, like shops, schools, health care or leisure services; economic exclusion which represents the high monetary costs of travel inhibiting access to facilities or employment and thus having an impact on incomes; time-based exclusion which refers to other demands on time, like combined work, household and child-care duties, reducing the time available for travel; fear-based exclusion which deals with the fears for personal safety precluding the use of public spaces and/or transport services and space exclusion which is the security or space management preventing given groups having access to public spaces, like first class waiting rooms at stations.

Lucas [5] proposed the definition of a "transport poor user", as the one whom some condition may happen such as when he/she has no transport alternative, which suits his/her physical conditions and capabilities; when the actual transport alternatives do not serve destinations where the user can fulfill his/her daily activity needs; when the weekly amount of money, which is spent on transport, brings the family with an income, which is below the poverty threshold. Moreover, when the user is pushed to spend long travel time, causing time poverty and/or social isolation and when factors like danger and safety characterize the travel conditions of the user.

It is important to clarify that not all socially excluded people are poor and that not all social exclusions concern the poor accessibility to transport facilities and services. However, in all countries, low-income people have fewer transport alternatives in addition to having low-quality transport services that offer travel with little comfort and low security [6]. There is an extensive literature on the wider socioeconomic inequality aspects of transport. In the book of Vasconcellos [7] the idea that the traditional transport planning has generated an unfair distribution of accessibility is supported and suggestions for new measures towards an equitable and sustainable urban environment are proposed. This idea is also supported by Martens [8] who sustains that governments have the duty of providing users with adequate transportation alternatives managing the mitigation of social disparities.

Banister's research shows [9] that "today's transport policy benefits the rich more than the poor. But it is the better-off who are travelling faster and further, leaving the poor in the slow lane and closer to home". The poor choose more the bus and they walk more, while the rich choose more the car and go by train. Investments in transportation systems should be more oriented to the limitation of this disparity, while, instead they "exacerbate it!".

This paper discusses the concept of social inclusion as it relates to transport, and how it is currently embedded within the Italian roads transport planning.

Through the support of a questionnaire submitted to tourists visiting the most popular tourist destinations in Campania region, in the south of Italy, it was possible to analyze their satisfaction with respect to the roads travelled during their journeys. Tourists were interviewed along some of the main roads managed by ANAS S.p.A. (Azienda Nazionale Autonoma delle Strade, National Autonomous Company of Roads), i.e. the Italian company managing road infrastructures.

The analysis revealed a difference between tourists with a low and those with a medium–high income. They perceived a different level of satisfaction with respect to road management and traffic management. This paper is organized as follows. In Sect. 2 a review of the contributions present in the literature on the relationship between social inclusion and transport is reported. Section 3 reports the case study; in Sect. 4 conclusions are described.

2 The Concept of Social Inclusion/Equity in Relation to Transportation Systems

Several special issues in transport related journals have been published on this topic. Hine [10] argues that the introduction of new information technologies, allowing the development of demand responsive transport, can make the system more inclusive since journeys will be matched to the users' needs.

The paper by Nash [11] deals with the issue of the Green Paper on Fair and Efficient Pricing in Transport. This document argues that tariffs should support transport costs. There are some costs that are not fully repaid such as environmental impacts, congestion, accidents, infrastructure, provision and maintenance. These excluded costs could be very high. The increase of these costs, however, could lead to social exclusion, especially for low-income people.

Lyons [12] highlights the role of accessibility in having an impact on exclusion. For example low access to places make them unsafe and intimidating, increasing the geographical exclusion of them.

Hine and Grieco [13] explain the importance of scatter or cluster identification in transport planning and a demand-sensitive transport system to meet the needs of socially excluded people. The most disadvantaged groups in transport are the older people, children, women, the disabled and low-income people. When the socially excluded are cluster it is possible to improve the bus lines and the bus times, when the excluded are scatter, transport on demand could improve their mobility. New information technologies foster the creation of a booking system that allows the pickup and drop off at home for people with low mobility in a cheap way thus reducing social exclusion.

Olvera et al. [14] analyze the case study of Dar es Salaam, the largest city in Tanzania. In that city there are numerous obstacles to the daily travel of the city's inhabitants, notably the poor. These barriers weight heavily on schedules, complicate access to services ever further, limit the use of urban space, and place considerable pressure on household budgets. Consequently, the poorest individuals tend to retreat into their neighborhood where the low-quality urban facilities are unable to assist in the development of human and social capital and economic opportunities, the alleviation of poverty or the prevention of social exclusion. Wu and Hine [15] analyze the Northern Ireland Citybus network and assess the spatial impact on population living in the area of interest due to a hypothetical network modification. The presence in the city of Belfast of the Protestant community and the Catholic community involves the use by the population of services that cross only the areas of the community they belong to for reasons of security and fear. Four scenarios have been proposed (including the current scenario) the outcome of this analysis is that the area served by Citybus is reduced in all options different from the current situation and in particular the areas excluded from the service are the poorest ones, thus increasing the social exclusion of low-income users, who cannot afford the private car.

Hodgson and Turner [16] propose the case study of Stockport in Greater Manchester, where the question of social exclusion has been managed by promoting citizens greater participation in the planning of local transport systems. The cities of Adswood and Bridgehall have obtained funding for regeneration, which is the reason why a planning process is started, in which the residents actively participate. The key points, identified by the citizens, are road safety and the physical environment of the roads (a green area is created in the cities). A minibus service is also implemented allowing not only to reach the local supermarket but also organizing trips for young people and children. Raje [17] analyzes the social exclusion question in the city of Bristol as a result of road pricing. The area subject to this measure deals with the city center and the main commercial area and excludes residential areas. Through focus groups and direct interviews, people interviewed believe that road pricing can be beneficial if revenues are spent to improve accessibility through more flexible and responsive public demand; discounts for taxi for people who need individual transport; discounts for particular categories of users; investments in planning software and online booking of minibuses.

Stanley and Brodrick [18] assume that the concept of social exclusion is not sufficient to encompass all social policy requirements in relation to transport, there being the need to use other theoretical concepts, especially in relation to well-being and community connectiveness. To build an efficient and effective transport system it is necessary to understand these relationships and realize how psychological factors can influence them. The document contains various definitions and measures of social exclusion, the most widely used is the Social Exclusion Unit (SEU). The SEU asserts that to reduce social exclusion, it is necessary to understand how people access to the different activities and improve the transport system according to the needs of the community.

Lucas et al. [19] contribute to the issue of social exclusion through the analysis of four case studies, ie a new service linking the suburbs and the city center in Leicester, in Cornwall, and in Manchester and a project to help people to bear the travel costs in the first weeks of work in West Midland. Through on board, postal or telephone surveys, users' opinions are collected, regarding these improvements, and through a Cost–Benefit Analysis (CBA), it is found that these interventions lead to a very substantial economic and time saving. Following these interventions it is easier to reach work, hospitals, places for shopping or leisure and visit old people.

Currie et al. [20] analyze the relationship between public transport, social exclusion and well-being. The research focuses on the metropolitan city of Melbourne, focus groups and consultations examine the disadvantages of the population in relation to transport and social life. Public transport is developed only in the city center, therefore people living in the suburbs, who do not own a car, are obliged to walk and this creates many disadvantages, which justify the number of car owners, which is very high and the car sharing is widespread in this area.

Loader and Stanley [21] report in their document the initiative that the Victoria government has adopted in the metropolitan city of Melbourne. The Bus Association Victoria, in order to solve the problem of public transport, has increased the number of buses and routes and has expanded the hours of service. In addition, the rates have been facilitated for the areas farthest from the center and discounts have been introduced on Sundays, which has led to an increase in weekend trips. The increase of petrol price has also led people, who previously preferred the use of cars, to choose public transport. Through interviews carried out after the interventions, it results that these interventions reduce the social exclusion of the people, who live in the suburbs, have increased social and employment opportunities, have led to a growth in the independence of young people and have contributed to the well-being of the population.

Priya and Uteng [22] summarize the four methods to study the relationship between transport and social exclusion present in the literature (studies on accessibility, qualitative studies, analysis of the potential of a virtual mobility and the activity-based modeling approach). The case study is the social exclusion in Norway due to the high cost of driving licenses. This involves a high social exclusion for people with low-income and within families, it is preferable to have a driver's license for sons rather than for daughters, entailing a disadvantage for girls to find work. Furthermore, the limited availability of public transport in the suburbs makes it necessary to own a car. Through surveys, submitted to the population through direct interviews or postal questionnaires, citizens express a preference for decreasing the price of the driving license rather than towards improving public transport, in this way it is believed that the social exclusion of women and non-western immigrants could decrease. Battellino [23] deals with the problem of public transport in New South Wales (NSW) in Australia. The transport supply does not fully meet the needs of the local communities and the demand often exceeds the supply. Existing services are almost exclusively for the elderly and disabled. The NSW Government has approve the Transport Community Project in which is established the expansion, by buses and cars driven by volunteers, of the public and private transport services in order to allow everyone to move easily.

Lucas and Musso [24], Macario [25] and Lucas and Porter [26] agree that authorities should engage the socially excluded within their planning programmes with the aim of defining solutions to address the question of transport-related social exclusion.

Brennan et al. [27] analyze how housing policies relates to the social inclusion of low-income people, mobility and accessibility in the outer suburbs of Perth, in the Western Australia. Low-income people are forced to live far from the center of the city because in the suburbs houses cost less, this affects the type of work they can perform, moreover in the suburbs there is less accessibility and this involves a dependence on cars or a performance of all activities in the surrounding area. The sale price of houses depends on the location, the characteristics of the dwelling and the accessibility to public transport and urban services. The most appreciated places are those near the center, the railways or near the coast. The proximity to shopping centers and educational facilities is seen negatively. However, people prefer to have larger lots rather than living in the city center. Carrier et al. [28] compute the level of NO_2 pollution in and around schools in Montreal and find out that schools are located in city blocks where there are fewer major roads than in, and generally similar concentrations of NO_2 to, the rest of the Island of Montreal. However, there are environmental and social inequalities as children from low-income families attend schools with a higher concentration of NO_2, in the surrounding environment and these schools are subject to concentrations higher than the city average.

Markett [29] evaluates the improvement of the lives of the elderly following the introduction of the policy that elders travel free on buses in Britain. The objective of this policy is to improve social inclusion, access to basic needs and increase the use of public transport. The results show that the targets are met by increasing the use of buses especially for people who do not have access to cars. Older people, who have shown poor use of buses, are those who do not have easy access to them, therefore fairness should be improved. Van der Kloof et al. [30] evaluate the impacts that the lessons on the use of the bicycle to immigrant and refugee women have on their participation in activities in the city of Amsterdam through quantitative surveys and a series of in-depth interviews. Especially non-Western immigrant and refugee women are the ones of the population groups most likely to experience accessibility problems and, subsequently, transport-related social exclusion. The bicycle offers considerable potential to increase the mobility of these women. The results show that the impacts of the bicycle lessons vary. Some participants use the bicycle for everyday purposes, while others still find it difficult to drive in traffic or have not yet purchased a bicycle. Respondents say that, the lessons have substantially improved women's feelings of self-esteem and self-confidence, they feel more independent and mentally stronger. In addition, bicycle lessons have made possible to be more informed about the activities of the neighborhood and the city. Maia et al. [31] report the research carried out on the residents of two low-income communities in the Recife metropolitan region of Brazil, a favela of Corque and a peripheral community of Alto Santa Terezinha (AST). Through focus groups, the transport needs and the accessibility of the residents of the two communities are analyzed. For both communities, health services and basic education are easily reachable on foot but the quality of services is very poor. Most respondents do not own a car, Corque participants prefer to walk and rarely use public transport, public transport is widely used at AST. In Corque the main problem is crime and the lack of quality of pedestrian areas, in AST instead the problem is to reach the top of the hill.

Alberts et al. [32] analyze the case of resettlement of urban suburbs in Chennai in India following the introduction of four bus lines and other services such as schools, nurseries, medical centers, gym, ration shops and a police outpost. The study focuses in particular on women who are most affected by the negative effects of resettlement and how they exercise agency in embedding spatial practices within their livelihood strategies to reconnect to the city. Through focus groups and participatory workshops, issues related to job accessibility, services etc. are discussed. The composition of the family has great influence, most of the women interviewed are housewives and move only in the neighborhood, women who instead need to work are led to move away and this involves costs and travel times. The provision of public transport offers access to more opportunities and participation in society thus contributing to social inclusion.

Accessibility and recreating relational spaces may both widen women's opportunities as well as overstretch their physical and financial resources.

Olvera et al. [33] report the growing development of motorcycle taxis in developing cities in Africa, India, Southeast Asia and Latin America. The case study analyzed is that of the city of Lomé in Togo. The presence of motorcycle taxis allows low-income people to move to areas, where public transport is not present, quickly and at an affordable price. Drivers of these vehicles are able to earn enough from the activity to meet their daily needs, but working conditions, health impacts and the risk of accidents mean that the activity is considered temporary, necessary to get out of poverty. It would be important to professionalize employment and thus improve its image, and to facilitate the purchase of a motorcycle would help improving the conditions of drivers.

Ikioda [34] focuses on the consequences of enlarging an urban highway in the city of Lagos. This road will connect Lagos with other important destinations in West Africa, its construction will allow the improvement of business in the city center. On the other hand, however, it causes serious damage to the Agboju and Alayabiagba markets, many traders find themselves without stalls and suffer from serious economic losses. A qualitative study with traders in two markets is used to explore the often ignored implications that large-scale transport development initiatives can have on the livelihoods of urban residents who may attach varying meanings to a road. The objective of improving the urban connection has proved to be a serious problem for groups of poor people living along the highway route. Esson et al. [35] analyze, through an in-depth qualitative research, the mobility of urban residents in different parts of the city of Accra, the capital of Ghana, in relation to their livelihood strategies. The study is conducted through focus groups and semi-structured interviews in four residential areas of the city, the discussion focuses on how three types of businesses (home-based enterprise operators, enterprise operators with a business located elsewhere and itinerant workers) interface with the means of transport for the purchase and sale of goods. The city of Accra lacks a secure transport system for people, this has led to a rapid growth of alternative means of transport such as shared taxis, tro-tros and okadas which in addition to promoting mobility are sources of livelihood for their drivers. It has also been established that the use of mobile phones has changed the way people move in relation to managing their business.

Lucas [36] blames that, although most European cities provide forms of fare subsidies to some low income groups, most do not take into account the effects of transport social exclusion and therefore something should be done in order to change this trend.

Boisjoly and Yengoh [37] highlight how the scarce participation of citizens in local transport planning decision-making processes produces technical plans that are not focused on the needs of the communities. The participatory processes of two boroughs of Montreal, in Canada are analyzed. Interviews are conducted with local planners and representatives of community groups (mainly disadvantaged groups) and planning documents are also viewed. The importance of collaboration between citizens and planners is highlighted in order to facilitate easier access to services and social inclusion. The results show that the presence of a skilled facilitator is the key to support the integration of diverse perspectives on transportation planning. It is also essential to provide community groups with resources to meaningfully participate in the process, thereby promoting social equity. Sterzer [38] studies the impact of the real estate market on mobility, and in particular the effect on low-income families that cannot afford the high cost of housing in accessible neighbourhoods but cannot even bear the high costs of mobility in less connected suburban areas. The case study is the metropolitan region of Munich. Interviews are conducted with low-income people who have recently moved. There is a strong dependence on public transport to get to work, schools and services, although public transport works well in Munich.

Li and Zhao [39] analyze the case study of migrant workers in central Beijing, China. For migrant workers, the jobs available are poorly qualified, salaries are low, good schools are inaccessible. Interviews are conducted with migrants and the local population. The mobility of migrants is limited, many of them walk or use electric bicycles to move around the neighborhood, there are few trips to visit family members and their social network is limited to people from the same hometown. However, the use of the mobile phone and the community initiatives such as community activities and volunteers have helped to improve their mobility.

3   The Case Study

Tourists were interviewed along some of the main roads, in the south of Italy, managed by ANAS S.p.A. (Azienda Nazionale Autonoma delle Strade, National Autonomous Company of Roads), i.e. the Italian company managing road infrastructures.

The idea of the research derives from the evidence that tourists choose the car as their main means of travel. Even in 2020, a year marked by the COVID-19 pandemic which generated a drop in holidays of about 45%, the car continued to be the most popular transport alternative to travel (73.9%), compared to other transport modes such as plane, train and bus. Even during the summer of the same year, users chose to travel by car. In fact, 81% of holiday trips took place by car, compared to 65.4% recorded during the summer of 2019 (ISTAT, 2021 – www.istat.it).

The choice of using the car to visit the Italian tourist destinations and, therefore, also those in the Campania region, arises from the fact that the road allows trips:

- always available, as there are no restrictions on traveling by road;
- continuous in time and space, in fact through the road it is always possible to travel and go everywhere;
- accessible to anyone because they are fair, regardless of social class and income.

In detail, through the design of a questionnaire, respondents were asked to indicate the route traveled during their trip with respect to which they could express their opinion (using a scale from 1 to 10) relating to four dimensions: road maintenance; road safety; traffic management and quality of service areas (see Fig. 1).

The most suitable road and, therefore, travelled by the tourists interviewed was the Motorway A2 "Autostrada del Mediterraneo" (32.9%), which crosses territories and landscapes not only of the Campania region, but also of the Basilicata and Calabria regions.

Then there is the road 163 "Amalfitana" (31.2%), which, connecting the towns of the Amalfi coast, has a route of about 50 km long, with numerous curves, and it has only one lane in each direction.

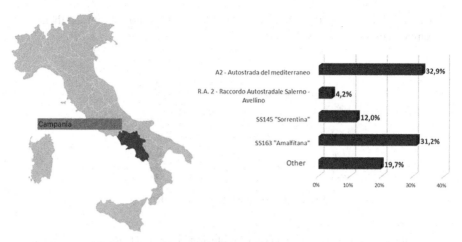

Fig. 1. The roads traveled and indicated by the respondents

3.1 The Survey

Overall, 405 were the respondents and the information collected allowed the estimation of the satisfaction levels, with a probability of 95%, close to the real value of the population itself, with an estimated standard error not exceeding ±5%.

For the data collection phase, the C.A.P.I. (Computer Assisted Personal Interview) method was the one adopted. Specifically, this approach allows direct contact between the interviewer and respondent; it favours the collaboration of the respondent.

The sample was mainly composed by men (64%), aged between 35 and 44 years (27.2%) (see Fig. 2).

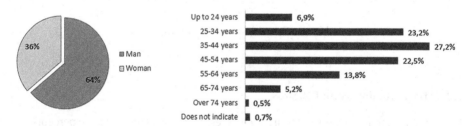

Fig. 2. The gender and age of the interviewees

Overall, 73.1% of the respondents declared they have a job and among them 51% were employed as a clerk (see Fig. 3).

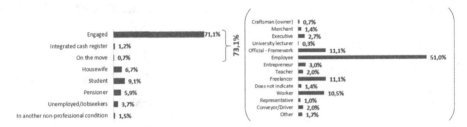

Fig. 3. The occupation the respondents

To analyze the issue of equity and social inclusion in relation to the world of transport, it was decided to divide the sample based on the "income" variable (see Fig. 4).

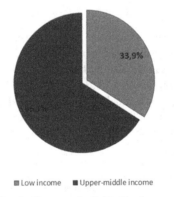

■ Low income   ■ Upper-middle income

Fig. 4. The sample divided by income

3.2 The Methodology and Results

Structural equation models (SEM) are used to test hypotheses and measure perceptions of impacts. SEM is a statistical modeling technique frequently used in the behavioral sciences. It can be viewed as a combination of factor analysis and multiple regression or as a combination of factor analysis and path analysis (Hox and Bechger, 1998).

In the social sciences it is common to study perceptions that are not directly measurable. They are indicated with the term "constructs" or with "latent variables". SEMs are models capable of modeling complex structures of causality relationships between latent variables starting from a set of real variables, called "manifest" (Kenneth A. Bollen, 1989). The objectives of the SEM are:

– Estimate latent variables as a synthesis of manifest variables;

– Estimate the relationships between latent variables.

To quantify a construct, questionnaires are filled out by individuals within a population. Through the questionnaires, stimuli are given to people who ask for opinions, feelings, etc. The responses serve to measure indicators (or measured variables). Once the indicators have been quantified, it is possible to reconstruct the latent variable that depends on them. SEM consists of two models:

- Structural model (or internal model): it specifies the dependence relationships between the latent variables;
- Measurement model (or external model): specifies the relationships between buildings and their indicators.

Latent variables are divided into endogenous and exogenous. Latent exogenous variables are independent, that is, they are constructs that are not explained by other constructs. In contrast, the endogenous latent variables are dependent, so they are explained by other latent variables.

In the structural model, each endogenous construct is a linear combination of exogenous constructs. The parameters to be estimated are the path-coefficients that bind the endogenous construct to each exogenous construct. Therefore, this model is generally a multiple regression model, unlike the measurement model which can predict even simple regression.

To study a model of structural equations it is possible to consider one of the following two approaches:

- CB-SEM (SEM based on covariance) based on a maximum likelihood estimation procedure;
- PLS-SEM: based on a partial least squares estimation algorithm (PLS).

The PLS-PM (Partial Least Square - Path Modeling) estimates through a system of interdependent equations based on simple and multiple regression the network of relationships between the manifest variables and their latent variables and between the latent variables within the model.

The aim is to provide an estimate of the latent variables so that they are as representative as possible of their block of manifest variables and, at the same time, able to best explain the causal relationships of the structural model.

The PLS-PM is an iterative procedure that allows estimating the external weights, the internal weights and the values of the latent variables, through the alternation of simple and multiple linear regressions. Estimates of the values of the latent variables are obtained through the alternation of internal and external estimates iterated until convergence.

Constructs are represented graphically by circles or ellipses while indices are represented by rectangles (see Fig. 5).

The measurement model is called formative when the construct is defined by the manifest variables. When the construct defines manifest variables, the measurement model is said to be reflexive. Reflexive models are typical of the social sciences because

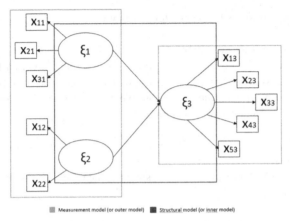

Measurement model (or outer model)   Structural model (or inner model)

Fig. 5. Structural Equation Models (SEM)

they best describe human attitudes. Furthermore, by adopting the reflexive measurement model, the constructs take on a double characteristic: they are both representative of their own block of manifest variables, and predictive towards any other adjacent constructs (see Fig. 6).

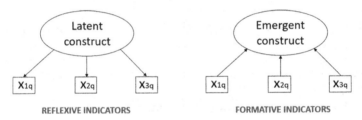

Fig. 6. Reflective model and training model

Once the model has been specified, through SEM it is possible to evaluate its goodness of fit to confirm it or, possibly, reject it. In this sense, SEM allows for a confirmatory analysis. Many researchers use SEM by combining the confirmatory approach with the exploratory approach. If the formulated model is not valid, it can be modified and then re-evaluated. To understand if the model is well structured, goodness of fit indices are used. If the value of each index is within its respective reference range, the model is supported.

The hypotheses underlying the SEM allow to correlate the constructs by means of equations whose coefficients can be estimated and whose significance can be verified. In this study it was decided to use the PLS-SEM approach.

For the data analysis it was therefore chosen to use the Structural Equations Model which represents, among other things, an international standard for the construction of Customer Satisfaction indicators.

During the survey, the hypothesis was formulated and verified according to which the four dimensions identified, namely road maintenance, road safety, traffic management and the quality of service areas (in the case of motorways) influence the general level of satisfaction of tourists with their travel experience (see Fig. 7).

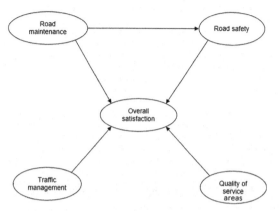

Fig. 7. Theoretical model connecting four dimensions of road management to the overall satisfaction of tourists concerning their travel experience

In line with the concept that the road is fair, accessible to anyone, regardless of social class and income, a further focus of analysis was carried out by dividing the sample of tourists interviewed on the basis of the income class they belonged to.

Tourists with medium–high income expressed a generally higher level of satisfaction with their travel experience (6.2/10) than those with low income (5.8/10). In detail, for both classes, road maintenance is the most satisfactory dimension among the four considered.

Therefore, the respondents with low income demonstrated to be more demanding in terms of the overall management of a street (see Table 1).

Table 1. The levels of satisfaction w.r.t. the four dimensions

	Tourists with medium-high income	Tourists with low income
Road maintenance	6.3	6.0
Road safety	6.2	5.7
Traffic management	5.9	5.4
Quality of service areas	5.9	5.7

A further difference that emerged between the two categories of tourists relates to the dimension that has the greatest impact on the overall satisfaction rating regarding the travel experience: for tourists with medium–high income this is traffic management (54.2%); while for tourists with low income it is road maintenance (45.4%), which represents a "strong point" in Anas' roads management (see Figs. 8 and 9).

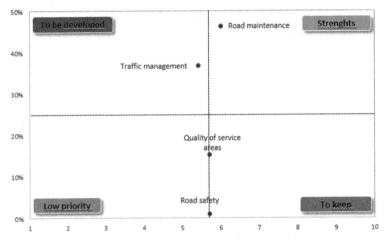

Fig. 8. Quadrant analysis of low income tourists

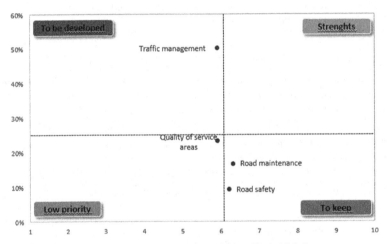

Fig. 9. Quadrant analysis tourists with medium–high income

4 Conclusions

At the centre of debates, there is always the issue of sustainability, resilience, and inclusion also in relation to mobility systems. Given the "nature" of roads, since they are accessible to everybody all, more policies should be introduced to make the other infrastructures more inclusive.

As emerged from the survey conducted, in the management and efficiency of the transport system and mobility in general, it would be appropriate to take into account the different needs of all the users of the transportation system, regardless of their social class and origin.

References

1. Silver, H.: Social exclusion and social solidarity: three paradigms. International Institute for Labour Studies (IILS), Discussion paper series no. 69, Genève (1994)
2. OECD Income inequality: Social inclusion and mobility. ITF Round Table Report 164 (2017). https://www.itf-oecd.org/income-inequality-social-inclusion-and-mobility-roundtable
3. Kenyon, S., Rafferty, J., Lyons, G.: Social exclusion and transport: a role for virtual accessibility in the alleviation of mobility related social exclusion? Journal of Political Policy **32**(3), 317–338 (2003)
4. Church, A., Frost, M., Sullivan, K.: Transport and social exclusion in London. Transport Policy **7**, 195–205 (2000)
5. Lucas, K.: Transport poverty and inequalities. European Transport Research Review **10** (17), (2018)
6. Lucas, K., Mattioli, G., Verlinghieri, E., Guzman, A.: Transport poverty and its adverse social consequences. Proceedings of the Institution of Civil Engineers - Transport **169**(6), 353–365 (2016)
7. Vasconcellos, E.: Urban Transport, Environment, and Equity: The Case for Developing Countries. Earthscan Publications (2001)
8. Martens, K.: Transport Justice: Designing fair transportation systems. Taylor & Francis Ltd. (2016)
9. Banister, D.: Inequality in Transport. Alexandrine Press (2018)
10. Hine, J.: Social exclusion and transport systems. Transport Policy **10** (14), (2003)
11. Nash, C.: Marginal cost and other pricing principles for user charging in transport: a comment. Transport Policy **10**, 345–348 (2003)
12. Lyons, G.: The introduction of social exclusion into the field of travel behaviour. Transport Policy **10**, 339–342 (2003)
13. Hine, J., Grieco, M.: Scatters and clusters in time and space: implications for delivering integrated and inclusive transport. Transport Policy **10**, 299–306 (2003)
14. Olvera, L.D., Guézéré, A., Plat, D., Pochet, P.: Earning a living, but at what price? being a motorcycle taxi driver in a Sub-Saharan African city. Journal of Transport Geography **55**, 165–174 (2016)
15. Wu, B.M., Hine, J.P.: A PTAL approach to measuring changes in bus service accessibility. Transport Policy **10**, 307–320 (2003)
16. Hodgson, F.C., Turner, J.: Participation not consumption: the need for new participatory practices to address transport and social exclusion. Transport Policy **10**, 265–272 (2003)
17. Rajé, F.: The impact of transport on social exclusion processes with specific emphasis on road user charging. Transport Policy **10**, 321–338 (2003)
18. Stanley, J., Vella-Brodrick, D.: The usefulness of social exclusion to inform social policy in transport. Transport Policy **16**, 90–96 (2009)
19. Lucas, K., Tyler, S., Christodoulou, G.: Assessing the 'value' of new transport initiatives in deprived neighbourhoods in the UK. Transport Policy **16**, 115–122 (2009)
20. Currie, G., et al.: Investigating links between transport disadvantage, social exclusion and well-being in Melbourne – Preliminary results. Transport Policy **16**, 97–105 (2009)
21. Loader, C., Stanley, J.: Growing bus patronage and addressing transport disadvantage - the melbourne experience. Transport Policy **16**, 106–114 (2009)
22. Priya, T., Uteng, A.: Dynamics of transport and social exclusion: effects of expensive driver's license. Transport Policy **16**, 130–139 (2009)
23. Battellino, H.: Transport for the transport disadvantaged: a review of service delivery models in New South Wales. Transport Policy **16**, 123–129 (2009)

24. Lucas, K., Musso, A.: Policies for social inclusion in transportation. Case Studies on Transport Policy **2**(2), 37–40 (2014)
25. Macario, R.: Virtual special issue on social exclusion. Case Studies on Transport Policy **2**(3), (2014)
26. Lucas, K., Porter, G.: Mobilities and livelihoods in urban developments contexts. Journal of Transport Geography **55**, 129–131 (2016)
27. Brennan, M., Olaru, D., Smith, B.: Are exclusion factors capitalised in housing prices? Case Studies on Transport Policy **2**, 50–60 (2014)
28. Carrier, M., Apparicio, P., Se´guin, A., Crouse, D.: Ambient air pollution concentration in montreal and environmental equity: are children at risk at school?. Case Studies on Transport Policy **2**, 61–69 (2014)
29. Mackett, R.: Has the policy of concessionary bus travel for older people in Britain been successful? Case Studies on Transport Policy **2**, 81–88 (2014)
30. Van der Kloof, A., Bastiaanssen, J., Martens, K.: Bicycle lessons, activity participation and empowerment. Case Studies on Transport Policy **2**, 89–95 (2014)
31. Maia, M.L., Lucas, K., Marinho, G., Santos, E., de Lima, J.H.: Access to the brazilian city—from the perspectives of low-income residents in recife. Journal of Transport Geography **55**, 132–141 (2016)
32. Alberts, A., Pfeffer, K., Baud, I.: Rebuilding women's livelihoods strategies at the city fringe: agency, spatial practices, and access to transportation from semmenchery, Chennai. J. Trans. Geogra. **55**, 142–151 (2016)
33. Olvera, L.D., Plat, D., Pochet, P.: Transportation conditions and access to services in a context of urban sprawl and deregulation. The case of Dar es Salaam, Transport Policy **10**, 287–298 (2003)
34. Ikioda, F.: The impact of road construction on market and street trading in Lagos. Journal of Transport Geography **55**, 175–181 (2016)
35. Esson, J., Gough, K.V., Simon, D., Amankwaa, E.F., Ninot, O., Yanksonc, P.W.K.: Livelihoods in motion: Linking transport, mobility and income-generating activities. J. Transp. Geogra. **55**, 182–188 (2016)
36. Boisjoly, G., Yengoh, G.T.: Opening the door to social equity: local and participatory approaches to transportation planning in Montreal. European Transport Research Review **9**, 43 (2017)
37. Sterzer, L.: Does competition in the housing market cause transport poverty? Interrela. Resi. Loca. choice mobility Euro. Transp. Res. Rev. **9**, 45 (2017)
38. Li, S., Zhao, P.: Restrained mobility in a high-accessible and migrant-rich area in downtown Beijing. Euro. Transp. Res. Rev. **10**, 4 (2018)

Challenges in the Implementation of the 2030 Agenda at the Local Scale. The Case Study of the Municipal Masterplan of Cagliari

Maddalena Floris and Francesca Leccis(✉) ⓘ

Università degli Studi di Cagliari, via Marengo 2, 09123 Cagliari, Italy
maddalenafloris@gmail.com, francescaleccis@unica.it

Abstract. The 2030 Agenda for Sustainable Development urges policy shift from a sectoral approach to a holistic one, which considers the interconnections among the economic, social and environmental dimensions of sustainable development and calls for integrated solutions. The Agenda identifies 17 Sustainable Development Goals, which are scaled at the national and regional level through the National Strategy for Sustainable Development and the Regional Strategy for Sustainable Development. This paper suggests a new methodological approach to advance the Sustainable Development Goals at the local level, by illustrating the procedure developed for the definition of the Preliminary environmental report of the Strategic environmental assessment of the Preliminary municipal masterplan of Cagliari, which localize the Sardinian Regional Strategy of Sustainable Development. The proposed methodology adopts the structure of the logical framework in order to provide a complete hierarchical relation among the objectives and the actions of the Preliminary municipal masterplan. The logical framework is articulated into four phases: the definition of the sustainability-oriented objectives, the analysis of policy consistency and coherence, the definition of the specific objectives and the definition of the actions. This contribution is centered on this last step and on the subsequent monitoring phase. In particular, impacts of the actions on the achievement of the sustainability-oriented objectives are assessed. In case they are found to be potentially negative, alternatives are provided. The monitoring system is constituted by a series of indicators that allow for the numerical measurement of a phenomenon in order to promptly identify negative impacts and take the appropriate corrective measures. The assessment of the actions is a key element in the definition of urban and regional plans, that allows for the development of special processes coherent with the Regional Strategy for Sustainable Development and able to contribute to the achievement of the Sustainable Development Goals. The proposed methodology is easily exportable in other Italian regional contexts and constitutes a fundamental reference framework for the integration of the Regional Strategy for Sustainable Development into the Strategic Environmental Assessment processes of territorial plans.

Keywords: 2030 agenda · Strategic environmental assessment · Monitoring

O. Gervasi et al. (Eds.): ICCSA 2022 Workshops, LNCS 13382, pp. 19–30, 2022.
https://doi.org/10.1007/978-3-031-10592-0_2

1 A New Paradigm for Development

The 2030 Agenda embodies a new paradigm for global development, based on the synergistic relation between sustainability and development [17]. This paradigm calls for a new model of international development, which combines economic progress, social justice and the preservation of natural resources, with the aim of building an equitable, inclusive and environmentally sustainable world [17].

This new concept of sustainable development relies on 17 Sustainable Development Goals (SDGs) (Fig. 1), further structured in 169 targets [18]. Progress in their implementation has to be monitored through the 231 indicators identified by the UN [17].

Fig. 1. The seventeen sustainable development goals [2].

One of the most innovative defining features of the 2030 Agenda is its universality, which, not only means that principles are universal and, as such, applicable to all countries and all people, but also that all the countries at all levels have to devote an effort, both individually and collectively, towards global sustainability [16]. For this reason, nations and administrative regions are called to develop National Sustainable Development Strategies (NSDS) and Regional Strategies for Sustainable Development (RSSD), respectively, while Local Governments are appointed to implement the Strategies at local level [12].

The Italian government approved the translation of the global agenda to the national level on 22nd December 2017 [11][1]. The Italian National Strategic Objectives are the result of a process of tailoring of the Agenda targets and they are monitored through a set of national indicators defined by the Italian National Institute of Statistics (ISTAT)

---

[1] CIPE: Delibera n. 108 del 22.12.2017. CIPE Resolution N. 108 of 22nd December 2017. Available at: https://ricerca-delibere.programmazioneeconomica.gov.it/108-22-dicembre-2017/, last access 11.04.2022.

[11]. The Sardinian regional government, in turn, approved the RSSD[2] on 8th October 2021 [15]. The Sardinian RSSD gears the National Strategic Objectives to the Sardinian context through the definition of the Strategic Regional Objectives (SROs). A series of actions have been identified to pursue the SROs and a system of indicators has been defined to monitor progresses in SRO achievement [15]. The implementation of the 2030 Agenda at the local level is here illustrated through the case study of the Municipality of Cagliari, the capital city of Sardinia (Fig. 2), which localized the Sardinian Regional Strategy of Sustainable Development in the Preliminary municipal masterplan (MMP) of the city.

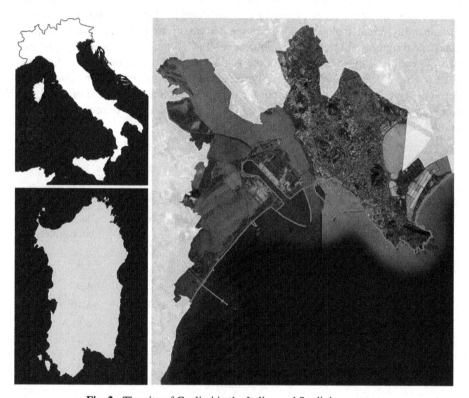

Fig. 2. The city of Cagliari in the Italian and Sardinian context.

This paper is structured into 3 sections: (i) a new paradigm for sustainability, (ii) methodology and case study, which is in turn organized into 2 subsections, and (iii) discussion and conclusion.

---

[2] RAS (Regione Autonoma della Sardegna): Deliberazione N. 39/56 del 08.10.2021. Strategia Regionale per lo Sviluppo Sostenibile. Indirizzi per l'attuazione. [Regional resolution N. 39/59 of 8th March 2021. RSSD. Guidelines for the implementation] Available at: https://delibere.regione.sardegna.it/protected/57125/0/def/ref/DBR57095/, last access 11.04.2022.

2 Methodology and Case Study

The applied methodology makes reference to the process of the Strategic Environmental Assessment (SEA), recognized as an efficient approach for the enhancement of the plan, because it allows for the balancing of socio-economic objectives and environmental concerns [8]. In particular, the methodology adopts the logical framework (LF) matrix, which enables the integration of the objectives and actions of the RSSD into the perspective plan, reflecting the SEA leading concepts of sustainability and endoprocedimentality and identification of alternatives [9]. The LF outlines a hierarchy of objective and actions [10], whose logic linkages are made explicit [19]. The matrix is constituted by four columns and n lines (Table 1). As illustrated in Table 1, columns represent: Sustainability-oriented objectives, Objectives deriving from the external analysis of the plans and programs in force, Specific objectives and Actions. Actions are separate into two sub-columns: those favorable for the achievement of the corresponding SpO and those potentially unfavorable for the achievement of the related SpO. Matrix completion develops from the left to the right, but far from being a linear sequence of steps, it is an iterative process, which might require to go back and forward to review and revise drafted elements in the light of the new ones [4].

Table 1. The structure of the logical framework.

Sustainability-oriented objectives	External consistency – related objectives	Specific objectives	Actions	
			favorable	Potentially unfavorable
SO.1	EC.1	SpO.1	A.1	A.8
			A.2	A.9
		SpO.2	A.3	A.10
			A.4	A.11
	EC.2	SpO.3	A.5	A.12
			A.6	A.13
		SpO.4	A.7	A.14
			...	...
...	...	...	...	...

Once every cell of the matrix is filled in, a set of indicators is defined to monitor and assess the advancement in the achievement of the objectives.

The next two sections illustrate the process of impact assessment of the actions and the definition of a set of indicators, respectively.

2.1 The Plan Actions and the Dualism with the Sustainability-Oriented Objectives

Endoprocedimentality mainly expresses through the internal coherence among the different level of the LF. However, internal coherence is not sufficient to guarantee the sustainability of the plan [21]. On the contrary, internal coherence needs to be flanked by a comprehensive analysis of the relation between the sustainability-oriented objectives and the MMP actions, since some actions defined for the achievement of a sustainability-oriented objective might entail potentially unfavorable impacts on other sustainability-oriented objectives.

Consequently, it is necessary to carefully analyze each action with regard to all the sustainability-oriented objectives, in order to identify potentially unfavorable impacts on sustainability-oriented objectives and, in this event, to seek non-conflicting alternatives.

Table 2 shows an example of the analyses of an action of the MMP of Cagliari with regard to some sustainability-oriented objectives, while Table 3 illustrates the negative impacts of the identified potentially unfavorable action with regard to some sustainability-oriented objectives and provides non-conflicting alternatives.

Table 2 shows the dualism of the MMP actions with regard to both the sustainability-oriented objectives and the environmental components.

With reference to the dualism of the MMP actions with regard to the sustainability-oriented objectives, it can be noticed that the action A_01, reported in the first column, "To locate new residential, commercial and productive activities in areas with less exposure to natural and man-made risks, excluding highly sensitive areas", can be potentially unfavorable for the achievement of the objectives SO_06 and SO_12, while the same action substantially contributes to the achievement of the objectives SO_03, SO_08, SO_14 and SO_15.

Concerning the dualism of the MMP actions with regard to the environmental components, it can be seen that, even within the same component, the same action A_01, has a dual attitude. For example, with respect to the component *Soil*, it can be potentially unfavorable for the achievement of the objective SO_06, while it substantially contributes to the achievement of the objective SO_08.

Similarly, as for the component *Landscape and historical and cultural heritage*, it can be potentially unfavorable for the achievement of the objective SO_12, while it substantially contributes to the achievement of the objective SO_14.

In total, notwithstanding the logical linkages between the sustainability-oriented objectives and the actions of the MMP of Cagliari explicated in the LF, as a result of this analysis, 33 actions are found to be in potential conflict with 13 sustainability-oriented objectives. In particular, conflicting relations are identified in the following environmental components: Air, Water, Soil, Flora, fauna and biodiversity, Landscape and historical and cultural heritage, Settlement system and demographic change, Transport and mobility and Noise.

Table 3 shows that the reason why the MMP action A_01 is considered potentially unfavorable for the achievement of the sustainability-oriented objectives SO_06 and SO_12 is that it might cause a loss of natural and semi-natural areas and it might undermine the current condition of landscape components with relevant environmental value, respectively. The assessment of the potential environmental impacts that the realization

Table 2. Excerpt from the assessment table of Cagliari MMP action *A_01* with regard to the sustainability-oriented objectives.

Action	Assessment	Sustainability-oriented objectives	Environmental component
A_01 To locate new residential, commercial and productive activities in areas with less exposure to natural and man-made risks, excluding highly sensitive areas	Potentially unfavorable	SO_06 To ensure biodiversity conservation, protection of agricultural and semi-natural areas and restoration and valorization of ecosystems services	Soil
		SO_12 To ensure protection, valorization and sustainable fruition of coastal areas, marine-coastal wetlands, urban areas, agricultural landscapes and hills of the city of Cagliari	Landscape and cultural heritage
	Favorable	SO_03 To reduce exposure to flood risk and to decrease floodings in the whole municipal area through the adoption of preventive measures like the collection, reuse and recycling of rainwater	Water
		SO_08 To reduce exposure to the risks of landslides and flooding and to ensure adequate safety levels in areas with high hydrogeological risk	Soil
		SO_14 To reuse, enhance and regenerate the built environment and the public space	Landscape and historical and cultural heritage

(*continued*)

Table 2. (*continued*)

Action	Assessment	Sustainability-oriented objectives	Environmental component
		SO_15 To protect and enhance the built environment and urban green areas and to limit soil consumption	Settlement system and demographic change

Table 3. Excerpt from the assessment and alternative provision table of Cagliari MMP action A_01.

MMP potentially unfavorable action	Sustainability-oriented objectives	Assessment	Alternatives
A_01 To locate new residential, commercial and productive activities in areas with less exposure to natural and man-made risks, excluding highly sensitive areas	SO_06 To ensure biodiversity conservation, protection of agricultural and semi-natural areas and restoration and valorization of ecosystems services SO_12 To ensure protection, valorization and sustainable fruition of coastal areas, marine-coastal wetlands, urban areas, agricultural landscapes and hills of the city of Cagliari	The realization of new volumetry might entail potentially negative impacts on the achievement of the sustainability-oriented objectives reported in the second column, because it might cause a loss of natural and semi-natural areas and might undermine the current condition of landscape components with relevant environmental value	Intervention of restoration and redevelopment of the built environment The need of extra volumetry should be meet by regenerating the existing public and private housing stock. In case the building of new volumetry is necessary, location must be studied carefully and adequate impact mitigation and compensation must be identified in order to limit negative effects on the landscape and on the environment

of an action might entail is essential for the definition of the alternatives [1]. In the example here illustrated, the analysis of the MMP action *A_01* leads to alternatives oriented to the restoration and regeneration of the built environment, in place of the realization of new volumetry.

2.2 The Monitoring Indicators as a Tool to Assess the Plan Actions

The evaluation process does not finish when the plan is adopted, but continues during its implementation through the monitoring activity, thus reinforcing the concept of the planning practice as an ongoing learning process [5, 20]. In this sense, the monitoring activity ensures the control of significant impacts on the environment MMP deriving from the realization of the plan activities and allows to ascertain whether the objectives are met [6, 14], so that it is possible to promptly identify negative impacts and take the appropriate corrective measures [3].

The monitoring activity is based on a series of indicators, which are parameters or a group of parameters that synthetically express the *status quo* of a phenomenon through a number. Plan monitoring, sanctioned by the article 10 of the EU Directive 2001/42/CE, is still often considered as an appendix of the assessment process and neglected by the working practice. One of the most frequent obstacles to the monitoring activity is constituted by technical and financial constraints of the public institutions [6, 7]. For this reason, it is crucial to identify a series of indicators which are not only able to adequately represent the monitored phenomenon with great communicative efficiency, but also easy to populate thanks to availability and updatability of data.

Indeed, according to the Organization for Economic Co-operation and Development [13, p.7], the ideal indicator should meet the following criteria:

- "provide a representative picture of environmental conditions, pressures on the environment or society's responses;
- be simple, easy to interpret and able to show trends over time;
- be responsive to changes in the environment and related human activities;
- provide a basis for international comparisons;
- be either national in scope or applicable to regional environmental issues of national significance;
- have a threshold or reference value against which to compare it so that users are able to assess
- the significance of the values associated with it.
- be theoretically well founded in technical and scientific terms;
- be based on international standards and international consensus about its validity;
- lend itself to being linked to economic models, forecasting and information systems".

In addition, data collected to inform the indicators should be [13, p.7]:

- "readily available or made available at a reasonable cost/benefit ratio;
- adequately documented and of known quality;
- updated at regular intervals in accordance with reliable procedures".

The indicators selected for the monitoring activity of Cagliari MMP are efficient tools to keep a check on the plan impacts in relation to the specific objectives (SpO) of the MMP. For each SpO a number of indicators of result are extracted from (i) the database of the Italian National Institute of Statistics (ISTAT) following the document in progress elaborated by Poliedra "Analisi del sistema degli Indicatori della Strategia Nazionale per lo Sviluppo Sostenibile e contributo a proposte di aggiornamento e revision" ["Analysis of the indicators of the NSSD and contribution for update and revision proposals"], (ii) the database of the Italian Institute for Environmental Protection and Research (ISPRA) on the basis of the XIV report on the urban environment and other publications concerning environmental issues, (iii) the list of indicators identified by the four Italian regions of Marche, Umbria, Liguria e Piemonte during a project promoted by CreiamoPA or, whether not included in any of the sources, new indicators are specifically defined to represent the efficiency and efficacy of the MMP in achieving the SpO.

The selected indicators are able to verify if the achievement of the SpO through the MMP actions is coherent with the territorial and environmental system or, vice versa, if the plan implementation includes interventions that impede the fulfilment of the SO previously defined. In this way, it is possible to promptly identify negative impacts and take the appropriate corrective measures.

Table 4 shows the set of indicators selected in the Preliminary environmental report of the Preliminary MMP of Cagliari with reference to the plan action *A_01*. The six columns of the table report: the name of the indicator, the unit of measurement, the numerical value on the baseline year, the baseline year and indications for benchmark setting.

Table 4. Excerpt from the table of the monitoring indicators related to A_01.

Indicator	Unit of measurement	Value	Baseline year	Indications for benchmark setting
Redeveloped public and private areas	m^2	NA	-	Increase in the m^2 of redeveloped public and private areas
Soil consumption in urban areas	ha	2073	2020	Reduction in the ha of soil consumption in urban areas
Redeveloped volumetry	m^3	NA	-	Increase in the m^3 of redeveloped volumetry
People living in areas with high and very high risk of landslide	N of people	641	2018	Reduction in the number of People living in areas with high and very high risk of landslide

3 Discussion and Conclusion

The proposed paper explores and addresses the challenges in the implementation of the 2030 Agenda at the local scale. In particular, it analytically analyzes the dualism of the plan actions with regard to both the sustainability-oriented objectives and the environmental components and it reflects on the monitoring indicators as a tool to control significant impacts on the environment deriving from the realization of the plan activities and to ascertain whether the plan objectives are met.

Examples from the definition of the preliminary environmental report of the SEA of the Preliminary MMP of Cagliari are reported in order to better illustrate the developed methodology and the critical reasoning.

The developed methodological approach, described in Sect. 2, is based on the SEA process and adopts the LF to integrate the objectives and actions of the RSSD into the perspective plan. In particular, the RSSD is integrated in terms of sustainability-oriented objectives, specific objectives and actions of the perspective plan.

Subsection 2.1 shows that Cagliari MMP actions, although logically linked with the respective objectives, have unfavorable impacts on other objectives of the LF. The conducted analysis highlights that this dualism is detectable both in objectives related to different environmental components and in objectives related to the same environmental component. This means that the adoption of the LF itself is not guarantee of sustainability. On the contrary, once it is constructed, it is necessary to conduct a meticulous assessment of the plan actions with regard to every sustainability-oriented objective. When unfavorable impacts are detected, alternatives must be provided to overcome the conflicts.

Subsection 2.2 illustrates that environmental impacts determined by the plan actions need to be monitored through a set of adequate indicators, so that negative impacts are promptly identified and appropriate corrective measures are taken in time. It also demonstrates that monitoring indicators are not just the answer to the request of a European directive to keep a check on the plan impacts, but constitute a powerful tool to monitor the actual achievement of the plan specific objectives.

This study carries an important implication concerning the definition of new MMP. Indeed, traditional SEA used to take into account exclusively environmental issues, ensuring sustainable exploitation of natural resources and biodiversity protection and conservation. Differently, thanks to the above illustrated approach, the new model of SEA includes both social justice and economic progress in the process of definition of MMP. According to the proposed methodology, preservation of natural resources is flanked by prosperity and fulfillment of people lives, because human progress occurs in harmony with nature. In this way, this new generation of MMP allows for the building of equitable, inclusive and environmentally sustainable cities, as aimed by the 2030 Agenda and the related NSSD and RSSD.

Moreover, this study puts in evidence that current Sardinian regional guidelines for the SEA of MMP are out of date and need to be updated according to the new holistic approach suggested by the 2030 Agenda, which calls for the integration of the three pillars of sustainability. To this end, it is necessary to coordinate technical expertise and administrative capacity through effective and continuous cooperation among regional, provincial and local authorities.

The proposed methodology has been developed within the definition of the preliminary environmental report of the SEA of the Preliminary MMP of Cagliari, which localize the Sardinian RSSD, but it is easily exportable in other Italian regional contexts and constitutes a fundamental reference framework for the integration of the Regional Strategy for Sustainable Development into the Strategic Environmental Assessment processes of municipal plans. In addition, this approach can also be adopted for the definition of territorial plans other than municipal plans. For example, it has already been applied for the definition of the plan of the Regional Park of Tepilora.

Further research might apply this methodology to the undertaking of SEA of different types of territorial plans such as local plans, metropolitan plans, regional plans, plans of regional and national parks, etc.

Funding. The study was implemented within the following Research Programs: i. "Investigating the relationships between knowledge-building and design and decision-making in spatial planning with geodesign", financed by the Fondazione di Sardegna; ii. "SOSLabs. Laboratori di ricerca-azione per la Sostenibilità urbana" ["SOSLabs. Research-action laboratories for urban sustainability"], financed by the Ministry of the Environment and of the Protection of the Territory and the Sea of the Italian Government within the "Bando per la promozione di progetti di ricerca a supporto dell'attuazione della Strategia Nazionale per lo Sviluppo Sostenibile - Bando Snsvs 2" ["Public selection for the promotion of research projects focusing on the implementation of the National Strategy for sustainable development – Public selection Snsvs 2"].

Contributions. Maddalena Floris and Francesca Leccis collaboratively designed this study, and jointly written the "Discussion and conclusion" section. Individual contributions are as follows: M.F.: 2.1, 2.2, F.L.: 1, 2.

References

1. Abis, E., Lecca, M.: La VAS del Piano urbanistico comunale di Alghero in adeguamento al Piano paesaggistico regionale della Sardegna. In: Zoppi, C. (ed.) a cura di, Valutazione e pianificazione delle trasformazioni territoriali nei processi di governance. Sostenibilità ed e-governance nella pianificazione del territorio. Franco Angeli, Milano (2012)
2. AER (Assembly of European Regions) Homepage: https://aer.eu/. Last accessed 26 March 2021
3. De Montis, A., Ledda, A., Caschili, S., Ganciu, A., Barra, M.: SEA effectiveness for landscape and master planning: An investigation in Sardinia. Environ. Impact Assess. Rev. **47**, 1–13 (2014)
4. EC (European Commission): Aid Delivery Methods. https://www.ars.toscana.it/files/oss_stili_vita/formazione/pcm_guidelines.pdf. last accessed 08 April 2022
5. Fundingsland Tetlow, M., Hanusch, M.: Strategic environmental assessment: the state of the art. Impact Assess Project Appraisal **30**(1), 15–24 (2012)
6. Gachechiladze-Bozhesku, M., Fischer, T.B.: Benefits of and barriers to SEA follow-up - theory and practice. Environ. Impact Assess. Rev. **34**, 22–30 (2012)
7. Hanusch, M., Glasson, J.: Much ado about SEA/SA monitoring: the performance of English regional spatial strategies, and some German comparisons. Environ. Impact Assess. Rev. **28**(8), 601–617 (2008)
8. Leone, F., Zoppi, C.: The delicate relationship between capitalization and impoverishment of cultural and landscape resources in the context of Strategic Environmental Assessment of municipal master plans: a case study concerning Tertenia, Sardinia, In: Atti della XVIII Conferenza Nazionale SIU. Italia '45-'45. Radici, Condizioni, Prospettive, Planum Publisher, Roma-Milano, pp. 1458–1467 (2015)
9. Leone, F., Zoppi, C.: Local development and protection of nature in coastal zones: a planning study for the sulcis area (Sardinia, Italy). Sustainability **11**(18), 5095 (2019). https://doi.org/10.3390/su11185095

10. Casas, G.L., Scorza, F.: Sustainable Planning: A Methodological Toolkit. In: Gervasi, O., et al. (eds.) ICCSA 2016. LNCS, vol. 9786, pp. 627–635. Springer, Cham (2016). https://doi.org/10.1007/978-3-319-42085-1_53
11. MiTE: (Ministero della Transizione Ecologica) Homepage. https://www.minambiente.it/. last accessed 31 March 2021
12. OECD: (Organisation for Economic Co-operation and Development) Homepage. https://www.oecd.org/. last accessed 31 March 2021
13. OECD: OECD core set of indicators for environmental performance reviews. A synthesis report by the group on the state of the environment; Ocde/Gd (93)179; Environment. monographs n° 83 (1993)
14. Partidário, M.R., e Arts, J.: Exploring the concept of strategic environmental assessment follow-up. Impact Assessment and Project Appraisal **23**(3), 246–257 (2005)
15. RAS: (Regione Autonoma della Sardegna) Homepage. http://www.regione.sardegna.it/. last accessed 05 April 2021
16. UNEP: Universality in the Post 2015 Sustainable Development Agenda, UNEP Post 2015 Note #9 (2015). https://www.ohchr.org/sites/default/files/Documents/Issues/MDGs/Post2015/OHCHR_UNEP.pdf. last accessed 06 April 2022
17. UNGA (General Assembly of the United Nation): Transforming our world: the 2030 Agenda for Sustainable Development. United Nations (2015)
18. UNSSC (United Nation System Staff College): The 2030 Agenda for Sustainable Development. UNSSC Knowledge Centre for Sustainable Development, Bonn (2017)
19. WEDC (Water, Engineering and Development Centre): An Introduction to the Logical Framework. WEDC, Loughborough University, Leicestershire (2011)
20. Zoppi, C.: Servizi pubblici e qualità della vita urbana. Il ruolo e il significato della partecipazione delle comunità locali ai processi decisionali, Gangemi editore (2003)
21. Zoppi, C.: Questioni problematiche per la VAS di un piano del sistema dei porti turistici della Sardegna. In Zoppi, C. (ed.) a cura di, Valutazione e pianificazione delle trasformazioni territoriali nei processi di governance. Sostenibilità ed e-governance nella pianificazione del territorio, Franco Angeli, Milano (2012)

Implementing Solutions for SECAP Transport Sector Towards Climate Neutrality

Luigi Santopietro[✉] and Francesco Scorza

School of Engineering, Laboratory of Urban and Regional Systems Engineering (LISUT),
University of Basilicata, Viale dell'Ateneo Lucano 10, 85100 Potenza, Italy
{luigi.santopietro,francesco.scorza}@unibas.it

Abstract. Transport sector is one of the pillars pursuits by the European Green Deal strategy in achieving the climate neutrality by 2050. One of the main aims is re-thinking transportation, as contributor to climate change, adopting a holistic approach towards the reduction of greenhouse gases (GHG) reduction. The authors define a methodological approach based on open-access data, for effective evaluation of CO_2 stock emitted by the private vehicle fleet for the Italian Municipalities. This approach is based on data describing the structure of the private vehicle fleet, distinguishing them according to vehicle class, age of construction or EURO classification. Hence, this framework supports the local administrators and local stakeholders in implementing place-based solutions for the reduction of the GHG emissions such as electric mobility, renovation of private vehicle fleet and support to sustainable mobility. The methodological approach was applied to three Municipalities in Southern Italy, highlighting common issues such as the relevant percentage of old vehicles and the lack of infrastructure serving sustainable mobility (bike lanes, electric recharge infrastructure, strengthening of public transport...). Results obtained represent an operative, support for local administrations in developing Sustainable Energy Action Plans in the framework of the Global Covenant of Mayors.

Keywords: Sustainable mobility · Covenant of mayors · SECAP · Voluntary-based planning · European policies

1 Introduction

European Union (EU) on December 2019 adopted the European Green Deal [1] as an ambitious package of measures to cut GHG gas emissions, in order to be the first climate-neutral continent. The European Council in March 2020 submitted its long-term strategy [2] to the UNFCCC presenting the European Climate Law and it has recognized that to meet the challenge of "net zero" GHG emission by 2050, actions should by undertaken by everyone in every aspect of society and the economy. The Green Deal Strategy (and its Acton Plan) re-thinks all the ways we contribute to climate change (manufacturing, transportation, heating) through a holistic approach, providing actions oriented to improve the well-being and the health of the European citizens. Transport sector is one of these pillars, contributing around 5% to EU GDP and employing more than 10 million people in Europe but at the same time, it is responsible of greenhouse gas and pollutant emissions, noise, road crashes and congestion. The Sustainable and Smart Mobility Strategy [3] facing these issues, chooses greening mobility as the new license for the transport sector to grow and support the transition to an efficient and interconnected multimodal transport system in Europe. In Sect. 2 is suggested a methodological approach based on open-access data, for effective evaluation of CO_2 stock emitted by the private vehicle fleet for the Italian Municipalities. In Sect. 3, the methodological approach was applied to three Municipalities in Southern Italy, highlighting common issues such as the relevant percentage of old vehicles and the lack of infrastructure serving sustainable mobility. In Sect. 4, results obtained represent a support for local administrations in providing and implementing solutions for Sustainable Energy Action Plans in the framework the Global Covenant of Mayors. Section 5 explains the conclusions and future perspectives of this research.

2   The Methodological Approach Applied to the Private Vehicle Fleet

The methodological approach proposed in this paper for the evaluation of CO_2 emission from the transport sector, is based on open-access data related to the fuel consumption using specific databases available in Italy. The database examined are:

- sales related to the annual oil consumption and the major oil products of the internal market, provided by the Italian Ministry of Ecological Transition. These data are divided for each Italian Province, specifying also the monthly sales;
- Vehicle fleet (cars, buses, two-wheelers, heavy and light-duty vehicles) in the territory of the Municipality and its Province searching on the Italian National Automotive Club (ACI) database;
- Vehicle fleet classification per year of registration and EURO classification provided by the Italian National Automotive Club (ACI) database;
- Data provided by UnipolSai and ACEA databases. The first was developed in 2018 by the Italian insurance company UnipolSai, the second was developed in 2019 by European Automobile Manufacturers' Association (ACEA)

The methodological approach is structured in two phases. The first is related to the computation of the fuel consumption (and related CO_2 emissions) for each Municipality classified per vehicles per type of power supply. The second phase is a validation of the first one, comparing results obtained by the methodological approach with UnipolSai and ACEA databases as meaningful check-step to the proposed methodology. The comparison of two phases highlights the level of accuracy and reliability of the methodological proposal.

The first phase is structured as follows:

1. The annual oil consumption per Province is divided for the number of vehicles per Province. The result is the fuel consumption expressed as the number of the fuel tons per Province vehicle.

2. ACI provides the vehicle fleet for each Italian Municipality but it does not classify the vehicles by type of power supply. In order to know this classification at Municipal level, it has computed the percentage of the vehicles divided per class (cars, buses, two-wheelers, heavy and light-duty vehicles) and type of power supply (gasoline, gasoline & lpg, gasoline and natural gas, diesel, lpg, electric) from the province classification of the vehicle fleet. This percentage has been considered constant for each Municipality inside the Province.
3. The percentages of the vehicles divided per class and type of power supply have been multiplied by the number of vehicles of the Municipality. The result is an estimation of the number of the vehicles classified for each class and type of power supply.
4. The fuel consumption per Province vehicle is multiplied by the number of the vehicles classified for each class and type of power supply. The result is the fuel consumption for each Municipality classified per vehicles per type of power supply.
5. The fuel consumption is transformed in CO_2 emission applying the standard factors proposed by Institute for Environmental Protection and Research (ISPRA) [4] in order to achieve the tons of CO_2 emitted for each type of power supply and for each class of vehicles.

The second phase of validation is based on the computation of CO_2 emissions by the following equation:

$$CO_2 \text{ emissions [ton]} = CO_2 \text{ average emission factor} \left[\frac{tonCO_2}{Km} \right] *$$
$$\text{Km driven (UnipolSai)*no. of total cars(methodological proposal)} \tag{1}$$

where the comparison is operated by the computation of Eq. 1 adopting the two CO_2 average emission factors suggested by UnipolSai and ACEA databases.

3   A Comparison of Three Small Municipalities

The methodological approach has been applied to three small Municipalities with specific features in Southern Italy (Basilicata Region): Castelsaraceno, Ginestra and Pietragalla. These three Municipalities are working on the development of their Sustainable Energy and Climate Action Plans (SECAPs), and the classification of the private vehicle fleet with related consumptions is part of the Baseline Emission Inventory (BEI) development. In detail the three Municipalities are:

• Castelsaraceno Municipality, (1274 inhabitants) is located in an inland area of Basilicata Region and the only transport infrastructure of the municipal territory is the road network, thus the CO_2 emissions has to be related only to the vehicle transport. Furthermore, the Municipality recently realized a tourism attraction according to the tourism development and since in August 2021 "The world's longest Tibetan bridge" operates in Castelsaraceno;
• Ginestra Municipality, (721 inhabitants) was selected because the 96% of its Municipal territory are forests or agricultural areas and as Castelsaraceno Municipality the only transport infrastructure is the road network. A particular feature is that Ginestra is one of *arbëreshe* Italian communities, a minority of ancient Albanian settlement;

- Pietragalla Municipality (3930 inhabitants) is one of industrial areas of Basilicata Region related to the production of building materials and food industries (olive oil and pasta). The Municipal territory is characterized by a main urban area with main public services and historical centre of Pietragalla, and three urban settlements dispersed in Municipal territory, where there are located other public services like schools. It was selected for the relevant contribution to transport emissions related to the mix of industrial activities and private transportation.

The methodological approach has been applied to the three Municipalities, classifying the private vehicle fleet according to the ACI year of registration compared to the relative percentage on overall private vehicle fleet and total cumulative count of private vehicles (see Fig. 1).

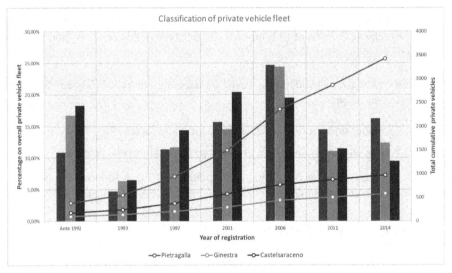

Fig. 1. Classification of vehicle fleet per year of registration to ACI compared to percentage on overall and total cumulative count of private vehicle fleet

Another classification of private vehicle fleet is the EURO classification, in order to understand which class of vehicle fleet needs intervention to produce less pollutant (see Fig. 2). An interesting remark coming from Figs. 1 and 2 is that EURO 5 and 6 vehicles represent for each of the three Municipalities a percentage under the 20% compared to the overall fleet.

In Fig. 3 are presented the total CO_2 emissions from the private vehicle fleet divided per classes and type of power supply as final step of the suggested methodology. Looking to the total CO_2 emissions, for each of the three Municipalities, diesel is the first power supply while other power supplies (i.e. Liquefied Petroleum Gas (LPG), Compressed Natural Gas (CNG) or Hybrid) are in percentage under the 10% of the total.

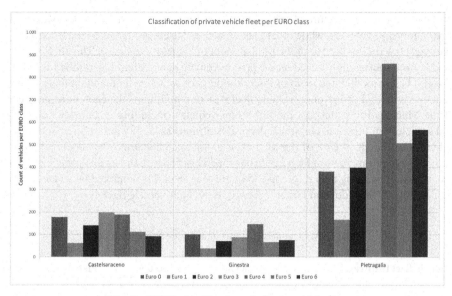

Fig. 2. EURO classification of private vehicle fleet

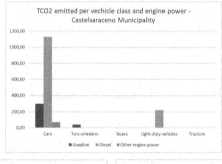

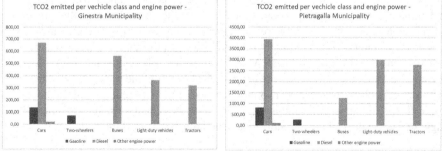

Fig. 3. Total CO_2 emissions from private vehicles of the three Municipalities divided per vehicle class and engine power

Considering the structure of vehicle fleet (see Table 1), cars are the majority class of it per number of vehicles, while other classes such as buses are characterized by percentages very low (under the 5% of the total amount of vehicles per class). This highlights a mode of transport mainly based on the private vehicle fleet, rather than public transport, also if it is remarkable that in all of three Municipalities for each inhabitant there is less than one vehicle. Furthermore, vehicle fleet structure highlights the economic structure of the Municipalities, through the light-duty vehicles (including essentially commercial vehicles) and tractors classes. Indeed, Castelsaraceno and Ginestra have light-duty vehicle class equal to 10% of the total class and it is characterized by an economy on craft and agriculture; contra Pietragalla has the industrial area and an economy based on production of building materials and food industries, and it is remarked by a percentage near to 20% of light-duty and tractor related to the total vehicle fleet.

Table 1. Vehicle fleet features of the three municipalities

Vehicle fleet features	Castelsaraceno	Ginestra	Pietragalla
Cars	831	459	2701
Two-wheelers	47	56	212
Buses	1	4	9
Light-duty vehicles	94	63	498
Tractors	0	3	26
Vehicle per inhabitants	0,770801	0,829404	0,887277

4 Improving Mobility in Sustainable Energy and Climate Action Plans

Sustainable Energy and Climate Action Plans (SECAPs) are voluntary plans developed by the Covenant of Mayors Signatories, in order to achieve and exceed the energy and climate targets submitted, towards the EU2050 objectives. The classification of the private vehicle fleet represents and related consumptions is an opportunity to investigate and promote interventions related to the transport sector. However, the planning of interventions is not the same for all Municipalities but it is related to specific features of each one Municipality, such as the geographical location, the transport infrastructure, the socio-economic structure or also the presence of tourist attractors that increase the traffic flows [5]. Thus, from the analysis of the vehicle fleet structure they have been suggested some possible interventions designed for the three Municipalities:

- For Castelsaraceno are suggested interventions on the renovation of private vehicle fleet (less of 10% of the cars are EURO 6) and promotion of transport by bus in order to reduce the touristic flows related to the operative period of Tibetan Bridge, that increases the number of visitors (about $50'000$ tourists for the period August-December 2021) and produces a variable emissions stock of 113 tCO_2 (see also [5]);

- For Ginestra are suggested interventions on the renovation of diesel vehicles (first producers of CO_2 emissions) with electric vehicles or supplied by LPG, CNG or hybrid and implementation of the transport infrastructure with green infrastructure based on bike lines and sustainable mobility oriented to the "net zero emissions";
- For Pietragalla is suggested the renovation of the vehicle fleet supporting the purchase of EURO 6 vehicles (supplied by LPG, CNG or hybrid) and electric vehicles. This renovation can be supported by Municipal financial support as the free recharge of electric vehicles or the reduction of ownership tax for LPG, CNG and hybrid vehicles. Furthermore, considering the urban settlements located in Municipal territory where there are public services as schools, these can be linked to the Pietragalla urban area, by a network of carpooling or car sharing

5 Conclusions

The adoption of the methodological approach to evaluate the structure of the private vehicle fleet and the total CO_2 emissions has allowed to establish a first assessment of the possible interventions oriented to reduce CO_2 emissions and greening the mobility demand. The analysis of the Municipal vehicle fleet highlighted a different interventions design, based on the specific features of each one Municipality. However, considering the private vehicle fleet of the three Municipalities, some common issues can be highlighted:

- A relevant number of vehicles powered by diesel motors and not in line with more recent normative (EURO 6) that need a restoration in order to achieve the foreword EU2030 objectives;
- The interventions provided should have as main target cars, considering that they are the first class for total CO_2 emissions of private vehicle fleet in all of the three Municipalities

In order to develop interventions related to the reduction of CO_2 emissions (not only referred to the transport sector), SECAPs represent an opportunity in supporting local actions related to energy and climate targets [6–8], and also a boost for the small Municipalities (as the three one considered in this research) in the domain of the planning. Also if previous researches remark the fruitful aspect of the sectorial approach [9–12], cities and territories should be evaluated as set of systems (such as green spaces, green infrastructures waterproofed soils, energy system [13], active mobility [14–17] etc.) achieving an "urban vision" [18]. Future perspectives of this research are related to the improvement of the methodological approach for the private vehicle fleet, the evaluation of touristic flows as the case of the Castelsaraceno, where the realization of a tourist attraction produced a surplus in terms of CO_2 transport emissions. Furthermore, interventions are related in designing interventions related to green infrastructure as the implementation of mitigation actions to reduce the CO_2 emissions.

References

1. European Commission: Communication from the Commission: The European Green Deal. Bruxelles (2019)
2. European Commission: Long-term low greenhouse gas emission development strategy of the European Union and its Member States. Bruxelles (2020)
3. European Commission: Putting European transport on track for the future. Brussels (2021)
4. Romano, D., et al.: Italian Greenhouse Gas Inventory 1990–2016. Institute for Environmental Protection and Research - Communications Area, Rome (2018)
5. Santopietro, L., Scorza, F., Murgante, B.: Multiple components in GHG stock of transport sector: technical improvements for SECAP baseline emissions inventory assessment. TeMA - J. L. Use, Mobil. Environ. **15**, 5–24 (2022). https://doi.org/10.6092/1970-9870/8391
6. Santopietro, L., Scorza, F., Rossi, A.: Small Municipalities Engaged in Sustainable and Climate Responsive Planning: Evidences from UE-CoM. In: Gervasi, O., et al. (eds.) ICCSA 2021. LNCS, vol. 12957, pp. 615–620. Springer, Cham (2021). https://doi.org/10.1007/978-3-030-87013-3_47
7. Bertoldi, P., Economidou, M., Palermo, V., Boza-Kiss, B., Todeschi, V.: How to finance energy renovation of residential buildings: review of current and emerging financing instruments in the EU. Wiley Interdiscip. Rev. Energy Environ. **10**, e384 (2021). https://doi.org/10.1002/WENE.384
8. Pietrapertosa, F., et al.: Urban climate change mitigation and adaptation planning: are Italian cities ready? Cities **91**, 93–105 (2019). https://doi.org/10.1016/j.cities.2018.11.009
9. Corrado, S., Giannini, B., Santopietro, L., Oliveto, G., Scorza, F.: Water Management and Municipal Climate Adaptation Plans: A Preliminary Assessment for Flood Risks Management at Urban Scale. In: Gervasi, O., et al. (eds.) ICCSA 2020. LNCS, vol. 12255, pp. 184–192. Springer, Cham (2020). https://doi.org/10.1007/978-3-030-58820-5_14
10. Santopietro, L., et al.: Geovisualization for Energy Planning. In: Gervasi, O., et al. (eds.) ICCSA 2020. LNCS, vol. 12252, pp. 479–487. Springer, Cham (2020). https://doi.org/10.1007/978-3-030-58811-3_35
11. Santopietro, L., Scorza, F.: A Place-Based Approach for the SECAP of Potenza Municipality: The Case of Green Spaces System. In: Gervasi, O., et al. (eds.) ICCSA 2020. LNCS, vol. 12255, pp. 226–234. Springer, Cham (2020). https://doi.org/10.1007/978-3-030-58820-5_18
12. Scorza, F., Santopietro, L., Giuzio, B., Amato, F., Murgante, B., Casas, G.L.: Conflicts Between Environmental Protection and Energy Regeneration of the Historic Heritage in the Case of the City of Matera: Tools for Assessing and Dimensioning of Sustainable Energy Action Plans (SEAP). In: Gervasi, O., et al. (eds.) ICCSA 2017. LNCS, vol. 10409, pp. 527–539. Springer, Cham (2017). https://doi.org/10.1007/978-3-319-62407-5_37
13. Scorza, F.: Towards self energy-management and sustainable citizens' engagement in local energy efficiency agenda. Int. J. Agric. Environ. Inf. Syst. **7**, 44–53 (2016). https://doi.org/10.4018/IJAEIS.2016010103
14. Scorza, F., Fortunato, G.: Cyclable cities: building feasible scenario through urban space morphology assessment. J. Urban Plan. Dev. **147**, 05021039 (2021). https://doi.org/10.1061/(asce)up.1943-5444.0000713
15. Scorza, F., Fortunato, G., Carbone, R., Murgante, B., Pontrandolfi, P.: Increasing urban walkability through citizens' participation processes. Sustain. **13**, 5835 (2021). https://doi.org/10.3390/su13115835
16. Fortunato, G., Scorza, F., Murgante, B.: Hybrid Oriented Sustainable Urban Development: A Pattern of Low-Carbon Access to Schools in the City of Potenza. In: Gervasi, O., et al. (eds.) ICCSA 2020. LNCS, vol. 12255, pp. 193–205. Springer, Cham (2020). https://doi.org/10.1007/978-3-030-58820-5_15

17. Scorza, F., Fortunato, G.: Active mobility oriented urban development: a morpho-syntactic scenario for mid-sized town. Eur. Plan. Stud. (2022). https://doi.org/10.1080/09654313.2022. 2077094

18. Scorza, F., Santopietro, L.: A systemic perspective for the sustainable energy and climate action plan (SECAP). Eur. Plan. Stud. 1–21 (2021). https://doi.org/10.1080/09654313.2021. 1954603

Tourism and Abandoned Inland Areas Development Demand: A Critical Appraisal

Rachele Gatto, Luigi Santopietro[(✉)] [ID], and Francesco Scorza[ID]

School of Engineering, Laboratory of Urban and Regional Systems Engineering (LISUT),
University of Basilicata, Viale dell'Ateneo Lucano 10, 85100 Potenza, Italy
rachelegatto@outlook.it, {luigi.santopietro,
francesco.scorza}@unibas.it

Abstract. Rural areas are those territories characterized by the depopulation phenomena in favor of central urban areas, constituting a generalized social cost linked to the abandonment of traditional land uses, hydrogeological risks, degradation and disappearance of traditions. The paper analyses relevant policies issues considering tourism as the main development perspective of such territories. According to a strategic view of the territory, local development projects focus on exploiting the potential of local production, creating daily actions, attracting tourists, promoting sustainable mobility, renewable energy and sustainable interventions, effective ecosystem management consequently reduction of social costs.

Keywords: Sustainable development · Inland areas · Tourism

1 Introduction

Rural inland areas are those territories significantly distant from urban centers and lacking of essential services (i.e. education, health and mobility) [1, 2] due to evolution processes of human settlement [3]. Rural areas are characterized by the depopulation phenomena in favor of central urban areas, constituting a generalized social cost linked to the abandonment of traditional land uses, hydrogeological risks, degradation and disappearance of traditions. The second post-war period, was characterized by the exodus from the countryside, causing a drop-in demand for public services, in the employment rate, and a reduction in the occupation of the territory. Consequences are that internal areas are not adequately exploited, there is insufficient maintenance and social problems are related to the lack of basic services [4, 5]. Through a polycentric interpretation of the territory [6–8], it is possible to explore the structure of the Italian country. A first infrastructure distinguishable, consists of a network of cities that extends over the whole territory constituting the center of essential services for the population. If we exclude the areas in close contact with the central urban center, the remaining part of the national territory is classified according to different degrees of peripherality. All areas that are more than 40 min away from the primary center are considered peripheral [9]. The peripheral areas have not been adopted the same public policies as the primary centers during the past. This is one of the criteria used to classify an aspect of rural in-land areas [10].

The research aims to analyze the results of the national guideline for the repopulation of places through: Sect. 1 - the definition of a national statistical-demographic framework in order to verify the feasibility of the proposal in relation to future scenarios; Sect. 2 - the cross-reading of the interventions carried out to verify the compliance of the objectives; Sect. 3 – The case study of Coletta di Castelbianco; Sect. 4 - Conclusion and discussion.

2 Depopulation and Italian Trends

Internal depopulation is an alarming phenomenon that has taken a back seat during the 1980s due to international migration and attention to the problems of the city, but still today it is important to talk about this. According to ISTAT data, in the year 2018 inter-municipal residence transfers are estimated at 1 million and 359 thousand. In the South of Italy, the balances are everywhere negative and the loss net population of the area is 65 thousand individuals. Only 5% of the Italian territory hosts 33% of people. In contrast, municipalities with low urbanization cover more than 70% of the country but host less than 25% of people. In total there are 6,943 municipalities in the national territory below 10,000 inhabitants in 2001. Depopulation includes complex socio-economic dynamics. The reasons for the move are studies opportunities and work; family reasons for inter-provincial ones; natural hazards.

The economic situation of Italy in the current period does not give any prospect of imminent growth as shows the trend of economic growth rates, considering the public debt and demographic data.

According to estimates and ISTAT data, Italian GDP is estimated to reach +0.1% at the end of 2019, placing last on the European scene if we consider that Ireland is at + 5.6%. Investments make up about 18% of GDP.

At the beginning of 2019, according to ISTAT data, it is estimated that the population more than 90 thousand out of 60 million residents (-1.5 per thousand), therefore an increase in the percentage of elderly population.

This implies a reduced capacity of the municipalities to invest large sums in ambitious requalification projects. However, a margin of growth is not excluded through lucid strategies and intervention policies.

Through a careful analysis of the places it is possible to recognize potentialities capable of stimulating the demand of investors and stakeholders and start a process of requalification with good prospects of economic recovery in the medium-long term. A particular case may be the redevelopment of places that are in a position considered strategic, but this is not guarantee an economically prosperous solution.

Other areas, even if they have interesting artifacts or potential environments, do not meet the minimum conditions for an intervention in economic terms.

An example is the ancient villages, especially in the south of the country, there are no convincing economic prospects based on the action of private operators.

Given the scarcity of investments and available resources, huge infrastructure works to improve the accessibility of inland areas are not taken into consideration because they represent a very risky investment with low return rate. Activating or triggering economic development processes based on local economies could prove effective in the short term, but does not ensure long-term effectiveness given the general frame of socio-economic trends.

Therefore, tourism as a driving force for triggering processes appears to be an attractive alternative with reduced short-term return of economic costs and an activity that has always yielded in our country rich in variety and beauty recognized all over the world [11–14].

The enhancement of the territory whose aim is tourism, concentrates activity and resources related on tourism itself. It is possible a positive variation of the residents of the area, but this does not imply a relevant endogenous development process. So, although there is economic growth, it could happen that there is a high risk that the problems associated with inadequate land use persist. An example would be the case of the 10 tourists who overwhelmed by an avalanche of mud in the Raganello gorges having one excursion were hit by an avalanche of mud due to the washing of the ground following the flood.

2.1 Strategies

The repopulation strategies adopted so far show a common line of action based on a more or less consolidated view of the internal areas. There are characteristics of the place that cannot be overlooked and are involved in the design process [15–17]. The strategies such as the selected proposal of this research start from the assumption that re-inhabiting the internal areas is the most suitable solution to overcome the problems caused by depopulation. They are distributed throughout the national territory and are concentrated on the Apennine and Alpine belt of national morphology. These areas are recognized for being difficult to access. It is the obvious and not negligible assumption of the territory.

The four projects, selected from the publication of "**Archipelago Italy, at the 2018 Architecture Biennale**" [18], are presented according to a renewed interpretation.

Archipelago Italia investigated how contemporary architecture approaches marginal areas, collecting a series of examples that stand out for their ability to dialogue with the local context and needs for the revitalization of territories.

The cases examined, in fact, were selected according to the type of key intervention to highlight the logic and processes that structure the hypothetical modus operandi. The hypothetical actors, the predominant actions that intervene in the project are extracted to be inserted in a scheme of relationships. Each case has its own structure and internal logic derived both from the potential of the territory and the built, from public or private clients, and from the analysis by the designer.

The selection criteria include: area located in the peripheral area as indicated by the Department of Development and Internal Cohesion (DPS); objective and purpose of the project for the territory and the development of the internal areas; presence of problems in the environmental and socio-demographic fields;

A further typological selection was carried out according to the projects that distinguished themselves in their field of action taking into consideration the purpose of the intervention and the subject dealt with.

Through the study and the deepening of the projects it is possible to identify four lines of action:

- intervention aimed at the enhancement of the territory with a tourist purpose;
- intervention to re-populate the abandoned places addressed towards a specific target of users;
- local interventions for urban development;
- urban and private recovery operations for a large user base;

Actions develop along a different timeline with diversified economic sources. The following selected proposal illustrate the strategy adopted for the redevelopment of the area with positive and negative implications and processes still under development.

3   The Case Study of Colletta di Castelbianco

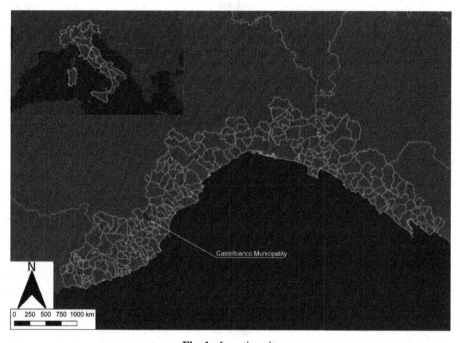

Fig. 1. Location site

The village of Colletta (see Fig. 1) was completely abandoned about two hundred years ago. During the second half of the nineties, it was the subject of intervention by the architect Giancarlo de Carlo on the initiative of a group of private investors.

Currently the village, after more than 20 years, has apartments for rent for short and long periods. Given the evocative landscape and the essence of the village, the project aims to re-inhabit this village in an innovative way by integrating the new telematic systems. Allow, therefore, those who will live there to work at a distance, isolated and enjoy the nature. This category of people are called "White eagles". The project is addressed to a specific category of users given the identifying characteristics of the space. The project follows the logic of the "crustacean", that is, to adapt the existing structure to the new typology of spaces focusing on the connection of the different environments. [19] The architect welcomes the challenge proposed by private investors in the transformation of the village to try to repopulate it and at the same time obtain an economic return. The project explores and manipulates the possibilities offered by the existing emerging a new theory that is detached from that of the "vertebrate" that had been adopted until then during the modern period. The structure that adapts to the space and not the space that adapts to the structure, revolutionizing the concept [19].

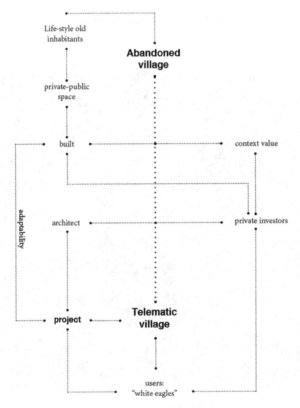

Fig. 2. Line of action

The project examined (see Fig. 2) is reported in their essential structure through the components that most influenced the design strategy and indirectly touched upon the design choices.

The guidelines for the in-land areas are based on a reading of the territory mainly for national statistical indexes and all the characters that highlight the polycentric structure comparing essential collective services for the city.

Obviously are involved the requests of the actors with the ultimate goal of repopulating these territories. The interpretation of the territory influences the design choices that will be mainly oriented to an economic "trigger" by setting up an engine of development such as tourism or retail. Tourist could mediate the phenomenon.

Tourism is one of the appropriate solutions for in-land rural areas, but a failure to control development that focuses on the number of visitors and not on the quality of the services offered can negatively impact the environment and the landscape. Faced with the growing increase in global mass tourism, this can be a risky and credible prospect. The moment the tourism is not integrated with a system of equilibrium of the inhabitants of the place the place itself will be disposable manifesting deficiencies in the care of the territory.

The almost total absence of public investments and the scarcity of actions on the landscape constitute a further junction point.

4 Discussions and Conclusions

The strategy adopted in the first case focuses on the enhancement of the territory. Therefore, it is mainly addressed to the promotion of tourism. The second case, although the project addresses a complex issue, the re-population strategy is addressed to a particular target of users by creating a new population center. The third case analyzed is an intervention mainly carried out by the private individual who follows the requests of the client but at the same time has the strength to generate urban development. The last case deals with securing the existing building by creating a new urbanity for a specific type of user.

Although the characteristics of the landscape are mentioned and all the problems that derive from it, none focuses on the analysis and deepening of value. It is assumed that action on the territory for repopulation can mediate all the problems caused by it.

All the projects present a component aimed at increasing tourism, a source of development together with the identification of a specific user target.

That tourism is an engine for the economy is a fact, represents a resource for the country if we consider that it constitutes 6% of national GDP. But what happens if a territory is purely conceived as a tourist place? A useful index to monitor the phenomenon could be the percentage of resident population compared to the average tourist presence.

In this case, directing the offer to a specific type of tourist could mediate the phenomenon.

Tourism is one of the appropriate solutions for in-land rural areas, but a failure to control development that focuses on the number of visitors and not on the quality of the services offered can negatively impact the environment and the landscape. Faced with the growing increase in global mass tourism, this can be a risky and credible prospect. The moment the tourism is not integrated with a system of equilibrium of the inhabitants of the place and the place itself will be disposable manifesting deficiencies in the care of the territory.

According to a strategic view of the territory [15, 20–22], local development projects focus on exploiting the potential of local production, creating daily actions, attracting tourists, promoting sustainable mobility [23–26], renewable energy and sustainable interventions [27–30], effective ecosystem management [31, 32] consequently reduction of social costs (hydro-geological structure; soil maintenance; protection of biological diversity).

References

1. Carbone, R., et al.: Using Open Data and Open Tools in Defining Strategies for the Enhancement of Basilicata Region. In: Gervasi, O., et al. (eds.) ICCSA 2018. LNCS, vol. 10964, pp. 725–733. Springer, Cham (2018). https://doi.org/10.1007/978-3-319-95174-4_55
2. Casas, G.L., Lombardo, S., Murgante, B., Pontrandolfi, P., Scorza, F.: Open data for territorial specialization assessment territorial specialization in attracting local development funds: an assessment. Procedure based on open data and open tools. TeMA - J. L. Use. Mobil. Environ. (2014). https://doi.org/10.6092/1970-9870/2557
3. Paternariato: accordo di: Strategia nazionale per le Aree interne: definizione, obiettivi, strumenti e. 4–7 (2020)
4. Scorza, F., Pilogallo, A., Saganeiti, L., Murgante, B., Pontrandolfi, P.: Comparing the territorial performances of renewable energy sources' plants with an integrated ecosystem services loss assessment: A case study from the Basilicata region (Italy). Sustain. Cities Soc. **56**, 102082 (2020). https://doi.org/10.1016/j.scs.2020.102082
5. Scorza, F., Casas, G.L.: Territorial Specialization in Attracting Local Development Funds: An Assessment Procedure Based on Open Data and Open Tools. In: Murgante, B., et al. (eds.) ICCSA 2014. LNCS, vol. 8580, pp. 750–757. Springer, Cham (2014). https://doi.org/10.1007/978-3-319-09129-7_54
6. Curatella, L., Scorza, F.: Polycentrism and Insularity Metrics for In-Land Areas. In: Gervasi, O., et al. (eds.) ICCSA 2020. LNCS, vol. 12255, pp. 253–261. Springer, Cham (2020). https://doi.org/10.1007/978-3-030-58820-5_20
7. Curatella, L., Scorza, F.: Una valutazione della struttura policentrica dell'insediamento nella regione basilicata. LaborEst. **0**, 37–42 (2020). https://doi.org/10.19254/LaborEst.20.06
8. Corrado, S., Scorza, F.: Machine learning based approach to assess territorial marginality. In: Lecture Notes in Computer Science. Springer (2022)
9. Acierno, A.: Pianificare paesaggi marginali: le aree interne del cilento. BDC. Boll. Del Cent. Calza Bini. **15**, 211–231 (2015). https://doi.org/10.6092/2284-4732/3779
10. Casas, G.L., Scorza, F.: Discrete Spatial Assessment of Multi-parameter Phenomena in Low Density Region: The Val D'Agri Case. In: Gervasi, O., et al. (eds.) ICCSA 2015. LNCS, vol. 9157, pp. 813–824. Springer, Cham (2015). https://doi.org/10.1007/978-3-319-21470-2_59
11. Scorza, F., Pilogallo, A., Las Casas, G.: Investigating Tourism Attractiveness in Inland Areas: Ecosystem Services, Open Data and Smart Specializations. In: Calabrò, F., Della Spina, L., Bevilacqua, C. (eds.) ISHT 2018. SIST, vol. 100, pp. 30–38. Springer, Cham (2019). https://doi.org/10.1007/978-3-319-92099-3_4
12. Pilogallo, A., Saganeiti, L., Scorza, F., Las Casas, G.: Tourism Attractiveness: Main Components for a Spacial Appraisal of Major Destinations According with Ecosystem Services Approach. In: Gervasi, O., et al. (eds.) ICCSA 2018. LNCS, vol. 10964, pp. 712–724. Springer, Cham (2018). https://doi.org/10.1007/978-3-319-95174-4_54
13. Pilogallo, A., et al.: Geotourism as a specialization in the territorial context of the basilicata region (Southern Italy). Geoheritage **11**(4), 1435–1445 (2019). https://doi.org/10.1007/s12371-019-00396-9
14. Scorza, F., Fortino, Y., Giuzio, B., Murgante, B., Las Casas, G.: Measuring Territorial Specialization in Tourism Sector: The Basilicata Region Case Study. In: Gervasi, O., et al. (eds.) ICCSA 2017. LNCS, vol. 10409, pp. 540–553. Springer, Cham (2017). https://doi.org/10.1007/978-3-319-62407-5_38
15. Casas, G.L., Scorza, F.: Sustainable Planning: A Methodological Toolkit. In: Gervasi, O., et al. (eds.) ICCSA 2016. LNCS, vol. 9786, pp. 627–635. Springer, Cham (2016). https://doi.org/10.1007/978-3-319-42085-1_53

16. Dvarioniene, J., Grecu, V., Lai, S., Scorza, F.: Four Perspectives of Applied Sustainability: Research Implications and Possible Integrations. In: Gervasi, O., et al. (eds.) ICCSA 2017. LNCS, vol. 10409, pp. 554–563. Springer, Cham (2017). https://doi.org/10.1007/978-3-319-62407-5_39

17. Las Casas, G., Scorza, F., Murgante, B.: Razionalità a-priori: una proposta verso una pianificazione antifragile. Sci. Reg. Ital. J. Reg. Sci. **18**, 329–338 (2019). https://doi.org/10.14650/93656

18. Cucinella, M.: Arcipelago Italia Progetti per il futuro dei territori interni del Paese. Padiglione Italia alla Biennale Architettura 2018. (2018)

19. De Carlo, G.: Overview of plans to restore abandoned Italian village. Archit. Rev. **197**, 83–88 (1995)

20. Las Casas, G., Scorza, F.: A Renewed Rational Approach from Liquid Society Towards Antifragile Planning. In: Gervasi, O., et al. (eds.) ICCSA 2017. LNCS, vol. 10409, pp. 517–526. Springer, Cham (2017). https://doi.org/10.1007/978-3-319-62407-5_36

21. Pontrandolfi, P., Scorza, F.: Sustainable Urban Regeneration Policy Making: Inclusive Participation Practice. In: Gervasi, O., et al. (eds.) ICCSA 2016. LNCS, vol. 9788, pp. 552–560. Springer, Cham (2016). https://doi.org/10.1007/978-3-319-42111-7_44

22. Scorza, F., Casas, G.L., Murgante, B.: Overcoming Interoperability Weaknesses in e-Government Processes: Organizing and Sharing Knowledge in Regional Development Programs Using Ontologies. In: Lytras, M.D., Ordonez de Pablos, P., Ziderman, A., Roulstone, A., Maurer, H., Imber, J.B. (eds.) WSKS 2010. CCIS, vol. 112, pp. 243–253. Springer, Heidelberg (2010). https://doi.org/10.1007/978-3-642-16324-1_26

23. Scorza, F., Fortunato, G.: Cyclable cities: building feasible scenario through urban space morphology assessment. J. Urban Plan. Dev. **147**, 05021039 (2021). https://doi.org/10.1061/(asce)up.1943-5444.0000713

24. Fortunato, G., Scorza, F., Murgante, B.: Hybrid Oriented Sustainable Urban Development: A Pattern of Low-Carbon Access to Schools in the City of Potenza. In: Gervasi, O., et al. (eds.) ICCSA 2020. LNCS, vol. 12255, pp. 193–205. Springer, Cham (2020). https://doi.org/10.1007/978-3-030-58820-5_15

25. Scorza, F., Fortunato, G.: Active mobility oriented urban development: a morpho-syntactic scenario for mid-sized town. Eur. Plan. Stud. (2022). https://doi.org/10.1080/09654313.2022.2077094

26. Scorza, F., Fortunato, G., Carbone, R., Murgante, B., Pontrandolfi, P.: Increasing urban walkability through citizens' participation processes. Sustain. **13**, 5835 (2021). https://doi.org/10.3390/su13115835

27. Scorza, F., Santopietro, L.: A systemic perspective for the sustainable energy and climate action plan (SECAP). Eur. Plan. Stud. 1–21 (2021). https://doi.org/10.1080/09654313.2021.1954603

28. Santopietro, L., Scorza, F.: The Italian experience of the covenant of mayors: A territorial evaluation. Sustain. **13**, 1–23 (2021). https://doi.org/10.3390/su13031289

29. Santopietro, L., Scorza, F., Murgante, B.: Multiple components in GHG stock of transport sector: technical improvements for SECAP baseline emissions inventory assessment. TeMA - J. L. Use. Mobil. Environ. **15**, 5–24 (2022). https://doi.org/10.6092/1970-9870/8391

30. Scorza, F.: Towards self energy-management and sustainable citizens' engagement in local energy efficiency agenda. Int. J. Agric. Environ. Inf. Syst. **7**, 44–53 (2016). https://doi.org/10.4018/IJAEIS.2016010103

31. Pilogallo, A., Scorza, F.: Mapping regulation ecosystem services specialization in Italy. J. Urban Plan. Dev. **148**, 4021072 (2022). https://doi.org/10.1061/(asce)up.1943-5444.0000801

32. Pilogallo, A., Saganeiti, L., Scorza, F., Murgante, B.: Ecosystem services' based impact assessment for low carbon transition processes. tema-journal l. use mobil. Environ. (2019)

Roghudi: Developing Knowledge of the Places in an Abandoned Inland Municipality

Rachele Gatto, Luigi Santopietro$^{(\boxtimes)}$ 🆔, and Francesco Scorza🆔

School of Engineering, Laboratory of Urban and Regional Systems Engineering (LISUT), University of Basilicata, Viale dell'Ateneo Lucano 10, 85100 Potenza, Italy

`{luigi.santopietro,francesco.scorza}@unibas.it`

Abstract. Inland rural regions are territories quite distant from the welfare of urban centers and are positioned far away from the established infrastructure network of the country. Demographic trends, despite the availability of natural resources, entail marginalization, abandonment, and depopulation mainly due to socio-economic changes. The considerable social cost of traditions that disappear also implies, for example, degradation of land use and hydrogeological instability. In recent years, different types of strategies aimed at reversing such demographic trend, mostly based on tourism economy, but sometimes they revealed cons as destructive as abandonment itself. The case study of Roghudi, gave us the opportunity to remark the importance of perceiving landscape as starting phase of the design process. Formal and informal knowledge of the places, are assumed as a key to read values of inland abandoned places, in order to structure a development scenario recovering the balance between man and nature.

Keywords: Landscape urbanism · Inland areas · Rural areas · Abandonment

1 Introduction

On an ever-increasing number of degraded and abandoned territories, connected with the implementation of national environmental programs, new territorial issues are opened. James Corner in landscape architecture, in order to engage policies and programs, tackle the notion of landscape shifting from being a manifestation of culture to an instrument of education [1].

For over two decades, mappings the ecosystems values [2–4] are the basic tools to open new frontiers in strategic local development [5–8] planning proposing new methodological approaches linking environmental, social-economic and temporal dynamics [9]. Considering the landscape as a set of elements and structures that change over time in close relation to each other, his vision changed. Along this perspective emerges the awareness of the landscape seen as a public space, where landscapers acquire an increasingly important role in urban planning [10]. The intertwining of ecology, landscape and urban planning moves research into a new field called Landscape Urbanism. Widespread thanks to the contribution of Charles Waldheim and James Corner since the late 1990s. Landscape urbanism describes a disciplinary realignment currently underway

O. Gervasi et al. (Eds.): ICCSA 2022 Workshops, LNCS 13382, pp. 48–53, 2022.
https://doi.org/10.1007/978-3-031-10592-0_5

in which landscape replaces architecture as the basic building block of contemporary urbanism. For many, across a range of disciplines, landscape has become both the lens through which the contemporary city is represented and the medium through which is constructed [11].

The new paradigms are created by a first recognition of reality as a complex system of social dynamics, changes in space over time. The relationship is a constant that affects the interaction between human activities and the landscape where space is the background of social activities that can be foreseen but also not foreseen. The protagonist is therefore the landscape and the place understood as the place of the relationship. Is abandoned the idea of the *genius loci* understood as a static character and where the presumed identity of the place predominates in favor of a *genius itineris* [9]. Landscape urbanism therefore provides the tools, drawing from its interdisciplinary lexicon, to formulate a project in contemporary space. Promote an ecological approach to the project, first of all to understand the space and then to formulate a dynamic and non-static system. The protagonists are the places in a state of neglect and discomfort where there are no conditions for combining a future anthropic repopulation, but only a strategy to cure the landscape, which seemed inevitably marked by degradation. The symbiosis between architecture and landscape architecture is articulated by the network together with economy, between form and social, and provide an alternative to the crisis condition of the territories also marked by climate change that took the modern movement by surprise. Although the theory has not found much success due to a perspective anchored to the margins of growth and development, landscape urbanism is proposed as a realistic alternative to the future for a construction of healthier and more sustainable spaces [6].

Good intentions aside, the urban planning of the landscape presents some enigmatic points that do not favor the reading and the exact understanding of the method of action. The methodology used for urban planning up to the nineties, even if static and limiting that used tools such as zooning, provided a clear and ineluctable model. The contradictions and conjectures advanced in the 90s persist in the modern era even if the advanced questions no longer arise from the rigid scheme of traditional urbanism. In fact, in the project *"Parc de la Villette" by Rem Koolhaas* it is possible to notice a change in urban planning that is composed of dynamic and de-hierarchical flows.

This paper addresses a structural reading of the marginal territories [12, 13] through the elaboration of a conceptual knowledge structure, better described in Sect. 2. In Sect. 3 Roghudi Municipality is proposed as case study while in Sect. 4, open discussions remark the importance of perceiving landscape as starting phase of the design process.

2 Perception, Knowledge, Design

The purpose of an approach does not propose a model of action but a methodology that is inserted before the design itself. An interaction between more or less defined variables that propose a reading of the territory far from the objective of establishing a productive activity or creating obligatory urban lines for a specific type of user. Given the more or less common characteristics of the internal areas, the algorithm starts from assumptions related to the morphology of the territory and therefore a large-scale vision of the whole site. The goal is to provide a different interpretation that stands out from the national strategy to imagine new developments in the territory. The interdependent variables between them do not follow a given flow in a hierarchical order but navigate together and take on different meanings in relation to the case study.

Starting from urban ecology, therefore, a type of approach oriented towards the care of the territory is formulated to improve the quality of the livability of the environment and mediate the problems caused by depopulation. Given its "address", this does not provide a static and unidirectional methodology and does not replace the designer's interpretation, which in this case is he who selects and defined better the processes. The open strategy considers an essential truth: time. The margin within which dynamics will certainly develop (Fig. 1).

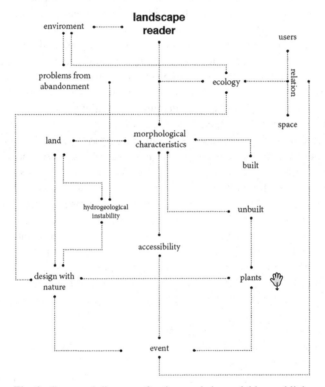

Fig. 1. Structural diagram of action made by variables and links

3   Landscape as Process

The maps and observations of the territory are part of a complex relationship network where the individual elements and themes develop according to an un-predictable and non-linear trend in a relationship of interdependence. This line of action is made by several variables such as: land form, landslides, accessibility, use, plants and design with nature.

Fig. 2. Roghudi municipality landscape

In order to apply the theoretical notion exposed to a real case study, the municipality of Roghudi (see Fig. 2) is the appropriate example for this purpose. At the extreme southern border of the Italian boot, an archipelago of villages on the slopes of the Aspromonte witnesses a gradual and progressive depopulation. Roghudi, the ghost town of the surroundings, has some very peculiar characteristics for a land-scape intervention aimed above all at remedying the hydro-geological instability through the natural vocation redesign of the landscape that presents critical points. This case study represents an opportunity for reflection on the modality of intervention in the inland rural areas starting from the point of view of the landscape. The town is part of the "Grecanica region" mainly composed by Bova, Roghudi Vecchio, Gallicianò, Condofuri, Roccaforte del Greco in an infrastructure network.

In the process of building knowledge of the places, the network of relationships between material things and immaterial things structures the schedule. Material and immaterial are linked by a transversal reading at different scales of the place examined. Material, we can define, all that is visible and perceptible that materializes in a form. Immaterial is configured as the network between actors and actions in the space that can be identified and associated through elements on the territory, however they do not express and define the identifying characteristics.

The methodology that draws inspiration from the paradigms of landscape urbanism and the ecology of the landscape involves multiple scales, starting from the local one that interfaces with the ecosystem of the place. The knowledge phase consists of a part of direct observation of the space, gathering useful information on how public places are lived. Four categories of uses can be defined around Roghudi. Although the Municipality is officially abandoned and so there is no permanent presence of the inhabitants, some elements suggest sporadic practices within the territory. These customs are not formalizable or recognizable through a plan, but it can be perceived only by observing the territory.

To distinguish the different practices that take place, it is appropriate to insert classification criteria such as the time spent during the day, the type in relation to the actions that take place and the agents provocateurs. The main street of Roccaforte del Greco delimited by private dwellings is the place where the collective and social dimension of the inhabited area is usually manifested.

Public space is the place where ordinary collective practices take place characterized by socially recognized, temporary and reversible actions. It can be perceived as a place of exchange, a place of passage, a scenario for exchanging ideas and knowledge but also a place for hosting community events such as public events or celebrations. The traffic, the elements of the private subjects drawn at the edge of the road (lying linen, planting, lighting, religious signs, near the entrance of the houses) indicate an active and continuous use.

4 Open Remarks

The methodology represented does not want to constitute a single and general reading to be applied to all peripheral areas. It constitutes a possible guideline for territorial analysis and understanding territories. Main while, the inland rural area presents common characteristics that reveals specific problems related depending on the environment and interactions between anthropic and natural components of the landscape,.one of these is the hydrogeological instability, also caused by the depopulation process. So, landslides and floods are often present and constitute a cost for the territory and the population that lives in the places, albeit sporadically. The morphology of the territory, in Italy, can be seen as influencing the isolation and marginality of places due to difficult access. Within the proposed strategy, there are keywords that we will call project variables:

- The morphology, understood as a form, can be examined according to two variables belonging to two different elements;
- The soil is a complex physical resource not only for the physical-chemical and biological processes that develop within it;
- the built environment as result of the transformations that man has operated.

McHarg in "Design with nature" recognizes the initial phase of observation of the territory as an important moment. Designing with nature consists of a series of controlled actions that start from the territory and incorporate a series of integrated disciplines that enrich the formal vocabulary and provide the necessary knowledge to design in a conscious manner considering the variables in the perspective of social sustainability, economic, environmental.

References

1. Kullmann, K.: Design with (human) nature: recovering the creative instrumentality of social data in urban design. J. Urban Des. **24**, 165–182 (2019). https://doi.org/10.1080/13574809. 2018.1433530
2. Pilogallo, A., Saganeiti, L., Scorza, F., Las Casas, G.: Tourism attractiveness: main components for a spacial appraisal of major destinations according with ecosystem services approach. In: Gervasi, O., et al. (eds.) ICCSA 2018. LNCS, vol. 10964, pp. 712–724. Springer, Cham (2018). https://doi.org/10.1007/978-3-319-95174-4_54
3. Pilogallo, A., Saganeiti, L., Scorza, F., Murgante, B.: Ecosystem services' based impact assessment for low carbon transition processes. TEMA-J. L. Use Mobil. Environ. **12**, 127–138 (2019)
4. Pilogallo, A., Scorza, F.: Mapping regulation ecosystem services specialization in Italy. J. Urban Plan. Dev. **148**, 4021072 (2022)
5. Scorza, F., Saganeiti, L., Pilogallo, A., Murgante, B.: Ghost planning: the inefficiency of energy sector policies in a low population density region. Arch. Di Stud. Urbani E Reg. **127**(Suppl. 1), 34–55 (2020)
6. Las Casas, G., Scorza, F., Murgante, B.: New urban agenda and open challenges for urban and regional planning. In: Calabrò, F., Della Spina, L., Bevilacqua, C. (eds.) ISHT 2018. SIST, vol. 100, pp. 282–288. Springer, Cham (2019). https://doi.org/10.1007/978-3-319-92099-3_33
7. Las Casas, G., Scorza, F.: A renewed rational approach from liquid society towards anti-fragile planning. In: Gervasi, O., et al. (eds.) ICCSA 2017. LNCS, vol. 10409, pp. 517–526. Springer, Cham (2017). https://doi.org/10.1007/978-3-319-62407-5_36
8. Las Casas, G., Scorza, F., Murgante, B.: Conflicts and sustainable planning: peculiar instances coming from val d'agri structural inter-municipal plan. In: Papa, R., Fistola, R., Gargiulo, C. (eds.) Smart Planning: Sustainability and Mobility in the Age of Change. GET, pp. 163–177. Springer, Cham (2018). https://doi.org/10.1007/978-3-319-77682-8_10
9. Padoa-schioppa, C.: La mente ecologica del Landscape Urbanism. Paesaggi Costieri **15**, 230–239 (2017). https://doi.org/10.13128/RV-22012
10. Corner, J.: Recovering Landscape : Essays in Contemporary Landscape Architecture. Princeton Architectural Press (1999)
11. Waldheim, C., Waldheim, J.E.I.P.C.L.A.C., Berger, A.: The Landscape Urbanism Reader. Princeton Architectural Press (2006)
12. Scorza, F., Santopietro, L., Giuzio, B., Amato, F., Murgante, B., Casas, G.L.: Conflicts between environmental protection and energy regeneration of the historic heritage in the case of the city of matera: tools for assessing and dimensioning of sustainable energy action plans (SEAP). In: Gervasi, O., et al. (eds.) ICCSA 2017. LNCS, vol. 10409, pp. 527–539. Springer, Cham (2017). https://doi.org/10.1007/978-3-319-62407-5_37
13. Casas, G.L., Scorza, F.: Discrete spatial assessment of multi-parameter phenomena in low density region: the Val D'Agri case. In: Gervasi, O., et al. (eds.) ICCSA 2015. LNCS, vol. 9157, pp. 813–824. Springer, Cham (2015). https://doi.org/10.1007/978-3-319-21470-2_59

A First Financial Assessment of SEAP Public Energy Interventions Performance Through Municipal Budget

Luigi Santopietro[1]([⊠]) [ID], Silvia Solimene[2] [ID], Ferdinando Di Carlo[3] [ID],
Manuela Lucchese[4] [ID], Francesco Scorza[1] [ID], and Beniamino Murgante[1] [ID]

[1] School of Engineering, Laboratory of Urban and Regional Systems Engineering (LISUT),
University of Basilicata, Viale dell'Ateneo Lucano 10, 85100 Potenza, Italy
{luigi.santopietro,francesco.scorza,
Beniamino.murgante}@unibas.it
[2] School of Engineering, University of Basilicata, Viale dell'Ateneo Lucano 10, 85100 Potenza,
Italy
silvia.solimene@unibas.it
[3] Department of Mathematics, Computer Science and Economics, University of Basilicata,
Viale dell'Ateneo Lucano 10, 85100 Potenza, Italy
ferdinando.dicarlo@unibas.it
[4] Department of Economics, University of Campania "Luigi Vanvitelli", Capua, Italy
manuela.lucchese@unicampania.it

Abstract. The European volunteer initiative of local administrators Covenant of Mayors (CoM) launched in 2008, set by 2020 the first deadline in achieving the emission reduction target of 20% CO_2 compared to 1990 levels. Each CoM signatory developed a Sustainable Energy Action Plan (SEAP), designing energy efficiency interventions. This first CoM commitment period (2008–2020) has highlighted a relevant engagement (63% of the total CoM signatories) of "small" Municipalities (i.e. under 10, 000 inhabitants), particularly in Italy and Spain. The aim of the research, is to propose a monitoring methodology for the assessment of the impacts of SECAP in local Municipality comparing CO_2 emission achievements with municipal budget analysis. Focusing on three Italian small Municipalities (two CoM signatories and one no-CoM), the research explores investments related to the public energy efficiency interventions on the Municipal budget. The selected case studies allowed to verify if SECAP represents or not an effective driver to boost energy transition in small municipalities. In this view achieved results have been compared, in order to highlight the main outcomes, and emphasizes how is the impact of the CoM initiative and how are the differences in terms of expenditure allocated and interventions planned by three sample Municipalities.

Keywords: SEAP · Municipal budget · Energy efficiency · Small municipalities

1   Introduction

The European initiative of Covenant of Mayors (CoM) is a voluntary initiative started in 2008, gathering European Mayors and local administrators with the ambition to tackle the "20-20-20" targets provided by 2020 climate & energy package [1]. The initiative in 2016 expanded its geographical coverage from European countries to worldwide, becoming the Global Covenant of Mayors (GCoM). GCoM is the result of the joining between CoM and Compact of Mayors, coupling energy targets with climate ones. Thus, looking at the temporal coverage of the CoM it is possible to distinguish two seasons characterized by different commitments: the first (2008–2020) pursued the targets provided by the 2020 climate & energy package, while the second (2020-ongoing) is pursuing the targets provided by the European Green Deal [2]. In this scenario, previous research [3, 4] highlighted that the majority of CoM signatories are "small" Municipalities (i.e. under 10.000 inhabitants) classified as XS Signatories by CoM; and coming from Italy and Spain. These CoM Signatories developed in the first period a Sustainable Energy Action Plan (SEAP) and now are developing a Sustainable Energy and Climate Action Plan (SECAP). These plans contain structured public and private interventions, related to energy efficiency and climate adaptation/mitigation related to a set of sectors (for example residential buildings, transport, and public lighting). In order to evaluate these interventions also from a financial perspective, the Municipalities' budgets have been analysed. In detail, this research focuses on three small municipalities in Basilicata Region (Italy): Castelsaraceno, Ginestra and Pietragalla. These are three small Municipalities, where Castelsaraceno and Pietragalla are CoM Municipalities while Ginestra is no-COM and is ongoing to become a CoM signatory. The aim of the research is to investigate the impact of the CoM initiative on Municipalities compared to non-CoM ones, in supporting and developing public energy efficiency investments. The structure of the research provided in Sect. 2, details of the databases investigated for the analysis of the Municipal budgets highlighting the share of public investments according to the CoM membership; Sect. 3 is related to the comparison of the investments planned in Municipal budgets related; Sect. 4 the main outcomes have presented an opening to the future perspectives of the research.

2   Dataset Investigated

Italian Local Governments (these include municipalities, provinces, mountain communities or associations) draw up their annual budget, which is the main vehicle for authorising expenditure [5]. However, in the last decade, several legislative initiatives have profoundly changed the accounting system of Italian Local Governments (LGs), first among equals, the Decree 118/2011. In order to achieve the aim of this research, the authors analysed the budget data in two different time frames: the first for the years from 2005–2015 and the second from 2016–2021. Although the reform has largely changed the presentation of balance sheet items, we have identified some similarities between macro-categories, allowing comparisons to be easily made (see Table 1).

The authors selected three databases detailing the public interventions and investments for Castelsaraceno, Ginestra and Pietragalla. Databases are:

Table 1. Comparison of municipalities budget items (Source: "Open Bilanci" database)

Categories in the first-time frame (2005–2015)		Categories in the second time frame (2016–2021)	
Education	Expenditure for school services and maintenance of buildings owned-excluding kindergartens	*Education and the right to study*	Amount of all expenditure on education and school buildings (excluding kindergartens)
Public lighting	Expenses for public lighting installations	*Energy and diversification of energy sources*	Expenditure on administration and operation of activities and services relating to the use of energy sources, including electricity and natural gas
Public buildings	Expenditure on public housing, on the operation of offices, on the provision of benefits to citizens in need, and on the construction and maintenance of facilities	*Public and local housing and social housing plans*	Expenses for the construction, purchase and renovation of public and social housing

1. "Open Bilanci" a public web-database with a temporal coverage from 2005–2021 where Italian municipal budgets are collected and detailed in terms of investments, expenditure and interventions related to several sectors (road maintenance, public lighting and public buildings.)
2. "Open CUP" a public web-database with a temporal coverage since the 1990s, where there are all public investments planned by Italian Municipalities. These investments are detailed in terms of financial support (public and private), and sectors
3. CoM database, provided by CoM official website, where it is possible to examine CoM signatories and perform advanced searches on them such as the region of origin, population, SECAP sectors, and CO_2 emissions target.

Examining the "Open Bilanci" database, the cash management principle has been selected for data collection. It considers the revenue and expenditure that the municipality has received (collections) and paid (payments) during the year, regardless of the year in which the receivables (assessments) and payables (commitments) arose. In particular, we have chosen to analyse the investment expenditure item, which details the payments actually made for each mission or intervention, i.e. it consists of all the costs that the municipality incurs for the purchase of real estate or the construction of infrastructure and long-term projects in the municipality. The result also includes the so-called *residual liabilities*, which represent the debts of the municipal authority, i.e. expenditure committed but not paid during the year.

"OpenCUP" makes data available to all public and private bodies, in an open format. This data relates to public investment decisions obtained with national, community or regional public funds or with private resources registered with the Unique Project Code (CUP). The CUP is the code that identifies a public investment project and is the key tool for the functioning of the Public Investment Monitoring System (MIP).

Analyzing the CoM database, in May 2022, it counts 10977 Signatory and 71% of them have submitted to CoM an Action Plan. Considering the Signatories with an Action Plan submitted, 67% of them are classified by CoM as XS Municipalities (i.e. with a resident population under 10000 inhabitants). This majority of XS Municipalities is proved considering that Italy is at first place among CoM Countries in terms of XS CoM Signatories (no. 3999), followed by Spain (no. 2288). Italy and Spain both represent over 90% of the whole XS Municipality class. However, this relevant engagement of XS Municipalities has set a CO_2 emissions target reduction in the range of 20–30%, close to the 20% of 20-20-20 target, but far from the current target (55%) provided by the European Green Deal. In order to understand how the relevance of public interventions is planned by the CoM signatories, the authors evaluated the occurrences of the SEAP/SECAP sectors. Results from the CoM database, highlight that XS Signatories have a preferential interest in developing actions related to sectors basically "public" like public lighting or municipal building equipment facilities. Instead, considering "private" sectors (involving not only public actors but also a private company, stakeholders etc..), there is a relevant development of interventions related to the improvement of the energy production (including r.e.s. technologies) and energy efficiency of the buildings toward the green transition.

3 The Comparison of the Public Investments in the Municipal Budget

The authors have selected three small municipalities Castelsaraceno, Ginestra and Pietragalla, located in Basilicata Region, Southern Italy (see Fig. 1).

These Municipalities have been selected according to specific features:

- Castelsaraceno is located in an inland area of Basilicata Region between two National parks (Pollino and Appennino Lucano Val d'Agri Lagonegrese National Parks) linked since August 2021 by the "The world's longest Tibetan bridge". It is a CoM signatory since 2012 and it developed its SEAP in 2013. In 2016 has developed its monitoring report while now is working on its SECAP.
- Ginestra is a "young" Italian Municipality founded in 1965. It is an ethnic-linguistic Italo-Albanian (Arbëreshe) minority in Basilicata and one of the Italian "Wine City" characterized by the production of three certified Italian wines from the local grapes of Aglianico. It is engaged in developing public interventions related to energy efficiency and now it is signing to CoM intending to develop its SECAP
- Pietragalla is a CoM signatory since 2013 and in 2019 has submitted its SEAP. Despite it is a small municipality, it has one of the main industrial areas in the Basilicata Region,

characterized by the food industry (olive oil and pasta) and building materials industry. Now it is working on its monitoring report, checking the interventions provided, and at the same time it is working on its SECAP.

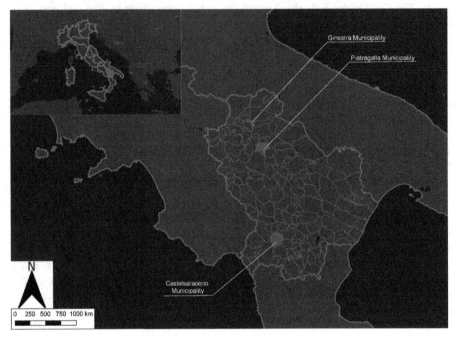

Fig. 1. The three small municipalities selected

Public investments have been analyzed through municipal budgets of the three Municipalities, moreover for CoM Municipalities (Castelsaraceno and Pietragalla) such investments have been identified in their SEAPs, in order to make explicit the link between the planning dimension (the SEAP) and the financial one. Furthermore, for Castelsaraceno Municipality it was possible to verify the implementation of the public interventions planned through the Monitoring Report submitted in 2016.

The data concerning investments in Municipal budgets from "Open Bilanci" and those related to public energy efficiency interventions from "Open CUP", have been classified in the three macro-categories previously defined: education, public lighting and public buildings. Education includes investments in energy efficiency interventions in schools related to the installation of Renewable Energy Sources (RES) technologies and improvements in building energy performance; public lighting is referred to as the expenditure's investment of street lamps and public buildings are related to the investments on the renovation (including energy efficiency interventions) of the public buildings. All these technological solutions produce a territorial impact, that should be take n into account in order to balance the different interventions sector according to territorial characteristics [6–8].

Data related to the investments have been collected for the period (2005–2021) and presented in Fig. 2. Comparing the stock of investments, Castelsaraceno and Pietragalla have managed an averagely over 100, 000 € per year, while Ginestra is on averagely under 100, 000 € per year. Considering the two CoM Municipalities (Castelsaraceno since 2012 and Pietragalla since 2013), the effects of the SEAP actions are remarked by the increase in the investments related to education and public lighting.

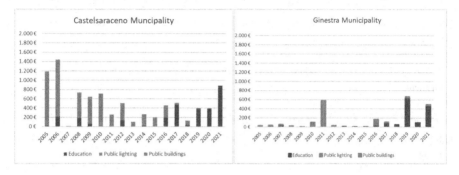

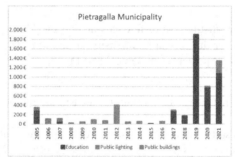

Fig. 2. Investments per year (for the period 2005–2021) expressed in thousand euros for the three municipalities

For the cases of Castelsaraceno and Pietragalla, the public interventions related to energy efficiency that increased the stock of investments related to the public energy efficiency interventions are included in the SECAPs These energy efficiency interventions can be distinguishable in four SEAP sectors (local electricity production, public lighting, building equipment facilities and transport). These sectors are reported in Table 2, structuring the overall targets of interventions provided in terms of CO_2 emission reduction expected [ton/year], energy reduction expected [MWh] and the total amount of investments [€].

Considering the only monitoring report available for Castelsaraceno Municipality, on 20 energy efficiency interventions planned, in 2016 only one was completed while four interventions were partially completed (i.e. 25% of the interventions have been realized).

Table 2. Targets related to public interventions provided for Castelsaraceno and Pietragalla SEAPs

Municipality	Castelsaraceno municipality			Pietragalla municipality		
Sector	CO_2 emission reduction expected [ton/year]	Energy reduction expected [MWh]	The total amount of interventions [€]	CO_2 emission reduction expected [ton/year]	Energy reduction expected [MWh]	The total amount of interventions [€]
Local electricity production	69.24	108	315, 000	239.68	560	n.a.
Building equipment facilities	237.01	214	251, 954	22	2	73, 710
Transport	161.85	554	69, 000	0	0	0
Public lighting	0	0	0	141	330	250, 000

A simple way to better distinguish differences among the Municipalities selected as case studies is to consider the per-capita intensity of investments and the territorial density of the investments, as presented in Table 3 and Fig. 3.

Table 3. Territorial indexes of investments for the three Municipalities

Municipality	Municipal surface [Km^2]	The total amount of investment for the period 2005–2021 [thousand €]	Yearly average investments per inhabitant for the period 2005–2021 [€/inhabitant]	Investments per Municipal surface for the period 2005–2021 [€/Km^2]
Castelsaraceno	75	8,878	7,142	118,717
Ginestra	13	2,451	3,400	184,015
Pietragalla	66	5,872	1,494	88,833

In addition to the static assessment of investment expenditure in absolute values, a dynamic analysis of investment expenditure was also conducted. The percentage variation of investment expenditure was analysed using two distinct time frames as a reference: the first from 2005 to 2012 and the second from 2013 to 2021. The year 2012 was chosen because it is the year of adhesion to the CoM of the Municipality of Pietragalla and for comparative purposes, the same period was also used for the Municipality of Castelsaraceno (signatory of the CoM the following year) and for the Municipality of Ginestra.

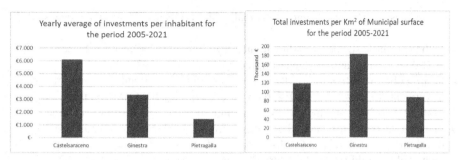

Fig. 3. The yearly average of investments per inhabitant and total investment per Km^2 of municipal surface for the period 2005–2021

This evaluation also confirms the positive impact of the CoM adhesion for the first two Municipalities:

- On average, the Municipality of Pietragalla, from an investment expenditure growth of 75% from 2005 to 2012, increased its investment expenditure by 263% after their CoM adhesion;
- On average, the Municipality of Castelsaraceno, from a decrease in investment of − 6% in previous years, increased its investment expenditure by about 50%.
- For the Municipality of Ginestra, considering the same time frame although it is not a signatory of the CoM, it was identified that investments decreased from 4.56% to 3.50%. It is important to note that the values considered are influenced by significant revenues from external financing.

4   Discussions and Conclusions

In order to achieve the research aims, an assessment of the investment expenditure of the selected Municipalities was carried out by selecting the year of adhesion to the CoM as the reference year.

In the case of Pietragalla Municipality the year selected as a reference is 2012.

- Considering Fig. 2, investment expenditure related to education shows an increasing trend. In detail, this macro-category contains an item called 'Assistance, transport and canteen', which for this municipality is one of the drivers for investment decisions in this sector. This can be a support in providing more public services from Municipalities to citizens;
- The public lighting sector, shows a clear increase in the year of CoM adhesion. In the previous year, on average, investment expenditure did not exceed 100, 000, whereas in 2012, more than 400, 000 euros were invested. Investment expenditure decreases and it has increased only since 2021;
- In the area of public buildings, there is an increasing trend in the years before the CoM, and in the opposite direction in subsequent years there is a lack of investment in this category.

In the case of Castelsaraceno Municipality, the year selected as a reference is 2013.

- In the education sector, according to the Fig. 2, the trend has increased since the year of CoM adhesion, and the highest figure was reached in 2021;
- In the Public Lighting sector, there was a discontinuous trend. The year of highest investments turns out to be 2014, the year after joining the CoM. While in the years from 2015 to 2021, no investment expenditure related to this sector is recorded;
- In the public buildings sector, there was an inverse trend to the CoM signature. Indeed, it was an upward trend pre-CoM signature and a reduction in investment expenditure in the public buildings sector after the CoM signature.

In the case of Ginestra Municipality, ongoing submitting to CoM, it was compared with Castelsaraceno and Pietragalla, in order to highlight any differences.

- In the education sector, since 2018 it has significantly increased investments compared to the previous years;
- In the public lighting sector, the trend shows that 2011 is the only year in which the amount invested is particularly significant, in the years before and after these figures, investments are rather low;
- the public building sector has a trend near to the public lighting sector. Indeed, 2016 is the year with the largest investments stock.

This first assessment of investments related to public energy efficiency interventions highlighted a positive impact of the CoM initiative on small Municipalities, as remarked by the Castelsaraceno Municipality. Furthermore, the CoM initiative promoted investment policies in energy efficiency, supporting the weaknesses in terms of technical capacity of small municipalities and implementing CO_2 reduction interventions oriented toward the EU 2050 targets. Considering the voluntary approach pursued by CoM, the increase of investments remarks a positive impact in terms of incentive to plan interventions in reducing energy consumption and support the build of a "green awareness" of citizens through these interventions. On the other hand, the data on municipal budges are a meaningful tool to improve the monitoring capacity for SEAP implementation and could be considered as additional indicators to be included in the CoM Monitoring Reports.

The comparison of two CoM Municipalities with one non-CoM remarked also some interesting future perspectives to be investigated:

- The research focused on the public investments related to three categories (education, public lighting and public buildings) but in order to achieve an "urban vision" (see also [9]) of the SEAP impacts, is useful to investigate also on other intervention categories (including private investments (i.e. the transport sector (see also [10–12] that is one of main SEAP sector [13, 14], especially for those small Municipalities with tourism specialization [15, 16]);
- This assessment can be extended to other CoM and non-CoM Municipalities in order to understand what categories (public or private) drive the investments toward the EU2050 targets and whether other EU funded programs contributes[17, 18];

- Considering the same investments stock, a comparison among CoM signatories of other population sizes (i.e. over 10,000 inhabitants) can define a performance assessment in terms of expenditure reduction and consumption reduction achieved.

References

1. European Commission: 2020 climate & energy package | Climate Action. https://ec.europa.eu/clima/policies/strategies/2020_en (2020). Accessed 1 Dec 2020
2. European Commission: The European Green Deal. Brussels (2020)
3. Santopietro, L., Scorza, F., Rossi, A.: Small municipalities engaged in sustainable and climate responsive planning: evidences from UE-CoM. In: Gervasi, O., et al. (eds.) ICCSA 2021. LNCS, vol. 12957, pp. 615–620. Springer, Cham (2021). https://doi.org/10.1007/978-3-030-87013-3_47
4. Santopietro, L., Scorza, F.: The Italian experience of the covenant of mayors: a territorial evaluation. Sustain. **13**, 1–23 (2021). https://doi.org/10.3390/su13031289
5. Rossi, F.M.: Public sector accounting and auditing in Italy. In: Brusca, I., Caperchione, E., Cohen, S., Rossi, F.M. (eds.) Public Sector Accounting and Auditing in Europe. ISGPM, pp. 125–141. Palgrave Macmillan UK, London (2015). https://doi.org/10.1057/9781137461346_9
6. Saganeiti, L., Pilogallo, A., Faruolo, G., Scorza, F., Murgante, B.: Energy landscape fragmentation: Basilicata region (Italy) study case. In: Misra, S., et al. (eds.) ICCSA 2019. LNCS, vol. 11621, pp. 692–700. Springer, Cham (2019). https://doi.org/10.1007/978-3-030-24302-9_50
7. Saganeiti, L., Pilogallo, A., Faruolo, G., Scorza, F., Murgante, B.: Territorial fragmentation and renewable energy source plants: which relationship? Sustainability **12**, 1828 (2020). https://doi.org/10.3390/su12051828
8. Scorza, F., Saganeiti, L., Pilogallo, A., Murgante, B.: Ghost planning: the inefficiency of energy sector policies in a low population density region. Arch. DI Stud. Urbani E Reg. **127**, 34–55 (2020)
9. Scorza, F., Santopietro, L.: A systemic perspective for the Sustainable Energy and Climate Action Plan (SECAP). Eur. Plan. Stud. 1–21 (2021). https://doi.org/10.1080/09654313.2021.1954603
10. Scorza, F., Fortunato, G.: Active mobility oriented urban development: a morpho-syntactic scenario for mid-sized town. Eur. Plan. Stud. **30**, 1–25 (2022) https://doi.org/10.1080/09654313.2022.2077094
11. Scorza, F., Fortunato, G.: Cyclable cities: building feasible scenario through urban space morphology assessment. J. Urban Plan. Dev. **147**, 05021039 (2021). https://doi.org/10.1061/(asce)up.1943-5444.0000713
12. Fortunato, G., Scorza, F., Murgante, B.: Cyclable city: a territorial assessment procedure for disruptive policy-making on urban mobility. In: Misra, S., et al. (eds.) ICCSA 2019. LNCS, vol. 11624, pp. 291–307. Springer, Cham (2019). https://doi.org/10.1007/978-3-030-24311-1_21
13. Croci, E., Lucchitta, B., Janssens-Maenhout, G., Martelli, S., Molteni, T.: Urban CO_2 mitigation strategies under the Covenant of Mayors: An assessment of 124 European cities. J. Clean. Prod. **169**, 161–177 (2017). https://doi.org/10.1016/j.jclepro.2017.05.165
14. Kona, A., et al.: Covenant of Mayors in figures: 8-year assessment. Publications Office of the European Union, Luxembourg (2017). https://doi.org/10.2760/64731

15. Santopietro, L., Scorza, F., Murgante, B.: Multiple components in GHG stock of transport sector: Technical improvements for SECAP Baseline Emissions Inventory assessment. TeMA J. L. Use Mobil. Environ. **15**, 5–24 (2022). https://doi.org/10.6092/1970-9870/8391

16. Pilogallo, A., Saganeiti, L., Scorza, F., Las Casas, G.: Tourism attractiveness: main components for a spacial appraisal of major destinations according with ecosystem services approach. In: Gervasi, O., et al. (eds.) ICCSA 2018. LNCS, vol. 10964, pp. 712–724. Springer, Cham (2018). https://doi.org/10.1007/978-3-319-95174-4_54

17. Scorza, F.: Improving EU cohesion policy: the spatial distribution analysis of regional development investments funded by EU structural funds 2007/2013 in Italy. In: Murgante, B., et al. (eds.) ICCSA 2013. LNCS, vol. 7973, pp. 582–593. Springer, Heidelberg (2013). https://doi.org/10.1007/978-3-642-39646-5_42

18. Scorza, F., Casas, G.L.: Territorial specialization in attracting local development funds: an assessment procedure based on open data and open tools. In: Murgante, B., et al. (eds.) ICCSA 2014. LNCS, vol. 8580, pp. 750–757. Springer, Cham (2014). https://doi.org/10.1007/978-3-319-09129-7_54

International Workshop on Specifics of Smart Cities Development in Europe (SPEED 2022)

A Preliminary Survey on Smart Specialization Platforms: Evaluation of European Best Practices

Simone Chiordi[1] , Giulia Desogus[2] , Chiara Garau[2]([✉]) , Paolo Nesi[1] ,
and Paola Zamperlin[3]

[1] Distributed Systems and Internet Technologies Lab (DISIT), University of Florence, Via di S. Marta 3, 50139 Florence, Italy
[2] Department of Civil and Environmental Engineering and Architecture (DICAAR), University of Cagliari, via Marengo 2, 09123 Cagliari, Italy
cgarau@unica.it
[3] Department of Civilisations and Forms of Knowledge, University of Pisa, via Pasquale Paoli 43, 56126 Pisa, Italy

Abstract. In July 2021, the World Economic Forum, in collaboration with the G20 Global Smart Cities Alliance, presented a study on the status of technology governance in cities, outlining the fundamental conditions that all smart cities, regardless of their strategic aims, must achieve. A decision support system based on a model that enables interoperability across multiple urban sectors should ensure these requirements, which serve as the foundation for effective technological governance. To accomplish this, many European cities have based their urban strategies on smart specialisation on open web platforms that systematise different sectors to create smart cities. From these premises, the purpose of this paper is threefold: (i) investigate the relationship between smart urban development and the use of open data platforms; (ii) understand how these are useful for defining actions and strategies that facilitate the planning of a smart city, and (iii) understand, if it is possible, to find platform's common characteristics that allow cooperation of intentions between European Union cities. To this goal, the authors make a systematic and cross-reading of some European platforms' good practices in smart city solutions and projects, highlighting the scope of the smart city and sustainability/financing, the open data exploitation and the technical characteristics. In this regard, an analytical approach is proposed, underlining the originality and value of this research to strengthen the smart Governance model based on open web platforms.

This paper is the result of the joint work of the authors. 'Results', 'Open data exploitation' and Technical characteristics" were written jointly by the authors. Simone Chiordi wrote the 'Introduction'. Giulia Desogus wrote 'The role of EU in open data platforms: legislation on Smart City and Artificial Intelligence'. Chiara Garau wrote 'Methodological approach and application to case studies', 'Amsterdam Smart City (ASC)', 'Helsinki Smart Region (HSR)'. Paolo Nesi wrote 'Discussion and Conclusions' and Paola Zamperlin wrote 'Copen-hagen Smart City (CSC)', 'Florence Smart City (FSC)', and 'Scope of the smart city and sustainability/financing'. Paolo Nesi coordinated and supervised the paper.

O. Gervasi et al. (Eds.): ICCSA 2022 Workshops, LNCS 13382, pp. 67–84, 2022.
https://doi.org/10.1007/978-3-031-10592-0_7

Keywords: Open data platforms · Urban strategies · Smart specialization platforms; Smart city · Decision support system · Technological governance

1 Introduction

Over the last decades, cities have invested in smart applications to provide better services to citizens and businesses. Concepts such as smart mobility, smart waste management, smart water, smart building, smart energy have evolved to signify the extensive use of IoT (Internet of Thing) in better managing city assets [1]. Connected sensors that collect data can help cities optimise their physical infrastructure's performance and are a key part of what it takes to build a smart city [2–4].

Implementing these solutions has helped the cities become more efficient and open but not yet smart. A key trend is moving to the next generation of smart cities where the focus is no anymore on the infrastructure but on sharing and managing data to enable better decision-making for all stakeholders' government, business, and residents [5–9]. Smart cities of tomorrow are evolving as intelligent, connected ecosystems that involve not just government but citizens, visitors, and businesses. This new information-sharing partnership between the city, residents and businesses can be considered a '*city-as-a-platform*'. In this context, smart cities enable more innovative things and smarter decisions. A truly smart city uses technology to promote better decision-making for city officials and its residents. The use of open web platforms allows cities to (i) manage data in an organised and systematic way, (ii) to advance as ecosystems of technological transformation and (iii) to be part of a network of cities of different maturity levels which can act as a catalyst for the motivation and engagement of their decision-makers and ambassadors of transformation.

However, in the past years, various pioneering cities in the use of platforms have been involved in (partially) sponsored city initiatives by a large tech company to promote their proprietary digital city platforms [10]. This has provoked a lot of longer-term consequences. Indeed, as initial platforms are proprietary and do not follow any standards, it becomes more difficult at a later stage to switch to different urban data platform providers as existing applications and systems have to be adapted or redeveloped. This situation is often referred to as '*vendor lock-in*'. Local authorities soon find themselves restricted to one company's IT system and products for many years. This also forms a significant barrier to entry for smaller technology providers excluded from these opportunities. Additional barriers also exist for small technology providers trying to engage in this market. Small technology providers must adapt and integrate their solutions if a local authority presents a specific technical system. This adds high cost and complexity to each implementation and limits the company's ability to expand and scale its solutions to other similar cities and communities. In recent years, to solve these problems, more and more cities have selected standards-based platforms for which multiple vendor implementations exist. This makes it easier in future to switch to a different vendor without breaking many existing dependencies. Standards-based ecosystems are often richer in terms of what they offer as market opportunities for a participating product, service and solution providers increase.

Open standards for urban data platforms have also been recently emerging. Key aspects that are currently standardised include data models and Application Programming Interfaces (APIs) for integrating IoT data sources and developing smart city services on the platforms. Examples of such emerging standards are NGSI-LD (Next Generation Service Interfaces-Linked Data) by the European Telecommunications Standards Institute (ETSI) for context information management [11], FIWARE data models also in NGSI [12], and the TM Forum business ecosystem APIs for ecosystem transaction management [13]. Multiple vendor implementations of urban data platforms around the aforementioned standards are now available. This also includes open-source implementation such as that supported by the FIWARE Foundation. An interesting aspect is that funding support is now available for public sector organisations to adopt such standards-compliant data platform components through the Connecting Europe Facility (CEF) [14]. Open technologies do not stop at urban data platforms but can also extend to the necessary connectivity layer in a future city. Recently emerging low-power, wide-area network technologies such as LoRaWAN [15] have made IoT connectivity affordable for cities, with some limitations with respect to the more expensive emerging 5G solutions. While they previously had to rely on network operators or external organisations to provide wide-area connectivity services, they can now own their network at a fraction of the average cost. In this way, cities are rapidly transforming their services to address current societal, environmental and economic challenges. Vertical smart solutions are being progressively replaced by solutions capable of exploiting a considerable range of data channels. This significantly reduces the barrier to smart city experimentation. In addition, accessible community-provided networks, such as The Things Network (TTN), enable cities to benefit from connectivity services provided by their citizens and tech communities, at relevant costs, which lead in most cases the cities to create their own network.

For these reasons, the authors will focus on digital platforms by answering the question, 'Which aspects of open web platforms can help a city move towards a smart city?' Secondly, the authors deepen this theme by analysing, in more detail, the platforms of European cities that have been useful for improving their urban strategies by answering the questions 'Why are open web platforms useful for defining actions and strategies that facilitate the planning of a smart city?' and 'Are there common features of the platforms that allow the cooperation of intentions between cities?'

To accomplish this, the paper begins with a theoretical study on open data platform EU legislation in Artificial Intelligence (AI) and smart city (Sect. 2). Subsequently, the paper focuses on European best practices (Sect. 3) through a content analysis between Smart Specialization Platforms (Sect. 3.1). In Sect. 3.2 the scope of the smart city and sustainability/financing, the open data exploitation and the technical characteristics are shown as a result. Finally, the results are discussed and the research's future directions (Sect. 4).

2 The Role of EU in Open Data Platforms: Legislation on Smart City and Artificial Intelligence

Today, each city/area still has its smart specialisation criteria requiring a highly tailored solution. Only a flexible and dynamic platform can put a city in complete control of its operational objectives. Cities are abandoning an approach based on data sources and becoming aware of actual data channels where information and actions flow in multiple directions. Multi-directional flows are vital in implementing city operating systems involving daily tuning to deal with current challenges. Cities are becoming smarter also due to regulatory pushes from international bodies and organisations such as the European Commission (Table 1).

As Table 1 shows, connectivity and interoperability are considered the most fundamental building block of digital transformation. It enables data to flow, people to collaborate wherever they are, and connects more objects to the Internet, transforming manufacturing, mobility and logistic chains.

However, the digital landscape is becoming more diverse, challenging cross-border interoperability and interconnectivity. As a result, Europeans still face barriers when using (cross-border) online tools and services. This means that citizens miss out on goods and services and businesses miss out on market potential, while governments cannot fully benefit from digital technologies. The EU's Digital Single Market aims to overcome these challenges by creating the right environment for flourishing digital networks and services. This is not only achieved by setting the right regulatory conditions, but also by providing cross-border digital infrastructures and services. Furthermore, a sense of belonging to a European Commission initiative (see Table 1) and corresponding network helps to activate local initiatives, enabling cities to progress towards meeting their objectives. It also stimulates a pan-European culture of working together to solve the 'European way' challenges, thereby putting the citizen at the centre as the ultimate beneficiary. A key trend in the smart cities sector is working beyond and across organisational boundaries and joining initiatives and networks at the European and international levels. The basic reason behind this trend is that: a city is smart when it acquires the capacity to evolve, learn, adapt and innovate continuously. A key challenge, which emerged as fragmented smart cities initiatives were implemented worldwide, was the realisation that in most cases, innovation resulting from publicly-funded projects usually hit a dead-end soon after the funding stopped, with frustration on both the demand and supply side. In this context, no system can scale and spread because there are no standards, and there are no standards because there is no widespread deployment. In this regard a growing trend is observed towards establishing of a global market that makes it possible to share solutions among cities that are facing similar challenges, while respecting their different cultural, economic, social, and technical structures. In order for this to happen, each smart city should develop based on a foundation that enables seamless sharing and reusing of digital, data-driven solutions, thereby reducing the cost of innovation, increasing the return on investment, and – thanks to the use of open standards and APIs – avoiding vendor lock-in. About that, in July 2021 the World Economic Forum, in cooperation with of the G20 Global Smart Cities Alliance, released a report on the state of technology governance in cities title "Governing Smart Cities: Policy Benchmarks for Ethical and Responsible Smart City Development" [24]. The report provides a benchmark in defining ethical and responsible governance policies for smart city programmes, based on findings coming from interviews and surveys with city government officials and policy experts of 36 Pioneer Cities across 22 Countries. The G20 Global Smart Cities Alliance proposes a political roadmap organized around five fundamental

Table 1. EU legislation in smart solutions and artificial intelligence (AI)

Name and Link	Synthetic description
2021 Artificial intelligence ACT [16]	The European Commission proposes a regulation laying down harmonised rules on Artificial Intelligence and amending certain union legislative acts
2021 European interoperability framework for smart cities and communities (EIF4SCC) [17]	The EIF4SCC aims to provide the local administration with definitions, principles, recommendations, and examples from all over Europe and beyond. It is a standard model to facilitate common public services in all cities and regions
2020 Shaping Europe's digital future [18]	Shaping Europe's Digital Future sets out as a key action to develop a 'reinforced EU governments' interoperability strategy' by 2021, aiming to foster coordination and the adoption of common standards for public services and data flows
2020 Smart cities marketplace [19]	It is a platform that aims to bring cities, industries, SMEs, investors, researchers and other smart city actors together. The goal is to have access to knowledge on Smart Cities to shape an idea of a bankable project, suitable for attracting public and private investors and which allows for an individual exchange between project promoters and community members for financial agreements and projects
2019 Join, boost, sustain [20]	The 'Join, Boost, Sustain' movement aims to support the scaling up of open, interoperable, cross-sector and cross-border digital platforms and digital solutions across the EU
2016 ISA^2 - Interoperability solutions for public administrations, businesses and citizens [21]	In January 2016, the five-year ISA2 programme on interoperability solutions and common frameworks for European public administrations, businesses and citizens was launched to promote the ICT-based modernisation of the public sector in Europe and to facilitate addressing the needs of businesses and citizens via improved interoperability of European public administrations
2015 A digital single market strategy for Europe [22]	Section 4.1 (Building a data economy) of the Communication 'A Digital Single Market Strategy for Europe' states that the Commission 'will encourage access to public data to help drive innovation

(continued)

Table 1. (*continued*)

Name and Link	Synthetic description
2014 Connecting europe facility [23]	The CEF building blocks offer basic capabilities that can be used in any European project to facilitate the delivery of digital public services across borders. The CEF building blocks are interoperability agreements between European Union member states. The aim of the building blocks is thus to ensure interoperability between IT systems so that citizens, businesses and administrations can benefit from seamless digital public services wherever they may be in Europe

principles, as a baseline for robust technology governance: equity, inclusivity and social impact; security and resilience; privacy and transparency; openness and interoperability; operational and financial sustainability. These principles encompass basic requirements that all smart cities should meet, no matter about their strategic objectives. In other words, if a city considering environmental sustainability as strategic invests in smart lighting to reduce its carbon footprint, it must also ensure security for citizens with street lights on when needed. According to the proposed roadmap, good models embody policies such as: "*Building accessibility standards into procurement to ensure digital-related services are accessible to those with disabilities; defining processes to assess privacy implications of new urban technology deployments; defining key accountability measures to be taken in order to protect the assets of cities and their citizens; setting out planning policies that improve coordination among city stakeholders and reduce the cost and complexity of digital infrastructure roll-out; developing a model policy for open data strategy in a city*". At the same time, the European Telecommunications Standards Institute published the standard ETSI TS 103 463 V1.1.1, Access, Terminals, Transmission and Multiplexing (ATTM) [25]. Key Performance Indicators for Sustainable Digital Multiservice Cities) define smart cities indicators in Europe. The set of indicators is based on the work delivered by the EU-funded project CITYkeys (http://www.citykeys-project.eu/). It expresses smart development in terms of people (social sustainability), planet (environmental sustainability), prosperity (economic sustainability), governance (developing and implementing) and propagation (potential for up-scaling and application in another context). According to the project results, such a performance measurement framework can be useful in cities as a support system during the agenda-setting process, for identifying tasks that could be performed better and more efficiently, for benchmarking differences and similarities in particular when it is necessary to establish a connection between district development and individual projects. European cities involved in the CITYkeys project revealed that they use city-level performance measurement to support decision-making, upscale and progress from experimental projects towards large-scale implementation, and manage resources. Furthermore, municipalities can use a performance measurement system to provide requirements for procurement procedures based on the actual situation and the need to meet city targets.

From the indications of the EU, the drive towards a connective smart city based on interoperability that starts from the guided and standardised use of Artificial Intelligence will lead cities to more investment in new technologies. For that reason, in planning platforms architecture, the basic level includes and integrates all existing networks, infrastructure and functions of the city that will be interconnected: urban transport, waste, municipal energy consumption, municipal/public parking spaces, green/urban areas, water supply networks, utilities networks. To understand the importance of open data platforms in the active management of smart cities, the authors, in the next section, analyse four successful European examples.

3 European Best Practices: Research Methodology for the Analysis of Smart Specialization Platforms

3.1 Methodological Approach and Application to Case Studies

This section examines some good European practices in smart city solutions and projects, trying to (i) investigate the relationship between smart urban development and the use of open data platforms; (ii) understand how these are useful for defining actions and strategies that facilitate the planning of a smart city and (iii) understand if it is possible to find platform's common characteristics that allow cooperation of intentions between European Union cities. To do this, the authors analyse the contents of the open web platforms of four European cities: Amsterdam, Helsinki, Copenhagen and Florence (Fig. 1), which have demonstrated interoperability and connectivity across multiple urban sectors and have implemented urban strategies on smart specialisation through their platforms. This will be done through a specific analysis of the contents that highlights the scope of the smart city and sustainability/financing, the open data exploitation and the technical characteristics.

3.1.1 Amsterdam Smart City (ASC)

The Amsterdam Smart City programme is a public-private initiative consisting of twenty permanent partners, including governments, academic institutions, social organisations and innovative companies active in the metropolitan area of Amsterdam [26–28]. It involves 32 territorial projects focused on the energy transition and connectivity [29]. Amsterdam was the first European municipality to launch a Smart City programme based on a model that enables bottom-up projects in various sectors, including circular economy, digital connectivity, energy, health, mobility and jobs of the future [30–32]. ASC also won several awards as the most successful smart city in the world (Chief Digital Officer Club in 2014, World Smart Cities Awards in 2012 and the European City Star Award in 2011). One of the main aspects of ASC is the role of governance, which, when combined with the aim of efficiency, environmental performance and quality of life, has the potential to promote public engagement [29]. As Jameson et al. (2019) underline,

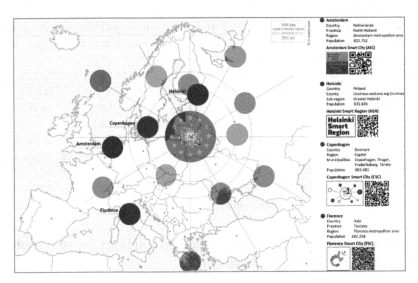

Fig. 1. Map of the cities analysed and links of smart initiatives

this aspect epitomises the split "between 'smart city' policies in urban planning and governance, where datafication is framed as a purely economic and technical phenomenon, and social policy, which frames problems as social and political" [30, p. 1].

ASC launched an open web platform in 2016 to expand its scope and professionalise the programme. Using a website as an online platform [24], ASC hopes to reach a broader audience and facilitate cooperation between the various partners to increase exchanges of ideas and opportunities, sharing projects and best practices, highlighting the most current issues and updates on the subject and organising multidisciplinary events and workshops [24, 33]. The open web platform has two roles: a "connector and an information exchanger. Firstly, the website as a connector means that it helps people, not only in the city of Amsterdam but also around the world, to get in touch with others, to contribute to urban innovation, and to gather related information about projects that are currently going on". Secondly, "the website as an information exchanger indicates that it facilitates suppliers and demanders to share their ideas, information, knowledge, and projects" [33, p. 246).

The platform is divided into six channels [24]: (i) Circular City. Amsterdam has established a circular economy innovation program to implement material reuse strategies by converting waste into electricity, urban heating and building materials; (ii) Energy. The city of Amsterdam has the ambition to provide every citizen with a solar panel in the next few years; (iii) Mobility. Amsterdam is considered the cycling capital of the world; 32% of traffic movement in Amsterdam takes place by bicycle, and 63% of its inhabitants use bicycles daily. Since 2008, car sharing has increased by 376%; (iv) Citizens & Living. To keep Amsterdam liveable and to find innovative tourism initiatives, the municipality works with its citizens; (v) Digital City. People are more connected, and technology has become part of the daily life of the citizens of Amsterdam; (vi) Smart City Academy provides available knowledge on smart city projects and helps with project development.

Professors, teachers and students study starting, managing, collaborating and scaling smart city projects. Through this system of channels, ASC open platform has made information more transparent for all actors by moderating all data entered by all people who join the platform. In this way, everyone can easily access information and "all actors should be able to choose a wide range of information that can support their decisions and further interact with other actors in several projects" [33, p. 247).

3.1.2 Helsinki Smart Region (HSR)

Helsinki Smart Region is a regional strategy of smart specialisation that promotes the participation of different actors in the European Union's international networks and cooperation projects. Indeed, HSR is linked to the EU initiative "Smart Specialization Platform" [34], which assists EU countries and regions in developing and implementing their smart specialisation strategies. The purpose is to improve regional innovation potential and to foster international collaborations by prioritising sustainable growth via the effective use of the Region's economic, environmental and social resources [35, 36]. The strategy is not limited to the Finnish capital of Helsinki (over 650,000 inhabitants). Still, it expands to the entire Helsinki-Uusimaa region, with 26 rapidly growing municipalities, even very small ones of about 2,000 inhabitants [40]. Hielkema et al. (2013), in "Developing the Helsinki Smart City", argue that "removing boundaries between municipalities and municipal organisations helps to create new integrated services" [37 p. 191]. This creates strength for the HSR project because it allows, on the one hand, to test smart and digital pilot solutions for cities and municipalities of different sizes and, on the other hand, to create a network of co-utility between territories with different socio-economic characteristics (urban, agricultural, pastoral ones).

HSR's smart specialisation is based on the close connection of different actors (large companies and start-ups, public sector, research and education centres) that create smart innovations together and in continuous contact with the population [41]. This strategy is based on innovative ecosystems [38] based on regional strengths where actors play a central role. HSR focuses "on the regional innovation ecosystem and the use of ecosystem thinking to consider which actor groups are relevant in societal change processes" [39, p. 9]. These ecosystems address three main themes [40]: (i) Citizens' City: citizens creating agile and user-centred solutions together with companies and institutions. The region provides real-time open data that citizens use to create new businesses. This was made systemic by the HSR project, which facilitated the development of significant technologies and social innovations. This theme covers areas such as transportation, housing, urban planning and healthcare; (ii) Climate neutrality; the region, by developing new infrastructure and construction service models, has set the goal of carbon-neutral by 2035. The issue of climate neutrality covers areas such as circular economy solutions, new forms of energy, bioeconomy innovations and new materials; (iii) Industrial modernisation: Helsinki-Uusimaa produces various products using, for example, industrial IoT and mobile technologies. HSR, through various innovation activities in different fields, develops cutting-edge technologies for the industry and future processes. Areas covered by the theme include, for example, new industrial processes, health technologies, robotics and travel.

Through these smart development themes, the Region has applied the concept of European Union Smart Specialization in territorial development. This produced, in recent years, the rapid growth of the innovation, digitality and technological security industries as the main support points of the entire HSR system. In conjunction, "knowledge creation takes place in the region's universities and research institutes, public administration, third sector and private companies. The expertise of the people working for these actors gives birth to a strong science and research base, new technology and skill" [40, p. 2]. Finally, this system is put into practice by the implementation of pilot projects in each theme (Citizens' City, Climate neutrality and Industrial modernisation).

3.1.3 Copenhagen Smart City (CSC)

Copenhagen, the capital of Denmark, situated on the east coast of Zealand, aims to become the world's first carbon-neutral capital by 2025 and is achieving the ambitious goal through smart city initiatives. It is one of the 20 cities included in the Nordic Smart City Network, a collaboration initiative joining five countries with the aim to explore the Nordic way to create smart, sustainable, and liveable cities.

In 2014 Copenhagen won the World Smart Cities Award [41] for its Copenhagen Connecting (CC), a project based on the intelligent use of data (wireless data from mobile phones, GPS in buses and sensors in sewers and garbage cans, etc.) to create a greener city, a better quality of life and a better business climate. This plan assists Copenhagen politicians in achieving the city's goals of reducing congestion, air pollution and CO_2 emissions. The concept is scalable and replicable and designed to avoid vendor lock-in and includes as key benefits a better use of resources, reliable and cost-effective services that meet the needs of citizens, engage businesses and open up new business opportunities.

The City has provided itself with a smart plan (CC Plan, in cooperation with private companies such as Rambøll and the University of Copenhagen, the University of Aalborg, the Technical University of Denmark (DTU) and the IT University of Copenhagen), and investments to implement it. For example, it has invested 34 million euros in new street lamps and over 13 million euros in new traffic lights and intelligent traffic management. A unique starting point for the implementation of the smart strategy in Copenhagen and for the development of smart solutions was the political decision to define a new government program, the Danish Basic Data Program, that included free access to public data sources (high-quality basic data: https://www.opendata.dk/city-of-copenhagen) collected and archived by the Danish authorities in order to promote innovation and address the challenges of urbanisation and climate change, such as traffic congestion and flooding in urban areas.

Copenhagen's smart city approach is firmly anchored in the three main objectives of achieving carbon neutrality by 2025; creating a greener, more sustainable, and the more liveable capital city; and supporting economic growth. Among the various projects launched to achieve its targets, one prominent example is the Strategic Climate Action Plan, which encompasses many diversified initiatives. Climate action and traffic systems receive the most significant share of funds.

The leadership role that Copenhagen has earned worldwide in smart innovation has contributed to the creation of Greater Copenhagen, a collaborative organisation founded in 2015, including Region Skåne, Region Halland, Region Hovedstaden, Region Sjælland and all 85 Danish and Swedish municipalities in the region (encompassing 4.4 million citizens in Southern Sweden and Eastern Denmark). Greater Copenhagen's efforts are directed at five key areas, which are essential to the framework for future growth and welfare: Green Transition, Labour market, Infrastructure, Digitalisation, and Life Science.

3.1.4 Florence Smart City (FSC)

Florence is a medium-sized Italian city (about 380,000 inhabitants, metro area of 1.5 million) with an intense tourist and commercial vocation (14 million of tourists per year). In 2020, it got the first place in the ranking of smart Italian cities according to the ICityRank report, research conducted by the Public Administration Forum, resulting in decades of policy and governance actions [42].

Together with San Sebastian (ES) and Bristol (UK), it is one of the three leading cities in the European project Replicate, which allowed an exchange of experiences and a sharing of problems and solutions with geographically different realities, thanks to the former STEEP EC project [43]. The three partner cities of Replicate project agreed on the need to adopt a comprehensive Smart City Plan [44], which includes the whole set of necessary actions following a holistic approach. Key factors were detected: a) strong collaboration of all the stakeholders across the value chain: public administrations, technology experts, companies, end-users, etc.; b) the city must be considered a complex system of processes strictly interconnected; c) building up a Smart City requires time, resources, clear vision and strong leadership.

Open Innovation for engaging the stakeholders, open standards to ensure interoperability, and open-source to maximise uptake and impact is another component of the Florence Smart City strategy. Open data is an opportunity for growth and support in decision-making, not only for statistical purposes but because it makes a city responsive, placing knowledge at the heart of the city government and sharing it with all the players (if you can measure it, you can manage it). To date, about 1,900 open datasets are published on the official website of the municipality of Florence [45].

That of Florence is the result of an ongoing process that has involved public administrations at various levels of governance, universities and research centres, private investors and stakeholders. A significant step along this path was the creation, in the context of the Replicate EU project of the first SCCR (Smart City Control Room) by collecting a relevant amount of data, performing big data analytics, and elaborating What-If scenarios to provide a vast set of dashboards starting from the main panel that is 24/7 accessible to city operators, where each tile/widget is autonomously updated and interactive to bring the user to a set of more detailed views on data and maps. This first SCCR taken advantage of other important open-source solutions (see the national projects Sii-Mobility, Km4City and European RESOLUTE H2020) up to the release of Snap4City framework [46, 47]. This solution is fully GDPR compliant and supports Living Lab implementation and management of IoT Applications, community and Multi Organization solutions, resources, heatmaps, AI and predictive models, traffic flow reconstruction (from Sii-Mobility), routing algorithms (from Sii-Mobility), What-IF simulation models, knowledge base and federated Smart City API, scalable processes, scalable data analytics, user profiles, Mobile Apps, IoT MultiBroker and MultiProtocol, Digital Twin local and global, BIM, etc. Being completely open-source, modular and scalable, this solution has had the advantage of growing with the needs of the city by adding components, reconfiguring and exploiting the components already present on the territory, without any Vendor-lock-in, protocol-lock-in, technology-lock-in and solution lock-in.

These premises highlight a vital connection between open data platforms and smart urban development. Made through artificial intelligence, these platforms can be connected with the reality of the city. Furthermore, using different data, the platforms manage to interpret the needs of citizens in other fields. By combining them, they create a dynamic interoperability capable of giving the city networks a real connection. To go into the details of the connectivity of the platforms, the following paragraph describes the results of the research with more focus on the smart city and sustainability/financing, the open data exploitation and the technical characteristics.

3.2 Results

To evaluate the positive outcomes of open web platform in smart urban development, this section defines three benefits that emerged from the study of the platforms in Amsterdam, Helsinki, Copenhagen and Florence: (i) the scope of the smart city and sustainability/financing, (ii) the open data exploitation and (iii) the technical characteristics. This section, reads these results in the context of Smart Cities. In fact, not all cities/areas are becoming smart in the same manner and are smart at the same level, because platforms services are typically different. However, as seen in the previous section, in most cases, the selected cities are deciding on addressing a selection of smart services, for example smart parking, smart waste management, smart lighting, etc., according to their needs and strategies.

3.2.1 Scope of the Smart City and Sustainability/Financing

Smart cities projects have demonstrated a positive impact on improving the environmental conditions and liveability of cities and the economic returns for citizens and public administrations. A key aspect of selected smart cities projects is to rely on revenue streams for economic sustainability coming from different sources. Deloitte, a network of companies in audit, consulting, financial advisory, risk advisory, tax and legal fields, [48] tries to list them as follows: (i) Financing model payments: payments received that match agreed cost (including finance) amounts, allowing full coverage of expenditure and agreed on returns; (ii) Availability payments: payments received that are linked with the performance of the private sector operator and availability of the service/asset in line with agreed performance standards. (iii) Savings sharing: certain services will generate savings for the public sector. If quantifiable and accountable, those savings can generate a budget to help fund the associated assets/service; (iv) Shadow tolls: the public sector makes payments to the private sector based on usage of the service/asset. In some cases, recurring payments may reduce risk; (v) User fees/charges: users pay directly for services (e.g., road tolls). This tends to be riskier than public sector payments as it is more difficult to quantify in advance with any certainty; (vi) Rate type payments: the public sector collects revenues from the public and utilises these to pay the private sector for specific services/assets (e.g., power generation/water utilities); (vii) "Pay-as-you-go": users are charged for each use of the service. Can be collected using the billing system of mobile operators; (viii) Subscription: user pays a fixed amount for service irrespective of the level of usage; (ix) Advertising-based: revenue streams are generated by selling advertising on asset space, rather than collecting from individual users. This allows service providers to provide service free (or inexpensively) to users; the above issues have been investigated during the elaboration of the feasibility study for the Cyprus Smart City platform [49].

3.2.2 Open Data Exploitation

Considering the different domains (government service, health service, security-safety issues, mobility, energy, waste, etc.) in which a smart city can generate revenues, an important impact on results is related to smartening public services like lighting, parking, waste management without forgetting the relevance of accessible Data storage. In fact, Open Data and citizens' engagement in their use can improve the quality of public services and bring to develop new applications and digital services that exploit the reuse of public data.

Due to this huge amount of data coming from different domains, the risk is to create separate data silos that do not allow to correctly evaluate project returns and exploit the full potential of smart city applications. Recently, cities are becoming more aware of multiple directions data channels and are abandoning an approach based on simply connecting data sources. Efficient management and exploitation of multi-directional flows are becoming key points to optimising results and dealing with current challenges. Thus, cities operating systems must be able to work with them.

A well-designed smart city platform allows collecting, aggregating, and analysing data to support decision-making with effective advice considering all the dimensions involved. For instance, resulting benefits from smart light, waste management and smart parking can be traced back to better environmental conditions due to traffic reduction, reduction of time spent in commuting and routing (public services as ambulances, fire brigade, services, logistic), reduction of energy resources and therefore a reduction of costs for citizens and for city administrators.

The key trends in smart waste management solutions leverage IoT technologies to monitor trash bins or just monitoring the collected waste from bins, collect data such as level of filling, data and time of latest waste collection and generate alerts in case of fire, vandalism or unauthorized bin movements. This data allows us to predict when the bin will be full and allows an efficient truck routing for the waste collection. This solution can improve city services with relevant savings on fuel expenses and maintenance costs, optimising the trips for waste collection dynamically.

Many cities are implementing smart street lights due to more tangible and instant cost reductions. Smart street lights (e.g., Copenhagen Smart City) save energy and make public spaces safer at night and provide helpful support for additional IoT tools like air quality sensors, surveillance cameras, smart light management for police and critical conditions, and Wi-Fi hotspots. Data collected by smart street lamps (such as people and traffic flows) can be marketed to recover costs for installation. Additionally, light remote control and activations by motion-sensing could save up to 20% in energy consumption.

3.2.3 Technical Characteristics

In the context of Smart City applications (web and mobile), most of the early solutions have been based on GIS (Geographical Information Systems) which provide standard solutions for managing geolocalised entities such as maps, shapes, etc., by using protocols such as WFS (Web Feature Service), WMS (Web Map Service). GIS-based solutions are discharging the complexity on the client side since the GIS servers are typically not capable of satisfying a huge number of requests simultaneously and neither to provide smart services. Other solutions are providing data via Open Data platforms such as CKAN (Comprehensive Knowledge Archive Network), which presents API to access the single data set file as well as a collection of APIs provided by multiple stakeholders in the city/area, and the possibility of exchanging these descriptions via harvesting protocols. IoT solutions based on IoT brokers for the smart city have also been proposed; for example, FIWARE based-solutions, which expose NGSI REST API, are provided to the Web and mobile clients to access at the data, typically last values and not historical values, directly accessing to IoT sensor data and not too sophisticated data structures neither via semantic queries [50].

In selected cities, there is a strong push on data and services aggregation to exploit higher-level machine learning business intelligence tools and control room dashboards, also provide smarter mobile apps that offer smarter services using a wider range of data. Therefore, it is pretty frequent to use Smart City API to provide and create services and data for web and mobile applications. Examples of Smart City APIs are Km4City (Knowledge Model for the City) API, and E015 (Digital Ecosystem E015: this name was given for expo 2015, then this changed as API distribution/sharing environments). Therefore, to develop smart city solutions, the usage of Smart City API can be the way to provide smarter applications that can take into account multiple aggregated data sources and data analytics, such as reasoning and predictions on parking, traffic flow, and people flow, weather, etc. On the other hand, most of the Smart City API services are focused on a single city/area and expose a limited number of services contextualised on the same geographic area, for example info-mobility, point of interest (POI), routing, smart light, smart parking, etc. This means that in most cases, passing from one city/area to another, the users have to get other applications to get the same services. This also happens for the lack of interoperability among the Smart City API, SCAPI, at the semantic level.

4   Discussion and Conclusions

This paper presented a detailed review of four open web platforms through an analysis that analysed the scope of the smart city and sustainability/financing, open data exploitation and technical characteristics.

In general, the paper investigated the relationship between smart urban development and the use of open data platforms. The results obtained reveal that the cities that use open data platforms to accelerate their intelligent growth, rely on Artificial Intelligence (AI), seen as a fast-evolving family of technologies that can bring a wide array of economic and societal benefits across the entire spectrum of industries and social activities.

This study and the related analyses demonstrate that this approach aims to enhance urban living by integrating more sustainable solutions and addressing city-specific challenges across various policy sectors, including energy, mobility and transport, and ICT. It builds on the engagement of the public, industry and other interested groups to develop innovative solutions and participate in city governance.

Subsequently, the research has shown that for a controlled and dynamic management, the smart city requires planned planning actions that connect, at the same time, several sectors. This characteristic, typical of the platforms analysed in Sect. 2, allows for defining actions and strategies that facilitate city management. In fact, the platforms allow a functional connection between different sectors that helps administrations to make planned decisions in the urban ecosystem.

Moreover, the analyses have shown that there are different characteristics that the platforms can implement to allow cooperation of intentions between different European cities. This is highlighted by the European Union, which defines standards and regulations that serve to standardise these platforms as much as possible. Furthermore, to ensuring that public and private organisations can work together, the research shows that a key feature for the use of these open data platforms is interoperability (e.g. interconnection ser-vices, data integration services, controlled vocabularies and common code lists to de-scribe data exchanges, organisational interoperability).

Furthermore, this analysis has been included in the broader discourse of Smart Cities, which, through the EU regulatory guidelines, increasingly use Artificial Intelligence to implement open data platforms. The analysis highlighted that Smart Cities are more and more understood as innovation ecosystems in which, if adopted across Europe and beyond, the open source-open data framework could set the foundations for a new digital single market, where local authorities and technology providers of all sizes can easily exchange data and digital goods and services in a fair data economy. With this digital market in place, local authorities will have access to a catalogue of digital services, quickly testing and procuring the best solutions for their citizens' needs and placing demands on the market based on their strategic goals.

But the benefits of this single digital market will only be realised if the minimal interoperability and connectivity mechanisms are adopted at scale. For this to happen, national governments are more and more prioritising the digital transformation of local authorities and creating an environment that rewards participation and minimises innovation risks. Funding, policies, legal frameworks and licensing models must also be in place to increase market confidence and trust between buyers and sellers.

This study provided a detailed framework for the use of Smart Specialization Platforms in cities. However, the next step in this theoretical research is to build a platform architecture model that should be implemented to meet the needs of different cities across Europe. Second, a preliminary analysis should be implemented to a single EU platform's social, urban, economic, and political gain. These new evaluations are welcome in further studies.

Acknowledgements. This study was supported by the "CYPRUS Smart City Platform" PI: BK PLUS Europe (Tender procedure No.: 02/2021/A/Δ/ΥΦΕΚΨΠ) Ministry of Research, Innovation and Digital Policies, Cyprus.

References

1. Rashid, A., et al.: RES-Q an Ongoing Project on Municipal Solid Waste Management Program for the Protection of the Saniq River Basin in Southern Lebanon. In: International Conference on Computational Science and Its Applications, pp. 536–550. Springer, Cham (2021)
2. Garau, C., Nesi, P., Paoli, I., Paolucci, M., Zamperlin, P.: A big data platform for smart and sustainable cities: environmental monitoring case studies in Europe. In: International Conference on Computational Science and Its Applications, pp. 393–406. Springer, Cham (2020)
3. Azzari, M., Garau, C., Nesi, P., Paolucci, M., Zamperlin, P.: Smart city governance strategies to better move towards a smart urbanism. In: International Conference on Computational Science and Its Applications, pp. 639–653. Springer, Cham (2018)
4. Desogus, G., Mistretta, P., Garau, C.: Smart islands: a systematic review on urban policies and smart governance. In: Misra, S., et al. (eds.) ICCSA 2019. LNCS, vol. 11624, pp. 137–151. Springer, Cham (2019). https://doi.org/10.1007/978-3-030-24311-1_10
5. Rassu N., et al.: Accessibility to local public transport in Cagliari with focus on the elderly. In: International Conference on Computational Science and Its Applications, pp. 690–705. Springer, Cham (2020)
6. Campisi, T., et al.: A new vision on smart and resilient urban mobility in the aftermath of the pandemic: key factors on european transport policies. In: Gervasi, O., et al. (eds.) Computational Science and Its Applications – ICCSA 2021: 21st International Conference, Cagliari, Italy, September 13–16, 2021, Proceedings, Part X, pp. 603–618. Springer International Publishing, Cham (2021). https://doi.org/10.1007/978-3-030-87016-4_43
7. Garau, C., Desogus, G., Zamperlin, P.: Governing technology-based urbanism: degeneration to technocracy or development to progressive planning? In: Aurigi, A., Willis, K.S. (eds.) The Routledge Companion to Smart Cities Routledge, pp. 157–173. (2020) https://doi.org/10.4324/9781315178387
8. Mistretta, P., Garau, C.: Città e sfide. Conflitti e Utopie Strategie di impresa e Politiche del territorio. Successi e criticità dei modelli di governance. CUEC, Cagliari (2013)
9. Garau, C., Desogus, G., Stratigea, A.: Monitoring sustainability performance of insular territories against SDGs: the mediterranean case study region. J. Urban Plann. Dev. **148**(1), 05021069 (2021)
10. Mannaro, K., Baralla, G., Garau, C.: A goal-oriented framework for analyzing and modeling city dashboards in smart cities. In: Bisello, A., Vettorato, D., Laconte, P., Costa, S. (eds.) Smart and Sustainable Planning for Cities and Regions: Results of SSPCR 2017, pp. 179–195. Springer International Publishing, Cham (2018). https://doi.org/10.1007/978-3-319-75774-2_13
11. EU standards: CEF Context Broker T01 - Update of the ETSI NGSI-LD Specifications. https://ec.europa.eu/digital-building-blocks/wikis/display/CEFDIGITAL/EU+Standards (2020). Accessed 4 April 2022
12. FIWARE: Smart Data Models. https://www.fiware.org/smart-data-models/ (2020). Accessed 4 April 2022
13. Claassen, A.:. My API story: Business API Ecosystem. https://inform.tmforum.org/digital-ecosystems-open-apis/2019/04/api-story-business-api-ecosystem/ (2029). Accessed 4 April 2022

14. CEF: Connecting Europe Facility. https://ec.europa.eu/inea/en/connecting-europe-facility (2021). Accessed 4 April 2022
15. LoRaWAN: What is LoRaWAN® Specification. https://lora-alliance.org/about-lorawan/ (2022). Accessed 4 April 2022
16. Artificial Intelligence ACT: Proposal for a regulation of the European Parliament and of the council laying down harmonised rules on artificial intelligence and amending certain union legislative acts. https://eur-lex.europa.eu/legal-content/EN/TXT/?uri=CELEX%3A52021PC 0206 (2021). Accessed 11 April 2022
17. EIF4SCC: Proposal for a European Interoperability Framework for Smart Cities and Communities. https://op.europa.eu/en/publication-detail/-/publication/f69284c4-eacb-11eb-93a8-01aa75ed71a1/language-en (2021). Accessed 11 April 2022
18. Shaping Europe's digital future: Communication from the commission to the European parliament, the council, the European economic and social committee and the committee of the regions shaping Europe's digital future. https://eur-lex.europa.eu/legal-content/en/TXT/?uri=CELEX:52020DC0067 (2020). Accessed 11 April 2022
19. Smart Cities Marketplace: https://smart-cities-marketplace.ec.europa.eu/ (2020). Accessed 11 April 2022
20. Join, Boost, Sustain: The European way of digital transformation in cities and communities. https://digital-strategy.ec.europa.eu/en/news/join-boost-sustain-european-way-digital-transformation-cities-and-communities (2019). Accessed 11 April 2022
21. https://ec.europa.eu/isa2/home_en (2016)
22. Digital Single Market Strategy for Europe: Communication from the commission to the European parliament, the council, the European Economic and Social Committee and the Committee of the Regions. https://eur-lex.europa.eu/legal-content/EN/TXT/?uri=celex%3A5 2015DC0192 (2015). Accessed 11 April 2022
23. Connecting Europe Facility: https://ec.europa.eu/inea/en/connecting-europe-facility (2014). Accessed 11 April 2022
24. White Paper: Governing Smart Cities: Policy Benchmarks for Ethical and Responsible Smart City Development. https://www3.weforum.org/docs/WEF_Governing_Smart_Cities_2021.pdf (2021). Accessed 4 April 2022
25. ETSI TS 103 463. V1.1.: Access, Terminals, Transmission and Multiplexing (ATTM); Key Performance Indicators for Sustainable Digital Multiservice Cities. https://www.etsi.org/deliver/etsi_ts/103400_103499/103463/01.01.01_60/ts_103463v010101p.pdf (2017). Accessed 4 April 2022
26. Amsterdam Smart City: https://amsterdamsmartcity.com/ (2022). Accessed 11 April 2022
27. Amsterdam Economic Board: https://amsterdameconomicboard.com/ (2022). Accessed 11 April 2022
28. Mora, L., Deakin, M., Reid, A., Angelidou, M.: How to overcome the dichotomous nature of smart city research: proposed methodology and results of a pilot study. J. Urban Technol. **26**(2), 89–128 (2018)
29. Angelidou, M.: Smart city policies: a spatial approach. Cities **41**, S3–S11 (2014). https://doi.org/10.1016/j.cities.2014.06.007
30. Papa, R., Gargiulo, C., Franco, S., Russo, L.: Urban Smartness Vs Urban Competitive: un confronto tra le classifiche delle città italiane. INPUT 2014 - smart city: planning for energy, transportation and sustainability of the urban system. Tema. J. Land Use, Mobility Environ. 771–782 (2014) https://doi.org/10.6092/1970-9870/2555
31. Capra, C.F.: The smart city and its citizens: governance and citizen participation in amsterdam smart city. Int. J. E-Plann. Res. **5**(1), 20–38 (2016). https://doi.org/10.4018/IJEPR.201601 0102

32. Jameson, S., Richter, C., Taylor, L.: People's strategies for perceived surveillance in Amsterdam Smart City. Urban Geogr. **40**(10), 1467–1484 (2019). https://doi.org/10.1080/02723638. 2019.1614369

33. Putra, Z.D.W., Van der Knaap, W.G.M.: Urban innovation system and the role of an open web-based platform: the case of Amsterdam smart city. J. Reg. City Plann. **29**(3), 234 (2018). https://doi.org/10.5614/jrcp.2018.29.3.4

34. Smart Specialisation Platform: Strategies for research and innovation-driven growth. https:// s3platform.jrc.ec.europa.eu/ (2022). Accessed 11 April 2022

35. Helsinki Smart Region: https://helsinkismart.fi/ (2022). Accessed 11 April 2022

36. Helsinki-Uusimaa Region: https://www.uudenmaanliitto.fi/en/helsinki-uusimaa_region/hel sinki-uusimaa_region_facts (2022). Accessed 11 April 2022

37. Hielkema, H., Hongisto, P.: Developing the Helsinki smart city: the role of competitions for open data applications. J. Knowl. Econ. **4**(2), 190–204 (2013). https://doi.org/10.1007/s13 132-012-0087-6

38. European Innovation Ecosystems: Policy, strategy, how to apply and work programmes. https://ec.europa.eu/info/research-and-innovation/funding/funding-opportunities/funding-programmes-and-open-calls/horizon-europe/european-innovation-ecosystems_en   (2022). Accessed 11 April 2022

39. Markkula, M., Kune, H.: Making smart regions smarter: smart specialization and the role of universities in regional innovation ecosystems. Technol. Innovation Manag. Rev. **5**(10), 7–15 (2015). https://doi.org/10.22215/timreview/932

40. STRATEGY UPDATE 2018–2020: https://s3platform-legacy.jrc.ec.europa.eu/documents/ 20182/261578/Background+document_Helsinki+Smart+in+English.pdf/96270e35-47fb-4882-a1f8-14b9d6abfaa3 (2018). Accessed 11 April 2022

41. Smart City Expo World Congress: https://www.smartcityexpo.com/ (2014). Accessed 11 April 2022

42. ICity Rank: https://www.forumpa.it/icity-rank/ (2020). Accessed 11 April 2022

43. System Thinking for Efficiency Energy Planning: https://cordis.europa.eu/project/id/314277 (2015). Accessed 4 April 2022

44. Smart Florence Plan: https://ambiente.comune.fi.it/sites/ambiente.comune.fi.it/files/2019-11/ Smart_City_Plan_eng.pdf (2019). Accessed 11 April 2022

45. Comune di Firenze Open Data: https://opendata.comune.fi.it/ (2022). Accessed 11 April 2022

46. Snap4City: https://www.snap4city.org (2022). Accessed 11 April 2022

47. SELECT for Cities: Knowledge Hub. EU Select4Cities Pre-Commercial Procurement. https:// www.select4cities.eu/ (2022). Accessed 11 April 2022

48. DELOITTE: https://www2.deloitte.com/it/it.html (2022). Accessed 11 April 2022

49. Smart Specialisation Platform. https://s3platform.jrc.ec.europa.eu/region-page-test/-/region s/CY (2020). Accessed 11 April 2022

50. IoTOrionFiWare: https://fiware-orion.readthedocs.io/en/master/ (2022). Accessed 11 April 2022

Industry 4.0 Technologies and Italian Urban System: Between Smart Development and Increasing Inequalities

Michela Lazzeroni◉ and Paola Zamperlin(✉)◉

Department of Civilisations and Forms of Knowledge, University of Pisa, via Pasquale Paoli, 15-56126 Pisa, Italy
paola.zamperlin@unipi.it

Abstract. The growing diffusion of new digital technologies are leading to profound changes and disruptions in various areas of human life (personal, social, economic, environmental, …). The scale and intensity of these changes call for an analysis of their impact both towards development opportunities, and negative effects related to potential spatial inequalities. The aim of this paper is to understand how much the 4.0 technologies (IoT, 5G, sensors, robotics, AI, Big Data, etc.) have penetrated the Italian urban system, and whether this technological enhancement involves a widespread improvement in general conditions or, on the contrary, precedes an increase in the gap between smart cities and struggling cities. In addition to undoubted advantages coming from big data availability for waste management, air pollution control, energy efficiency, mobility management and overall urban planning, it is important to assess economic, social and territorial disparities, as possible effect of incorrect planning, lack of investments, inadequate policies and/or linked to specific geographic characteristics and different urban visions. After an initial theoretical framework on the Italian urban system, characterized by a high number of small and medium-sized cities with different responses to smart policies, the paper focusses on the distribution of 4.0 technology patents acquired in Italy between 2016 and 2021, considered at a NUTS 3 level. This methodology allows on the one hand to consider how responsive cities are and on the other to compare this response with general KPIs of the urban contexts.

Keywords: Industry 4.0 technologies · Smart development · Patents · Italian urban systems · Territorial disparities

1 Introduction

This paper intends to present the main goals, methodology and first results of a wider research project, aimed at representing the impact of the fourth industrial revolution, through historical-economic, historical-political, socio-cultural and geographic approaches. The dynamics of Industry 4.0 have so far been studied mainly by technological disciplines, which deal with developing enabling technologies and extending their

O. Gervasi et al. (Eds.): ICCSA 2022 Workshops, LNCS 13382, pp. 85–92, 2022.
https://doi.org/10.1007/978-3-031-10592-0_8

application, and the economic ones, which analyze the effects on regional and industrial competitiveness, on productivity, work organization [1]. However, the complexity of the phenomenon and the extent of its impact, also from a social and cultural point of view, recalls the need of the contribution of various disciplines and systemic interpretations to understand the connections between different spheres and outline future scenarios. In this context, the geographic approach can contribute because it helps to observe the territorial contexts where technologies develop, the concentration and diffusion processes, the places where they arrive or do not. In this sense, technologies are powerful agents for territorial transformation and for the generation of new spatialities and multiscalar connections.

This paper focuses on the geographical perspective, showing some initial reflections and results about the impact of Industry 4.0 technologies on the dynamics of smartness in the Italian urban system. In particular, the empirical work analyses the spatial distribution of 4.0 technology patents obtained by Italian inventors between 2016 and 2021, considered at a NUTS 3 level. The results show the asymmetry among different areas in Italy and also among systems characterized by large cities and others where small and medium-sized ones are present. This comparative analysis also allows to outline a new picture of the geographies of inequalities linked to Industry 4.0 technologies and to reflect on the policies connected to them, which should consider different response capacities of territorial contexts to smart paradigm and to current technological paths.

2 Theoretical Framework

The relevance of changes that have taken place in production systems and spaces, in the way the job market is organized, in the qualification of human resources [2, 3], as a consequence of the diffusion of the advanced latest technologies (robotics, 3D technologies, Artificial Intelligence, IoT, IoE, LBS, etc.), tends to justify the use of expressions such as the fourth industrial revolution. What distinguishes this revolution from the previous one is the speed with which technological changes take place, the extent and intensity of connections and transformations, the impact it is determining both in production processes and in work 4.0 [4, 5].

The complexity and pervasiveness of the changes that Industry 4.0 technologies are determining on the economic and productive system on the one hand and on social dynamics on the other, oblige to focus attention on what the impact of these changes can be both in positive terms, such as development opportunities, and in negative terms, such as the amplification of social inequalities or marginalization phenomena at different territorial scales [6].

From a geographical point of view, the focus is on how territorial systems and cities are strengthened and at the same time transformed by new technologies, both in terms of forms and landscapes and in terms of economic, social and cultural components. Internet networks, investments in sensors and 5G technologies, robotics, online platforms, are all technologies that are changing not only production spaces and, more generally, cities, making them increasingly smart and more connected systems in which physical and digital spaces, individuals and networks, multiple flows and identities intertwine.

Although the advantages of their diffusion are clear, Industry 4.0 technologies and their applications in cities, however, may increase not only social gaps but also disparities at different territorial scales: for example between advanced and emerging countries, or between metropolitan and peripheral ones, or among the different parts of cities [7]. The problem of technological and territorial gaps represents an important issue in the scientific and political debate; therefore, it appears important for understanding if Industry 4.0 may activate diffused smart development among regions or, on the contrary, contribute to a persistent divide between technology leaders and laggards [8].

Since it is assumed that the "smartness" degree of a territory is expressed by the improvement of the quality of life of its inhabitants, it will be important to analyse what its response is at the introduction of these technologies and whether they play a role in increasing social inequalities or, on the contrary, in the reduction of the pre-existing gaps, with evident repercussions in the political and territorial governance choices [9]. In this regard, the recent literature on innovation studies argues the need to rethink policies finalised to reduce inequalities and improve the different types of regions, through the promotion of place-sensitive development logics and the integration of various actions [10]. The objective is to intervene on standard contextual factors (education, employment, infrastructures, etc.), but also on the absorptive capacity of technologies by local systems and on specific innovative potentials, in terms of digital connectivity, technological competences, combination between advanced technologies and manufacturing sectors.

3 Main Goals and Methodological Approach

The reflections presented in this paper are part of a wider research, aimed at representing the impact of the fourth industrial revolution through the analysis of empirical evidence and the use of key performance indicators, according to differentiated theoretical and methodological perspectives. These representations will contribute to the identification of increasing opportunities, linked to the Industry 4.0 paradigm, and emerging divergences in the world of work, in society and in the territories. In particular, the main goal is to emphasize the geographical perspective, presenting some initial methodological reflections on the impact of Industry 4.0 technologies in the dynamics of "smartness" concerning the Italian urban system, with particular regard to the different answers of cities and to the formation of disparities between areas of the country and between cities of various sizes.

From a methodological point of view, in other works we have elaborated some data (source ISTAT) regarding technological investments, innovative projects and interventions on digital skills carried out or planned for the future [11]. Figure 1 represents the comparison among the 14 Italian metropolitan cities, both in terms of the number of enterprises investing in projects of innovation and in the second map related to the category of investments in digital and technological sectors. Analysing the first map, it is possible to highlight three distinct groups: a) with the highest values, we can group the areas of Milan, Rome and Turin; b) Naples, Florence, Bologna, Bari and Venice belong to a second group with intermediate values; c) the remaining metropolitan cities, Genoa, Palermo, Catania, Messina, Cagliari and Reggio di Calabria have the lowest values of digital investments.

The map on the right represents the total number of investments made, classified by different types of investment. It shows a strong propensity towards infrastructure (optic fiber and 4-5G connectivity in all cases hold the majority share of the investment), which is at the same time an indication of a primary need of firms and also of a gap in terms of the digital accessibility.

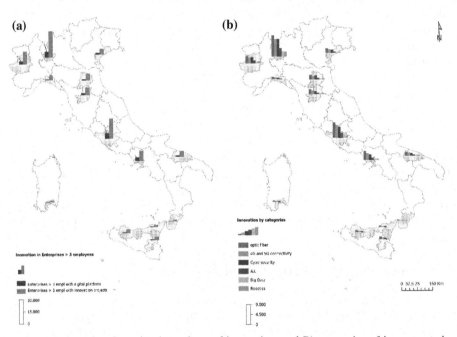

Fig. 1. A) Enterprises investing in projects of innovation, and B) categories of investments in digital sector, grouped by metropolitan cities. Source: ISTAT

Considering some European studies on a regional scale (NUT-2) [8, 12], in this paper we have tried to reflect on the geographical distribution of Industry 4.0 technologies, exploring the number of the European Patent Office (EPO) patent applications across NUT-3 areas in Italy between 2016–2021. Patent data has long been used in the literature and at European level to analyse innovative performance of regions and their capacity to produce and apply technologies. In this work we focus our attention on patents related to Industry 4.0 technologies, considering both the EPO classification (2017; 2020) [13] and a more restricted selection of Cooperative Patent Classification (CPC) classes, which is elaborated using specific keywords according to a methodology proposed by other recent studies [14]. Patents are allocated to NUT-3 Italian provinces considering the inventor's location and technological class of the patent.

This methodology of analysis based on patents in 4.0 technologies allows us to add a further step in the understanding of spatial patterns in the creation and diffusion of smart technologies and of the geography of the Fourth Industrial Revolution.

4   Results

As a general statement, the Italian urban system is characterized by a high distribution of small and medium-sized centers compared to a small number of large cities. According to previous studies [15], the asymmetry of metropolitan areas emerges in Italy: Rome, Milan and Naples, for example, have critical housing densities, with all the problems that arise, and a significant gap is highlighted between the metropolitan cities of the center-north and the south of the peninsula in terms of some smart components.

The area of origin of the patents (Fig. 2, Fig. 3, and Fig. 4) is aligned with a general picture of division between North and South and confirms some results emerged from the distribution of investments in innovation projects and digital sector (Fig. 1).

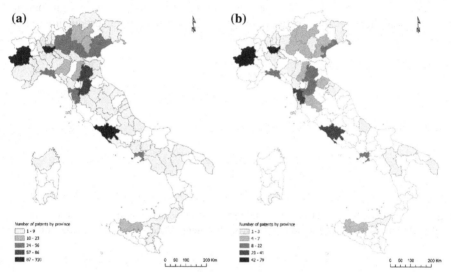

Fig. 2. Italian patents related to Industry 4.0 technologies issued between 2016–2021: A) according to EPO classification, and B) according to CPC restricted selection (Martinelli *et al.*, 2021). Source: Data of the European Patent Office, elaboration by the authors.

As can be seen, the classification proposed by EPO includes a greater number of patents (just under 400) with a marked concentration in the central and northern provinces, with the slight exceptions of Naples and Palermo (in ninth and twenty-first place, see Fig. 3). Milano, Torino and Roma are attested with significantly higher values compared to the other provincial averages; these data confirms the relevance of these three areas in the ability to produce new technologies, in connection with their economic development, the concentration of universities and research centers and qualified human resources, the demand for innovation of the local ecosystem. The provinces included in Lombardia, Veneto, Emilia Romagna regions, which are the most industrialized areas of the country and present a tradition in small and medium-sized manufacturing, have a more homogeneous and continuous distribution. As can be seen from Fig. 3, other Italian metropolitan areas emerge, such as Bologna, Florence and Genoa, but also provinces with smaller cities oriented towards Industry 4.0, thanks to the push of the university research activity (such as Pisa, Padua or Trento) or of a manufacturing context more oriented towards technological changes (such as Bergamo, Brescia, Treviso, Parma). Despite the phenomenon of territorial polarization, the EPO classification reveals a widespread presence of patent production in Italy, which however excludes the provinces that are geographically more marginal or specialized in other activities such as agriculture and tourism.

The second classification, which is more restrictive, considers a number of patents equal to approximately one quarter of the previous one. As can be seen from the map, the distribution is spatially more selective and strongly unequal between areas of the center/north and south. This classification strengthens metropolitan areas and those that rely on a high-level university or specialized in scientific-technological disciplines. A university city like Pisa (Fig. 4) emerges from the previous picture, a sign that the presence of higher education institutes in the area also impacts in the production of new technologies.

Fig. 3. Italian patents related to Industry 4.0 technologies issued between 2016–2021 according to EPO classification. Source: Data of the European Patent Office, elaboration by the authors.

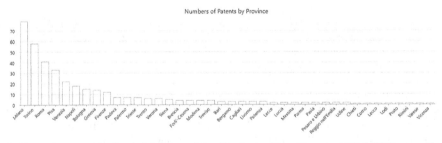

Fig. 4. Italian patents related to Industry 4.0 technologies issued between 2016–2021 according to CPC restricted selection (Martinelli *et al.*, 2021). Source: Data of the European Patent Office, elaboration by the authors.

In fact, all the provinces characterized by a marginality linked to the predominantly mountainous territorial configuration and/or in an internal area position are excluded from the innovation processes that go through patents. The picture that emerges from Fig. 2B is definitely alarming: large areas of the southern center and islands are not affected by the phenomenon. The only exception is Naples, which is confirmed to be a growing area for which the outcomes of recent years investment policies and the creation of technological districts emerge.

5 Conclusions

The comparative analysis of the impact of the growing diffusion of Industry 4.0 technologies and smart dynamics in the Italian urban system allows us not only to outline a picture of the differences, but also to reflect on the policies connected to them, which often have replicated initiatives without considering the different territorial characteristics and the different response capacities of urban contexts.

The analysis proposed here required the extraction of patents attributable to Industry 4.0 from the dataset of the European Patent Office, according to two different classifications. The results, although differing in quantity and quality of the data, converge in outlining a strong gap between the leading areas of the country and a south that struggles to reach the development levels of the center-north. In addition to highlighting the critical differences in geographical location of Industry 4.0 technologies, this research confirms the role of the accumulative effects derived from the concentration of the technological capabilities and of the spatial proximity to the knowledge production centers or to advanced firms. The factors of socio-economic marginality and those of a geographical one (morphology, position, etc.) further explain the picture of differences, even within the most advanced regions.

The aim of the next research will be to understand whether the need to rapidly adopt Industry 4.0 solutions will help to increase the gap between developed and marginal areas, or if on the contrary it will accelerate development processes in the short and medium term. The risk is linked to persistent or increasing divergences among different parts of Italy and policies may be important to ensure the diffusion of the benefits of Industry 4.0 and to manage the impact of advanced technologies in the different territorial contexts, including peripheral ones. In particular, it seems crucial to promote place-based policies, in terms of advanced infrastructures, technologies, support for businesses, material and digital accessibility, smart services, accompanied by territorial animation projects, enhancement of the quality of life, promotion of research, training and new entrepreneurship, which aims to achieve a dynamic of counter-trend and reduce inequalities..

Acknowledgments. This study was supported by the University of Pisa, Project PRA_2020_15 "The impact of the fourth industrial revolution between opportunities and inequalities".

References

1. De Propis, L., Bailey, D. (eds.) Industry 4.0 and Regional Transformation. Routledge, London (2020)
2. Brynjolfsson, E., McAfee, A.: The Second Machine Age Work, Progress, and Prosperity in a Time of Brilliant Technologies. WW Norto, New York (2014)

3. Cipriani, A., Gramolati, A., Mari, G.: Il lavoro 4.0. In: La Quarta Rivoluzione Industriale e le Trasformazioni Delle Attività Lavorative. Firenze University Press, Firenze (2018)

4. Schwab, K.: The Fourth Industrial Revolution. World Economic Forum, Geneva (2016)

5. Marsh, P.: The New Industrial Revolution. Consumers, Globalization and the End of Mass Production. Yale University Press, New Haven (2012)

6. Balland, P., Boschma, R.: Mapping the potentials of regions in Europe to contribute to new knowledge production in Industry 4.0 technologies. Reg. Stud. **55**(10–11), 1652–1666 (2021)

7. Lazzeroni, M., Vanolo, A.: La nuova rivoluzione industriale tra smartness e crisi: le prospettive della geografia. In: Lazzeroni, M., Morazzoni, M. (eds.) Interpretare la quarta rivoluzione industriale: la geografia in dialogo con le altre discipline, pp. 87–100, 2020

8. Corradini, C., Santini, E., Vecciolini, C.: The geography of Industry 4.0 technologies across European regions. Reg. Stud. **55**(10–11), 1667–1680 (2021)

9. Azzari, M., Garau, C., Nesi, P., Paolucci, M., Zamperlin, P.: Smart city governance strategies to better move towards a smart urbanism. In: Gervasi, O., et al. (eds.) Computational Science and Its Applications – ICCSA 2018. Lecture Notes in Computer Science, vol. 10962, pp. 639–653. Springer, Cham (2018). https://doi.org/10.1007/978-3-319-95168-3_43

10. Iammarino, S., Rodriguez-Pose, A., Storper, M.: Regional inequality in Europe: evidence, theory and policy implications. J. Econ. Geogr. **19**, 273–298 (2019). https://doi.org/10.1093/jeg/lby021

11. Lazzeroni, E.M., Zamperlin, P.: Nuovi paradigmi tecnologici e impatto sui sistemi urbani tra convergenze e fratture. In: Dini, F., Martellozzo, F., Randelli, F., Romei, P. (eds.) Oltre la globalizzazione – Feedback, Società di Studi Geografici. Memorie geografiche NS 19, pp. 13–20. Firenze University Press, Firenze (2021)

12. Capello, R., Lenzi, C.: 4.0 technological revolution and economic competitiveness: unexpected opportunities for peripheral areas. Scienze Regionali, Italian J. Reg. Sci. **1**(2022), 13–36 (2022). https://doi.org/10.14650/103209

13. EPO: Patents and the Fourth Industrial Revolution. The global technology trends enabling the data-driven economy (2017 and 2020)

14. Martinelli, A., Mina, A., Moggi, M.: The enabling technologies of industry 4.0: examining the seeds of the fourth industrial revolution. Ind. Corportate Change **30**(1), 161–188 (2021)

15. Zamperlin, P., Garau, C.: Smart region: analisi e rappresentazione della smartness delle città metropolitane italiane. Bollettino AIC **161**, 59–71 (2017). https://doi.org/10.13137/2282-572X/21828

Measuring Urban Competitiveness Through the Lens of Sustainability: An Application at the Urban Districts Level in the City of Naples (Italy)

Sabrina Sgambati, Gerardo Carpentieri[(✉)], and Carmela Gargiulo

Department of Civil, Building and Environmental Engineering, University of Naples Federico II, P.le Tecchio 80, 80125 Naples, Italy
{sabrina.sgamabati,gerardo.carpentieri,gargiulo}@unina.it

Abstract. Urban competitiveness, the study of which has broadened significantly in recent decades, is the ability of a city to attract investments, people and new activities. It depends on a multitude of closely interrelated factors that characterise urban areas. The multidimensional approach, which is typical of urban competitiveness studies, allows the attitude to sustainability to be considered as one of the possible measures of competitiveness. This work aims to evaluate, at the local level, the relationship between urban competitiveness and the achievement of the Sustainable Development Goals adopted with Agenda 2030. The paper proposes a composite index structured in several dimensions that are useful to compare the competitive performance of cities' districts in relation to social, economic and environmental sustainability features, providing a multidimensional ranking. The application phase focuses on the municipality of Naples, in Italy, chosen for the heterogeneity of its districts. The overall competitive performance of the city's districts is highlighted, and their strengths and shortcomings in the different dimensions are considered. The results aim to emphasise the main components of competitiveness of the Neapolitan districts and support decision-makers in improving competitiveness in line with the Sustainable Development Goals.

Keywords: Urban competitiveness · Sustainable development goals · Urban districts

1 Introduction

Since the end of the last century, with the advent of globalisation, the progressive liberalisation of markets and the territorial relocation of businesses, the concept of competitiveness has taken on an increasingly important role, including in the context of the governance of urban and territorial transformations [1, 2]. It is now common for cities, regions and nations to assess, improve and publicise their competitive standing with other places [3, 41]. The use of the concept of competitiveness at the territorial level has led to a wide-reaching debate in the scientific community, sparking dissent among

© The Author(s), under exclusive license to Springer Nature Switzerland AG 2022
O. Gervasi et al. (Eds.): ICCSA 2022 Workshops, LNCS 13382, pp. 93–108, 2022.
https://doi.org/10.1007/978-3-031-10592-0_9

scholars such as Krugman and Lall, who underlined how the application of the concept of economic competitiveness on a territorial scale generates both conceptual and applicative criticism. These statements are mainly based on an assessment of the numerous differences between companies and territorial contexts from the point of view of both the organisational structure and the objectives pursued. A rigid transfer of the concept of competitiveness from economic activities to territorial contexts risks not adequately taking into account the complexity of the latter. Therefore, the innumerable elements and relationships which compose these contexts may be neglected, making such analyses unreliable or even harmful in supporting choices [4, 5].

Later studies have further investigated these critical issues, providing a different interpretative key. This has highlighted the need to apply the concept of competitiveness to urban and territorial systems [6–8]. Further advancement is provided by Camagni (2002), who states that it is possible to consider phenomena such as globalisation and internationalisation as part of a shared heritage because all regions can be affected by the possible benefits and threats deriving from these phenomena depending on their extrinsic characteristics [9]. This highlights how the specificities of each region can be essential elements of the competition between different territorial entities [10]. These characteristics include aspects such as human capital, innovation capacities, geomorphological characteristics of the region, types of infrastructures and all the other factors [11, 12] that contribute to the multidimensional nature of urban competitiveness. The economic and social importance of this competition has made competitiveness a topic of great interest, especially for those involved in the governance of urban and regional transformations.

The multidimensional approach, which is typical of urban competitiveness studies, allows considering sustainability as one of the main components of competitiveness. In this regard, this work examines the relationship between urban competitiveness and the achievement of the Sustainable Development Goals adopted by the United Nation with the document Agenda 2030. This relationship takes on particular implications at the city scale. The paper aims at developing a composite index structured in several dimensions useful to compare the competitive performance of cities' districts in terms of social, economic and environmental sustainability. The index has been tested through an application to the municipality of Naples, in Italy. The city was chosen for the heterogeneity of its districts which differently contribute to the overall level of competitiveness of the municipality. The objective is to emphasize the competitive advantage provided by the city's districts and highlight their strengths and shortcomings in the different dimensions considered. The results aim to emphasise the main components of competitiveness of the Neapolitan districts and support decision-makers in improving competitiveness in line with the Sustainable Development Goals.

2   The Multidimensionality of Urban Competitiveness

The growing interest in advancing the research which tries to integrate the themes of competitiveness and urban development is motivated by the central role that cities play in modern society [13]. These territorial contexts have become the reference point for global economic and social development [14]. In recent years, cities all over the world have started a competition among themselves in order to offer the best conditions to attract investments, citizens and new skills. In this context of global competition, the traditional approach that envisaged the exclusive study of the relationships between a city and its neighbouring territorial context is now outdated. Today, thanks to new communication and transport technologies, cities are able to interact, materially and immaterially, with other territorial entities, even ones that are geographically distant. This has enabled urban entities, located a considerable distance away from each other, to compete in the most diverse sectors, from the production of goods and the provision of specific services to environmental protection.

Large cities such as New York, London and Tokyo are increasingly orienting their future development choices by pursuing the priority objective of dealing with competition from other international urban entities of the same size, neglecting internal competition within their respective national borders [15]. In Europe, with the creation of the European common market and the free movement of goods and people, cities have become more attentive to the opportunities and threats arising from the European integration process in order to affirm their European leadership in the various sectors of competition. In Asia, in order for the city of Hong Kong to increase its importance as a reference economic-financial centre for the continent, it must compete with other Asian cities that aim to play the same role, such as Guangzhou and Shanghai [16–19].

One of the most common definitions of urban competitiveness in the literature states that this concept represents a city's ability to confirm and/or improve its competitiveness within a specific area or context (regional, national or international) [20]. Urban competition takes place between similar territorial contexts that pursue the same objectives in order to preserve the resources and improve the well-being of the members of their cities through optimal management of the many external and internal factors that can influence the cities' development.

Before the concept of competitiveness reached its full application in the urban planning field, numerous scholars sought to develop an adequate theoretical support base. In the first studies on territorial competitiveness, only the economic aspects capable of making a specific urban context attractive for companies, investors and the marketing of the goods produced were taken into consideration [21]. Kresl (1999) states that a vision of urban competitiveness aimed at identifying the factors capable of attracting productive investments is made up of two components: the economic and the strategic [22]. The first includes aspects related to production, infrastructure, location, economic structure and urban services. The second component includes aspects such as government efficiency, urban development strategy, cooperation between the public and private sectors and institutional flexibility. Factors that are not preparatory to businesses are excluded from this type of consideration.

Martin and Simmie (2008) contribute to broadening the scientific debate on this issue, defining urban competitiveness as "the ability of cities to continually upgrade their business environment, skill base, and physical, social and cultural infrastructures, so as to attract and retain high-growth, innovative and profitable firms, and an educated, creative and entrepreneurial workforce, to thereby enable it to achieve a high rate of productivity, high employment rate, high wages, high GDP per capita, and low levels of income inequality and social exclusion" [23].

Further in-depth studies have expanded the field of study with the inclusion of other tangible and intangible aspects (environmental, cultural, technological, human capital, artistic beauty, etc.) that can, directly and indirectly, influence the localisation choices of both businesses and citizens choosing an urban environment in which to reside and/or invest in order to satisfy their needs and aspirations [24, 25].

Over the years, different scientific disciplines have paid particular attention to developing (quantitative and/or qualitative) methods that can provide a measure of the level of competition between cities. This has been motivated primarily by the interest of public and private decision-makers in identifying adequate information support to guide future development choices [26]. Measuring the level of competitiveness of a territorial system (region, province, metropolitan city and city) is very complicated. The phenomena which typify such systems are characterised by a multiplicity of "facets" (such as the degree of well-being, quality of life, infrastructural endowment, services, etc.) and therefore can be difficult to measure [27, 28].

In assessing cities' level of competitiveness, the analyses obtained through measurement tools which use single indicators cannot be considered exhaustive. There is a need to use large sets of indicators that can measure a great number of characteristic aspects.

For cities, it is now evident that satisfying individual and collective needs in order to improve citizens' quality of life is crucial element of urban competitiveness [29]. These new needs have gradually transformed the competitive priorities of cities from exclusive support of the productive sector (such as technical infrastructures or investment incentives) to the promotion of development oriented towards the well-being of the individual from a sustainable perspective. This evolution of the concept of urban competitiveness was well summarised by Porter, who formulated four development phases for this theme [30]: 1) competitiveness aimed at the promotion of production, 2) competitiveness aimed at encouraging investments, 3) competitiveness aimed at innovation and 4) competitiveness aimed at improving quality of life.

3   Urban Competitiveness and Sustainable Cities

The current trends of urban population growth, changing lifestyles, unsustainable production patterns and consumption of services and goods increase the pressures on the social and environmental components of cities. By 2030, the global share of the urban population is projected to rise to 60% and it is estimated that a third of the global population will be living in cities with at least half a million inhabitants [30]. Satisfying the basic needs of urban populations while ensuring the integrity of the environment, and promoting economic development and social inclusion is one of the principal targets of our time. Urban communities face many problems that make sustainable development a difficult target to achieve but a necessary goal.

In the context of competitiveness aimed at the governance of urban and regional transformations, scientific literature and professional practice have highlighted how it is possible to achieve an improvement in the ability to compete through implementing specific infrastructural and functional solutions that can intervene in both critical issues and in the improvement of the characteristics on which the competition is based [31]. However, in estimating the competitive advantages deriving from the implementation of specific solutions, it must be taken into account that their effectiveness is also linked to the local characteristics of the territorial context of intervention and to those of the supra-urban context within which the competition takes place. Furthermore, it is also necessary to consider the possible impacts of external events (economic crises, climate change, difficulties in the procurement of resources, health emergencies, etc.), which can significantly reduce their effectiveness [32]. The occurrence of these local and global events can also affect the full functioning of a city, with possible negative repercussions for all components of the urban system. In order to minimise these criticalities that influence urban competitiveness, it is important to intervene through a sustainable approach [33, 34].

The direct and indirect benefits that can be generated through the implementation of solutions aimed at improving urban sustainability are manifold. Different researchers have shown that making a city sustainable reduces the negative environmental, social and economic consequences of calamitous events. The implementation of interventions capable of influencing the mitigation of and/or adaptation to natural and anthropogenic phenomena and, at the same time, influencing sustainable development can allow cities to achieve better performance in economic, social and environmental terms compared to other similar regional contexts, in both ordinary and extraordinary conditions [35].

For cities, improving their ability to promote social, economic and environmental sustainability can also allow them to attract new citizens and more investment [36]. The advantages of living and carrying out economic and social activities in a city that has invested in sustainability can motivate individuals' and economic operators' choices of location.

On the basis of these considerations, over the years, an increasing number of studies aimed at ranking urban competitiveness have given greater weight to aspects related to sustainability. Orienting the governance of urban transformations towards the implementation of intervention solutions aimed at improving urban sustainability offers the opportunity for cities to improve the quality of life and safety of their citizens and economic operators [37]. Being able to live and work in a regional context that offers adequate guarantees in terms of safety, services, job opportunities and environmental quality is now a fundamental element of localisation and investment choices [38]. From the point of view of companies and investors, locating one's business in an area where disasters can compromise the functionality of the settlement system constitutes an unsustainable risk factor for a private economic operator [23].

4 GIS-Based Methodology

4.1 The Components of Urban Competitiveness

This research intends to analyse the competitiveness of urban districts in relation to sustainability, as it was intended in Agenda 2030 [39]. One of the expected results is the construction of a ranking.

Urban competitiveness is a multidimensional concept made up of different components. Therefore, its study requires a systemic and integrated approach. First, we have to consider which urban features are most meaningful and effective in gaining a competitive advantage. This consideration hinges on two factors. On the one hand, the choice of urban characteristics depends on the general framework of the research, which, in this case, aims at analysing the relationship between competitiveness and the achievement of Agenda 2030 sustainability objectives. On the other hand, the selected urban characteristics must reflect the territorial scale of the study, in this case, the local level.

Considering the intersection between sustainability and competitiveness, intended as the ability to attract investments, business, activities and people, we identified seven categories encapsulating a certain number of variables. The categories refer to some of the Sustainable Development Goals (SDGs) that we considered significant for improving the competitiveness of cities' districts from an urban planning perspective. Specifically, they refer to:

– Goal 3: Good health and well-being;
– Goal 4: Quality education;
– Goal 8: Decent work and economic growth;
– Goal 10: Reduced inequalities;
– Goal 11: Sustainable cities and communities;
– Goal 12: Responsible consumption and production;
– Goal 13: Climate action.

SDG 3 is aligned with indicators linked to the overall level of well-being of the population. This has a considerable influence on districts' competitiveness, since districts that can ensure high-quality health services, sports facilities and a better quality of life are, in general, the most attractive. Goal 4 is linked to the level of education of people—which is a social component of competitiveness—and to the availability and accessibility of schools and educational services. Goal 8 relates to urban competitiveness in terms of the distribution of job opportunities and the quality of working life (e.g., travel time to work, number of commercial activities, etc.). Goal 10 is connected to the necessity of eliminating disparities among territories, favouring social justice and reducing marginalisation to build more inclusive and attractive districts. This is also linked to Goal 11, which addresses making urban areas places of prosperity and growth. Goal 12 entails indicators linked to sustainable energy and resources consumption. Urban areas have a key role in this sector, and cities that are successful in saving energy are competitive. Finally, Goal 13 is connected to climate resilience: Climate compatible cities attract more business and investments and guarantee safety for their inhabitants.

4.2 The Indicators

The categories consist of a flexible number of indicators which reflect the characteristics that make a city competitive at an international level. We selected 39 indicators on the basis of their meaningfulness and the availability, accessibility, measurability and coverage of data.

The normalisation of indicators was necessary to make characteristics comparable and aggregable. We used the min-max method (1) because it is applicable to indicators with positive, negative or zero values and because it allows one to widen the variability of indicators lying within a small interval:

$$y_{SCi} = \frac{x_{SCi} - min(x_{SCi})}{max(x_{SCi}) - min(x_{SCi})} \tag{1}$$

where S indicates the statistical unit, C the category and i the indicator.

The distances created with normalisation represent the absolute measurements of the gap between each single statistical unit and the "ideal" one. We considered negative those indicators that have a negative impact on competitiveness.

For the finalisation of the dataset, a correlation analysis is also necessary to evaluate the relationships between indicators and verify their impact on the overall structure of indicators.

4.3 Building a SDG Urban Competitiveness Index

We proceeded with the aggregation of normalised indicators belonging to the different categories. In the literature, there are numerous criteria for weighting and then aggregating variables, ranging from systems of weights attributable ex ante to criteria that infer the meaningfulness of indicators from the analysis of the data (e.g., implementing multivariate statistical analysis). However, sometimes these methods of aggregation implicitly have a degree of subjectivity. We did not develop a system of weights since this paper represents a first approach to the research. Furthermore, we wanted to develop an innovative application to the district scale. Therefore, we put forward the hypothesis of interchangeability between dimensions, giving equal importance to different indicators.

Hence, we used simple averages to calculate a partial indicator of competitiveness for single categories (SC) (2). This operation is conceptually equivalent to putting all indicators on an equal footing.

$$M_{SCj} = \frac{x_{SC1} + x_{SC2} + \ldots + x_{SCn}}{n} = \frac{\sum_{I=1}^{n} x_{SCI}}{n} \tag{2}$$

Subsequently, in order to obtain a general measurement of competitiveness, we proceeded with the aggregation of the M_{scj} indexes, which represent the competitiveness of statistical units within single categories. We obtained a composite index that represents the competitiveness of districts as a result of their performance in sustainable development.

$$I_{UCSDG} = \frac{M_{S1} + M_{S1} + \ldots + M_{SM}}{m} = \frac{\sum_{C=1}^{m} M_{SC}}{m} \tag{3}$$

While M_{scj} indicates the level of competitiveness in the C category, I_{UCSDG} shows the level of competitiveness of the S district, taking into account all the categories of the model. The results can be represented in GIS and in bar graphs.

Table 1. The system of indicators.

Sustainable Development Goals	ID	Indicator
Goal 3: Good health and well-being	01	Infant mortality
	02	Disease mortality
	03	Inadequate hospitalisation
	04	Public hospitals
	05	Integrated home care
	06	Infantile vaccination coverage
	07	Health index
	08	Incidence of disease
Goal 4: Quality education	09	Absence of education
	10	Tertiary education
	11	Gender education gap
	12	Gender work gap
Goal 8: Decent work and economic growth	13	Employment rate
	14	Firms
	15	Employees
Goal 10: Reduced inequalities	16	Average income per capita
	17	Born from working mothers
	18	Adolescent fertility rate
	19	Dependent drug users
Goal 11: Sustainable cities and communities	20	State of conservation of buildings
	21	Public busses density
	22	Railway density
	23	Cultural facilities
	24	Schools
	25	Areas of historical, artistic and cultural interest
	26	Public areas
	27	Urban safety
	28	Road deaths
Goal 12: Responsible consumption and production	29	Residential energy consumption
	30	Non-residential energy consumption

(continued)

Table 1. (*continued*)

Sustainable Development Goals	ID	Indicator
Goal 13: Climate action	31	Protected areas
	32	Forest fires
	33	Contaminated sites
	34	Green urban areas

5   The Application

For the application of the proposed methodology, we chose the municipality of Naples, Italy. This case study was selected because of the wide heterogeneity of resources and characteristics of the 31 districts of the city. Naples is the third most populous city in Italy, with about 900,000 inhabitants, an average population density of 8,000 inhabitants/Km^2 and a municipal area of 112 Km^2. The urban structure of the city can be divided in three main urban zones: the "periphery zone", which includes districts that took shape during the 80s and some ex-industrial areas in the east area; the "inner zone", which includes the most populous residential area and the principal business districts; and the "central zone", which is the most densely populated area and the historical area of the city that coincides with the UNESCO perimeter.

Due to this heterogeneity, we expected that some districts would be more competitive in certain categories of "sustainable competitiveness", while other districts would

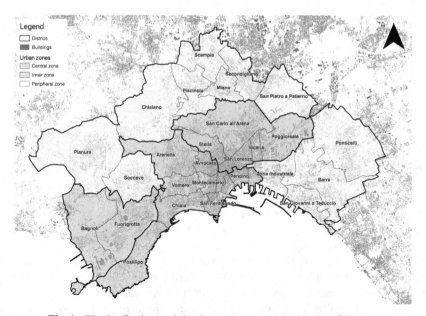

Fig. 1. The 31 districts and the three urban zones in the city of Naples.

distinguish themselves in different categories. We also expected interesting results from the combination of the single categories of competitiveness (Fig. 1).

5.1 The Set of Indicators

To define the final set of indicators, we considered 0.8 as the threshold value for correlation coefficients in deleting indicators that were too correlated. This led to a restricted set of 34 indicators, listed in Table 1. The indicators were divided into the seven SDG categories.

5.2 Results and Discussion

Through applying the proposed methodology, we obtained the final score for competitiveness of each district in the city of Naples. The normalised value of competitiveness for the city is 41.72 on 100. Chiaia is the district with the maximum value of competitiveness (100) and Miano is the district with the minimum value (0).

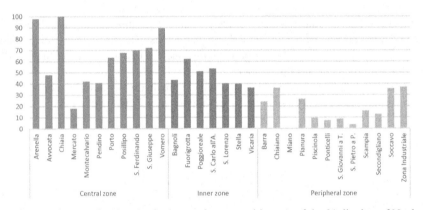

Fig. 2. Bar diagram showing the final score for competitiveness of the 31 districts of Naples.

The results shown in Fig. 2 reveal that the peripheral districts are less competitive than the central districts. Specifically, the less competitive districts are those located in the north of the peripheral zone (Miano, Piscinola, San Pietro a Patierno, Secondigliano and Scampia) and in the east of this zone (Ponticelli and San Giovanni a Teduccio). The most competitive districts of the city are Chiaia, Arenella and Vomero. The district with the lowest score for competitiveness in the central zone is Mercato.

The objective of this application is not only to evaluate the competitiveness of the city of Naples but also to highlight the shortcomings and the favourable aspects of each district in different sectors, in order to support decision-makers in improving sustainability and competitiveness. Therefore, it is worth discussing the scores obtained in the different categories that correspond to the SDGs of Agenda 2030. Regarding "good health and well-being" (Fig. 3a), the distribution of scores is more uniform. This can be traced back to a uniform distribution of health services and homogenous accessibility

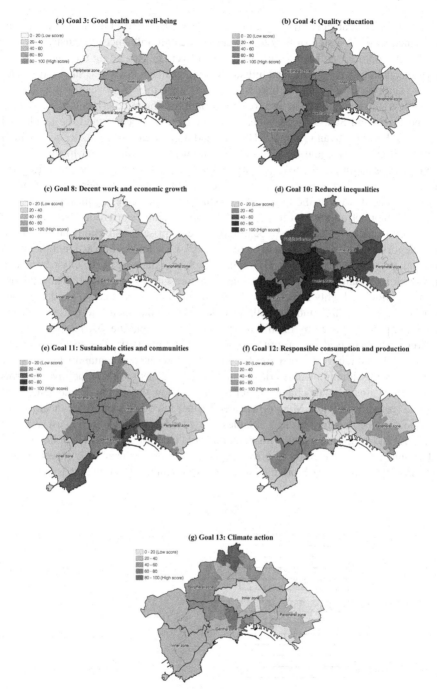

Fig. 3. A representation of the results obtained for each SDG category for the 31 districts in the city of Naples.

to healthcare. The category "quality education" (Fig. 3b) reflects the same trend of "reduced inequalities", a sign of how the level of education influences the distribution of social and economic well-being and, so, competitiveness. Regarding the category "reduced inequalities", the coastal and hillside districts (Chiaia, Posillipo, San Ferdinando, Vomero and Arenella) score the highest (Fig. 3d) since they host wealthy populations and are less subjected to gender and social inequalities. The middle-income districts are Montecalvario and San Giuseppe, located in the historical centre, and the residential districts of Fuorigrotta and Bagnoli. The east and north areas are characterised by high levels of poverty and inequalities. The only exception is the districts of the historic centre, where perhaps the proximity to university facilities supports tertiary education. Regarding the category "decent work and economic growth", Chiaia, Vomero and Arenella, along with the district of the city centre, distinguish themselves again for their wide range of job opportunities and low rate of unemployment. Fuorigrotta also achieves a high score because of its high concentration of enterprises, institutions and workers. The category "sustainable cities and communities", which takes into account the urban structure, presents a peak for San Giuseppe, which is at the core of the city centre, and a depression for San Pietro a Patierno, due to the presence of the airport. The category "climate action" is highly affected by the distribution of green areas. This determines the primacy of Chiaiano and Arenella in this category, thanks to the presence of the Camaldoli park, followed by the hill district of Posillipo and the district of San Carlo all'Arena, characterised by the presence of Capodimonte park. The eastern districts, along with Bagnoli, have lower scores because of the presence of contaminated sites due to the decommissioning of industrial plants. Soccavo is also less competitive in terms of the fight against climate change. Figures 4 and 5 show the results for the districts of Mercato (central zone) and Miano (peripheral zone) in comparison to the mean values of the SDG categories for the city of Naples. The two districts have the lowest scores in the central and peripheral zones. This diagram could therefore be useful to policymakers and technicians to help identify priority categories to improve the urban competitiveness of districts with an approach oriented towards sustainability development.

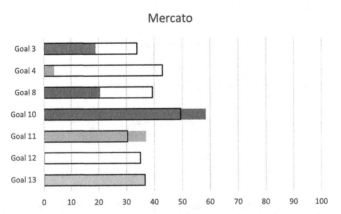

Fig. 4. The results for the SDG categories for the Mercato district in the central zone of Naples (in black the values of the SDG categories for the greater city).

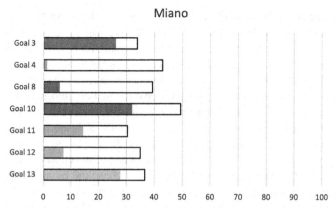

Fig. 5. The results for the SDG categories for the Miano district in the peripheral zone of Naples (in black the values of the SDG categories for the greater city).

6 Conclusion

The study of competitiveness has significantly broadened in recent decades, becoming a pivotal aspect of the governance of territorial and urban transformation. Due to the increasing importance of the urban contexts in global growth, urban areas are now competing with each other to attract resources, investments, people and activities. Cities are able to compete in many sectors thanks to the opportunities offered by communication and transport technologies, and different aspects contribute to their attractiveness. Scholars agree that numerous features influence the localisation of new business and the choices of citizens and users. In this sense, urban competitiveness is made up of different interrelated components that make it multidimensional.

The multidimensional approach, typical of urban competitiveness studies, allows sustainability to be considered as one of the components influencing the attractiveness and magnetism of urban areas. Satisfying the basic needs of citizens, promoting equal economic development, ensuring a high-quality environment and mitigating and adapting to climate change are some of the principal targets of the model of urban sustainability, with an evident impact on the competitiveness of urban areas. As a matter of fact, the achievement of sustainability goals and the implementation of sustainable actions can support cities' performance in economic, social and environmental terms. Orienting urban development towards sustainability offers the opportunity for cities to improve the quality of life and safety of their citizens and economic operators.

In recent decades, an increasing number of studies aimed at ranking the competitiveness of cities have given greater weight to aspects related to sustainability. Many urban sustainability rankings have also been proposed by the scientific community, a sign of how cities are called upon to compete by developing their own strategies to face the challenges of sustainability [40]. Although many of these studies focus on the regional or metropolitan scale, we found it interesting to consider the resources for sustainability at the district scale to measure urban competitiveness according to the peculiarities of single districts.

Given this scientific framework, it is worth analysing the competitiveness of urban districts according to their level of sustainability. In order to achieve this objective, we developed a simple methodology to compare the competitiveness of the districts of a city in terms of sustainability. To build the system of components and indicators useful for the comparison, we referred to some of the SDGs of Agenda 2030 since they represent objectives that are shared by many countries. We defined an algorithm to calculate a composite index that measures a district's competitiveness in relation to its sustainable features, and we implemented the algorithm in GIS. The result was a multidimensional ranking that can be visualised on digital maps or on radar graphs, enabling a comparison of both a city's overall score and its performance in one of the chosen components.

For the application of the proposed method, we chose the municipality of Naples in Italy, which is characterised by the high heterogeneity of its districts in terms of resources, vocations and sustainable development. We found a great disparity between central districts and suburban areas. Specifically, the less competitive districts are the northern suburbs (such as Scampia, Miano, San Pietro a Patierno and Secondigliano), which are affected by social and economic problems, together with the eastern suburbs (such as Barra, Ponticelli and San Giovanni), whose marginality is the result of the decommissioning of industrial sites and the lack of adequate governance of urban transformation. The most competitive districts are Chiaia, Vomero and Arenella, followed by San Giuseppe, San Ferdinando and Posillipo, which are known to be the wealthiest districts in the city. We also studied the differences among the different components in order to highlight the strengths and weaknesses of the districts. The aim of this was to support decision-makers in improving sustainability and competitiveness.

This study aimed to provide a basic comparison of the sustainability characteristics of districts for competitiveness purposes. In this sense, it represents the first step of a wider study on the subject that will focus on the integration of sustainable development and competitive advantages. Future developments of the research will regard the structure of the methodology especially for what concerns the system of weightings. Furthermore, another application to a different city may confirm the replicability of the Index also for other contexts.

References

1. Feurer, R., Chaharbaghi, K.: Defining competitiveness. Manag. Decis. **32**(2), 49–58 (1994). https://doi.org/10.1108/00251749410054819
2. Sassen, S.: Cities in a world economy. Sage Publications (2018). ISBN: 9781506362618
3. Malecki, E.: Jockeying for position: what it means and why it matters to regional development policy when places compete. Reg. Stud. **38**(9), 1101–1120 (2004). https://doi.org/10.1080/0034340042000292665
4. Krugman, P.: Competitiveness: a dangerous obsession. Foreign Aff. **73**, 28 (1994)
5. Lall, S.: Competitiveness indices and developing countries: an economic evaluation of the global competitiveness report. World Dev. **29**(9), 1501–1525 (2001). https://doi.org/10.1016/S0305-750X(01)00051-1
6. Werker, C., Athreye, S.: Marshall's disciples: knowledge and innovation driving regional economic development and growth. J. Evol. Econ. **14**(5), 505–523 (2004). https://doi.org/10.1007/s00191-004-0237-5

7. Malecki, E.J.: Hard and soft networks for urban competitiveness. Urban studies **39**(5–6), 929–945 (2002). https://doi.org/10.1080/00420980220128381
8. Porter, M.E.: Clusters and the New Economics of Competition, vol. 76, No. 6, pp. 77–90. Harvard Business Review, Boston (1998)
9. Camagni, R.: On the concept of territorial competitiveness: sound or misleading? Urban studies **39**(13), 2395–2411 (2002)
10. Audretsch, D.B., Keilbach, M.: Entrepreneurship and regional growth: an evolutionary interpretation. J. Evol. Econ. **14**(5), 605–616 (2004). https://doi.org/10.1007/s00191-004-0228-6
11. Turok, I.: Cities, regions and competitiveness. Reg. Stud. **38**(9), 1069–1083 (2004). https://doi.org/10.1080/0034340042000292647
12. Papa, R., Gargiulo, C., Franco, S., Russo, L.: Urban Smartness Vs Urban Competitiveness: A Comparison of Italian Cities Rankings. TeMA - Journal of Land Use, Mobility and Environment. (2014). https://doi.org/10.6092/1970-9870/2555
13. Bruneckienė, J., Činčikaitė, R., Kilijonienė, A.: The specifics of measurement the urban competitiveness at the national and international level. Inžinerinė ekonomika, 256-270 (2012). https://doi.org/10.5755/j01.ee.23.3.1272
14. Papa, R., Gargiulo, C., Franco, S., Russo, L.: The Evolution of Urban Competitiveness in Italy from 1995 to 2013 (2014)
15. Jensen-Butler, C.: Cities in competition: equity issues. Urban studies **36**(5–6), 865–891 (1999). https://doi.org/10.1080/0042098993259
16. Economist Intelligence Unit: Democracy index 2011: Democracy under stress (2012)
17. Godfrey, B.J., Zhou, Y.: Ranking world cities: multinational corporations and the global urban hierarchy. Urban Geogr. **20**(3), 268–281 (1999). https://doi.org/10.2747/0272-3638.20.3.268
18. Jessop, B., Sum, N.L.: An entrepreneurial city in action: Hong Kong's emerging strategies in and for (inter) urban competition. Urban studies **37**(12), 2287–2313 (2000). https://doi.org/10.1080/00420980020002814
19. Xu, J., Yeh, A.G.: City repositioning and competitiveness building in regional development: New development strategies in Guangzhou, China. Int. J. Urban Reg. Res. **29**(2), 283–308 (2005). https://doi.org/10.1111/j.1468-2427.2005.00585.x
20. Jiang, Y., Shen, J.: Measuring the urban competitiveness of Chinese cities in 2000. Cities **27**(5), 307–314 (2010). https://doi.org/10.1016/j.cities.2010.02.004
21. Deas, I., Giordano, B.: Conceptualising and measuring urban competitiveness in major English cities: an exploratory approach. Environ Plan A **33**(8), 1411–1429 (2001). https://doi.org/10.1068/a33142
22. Kresl, P.K., Singh, B.: Competitiveness and the urban economy: twenty-four large US metropolitan areas. Urban studies **36**(5–6), 1017–1027 (1999). https://doi.org/10.1080/0042098993330
23. Martin, R., Simmie, J.: The theoretical bases of urban competitiveness: does proximity matter? Revue dEconomie Regionale Urbaine **3**, 333–351 (2008)
24. Sáez, L., Periáñez, I., Heras-Saizarbitoria, I.: Measuring urban competitiveness: ranking European large urban zones. J. Place Manag. Dev. (2017). https://doi.org/10.1108/JPMD-07-2017-0066
25. Buck, N.H., Gordon, I., Harding, A., Turok, I. (eds.) Changing cities: Rethinking urban competitiveness, cohesion, and governance. Macmillan International Higher Education (2005). ISBN 978-1-4039-0680-9. https://doi.org/10.1007/978-0-230-21203-9
26. Cheshire, P.: Spatial policies, planning and urban competitiveness: the particular case of London. Edward Elgar, Cheltenham (2009)
27. Rogerson, R.J.: Quality of life and city competitiveness. Urban studies **36**(5–6), 969–985 (1999). https://doi.org/10.1080/0042098993303

28. Donald, B.: Economic competitiveness and quality of life in city regions: compatible concepts?. Canadian Journal of Urban Research, 259–274 (2001)
29. Biagi, B., Ladu, M.G., Meleddu, M.: Urban quality of life and capabilities: an experimental study. Ecol. Econ. **150**, 137–152 (2018). https://doi.org/10.1016/j.ecolecon.2018.04.011
30. Ni, P., Kamiya, M.: The Global Urban Competitiveness Report–2019–20 (2020)
31. Eraydin, A.: "Resilience Thinking" for Planning. In: Resilience thinking in urban planning, 17–37. Springer, Dordrecht (2013). https://doi.org/10.1007/978-94-007-5476-8_2
32. Leichenko, R.: Climate change and urban resilience. Current opinion in environmental sustainability **3**(3), 164–168 (2011). https://doi.org/10.1016/j.cosust.2010.12.014
33. Book, K., Eskilsson, L., Khan, J.: Governing the balance between sustainability and competitiveness in urban planning: the case of the Orestad model. Environ. Policy Gov. **20**(6), 382–396 (2010)
34. Mazzeo, G.: Planning assignments of the Italian metropolitan cities. Early trends. TeMA-Journal of Land Use, Mobility and Environment **10**(1), 57–76 (2017)
35. Monfaredzadeh, T., Berardi, U.: Beneath the smart city: dichotomy between sustainability and competitiveness. Int. J. Sustain. Build. Technol. Urban Dev. **6**(3), 140–156 (2015). https://doi.org/10.1080/2093761X.2015.1057875
36. Hu, R.: Sustainability and competitiveness in Australian cities. Sustainability **7**(2), 1840–1860 (2015). https://doi.org/10.3390/su7021840
37. Birkmann, J., Garschagen, M., Kraas, F., Quang, N.: Adaptive urban governance: new challenges for the second generation of urban adaptation strategies to climate change. Sustain. Sci. **5**(2), 185–206 (2010). https://doi.org/10.1007/s11625-010-0111-3
38. Esmaeilpoorarabi, N., Yigitcanlar, T., Guaralda, M.: Place quality and urban competitiveness symbiosis? A position paper. Int. J. Knowl. Based Dev. **7**(1), 4–21 (2016)
39. UN: Transforming Our World: The 2030 Agenda for Sustainable Development. UN, New York (2015). https://unric.org/it/wp-content/uploads/sites/3/2019/11/Agenda-2030-Onu-italia.pdf
40. Carpentieri, G., Guida, C., Fevola, O., Sgambati, S.: The Covid-19 pandemic from the elderly perspective in urban areas: an evaluation of urban green areas in 10 European capitals. TeMA-J. Land Use, Mobility Environ. **13**(3), 389–408 (2020)
41. Sgambati, S., Gargiulo, C.: The evolution of urban competitiveness studies over the past 30 years. A bibliometric analysis. Cities **128**, 103811 (2022)

Lack of Correlation Between Land Use and Pollutant Emissions: The Case of Pavia Province

Roberto De Lotto[✉], Marilisa Moretti, Elisabetta M. Venco, Riccardo Bellati, and Melissa Monastra

Department of Civil Engineering and Architecture, DICAr – University of Pavia, via Ferrata 3, 27100 Pavia, Italy
uplab@unipv.it

Abstract. Air quality is a major concern in highly urbanised and industrialised regions, as well as rural areas. Air pollutant concentrations often exhibit significant spatial and temporal variability, depending on local sources, climate conditions and the characteristics of the built and natural environment. The strong relationship between emissions and human activities is well known: residential functions, infrastructure systems and industrial plants are the main emission sources of different pollutants, especially for PM2.5. Agriculture also produces pollutants. By contrast, forests usually act as adsorption sinks, reducing the pollution concentration. Therefore, pollutant emissions and concentration patterns present significant spatial variability due to different land uses. Moreover, the correlation between urban and territorial functions and pollution varies, sometimes by a significant amount, with different regions and scales leaving a significant gap for urban planning. The presented research aims at describing the potential correlation between different land uses and the emissions and concentrations of air pollutants, as a starting point for more in-depth studies in relation to urban and territorial transformations, the sustainable renewal of dismissed areas and the revitalisation of rural areas. By considering a territorial scale for the analysis (Pavia Province in northern Italy), we intend to underline the links (linear, direct, indirect) between land uses (residential, agricultural, and industrial) and the main air pollutants (CO2eq), as well as the degree of intensity.

Keywords: Land Use · Pollutant emissions · Correlation analysis

1 Introduction

The United Nations Framework Convention on Climate Change states that land use plays a key role in the production of greenhouse gases, indeed human activities can lead to the production of pollutants in the atmosphere, or their absorption [1].

In both developed and developing countries, air pollution causes significant threats to human health, the environment, social and economic activities. The issue of air quality is receiving increasing attention in an urban context, as well as in less urbanised contexts, such as the so-called rural-urban areas and the countryside regions [2–7].

O. Gervasi et al. (Eds.): ICCSA 2022 Workshops, LNCS 13382, pp. 109–124, 2022.
https://doi.org/10.1007/978-3-031-10592-0_10

The variations in spatial distribution of air pollutants have become a widespread concern in several fields such as urban and rural planning, environmental science, and medicine [8–11].

In 2018, global emissions from agriculture were 4 billion tons of CO2eq from agricultural and livestock activities; land use change CO2eq emissions are mainly from deforestation and the burning of organic soils [12]. Moreover, agricultural activities contribute to increasing CH_4 and N_2O emissions [13–15].

In the last 5 years, in Italy, the interaction between pollution, fuel consumption and weather conditions has been particularly accentuated. In 2017, there was an increase for both PM10 and PM2.5, exceeding the WHO reference thresholds: PM2.5 annual limit = 10 μg/cbm; PM10 annual limit = 20 μg/cbm - O_3: 8 h limit = 100 μg/cbm [16, 17].

The authors have focussed on analysing the role played by land use and, therefore, human activities on the production of pollutants in the Lombardy Region (Italy). In particular, the chosen study area is Pavia province, in the southwestern part of the Lombardy Region. It is a highly urbanised plain with a high population density and small to middle size cities (only two cities have more than 60,000 inhabitants, one has almost 40,000 inhabitants, and a few have 10–15 thousand inhabitants, but most municipalities have less than 1000 inhabitants). Importantly, there is little settlement sprawl, intensive agriculture and livestock management, and high emission levels of different pollutants.

Air pollution levels in Lombardy remain high and above the European average. Some pollutants have slightly increased their concentrations in the last two years due to meteorological and climatic variations. The meteorological situation of this area is peculiar (atmospheric stability with low winds and thermal inversion) and this affects the concentration levels, the diffusion and dispersion of pollutants in the air [18].

This phenomenon is particularly relevant in the cities of the Po Valley, in which the Province of Pavia is part of the study [19].

The paper aims to verify, at a local level, the provincial/regional trends of the relationship between land use and polluting emissions using correlation analysis of demographic, economic, environmental, and territorial indicators at a provincial level and in the most emissive municipalities.

1.1 Study Area: Pavia Province

The choice of the study area fell on the Lombardy Region and on Pavia province, which covers an area of 2,964.7 sqkm. Its geographical and physical characteristics make it one of the most disadvantaged areas in Europe, in terms of air quality: the closed geographic conformation, the poor ventilation of the area, the frequent thermal inversions and the modest mixing height all favour the stagnation of pollutants and hinder their dispersion [20]. The high anthropisation and the high rate of industrialisation of the region further contribute to the degree of pollution.

The most active emission sources in Lombardy appear to be civil combustion processes, production processes and agriculture [21].

The Lombard industrial system is characterised by a wide variety of economic activities and industry is a significant emissive source of volatile organic compounds (VOC) and particulates (PM2.5 and PM10), in quantities that vary according to the processing.

In the residential sector in Lombardy there are about 3.3 million installations, the majority being fuelled by methane gas and resulting in emissions of sulphur dioxides SO_2, carbon oxides CO and nitrogen oxides NOx, which are the main causes of the heavy pollution characteristics, especially of large cities in the winter period [22]. Moreover, Lombardy ranks as one of the main agricultural regions of Europe and the progress that this sector has seen has led to great growth in agriculture and, consequently, caused an impact on the environment, making it one of the main causes of pollution in the Po Valley [23]. Figure 1 represents the emission contributions, in terms of CO2eq, of the provinces of Lombardy.

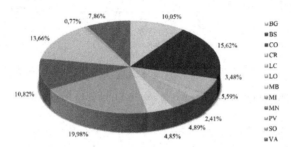

Fig. 1. CO2eq contribution of each province in the Lombardy Region (source: authors)

The provinces that produce the largest quantities of CO_2 equivalent emissions and, therefore, contribute the most to the greenhouse effect are those of Milan (20%), Brescia (16%) and Pavia (14%). The province of Milan is characterised by a medium-high territorial extension and the highest population density in the region. The province of Brescia is the province with the largest extension in the region. The province of Pavia is characterised by medium-high territorial extension and by minimal sources of absorption, being a mainly agricultural territory.

Figure 2 shows the estimates of the emissions produced by each macrosector. The 11 macrosectors considered by INEMAR are: public power plants, cogeneration and district heating, energy production (electricity, cogeneration and district heating) and transformation of fuels; non-industrial combustion plants (commercial, residential, agriculture); combustion in industry; production processes; extraction and distribution of fossil fuels; use of solvents; road transport; other moving sources and machinery; waste treatment and disposal; agriculture; other sources and absorption percentage in each province [24]. Pavia province is characterised by a high emission contribution of macrosector 1, a low emission contribution of macrosector 2 and a medium-high emission contribution of macrosector 10, being a mainly agricultural territory. It has minimal absorption because there is scarcely any vegetation in the territories.

In high-density urban environments, the soil is an important regulator of climate and microclimate and is related to air quality. Knowledge of the dynamics relating to land uses is strategic for territorial planning: it allows a fully understanding of the current situation of the territory and, at the same time, allows monitoring the in-progress changes and predicting the possible future changes.

Land use status indicators are obtained with a quantitative geographic approach.

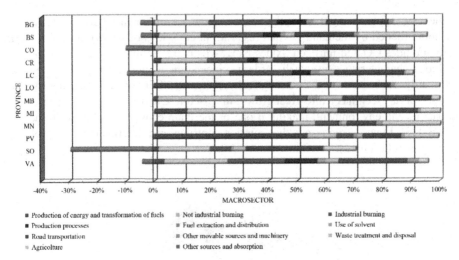

Fig. 2. CO2eq contribution of each province in the Lombardy Region for each macrosector (source: authors)

Geographical elements in an urban context are surfaces, perimeters and percent-age distributions on an overall area: they are objective values that can be used as quantitative indicators and analysed through the theme of land use in Lombardy (Fig. 3), which is concretised in the database DUSAF [25].

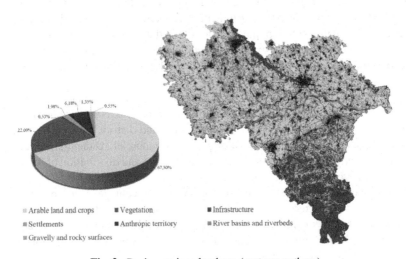

Fig. 3. Pavia province land use (source: authors)

The surface of the province of Pavia:

– 67.30% is occupied by arable land and has a percentage of emissions from agriculture of 10.4% (1,105 kt/year);

- 22.09% is occupied by vegetation and has an absorption rate of -0.7%;
- it has the lowest percentage of territory used for infrastructure in the region (0.53%), producing 13.8% of the total road transport emissions (1460 kt/year), the lowest percentage in Lombardy.

2 Data and Methodology

The population of Pavia province forms 5% of the Lombard population; its 534,691 inhabitants are concentrated mostly in the cities of Pavia, Voghera and Vigevano (31% of the total); in 10 of the 186 municipalities there is the 50% of the entire population, while the rest is spread over the remaining municipalities. The municipalities that do not have a population exceeding 5,000 inhabitants account for 88% and only 13 of these are cities. The average population density of the province of Pavia is about 184 inhabitants/sq km and is below the regional average (422 inhabitants/sq km).

Economic growth and, therefore, the growth of GDP (Gross Domestic Product, the most used indicator to evaluate the wealth produced by a country) consequently leads to an increase in emissions due to production activities, construction and transport. It is necessary to combine economic growth with an improvement in environmental quality, thus creating the so-called decoupling between the growth of a country's wealth and its negative impacts on the environment. The province of Pavia is one of the provinces that contributes the least to the growth of Lombardy's GDP, in fact its contribution is only 4%.

The definition of 'emission' given by INEMAR is "the quantity of pollutant introduced into the atmosphere, from a certain polluting source and over a certain period of time; generally, it is expressed in tons/year" [26]. To evaluate the contribution of the various pollutants emitted from various sources, the inventories of the emissions are used which allow us to identify, for each source, the type of pollutant, the quantity emitted and the location. The Lombardy Region inventory of atmospheric emissions INEMAR of ARPA LOMBARDIA, is currently available for the year 2017. Consequently, all of the data in this research is derived from this database [26].

For diffuse emissions it is not possible to obtain a direct measurement and it is, therefore, necessary to estimate them from statistical data and appropriate emission factors, in accordance with the methodologies adopted at national (ENEA-ANPA) and international (Corinair) level [27]. INEMAR makes these estimates on the basis of an indicator that characterises the activity of the source and an emission factor, specific to the type of source, industrial process and purification technology adopted. Therefore, this method is based on a linear relationship between the activity of the source and the emission, according to a relationship that, at a general level, can be traced back to the following [28]:

$$Ei = A \times FEi \tag{1}$$

where:

- Ei = emission of the pollutant i (t/year);
- A = activity indicator;

– FEi = pollutant emission factor I.

The Lombardy Emissions Inventory considers the following air pollutants: sulphur dioxide (SO_2), nitrogen dioxide (NO_2), nitrogen monoxide (NO), Volatile Organic Compounds (VOCs), carbon monoxide (CO), ammonia (NH_3), and fine particulate matter (PM10 and PM 2.5). In addition, there are also aggregate pollutants, obtained from the combination of the emission data of individual pollutants, and one of these is CO_2 equivalent: the emissions of 'CO2eq' represents the total emissions of greenhouse gases, weighted based on their contribution to the greenhouse effect. The estimate of aggregate greenhouse gas emissions is based on the following equation [29]:

$$CO2eq = \Sigma i\, GWPi \times Ei \tag{2}$$

where:

- CO2eq = CO_2 equivalent emissions in kt/year;
- GWPi = 'Global Warming Potential', coefficient IPCC equal to 1.000, 0.025 and 0.298 for CO_2, CH_4 and N_2O, respectively [26];
- Ei = CO_2 emissions (in kt/year), CH_4 and N_2O (in t/year).

For the presented research, we consider all the previous pollutants, as well as CO_2, PAH, PTS, N_2O, and CH_4 as well as the most common elements derived from combustion phenomena and anthropogenic activities.

Moreover, correlation analysis is used to establish a relationship or an association between two quantitative variables [29–31]. For the presented research, we used it to highlight (if present) the relations between air pollution (considering greenhouse gases and other pollutants) and human activities (mainly agricultural and industrial activities, and urban settlements as a whole).

3   Correlation Analysis Output

3.1   Provincial Level

The first analysis was performed on the entire Province, considering the different air pollutants [26], the population, the population density, and GDP. The correlation analysis was then completed (Fig. 4).

	PAHs	PM10	PTS	PM2.5	SO₂	N₂O	NH₃	NOx	VOCs	CH₄	CO	CO₂	CO₂ eq.	Population	Population Density	GDP
PAHs		0.65	0.59	0.68	0.98	0.30	0.18	0.87	0.59	0.17	0.48	0.59	0.59	0.10	0.07	0.08
PM10			0.99	1.00	0.55	0.54	0.42	0.78	0.93	0.51	0.90	0.50	0.52	0.68	0.41	0.65
PTS				0.98	0.48	0.57	0.48	0.74	0.95	0.60	0.90	0.45	0.47	0.72	0.42	0.69
PM2.5					0.58	0.53	0.39	0.79	0.91	0.49	0.89	0.52	0.53	0.65	0.38	0.61
SO₂						0.23	0.09	0.83	0.49	0.06	0.40	0.60	0.60	0.03	0.04	0.02
N₂O							0.62	0.64	0.58	0.51	0.53	0.69	0.71	0.37	0.18	0.34
NH₃								0.28	0.49	0.63	0.39	0.11	0.13	0.33	0.19	0.30
NOx									0.73	0.28	0.68	0.84	0.84	0.35	0.22	0.33
VOCs										0.67	0.87	0.46	0.48	0.72	0.37	0.69
CH₄											0.45	0.12	0.16	0.44	0.20	0.41
CO												0.43	0.45	0.80	0.49	0.77
CO₂													1.00	0.18	0.10	0.16
CO₂ eq.														0.20	0.11	0.19
Population															0.69	0.99
Population Density																0.68
GDP																

Fig. 4. Correlation Analysis among air pollutants and territorial descriptors at province level (source: authors)

All the results show a direct correlation among the elements.

Moreover, in order to obtain an effective visualisation, the elements were classified using their correlation index (Fig. 5).

	PM10	PTS	PM2.5	VOCs	CO	NOx	Population	N₂O	Population Density	CO₂ eq.	PAHs	CO₂	SO₂	CH₄	NH₃	GDP
PM10		0.99	1.00	0.93	0.90	0.78	0.68	0.54	0.41	0.52	0.65	0.50	0.55	0.51	0.42	0.65
PTS			0.98	0.95	0.90	0.74	0.72	0.57	0.42	0.47	0.59	0.45	0.48	0.60	0.48	0.69
PM2.5				0.91	0.89	0.79	0.65	0.53	0.38	0.53	0.68	0.52	0.58	0.49	0.38	0.61
VOCs					0.87	0.73	0.72	0.58	0.37	0.48	0.59	0.46	0.49	0.67	0.49	0.69
CO						0.68	0.80	0.53	0.49	0.45	0.49	0.43	0.40	0.45	0.39	0.77
NOx							0.35	0.64	0.22	0.84	0.87	0.84	0.83	0.28	0.27	0.33
Population								0.37	0.69	0.20	0.10	0.18	0.03	0.44	0.33	0.99
N₂O									0.18	0.70	0.30	0.69	0.23	0.51	0.63	0.35
Population Density										0.11	0.07	0.10	0.04	0.20	0.19	0.68
CO₂ eq.											0.59	1.00	0.60	0.16	0.13	0.19
PAHs												0.59	0.98	0.17	0.18	0.08
CO₂													0.60	0.12	0.11	0.16
SO₂														0.06	0.08	0.02
CH₄															0.63	0.41
NH₃																0.30
GDP																

Fig. 5. Correlation analysis among air pollutants and territorial descriptors at province level. Classification based on correlation coefficient (source: authors)

Figure 6 highlights the massive presence of strong positive correlations. Few pairs of elements show a mild positive correlation (which means there is not so strong a dependence between them, e.g. NH_3 and PTS or CO_2 and PM10).

Moreover, as expected, it can be seen that, as emissions increase, income also increases; as the population and population density increase, emissions also increase.

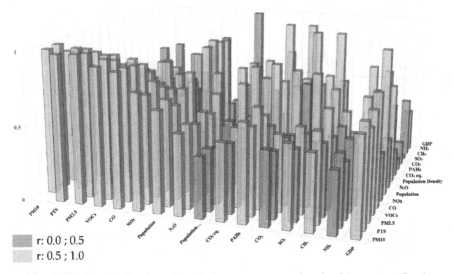

r: 0.0 ; 0.5
r: 0.5 ; 1.0

Fig. 6. Graphic visualisation of correlation outputs at province level (source: authors)

3.2 Municipal Level

Considering the municipal dimension, as a first step, we analysed the most emissive (in relation to CO2eq) municipalities and highlighted seven realities that were far away from all the others (the next municipality only produced 9.28 kiloton/year of CO2eq). The main features of each municipality are different, with respect to population density, spatial dimension, and GDP. Due to the distribution of their urban functions, they are the most emissive entities in the province.

As already performed for the entire province, we correlated all of the air pollutants, population, population densities and GDP (Table 1, Table 2 and Fig. 7).

Table 1. Data on pollutants of the seven most emissive municipalities (source: authors)

Municipality	PAHs (kg/year)	PM10 (t/year)	PTS (t/year)	PM2.5 (t/year)	SO₂ (t/year)	N₂O (t/year)	NH₃ (t/year)	NOx (t/year)	VOCs (t/year)	CH₄ (t/year)	CO (t/year)	CO₂ (kt/year)
Ferrera Erbognone	6.0	14.3	17.5	13.6	15.1	68.6	36.8	863.1	242.5	400.6	82.3	2.838.8
Mortara	117.8	44.8	60.3	38.4	24.0	29.7	247.1	588.1	637.3	1,251.6	464.4	81.2
Parona	66.2	12.4	15.4	9.5	171.4	20.7	24.8	447.4	235.6	192.4	166.9	229.2
Pavia	20.1	53.6	74.9	44.5	4.9	22.6	109.7	468.0	924.2	1,151.9	695.7	290.0
Sannazzaro De'Burgondi	601.1	75.9	82.1	70.8	3,380	29.2	82.6	1,918.9	1,105	449.0	667.4	2,223.6
Vigevano	24.6	50.8	65.0	42.9	11.7	20.4	107.7	382.7	980.3	1,161.0	645.3	230.5
Voghera	8.9	40.4	45.7	36.4	7.1	34.3	83.9	448.1	538.0	289.2	880.6	855.2

Table 2. Data on CO_2 eq. and territorial descriptors of the 7 most emissive municipalities (source: authors)

Municipality	CO_2 eq. (kt/year)	Population (inhab.)	Population Density (inhab./kmq)	GDP (€)
Ferrera Erbognone	2.869,72	1.171,00	59,90	15.442.841,00
Mortara	126,62	15.543,00	298,20	228.606.170,00
Parona	240,81	1.975,00	211,50	26.400.225,00
Pavia	350,58	71.297,00	1.134,20	1.502.659.302,00
Sannazzaro De'Burgondi	2.245,46	5.533,00	237,30	77.957.469,00
Vigevano	287,35	63.268,00	768,00	970.129.252,00
Voghera	886,22	39.356,00	621,90	637.341.042,00

	PAHs	PM10	PTS	PM2.5	SO₂	N₂O	NH₃	NOx	VOCs	CH₄	CO	CO₂	CO₂ eq.	Population	Population Density	GDP
PAHs		0.66	0.52	0.72	0.98	-0.14	0.03	0.94	0.53	-0.17	0.19	0.41	0.40	-0.40	-0.33	-0.38
PM10			0.97	0.99	0.65	-0.44	0.41	0.53	0.96	0.42	0.76	-0.03	-0.02	0.38	0.40	0.36
PTS				0.95	0.49	-0.49	0.52	0.37	0.97	0.60	0.75	-0.17	-0.16	0.52	0.54	0.51
PM2.5					0.71	-0.38	0.36	0.60	0.93	0.34	0.74	0.06	0.07	0.30	0.32	0.28
SO₂						-0.09	-0.12	0.95	0.53	-0.26	0.20	0.49	0.49	-0.36	-0.30	-0.34
N₂O							-0.27	0.20	-0.51	-0.35	-0.49	0.80	0.80	-0.46	-0.53	-0.43
NH₃								-0.12	0.35	0.77	0.31	-0.46	-0.46	0.21	0.18	0.18
NOx									0.39	-0.28	0.03	0.70	0.69	-0.49	-0.44	-0.46
VOCs										0.54	0.71	-0.12	-0.12	0.54	0.54	0.52
CH₄											0.28	-0.51	-0.50	0.62	0.56	0.60
CO												-0.29	-0.29	0.66	0.68	0.61
CO₂													1.00	-0.53	-0.55	-0.50
CO₂ eq.														-0.52	-0.54	-0.49
Population															0.97	0.98
Population Density																0.99
GDP																

Fig. 7. Correlation analysis among air pollutants and territorial descriptors for the seven most emissive municipalities (source: authors)

Moreover, we defined the ranking of the correlation index (Fig. 8).

	PM10	PM2.5	PTS	VOCs	CO	SO₂	PAHs	NOx	CO₂	CH₄	Population Density	GDP	Population	NH₃	CO₂ eq.	N₂O
PM10		0.99	0.97	0.96	0.76	0.65	0.66	0.53	-0.03	0.42	0.40	0.36	0.38	0.41	-0.02	-0.44
PM2.5			0.95	0.93	0.74	0.71	0.72	0.60	0.06	0.34	0.32	0.28	0.30	0.36	0.07	-0.38
PTS				0.97	0.75	0.49	0.52	0.37	-0.17	0.60	0.54	0.51	0.52	0.52	-0.16	-0.49
VOCs					0.71	0.53	0.53	0.39	-0.12	0.54	0.54	0.52	0.54	0.52	-0.12	-0.51
CO						0.20	0.19	0.03	-0.29	0.28	0.68	0.61	0.66	0.31	-0.29	-0.49
SO₂							0.98	0.95	0.49	-0.26	-0.30	-0.34	-0.36	-0.12	0.49	-0.09
PAHs								0.94	0.41	-0.26	-0.33	-0.38	-0.40	0.03	0.40	-0.14
NOx									0.70	-0.28	-0.44	-0.46	-0.49	-0.12	0.69	0.20
CO₂										-0.51	-0.55	-0.50	-0.53	-0.46	1.00	0.80
CH₄											0.56	0.60	0.62	0.77	-0.50	-0.35
Population Density												0.99	0.97	0.18	-0.54	-0.53
GDP													0.18	0.18	-0.49	-0.43
Population														0.18	-0.52	-0.46
NH₃															-0.46	-0.27
CO₂ eq.																0.80
N₂O																

Fig. 8. Correlation analysis among air pollutants and territorial descriptors for the seven most emissive municipalities. Classification based on correlation coefficient (source: authors)

Figure 9 shows the different correlation indexes obtained. There are different kinds of correlations: strong positive (i.e. NOx and PAH), mild positive (i.e. SO_2 and CO_2), mild negative (SO_2 and population density) and strong negative (i.e. population density and N_2O).

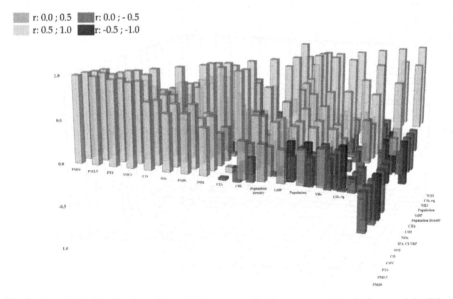

Fig. 9. Graphical visualisation of correlation outputs for the seven most emissive municipalities (source: authors)

Agricultural Areas. For each municipality, we assumed that CO2eq was the most representative pollution parameter in the context of the real pollution situation, in relation to the agricultural function (expressed in square metres). As shown in Table 3 and Fig. 10, there is a negative correlation between agricultural area and CO2eq.

Table 3. Correlation between CO2eq and agricultural area for the seven most emissive municipalities

Municipality	Agricultural area (sqm)	CO_2 eq. (kt/year)	r
Ferrera Erbognone	11,155,741.44	2.869.72	−0.44
Mortara	38,189,181.16	126.62	
Parona	4,129,459.89	240.81	
Pavia	29,322,650.69	350.58	
Sannazzaro de' Burgondi	11,615,745.83	2,245.46	
Vigevano	28,626,280.19	287.35	
Voghera	46,643,247.56	886.22	

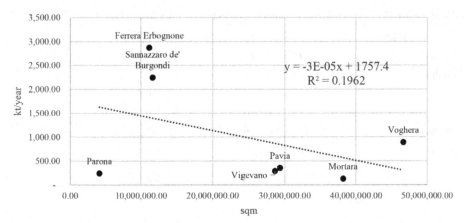

Fig. 10. Scatterplot of correlation between CO2eq and agricultural area for the seven most emissive municipalities (source: authors)

Moreover, we performed the correlation with all of the air pollutants, starting from specific data related to each function. The results shown in Table 4 are in line with those expected, particularly for NH_3 and CO_2.

Urban Settlements. For each municipality, we assumed CO2eq as the pollution parameter representative of the context and of the real pollution situation, in relation to urban settlement areas (expressed in square metres). Residential, tertiary, and commercial functions and public services and facilities were included. As shown in Table 5 and Fig. 11, there is a negative correlation between areas of urban settlement and CO2eq.

Table 4. Correlation coefficients between air pollutants and agricultural area for the most emissive municipalities (source: authors)

Municipality	Agricultural area (sqm)	PAHs (kg/year)	PM10 (t/year)	PTS(t/year)	PM2.5 (t/year)	SO₂(t/year)	N₂O(t/year)	NH₃(t/year)	NOx(t/year)	VOCs (t/year)	CH₄(t/year)	CO(t/year)	CO₂(kt/year)
Ferrera Erbognone	11.155.741,4	6	14,3	17,5	13,6	15,1	68,6	36,8	863,1	242,5	400,6	82,3	2.838,8
Mortara	38.189.181,1	117,8	44,8	60,3	38,4	24,0	29,7	247,1	588,1	637,3	1.251,6	464,4	81,2
Parona	4.129.459,9	66,2	12,4	15,4	9,5	171,4	20,7	24,8	447,4	235,6	192,4	166,9	229,2
Pavia	29.322.650,7	20,1	53,6	74,9	44,5	4,9	22,6	109,7	468,0	924,2	1.151,9	695,7	290
Sannazzaro De'Burgondi	11.615.745,8	601,1	75,9	82,1	70,8	3.380	29,2	82,6	1.918,9	1.105	449	667,4	2.223,6
Vigevano	28.626.280,2	24,6	50,8	65	42,9	11,7	20,4	107,7	382,7	980,3	1.161	645,3	230,5
Voghera	46.643.247,6	8,9	40,4	45,7	36,4	7,1	34,3	83,9	448,1	538,0	289,2	880,6	855,2
Correlation between Agricultural land and indicator	Agricultural area	-0,34	0,30	0,38	0,26	-0,38	-0,19	0,63	-0,43	0,24	0,46	0,71	-0,45

Correlation coefficient

Table 5. Correlation between CO2eq and urban settlements area for the seven most emissive municipalities

Municipality	Agricultural land (sqm)	CO2eq (kt/year)	r
Ferrera Erbognone	734,689.37	2,869.72	−0.45
Mortara	4,181,058.73	126.62	
Parona	627,983.42	240.81	
Pavia	11,352,391.73	350.58	
Sannazzaro de' Burgondi	4,566,901.56	2,245.46	
Vigevano	12,430,334.36	287.35	
Voghera	46,643,247.56	886.22	

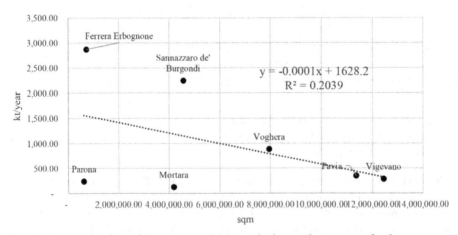

Fig. 11. Scatterplot of correlation between CO2eq and urban settlement areas for the seven most emissive municipalities (source: authors)

Correlation was performed for all the air pollutants. The results, shown in Table 6, are quite peculiar because they show that direct or indirect correlations were not in line with what was expected (i.e. CO_2 or PM2.5 and PM10, for which strong direct correlations were expected).

Table 6. Correlation coefficients between air pollutants and urban settlement areas for the seven most emissive municipalities (source: authors)

Municipality	Urban settlements area (sqm)	PAHs (kg/year)	PM10 (t/year)	PTS(t/year)	PM2.5 (t/year)	SO₂(t/year)	N₂O(t/year)	NH₃(t/year)	NOx(t/year)	VOCs (t/year)	CH₄(t/year)	CO(t/year)	CO₂(kt/year)
Ferrera Erbognone	734.689,37	6	14,3	17,5	13,6	15,1	68,6	36,8	863,1	242,5	400,6	82,3	2.838,8
Mortara	4.181.058,73	117,8	44,8	60,3	38,4	24,0	29,7	247,1	588,1	637,3	1.251,6	464,4	81,2
Parona	627.983,42	66,2	12,4	15,4	9,5	171,4	20,7	24,8	447,4	235,6	192,4	166,9	229,2
Pavia	11.352.391,73	20,1	53,6	74,9	44,5	4,9	22,6	109,7	468,0	924,2	1.151,9	695,7	290
Sannazzaro De'Burgondi	4.566.901,56	601,1	75,9	82,1	70,8	3.380	29,2	82,6	1.918,9	1.105	449	667,4	2.223,6
Vigevano	12.430.334,36	24,6	50,8	65	42,9	11,7	20,4	107,7	382,7	980,3	1.161	645,3	230,5
Voghera	46.643.247,56	8,9	40,4	45,7	36,4	7,1	34,3	83,9	448,1	538,0	289,2	880,6	855,2
Correlation between	Correlation coefficient												
Agricultural land and indicator	Urban settlements area area	-0,42	0,20	0,40	0,10	-0,51	-0,53	0,70	-0,59	0,30	0,84	0,32	-0,81

Industrial Sites. For each municipality, we assumed CO2eq as the pollution parameter most representative of the context and of the real pollution situation in relation to the industrial sites (expressed in square metres). As shown in Table 7 and Fig. 12, there is an irrelevant negative correlation between industrial sites and CO2eq.

Table 7. Correlation between CO2eq and industrial sites for the seven most emissive municipalities

Municipality	Industrial sites	CO2eq (kt/year)	r
Ferrera Erbognone	1,913,019.42	2,869.72	−0.018
Mortara	2,003,151.37	126.62	
Parona	999,895.96	240.81	
Pavia	2,577,443.08	350.58	
Sannazzaro de' Burgondi	2,248,542.33	2,245.46	
Vigevano	3,135,846.70	287.35	
Voghera	2,863,940.06	886.22	

Moreover, we performed the correlation with all the air pollutants. The results, shown in Table 8, are quite peculiar because they show some direct or indirect correlation, which is not in line with what was expected.

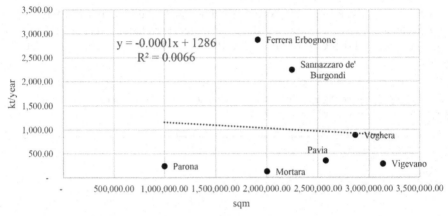

Fig. 12. Scatterplot of correlation between CO2eq and industrial sites for the seven most emissive municipalities (source: authors)

Table 8. Correlation coefficients between air pollutants and industrial sites for the seven most emissive municipalities (source: authors)

Municipality	Industrial settlements area (sqm)	PAHs (kg/year)	PM10 (t/year)	PTS(t/ year)	PM2.5 (t/year)	SO₂(t/ year)	N₂O(t/ year)	NH₃(t/ year)	NOx(t /year)	VOCs (t/year)	CH₄(t/ year)	CO(t/ year)	CO₂(k t/year)
Ferrera Erbognone	1.913.019,42	6	14,3	17,5	13,6	15,1	68,6	36,8	863,1	242,5	400,6	82,3	2.838, 8
Mortara	2.003.151,37	117,8	44,8	60,3	38,4	24,0	29,7	247,1	588,1	637,3	1.251, 6	464,4	81,2
Parona	999.895,96	66,2	12,4	15,4	9,5	171,4	20,7	24,8	447,4	235,6	192,4	166,9	229,2
Pavia	2.577.443,08	20,1	53,6	74,9	44,5	4,9	22,6	109,7	468,0	924,2	1.151, 9	695,7	290
Sannazzaro De'Burgondi	2.248.542,33	601,1	75,9	82,1	70,8	3.380	29,2	82,6	1.918, 9	1.105	449	667,4	2.223, 6
Vigevano	3.135.846,70	24,6	50,8	65	42,9	11,7	20,4	107,7	382,7	980,3	1.161	645,3	230,5
Voghera	2.863.940,06	8,9	40,4	45,7	36,4	7,1	34,3	83,9	448,1	538,0	289,2	880,6	855,2
Correlation between Agricultural land and indicator	Industrial settlements area area	-0,09	0,59	0,62	0,56	-0,04	-0,13	0,26	-0,10	0,65	0,46	0,80	-0,09

Correlation coefficient

4   Discussion and Conclusion

The presented correlation analysis aimed to highlight evidence among the human activities and pollutant emissions in the Province of Pavia and in the most polluted Municipalities of the selected territory, in terms of equivalent CO_2. The human activities were synthesised with the extension (in sqm) of land use: agricultural land, urban settlement areas and industrial areas. The source of territorial data is the Geoportale of Lombardy Region (open source data) that considers groups of activities based on their similarity (i.e. industrial land and artisan areas are combined).

The correlation between the global pollutants for the whole province territory (Fig. 4), allows us to be confident about the research hypothesis. At the moment, open source data is not available (at municipality level) that is able to combine every single activity with the specific emissions. These data are only available at the Province level.

It is well known that the total pollutant emissions depend on the intensity of land use and on. Specific uses that the GIS data may not trace, e.g. certain industrial activities in Sannazzaro de' Burgondi have very high emissions even if the extension of the industrial area is not huge. So, it is foreseeable that the relation analysis among parameters could have some nonlinear behaviour.

What emerged as a novelty in the analysis is the total lack of correlation between land uses and total emissions (Fig. 10, Fig. 11, and Fig. 12). The correlation is not only weak, but also negative, and this result is absolutely surprising. The reasons for this could depend on the low sensitivity of the single activity extension with the global data (Table 3, Table 5, and Table 7). At the Lombardy Region scale, agriculture is the driving force for the 6% of PM10, and industrial activities are driving forces for around 10% of PM10. In Table 4, the correlation index r between agricultural land and PM10 is positive but low ($r = 0.3$) and, in Table 8, the correlation index between industrial settlements and PM10 is 0.59. The behaviour of these two parameters makes sense, considering the linear impact of correlation and the global emissions. It is quite surprising that the correlation among various settlements and the total equivalent CO_2 is always negative.

The next steps of the research will be: a) analysis of the regression index; b) comparison between correlation indexes and regression indexes; c) comparison among global data coming from different provinces of the Lombardy Region, in order to check the strength of the results.

References

1. UNFCCC Homepage: https://unfccc.int/topics/land-use/the-big-picture/introduction-to-land-use. Last accessed 10 April 2011
2. Babiy, A.P., Kharytonov, M.M., Gritsan, N.P.: Connection between emissions and concentrations of atmospheric pollutants. In: Melas, D., Syrakov, D. (eds.) Air Pollution Processes in Regional Scale. NATO Science Series, vol 30. Springer, Dordrecht (2003)
3. Janssen, S., Dumont, G., Fierens, F., Mensink, C.: Spatial interpolation of air pollution measurements using CORINE land cover data. Atmos. Environ. **42**(20), 4884–4903 (2008)
4. Xu, G., et al.: Examining the impacts of land use on air quality from a spatio-temporal perspective in wuhan, China. Atmosphere **7**(62), (2016)
5. Zheng, S., Zhou, X., Singh, R.P., Wu, Y., Ye, Y., Wu, C. The spatiotemporal distribution of air pollutants and their relationship with land-use patterns in hangzhou City, China. Atmosphere **8**(110), (2017)
6. Bashir, M.F., et al. Correlation between environmental pollution indicators and COVID-19 pandemic: a brief study in californian context. Environmental Research 187 (2020)
7. Zimmerman, N., et al.: Improving correlations between land use and air pollutant concentrations using wavelet analysis: insights from a low-cost sensor network. Aerosol Air Qual. Res. **20**, 314–328 (2020)
8. Weng, Q., Yang, S.: Urban air pollution patterns, land use, and thermal landscape: an examination of the linkage using GIS. Environ Monit Assess **117**, 463–489 (2006)
9. Zou, B., Wilson, J.G., Zhan, F.B., Zeng, Y.: Spatially differentiated and source-specific population exposure to ambient urban air pollution. Atmos. Environ. **43**, 3981–3988 (2009)

10. Yang, J., Shi, B., Shi, Y., Marvin, S., Zheng, Y., Xia, G.: Air pollution dispersal in high density urban areas: Research on the triadic relation of wind, air pollution, and urban form. Sustainable Cities and Society **54** (2020)

11. Han, L., Zhao, J., Gao, Y., Gu, Z., Xin, K., Zhang, J.: Spatial distribution characteristics of PM2.5 and PM10 in Xi'an City predicted by land use regression models. Sustainable Cities and Society **61** (2020)

12. FAO: Emissions due to agriculture. Global, regional and country trends 2000–2018. FAOSTAT Analytical Brief Series. No 18. Rome

13. Cloy, M.J., et al.: Impacts of agriculture upon greenhouse gas budgets. In: Hester, R.E., Harrison, R.M. (eds.) Environmental Impacts of Modern Agriculture. Issues in Environmental Science and Technology 34, pp. 57–82. Royal Society of Chemistry, Cambridge (2012)

14. Feliciano, D., Slee, B., Hunter, C., Smith, P.: Estimating the contribution of rural land uses to greenhouse gas emissions: A case study of North East Scotland. Environ. Sci. Policy **25**, 36–49 (2013)

15. Pezzagno, M., Richiedei, A., Tira, M.: Spatial planning policy for sustainability: analysis connecting land use and GHG emission in rural areas. Sustainability **12** (2020)

16. WHO Homepage: https://www.who.int/news-room/feature-stories/detail/what-are-the-who-air-quality-guideline. Last accessed 10 April 2022

17. Feng, H., Zou, B., Tang, Y.: Scale and region-dependence in landscape-PM2.5 correlation: implications for urban planning. Remote Sens. 9 (2017)

18. Briganti, G.: Un'introduzione Allo Studio Della Dispersione di Inquinanti in Atmosfera in Condizioni di Calma di Vento. ENEA: Pisa, Italy (2007)

19. Istat: SDGs 2021 Report. Statistical information for Agenda 2030 in Italy. Available online: https://www.istat.it/storage/rapporti-tematici/sdgs/2021/Rapporto-SDGs-2021.pdf

20. Caserini, S., Giani, P., Caspani, F., Santoro, D., Cacciamani, C., Lonati, G.: Influence of climate change on the frequency of lapse rate inversion and stagnation events in Po valley: historical trend and future projections. Ingegneria dell'Ambiente **3**(1) (2016)

21. Quality report of the air of the province of Pavia: https://www.arpalombardia.it/qariafiles/Rel azioniAnnuali/RQA_PV_2020.pdf

22. Maranzano, P.: Air Quality in Lombardy, Italy: an overview of the environmental monitoring system of ARPA Lombardia. Earth **3**(1), 172–203 (2022)

23. European Commission: Closing the mineral cycles at farm level. Good practices to reduce nutrient loss in the Lombardy region (Italy). available online https://ec.europa.eu/enviro nment/water/water-nitrates/pdf/leaflets/Leaflet_Lombardy_EN.pdf

24. INEMAR Homepage: https://www.inemar.eu/xwiki/bin/view/Inemar/HomeLombardia. Last accessed 01 April 2022

25. Geoportale Lombardia Homepage: https://www.geoportale.regione.lombardia.it/en-GB/home. Last accessed 02 April 2022

26. INEMAR Homepage: https://www.inemar.eu/xwiki/bin/view/Inemar/. Last accessed 10 April 2022

27. Corinair: https://www.eea.europa.eu/help/glossary/eea-glossary/corinair. Last accessed 10 April 2022

28. INEMAR Emission factors: https://www.inemar.eu/xwiki/bin/view/InemarDatiWeb/I+fat tori+di+emissione. Last accessed 10 April 2022

29. Gogtay, N.J., Thatte, U.M.: Principles of Correlation Analysis. J Assoc Physicians India. **65**(3), 78–81 (2017)

30. Bouslaugh, S., Watters, P.A.: Statistics in a Nutshell, 1st ed., pp. 176–179. O'Really Media, Sebastopol, USA (2008)

31. Nettleton, D.: Commercial Data Mining: Processing, Analysis and Modeling for Predictive Analytics Projects (2014)

Smart Solution for a Smart City: Using Open Source Maps in Municipal Waste Management

Ingrid Majerova(✉) , Radim Dolak , and Martin Murys

School of Business Administration in Karvina, Silesian University in Opava, Univerzitni nam.
1934/3, 73340 Karvina, Czech Republic
majerova@opf.slu.cz

Abstract. E-Government as an approach using smart technologies, has been analyzed in recent decades not only at the (inter)national level, but also at regional or municipal level. Electronic access to information and services provided by public administrations begins (and in many cases ends) at the level of municipalities, which should provide the widest possible range of their e-services to increase the quality of life of their citizens. In addition to traditional e-services in the form of providing information about municipal activities or processing documents, many municipalities in the Czech Republic also try to provide their citizens with e-Government in the field of cultural, social, and environmental, including the issue of waste management. The aim of this paper was to create an application for the inhabitants of one Czech municipality – the statutory city of Karvina, that will allow them to find out very quickly and easily where the containers for separated waste are located in their vicinity. Through the Joomla content management system, the website was created, the main element of which is a map supplement. On this map, there are marked container stations where, in addition to containers for municipal waste, paper, glass, and plastic, containers for metal, textiles, oils or electrical waste can be found.

Keywords: Content management system · E-government · Maps · Municipal waste management · Opensource · Smart city

1 Introduction

Municipal authorities increasingly choose to establish their online presence, by using technological management solutions, which ensure that the information they have, the content they produce and the services they provide are promptly available to citizens and businesses. This strategy of using information technologies in public administration at the national, regional and local level to improve the quality of services that governments provide to citizens and businesses is known as e-Government [1]. This e-Government agenda remains one of the most important innovation drives facing the public administrations of the 21st century [2].

Within this, the European Commission encourages and leverages the transformative, innovative, and collaborative potential of open source within its open source software strategy 2020–2023. This strategy puts a special emphasis on the sharing and reuse of software solutions, knowledge and expertise, as well as on increasing the use of open source in information technologies and other strategic areas [3]. Based on this approach, many municipal public administrations have adopted Open source Content Management Systems (CMS) for their websites, greatly reducing operating costs and ensuring scalability, advanced performance, and privacy to the users. CMSs represent one of the most powerful online content management tools today, by allowing one to create a web page in a short time, control who has access to information and who creates, alters, and stores content on the platform [4]. One of the most intuitive and versatile CMS's on the market is Joomla, used also by international and national organizations such as Harvard University, IKEA, Lipton, Danone, Porsche, or Peugeot [5].

The possibilities of using CMS based on open source software (OSS), such as the mentioned Joomla, are many in public administration; one of these areas is municipal waste management. In the last decades, waste represents difficult problems and requires the integration of various processes and measures into an intelligent (smart) and comprehensive plan [6]. Some major classes of waste include municipal, hazardous, industrial, medical, universal, construction and demolition, radioactive, mining, and agricultural [7]. Municipal waste consists mainly of waste generated by households, although it also includes similar waste from sources such as shops, offices and public institutions [8]. It is extremely heterogenous and includes durable, non-durable, packaging, and containers, food waste, yard wastes, and miscellaneous inorganic wastes [7]. Totals of European municipal waste generation vary considerably, ranging from 282 kg per capita in Romania to 845 kg per capita in Denmark [8]. Variations reflect differences in consumption patterns and economic wealth, but also depend on how municipal waste is collected and managed [9]. The waste should be collected, separated, stored, transported, transferred, processed, and treated; the administration of which is the main objective of municipal waste management [10]. Waste management is a rapidly developing area of the national, regional, and local economy [11]. The Czech Republic has been also done quite a significant move forward in waste management from its accession to the European Union (2004), among other things in the area of supplied e-services to its citizens.

In view of the above, it was the intention of the authors of this paper to create an application for the citizens of one municipality in the Czech Republic, the Statutory city of Karvina in the Moravian-Silesian region. This will allow inhabitants to find out very quickly and easily where the containers for separated municipal waste are located in their vicinity. Through Joomla CMS, a website was created, the main element of which is a map supplement. On this map, there are marked container stations where, in addition to containers for municipal waste, paper, glass, and plastic, containers for metal, textiles, oils or electrical waste can be found.

Motivation to write this paper went hand in hand with its objective and was to promote the use of open source software at the municipal level. The creation of one from many possible websites can bring the benefits of local e-Government and its services closer to their citizens. Thus, they can actively and intuitively use the created map in the field of waste management. The result of this paper also became the inspiration and basis for the creation of other city websites in the leisure area.

This paper is organized as follows. Section 2 describes the state of knowledge in the field of e-Government in relation with municipal waste management. Examples of the use of open source software in domestic and foreign public administration are given in Sect. 3. The fourth part describes the creation of the map supplement itself and the next section presents the result - an interactive map of container sites. The last sixth part of the paper is a summary of the solved issue.

2   Current State of Knowledge

Smart e-Government is a rising conception that refers to developing Information and Communications Technologies (ICTs) in public sectors in order to achieve administrative efficiency [12], service improvement, and citizen centricity [13]. ICTs have become an essential tool for public and private organizations that make significant investments to support their activities. In the case of public administration from the mid-90´s, governments have started using ICT especially the Internet to provide better services to citizens. E-Government combines the intensive use of ICT with forms of management, planning and management, aimed at creating a more efficient and effective public sector to meet the needs of citizens optimally, by developing new electronic services (e-Services) [14]. Naser and Concha [15] claimed that e-Government is a tool of enormous potential in terms of public administration and democratic management. The e-Government bases its application in public administration, having as purpose to contribute to the use of ICT for the following: i) improving services and the availability of information, ii) improving and simplifying the processes of institutional support, and iii) facilitate the establishment of communication channels, which can increase transparency and citizen participation.

Przeybilovicz et al. [16] investigated the characteristics of the infrastructure and use of information and communication technologies of Brazilian municipalities reflecting on the possibility of developing e-Government and smart cities actions. The authors used the quantitative study of cluster analysis and identified four clusters: the technology-less, the concerned-on citizen, the concerned-on legislation, and the ICT supported. Although information technology has become one of the core elements of managerial reform and electronic government may figure prominently in future governance, there are some barriers and legal issues to the progress of municipal e-Government. Moon [17], in his study of US municipalities, identified widely shared barriers as a lack of financial, technical, and the privacy personnel capacities and legal issue. This study also indicates that the size of the city and manager-council government are positively associated with the adoption of a municipal Web site, as well as its longevity.

Zhang and Zhu [18] collected responses from more than thousands of urban and rural residents in China (Chongqing Municipality). Using a structural equation model, they obtained the result showing differences between use of e-Government within urban and rural groups as well as providing the e-services to them. Similarly, Bayona and Morales [19] studied the provision of e-services in small cities that belong to a small province of Ecuador. The results show that there is a difference between the e-services that offer the municipalities with different sizes, and it is necessary to improve them. According to Urs [20], most public services in Romania are provided by local public institutions, especially city halls. E-Government development is not a priority at central level, and that essential national technological infrastructure is underdeveloped or nonexistent. Due to these shortcomings, even online services that work well in a local context will be difficult to replicate or integrate at the country level.

As significant determinants for successful development of electronic government initiatives at a municipal level, the importance of the infrastructure, the political capital of the mayor and the financial independence of the municipality was identified. Gonzalez-Bustamante et al. [21] analyzed the above level of electronic government and its determinants in the 188 municipalities of the five most densely populated regions in Chile. The factors analyzed are related to the dimensions distinguished by theory as necessary for the implementation of strategies of electronic government.

Another work has been implemented to simplify and improve co-existence between government and citizens. Bayona and Morales [19] presented a preliminary comparison of local e-government maturity levels between municipalities in some countries in Latin America. Successful models show significant progress in terms of citizen satisfaction, reduced bureaucratic attitudes in public institutions, and a significant saving of resources. Bernhard et al. [22] investigated the relationship between the degree of government in Swedish municipalities and perceived satisfaction among citizens in general. Using a large-scale quantitative study, these results were shown: There is a relationship between the degree of digitalization in a municipality and the perceived satisfaction among its citizens. Furthermore, this relationship is in parity with or even stronger than the relationship between citizen satisfaction and other crucial factors, such as educational level or median income. Similar results have been described by Budding et al. [23]. According to these authors, electronic service delivery has become an important issue in many municipalities, and using the Internet for service delivery is seen as an important element of municipal e-government in the Netherlands. They ascertained the strong relationship of municipal e-government adoption with demographic characteristics, such as population, population density, and both older age and younger age groups. In contrast, they did not find an influence of education and income.

Governments around the world are increasingly relying on information technology, in particular the Internet, as a mean of communication with their citizens. Rooks et al. [24] stated, that the use of government websites is one of the fastest growing activities on the Internet. This set of technological processes is trying to change both the provision of public services such as the scope of interactions between citizens and the government [25]. The use of the Internet has allowed to overcome many of the technical barriers that impede smooth relations between citizens and the municipal public administration, allowing the disclosure of more detailed information, the increase in frequency and timeliness of the information provided, and decreasing costs of printing and distribution of information [26]. The adoption of e-Government is the result of the high degree of computer use and the growing number of people and organizations with access to the broadband Internet [27]. With the Internet, citizens are looking for more information about what is going on in their cities and are looking for more ways to hold their government representatives accountable. One of the best ways to provide transparency and make it easier for citizens to obtain the city services they require is to become an "open source city". An open source city is one that uses a variety of new tools, including apps, to make information available to citizens and interact with them as well [28].

3   Use of OSS and CMS in Foreign and Domestic Public Administration

The European society as a whole will benefit from the adoption of and OSS in the public sector: the citizen will not be required to buy proprietary software for accessing the information and services provided by the public administration. That, in turn, will increase the accessibility of public services. Public administration will increase trust and confidence by using recognized, transparent, and secure technologies [29].

3.1   Open Source in Public Administration

Thanks to the features of open source software, its use is associated with several advantages not only in the private sphere, but also especially in the public sphere [30]. The most obvious positive is the reduction of financial costs; OSS is available free of charge and thus eliminates the costs associated with the purchase of proprietary software and licenses to use it. Another advantage is the reduction of the risk of vendor lock-in. Related to this, the existence of open formats guarantees maximum compatibility and interconnectivity of systems, especially within e-Government, which is based on mutual reading and data exchange. It is the opposite of proprietary software, where each producer can come up with their own formats, making it impossible for other users who do not have their software to open these files. Significant benefits can also be observed in terms of quality and safety. Due to the openness of the OSS code, the institutions concerned may be able to examine it and check that the software is properly programmed for stability or security vulnerabilities. At the same time, thanks to the openness of the code, they can make any changes and adapt it to the needs of a particular institution.

The advantages of open source are used by public institutions both abroad and in the Czech Republic. One of the most well-known users of OSS in the public sector is the municipality of Munich. It started a plan to migrate to OSS in 2003 with the aim of finishing the migration of all its 14.000 workstations by the end of 2012 [29]. The municipality calculated that the current cost of its migration project is 11.7 million euros, while upgrading to a comparable environment based on Microsoft Windows and Office would have required 15.52 million, excluding costs of 2.8 million euros for license fees for upgrades recurring every three to four years for a Microsoft infrastructure [31]. OSS has been used by the French state police since 2005. Specifically, it was initially a transition from the Microsoft Office suite to OpenOffice. However, the transfer from Microsoft Explorer to Mozzila Firefox and the transfer of the mail client from Microsoft Outlook to Thunderbird gradually took place. In the last phase of moving to OSS, almost a hundred thousand computers were running the Ubuntu operating system, which is one of the many available Linux distributions. The total financial savings associated with the purchase of licenses were estimated at almost 50 million euros in the first five years since migration [32]. The Lithuanian police, which as the police in France, gradually switched from the MS Office package to LibreOffice and subsequently from the Windows operating system to the Ubuntu system, is also an almost identical case. The transfer involved a total of 8,000 computers [30]. An interesting example is the situation in Bulgaria, where the government passed a law in 2016 that stipulates that all new software acquired for government purposes must be open source basis [33]. In the

United States, a website has been set up that requires the source code of at least 20% of newly developed and deployed software within government agencies and institutions. The goal is to increase the reusability of existing software solutions and reduce duplicate software purchases. At the same time, this should lead to more innovation in government software. Financial savings are also significant: Federal IT savings could reach 3.7 billion US dollars from open source [34]. Since 2017, the public authorities in the capital of Albania have also switched to LibreOffice. Therefore, the Tirana authorities want to make the services more accessible to the population and, at the same time ensure the availability of their data and systems in the future. Migration affects about a thousand computers [35].

There are also numerous open source solutions available in public administration in the Czech Republic [30]. For example, the Czech POINT system itself uses SUSE Linux Enterprise Server for server operating systems and the open source Zabbix tool is used to monitor system operation. Many other departments of the Ministry of the Interior also use OSS for their systems. The Central Information Systems Department uses Linux operating systems, Firebird and Postgres databases, and Python and Java programming languages. The Department of the Chief Architect of e-Government manages the National Open Data Catalog, which is based exclusively on open source technologies and open standards; it uses the Ubuntu operating system, the Apache Solr search tool, the Nginx web server, and more. The Open Data Portal itself is created using the GitHub platform, which offers free hosting for open-source projects. On the portal you can find, for example, city plans, 3D building models, green passports, and many other documents. Open source tools are also used within the Czech Telecommunication Office; these include Debian, Apache, and Nginx web servers, PostgreSQL databases, Zabbix traffic monitoring and more. The pioneer of municipal use of OSS in the Czech Republic is the municipality of Grygov, where open source is used almost everywhere since 2006. Using open source has helped to reduce IT costs, and moreover, it allows Grygov to offer reliable and innovative e-government services [36].

Within the Czech Republic, there are also several initiatives aimed at promoting open-source technologies in public administration. One of them is the Open-Source Alliance, which was established to create optimal conditions for the use of open-source products in the field of government. Further, the NGO Open Cities, with seventeen municipalities as members, strives for maximum openness to their citizens and achieve this using various open source tools. Several projects have already been or are being set up within it: a solution for submitting applications for municipal subsidies and their administration, a tool for displaying the results of local council voting, or a modifiable template for creating city pages based on the WordPress content management system.

3.2 Content Management System in Public Administration

Most content management systems, which create and manage content on the Web, also operate on an open source basis. Currently, the CMS's represent one of the management technologies that best responds to this public administration needs, by representing a system that incorporates a whole panoply of tools that extend from the Web page to the most varied applications of content management [4]. Specifically, in public administration, content management promotes a substantial increase in flexibility through remote and updated network access, as well as more selective control of which metadata should be used to steer information rightly, rules that regulate access, search possibilities, and the integration of different information systems [37].

The advantage of these solutions is their simple installation and management. These are basically web page interfaces and templates that are already pre-created and available as soon as they are installed. This eliminates the need to create the own pages from scratch. After installing the CMS, it is possible to get universal websites that can be further customized through templates or by installing add-ons. Web administration is handled by a simple interface, as well as content editing and publishing. Webmasters and content creators may not have a knowledge of the HTML, CSS, PHP, or Javascript languages commonly used when working with websites.

Choosing a specific CMS is possible from dozens of different options, where the OSS-based operation allows to be downloaded and tested for free. The most widely used CMS in the world is WordPress. Its share of the CMS market is around 65% [38]. According to statistics, WordPress is used on a third of websites on the Internet. Second is Shopify (less than 7%), followed by Wix (3.3%) and Squarespace (less than 3%). Joomla is in fifth place with a share of about 2.5% now (a decrease from second place since 2020), but it was the market leader until WordPress came along. The mass popularity of blogs has caused less interest in systems other than WordPress. However, other CMS still use a large number of websites around the world. In the case of Joomla, there are almost two million websites. Here, the installation, administration, and creation of content is very simple and can be done even by a person without experience with the operation of the website. Unlike WordPress, which is focused on creating blogs, Joomla is also suitable for more complex websites. The advantage is also a lower risk of hacker attacks, which focus more on the more widespread WordPress. Other positions within the CMS market are Drupal (1.9%), Adobe Systems (1.6%), Google Systems (1.5%) or Bitrix (1.2%).

Regarding the practical use by CMS, the study of Louraço and Marques [4] aims to analyze the acceptance of CMSs by professionals from municipalities belonging to the Comunidade Intermunicipal da Lezíria do Tejo. WordPress is used by the official Swedish website or the White House website. Destefanis et al. [39] showed that the number of Italian public administrations that use Open Source CMS is increasing about 5% per year. Joomla was used in more than half of municipalities in 2012. Joomla is a key CSM tool for the design of municipal websites of the MuNet program that the Organization of American States has implemented in several countries of Latin America, specifically the municipalities of Patzún (Guatemela), David or San Miguelito in Panama are examples [40].

4   Problem Solving

For the implementation of OSS has been selected one Czech municipality (Statutory city of Karvina), which is trying to digitize its public administration and introduce smart elements within the framework of improving its municipal e-Government. The solved issue was focused on the area of waste management, namely providing e-services in the field of waste containers. This was selected based on a survey of the city's website, where sufficient user-friendly and clear information were absent.

4.1 The Study Area and Open Source Tool

The Statutory city of Karvina, located in the border Moravian-Silesian Region on the territory of historic Teschen Silesia, was chosen to implement the open source tool. It is a city with a strong spa and mining tradition dating back to the late 18th century. At the same time, a university, namely the School of Business Administration of the Silesian University in Opava, is located here. The city of Karvina is divided into nine city districts and has approximately 52,000 inhabitants, not only Czech but also Polish and Slovak origin.

As the city presents itself as a municipality in which smart elements are being introduced, including the expansion of digitization and e-Government, its website has been explored and ascertained that in some areas (maps of parks, sports grounds, playgrounds or waste containers) the introduction of "smart" elements is at a very low level. Therefore, the area of waste management was chosen, because the information on the location of containers for separated waste was only given in the form of tables with given street addresses. One possible way to expand or improve the presentation of this information was to show the location of individual containers using the interactive maps based on open source.

In the city Karvina, there are 274 container sites. There are usually one to six containers for municipal waste and one to three containers for plastics, paper, and glass in the designated places. Individual containers for bio-waste, metals, textiles, small electronics, and used respirators can also be found at several selected places. Larger kitchen appliances, consumer electronics, cooling systems, garden tools, and implements are then taken by the residents to the collection yard, or they have a high-volume container delivered for a fee. Since 1965, the company Technical Services Karvina has been taking care of the collection, transport, and disposal of waste in the city, as well as the operation of the collection yard.

To create a website, it was most appropriate to use an open source CMS. With its help, it is easy and without the necessary financial investment to create a website that will meet the requirements for an information website about containers, i.e. the presence of a map supplement.

For the purposes of this paper, Joomla CMS was chosen as a proven tool for creating and managing websites. This tool is the most suitable for the purpose of creating a website of waste management, the main part of which is a map of container sites. Joomla offers a relatively large number of different map accessories, which are usually available for free. Another reason to choose this system is the user interface for web administration. It is clear, friendly, and improves with each new version of the system. Web administration can be performed from a computer, but also from a mobile phone or tablet. At the same time, most of the available templates are responsive, so the web view adapts to the screen dimensions of the device on which the web is browsing. The look of the site can be changed in a few steps, as well as adding the additional features such as maps, galleries, discussions, and more [41]. Other Joomla features include content approval for subsequent publication, user group management, content publishing scheduling, automatic web content search, banner management, add-on installation support, or multilingual support.

4.2 Process of Installation

Before the installation and subsequent use of the content management system, it was necessary to ensure that several requirements were met. The so-called hosting is necessary for the operation of the content management system, which is a virtual space on a web server on which the created web pages are placed. In the case of Joomla, hosting is required to support the PHP scripting language in which Joomla is written. In addition, MySQL database support is required for data storage purposes. Another requirement is the use of an open source Apache Web server, which processes PHP instructions to work with the database and for displaying web pages. The last requirement is support for XML and a software library for data compression called *zlib* [41].

There are several ways to get web hosting that meets the above requirements. The first way is to use the web hosting services of a specialized company. This eliminates the need for customers to install it by themselves, and, conversely, they can use the functions for automatic system installation, or rent hosting with an already pre-installed CMS. The second option is to have own web server. However, this is a rather demanding solution, which is why companies or organizations often resort to renting web hosting services that provide all the operational issues. Another way to use Joomla CMS is the possibility of the cloud. On the official Joomla website, it is possible to create a fully functional website for free using a cloud platform. The last variant for Joomla installation and operation is the so-called local installation, where Joomla is installed directly on a personal computer. This variant is suitable for creating and testing a website. For our purposes, this last method of content management system installation was chosen, and after testing and launching online was transferred to the web hosting form.

Before the CMS installation itself, it was necessary to install a server application on the computer; the XAMPP software package was used for this purpose. It contains the OSS, which is necessary for creation of a local web server (Apache server application, MariaDB database, and PHP scripting language). In addition to these parts, the MySQL database and phpMyAdmin to work with the database were needed to install. In the next step, the installation location was selected, and then the installation itself was performed. The next step before installing the content management system was to create a database called *joomladb*, in which the website data will be stored, using the phpMyAdmin utility, as a part of the XAMPP package.

The installation of the Joomla CMS itself took place in three steps - filling in the site name and login details for the administrator; setting up the database (type, host name, username, and password); and last but not least, a summary of the settings using templates. Finally, to complete the installation and gain access to the site, it was necessary to delete the installation folder, which is a security feature.

4.3 Selection of the Map Supplement, Customization and Allocation of Website

After the CMS was installed, it was possible to start creating an application. The main component of the generated waste management page is a map with the location of container sites. Basically, the Joomla system does not contain an add-on for embedding maps on the web, so it was necessary to add this feature additionally. Total of 7,619 of these features are available and include extensions for uploading photo galleries and presentations, supporting social networks, writing and publishing articles, as well as extensions that do not relate to web content. These are various modules for web administration, traffic analysis, web navigation, or security management.

Dozens of different maps embedding add-ons can be found in the Maps and Weather extension tab, the most suitable of which are listed in Table 1. The main criterion for selecting this add-on is whether it uses Google Maps or OpenStreetMap to render the map. Using Google Maps and exceeding the monthly limit of possible map loads, the service is charged. On contrary, using OpenStreetMap is completely free. Other criteria taken into account by choosing a map add-on, include the possibility of customizing map markers, the presence of a manual or documentation, or language support for the add-on.

Table 1. Comparison of the map supplement.

Title of supplement	Free	Support of OpenStreetMap	Manual	Support of Czech language
My Maps Location	No	Yes	Yes	No
Hotspots Pro	No	No	Yes	No
GMapFP	Yes	No	Yes	No
Phoca Maps	Yes	Yes	Yes	Yes
Phoca Maps	Yes	No	Yes	No

Among the twenty most used map add-ons, there are only two that use Open-StreetMap, the others are focused only on Google Maps. Of these two supplements, one is paid and one is available for free. The paid add-on My Maps Location from JoomUnited developers offers a module with options for customizing the appearance and layout of the map, a sophisticated search system. The second add-on is Phoca Maps (made by Czech developer Jan Pavelka). Unlike My Maps Location, it is available for free. It is a simpler add-on in terms of a number of different customization options, settings, and functions, but it is sufficient for the needs of the application. Its interface is clear, the advantage is also the presence of the Czech localization. To install add-ons, content creation, graphic design of the website, and other activities, it is necessary to access the website from the position of administrator.

The next step was to create a map in which container station markers were later inserted, using the forms. Maps can be created with this add-on and can be used at the same time, each with its own settings and custom markers. Creating a map involved specifying its name, initial coordinates, zoom level, dimensions, and description. The last step before placing the map on the website, was to create map markers that will indicate the location of the container sites.

During the installation of the CMS, a basic template with a preset appearance and structure of the pages was set. The form (Logo) allowed to insert an image into the site header. The last step in creating the site was to insert the map plugin itself.

At the time when the website was created, it had to be placed on the internet to make it available to visitors online. Therefore, it was necessary to transfer it from the local server to the actual online hosting. For the selected free hosting (Endora), a third-order domain was used, and the address of the website was used: containerykarvina.tode.cz. Further, it was necessary to pack the folder with the content management system files in a zip file. Then the created database was exported, a zip file with a prepared content management system was uploaded to the Endora website, unpacked, and a new database was created. The database server address had to be rewritten to the Endora server address (received after domain registration) and saved. After that, the whole process of moving the website from the local server to online hosting was completed, and the finished website was made available.

5   Result: Final Website

The result of all steps discussed in the previous section, was the creation of an application based on the Joomla content management system with a map complement of container sites. The intention was to support the smart municipal waste management of

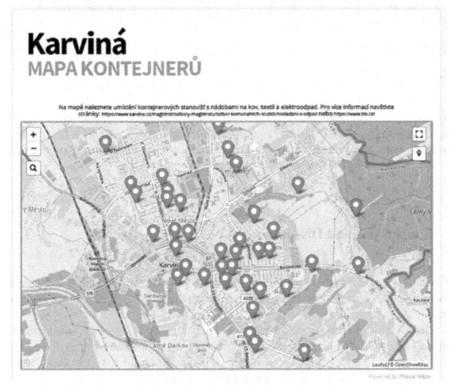

Fig. 1. Final web site with the map (maps of containers).

the Statutory City of Karvina using the e-map of containers. The map shows the container locations where, in addition to containers for municipal, paper, glass and plastic waste, containers for metal, textile, oil or electrical waste can be also found (see Fig. 1).

By clicking on a specific brand, the details of the brand with the name of the site will be opened, namely address and quantity of each container (see Fig. 2). There can be found the name of the street with the house number and the kinds of containers - if they are available (and how many) or not. The map also includes links to the pages of the Department of Municipal Services and to the pages of Karvina Technical Services, in case of need to contact the institution.

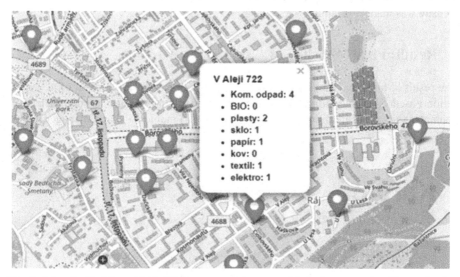

Fig. 2. Map details (Notes: V Aleji 722 – name of the street with the house number, Kom. odpad – municipal waste, BIO – bio waste, plasty – plastic waste, sklo – glass waste, papír – paper waste, kov – metal waste, textile – textile waste, elektro – electrical waste).

6 Conclusions and Discussion

E-Government also usually represents an alternative instrument that offers new means or methods of work for those who can and/or want to use them, although it is apparent that more duties are prescribed for public administration and businesses rather than for citizens [42].

The potential of open source solutions used in public administration is considerable, not only can it bring big financial savings, but thanks to the use of open formats it will also ensure better interconnectivity of various e-government systems and better availability of services for citizens. Thanks to the openness of the source code of open source software, public administration institutions can then check the quality and level of security of individual tools as well as make any adjustments to their own needs.

Based on the stated objective of this paper, the use of open source tools within smart solutions in public administration (namely waste management) of the statutory city of Karvina, the content management system Joomla was selected, which was proved to be effective for the creation of the website. Its advantage is easy installation and administration; at the same time its possibilities and functions can be very well expanded with the help of various paid and unpaid accessories. Another positive feature of this add-on is the ability to use OpenStreetMap, unlike most other add-ons focused exclusively on Google Maps. However, in general, the Joomla content management system and the selected Phoca Maps add-on are more than sufficient.

Using the Joomla content management system, the map of container sites within the municipality waste management was created. The map shows container stations which, in addition to containers for municipal, paper, glass, and plastic waste, also displays containers for metal, textile, or electrical waste. The resulting website is available to users at the address: www.kontejnerykarvina.tode.cz.

Limitation of this paper can be seen in the used system: the absence of importing map markers into the map add-on Phoca Maps. When the insertion of larger number of markers into the map are needed, this can be a problem. However, some paid add-ons offer solutions of this problem, as well as more advanced branding options.

In the future, the application could be expanded in terms of content, such as statistical tables and figures of the total waste collected per year. Dozens of different supplements can be found for this agenda. Another option is to extend the focus of the application to other facilities managed by the Department of Municipal Services: maps of parks, sports grounds, or children's playgrounds, etc.

This website (and others of this type) can also serve as inspiration for the implementation of this e-Government tool for other cities in all areas of providing e-information to their citizens. In general, the use of open source content management systems can be recommended as a tool to simplify or support the implementation of processes within e-services.

Acknowledgement. This study has been supported by the grant project CZ.02.1.01/0.0/0.0/17_049/0008452 "Smart Technologies to Improve the Quality of Life in Cities and Regions".

References

1. Hartman, E.: Master Your Content Using the Content Management Lifecycle. CMS. https://www.shorturl.at/imnC5/ (2019). Accessed 21 Feb 2022
2. van Loon, A., Toshkov, D.: Adopting open source software in public administration: The importance of boundary spanners and political commitment. http://www.dimiter.eu/Publications_files/Van_Loon_and_Toshkov_2015.pdf (2015) Accessed 21 Feb 2022
3. EC: European Commission. Open source software strategy 2020–2023. https://ec.europa.eu/info/departments/informatics/open-source-software-strategy_en (2020). Accessed 21 Feb 2022

4. Louraço, D., Marques, C.G.: The acceptance of content management systems in portuguese municipalities: a study in the intermunicipal community of Lezíria do Tejo. In: Rocha, Á., Adeli, H., Dzemyda, G., Moreira, F., Ramalho Correia, A.M. (eds.) WorldCIST 2021. AISC, vol. 1366, pp. 503–512. Springer, Cham (2021). https://doi.org/10.1007/978-3-030-72651-5_48

5. Louraço, D., Marques, C.G.: CMS in public administration: a comparative analysis. J. Inf. Syst. Eng. Manag. **7**(1), 11688 (2022)

6. Bilitewski, B., Härdtle, G., Marek, K.: Waste Management. Springer Berlin Heidelberg, Berlin, Heidelberg (1997). https://doi.org/10.1007/978-3-662-03382-1

7. Pichtel, J.: Waste Management Practices: Municipal, Hazardous, and Industrial. CRC Press, Florida (2014)

8. Eurostat Glossary: Municipal waste. https://ec.europa.eu/eurostat/statistics-explained/index.php?title=Glossary:Municipal_waste (2022). Accessed 27 Feb 2022

9. EC: European Commission: Municipal waste statistic. https://ec.europa.eu/eurostat/statistics-explained/index.php?title=Municipal_waste_statistics (2022). Accessed 27 Feb 2022

10. Tchobanoglous, G.: Solid waste management. Environmental Engineering: Environmental Health and Safety for Municipal Infrastructure, Land Use And Planning, and industry. Wiley, New Jersey (2009)

11. MECR: Waste management. Ministry of the Environment of the Czech Republic. https://www.mzp.cz/cz/odpadove_hospodarstvi (2022). Accessed 27 Feb 2022

12. Gustafsson, K., Fiedler, M.: E-Government: Services, Needs and user Satisfaction. Blekinge Institute of Technology, School of Engineering, Sweden, Karlskrona (2004)

13. Zhu, Z., Kou, G.: Linking smart governance to future generations: a study on the use of local e-Government service among undergraduate students in a Chinese municipality. Informatics **6**(4), 45 (2019)

14. Justice, J., Melitski, J., Smith, D.: E-government as an instrument of fiscal accountability and responsiveness: do the best practitioners employ the best practices? Am. Rev. Public Adm. **36**(3), 301–322 (2006)

15. Naser, A., Concha, G.: El gobierno electrónico en la gestión pública, Instituto Latinoamericano y del Caribe de Planificación Económica y Social (ILPES), Naciones Unidad, CEPAL, Santiago de Chile https://repositorio.cepal.org/handle/11362/7330 (2011). Accessed 01 Mar 2011

16. Przeybilovicz, E., Cunha, M., Meirelles, F.: The use of information and communication technology to characterize municipalities: who they are and what they need to develop e-government and smart city initiatives. Revista de Administracao Publica, 630–649 (2018)

17. Moon, M.J.: The evolution of e-Government among municipalities: rhetoric or reality? Public Adm. Rev. **62**(4), 424–433 (2002)

18. Zhang, B., Zhu, Y.: Comparing attitudes towards adoption of e-Government between urban users and rural users: an empirical study in Chongqing municipality, China. Behav. Inf. Technol. **40**(11), 1154–1168 (2021)

19. Bayona, S.O., Morales, L.V.: Maturity model for local e-Government: a case study. In: Proceedings of the 8th International Conference on Computer Modeling and Simulation (ICCMS'17), pp. 78–83. Association for Computing Machinery, USA, New York (2017)

20. Urs, N.: E-government development in Romanian local municipalities: a complicated story of success and hardships. Transylv. Rev. Adm. Sci. **55**, 118–129 (2018)

21. Gonzalez-Bustamante, B., Carvajal, A., Gonzalez, A.: Determinants of e-government in the municipalities: evidence from the Chilean case. Gest. Polít. Pública **29**(1), 97–129 (2020)

22. Bernhard, I., et al.: Degree of digitalization and citizen satisfaction: a study of the role of local e-government in Sweden. Electron. J. Gov. **16**(1), 59–71 (2018)

23. Budding, T., Faber, B., Gradus, R.: Assessing electronic service delivery in municipalities: determinants and financial consequences of e-government implementation. Local Gov. Stud. **44**(5), 697–718 (2018)
24. Rooks, G., Matzat, U., Sadowski, B.: An empirical test of stage models of e-government development: evidence from Dutch municipalities. Inf. Soc. **33**(4), 215–225 (2017)
25. Torres, L., Pina, V., Royo, S.: E-government and the transformation of public administrations in EU countries: beyond NPM or just a second wave of reforms? Online Inf. Rev. **29**(5), 531–553 (2005)
26. Pina, V., Torres, L., Royo, S.: Is E-government leading global convergence towards account-able governments?. In: Proceedings of the XIV Congress of AECA, pp. 1–8. Valencia, Spain (2007)
27. Alcaide, L., Rodríguez, M., López, A.: Investigación metodológica en gobierno electrónico: Evaluación de publicaciones periódicas ISI (2000–2006). In: Proceedings of the XIV Congress of AECA, pp. 1–8. Spain, Valencia (2007)
28. Harper, L.: 10 tools to help open source cities maintain transparency. https://opensource.com/government/13/10/tools-open-source-cities (2013). Accessed 10 Mar 2022
29. Kovács, G., Drozdik, S., Zuliani, P., Succi, G.: Open source software for the public administra-tion. In: Proceedings of the 6 th International Workshop on Computer Science and Information Technologies, CSIT'2004, pp. 1–8. Hungary, Budapest (2004)
30. Murys, M.: Selection and implementation of an open source tool for a selected area of public administration of the city Karvina. Silesian University in Opava, Business School in Karvina. https://is.slu.cz/th/ojru4/. Accessed 11 Mar 2022
31. von Eitzen, C.: LiMux: cheaper and more robust than Windows. http://www.h-online.com/open/news/item/LiMux-Cheaper-and-more-robust-than-Windows-1485895.html   (2012). Accessed 11 Mar 2022
32. Paul, R.: French police: we saved millions of euros by adopting Ubuntu. https://arstechnica.com/information-technology/2009/03/french-police-saves-millions-of-euros-by-adopting-ubuntu/ (2009). Accessed 12 Mar 2022
33. Bozhanov, B.: Bulgaria got a law requiring open source. https://thepolicy.us/bulgaria-got-a-law-requiring-open-source-98bf626cf70a (2016). Accessed 12 Mar 2022
34. Repas, M.A.: Using Free, Open-Source Software in Local Governments: Streamlined Inter-nal Computing for Better Performance and Record Keeping. An ICMA Report. ICMA, Washington, DC (2010)
35. OSOR: Open source observatory. the municipality of Tirana goes free open source by using Nextcloud. https://joinup.ec.europa.eu/collection/open-source-observatory-osor/news/municipality-tirana-go (2017). Accessed 15 Mar 2022
36. Hillenius, G.: Czech municipality uses open source for nearly everything. https://joinup.ec.europa.eu/collection/open-source-observatory-osor/news/czech-municipality-uses-open (2012). Accessed 15 Mar 2022
37. Svärd, P.: E-Government development and its impact on information management. In: Enterprise Content Management. Records Management and Information Culture Amidst E-Government Development, pp. 1–10. Chandos Publishing, Cambridge (2017)
38. W3Techs: Usage statistics of content management systems. https://w3techs.com/technologies/overview/content_management (2022). Accessed 16 Mar 2022
39. Destefanis, G., Tonelli, R., Cocco, L., Concas, G., Marchesi, M.: A case study of the use of Open Source CMS in public administrations. In: 14th IEEE International Symposium on Web Systems Evolution (WSE), pp. 31–34. Trento, Italy (2012)
40. Lopez-Bachiller, J.: eGovernment - Joomla and Patzun Municipality at ICEGOV2012, Electronic Government World Conference. https://magazine.joomla.org/all-issues/december-2012/joomla-patzun-at-icegov2012 (2012), Accessed 16 Mar 2022

41. Tiggeler, E.: Joomla! Beginner's Guide Second Edition, 2nd edn. Packt Publishing, Birmingham (2014)
42. Špaček, D.: Trends of E-government in Czech municipal and regional self-government. Rev. Econ. Perspect. **12**(1), 42–67 (2012)

Smart Interventions for Smart Cities: Using Behavioral Economy in Increasing Revenue from Local Fees and Why It Might Sometimes Fail

Nikoleta Jakuš Muthová[ID], Mária Murray Svidroňová[(✉)] [ID], and Katarína Vitálišová[ID]

Faculty of Economics, Matej Bel University, Tajovského 10, 975 90 Banská Bystrica, Slovakia
{nikoleta.jakusmuthova,maria.murraysvidronova,
katarina.vitalisova}@umb.sk

Abstract. The collection of taxes and fees is one of the main functions of a modern local government, through which many public goods and services are provided. However, in many local governments, there is a need to address the problem of non-payers of local taxes or other local fees. Although taxpayers are usually sent reminders to pay local taxes or charges, or if they fail to pay, they will be referred for distrainment, there are still people who do not fulfill their obligations to the local government. Several studies have confirmed that the use of behavioral intervention can be a useful tool to reduce the proportion of non-payers, i.e., the taxpayers can be 'nudged' to pay their taxes on time and correctly. In this paper, we present the results of a behavioral intervention in the city of Banská Bystrica, Slovakia. The aim of the intervention was to increase the city's revenues from garbage disposal fees, dog fees and property tax by proactive communication – reminder (a letter) and leaflets with targeted framing. In October 2021, the city sent a total of 520 reminder letters as part of the intervention. The letters were divided into 4 groups of 130 tax subjects. The data was analyzed using Cramer's V. The results in this particular city show that the intervention did not produce the expected results; we discuss other examples of Slovak local governments that show the positive effect of behavioral interventions in the area of tax and fee collection.

Keywords: Behavioral intervention · Modern government · Smart city · Tax and fee collection

1 Introduction

The introduction of behavioral interventions into public policy making is now widespread. Not only at the national level, but also at the regional and local level, behavioral nudges and other forms of interventions have proven to be an effective and efficient way to influence the effectiveness of public policy in a variety of areas. The area of making tax and fee collection more efficient, which is the focus of this paper, is no exception.

O. Gervasi et al. (Eds.): ICCSA 2022 Workshops, LNCS 13382, pp. 141–156, 2022.
https://doi.org/10.1007/978-3-031-10592-0_12

When collecting taxes and fees, the responsible institutions are quite often faced with the problem of non-payers. The fact that there are people who refuse to pay compulsory taxes and fees has significant implications for the functioning of the public sector. First and foremost, it is associated with a shortfall in revenue in the respective budget, i.e., fewer resources are available to ensure that the tasks and functions of public administration at that level are carried out. This can negatively affect the level of service delivery. Revenue shortfalls therefore undermine the provision of public goods and the design and implementation of public policies, but they also have an impact on equity in terms of people's contribution to the generation of public resources.

Addressing this problem is also important because non-payment of taxes results in revenue shortfalls in local government budgets and has implications for the behavior of taxpayers themselves. Taxpayers who pay their taxes and fees may feel that they bear the tax burden, while non-payers benefit from public services in the same way as those who fulfil their obligations. This may be perceived as unfair and may negatively affect their behavior in terms of paying taxes and fees in the future.

Non-payment of local taxes and fees is therefore not only a legal problem in terms of compliance with legislation, an economic problem in terms of obtaining adequate resources to ensure the financing of the needs of the municipality or city, but also an ethical and moral problem in relation to the residents of the municipality who pay local taxes and fees.

Several studies have confirmed that the use of behavioral intervention can be a useful tool to reduce the proportion of non-payers, i.e., the taxpayers can be 'nudged' to pay their taxes on time and correctly [7, 9, 10, 12, 19]. The application of behavioral interventions to tackle problems with defaulters is usually done by sending out arrears notices that contain behavioral elements. Compared to standard reminders, the effectiveness of such reminders is generally higher. The behavioral approach is based on interventions that are called EAST: Easy, Attractive, Social and Timely [18]. It is essential to take this into account when designing an experiment in this area.

Therefore, in the first part of this paper we review behavioral interventions in the area of tax and fee collection. We then present a selected local government with a focus on its revenues from taxes and problems associated with tax and fee collection. We implemented the behavioral intervention in the form of a randomized controlled experiment, which is described in the Experiment design section, including the statistical methods used to evaluate the experiment. The next section presents the results of the experiment and a discussion with the results of similar experiments in other Slovak local governments. In the Conclusion we summarize the main points of the paper and point out the limits of our research.

2   Behavioral Interventions in the Services of Tax and Fee Collection

A number of local governments around the world are currently implementing behavioral interventions. Many times, it is the most efficient and least expensive way to nudge citizens to make the right decisions that will benefit the citizen, the local government and society as a whole.

In designing and implementing an experiment aimed at increasing tax and fee payment rates, one can take inspiration from the numerous studies that have emerged from successful previous experiments in this area.

Most of the experiments in tax and fee collection have taken the form of sending reminders to taxpayers. As a rule, a control group is defined to which a standard reminder is sent without any intervention. In addition to the control group, there are experimental (intervention) groups to which modified reminders are sent. The impact of alternative forms of behavioral interventions and which is most appropriate is examined. In doing so, the use of different methods of sending reminders or other related interventions may also be considered.

In 1995–1996, experiments were conducted in Minnesota, USA, to promote voluntary tax compliance [4]. The intervention took the form of reminder letters that included a morality-focused element and confronted taxpayers with perceived social norms. Taxpayers were divided into two groups, a control group that received a standard reminder letter and an intervention group that received a reminder letter containing an appeal to morality. In the area of income tax payments, the focus was on raising people's awareness that cheating on tax payments is not common, but rather an isolated phenomenon committed by only a minority of the population. The reason for focusing on this secondary objective was the results of a survey carried out two years prior to the intervention, which found that up to 20–50% of people in the state thought that they cheated on their taxes. In a letter using the social norm, taxpayers were informed that 93% of people pay their taxes on time. The results confirmed that tax collection was statistically significantly higher for recipients of the letter that included a reference to the social norm compared to the control group.

A behavioral intervention using reminder mailings was also carried out in Poland, where a field experiment was conducted to maximize the proportion of tax payers. They specifically targeted non-payers of income tax. The intervention groups received differently worded reminders. The experiment was carried out in cooperation with experts from the World Bank [9]. The reminders sent were formulated in different ways (Table 1). The research confirmed that the behavioral nudge letters were successful and resulted in a statistically significant increase in the proportion of tax payers.

Table 1. Wording of the letters sent to tax-payers. Source: own based on Hernandez et al. 2017.

Type of letter	Description of letter	Tone of the letter
Control group, status quo	Official letter used by the polish tax office	Neutral tone
Standard behavioral	Letter written in accordance with best practice in behavioral research using plain language and clear instructions	Neutral tone
Social norms	Variation of the standard behavioral letter, emphasizing that most citizens have already paid their tax	Soft tone
Public goods (benefits)	Variation of the standard behavioral letter, including a reminder that taxes pay for public goods	Soft tone
Public goods (loss)	Variation of the standard behavioral letter, including a reminder that not paying taxes harms the community	Soft tone
Deterrence	Variation of the standard behavioral letter, including a reminder of the steps the tax authority can take to punish noncompliance	Harsh tone
Deterrence + Distrainment order	Deterrence letter with a sample distrainment order sent to taxpayers ordering them to pay their taxes	Harsh tone
Omission	Variation of the standard behavioral letter and behavioral framework - non-payment as a deliberate choice	Harsh tone
Omission + Deterrence	Variation of the standard behavioral letter including deterring message and omission	Harsh tone
Omission + Taxpayer perspective	Variation of the omission and deterrence letter telling defaulters that they should have a feeling of dishonesty	Harsh tone

An evaluation of the experiment found that behavioral letters improved individuals' behavior compared to a control letter; letters written with a harsh tone were more effective than letters with a soft tone, which were even less effective than standard behavioral letters, although the effectiveness also depended on the characteristics of the individual payers. They also found that the method of letter delivery had no effect on taxpayers, and if the most effective version (omission + deterrence) was sent to the entire sample, it would generate 28 times the return over the cost of the intervention [9].

The authors of the experiment used reminders predominantly using the influence of social norms to remind taxpayers of the benefits of paying their taxes and to point out that most taxpayers were complying with their tax obligations. A total of 101 471 individuals, geographically distributed across different areas of England, Wales and Northern Ireland, took part in the experiment. Participants included people who owed between £400 and £100,000 in tax. It was found that all the letters sent to the intervention groups were successful and led to an increase in the proportion of taxpayers. In terms of increasing the number of tax payers, letters using social norms were the most successful. Messages pointing to the lack of public services due to budget shortfalls did not lead to significantly better results than messages pointing to the benefits of paying taxes in relation to the provision of public goods. This field experiment was replicated a year later to see if the effectiveness of these changes had diminished over time.

In the UK, it is also standard practice to send letters to taxpayers who fail to pay their taxes on time. Their experiment was also based on changing the wording of the letters sent. The new letters were successful and helped to increase tax collection, the most successful of which was a letter reminding taxpayers that they were part of a minority who had not yet paid their taxes [5].

Another experiment was conducted at the local authority level in London (London Borough of Lambeth) to increase the success rate of tax collection. This local authority is very heterogeneous, with only 57.1% of the population being of white ethnicity. The borough is also characterized by large disparities in income and wealth between residents. Taxpayers were divided into four groups. The first group received a classic tax calculation letter. The second group received a modified tax calculation letter, which was slightly modified as follows: at the top of the letter was key information - how much to pay, by when to pay, and a contact point where the taxpayer could go in case of confusion or miscalculation of the tax. The third group received a tax calculation letter, which additionally included the information that more than 95% of people in the local authority pay their taxes on time and correctly. The last group received letters that contained a combination of a simplified letter and a social norm. That is, immediately at the beginning of the letter there was key information and also the message that 95% of taxpayers in the local authority are paying their tax obligations properly. In this experiment, it was found that taking into account the social norm did not have a statistically significant effect; on the contrary, simplifying the letter to include the tax calculation proved to be a successful behavioral intervention. In this case, it succeeded in increasing the number of tax payers by 3.8%. The most successful result was achieved with a reminder letter that combined the social norm with simplified data, where it managed to increase the proportion of tax payers by 4.3% [10].

In 2019, Luts and Roy, in collaboration with IOTA (Intra-European Organisation of Tax Administration), carried out an experiment in Belgium targeting non-payers of income taxes at the national level. The experiment was carried out by sending various reminder letters to groups of taxpayers who had not paid their tax. Their aim was to see which of the reminder alternatives was the most effective in nudging the non-payers to pay the tax. They drafted seven versions of the letters that included different behavioral insights. The first of the letters used social norms formulated in such a way that 95% of taxes in Belgium are paid on time. Another letter informed taxpayers about the areas that are financed thanks to taxes (education, health, etc.) and a negative version of this letter. Other versions of the letters used, for example, status quo heuristics, loss aversion - they informed about the penalties that follow for not paying taxes, or were a combination of some of the letters, and there was also a basic version of the letter for the control group. By evaluating the experiment, they found that the most effective version contained information about the penalty, which increased payments by 20% compared to the control group, and the cost-benefit analysis also showed the cost-effectiveness of the project [14].

In 2016, Dwenger et al., using a natural experiment, investigated the impact of incentives on church tax payments in Germany. The authors used three schemes to motivate taxpayers, - simplification of tax payment; different ways to discourage non-payment of taxes; rewards for compliance such as social recognition, inclusion in a prize draw for cash prizes, or a combination of these. The authors conclude that intrinsic motivation affects compliance positively, while extrinsic motivation affects compliance negatively. This suggests that rewarding taxpayers for contributing to the financing of public goods (rather than punishing them for not paying taxes) creates a signal that a given tax system contains voluntary aspects and puts the legally binding obligation to pay taxes on the back burner [6].

In Guatemala, attempts have been made to address the high proportion of tax default-ers through behavioral interventions, as the local tax office estimated that up to 30% of taxpayers do not file their tax returns on time, which translates into a practical loss of tax revenue of approximately US $1.9 million USD [12]. This has obviously limited the ability to implement social programs for residents and has led to a deepening of poverty. The intervention targeted payers of value-added tax (VAT) on services, which is paid monthly in Guatemala. The authors examined two effects: a timing effect and a message text effect. Taxpayers were sent a text message designed to increase their VAT payments. Text messages were sent to recipients at two times - four days before the tax was due and twenty days after the tax was due. They tested three types of behavioral incentives: personalization of the messages, they made the messages more personal; simplification, they added a web link directly into the messages where the tax return could be filed; and deterrence, where the messages included information that if the return was not filed on time, the taxpayer would receive a fine. It was found that messages that were consistent with behavioral science findings and were sent before the due date had a significant positive impact on the number of tax returns filed. This effect persisted throughout the six-month duration of the study, confirming its lasting impact on individual taxpayer behavior. The number of tax returns in each group that received one of the reports increased by 1%. In contrast, messages sent after the VAT due date in any text form did not have such a significant positive effect. This finding documents that the timing of the intervention is very important. In the above experiment, the timeliness of the message was a more significant factor than the wording of the message itself. Another important finding is that the increase in tax returns filed did not translate into an increase in tax payments. It turned out that many taxpayers filed tax returns with zero tax payments.

Castro and Scartascini conducted a large-scale field experiment in a municipality in Argentina in which they sought to influence compliance rates in property tax payment by focusing on the different levels of compliance assurance, the reciprocity associated with the use of the tax revenue, and the impact of the attitudes of other taxpayers in the municipality. Participants were divided into control and intervention groups. Individuals in the intervention group were sent attachments along with the tax regulations containing information on tax enforcement and fines; on the behavior of other taxpayers; and on how tax revenues are used by the government. The results of the PROBIT statistical model conducted suggest that the information sent to deter taxpayers from not paying the tax (e.g., informing about tax recovery and fines) had a statistically positive and economically significant effect on compliance with the regulations. Sending such information increased tax compliance by almost 5 percentage points. On the other hand, information on how others in the municipality pay taxes or how the municipality uses the tax revenue did not have a statistically significant impact. However, the results suggest that information about what the collected resources will be used for, as well as how other taxpayers behave, is also relevant to some people's decisions about whether to pay taxes - e.g., after taking into account the individual characteristics of individuals, the results suggest that those who have complied with tax regulations in the past tended to react in the same direction to information about how others comply [3].

In Canada, they conducted an experiment on employers who were late in paying taxes in previous years. Letters guided them on how, where and when to complete their tax returns, resulting in a 4.2% increase in the first year and a 6.1% increase in the second year compared to the control group [15].

In Slovakia, behavioral experiments in the area of paying taxes and local fees are relatively new. The first experiment in Prievidza focused on sending reminders to debtors of the municipal garbage fee. The main aim of the experiment was to find out what effect a reminder in the form of a letter would have on the behavior of the debtors and also to find out what effect other moral norms and thank-you letters in the form of leaflets would have on them [17]. The authors point out that for objective reasons a random distribution could not be made, and therefore the economic department of the city of Prievidza ensured that they were divided into two groups according to gender and amount of debt, so that the groups were similar to each other. One group received a reminder and the other, the control group, did not. The frameworks chosen were the social norm and the thank you, which they named Intervention A (letter + social norm), Intervention B (letter only) and Intervention C (letter + thank you). The intervention that has proven to be the most effective was a reminder together with an injunctive social norm leaflet. It resulted in a 1.7 times higher probability for the debt to be paid. The results also indicate that a reminder is significantly more effective if targeted at debtors who only owe one payment - this group was three times more likely to pay their debt after being exposed to the intervention [17].

From the above review (which is not exhaustive, but covers several countries around the world and different outcomes), it is clear that the studies that have emerged from behavioral interventions conducted around the world can provide a starting point for the formulation of the intervention in our experiment, both in terms of the content and modality of the intervention implemented, and in terms of the methods that can be used to evaluate it.

2.1 Tax Collection in the Municipality of Banská Bystrica

The town of Banská Bystrica is both a district and regional seat of local government, with a population of 78,484 inhabitants it is the sixth largest town in Slovakia. Real estate taxes constitute a significant part of the city's income, almost one-fifth (Table 2).

Table 2. Percentage share of real estate tax on current tax revenues of the city of Banská Bystrica for the years 2015–2020. Source: own based on Banská Bystrica´s budgets.

Year	% share of real estate tax in current tax revenue
2015	19.43
2016	18.00
2017	17.10
2018	16.10
2019	15.56
2020	19.52

A list of defaulters is published by the city as of 31 December each year on its website, namely those whose arrears exceed € 160 in the case of a natural person and € 1,600 in the case of a legal entity.

The city sends a reminder to non-payers of taxes - a notice to pay every 2 years. If the debtors fail to pay the arrears even after the expiry of the deadline for payment set in the notice sent, the recovery of the arrears in the tax distrainment procedure is referred to an external bailiff.

In addition to the service of summonses and the referral of cases for distrainment, the names of debtors are published on an electronic notice board. The list of debtors is published in accordance with Article 52 of Act No 563/2009 Coll [1]. This is a list of tax debtors as of 31 December of the previous year whose aggregate amount of tax arrears exceeded € 160 for a natural person and € 1,600 for a legal person.

The City of Banská Bystrica registers approximately 4,440 real estate tax defaulters as of 18 October 2021 (Banská Bystrica, 2021). The total debt of natural persons amounts to approximately € 516,000. Arrears for municipal garbage for individuals amounted to approximately € 1,650,000. In this case, there are 10,455 defaulters.

Interviews with representatives of the City of Banská Bystrica revealed that default-ers are often from socially disadvantaged groups, which makes the recovery of arrears particularly challenging. The administration associated with sending notices and dis-trainment proceedings is also time-consuming, so the city is interested in trying to increase the efficiency of tax and fee collection and reduce the number of defaulters by using behavioral intervention.

3 Experiment Design

The main objective of the proposed experiment is to solve the problem of non-payers of local real estate tax and local fees in the city of Banská Bystrica. Using a behavioral intervention, we want to find out how the defaulters will react to different forms of behavioral nudges embedded in a leaflet that will be part of the tax payment reminder. We will evaluate the data collected from the experiment to see which form of intervention proves to be effective.

In order to meet the objective, we set 3 research questions (RQs):

RQ1: Did the implemented nudge help to change the behaviour of non-payers and contribute to the timely and correct payment of local taxes and fees in the city of Banská Bystrica, compared to the control group?

RQ2: Which of the three versions of the leaflet sent out most influenced the behaviour of non-payers in the desired direction?

RQ3: Which of the three versions of the leaflet sent out was not effective or did not influence the behaviour of non-payers in the desired direction?

When designing the leaflets, we drew on experiments carried out in the field of taxes and fees from around the world and in Slovakia.

The results of many experiments point to the effectiveness of behavioral interventions that use social and moral norms [7, 9, 13, 17]. An example of a moral norm is the statement, "9 out of 10 people already pay their taxes on time." In this way, taxpayers become more identified with their city, and a more significant change from the general social norm occurs. We also used this framing in the design of our behavioral intervention and the leaflet sent to the first group informs how other citizens behave: "Did you know that 9 out of 10 taxpayers in Banská Bystrica have already paid their real estate tax?" The leaflet encourages non-payers to join the paying majority.

The leaflet sent to the second group highlights social norms. The change from the first group is its focus on belonging to a group of people with the same surname. A similar social norm is used by the Brno City Transport Company, which informs its passengers about the most common names of passengers who do not buy tickets. In addition to self-interest, how others behave also influences the behavior of other individuals. A third version of the leaflet encourages defaulters to keep a good reputation and informs, "Did you know that people with the same surname as you pay their real estate tax on time? Be one of them".

The leaflet designed for the third group is intended to be a deterrent. It encourages defaulters to pay the tax they have been assessed to avoid distrainment proceedings. The leaflet works with the concept of loss aversion and informs defaulters that "There is a high likelihood that if you are found to default in paying your taxes, your case will be referred to distrainment proceedings and, among other things, your driver's license may be revoked or the arrears may be taken from your pension, wages or account." In the defaulter, this information is intended to induce a state known as fear of loss [11] and of the possible consequences resulting from non-payment of taxes.

A randomized controlled experiment was conducted by mailing leaflets including a simple infographic to reinforce their effect. The leaflets were sent to defaulters assigned to each intervention group (Intervention group 1 - Moral norm leaflet, Intervention group 2 - Social norm leaflet, Intervention group 3 - Fear of loss intervention leaflet), along with an invitation to pay the tax arrears. The first and second intervention groups were sent a leaflet with information about moral and social norms and how other residents comply with regulations and meet their tax obligations. The third intervention group was sent a deterrent leaflet informing them of the high likelihood of having their case referred to distrainment proceedings or having their driver's license revoked if they were found to have irregularities in paying taxes. Only a reminder, so no leaflet, was sent to the control group and this group will be used to compare effectiveness with the three intervention groups.

Taxpayers who had outstanding local tax (real estate tax, dog tax) and/or local municipal garbage charges were randomly allocated to the intervention groups. In this way, we eliminated predictable effects and each of the defaulters had an equal chance of being included in the sample. The sample consists of 520 taxpayers to whom the Banská Bystrica City Council sent notices for payment of tax arrears in October 2021.

We used the following methods to process the data:

- Descriptive statistics (e.g., the number of defaulters who paid the tax after the summons, the total value of summonses paid, etc.),
- Cramer's V to determine the degree of dependence (e.g., the existence of a statistically significant relationship between the version of the leaflet sent and the payment of the arrears, the amount of the arrears and the payment of the arrears, etc.).

4 Results and Discussion

The experiment collected basic data from all 520 taxpayers. The type of tax for which the taxpayer is in arrears (real estate tax, dog tax or municipal garbage tax), the amount of the arrears (also the amount of the paid and unpaid part of the arrears) and whether or not the taxpayer took the leaflet sent by the municipality. Out of a total of 520 tax subjects, 190 tax subjects were in arrears on property tax, 77 tax subjects were in arrears on dog tax and 253 tax subjects were in arrears on municipal garbage tax. Municipal garbage tax arrears represented the highest amount of total arrears in each group.

In the control group of the experiment, the value of the arrears totaled € 16,741.91. 75 arrears totaling € 8,471.26 were paid and 30 arrears totaling € 8,270.65 remained unpaid. In this group, no intervention was sent with the reminder.

In Intervention Group 1, a leaflet with a moral standard was sent to taxpayers together with the notice to pay the arrears. 66 notices were paid, representing 51%, the total amount of arrears paid was € 6,457.23 and the total amount of unpaid arrears was € 5,727.78.

In Intervention Group 2, a leaflet with a social standard was sent to taxpayers together with the notice to pay the arrears. Although the number of paid notices was higher than the number of unpaid notices in this group, the amount of € 4,487.28 paid is lower than the number of unpaid notices and represents 43.76% of the total amount of arrears.

In Intervention Group 3, taxpayers were sent a payment notice together with a leaflet informing them that there was a high probability of distrainment proceedings if irregularities in tax payments were detected. In Intervention Group 3, the total amount of arrears was € 11,591.22. During the course of the experiment, 53 notices were paid in this group, amounting to € 3,956.19. The collection success rate was 34.13%. Of all the groups, Intervention Group 3 had the lowest number of calls paid and therefore the highest number of outstanding calls, totaling € 7,635.03.

The results are summarized in Table 3.

Table 3. Experimental results in the control and intervention groups. Source: own.

	Control group			
	Amount in €	Amount in %	Number of calls	Number of calls in %
Calls paid	8,471.26	50.6	75	58%
Calls unpaid	8,270,65	49.4	55	42%
Total	16,741.91	100	130	100%
	Intervention group 1			
	Amount in €	Amount in %	Number of calls	Number of calls in %
Calls paid	6,457.23 €	52.99	66	51%
Calls unpaid	5,727.78 €	47.01	64	49%
Total	12,185.01 €	100	130	100%
	Intervention group 2			
	Amount in €	Amount in %	Number of calls	Number of calls in %
Calls paid	4,487.28 €	43.76	69	53%
Calls unpaid	5,767.88 €	56.24	61	47%
Total	10,255.16 €	100	130	100%
	Intervention group 3			
	Amount in €	Amount in %	Number of calls	Number of calls in %
Calls paid	3,956.19 €	34.13	53	41%
Calls unpaid	7,635.03 €	65.87	77	59%
Total	11,591.22 €	100	130	100%

On the basis of the data obtained from the experiment, we found that 188 out of 390, i.e., 48.20%, were paid arrears, to whom the intervention leaflet was sent with the reminder. In the control group that did not receive the leaflet with the reminder, 75 out of 130, i.e., 57.69%, of the arrears were paid. From these results, the behavioral intervention appears to have been unsuccessful, but we cannot know for sure whether the leaflet sent was the reason for the non-payment of the arrears. We therefore also statistically verified the association between the receipt of the reminder and the payment of the arrears. We used Cramer's V (Table 4) to find the correlations.

We found that receipt of the reminder affected the payment of arrears in each group. This was least in Intervention Group 3 ($p = 0.001$, Cramer's $V = 0.304$). We found that payment of arrears in Intervention Group 2 depended on the amount of arrears ($p = 0.021$, Cramer's $V = 0.243$), i.e., there was a low to medium dependence between the two groups.

To determine the percentage effectiveness of the behavioral intervention, we examined the number of reminders received and also how many of these reminders were paid. According to the results summarized in Table 5, the behavioral intervention was most effective in Intervention Group 2, in which we worked with the social norm. Of

Table 4. Interdependencies between selected data from the experiment. Source: own.

Variant of leaflet	Selected data	Selected data	P-value	Cramer's V
Control group - No leaflet	Payment of arrears	Reminder received	0.000	0.529
Intervention group 1 – Moral norm	Payment of arrears	Reminder received	0.000	0.509
Intervention group 2 – Social norm	Payment of arrears	Reminder received	0.000	0.518
		Amount of arrears	0.021	0.243
Intervention group 3 – Fear of loss	Payment of arrears	Reminder received	0.001	0.304

the 98 reminders received, 69 were paid, representing 70.41%. This was followed by Intervention Group 1, which was 12.71% less effective. In monetary terms, the arrears in Intervention Group 2 amounted to € 10,255.16, of which € 4,487.28, i.e., 43.76%, were paid.

Table 5. Interdependencies between selected data - effectiveness.

Variant of leaflet	Number of paid reminders	Number of reminders received	Effectiveness (%)	Comparison of effectiveness (%)		
Intervention group1	66	98	67.35		3.06	-12.71
Intervention group2	69	98	70.41	-3.06		-15.77
Intervention group3	53	97	54.64	12.71	15.77	

The total amount of arrears paid amounted to € 23,372. The total amount of arrears amounted to € 50,773.30. The arrears paid represent 46.03% of the total amount owed.

Although our experiment did not confirm the success of the behavioral intervention in the form of a nudge, we cannot know with certainty whether the leaflet sent was the real reason for the (non−)payment of the arrears in our observation period, i.e., from the sending of the reminder (October 2021) to the end of the experiment (November 2021). Other factors influenced the payment of the arrears, among which we can mention the difficulty in communicating with the city, the heterogeneity of the groups in the research sample, the lack of information about the research sample, the premature disclosure of information about the experiment, and last but not least the situation of COVID-19.

Communication with the city of Banská Bystrica was promising at the beginning, with both the mayor and the deputy-mayor pledging support for the experiment. However, when it came to the implementation of the experiment, officials from the economic department declared that they could not provide the necessary information and that participation in the experiment would be contrary to the legislation of the Slovak Republic. The research team had to argue with fact that similar experiments were conducted in the municipality of Prievidza and therefore there is nothing illegal. Apparently, the civil servants, overloaded with their duties, were resistant to participate in the research since it meant extra tasks for them. We might observe here so-called civil servant resistance [8, 16]. The civil servants eventually agreed to participate, but we also encountered resistance when evaluating the results and the deputy-mayor had to intervene to provide the data in a format that could be further worked with.

The heterogeneity of the groups was conditioned by the fact that the city of Banská Bystrica decided to combine three types of taxes and fees that were to be the subject of the experiment: real estate tax, dog tax and municipal garbage tax. The city divided the research sample of 520 defaulters into 4 groups (1 control, 3 intervention) and although they tried to maintain an approximately equal share of defaulters of each tax and fee, this distribution was no longer even with respect to the amount owed. For example, in each group there were between 61 and 70 non-payers for municipal garbage, but the total amount owed varied from €7,111 to €12,159. These differences could then be reflected both in the number of reminders paid and in the total amount owed, which skewed the results of the nudge.

Lack of information about the research sample - in processing the results of the experiment, we encountered the additional limitation of a lack of information about the research sample, such as gender, age, length of outstanding arrears, regularity of payment of fees, and whether they were in arrears in only one or more areas. If we had these data, it would be possible to better assess whether the individual is a 'regular defaulter' on whom no intervention is likely to be effective, or just an 'occasional defaulter' who could be nudged by an intervention to pay the arrears. However, this data was not provided by the city, whereas in Prievidza it helped to reveal other contexts. According to the results of the experiment in Prievidza, the most effective type of reminder to municipal garbage fee debtors was Intervention A, i.e., letter + social norm, and they also found that the intervention was more effective on men than on women, but this result is difficult to interpret as it may be related to income inequality or single-parent families with a more difficult economic situation.

Premature disclosure of information about the experiment was made by the city. As local elections are approaching, the city leadership used the information about the experiment as an opportunity to promote itself as an innovative smart city that engages in projects and research and uses the latest findings of behavioral economics. By publishing the information before the leaflets were sent out, they were able to influence non-payers in a negative direction in the sense that people do not like to be 'manipulated' [20], i.e., they chose to ignore the invitation with the leaflet and did not pay the tax/fee on purpose.

The COVID-19 pandemic, persisting from March 2020, could have a negative impact on the ability of individuals to pay local taxes and fees, in which case no intervention, however framed, would be effective.

Research in 2017 showed that messages with social norms or other behavioral nudges work, but cannot be applied everywhere and in every circumstance [7, 9]. In the case of the Guatemala intervention, there was no increase in tax payments [19]. Similarly, in Nebraska an informational nudge was not likely to be sufficient to substantially change tax reporting behavior [2]. Findings from studies in the UK suggest that it may be the case that interventions successful at the national level are not necessarily successful at the local level [7, 10]. Therefore, when introducing behavioral interventions, it is essential to take into account the particular characteristics of the area where the intervention will be implemented and to identify potential problems with the introduction of the intervention.

Although the experiment in Banská Bystrica did not bring the desired effect in the form of a higher number of paying tax subjects, we can include the UK, Canada (Ontario) and Slovakia (Prievidza), as well as other examples that we have presented in the theoretical section, among the countries that have successfully tried to improve tax collection from tax subjects and on-time tax payment.

At the same time, however, it should be said that relevant conclusions can only be formulated after a more detailed examination of the impact of heterogeneity in the composition of tax subjects in each intervention group. It is also necessary to consider the possibility of using another form of behavioral intervention, e.g., changing the wording of the call to the arrears office, simplifying the provision of a form of payment data for payment via QR codes, etc.

5   Conclusion

The main objective of the proposed experiment was to solve the problem of non-payers of local real estate tax and local fees in the city of Banská Bystrica. The intervention took the form of sending differently formulated leaflets to citizens assigned to the intervention groups. We expected that the share of tax defaulters would decrease as a result of this intervention (RQ1: Did the implemented nudge help to change the behaviour of non-payers and contribute to the timely and correct payment of local taxes and fees in the city of Banská Bystrica, compared to the control group?). On the basis of the data obtained from the experiment, we found that 188 out of 390, i.e., 48.20%, who were sent the intervention leaflet with the reminder, paid their arrears. In the control group that did not receive the leaflet with the reminder, 75 out of 130, i.e., 57.69%, of the arrears were paid. This expectation was not met and in the discussion we gave a number of reasons why this might have been the case. We consider the main reason to be the heterogeneity of the research sample. The fact that it was not only non-taxpayers, but also non-payers of local dog and municipal garbage fees were in the sample affected whether they paid or not (it makes a difference whether the taxpayer has to pay € 15 for the dog or € 150 for the garbage).

The aim of RQ2 (Which of the three versions of the leaflet sent out most influenced the behavior of non-payers in the desired direction?) was to determine the effectiveness of the behavioral intervention implemented. The experiment involved taxpayers who were in arrears in one of the local taxes and were therefore sent reminders or notices to pay their arrears. With the behavioral intervention, we wanted to nudge the tax subjects to make the right decision - to pay the arrears. To determine the percentage effectiveness of the behavioral intervention, we examined the number of reminders received and also how many of them were paid. According to the results, the behavioral intervention was most effective in Intervention Group 2, in which we worked with the social norm. Of the 98 reminders received, 69 were paid, which is 70.41%.

For RQ3 "Which of the three versions of the leaflet sent out was not effective or did not influence the behavior of the defaulters in the desired direction", it can be answered from the data obtained from the experiment that the intervention in Intervention Group 3 was the least effective. Out of a total of 130 taxpayers, 53 taxpayers (41%) paid their debt.

The presented research has its limitations, especially the focus of the analysis on only one municipality. The experiment was conducted on a relatively small research sample with a sizeable heterogeneity. In future research we will focus on examining the composition of types of arrears in the different groups. Nevertheless, it has shown several aspects why a behavioral intervention can fail and this can be an issue of further research. Why and when nudges do not meet expected results and what can we learn from such failures?

Acknowledgements. This work was supported by the Slovak Research and Development Agency [APVV – 18 – 0435].

References

1. Act on tax administration no. 563 (2009)
2. Anderson, J.E.: Paying the state use tax: is a "Nudge" enough? Public Finance Rev. **45**(2), 260–282 (2017). https://doi.org/10.1177/1091142115614390
3. Castro, L., Scartascini. C.: Tax compliance and enforcement in the pampas evidence from a field experiment. J. Eco. Behav. Organ. **116**, 65–82 (2015)
4. Coleman, S.: The Minnesota income tax compliance experiment: replication of the social norms experiment. https://papers.ssrn.com/sol3/papers.cfm?astract_id=1393292 (2007). Accessed 16 Mar 2022
5. Doshi, M.: How the British government got more citizens to pay their taxes on time. https://www.bloombergquint.com/politics/uk-the-nudge-unit-uses-behavioural-science-to-influe nce-policy-outcomes-such-as-improved-tax-collections-and-pension-enrolment   (2017). Accessed 13 Mar 2022
6. Dwenger, N., Kleven, H., Rasul, I., Rincke, J.: Extrinsic and intrinsic motivations for tax compliance: evidence from a field experiment in Germany. Am. Econ. J. Econ. Pol. **8**(3), 203–232 (2016)
7. Hallsworth, M., List, J.A., Metcalfe, R.D., Vlaev, I.: The behavioralist as tax collector: using natural field experiments to enhance tax compliance. J. Public Econ. **148**, 14–31 (2017)
8. Hemmer, A.: Civil servant suits. Yale Law J **124**, 758 (2014)
9. Hernandez, M., Jamison, J., Korczyc, E., Mazar, N., Sormani, R.: Applying behav-ioral insights to improve tax collection. https://openknowledge.worldbank.org/handle/10986/ 27528 (2017). Accessed 16 Mar 2022

10. John, P., Blumem, T.: Nudges that promote channel shift: a randomized evaluation of messages to encourage citizens to renew benefits online. Policy Internet **9**(2), 168–183 (2017)
11. Kahneman, D., Tversky, A.: Prospect theory: an analysis of decision under risk. Econometrica **47**(2), 263–291 (1979)
12. Kettle, S., Hernandez, M., Sanders, M., Hauser, O., Ruda, S.: Failure to CAPTCHA attention: null results from an honesty priming experiment in Guatemala. Behav. Sci. **7**(2), 28 (2017)
13. Kettle, S., Hernandez, M., Ruda, S., Sanders, M.: Behavioral Interventions in tax compliance. https://openknowledge.worldbank.org/handle/10986/24530 (2016). Accessed 13 Mar 2022
14. Luts, M., Roy, M.: Nudging in the Context of Taxation. Intra-European Organisation of Tax Administrations, IOTA. https://www.iotatax.org/sites/default/files/documents/iota_paper_b elgium_nudging_final.pdf (2019). Accessed 16 Mar 2022
15. OECD: Behavioral Insights and Public Policy. OECD Publishing, Paris (2017)
16. Shah, B.: Civil servant alarm. Chi.-Kent L. Rev. **94**, 627 (2019)
17. Sloboda, M., Pavlovský, P., Sičáková-Beblavá, E.: The effectiveness of behavioural interventions on increasing revenue from local fee. Rev. Beha. Finance **14**(1), 1–15 (2022)
18. The Behavioural Insights Team: EAST: Four simple ways to apply behavioural insights. https://www.bi.team/publications/east-four-simple-ways-to-apply-behavioural-ins ights/ (2014). Accessed 16 Mae 2022
19. The Behavioural Insights Team: Testing the optimal frequency of tax reminders in guatemala. https://www.bi.team/wp-content/uploads/2019/11/Guatemala-1-TR-Increase-dec laration-during-a-tax-amnesty.pdf (2018). Accessed 16 Mar 2022
20. Wilkinson, T.M.: Nudging and manipulation. Political Stud. **61**(2), 341–355 (2013)

A Traffic Model with Junction Constraints for Smart Cities Development

Sabrina Francesca Pellegrino[(✉)]

Dipartimento di Management, Finanza e Tecnologia,
Università LUM Giuseppe Degennaro, S.S. 100 Km 18,
Casamassima, 70010 Bari, Italy
pellegrino@lum.it

Abstract. Good environmental quality is the foundation for a good quality of life. Technologies of Smart Cities can adequately support the path of sustainability in urban areas and thus compete to raise the quality of life of citizens. In particular, sustainable urban development concept can be characterized in terms of CO_2 emissions. In order to address sustainable urban development, management and modeling traffic jam is a primary issue. We propose a mathematical model based on hyperbolic scalar conservation laws with non-local point constraint at the interface and a finite volume scheme to reproduce the capacity drop phenomenon at a road merge. We call capacity drop the situation in which the outflow through the junction is lower than the receiving capacity of the outgoing road, as too many vehicles trying to access the junction from the incoming roads hinder each other. The capability of representing such phenomenon by means of a non-local model allow us to obtain more accurate and detailed information by traffic data provided by sensors which can be used to propose a strategy to manage traffic flow near crossroads and to reduce the congestion in urban setting.

Keywords: Non-local point constraints · Traffic jam · Capacity drop · Smart cities · Sustainability

1 Introduction

In recent years, traffic related problems such as congestion and traffic jams have become a major issue in the cities all around the world and the increasing demand of mobility imposes the need of efficient traffic management solutions. This gave birth to a large number of traffic theories and mathematical models formulated with the aim of understanding and developing optimal transport networks with minimal congestion problems.

Supported by GNCS of Istituto Nazionale di Alta Matematica, by PRIN 2017 "Discontinuous dynamical systems: theory, numerics and applications" and by Regione Puglia, "Programma POR Puglia 2014/2020-Asse X-Azione 10.4 Research for Innovation-REFIN - (D1AB726C)".

© The Author(s), under exclusive license to Springer Nature Switzerland AG 2022
O. Gervasi et al. (Eds.): ICCSA 2022 Workshops, LNCS 13382, pp. 157–172, 2022.
https://doi.org/10.1007/978-3-031-10592-0_13

Managing urban expansion effectively is a global priority, especially in light of growing concerns about climate change. Many cities currently lack the necessary infrastructure to meet the travel needs of their citizens. The intelligent transport systems of the future will have to have less impact on emissions and more efficient and sustainable in terms of energy.

Smart city is a wide concept with connections to physical infrastructures and social factors [3,23]. One of the main aspects of smart cities is traffic control: indeed this issue is strictly related with pollution and economic problems, as businesses suffer from delivery delays and lost productivity and as a consequence, all of these aspects diminishes the city's quality of life.

Smart cities make use of technologies, such as sensors, camera and routers to dynamically alert riders and adjust control mechanisms [4,12,16].

Current trends for traffic control are based on the use of smart traffic lights and signals. From a mathematical point of view, these strategies can be thought as external controls [1,18]. However, most traffic signals are preprogrammed and do not support real-time conditions.

A different approach to deal with these problems is based on the implementation of non-local techniques. In fact, the use of non-local point constraints allows us to have a more realistic representation of the transient behavior between congested traffic and free flow [2,7]. Moreover, from a mathematical point of view, the introduction of a non-local constraint is largely adopted in different contexts in order to have a consistent behavior near discontinuities or interfaces, see for instance [5,6,13-15,20].

Macroscopic traffic models are typically based on systems of conservation laws and describe traffic flow in terms of density of vehicles and average velocity.

The main purpose of the paper is to summarize a non-local approach to model traffic jam and to reproduce the capacity drop phenomenon at a road merge proposed in [7,17,19,22]. This phenomenon expresses the fact that the outflow of a traffic jam is significantly lower than the maximum achievable flow at the same location, as too many vehicles trying to access the junction from the incoming roads hinder each other. More precisely, if the demand is higher than the maximum flow that can pass through the junction at a certain time, a congestion is formed. Empirical observations show that whenever a traffic jam occurs, the maximum outflow that materializes, called discharge flow, may be lower than the receiving capacity of the outgoing road. The capacity drop can then be defined as the difference between these two values, i.e. the receiving capacity and the discharge flow.

To model the capacity drop we introduce a non-local point constraint at junction which maximizes the vehicular passing flow. Additionally, we describe a numerical method based on the implementation of a finite volumes scheme and validate its performance by comparison with explicit solutions. Our tests make evidence that non-local point constraint allows for a more regular transition between capacity drop and capacity recovery, without putting control strategies into practice.

Indeed, non-local models can improve the results of the sensor's revelations: instead of evaluate the vehicles density in a fixed location, sensors could provide an averaged value in a suitable interval in real-time.

The paper is organized as follows. Section 2 describes the proposed methodology used to model and manage the traffic in presence of a crossroad. In particular, Sect. 2.1 briefly introduces the basic notation, describes the proposed non-local model for the capacity drop representation on a road network and outlines the main properties of the non-local model. While, Sect. 2.2 is devoted to the description of the finite volumes scheme. In Sect. 3 we present and discuss the numerical results. More precisely, we validate the finite volumes scheme and show the capability of the model to provide a hint to manage traffic at crossroads. Finally, Sect. 4 concludes the paper.

2   Methodology

The strategy we propose to represent the capacity drop at crossroads consists in the implementation of a nonlocal point constraint at a junction of a road merge. In the next sections, we briefly recall the basic notations and introduce the mathematical background for the construction of the model and then we describe a constrained finite volume scheme used for the simulations.

2.1   The Non-local Model for the Capacity Drop Representation

We consider a road network consisting of two incoming and one outgoing roads and a junction. The incoming roads are parametrized by the negative real line, here denoted by $\Omega_i = (-\infty, 0]$ for $i \in I = \{1, 2\}$, while the outgoing one is parametrized by the positive real line, denoted by $\Omega_3 = [0, \infty)$. In this way the junction is located at $x = 0$. For simplicity we fix the index $h \in H = \{1, 2, 3\}$ and we denote the network by $\mathcal{N} = \Pi_{h \in H} \Omega_h$.

On each road we describe the traffic evolution by the Lighthill-Whitham-Richards model [11, 21], namely by a scalar conservation law of the form

$$\partial_t \rho_h + \partial_x f_h(\rho_h) = 0, \qquad t > 0, \quad x \in \Omega_h, \tag{1}$$

where ρ_h is the density of vehicles and f_h is the flux along the h-th road. We fix the initial conditions

$$\rho_h(0, x) = \rho_{h,0}(x), \qquad x \in \Omega_h, \tag{2}$$

and we assume they are in $L^1 \cap \mathrm{BV}(\Omega_h; [0, \rho_{\max}])$. Moreover, we suppose that the roads have a common maximal density $\rho_{\max}$, admit a maximum point $\rho_{h,c}$, for $h = 1, 2, 3$, and finally, we require the conservation of the number of vehicles across the junction

$$f_3(\rho_3(t, 0^+)) = f_1(\rho_1(t, 0^-)) + f_2(\rho(t, 0^-)), \tag{3}$$

for a.e. $t > 0$.

We use the following definition of weak solution on the network.

Definition 1. *The vector function $\rho = (\rho_1, \rho_2, \rho_3)$, where $\rho_h : (0, \infty) \times \Omega_h \to [0, \rho_{\max}]$, $h \in H$, is a* weak solution *to (1)–(2), $h \in H$, in the network if*

- $\rho_h \in C^0((0, \infty); L^1(\Omega_h; [0, \rho_{\max}])) \cap \mathrm{BV}_{\mathrm{loc}}((0, \infty) \times \Omega_h; [0, \rho_{\max}])$, $h \in H$;
- *for $i \in I$, ρ_i is a weak entropy solution to (1)–(2)$_{h=i}$, namely for every $c \in [0, \rho_{\max}]$ and every nonnegative test function $\phi \in C^\infty(\mathbb{R} \times (-\infty, 0); \mathbb{R})$ with compact support*

$$\int_0^\infty \int_{\Omega_i} \left(|\rho_i - c| \, \partial_t \phi + \mathrm{sign}(\rho_i - c)(f_i(\rho_i) - f_i(c)) \partial_x \phi \right) \mathrm{d}x \, \mathrm{dt}$$
$$+ \int_{\Omega_i} |\rho_{i,0}(x) - c| \, \phi(0, x) \, \mathrm{d}x \geq 0;$$

- *ρ_3 is a weak entropy solution to (1)–(2)$_{h=3}$, namely for every $c \in [0, \rho_{\max}]$ and every nonnegative test function $\phi \in C^\infty(\mathbb{R} \times (0, \infty); \mathbb{R})$ with compact support*

$$\int_0^\infty \int_{\Omega_3} \left(|\rho_3 - c| \, \partial_t \phi + \mathrm{sign}(\rho_3 - c)(f_3(\rho_3) - f_3(c)) \partial_x \phi \right) \mathrm{d}x \, \mathrm{dt}$$
$$+ \int_{\Omega_3} |\rho_{3,0}(x) - c| \, \phi(0, x) \, \mathrm{d}x \geq 0;$$

- *the number of vehicles across the junction is conserved.*

This definition does not ensure uniqueness of the solution, therefore, to get it, we need to select a Riemann Solver at the junction. The choice is made by following ad hoc admissibility criteria, see [8,9].

We recall the definition of Riemann solver at the junction.

Definition 2. *We say that*

$$\mathcal{RS} = (\mathcal{RS}_1, \mathcal{RS}_2, \mathcal{RS}_3) : \Lambda \to \mathrm{BV}(\mathcal{N}; \Lambda), \qquad \Lambda = [0, \rho_{\max}]^3,$$

is a Riemann solver *at the junction if for any constant initial datum $\rho_0 = (\rho_{1,0}, \rho_{2,0}, \rho_{3,0}) \in \Lambda$ the map*

$$(t, \boldsymbol{x}) \mapsto \mathcal{RS}[\rho_0](\boldsymbol{x}/t) = (\mathcal{RS}_1[\rho_0](x_1/t), \mathcal{RS}_2[\rho_0](x_2/t), \mathcal{RS}_3[\rho_0](x_3/t))$$

is a self-similar weak solution to (1)–(2), $h \in H$, in the network.

The self-similar weak solution is obtained by solving three initial boundary value problems

$$\begin{cases} \partial_t \rho_h + \partial_x f_h(\rho_h) = 0, & t > 0, \, x \in \Omega_h, \\ \rho_h(0, x) = \rho_{h,0}, & x \in \Omega_h, \qquad h = 1, 2, 3. \\ \rho_h(t, 0) = \rho_{h,b}, & t > 0 \end{cases} \qquad (4)$$

The values $\rho_{h,b}$ are suitable boundary data chosen in order to ensure the conservation at the junction, to produce only waves with negative speed on incoming roads and positive speed on outgoing roads, to satisfy the *consistency property* $\mathcal{RS}[\rho_b] = \rho_b$ and to maximize the passing flow at the junction.

Now, we introduce some notions to select the boundary data maximizing the passing flow at the junction.

Definition 3 (Sect. 5.2.3 in [8]). *For $i \in I$, the* equilibrium sending capacity *of the i-th incoming road Ω_i is the map $\Delta_i : [0, \rho_{\max}] \to [0, f_i^{\max}]$, see Fig. 1, defined by*

$$\Delta_i(\rho) = \begin{cases} f_i^{\max} & \text{if } \rho \text{ is a good datum,} \\ f_i(\rho) & \text{otherwise.} \end{cases}$$

The equilibrium receiving capacity *of the outgoing road Ω_3 is the map $\Sigma_3 : [0, \rho_{\max}] \to [0, f_3^{\max}]$, see Fig. 1, defined by*

$$\Sigma_3(\rho) = \begin{cases} f_3^{\max} & \text{if } \rho \text{ is a good datum,} \\ f_3(\rho) & \text{otherwise.} \end{cases} \tag{5}$$

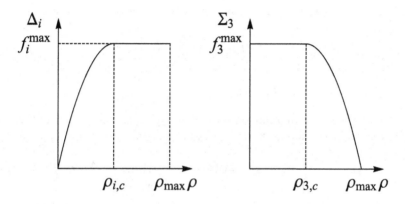

Fig. 1. The equilibrium demand and supply functions.

For the definition of a good and a bad datum, we refer the reader for instance to [8]. The equilibrium receiving represents the maximum flux that an incoming road can demand for a given initial condition, while the equilibrium sending capacity measures the maximum flux that an outgoing road can supply for a given initial condition.

Definition 4. *We fix a priority factor α which has the meaning of a* right of way *and a receiving capacity $Q(\rho)$ less than or equal to the equilibrium sending capacity $\Sigma_3(\rho_3)$. We define the* passing flow at the junction *as follows:*

$$\Gamma_1 = \begin{cases} \Delta_1 & \text{if } \Delta_1 + \Delta_2 \leq Q, \\ \begin{cases} \Delta_1 & \text{if } \alpha Q \geq \Delta_1, \\ \alpha Q & \text{if } Q - \Delta_2 < \alpha Q < \Delta_1, \\ Q - \Delta_2 & \text{if } \alpha Q \leq Q - \Delta_2, \end{cases} & \text{otehrwise} \end{cases} \tag{6}$$

and

$$\Gamma_2 = \begin{cases} \Delta_2 & \text{if } \Delta_1 + \Delta_2 \leq Q, \\ Q - \Gamma_1 & \text{otherwise.} \end{cases} \tag{7}$$

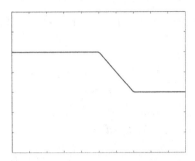

Fig. 2. The qualitative behavior of the constraint function g.

According with the previous rules, we can define the admissible boundary data as

$$\rho_{i,b} = \hat{\rho}_i(\Gamma_i) = \left(f_i\big|_{[\rho_{i,c},\rho_{\max}]}\right)^{-1}(\Gamma_i), \quad i = 1, 2, \tag{8}$$

and

$$\rho_{3,b} = \check{\rho}_3(\Gamma_1 + \Gamma_2) = \left(f_3\big|_{[0,\rho_{3,c}]}\right)^{-1}(\Gamma_1 + \Gamma_2) \tag{9}$$

We can notice that an admissible Riemann solver at the junction $\mathcal{R}_j$ realizes the maximum of the passing flow at the junction. Indeed, we have

$$\Gamma_1(\boldsymbol{\rho}_0) + \Gamma_2(\boldsymbol{\rho}_0) = \begin{cases} \Delta_1(\rho_{1,0}) + \Delta_2(\rho_{2,0}) & \text{if } \Delta_1(\rho_{1,0}) + \Delta_2(\rho_{2,0}) \leq Q(\boldsymbol{\rho}_0), \\ Q(\boldsymbol{\rho}_0), & \text{otherwise.} \end{cases}$$
$$\tag{10}$$

In order to reproduce the capacity drop phenomenon, we need to introduce a constraint on the junction. We assume that

$$f_3^{\max} < f_1^{\max} + f_2^{\max},$$

then, we define the *constraint function* $g : [0, f_1^{\max} + f_2^{\max}] \to [0, f_3^{\max}]$ in the following way:

$$g(s) = \begin{cases} f_3^{\max} & \text{if } s \leq f_3^{\max}, \\ f_3^{\max} + \frac{g_{\min} - f_3^{\max}}{b - f_3^{\max}}(s - f_3^{\max}) & \text{if } f_3^{\max} < s < b, \\ g_{\min} & \text{otherwise,} \end{cases} \tag{11}$$

where $b \in (f_3^{\max}, f_1^{\max} + f_2^{\max}]$ and $g_{\min} \in (0, f_3^{\max})$.

Figure 2 shows a possible behavior of the constraint function g. The aim of such function is to reduce the outflow through the junction whenever the total sending capacity overcomes the receiving capacity of the outgoing road.

Hence, the non-local model is based on the implementation of the non-local receiving capacity Q^{nl} in the definition of the admissible Riemann Solver, with

$$Q^{nl}(\boldsymbol{\rho}) = \min\left\{\Sigma_3\left(\rho_3(0+)\right), g\left(\Delta_1(\zeta_1) + \Delta_2(\zeta_2)\right)\right\}, \tag{12}$$

where ζ_i is a weighted average of the density of vehicles on Ω_i in a neighborhood of the junction, namely

$$\zeta_i = \int_{-\infty}^{0} w_i(x)\,\rho_i(x)\,\mathrm{d}x,$$

where $w_i \in L^\infty(\mathbb{R}_-; \mathbb{R}_+)$ is an increasing function with compact support in $[-\ell_i, 0]$ and $\|w_i\|_{L^1(\mathbb{R}_-)} = 1$, $i \in I$.

The admissible Riemann solver here constructed is non-local, as the evaluation of the flow at the junction does not depend on the total sending capacity at the same location, but takes into account a weighted average of the density of vehicles in a left neighborhood of the crossroad. This choice allows for a smooth representation of the transition between the situation in which a capacity drop happens and the case in which the capacity drop is reabsorbed. Additionally, the introduction of a weight function is driven by the fact that in real life the maximum achievable flow at the junction is more affected by the closest densities, while it does not take into account far densities.

In the next section we describe a finite volumes numerical scheme, which can be used to construct a numerical approximation of the solution for the Cauchy problem at a junction with capacity drop representation.

2.2 Finite Volumes Scheme for the Non-local Model

We describe here a constrained numerical method based on the implementation of a finite volume scheme for scalar conservation laws.

We fix a constant space step Δx. For $\ell \in \mathbb{Z}$ and $h \in H$, we set $x_\ell^h = \ell \Delta x$. We define the cell centers $x_{\ell + \frac{1}{2}}^h = (\ell + \frac{1}{2})\Delta x$ for $\ell \in \mathbb{Z}$ and consider the uniform spatial mesh on each Ω_h

$$\bigcup_{\ell \leq -1} [x_\ell^i, x_{\ell+1}^i), \quad i \in I, \qquad \bigcup_{\ell \geq 0} [x_\ell^3, x_{\ell+1}^3),$$

so that the position of the junction $x = 0$ corresponds to x_0^h for each road. Then we fix a constant time step Δt satisfying the CFL condition

$$\Delta t \max_{h \in H} L_h \leq \frac{\Delta x}{2},$$

where L_h is the Lipschitz constant of f_h. For $s \in \mathbb{N}$ we define the time discretization $t^s = s\Delta t$. At each time t^s, $\rho_{\ell + \frac{1}{2}}^{h,s}$ represents an approximation of the mean value of the solution on the interval $[x_\ell^h, x_{\ell+1}^h)$, $\ell \in \mathbb{Z}$, along the h-th road. We initialize the scheme by discretizing the initial conditions

$$\rho_{\ell + \frac{1}{2}}^{h,0} = \frac{1}{\Delta x} \int_{x_\ell^h}^{x_{\ell+1}^h} \rho_{h,0}(x)\,\mathrm{d}x,$$

for all $h \in H$ and for $\ell \leq -1$ if $h \in I$, $\ell \geq 0$ if $h = 3$.

For each $s \in \mathbb{N}$, at all cell interfaces x_ℓ^h with $\ell \neq 0$, we consider a monotone, consistent numerical flux $F_h(\rho_{\ell-1/2}^{h,s}, \rho_{\ell+1/2}^{h,s})$ corresponding to the flux f_h. At the junction x_0^h we take on each road Ω_h the Godunov flux G_h corresponding to the solution of the Riemann problem at the junction computed by the appropriate solver. We refer the reader to [19] for the definition and basic properties of the Godunov flux.

Then, the finite volumes scheme can be computed by a two-step procedure:

(i) find

$$(\hat{\rho}_1, \hat{\rho}_2, \check{\rho}_3) \text{ such that } f_i(\hat{\rho}_i) = \Gamma_i \text{ for } i \in \mathsf{I} \text{ and } f_3(\check{\rho}_3) = \Gamma_1 + \Gamma_2, \quad (13)$$

where Γ_1 and Γ_2 are defined in (6) and (7);

(ii) compute

$$\rho_{\ell+\frac{1}{2}}^{h,s+1} = \rho_{\ell+\frac{1}{2}}^{h,s} - \frac{\Delta t}{\Delta x}\left(\mathcal{F}_{\ell+1}^{h,s} - \mathcal{F}_{\ell}^{h,s}\right), \quad (14)$$

where

$$\mathcal{F}_\ell^{h,s} = \begin{cases} F_h\left(\rho_{\ell-1/2}^{h,s}, \rho_{\ell+1/2}^{h,s}\right) & \text{if } h \in \mathsf{I} \text{ and } \ell \leq -1 \quad \text{or} \quad h = 3 \text{ and } \ell \geq 1, \\ G_h\left(\rho_{-\frac{1}{2}}^{h,s}, \hat{\rho}_h\right) & \text{if } h \in \mathsf{I} \text{ and } \ell = 0, \\ G_h\left(\check{\rho}_3, \rho_{\frac{1}{2}}^{h,s}\right) & \text{if } h = 3 \text{ and } \ell = 0, \end{cases}$$

$$\quad (15)$$

and $F_h\left(\rho_{\ell-1/2}^{h,s}, \rho_{\ell+1/2}^{h,s}\right)$ is a monotone, consistent numerical flux, i.e. for all $h \in \mathsf{H}$

- F_h is Lipschitz continuous from $[0, \rho_{\max}]^2$ to $\mathbb{R}$,
- $F_h(a,a) = f_h(a)$ for any $a \in [0, \rho_{\max}]$,
- the map $(a,b) \in [0, \rho_{\max}]^2 \mapsto F_h(a,b) \in \mathbb{R}$ is non-decreasing with respect to a and non-increasing with respect to b.

In principle any monotone and consistent numerical flux might be used away from the junction, but we limit our attention to Godunov flux, because all admissible stationary solutions are exact solutions for such scheme.

The step (ii) is a standard marching scheme, while the step (i) is implicit: once per time step, we have to find a zero of a scalar nonlinear function. In our implementation, we compute efficiently the boundary data by using the Regula Falsi method on the interval of definition of the flux function.

Finally, we need to approximate the weighted average of the density ζ_i, $i \in \mathsf{I}$ as follows

$$Z_i^s = \Delta x \sum_{\ell \leq 0} w_i(x_{\ell+\frac{1}{2}}) \rho_{\ell+\frac{1}{2}}^{i,s}, \qquad i \in \mathsf{I}.$$

In what follows, we present and discuss the numerical results. As we will see, the proposed non-local model is able to represent the capacity drop phenomenon. Moreover, thanks to the study of the observation interval, we can find a way to manage traffic at crossroad in order to distribute vehicles on road network.

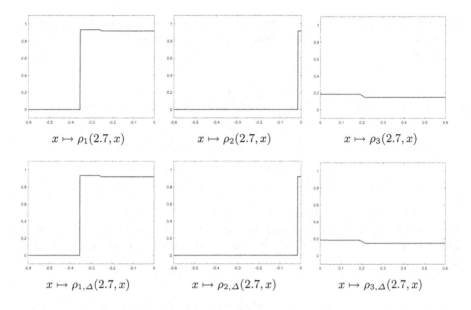

Fig. 3. With reference to the simulation of Sect. 3.1, the comparison between the explicit solution ρ and the numerical one ρ_Δ at time $t = 2.7$.

3 Numerical Results and Discussion

In this section we validate the implementation of the finite volume scheme presented in the previous section in the constrained setting. The validation of the scheme in the unconstrained case can be found in [19]. The validation consists in a comparison of the numerical approximation with an explicit solution computed in [7].

Additionally, we focus on a comparison between the proposed non-local model and the local one proposed in [10]. In this part we can notice that the capacity drop representation based on non-local point constraint allows to capture a more realistic behavior as the congestion disappears in finite time.

Finally, for a given constraint function g, we discuss the relation between the qualitative behavior of the numerical solution and the choice of the weight function w.

3.1 Validation of the Constrained Method

In order to show that the numerical scheme (13)–(14)–(15) is able to integrate in a coherent way the non-local point constraint at the junction, we validate it by comparison with the explicit solution computed in [7].

The parameters for the simulation are $\Delta x = 0.5 \times 10^{-4}$ and $\Delta t = 0.25 \times 10^{-4}$.

In Fig. 3 we compare the numerical and the explicit solution at time $t = 2.7$. We observe a good agreement of these profiles. We perform a convergence analysis for this test. We introduce the relative L^1-error respectively for the whole network, for the incoming and for the outgoing roads at a given time t^s as follows

$$E_{L^1}^{s,\mathcal{N}} = \frac{\sum_{h=1}^3 \sum_\ell |\rho_h(t^s, x_\ell) - \rho_\ell^{h,s}|}{\sum_{h=1}^3 \sum_\ell |\rho_h(t^s, x_\ell)|},$$

$$E_{L^1}^{s,\mathrm{I}} = \frac{\sum_{h=1}^2 \sum_\ell |\rho_i(t^s, x_\ell) - \rho_\ell^{i,s}|}{\sum_{i=1}^2 \sum_\ell |\rho_i(t^s, x_\ell)|},$$

$$E_{L^1}^{s,3} = \frac{\sum_\ell |\rho_3(t^s, x_\ell) - \rho_\ell^{3,s}|}{\sum_\ell |\rho_3(t^s, x_\ell)|}.$$

Table 1 depicts the relative L^1-error with respect to the space step at the fixed time $t = 2.7$. We observe that the rate of convergence is approximately 1. This means that the introduction of a non-local point constraint does not affect the accuracy of the scheme.

Table 1. Relative L^1-error at time $t = 2.7$ computed in Sect. 3.1

Number of cells per road	$E_{L^1}^{s,\mathcal{N}}$	Rate of convergence	$E_{L^1}^{s,\mathrm{I}}$	Rate of convergence	$E_{L^1}^{s,3}$	Rate of convergence
60	3.0860×10^{-2}	–	3.0882×10^{-2}	–	3.0783×10^{-2}	–
120	2.4713×10^{-2}	0.3205	2.7028×10^{-2}	0.1923	1.6441×10^{-2}	0.9048
600	5.4311×10^{-3}	0.7874	5.6482×10^{-3}	0.7792	4.6523×10^{-3}	0.8143
1200	2.6768×10^{-3}	0.8442	2.6246×10^{-3}	0.8565	2.8639×10^{-3}	0.7909
6000	9.3434×10^{-4}	0.8024	9.4064×10^{-4}	0.8115	9.1174×10^{-4}	0.7612
12000	5.8915×10^{-4}	0.7816	6.0521×10^{-4}	0.7867	5.3150×10^{-4}	0.7560

3.2   Local and Non-local Constrained Method at the Junction

We make a numerical comparison between the proposed non-local model and the local one proposed in [10].

As explained in the previous sections, local methods can suffer of the lack of consistency, and as a consequence the stationary solutions are not fixed points for the associated Riemann solver. Moreover, a local approach in suitable cases is not able to recover a traffic jam after that a capacity drop happens.

We perform a simulation analogous to the one made in [10]. We parametrize the incoming roads by the segment $[-12/5, 0]$ and the outgoing road by $[0, 12/5]$. We take

$$f(\rho) = \frac{9}{4 \cdot 10^6 \sqrt{5}} \rho \left(10^4 - \rho^2\right)^2,$$

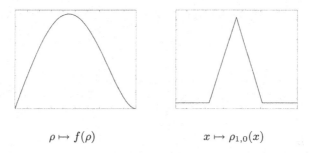

$$\rho \mapsto f(\rho) \qquad\qquad x \mapsto \rho_{1,0}(x)$$

Fig. 4. Flux and initial condition on the first incoming road considered in Sect. 3.2.

as flux for each road, see Fig. 4 on the left. As initial conditions, see Fig. 4 on the right, we fix

$$\rho_{1,0}(x) = \begin{cases} p_1 & \text{if } x \le x_1, \\ p_1 + \frac{p_2-p_1}{x_2-x_1}(x-x_1) & \text{if } x_1 < x \le x_2, \\ p_1 - \frac{p_2-p_1}{x_3-x_2}(x-x_3) & \text{if } x_2 < x \le x_3, \\ p_1 & \text{if } x_3 < x \le 0, \end{cases} \qquad p_{2,0} = p_1, \quad p_{3,0} = p_3,$$

where

$$p_1 = 14.5190, \qquad p_2 = 16.2511, \qquad p_3 = 38.0366,$$
$$x_1 = -2.3957, \qquad x_2 = -1.6588, \qquad x_3 = -0.9583.$$

We take

$$g(s) = \begin{cases} 2880 & \text{if } 0 \le s \le 2880, \\ 5760 - s & \text{if } 2880 < s < 3024, \\ 2736 & \text{if } 3024 \le s \le 5760, \end{cases}$$

as constraint function, and we choose the weight function $w(x) = 2(1 + x)\chi_{[-1,0]}(x)$. The parameters for the simulation are $\Delta x = 10^{-4}$, $\Delta t = (\sqrt{5}/45) \times 10^{-5}$ and $\alpha = 1/2$.

We compute and compare the approximate solutions corresponding to the local and the non-local model.

Figure 5 shows that, as observed in [10], even if the initial condition leads to a moderate congestion, the shock in the solution corresponding to the local model is never reabsorbed. On the other hand, the non-local model allows the congestion to be reabsorbed in finite time.

Figure 6 shows the dynamic of the shocks on Ω_1 in the solution corresponding to the local and the non-local model. On the x-axis we represent time and on the y-axis we represent the distance from the junction. We can observe that the non-local approach allows the traffic jam to disappear at a smoothly increasing rate while with the other approach the congestion keeps growing forever.

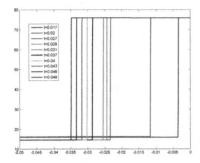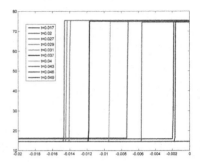

Fig. 5. With reference to Sect. 3.2. Left panel: The zoom of the profiles of solution on Ω_1 corresponding to the local model under consideration in a neighborhood of the junction as time evolves. Right panel: The zoom of the profiles of solution on Ω_1 corresponding to the non-local model in a neighborhood of the junction as time evolves.

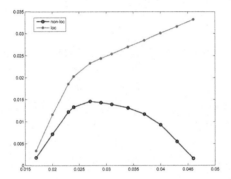

Fig. 6. With reference to Sect. 3.2, the dynamic of the shocks on Ω_1 in the solution corresponding to the local and the non-local model.

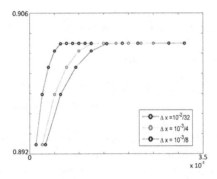

Fig. 7. With reference to Sect. 3.2, the changing of the value of the boundary datum on Ω_1 when the local Riemann solver is iterated.

Finally, we prove numerically that the local model proposed in [10] is not consistent. The lack of consistency means that the Riemann Solver provides not stable solutions. As a consequence, if we implement the solver in a finite volumes numerical scheme we do not observe the expected solution as it is destroyed after few iterations. Figure 7 plots the boundary value $\hat{\rho}_{1,b}$ of the first incoming road as time evolves for different space step. We can observe that after few iterations the method stabilizes itself around a value different by the boundary datum provided by the local solver.

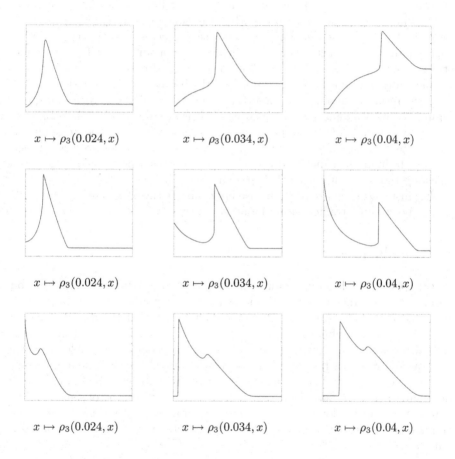

$x \mapsto \rho_3(0.024, x)$ $x \mapsto \rho_3(0.034, x)$ $x \mapsto \rho_3(0.04, x)$

$x \mapsto \rho_3(0.024, x)$ $x \mapsto \rho_3(0.034, x)$ $x \mapsto \rho_3(0.04, x)$

$x \mapsto \rho_3(0.024, x)$ $x \mapsto \rho_3(0.034, x)$ $x \mapsto \rho_3(0.04, x)$

Fig. 8. With reference to Sect. 3.3, the profiles of the solution on Ω_3 with varying observation interval supp(w): in the first line supp(w) = $[-0.98, 0]$, in the second line supp(w) = $[-1, 0]$, in the last line supp(w) = $[-1.2, 0]$.

3.3   Qualitative Behavior of the Solutions with Respect to the Observation Interval

We investigate, here, the role of the weight function w. To do this, we run simulations using the same setting and data as before, but letting the support of w vary.

We plot in Fig. 8 the profiles of the solutions on the outgoing road Ω_3 corresponding to $\min\{\text{supp}(w)\} \in \{-1.2, -1, -0.98\}$.

We find that the behavior of the solution changes continuously depending on the value of $\min\{\text{supp}(w)\}$. In particular, the first line shows that the capacity of the junction diminishes gradually, but the congestion last forever as in the local model. In the second line we can observe a capacity recovery after the capacity drop. This fact might be interpreted by a sort of "self-organization" strategy of the vehicles. In the last line the capacity drop becomes so small that it practically does not have any impact on the behavior of the solution.

Such result represents an important aspect in order to propose response strategies able to manage traffic near crossroads and to avoid traffic jams.

The peculiarity of the proposed non-local model relies in the possibility to let the observational interval to vary depending on the vehicles averaged density in order to limit the capacity drop phenomenon. This aspect could help drivers to choice the best route from their present location.

For instance, such result can be used to calibrate the parameters of the model and to positioning traffic sensors more efficiently.

4   Conclusions

In this paper, in the framework of smart cities, we propose a non-local constrained model and a finite volume scheme to reproduce the capacity drop phenomenon at a road merge. Our simulations show that the model converges numerically and is able to suggest a strategy to manage traffic at crossroads. Indeed, thanks to the implementation of a non-local model, we are able to provide more accurate results from sensors data revelation, which can take into account not only point values, but average values in suitable observational interval. The determination of the size of such interval and the best location of sensors in this new setting can be done by calibrating the parameters of the model with real traffic data. This represents a further step we intend to investigate to improve our results.

Acknowledgements. This paper has been supported by GNCS of Istituto Nazionale di Alta Matematica, by PRIN 2017 "Discontinuous dynamical systems: theory, numerics and applications" and by Regione Puglia, "Programma POR Puglia 2014/2020-Asse X-Azione 10.4 Research for Innovation-REFIN - (D1AB726C)".

References

1. Albi, G., Cristiani, E., Pareschi, L., Peri, D.: Mathematical models and methods for crowd dynamics control. In: Gibelli, L. (ed.) Crowd Dynamics, Volume 2. MSSET, pp. 159–197. Springer, Cham (2020). https://doi.org/10.1007/978-3-030-50450-2_8
2. Andreianov, B., Donadello, C., Razafison, U., Rosini, M.D.: Qualitative behaviour and numerical approximation of solutions to conservation laws with non-local point constraints on the flux and modeling of crowd dynamics at the bottlenecks. ESAIM: Math. Model. Numer. Anal. **50**(5), 1269–1287 (2016). https://doi.org/10.1051/m2an/2015078
3. Caragliu, A., Del Bo, C., Nijkamp, P.: Smart cities in Europe. J. Urban Technol. **18**(2), 65–82 (2011). https://doi.org/10.1080/10630732.2011.601117
4. Chiou, S.-W.: A data-driven traffic-responsive signal control for a smart city road network under uncertainty. In: García Márquez, F.P., Lev, B. (eds.) Introduction to Internet of Things in Management Science and Operations Research. ISORMS, vol. 311, pp. 119–146. Springer, Cham (2021). https://doi.org/10.1007/978-3-030-74644-5_6
5. Coclite, G.M., Fanizzi, A., Lopez, L., Maddalena, F., Pellegrino, S.F.: Numerical methods for the nonlocal wave equation of the peridynamics. Appl. Numer. Math. **155**, 119–139 (2020). https://doi.org/10.1016/j.apnum.2018.11.007
6. Coclite, G.M., Paparella, F., Pellegrino, S.F.: On a salt fingers model. Nonlinear Anal. **176**, 100–116 (2018). https://doi.org/10.1016/j.na.2018.06.007
7. Dal Santo, E., Donadello, C., Pellegrino, S.F., Rosini, M.D.: Representation of capacity drop at a road merge via point constraints in a first order traffic model. ESAIM: Math. Model. Numer. Anal. **53**(1), 1–34 (2019). https://doi.org/10.1051/m2an/2019002
8. Garavello, M., Piccoli, B.: Traffic flow on networks. In: AIMS Series on Applied Mathematics, vol. 1. MO, American Institute of Mathematical Sciences (AIMS), Springfield (2006)
9. Garavello, M., Piccoli, B.: Conservation laws on complex networks. Annales de l'Institut Henri Poincare (C) Non Linear Analysis **26**(5), 1925–1951 (2009). https://doi.org/10.1016/j.anihpc.2009.04.001
10. Haut, B., Bastin, G., Chitour, Y.: A macroscopic traffic model for road networks with a representation of the capacity drop phenomenon at the junctions. In: Proceedings 16th IFAC World Congress, Prague, Czech Republic. vol. 229, pp. Tu-M01-TP/3 (2005)
11. Lighthill, M.J., Whitham, G.B.: On kinematic waves. II. A theory of traffic flow on long crowded roads. Proc. Roy. Soc. London. Ser. A. **229**, 317–345 (1955). https://doi.org/10.1098/rspa.1955.0089
12. Liu, C., Ke, L.: Cloud assisted Internet of things intelligent transportation system and the traffic control system in the smart city. J. Control Decis. 1–14 (2022). https://doi.org/10.1080/23307706.2021.2024460
13. Lopez, L., Pellegrino, S.F.: A space-time discretization of a nonlinear peridynamic model on a 2D lamina. Comput. Math. with Appl. **116**, 161–175 (2022). https://doi.org/10.1016/j.camwa.2021.07.004
14. Lopez, L., Pellegrino, S.F.: A spectral method with volume penalization for a nonlinear peridynamic model. Int. J. Numer. Meth. Eng. **122**(3), 707–725 (2021). https://doi.org/10.1002/nme.6555
15. Lopez, L., Pellegrino, S.: Computation of eigenvalues for nonlocal models by spectral methods. J. Peridyn. Nonlocal Model. (2021). https://doi.org/10.1007/s42102-021-00069-8

16. Masek, P., et al.: A harmonized perspective on transportation management in smart cities: the novel IoT-driven environment for road traffic modeling. Sensors **16**(11), 1872 (2016). https://doi.org/10.3390/s16111872

17. Ngoduy, D.: Noise-induced instability of a class of stochastic higher order continuum traffic models. Transp. Res. B: Methodol. **150**, 260–278 (2021). https://doi.org/10.1016/j.trb.2021.06.013

18. Papamichail, I., Papageorgiou, M.: Traffic-responsive linked ramp-metering control. IEEE Trans. Intell. Transp. Syst. **9**(1), 111–121 (2008). https://doi.org/10.1109/TITS.2007.908724

19. Pellegrino, S.F.: On the implementation of a finite volumes scheme with monotone transmission conditions for scalar conservation laws on a star-shaped network. Appl. Numer. Math. **155**, 181–191 (2020). https://doi.org/10.1016/j.apnum.2019.09.011

20. Pellegrino, S.F.: Simulations on the peridynamic equation in continuum mechanics. In: Skiadas, C.H., Dimotikalis, Y. (eds.) CHAOS 2020. SPC, pp. 635–649. Springer, Cham (2021). https://doi.org/10.1007/978-3-030-70795-8_46

21. Richards, P.I.: Shock waves on the highway. Oper. Res. **4**, 42–51 (1956). https://doi.org/10.1287/opre.4.1.42

22. Torrisi, V., Ignaccolo, M., Inturri, G.: Analysis of road urban transport network capacity through a dynamic assignment model: validation of different measurement methods. Transp. Res. Procedia **27**, 1026–1033 (2017). https://doi.org/10.1016/j.trpro.2017.12.135, 20th EURO Working Group on Transportation Meeting, EWGT 2017, 4–6 September 2017, Budapest, Hungary

23. Willis, K., Aurigi, A.: The Routledge Companion to Smart Cities. Routledge, Taylor & Francis Group (2020)

Searching for Heterogeneous Geolocated Services via API Federation

Ala Arman, Pierfrancesco Bellini, and Paolo Nesi[✉]

DISIT Lab, DINFO Department, University of Florence, Florence, Italy
{ala.arman,pierfrancesco.bellini,paolo.nesi}@unifi.it
http://www.disit.org

Abstract. In the context of Smart City applications, the usage of Smart City APIs, for exposing services and data to web and mobile applications, is quite frequent. Most of the mobile solutions, using the Smart City APIs, are focused on a single city which can expose several services that are contextualized on a single geographic area. In fact, passing from one city/area to another, the users must change applications and services, and consequently, discontinuity problems could occur at the border. This also happens for the lack of interoperability among the Smart City APIs and related operators that may strongly differ, depending on the applicative levels at which they are developed. A large part of the services proposed via Smart City APIs are geo-localized, and as a result, may provide different results according to the GPS coordinates of the client context. In this paper, the *problem of the federation of smart city services is addressed by proposing a solution for federating smart city APIs, related knowledge-base, and ontology.* To this end, a solution to *autonomously federate API services* has been presented together with other requirements (e.g., *efficiency, overlapped* and *included* areas of competence, *distributed searches, security and privacy, scalability, interoperability* among different smart city application servers) which are typically neither all satisfied by classical Geographical Information System (GIS) solutions that federate the services at the level of database nor by those based on Internet of Things (IoT) Brokers. The solution is open-source and has been developed in the context of the Snap4City European platform enhancing the former Km4City Ontology and API of the *Sii-Mobility* national project (https://www.snap4city.org). The solution is presently in use in Snap4City federation of Smart City Services in Europe, among several cities/areas including, Florence, Tuscany, Bologna, Helsinki, Antwerp, Valencia, Dubrovnik, and Mostar, just to mention a few.

Keywords: Knowledge base · Smart city API · Smart city services · Federation of smart cities · FiWare · IoT Orion broker

1 Introduction

In the context of Smart Cities, not all cities/areas are becoming smart in the same manner and are smart at the same level because provided services are typically different [1]. In most cases, the cities decide to address only a selection of smart services (e.g., smart parking, smart education, smart gov., smart lighting), and not others, according to their needs and strategies. Therefore, vertical applications have been implemented for years and are not integrated in most of the cases. In the context of Smart City applications (web and mobile), most of the early solutions have been based on GIS and provide standard solutions for distributing geo-localized entities (e.g., maps, shapes), using protocols such as Web Feature Service (WFS), Web Map Service (WMS) [2]. Other solutions provide data via Open Data platforms such as the Comprehensive Knowledge Archive Network (CKAN) [3]. These solutions provide Application Programming Interfaces (APIs) to access a single dataset file as well as a collection of APIs provided by multiple stakeholders in the city/area and the possibility of exchanging these descriptions via harvesting protocols. IoT solutions, based on IoT brokers for the smart city, have been also proposed. For example, FIWARE-based solutions, which expose Next Generation Sensors Initiative (NGSI) REST APIs, are provided to the Web and mobile clients to access the data, typically last values (and not historical values), directly accessing IoT sensor data (and not sophisticated data structures via sematic queries) [4]. A strong push on the usage of Smart City APIs (SCAPIs) for providing and creating data and services for web and mobile applications has been recently observed (e.g., the Knowledge Model for the City (Km4City) API [5], E015 [6, 7]). Therefore, with the aim of developing smart city solutions, the usage of SCAPIs can be the way to provide smarter applications, considering multiple aggregated data sources and analytics (e.g., weather, reasoning, and predictions on parking, traffic and people flow [8]). On the other hand, most of the SCAPIs services are focused on a single city/area and expose a limited number of contextualized services in the same geographic area (e.g., info-mobility, Point of Interest (POI), routing, smart light, smart parking). In fact, in most cases, passing from one city/area to another, the users must get other applications to get the same services. This also happens due to the lack of interoperability among the SCAPIs at a semantic level that is not standardized and may strongly differ depending on the applicative levels at which they are developed.

In this paper, a solution for federating SCAPIs among geographic areas and contexts is presented. The development of the proposed solution for the smart city federation overcomes the problems of GIS and open data solutions. The main addressed problems are related to the possibility (i) to provide a network of geolocated services without constraining the providers to agree on the service shared with the other providers, (ii) to provide the clients a GIS/IoT list of results services without reporting eventual duplications on overlapped and/or duplicated services, (iii) not to pose limits to the size/shape of the geo-area and of the shared number of services, iv) to avoid addressing the problems of data privacy in a centralized structure, (v) to (or not) decide to join the network of services, (vi) to offer (non−)geolocalized information along with services in the network, and (vii) to provide a scalable and fault-tolerant solution for recovering services. The main cases are depicted in Fig. 1, where two regions of services may be overlapped, or one included in another. The services can be present in both (thus they are duplicated) or in one and even shared among them such as a passing road/path from one to another.

Therefore, the main contributions of this paper are: i) the possibility of federating Snap4City/GIS solution with FIWARE solutions based on IoT Orion Broker, and ii) the assessment of performance for the federated solutions and to the access private and public IoT devices. The validation of the presented solution has been performed by considering 4 large areas and smart city services (together with smaller areas) in place covering the Tuscany region of 3.5 million of inhabitants in the center of Italy, north of Italy (Garda area) and Sardegna island, Antwerp and north of Belgium, Helsinki and south of Finland, Spain (Valencia), Occitanie (Pont du Gard), Dubrovnik, and West Greek. To solve the above-mentioned problems, the solution reported in this paper has been completely developed open-source and presently used in a federation of Snap4City (https://www.snap4city.org) Smart City Services and APIs in Europe including federated services in different cities and regions (e.g., Florence, Tuscany region, Helsinki, Antwerp, Dubrovnik, Garda, Valencia, Pont du Gard, Greek) [9].

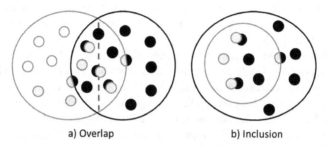

a) Overlap   b) Inclusion

Fig. 1. Overlapped and included areas of services, with duplicated, exclusive, and shared services of two areas.

The paper is organized as follows. Section 2 reports and discusses the related works. In Sect. 3, the requirements identified for federating SCAPIs are presented and analyzed. Section 4 presents the general architecture and solution of the proposed Snap4City federation smart city services which may cover single cities and regions, with area and service overlaps and flexibility. The same section also includes the formal presentation of the operational model of the federation of SCAPI enabling the solution, thus addressing both local and geo-distributed services and information. Section 5 briefly describes the Km4City Ontology and the developed web-based tool for the proposed solution. Section 6 presents the mechanism for propagating the queries of the SCAPI in the federated network, managing the exception, and combining the results. Section 7 provides a description of the validation and the experiments performed for the assessment of the performance of semantic queries and for those regarding IoT devices/sensors to access private/public city entities, via federated queries, by different user roles. Conclusions are drawn in Sect. 8.

2   Related Work

The first smart city applications have been developed by exploiting technologies of GIS solutions which the federation of services also allows data exchange [2]. The classical GIS interoperability is limited to a 1 : 1 exchange of geographical data; for example, exploiting protocols (e.g., WFS, WMS) for the exchange of Maps and geo-elements (e.g., paths, POIs, road elements, road graphs). A Web-service-based software for data dis-covery, download, visualization, and analysis has been proposed in [10] which included a middle layer, named HIS Central, mediating among clients and data located on dis-tributed GIS-based HydroServers. The solution is then focused on delivering GIS data and not full smart services. In [11], the CityPulse project has been proposed for real-time data stream analysis by exploiting semantic modeling. In [12], a wide review of IoT solutions for smart cities has been presented with current and future research directions. The paper has performed an extensive analysis of literature identifying major keywords and domains of applications, but only marginally addressing smart city interoperability. In the context of Smart Cities, the solutions for managing geographically distributed Big Data to provide Smart Services are more relevant [13], especially when they are capable to work on a large scale (i.e., spreading across sets of cities, intersects with the prob-lem of managing with the Big Data generated by dense and/or extensive environmental monitoring systems [14]).

Other solutions provide data via Open Data platforms (e.g., CKAN [3]) which pro-vides APIs to access the single dataset file and a collection of APIs provided by multiple stakeholders in the city/area and the possibility of exchanging these descriptions via har-vesting protocols. A similar approach has been proposed by $E015$ with their collection of SCAPIs and services in the north of Italy [6]. IoT solutions, based on IoT brokers, for the smart city, have been also proposed; for example, FIWARE-based solutions which expose NGSI Rest APIs are provided to web and mobile clients to access data (typically last values and not historical values), directly accessing IoT sensor data (and neither via sophisticated data structures nor semantic queries) [4, 15, 16]. They mainly move the complexity of the service to the Mobile Apps since the IoT broker only provides data, and thus, the business logic of the application must be elsewhere. Therefore, smart city applications may use those APIs for implementing their logic on the server and client sides. In most cases, mobile and Web Apps need to be updated when a new data type is added.

A review of SCAPIs can be recovered on [17, 18]. Examples of more complete SCAPIs are: Km4City API on a large range of SCAPIs to search and retrieve information and services [5], on DIMMER for the composition of smart city services exploiting service-oriented architecture [7], CitySDK which provides a set of smart city services without federation and Transport APIs on mobility. An early version of the SCAPI federation has been presented in [19].

3   Requirements and Analysis

In this section, the requirements that should be satisfied by a solution for federating SCAPI are reported and discussed. The solution should be a distributed system of SCAPIs to create a federation of City services. The federated network is conceptually a middle-ware, based on a set of SCAPI services (provided by Nodes), that is independently offered and maintained by a number of cities/areas. The federation approach should not be confused with a collection of APIs in a common basket to expose them uniformly in terms of definitions. It is, in fact, managed and offered by different organizations that provide the service to a single city/area (e.g., [3, 6, 20, 21]). Therefore, according to the definition of a federated SCAPI network of Nodes, the services, and in particular, each Node, should satisfy the following advanced requirements.

Req.1.   **not permanently replicate data** of other Nodes;

Req.2.   support **distributed search** on the network federated Nodes. The computational workload for providing results is distributed among the nodes which can work only on their own data;

Req.3.   be of **any size** in terms of geo area and data volume. The geospatial size and shape of each Node may be (i) of any form and multiple connected (so-called multi-polygon). A Node may manage one or more geo-areas even if they are distant and not neighbouring areas, (ii) partially overlapped with other Nodes, (iii) totally included in other Nodes, and (iv) disjoint and even far from each other;

Req.4.   **offer a different number/kind of services**. This allows a Node to provide different kinds of services without constraints and to autonomously decide the set of provided /removed services;

Req.5.   **contain (non−) georeferenced services.** There may exist services that are generic for a certain Node and not associated with a GPS position (e.g., global service of payment, global service to save the car position);

Req.6.   **respond to API** calls in terms of services in a **transparent manner, thus allowing clients to pass from one Node to another**. When federated nodes are geographically contiguous, requested results may take into account both areas and avoid duplications of results;

Req.7.   support access control to **prevent access to services by non-authorized users**. Users should be registered and authorized in multiple services/cities to freely access the protected data on both sides when authorization may arrive from a common Single Sign-On (SSO). This feature opens the path for multi-site operators, such as those for parking, car sharing, etc. This requirement implies a set of access rules to assure that the data is accessed only by authorized personnel at which the single Node may grant access independently, considering access authorization and GDPR compliance [22];

Req.8.   **join and abandon the network,** without the need for network restructuring, and modifications with an immediate effect when no service reloads or disrupts;

Req.9.   **provide query results in real time even in presence of a large number of Nodes**. The implementation should provide support for creating redundant solutions with high resilience and fault-tolerance;

Req.10. provide search query **results in a coherent format** with the expected response of the single services. For example, REST calls in some cases provide responses in JSON, XML, or HTML formats;

Req.11. interoperate with **Nodes based on data services**, for example, IoT Brokers, when they are supported by historical databases and geo-queries (as in FIWARE [4]);

Req.12. support **services based on IoT Devices.** This is possible if the Node is able to manage IoT Devices as an IoT Broker or the Knowledge Base, KB, exploited by the Node, is capable of modelling, indexing, and searching IoT Devices. To this end, the Km4City Ontology, by supporting the Industry 4.0 domain, has been extended to model IoT Devices by including a range of IoT Brokers, protocols, and devices;

Req.13.   support the **creation of disjoint federations of Nodes and the presence of independent services** which are not connected to any federation of Nodes.

Req.14.   support for an interactive user interface.

In Sect. 4, the architecture, Req.1 is satisfied by the solution because different Nodes/servers do not locally copy the data of the other services and only know about the presence of the other services. In fact, the nodes/servers keep their high-level descriptor, in terms of area of competence, as described in Sects. 4 and 5. Meeting Reqs.11,12, and13, by the solution, has been also demonstrated in Sect. 4. Reqs.2,3,4,8, and 9 are satisfied through validation and performance assessments in Sect. 7. Reqs. 5 and 6 are discussed in Sect. 7.1. In addition, Req.7 is satisfied and addressed at the level of single SCAPI, according to security aspects, as described in [22]. The evidence for the satisfaction of Req.10 has been described in Sect. 7.2. Also, Req. 14 is briefly highlighted in Sect. 5.1, while the actual implementation is accessible via https://www.snap4city.org and specifically via https://www.snap4city.org/MultiServiceMap/.

4   General Architecture of Federated Services and SCAPIs

To satisfy the above-described requirements, we have designed and implemented the solution reported in Fig. 2 in terms of its architecture. It is based on a network of federated Nodes exposing services via SCAPI. The Nodes, which are called Super, each of which (i) provides access to services via SCAPI formalism as REST API to client applications of the federated network and (ii) exploits SCAPI of the actual Smart City service providers and of other Supers. According to Req.11 on interoperability, the Nodes/Supers can be on the front of the SCAPI interface of two kinds of smart city servers: (i) *Snap4City/Km4City*, which provides GIS data via WFS/WMS, services via SCAPI, querying the smart city server with SPARQL queries, and exploiting the Km4City Ontology on the RDF store Virtuoso, and (ii) *SSM2ORION* (SuperServiceMap to Orion FIWARE), which converts the call on SCAPI to NGSI V2 Rest Calls, provides data information accessible from FIWARE solution, based on IoT Orion Context Broker, with storage support, using well known tools (e.g., Quantum Leap broker, CrateDB) as described in the following [4]. According to Fig. 2, Node (a) manages data of Area 1 by the Km4City RDF store and ServiceMap. Nodes (b) and (c), using the Km4City RDF stores and in a balancing and fault-tolerant approach, share the same geo-Areas 2*a* and 2*b*. Node (d) is covering Area 3 with an IoT Orion Broker FIWARE and a related storage. Some of the Nodes manage overlapped areas while Areas 4*a* and 4*b* are managed by an independent service. It is noted that some of the areas covered by Nodes contain multiple disjoint subareas. To avoid having a single point of failure, each Node includes a master of the distributed communication among Supers reporting the lists of Nodes/Supers and providing services to the clients. A central server, with the list of the connected Supers, is made accessible in one or more Web servers for the periodic update of Supers. Each Node/super has a representation of the multi-polygon addressed by the nodes (with their data/services) and thus of their partitioning over the nodes of the federated SCAPI network. In more details, each Node may be registered in the list of Supers with its descriptor of the multi-polygon area of competence.

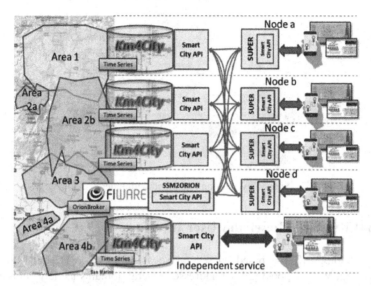

Fig. 2. General architecture of super and federated SCAPI network

The most relevant aspects and complexity of the procedure are mainly related with (i) identification of the Nodes to be involved, according to the requests received, with a complexity that may depend on the size of the node descriptors (number of polygons), (ii) distribution of query in each Super, with a complexity $O(1)$, which is based on the decreasingly sorted execution time of nodes, using a multithreading approach, and (iii) collection of results and their fusion, as the main complexity, to avoid duplicates and compounding the results, with a complexity, depending on the size S of the elements $O(S)$.

In Fig. 3, a simplified architecture is reported where the authentication and authorization layer which allows to satisfy Req.1. It is noted that, while any kind of data may be integrated via Data Connectors in Node-Red (including WFS/WMS of GIS via Snap4City tools), IoT Devices can be registered on the IoT Directory of Snap4City and connected via one or more IoT Brokers with different protocols. New IoT Devices must be registered, and each data access must be authorized according to the user authentication/authorization [22]. In the case of Federated Nodes, the authentication/authorization must satisfy the GDPR. In addition, the federation can also be performed at the level of authentication and SSO-SAML (Security Assertion Markup Language) of KeyCloak. Snap4City is then based on OpenID Connect and JWT Access Token while the role management is performed by using Lightweight Directory Access Protocol (LDAP) federation protocols.

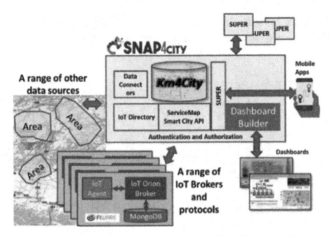

Fig. 3. Snap4City solution integrated with federated nodes

5   Km4City Data Model and User Interface

Km4City Ontology [23] is based on several vocabularies (e.g., DCTERMS, FOAF, SCHEMA.org, WGS84_pos) [24]. It addresses several domains namely, mobility and transport, energy, health, economy, and key performance indicators (KPIs), just to mention a few while modelling concepts such as POIs, road structure, and civic numbers. The Km4City Ontology I, based on 10 macro-classes/areas (e.g., Places, Administration, POIs). These concepts and relations may model a wide spectrum of applications (e.g., indoor routing, the automatic building of context-rich synoptics). Regarding the modeling of Data Analytics results, the Km4City ontology provides, for example, the Predictions macro-class together with a set of associated concepts (e.g., BusStopForecast) which enables the representation of the expected arrival/departure time of a given ride at a given stop [19].

5.1   User Interface Exploiting SCAPI: SuperServiceMap

In this section, we present details on the designed and developed a web-based tool to perform the queries via a graphic user interface, called SuperServiceMap, which is freely accessible via www.snap4city.org and depicted in Fig. 4. Using the selector in the center of the tool, the user can define to connect the user interface to a Super as well as to one of the SCAPI services of the single organization/node (e.g., Firenze, Helsinki, Valencia) which 18 of them are present now. The menu on the right comprises two tabs. One is dedicated to categories (e.g., Accommodation) and sub-categories (e.g., Camping, Farm, Hostel), associated with Regular Services, while the other contains categories (e.g., Area) and sub-categories (e.g., Gardens, Sports_facility) regarding Transversal Services. The user can select, in addition to the possibility of instant searching for a service category or a sub-category, a set of them, including Regular or Transversal. Also, it is possible to limit the search results, using N. Results, or filter them, using the Text Search and Search Range (e.g., 100(m)) together with the Service Model and Value Type [25] options.

The menu on the lower left is used to show the weather information (e.g., minimum/maximum temperature) in a region. The menu on the upper left is used to obtain information on Public Transportation, Address Search, and Events along with the possibility of text service search in a desired area. Considering the Public Transportation tab, it is possible to detect the current position of vehicles, using the associated Agency (and Line). The user can also see a Route (or all of them) of a Line and a Stop/station (or all of them) of a Route, together with detailed information on stops/stations. It is possible to Search Path, considering the Route Via (e.g., car, public_transport) and Start date&time options, and Search Geometry between two selected points. The interface also allows performing text search when constraining the search around a point or in a given area.

Fig. 4. SuperServiceMap tool (https://www.snap4city.org/MultiServiceMap/)

6 Federation of Enabled SCAPI via Network of Supers

In this subsection, the actions needed to enable the federation of Nodes are described by starting from the limitations and the improvements performed on former SCAPI as it was presented in [17]. The full list and semantic of input arguments for API is available on https://www.km4city.org/swagger/external/index.html.

6.1 Enhancing Smart City API on Geo-Distributed Services

The extension of the SCAPI has been performed on specific query and data types that may be shared over different areas managed by different nodes and API services in the network. In more detail, since an area can be overlapped with other areas, some of the geolocated elements can be completely located/duplicated in multiple areas, partially located into multiple areas (e.g., a national across multiple provinces or regions). Therefore, the most affected services are those related to Service discovery and information family of

APIs, that depending of values received from input arguments, performs a search for services (i) close to a given position (identified by a GPS location or service), (ii) within the boundaries of a bounding box described through the geospatial coordinates of its vertexes, (iii) within a shape of a given geographic area (which can be defined as a Well Known Text (WKT) shape format), with an arbitrary shape or the shape of a city, a province, etc., or iv) through the submission of a full-text to be matched in addition to or without geo restrictions. The key parameter through which the geographical area of interest is delimited is called Selection. It can be (i) a Point plus distance, (ii) two points, or (iii) a shape for which builds a geographic area.

More complex entities are those including a Path or a Shape in the Selection. For example, the Bus Lines may pass into the area of Selection even if they do not present any Stop into the area. Therefore, because of certain Selection, one could be interested to retrieve the Lists of Lines, Routes, Stops, etc. that are different from a geographical position or area. Among the most complex queries, those along paths need special attention (e.g., cycling path, bus-lines, routing paths). The identification of Services along a path implies to search for services that are close to the path within a certain distance. Otherwise, the perfect match on the path would be too selective. Therefore, the search along a path must be transformed to a search into a closed polyline which has the Selected path as mean point by point.

Queries to identify Shortest Route/Paths to compute the best route from a starting point to a destination through a modal or multimodal routing provide results only when both the start and the destination parameters are geospatial coordinates belonging to the same service Node/area. However, to get the results, it is also possible to provide the URI of the service where they locate, and/or the URI of the service where they wish to go. In this case, the following are checked: (i) the Node managing them (via cache or via request) and (ii) if there exists a Node that matches both the required source and destination; otherwise, an error is returned. The error management allows to split the problem in distinct routing queries towards the corresponding Node services.

The results of the queries are services expressed as a list of ServiceURI (services are stored as resources in the RDF store and identified through a URI that also is a Uniform Resource Locator (URL) from a Linked Data perspective). On the contrary, if it is not possible to identify the corresponding Super managing the entity, all nodes must be queried. To reduce this effort, the pairs ServiceURI and Node ID are cached for shortening time of future requests.

6.2 Exceptions in the Selection of Nodes to Be Queried by the Supers

With the aim of creating fault-tolerant redundant solutions, it possible to have different Super largely covering the same area. To maximize performance or making a priori balance on services, it is possible to define a priority, among the different Supers/nodes, based on the query/areas or on services or exclude some of them in specific cases. Nodes with the same priority are queried in random order. Thus, the above-described distribution of queries based on the area of competence, based on the API type and/or output format, can be overwritten by specific rules for each Super,. This mechanism can be used to redirect the requests to a specific node non-geolocated services as planned, according to Req.5.

6.3 Merging Node Results of Any Format

The results of Snap4City SCAPI can be provided in JSON or HTML [17], according to the request performed. When the result of a call is requested to be in JSON, a resulting message can be easily merged. On the contrary, if the result is requested in HTML, a final full Web page is provided (e.g., a set of geolocated services, each of which is represented by a clickable pin drawn on a map) with relative URLs to JavaScript, style sheets, images, etc. can be found. Also, the Super may need to combine multiple results by merging data of different Nodes with possibly different base URLs. Therefore, the HTML received from the Nodes must be first parsed, and then, relative URLs identified and replaced with full URLs by simply prefixing them with the base URL of the Node that has produced the Web page. Remarkably, operating this way, artifacts, located on a Node, are directly addressed and embedded in a Web Page that is provided by the Super, operating the server-side on the original Node, which leads to managing the Cross-Origin Resource Sharing (CORS) [26].

7 Performance Assessment and Validation

This section describes the results of the validation and performance assessment of the proposed solution for managing distributed geo services when addressing the problems derived from the overlap and inclusion of different areas and their geo services (e.g., locations, paths, shapes), as depicted in Fig. 1. Considering both scenarios, we compared the performance of results when direct and federated queries are formulated. The queries have been performed by searching for (i) all regular services (i.e., single points as POIs), including 20 categories and 540 sub-categories, and (ii) a regular service TransferServiceAndRenting with 47 associated sub-categories (e.g., Tramline, Urban_bus). For the assessment, we focused on measuring the Response Time (RT) and Number of Results (NoR), by identifying circular areas with different diameters, ranging from 1 to 100(Km).

7.1 Case (a) for Overlapped Areas

This case has been assessed in real conditions at the border of two adjacent regions, with two overlapping KBs, in terms of services modeled by Km4City (as tenants on Snap4City.org platform), namely, Florence, and Garda Lake. Figure 5 reports the query results, all presented in clusters, when searching for all regular services, including all categories and sub-categories, when the radius is equal to 50 (km), and the center has been placed on the center of the overlapped area, at the border (in yellow) of two provinces of Florence and Bologna.

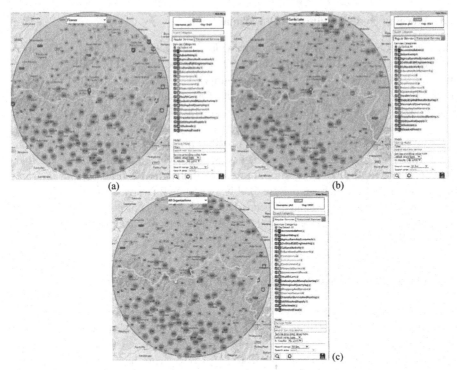

Fig. 5. Results for query on all Regular Services on an overlapped area (case (a) of Fig. 1), when search radius is equal to 50 (km), only Firenze KB (a), only Garda Lake KB (b), and full query results on the federated network (c) (GPS Center location (Lat,Lon): 44.122657449923224, 11.212175488471985). (Color figure online)

Table 1 reports the results of the performance assessment for the described Case (a) scenario. For example, when the search radius is equal to 50 (km), the NoR for Regular Services, considering Florence and Garda Lake regions, are respectively equal to 80546 and 23213 entities. The number of results for the same search via Super is equal to 91483 entities which is slightly different than the sum of results (80546 + 23213 = 103759) due to the presence of 12276 duplicated data (NoD, Number of Duplicates). For example, bus-stops of lines that connecting Florence and Bologna/Garda Lake regions must be available in both areas. Regarding the RT, it can be observed that, the Super has a better performance when the two regions are considered separately. For example, when searching for all Regular services and the search radius is equal to 50 (km), the response time, is 104640 (ms), using the Super is which less than the sum (87600 (ms) + 78660 (ms)), and more than the max of the two RTs, Max_NoR, (87600, 78660). It is noted that the RT for super also includes the time for eliminating the duplications.

Table 1. Performance results for the case (A) of Fig. 1. (overlapped regions): single nodes (Florence, Gard Lake) vs. super.

Query/kind	Search Radius (km)	Node/Organization/Region				Super	
		Florence		Garda Lake			
		NoR	RT (ms)	NoR	RT (ms)	NoR	RT (ms)
Get Regular Services (case A1)	1	0	1578	11	3160	11	3050
	5	47	1592	143	1106	159	1334
	10	260	1622	362	2570	485	2940
	50	80546	87600	23213	78660	91483	104640
	100	139279	270180	48259	191580	154774	271500
Get TransferServiceAndRenting service (case A2)	1	0	1661	11	3100	11	3100
	5	31	1437	125	1128	125	1576
	10	150	1623	339	2650	352	2670
	50	18720	78900	17856	79140	24281	90360
	100	40163	212160	42393	189900	49769	236040

Considering Fig. 6, it can be observed that the performance of the solution is very good in terms of RT if the query at the border is in the range of 10 (km) (which is very realistic for the smart city and rural services, in Europe), even in the presence of a high number of duplications (NoDs) and a very high NoR. When the range of the query is very large (e.g., $50 - 100$ (km)), the number of resulting objects and duplications may be very high and thus the RT to get all results from Super is still comparable with respect to the RT of the service providing the majority of the results.

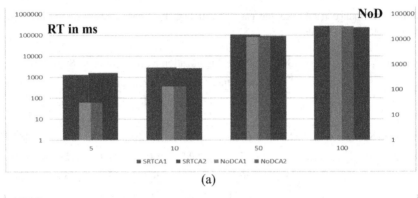

(a)

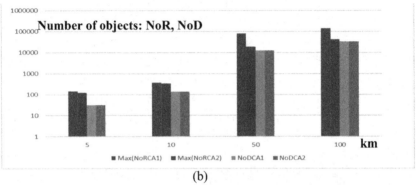

(b)

Fig. 6. Comparative trends to get regular (case $A1$) and transversal services (case $A2$) in overlapped areas w.r.t. to the range in km. (a) reports in Log Scales the trends of RT for super case $A1$ and case $A2$ respectively, $SRTCA1$, and $SRTCA2$, where on the right the data regarding the NoD; (b) reports the comparison of in Log scale of the trend of the NoR and NoD for Cases $A1$ and $A2$ respectively.

7.2 Case (B) for Inclusion Areas

Considering different search radiuses, this case has been also addressed in real conditions by examining **three** regions namely: Garda Lake, Snap4eu, and DISIT (managed by different organizations), where the KBs of Snap4eu and DISIT, in terms of services modelled by Km4City (as tenants on Snap4City.org platform), is included in the KB of Garda Lake. Figure 7 shows an example of the described scenario when the search radius is equal to 100 (km).

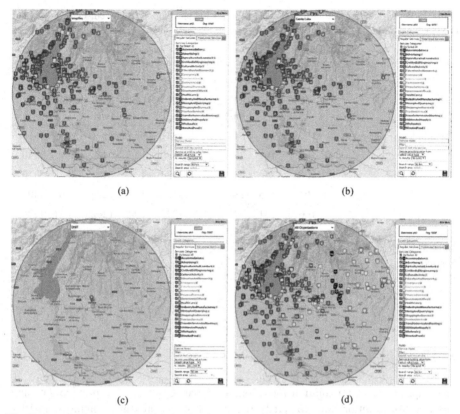

(a)   (b)

(c)   (d)

Fig. 7. Results for query on Regular Services on an inclusion area (case (b) of Fig. 1), when search radius is equal to 50 (km), considering, only snap4eu KB (a), only Garda Lake KB (b), DISIT (c), and full query results on the federated network (d).

We compared the results when the queries are performed on the federated network (Super). Table 2 reports the validation and performance assessment results for the above-mentioned scenario. As on can see, for example, when the search radius is equal to 100 (km), the NoR for Regular Services, considering Snap4eu, Garda Lake, and DISIT regions, are respectively equal to 231, 4385, and 2086. The NoR for the same search, the Super find 4621 results which is much smaller than the sum $(231 + 4385 + 2086)$ of the results coming from the single organizations: Snap4eu, Garda Lake, and DISIT. Regarding the RT, we can see that, using the Super provides a response time comparable with the larger service. For example, when searching Regular services and the search radius is equal to 50 (km), the RT for super is 440 (ms), which is comparable with 322 (ms) presented by the GardaLake service which provided the majority of the results.

Table 2. Performance results for the case (b) of inclusion regions (Snap4eu, Gard Lake, and DISIT): single nodes vs super.

Query/kind	Search radius (*km*)	Node/Organization/Region						Super	
		Snap4eu		Garda Lake		DISIT			
		NoR	RT (*ms*)	NoR	RT (*ms*)	NoR	RT (*ms*)	NoR	RT (*ms*)
Get all regular services (case B1)	1	11	64	9	1541	0	81	20	1513
	5	19	76	16	1880	1	944	36	2140
	10	25	65	22	3220	1	646	48	3310
	50	125	186	430	322	1	127	556	440
	100	231	197	4385	12900	2086	12425	4621	12760
Get TransferServiceAndRenting service (case B2)	1	0	61	0	1705	0	117	0	1813
	5	0	62	0	1816	0	1326	0	1770
	10	0	62	0	3290	0	688	0	3090
	50	11	66	57	993	0	160	68	1103
	100	11	75	3102	13820	2081	12790	3113	13980

8 Conclusions

This paper presented a solution for federating Smart CityAPIs that provide data and services. The solution aims to satisfy requirements that presently cannot be met by traditional solutions based on GIS or IoT Brokers. The proposed solution, while avoids migrating data, provides federation at level of APIs, involves nodes of any size (in terms of geo area and number of content/entities), and combines them autonomously so that each of them may (not) decide to join an area/content. It also leaves the possibility of having different kind of services, enables the movements among federated areas, respects privacies according to GDPR, and combines services with IoT Brokers NGSI of FiWare and GIS via WFS/WMS, by using Snap4City tools. Moreover, the proposed solution provides scalable performance in data access even in the case of private devices, etc. It finally allows the creation of separate clusters of federated APIs and standalone solutions. The main results include the formalization of decisions for the propagation of queries, optimizing the composition of results in an efficient manner, the possibility of federating Snap4City solutions with native FiWare solutions based on IoT Orion Broker, the assessment of performance for the federated solution, and access private and public IoT devices. To design, implementation, and validation of the solution, we enhanced the former Km4City Smart City API and ontology to improve the semantic queries that can be overlapped among different areas. We also developed an adapter from/to NGSI V2 of IoT Brokers FiWare and Smart City API. The validation has shown that the solution is scalable and viable in terms of performance by removing the duplications at a reasonable expense, for urban and rural areas, even in presence of a large number of duplications. When the range of the query is very large (e.g., $50 - 100(km)$), the number of resulting objects is high, while the response time of federated solution is still comparable with respect to the response time of the service providing the majority of the results.

Future work on this research line should address the new emerging protocol of NGSI-LD that is going to bring semantic descriptions into the messages. It is presently based on a non-consolidated but still interesting set of data models. Therefore, the connection of FiWare brokers based on NGSI-LD could allow to extend some of the semantic reasoning also to those nodes.

Acknowledgments. The authors would like to thank the European Union's Horizon 2020 research and innovation program for funding the Select4Cities PCP project (supported within the Snap4City framework) under the grant agreement No. 688196, and all the companies and partners involved. Snap4City and Km4City are 100% open-source technologies and the platform of DISIT Lab can be accessed at https://www.snap4city.org.

References

1. Hernández-Muñoz, J.M., et al.: Smart cities at the forefront of the future internet. In: Domingue, J., et al. (eds.) FIA 2011. LNCS, vol. 6656, pp. 447–462. Springer, Heidelberg (2011). https://doi.org/10.1007/978-3-642-20898-0_32
2. Cinquini, L., et al.: The earth system grid federation: an open infrastructure for access to distributed geospatial data. Futur. Gener. Comput. Syst. **36**, 400–417 (2014). https://doi.org/10.1016/j.future.2013.07.002
3. Herrera-Cubides, J.F., Gaona-García, P.A., Gordillo Orjuela, K.: A view of the web of data. case study: use of services CKAN. Ingeniería. **22**, 46–64 (2017). https://doi.org/10.14483/udistrital.jour.reving.2017.1.a07
4. IoT Orion Broker FiWare with Persistence. https://github.com/FIWARE/tutorials.Time-Series-Data. Accessed 25 Feb 2022
5. Badii, C., Bellini, P., Cenni, D., Difino, A., Nesi, P., Paolucci, M.: Analysis and assessment of a Knowledge based smart city architecture providing service APIs. Futur. Gener. Comput. Syst. **75**, 14–29 (2017). https://doi.org/10.1016/j.future.2017.05.001
6. Zuccalà, M., Verga, E.S.: Enabling energy smart cities through urban sharing ecosystems. Energy Procedia. **111**, 826–835 (2017). https://doi.org/10.1016/j.egypro.2017.03.245
7. Krylovskiy, A., Jahn, M., Patti, E.: Designing a smart city internet of things platform with microservice architecture. In: 2015 3rd International Conference on Future Internet of Things and Cloud, pp. 25–30 (2015). https://doi.org/10.1109/FiCloud.2015.55
8. Arman, A., Bellini, P., Nesi, P., Paolucci, M.: Analyzing public transportation offer wrt mobility demand. In: Proceedings of the 1st ACM International Workshop on Technology Enablers and Innovative Applications for Smart Cities and Communities, pp. 30–37 (2019)
9. Badii, C., et al.: Snap4City: a scalable IOT/IOE platform for developing smart city applications. In: 2018 IEEE SmartWorld, Ubiquitous Intelligence Computing, Advanced Trusted Computing, Scalable Computing Communications, Cloud Big Data Computing, Internet of People and Smart City Innovation (SmartWorld/SCALCOM/UIC/ATC/CBDCom/IOP/SCI), pp. 2109–2116 (2018). https://doi.org/10.1109/SmartWorld.2018.00353
10. Ames, D.P., Horsburgh, J.S., Cao, Y., Kadlec, J., Whiteaker, T., Valentine, D.: HydroDesktop: web services-based software for hydrologic data discovery, download, visualization, and analysis. Environ. Model. Softw. **37**, 146–156 (2012). https://doi.org/10.1016/j.envsoft.2012.03.013

11. Kolozali, Ş, et al.: Observing the pulse of a city: a smart city framework for real-time discovery, federation, and aggregation of data streams. IEEE Internet Things J. **6**, 2651–2668 (2019). https://doi.org/10.1109/JIOT.2018.2872606

12. González-Zamar, M.-D., Abad-Segura, E., Vázquez-Cano, E., López-Meneses, E.: IoT technology applications-based smart cities: research analysis. Electronics **9**, 1246 (2020). https://doi.org/10.3390/electronics9081246

13. Anttiroiko, A.-V., Valkama, P., Bailey, S.J.: Smart cities in the new service economy: building platforms for smart services. AI & Soc. **29**, 323–334 (2014)

14. Vitolo, C., Elkhatib, Y., Reusser, D., Macleod, C.J.A., Buytaert, W.: Web technologies for environmental big data. Environ. Model. Softw. **63**, 185–198 (2015). https://doi.org/10.1016/j.envsoft.2014.10.007

15. Latre, S., Leroux, P., Coenen, T., Braem, B., Ballon, P., Demeester, P.: City of things: an integrated and multi-technology testbed for IoT smart city experiments. In: 2016 IEEE International Smart Cities Conference (ISC2), pp. 1–8 (2016). https://doi.org/10.1109/ISC2.2016.7580875

16. Salhofer, P., Buchsbaum, J., Janusch, M.: Building a fiware smart city platform. In: Proceedings of the 52nd Hawaii International Conference on System Sciences (2019)

17. Nesi, P., Badii, C., Bellini, P., Cenni, D., Martelli, G., Paolucci, M.: Km4City smart city API: an integrated support for mobility services. In: 2016 IEEE International Conference on Smart Computing (SMARTCOMP), pp. 1–8 (2016). https://doi.org/10.1109/SMARTCOMP.2016.7501702

18. Namiot, D., Sneps-Sneppe, M.: On software standards for smart cities: API or DPI. In: Proceedings of the 2014 ITU Kaleidoscope Academic Conference: Living in a Converged World - Impossible Without Standards?, pp. 169–174 (2014). https://doi.org/10.1109/Kaleidoscope.2014.6858494

19. Bellini, P., Nesi, D., Nesi, P., Soderi, M.: Federation of smart city services via APIs. In: 2020 IEEE International Conference on Smart Computing (SMARTCOMP), pp. 356–361 (2020). https://doi.org/10.1109/SMARTCOMP50058.2020.00077

20. Soto, J.Á.C., et al.: Towards a federation of smart city services. In: International Conference on Recent Advances in Computer Systems, pp. 163–168. Atlantis Press (2015)

21. Bonino, D., et al.: ALMANAC: internet of things for smart cities. In: 2015 3rd International Conference on Future Internet of Things and Cloud, pp. 309–316 (2015). https://doi.org/10.1109/FiCloud.2015.32

22. Badii, C., Bellini, P., Difino, A., Nesi, P.: Smart city IoT platform respecting GDPR privacy and security aspects. IEEE Access. **8**, 23601–23623 (2020). https://doi.org/10.1109/ACCESS.2020.2968741

23. Km4City ontology. https://www.snap4city.org/drupal/node/19, https://www.snap4city.org/download/video/DISIT-km4city-City-Ontology-eng-v5-1.pdf. Accessed 25 Feb 2022

24. Bellini, P., Benigni, M., Billero, R., Nesi, P., Rauch, N.: Km4City ontology building vs data harvesting and cleaning for smart-city services. J. Vis. Lang. Comput. **25**, 827–839 (2014). https://doi.org/10.1016/j.jvlc.2014.10.023

25. Arman, A., Bellini, P., Bologna, D., Nesi, P., Pantaleo, G., Paolucci, M.: Automating IoT data ingestion enabling visual representation. Sensors. **21**, 8429 (2021). https://doi.org/10.3390/s21248429

26. doc: RFC 6454: The Web Origin Concept. https://www.hjp.at/doc/rfc/rfc6454.html. Accessed 25 Feb 2022

Communication as a Part of Smart Governance in Local Municipalities

Katarína Vitálišová(✉) ⓘ, Kamila Borseková ⓘ, Anna Vaňová ⓘ, Darina Rojíková, and Peter Laco ⓘ

Faculty of Economics, Matej Bel University, Tajovského 10, 975 90 Banská Bystrica, Slovakia
{katarina.vitalisova,kamila.borsekova,anna.vanova,
darina.rojikova,peter.laco}@umb.sk

Abstract. The problem of many Central and Eastern European countries is very fragmented structure of public administration at the local level. It is also a specific of the Slovak Republic with 95,23% of local municipalities with less as 5000 inhabitants. The size of municipality (number of inhabitants, cad aster) influences significantly the total sum of funds needed to realize all original competences, as well as to implement innovative tools of local governance. The aim of the paper is to define the specifics of communication as a part of local governance implemented by small local municipalities and to propose how the communication can be developed in line with the concept of smart governance reflecting the human and financial limits of smaller municipalities. The paper presents selected findings of primary research on the utilization of traditional and digital tools in local governance realized by the Delphi method and compares them with the results of secondary research in the municipalities of the Slovak Republic with less than 5 000 inhabitants.

Keywords: Communication · Municipalities · Smart governance

1 Introduction

Communication of local municipality with all stakeholders in the territory, their participation in the development, cooperation and partnership are the main preconditions for an integrated approach to a dynamic and progressive development of the territory [1, 2]. The aim of communication in local municipalities is to inform stakeholders, to influence their behavior and engage them into the development activities. The smooth communication process with stakeholders helps initiate their participation and integration into the local development activities and persuade them about its necessity and benefits [3, 4].

The paper aims to define the specifics of communication as a part of local governance implemented by small local municipalities and to propose how the communication can be developed in line with the concept of smart governance reflecting the human and financial limits of smaller municipalities.

This aim will be achieved using several methods. We start with detailed characteristics of communication of local municipality that is defined from different point of views.

© The Author(s), under exclusive license to Springer Nature Switzerland AG 2022
O. Gervasi et al. (Eds.): ICCSA 2022 Workshops, LNCS 13382, pp. 191–203, 2022.
https://doi.org/10.1007/978-3-031-10592-0_15

The analysis focuses, firstly, on the identification of the communication tools in small municipalities as a part of smart governance and subsequently, it compares the utilization of the tools with the recommended communication tools by experts from academia and practice. Based on comparison of both approaches the papers define the potential pathway how to improve the communication in more smart way.

The paper composes of 3 main parts. The theoretical part explains the specifics of communication in the local municipalities in context of using new modern communication technologies. The second chapter presents the results of primary research on the utilization of traditional and digital tools in local governance realized by the Delphi method and compares them with the results of secondary research in the municipalities of the Slovak Republic with less than 5 000 inhabitants. In conclusions, we present some recommendations how the communication of small local municipalities can be developed in line with the concept of smart governance.

2 Communication of Local Municipality

Communication in the local municipality can be defined from different point of views. From the marketing point of view, the communication is created by a set of tools to inform about local municipality, persuade about its advantages and to motivate final market or markets to "buy" products of the municipality. To do it effectively, the important purpose of communication is to awake interest and raise awareness in public to co-solve problems in municipality and co-create tailored solutions with the aim to achieve "win-win" situation for involved stakeholders reflected in prosperity of the territory [5, 6]. Well-prepared communication plan towards municipal stakeholders can be a great source of information in defining stakeholders' needs and wishes, so then can be subsequently integrated into the development activities.

Communication of local municipality is closely connected with the communication of city. It performs in three ways [7–11]. The first way of communication is related to the physical elements and activities of the city, which include architecture, city design, infrastructure, but also the behavior of the city, e.g. municipal institutions and residents. This way of communication is indicated as primary or physical communication. The second method of communication involves formal communication through various traditional and modern forms of marketing communication. The third method of communication (tertiary communication) concerns the oral presentation of information about the city through the city's consumers (residents, entrepreneurs, visitors, etc.) and is based on their personal experience. Tertiary communication is an uncontrolled way of communication, as it is largely beyond the control of urban management. As tertiary communication primarily affects the image of the city, which in turn affects the city branding, it can bring great benefits but also cause quite a lot of problems, especially when consumers of the area have a negative experience with the city [12]. In the paper, we focus on the communication realized by local municipalities towards stakeholders, it means the second way of communication. Nowadays, these forms of communication are often associated with using internet, social media, web and mobile applications, etc.

However, because of the diversified structure of target audience in towns and cities, the communication should mix the traditional promotion mix with the new ones. From the traditional ones belong to the most used tools in public relations in a form of press conferences, press articles, news, professional conferences and seminars, sponsorship, or event organizing [13, 14]. Personal communication, or in commerce marketing personal selling, is embodied in each provided information or service by local municipalities. The less use communication tools are various forms of sales promotion as delivering local services for free, gifts for customers, free admission to cultural events, theatres, etc. The local municipalities have preferred the advertising forms in printed form as brochures, leaflets.

However, the fast development of modern technologies has brought a lot of new possibilities in communication of municipalities. These changes are reported also by Eurostat. According to statistics, the internet access of EU households has risen from 84% in 2016 to 92% in 2021. 44% of citizens in the European Union reported that they had obtained information from the websites of public authorities during the last 12 months. This was considerably higher than the 33% of citizens reporting the same in 2008. Nevertheless, the development of e-Government and the availability of online information for citizens vary considerably across the EU Member States, as well as the share of citizens that use the internet in general. In 2019, a large part of the citizens in the Nordic countries had used the websites of public authorities to obtain information: 89% of citizens in Denmark, 84% of citizens in Finland and 79% of citizens in Sweden reported to have done this in the last 12 months. These shares were high also in the Netherlands (76%) and in Estonia (69%). In contrast, only 9% of citizens in Romania had obtained information from public authorities through their websites. This was also not common in Italy (19%) and Bulgaria (20%) [15, 16].

It is questionable what is the cause of these differences. We can anticipate the economic, cultural, social, and other differences that currently exist between individual EU countries. Anyway, we assume that one of the important reasons are activities of municipalities and local government in the on-line world. The information provided on websites and social networks, as well as the possibilities of interactive communication, enable citizens to obtain useful and important information. Therefore, it is important to be aware of what important factors local governments websites should meet.

In cites, the most often used new communication tools are websites, that are relatively cheap, widely available, and easily up-to-date, as well as social media [17–20]. During recent years, different website evaluation approaches have been introduced. To the important features of websites belong the website usability [21, 22], content [23], website accessibility [24], design [25], functionality, or technical aspects of websites.

Factors influencing a website evaluation by visitors seems to be different to factors that are important for website owners and developers. As described in Laco [26], the most important criterion for website visitors is security. Visitors need to feel safe browsing all pages and components of the site, otherwise they leave immediately. During last years, we can see rising importance of another criterion that is advertising. Visitors are already overwhelmed by annoying advertising or spamming, and they are becoming more and more sensitive to it. Another important criterion is content itself, its quality, structure, and relevance. Functionality of webpages is also a necessity to keep visitors at the site. Broken links, images or other components cause dissatisfaction and embarrassment for website visitors. Loading time, or in other words speed, has also proven to be one of the deciding factors, especially if visitors have an alternative site to which they can browse. Nearly half of web visitors expect a site to load in 2 s or less, and they will potentially leave a site that isn't loaded within 3 s. The last crucial factor is simple and clear navigation. Real practice shows that creating and maintaining simple navigation is not easy at all. As website navigation is key to retaining visitors, it is important to use all possible tools to keep visitors informed where in the website structure they are and where they can go next. Simplicity is one of the best approaches when considering the user experience and the usability of the website.

The following factors have been marked as relatively less, but still important for website visitors. It is for example, correct display of webpages on any screen. Responsive web design is a necessity in today's world full of devices with absolutely different screen resolutions and various web browsers. The current trend can be called "mobile first", but all platforms still need to be considered. Websites must also be "searchable" in both external and internal meanings. Website must be easy to be found in the whole internet – via Google mostly. Visitors expect to have also site search possibility as they navigate from one page to another within the specific website. One of the most surprising findings is the fact that design (colours, fonts, images, …) of the webpages is relatively even less important for web visitors, but again still need to be carefully handled. It must be consistent with other factors, especially it has to support simple navigation and cannot cause long loading time due to rich multimedia content like large images of videos. Usability and the utility, not the visual design, determine the success or failure of a website. Since the visitor of the page is the only person who clicks the mouse and therefore decides everything, user-centric design has established as a standard approach for successful web design. For specific groups of visitors' language versions as well as interactivity possibilities are important too.

Website owners and developers focus mostly on website traffic, as a key performance indicator. It is very easy to be measured, but not easy to be achieved at all. Second important factor is functionality of all pages in a website. Third important is design, followed by easy-to-remember domain, simple and intuitive navigation, speed, correct display, language versions and interactivity.

The processes associated with the development and maintenance of the website depend primarily on the decision of the level of outsourcing. According to results published in Laco [26] in most cases the website is created by external company, usually marketing agency. This brings professional design and great first impression of a website. In a large number of cases, website was created by an external company, but it is updated by internal employees. This approach comes with significant benefit of flexible update possibilities. Popular and easy-to-use content management systems make website management processes much more accessible even for non-technical people than in the past. This is probably one of the reasons why in approximately one third of cases, websites were both created and updated by internal employees.

The second mentioned innovation in communication are social media. They include internet, mobile communication channels, and tools through which users can share opinions and textual, audiovisual, and visual content. Social networks involve the building of communities and networks and the encouragement of their users to participate and engage [27, 28]. Kollárová [29] divides social media into three platforms: social networks (Facebook, Google+, LinkedIn, etc.); blogs (WordPress, Blogger), and discussion forums (Google Groups, Yahoo Groups, Answers). Few other platforms could be involved, namely: microblogs (Twitter, Posterous, Tumbrl, etc.); on-line rating sites (TripAdvisor, Zagat, Google Places); social bookmarking (StumbleUpon, Delicious, Digg); podcasting; social knowledge and Wiki (Wikipedia, Quora); geolocation services (FourSquare); shared multimedia (YouTube, Instagram, Last.fm, Slideshare).

Social media provide a lot of opportunities for interaction with citizens through plug-in applications, groups and fan pages. Each social network is specific and with its specific users. Social media give the users a chance to share their ideas, contents and relationships online. The user can create, comment and post their own content and share it with the others. The users' posts can have the form of a text, a video, animation, images, photos, etc. The concept of social networking creates vast possibilities for presentation. Creative and interactive communication brings the product, place or brand to attention. On the other hand, customers can attach videos, photos or comments to their profiles. Besides, they can have discussions managed and possibly entered by the discussion group administrators. In this way, information is spread to people who would probably not get it otherwise [30].

Moreover, the progressive development opens still new and new possibilities how to improve the communication. There are various possibilities of chat and audiovisual communication in a form of video conferences, discussion forums, IP telephoning, instant messaging (ICQ, g-talk, skype). All these technology options make communication faster and allow better cooperation between various entities. The great advantage is a quick, immediate response. Chat allows electronic communication between the Internet users in real time, or on-line discussions with several users at the same time.

Another example is a mobile communication. The advantage of mobile marketing communication is a possibility of accurate targeting of a campaign (information about the consumer's identity, behaviour, personal preferences and geographic location), the ability to mediate direct interaction between the advertiser and recipient, high operability in real time, simple and quick updating, high user comfort, low cost, large scale use and, last but not least, simple measurability [14, 31].

3 Material and Methods

The paper aim to define the specifics of communication as a part of local governance implemented by small local municipalities and to propose how the communication can be developed in line with the concept of smart governance reflecting the human and financial limits of smaller municipalities.

Research on the communication tools as a part of smart governance from the theoretical point of view was done by using the Delphi method among 33 experts during the second half of 2020 in two rounds. The experts involved in the research sample were identified by the authors' analysis of the academic papers and strategic documents of municipalities in Slovakia. In the first round, 278 experts were invited to participate. We received responses from 33 experts who were involved in the next steps of research. That is why we assume that they are perfectly oriented in the topic and that their knowledge covers the research problem in a complex way.

The experts who participated in the research were mainly from the fields of regional development (39,39%), strategic planning (27,27%), and public administration (15,15%), politics (6,06%) and other (3,03%). They come from academia (85%) and from practice (15%). 49% of the experts came from Slovakia, 18% from Poland, 9% from Italy, as well as from the Czech Republic. Other experts come from Hungary, Belgium, Finland, and Japan (Fig. 1).

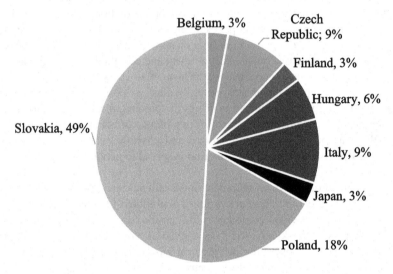

Fig. 1. The structure of experts involved in the research according to country

The next part of the research is a secondary research in a form of observing the strategical documents of municipalities, websites and other official information of the local municipalities with less than 5000 inhabitants in the Slovak Republic during first half of 2021. The research sample was 253 local municipalities. The structure of research sample by the number of inhabitants presents Fig. 2. By Chi quadrat test the research sample is representative by the large of the municipality as well as by the localization in the Slovak parts – West Slovakia, Central Slovakia and East Slovakia.

From both researches, we selected the data that are directly associated with the used communication forms of the local municipalities. To process data we used the MS Excel, statistical program SPSS. We used the methods of descriptive statistics and correlations analysis.

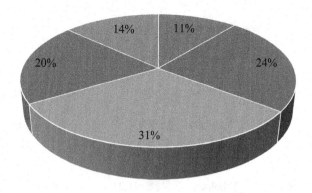

- to 199 inhabitants   - 200 - 499 inhabitants   - 500 - 999 inhabitants
- 1000 - 1999 inhabitants - 2000 - 4999 inhabitants

Fig. 2. The structure of researched local municipalities by number of inhabitants

4 Research Results and Discussion

The structure of Slovak municipalities was established in 1990 by no. 369/1990 Coll. on municipalities amended and its importance was confirmed also by the Constitution of the Slovak Republic in 1993 [32]. The main role of the municipality is to care about the comprehensive development of its territory and the population living in it.

In Slovakia, a one-tired municipal government was established beside the cities of Bratislava and Košice (cities over 100 thousand inhabitants) with two-layers of self-government – city and city district. The structure of the Slovak cities by the number of citizens is very fragmented. 84,81% of Slovak municipalities has less as 1 999 inhabitants, and 95,23% has less than 4 999 inhabitants. The large of a local municipality influences significantly the funds that municipality receives and is able to collect, and thus is reflected in the ability to fulfill the original tasks defined by law. Smaller municipalities, lower funds. By other words, in Slovakia, many of the municipalities are very small, are limited in sense of human and financial resources, as well as in communication forms used to inform and engage the local stakeholders.

In the research, we map the traditional and modern forms of communication which use the local municipalities up to 5000 inhabitants. By investigation of municipal websites and strategical documents we identified the most used tools of communication, which are illustrated in Fig. 3.

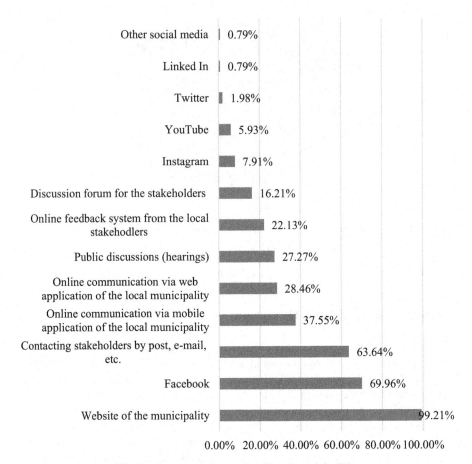

Fig. 3. Communication tools of local municipalities

The most used communication tool is a municipal website. It is followed by Facebook – the official profile of local municipality. This result confirms that Facebook is the most used social media in Slovakia. The third most used activity is contacting stakeholders by post, e-mail etc., by other words direct mail. All other activities are used by less than 38% of local municipalities. The least used forms of communication are Instagram, Twitter, Youtube and Linked In – so various types of social media.

The utilization of communication tools by local municipalities by size categories presents Fig. 4. The figure shows that in first four communication tools are the most active local municipalities with size 1000–1999 inhabitants. In the majority of other communication tools are dominant in the local municipalities with 2000–4999 inhabitants.

In the next step, we compare the tools which are the most often used by the local municipalities by the importance of the communication tools evaluated by experts (Table 1).

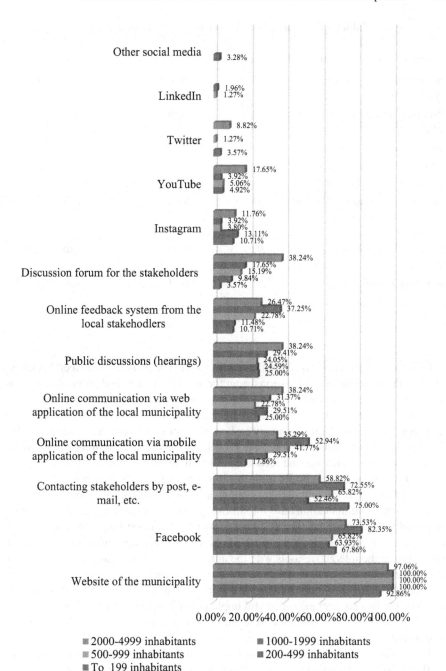

Fig. 4. Communication tools of local municipalities by the size categories

Table 1. Importance of the communication tools by experts

Importance of communication tools	Average value	Standard deviation	Min.	Max.
Online feed-back system from the stakeholders	4,39	0,86	3,53	5,26
Discussion forum for the stakeholders	4,33	0,69	3,64	5,03
Public discussions (hearings)	4,06	0,86	3,20	4,92
Online communication via web applications of the municipality	4,03	0,92	3,11	4,95
Online communication via mobile phone applications of the municipality	4,03	1,05	2,98	5,08
Online communication via social networks	4,00	0,90	3,10	4,90
Website of the city	3,91	0,91	3,00	4,82
Contacting stakeholders by post, e-mail, etc.	2,88	1,18	1,69	4,06

By experts, the modern local municipalities should use mainly online feed-back system from the stakeholders, discussion forum for the stakeholders and public discussions (hearings). To the other tools, almost with the same evaluation, belongs online communication via web applications of the municipality, online communication via mobile phone applications of the municipality and online communication via social networks. The experts confirm that it is more important to use interactive communication tools, i.e. two-way communication and feedback, as just to inform the stakeholders.

When we compare the results from the municipalities and from experts, there is an obvious difference in perception of communication tools. The local municipalities use more often the communication tools for informing and absents the support of interaction. That is why the communication as a tool of local governance loses the real meaning because it covers just the first stage of stakeholders' participation. On the other hand, the experts prefer the interactive tools with the aim to involve and engage the stakeholders into the local governance. It is desirable to re-orient the communication strategy of local municipality on the tools preferred by the experts. The interactive communication tools are a medium that support the successful implementation of smart governance based on a tricky balance of implementation of technological and social innovations relevant to the stakeholder's needs and expectation.

As we already mentioned, the research was focused on the local municipalities with less than 5 000 inhabitants. The possibilities to realise some communication strategy are limited because of the financial and human resources. However, due to the progressive IT development, there opens new options also for these municipalities.

Firstly, the most used tool of local municipalities is a website. As we mentioned in the theoretical review, there are a lot of requirements for a well-designed website. To some practical tips belongs five quality components defined by Nielsen (2012). The important is learnability – the website has to be easy for users to accomplish basic tasks the first time they encounter the design. The second component is an efficiency – once users have learned the design, how quickly can they perform tasks – as shorter as better. The next factor is memorability – when users return to the design after a period of not using it, how easily can they re-establish proficiency. The last feature that must be minimalised is how many errors do users make, how severe are these errors, and how easily can they recover from the errors. It is important to research also the satisfaction of users, by other words, how pleasant is it to use the design.

The possibility how to use the website more interactively is also a chatbot artificial intelligence module. It is a smart tool for communication with citizens. The essence of the chatbot is interactive personalized communication between local government and residents on the main topics of the municipality such as news, invitations to cultural events, changes in the organization of transport, notifications of repairs, comments on the official board and information from the city council. By chatbot, citizens are able to choose the information they prefer to receive via "chat" in the Messenger application as well as in a web chat.

Other option, usually also financially convenient, for local municipalities are a mobile and web application. They are sold in specific packages of services reflecting the municipal requirements. In Slovakia, there are a few examples as applications SOM (I am), V obraze (I am in), Virtuálne (Virtual).

Moreover, in smaller local municipalities, the potential of the personal forms of communications should be exploited. They include various forms of public discussions and hearings, as well as events organizing for local stakeholders, or some specific activities supporting the co-creation and co-production of public services and local policy decision-making (e.g. hackathons, workshops based on the ideas of living labs).

5 Conclusions

The paper aimed to define the specifics of communication as a part of local governance implemented by small local municipalities and to propose how the communication can be developed in line with the concept of smart governance reflecting the human and financial limits of smaller municipalities.

The paper compares the used communication tools of local municipalities with the experts' opinion on their importance. The main finding is that the local municipalities prefer the utilization of the one-way forms of communication, what is in opposite to the experts. They recommend focusing on interactive communication tools. Moreover, we present also a few examples of new possibilities for smaller local municipalities given by IT progress. However, we consider as a very important to combine the modern IT communication tools with the physical ones, which are in small local municipalities extremely important.

The research showed that all the tools of communication are important and optimal way is to mix them with aim to achieve the multichannel communication with stakeholders which significantly influence the forms of interaction and cooperation in co-creating and co-producing of public services and local policy decision-making.

The presented research results open potential new research areas. As the first step, more sophisticated methods can be used to generalise the correlations between the research aspects. Secondly, the next research could answer the research questions, e.g. how are the differences between the communication of small and big cities, not only from the type of tools, but also content, frequency of communication etc., or how is the effectiveness of the communication tools to various groups of stakeholders. Because it is quite complex issue that was strongly foster and developed during corona phenomenon, it could be beneficial also its effect on the way of communication in cities and villages as a part of smart governance.

Acknowledgement. The paper presents the partial outputs of project VEGA 1/0213/20 Smart Governance in Local Municipalities.

References

1. Vaňová, A., Foret, M.: The partnership for local development. In: Proceedings of International Scientific Conference Nové trendy – nové nápady, p. 412–419. SVŠE Znojmo, Znojmo (2009)
2. Turečková, K., Nevima, J.: Smart approach in regional development. In: Proceedings of MIRDEC-12th, International Academic Conference Multidisciplinary and Interdisciplinary Studies on Social Sciences, pp. 77–84. University of Washington Rome Center, Rome (2019)
3. Vitálišová, K., Borseková, K., Vaňová, A.: Problems and perspectives in communication of citizens and local municipalities in the Slovak Republic. In: Höhn, E., Poliak, P. (eds.) Foreign Languages and Cultures in Theory and Practice, pp. 377–387. Matej Bel University, Faculty of Arts, Banská Bystrica (2016)
4. Turečková, K., Nevima, J.: The cost benefit analysis for the concept of a smart city: how to measure the efficiency of smart solutions? Sustainability 12(7), 1–17 (2020)
5. Vaňová, A.: Strategic Marketing Planning of Territorial Development. Matej Bel University Faculty of Economics, Banská Bystrica (2006)
6. Vitálišová, K.: Relationships Marketing in Local Municipalities. Matej Bel University Faculty of Economics, Banská Bystrica (2015)
7. Kavaratzis, M.: From city marketing to city branding: towards a theoretical framework for developing city brands. Place Branding 1(1), 58–73 (2004)
8. Kavaratzis, M.: From City Marketing to City Branding: An Interdisciplinary Analysis with Reference to Amsterdam, Budapest and Athens, Doctoral Thesis. University of Groningen (2008)
9. Kavaratzis, M.: The dishonest relationship between city marketing and culture: reflections on the theory and the case of Budapest. J. Town City Manage. 1(4), 334–345 (2011)
10. Braun, E.: City Marketing: Towards an Integrated Approach. Haveka, Rotterdam (2008)
11. Cavia, J.F.: Place branding: a communication perspective. Commun. Soc. 31(4), 1–7 (2018)
12. Baker, B.: Place Branding for Small Cities, Regions and Downtowns: The Essentials for Successful Destinations. Independently Published (2019)
13. Rojíková, D., Borseková, K., Vitálišová, K., Vaňová, A.: Digital transformation of city branding: comparison of the role of digital communication in branding of selected cities in Europe and Slovakia (2022, in print)
14. Vaňová, A., Vitálišová, K., Boseková, K.: Marketing Places. Belianum, Banská Bystrica (2017)

15. Eurostat: Digital economy and society statistics – households and individuals https://ec.europa.eu/eurostat/statistics-explained/index.php?title=Digtal_economy_and_society_statistics_-_households_and_individuals#Internet_access. Accessed 21 March 2022
16. Eurostat: e-Government – more citizens consult information online. https://ec.europa.eu/eurostat/web/products-eurostat-news/-/edn-20200307-1 (2020). Accessed 21 March 2022
17. Smith, B.G.: Beyond promotion: conceptualizing public relations in integrated marketing communications. Int. J. Integr. Mark. Commun. **2**, 47–57 (2010)
18. Kotler, P., Keller, K.L.: Marketing Management. Grada, Praha (2013)
19. Labanauskaitė, D., Fiore, M., Stašys, R.: Use of E-marketing tools as communication management in the tourism industry. Tourism Manage. Perspect. **34**, 100652 (2020)
20. Turečková, K.: Sectoral industrial agglomeration and network externalities: concept of ICT sector. In: Proceedings of 5th International Conference on Applied Social Science, pp. 50–55. IERI, USA (2015)
21. Alva, M.E.O., Martínez P., A.B., Cueva L., J.M., Sagástegui Ch., T.H., López P., B.: Comparison of methods and existing tools for the measurement of usability in the web. In: Lovelle, J.M.C., Rodríguez, B.M.G., Gayo, J.E.L., del Puerto Paule Ruiz, M., Aguilar, L.J. (eds.) ICWE 2003. LNCS, vol. 2722, pp. 386–389. Springer, Heidelberg (2003). https://doi.org/10.1007/3-540-45068-8_70
22. Tezza, R., Bornia, A., De Andrade, D.: Measuring web usability using item response theory: principles, features and opportunities. Interact. Comput. **23**(2), 167–175 (2011)
23. Robbins, S., Stylianou, A.: Global corporate web sites: an empirical investigation of content and design. Inform. Manage. **40**(3), 205–212 (2003)
24. Leporini, B., Paternò, F.: Criteria for usability of accessible web sites. In: Carbonell, N., Stephanidis, C. (eds.) UI4ALL 2002. LNCS, vol. 2615, pp. 43–55. Springer, Heidelberg (2003). https://doi.org/10.1007/3-540-36572-9_3
25. Palmer, J.W.: Web site usability, design, and performance metrics. Inform. Syst. Res. **13**(2), 151–167 (2002)
26. Laco, P.: Hodnotenie podnikových internetových stránok. Banská Bystrica. Belianum (2018)
27. Papasolomou, I., Melanthiou, Y.: Social media: marketing public relations' new best friend. J. Promot. Manage. **18**(3), 319–328 (2012)
28. Chaffey, D., Smith, P.R.: eMarketing eXcellence: Planning and Optimizing your Digital Marketing. Routledge, Oxon (2013)
29. Kollárová, D.: Podpora predaja pri komunikácii s vybranými cieľovými skupinami. Univerzita sv. Cyrila a Metoda v Trnave, Trnava (2014)
30. Rojíková, D., Vaňová, A., Vitálišová, K., Borseková, K.: The role of social media in city branding in contemporary business concepts and strategies in the new era. In: 14th Annual Conference of the EuroMed Academy of Business: Conference Readings, pp. 639–652. EuroMed press (2021)
31. Vitálišová, K., Vaňová, A., Borseková, K., Rojíková, D.: Promotion as a tool of smart governance in cities. In: Paiva, S., Lopes, S.I., Zitouni, R., Gupta, N., Lopes, S.F., Yonezawa, T. (eds.) SmartCity360° 2020. LNICSSITE, vol. 372, pp. 497–510. Springer, Cham (2021). https://doi.org/10.1007/978-3-030-76063-2_33
32. Act of NCSR no. 90/2001 Coll. on the Constitution of the Slovak Republic amended

The Market Concentration as the Public Services Contracting Out Efficiency Factor at the Local Government Level: The Case of Slovakia

Beáta Mikušová Meričková(✉) ⓘD, Daniela Mališová ⓘD, and Kristína Murínová

Faculty of Economics, Matej Bel University, Tajovského 10, Banská Bystrica 974 01, Slovakia
beata.mikusovamerickova@umb.sk

Abstract. The changes in market concentration in recent years point to the fact that the intensity of competition is declining and the number of large players with a high market share is increasing. Therefore, the market concentration has the effect of restricting competition. The direct impact of market concentration is also felt at the local government level. Municipalities provide local public services in public–private-mix delivery system, many services are contracted out. The aim of the paper is to analyze the market concentration as the public services contracting out efficiency factor at the local government level. Paper analyzes contracting out collection and removal of municipal solid waste in 18 districts of central Slovakia. The degree of market concentration assessed using the CR and HHI indexes is confirmed. The results of the analysis showed that the private market of municipal solid waste collection and removal services in central Slovakia is highly concentrated. None of the monitored districts recorded a HHI index value lower than 2,500, which we perceive critically. The dominant players influence the price of the service. That could be the reason of new trend in local public services delivery – remunicipalisation in urban and local planning.

Keywords: Market concentration · Public services · Local government · Contracting out · Remunicipalisation · Urban and local planning

1 Introduction

Market concentration has been present in European countries since the 1960s 20th century. From an economic point of view, market concentration is associated with competition and refers to the merging (concentration) of companies in a market economy [25]. As a result of the growing range of private sector activities in the provision of public services, these economic impacts also affect the public sector. For this reason, the aim of the paper is to analyze the market concentration as the public services contracting out efficiency factor at the local government level.

At the level of local governments, the concept of market concentration is linked at the same time as the concept of decentralization. Government fragmentation limits efficiency [19, 20] gains by reducing administrative capacity and economies of scale. It is the problem of local savings in the range of local services that has intensified in recent decades due to the transformation of public services [16, 29]. The local self-government (municipality) is itself responsible for providing local services. We distinguish the form of the approach to provisioning internally if the municipality provides the service at its own expense, or external if the municipality uses external institutions to provide the service (for example, the form of outsourcing). Alternatively, the municipality may use the intersection between internal and external forms – contracting – to provide services.

In this context, we state that it is common practice in the public sector to provide public services at the municipal level by contracting services. Contracting services [31] are an alternative form of public service provision in which the functions of service provider and producer are separated [27]. Thus, the public sector is not a direct producer of the service, this service is provided by a private player based on a contractual relationship. We agree with Brooks' approach [8], according to which contracting is the process by which a private sector firm enters a contract with a government unit to produce a particular service. Under this agreement, the private sector creates the service and is paid for by the government unit. Typical examples of contracted services at the municipal level are waste collection and removal services, maintenance of public lighting, public greenery, and cemetery management.

2 Market Concentration and Its Impact on Public Service Delivery: Literature Review

The results published in domestic and foreign studies are the starting point for examining market concentration in Slovakia. Studies [17] increasingly focus on contracting factors such as transaction costs or market concentration, which often show results to the detriment of higher cost-effectiveness of local public service contracting. The main challenge is to create economies of scale, given the developments in the provision of services and their economic complexity.

The issue of economies of scale in waste management [3, 4, 24], especially in solid waste collection. Based on their detailed review of the literature, we find that economies of scale are present in municipalities with 20,000 to 50,000 inhabitants and that continuous economies of scale are present above 50,000 inhabitants. Economies of scale in smaller municipalities may be present, but to a lesser extent. However, economies of scale may not be present when recycling waste. This is mainly due to increased processing fees. The authors state that economies of scale in the collection and treatment of solid waste are less relevant than in the case of other services, such as the provision of education services.

Another approach to market concentrations in the provision of waste collection services [12] is in reverse privatization, which consisted of municipalities taking control of the provision of services. The analysis of this approach was performed in the period 2003–2015 in German municipalities, while the authors use CR and HHI indexes. From the results, we find that municipalities in response to the concentrated market more often switch to internal service provision (insourcing). Following this, municipalities also copy the provision of services according to the model of their neighbor, i.e. in the event that a close neighbor (municipality) applies insourcing, it is likely that its surrounding municipalities will also apply it. The authors state that this is an induced vertical connection between municipalities. However, such behavior may lead to a reverse privatization spiral, which is associated with a high market share of municipalities, the exit of small private players and an increase in the dominance of large private players, further increasing market concentration. The authors add that the effective outcome of such cyclicality is debatable.

In contrast, reverse privatization [21] reflects the complexity of public service delivery in the world. It is a dynamic process that often involves shifting from alternative provision back to the original forms of service provision. However, we note that both the internal interest and the structure of the market need to be taken into account, both in the internal and external provision of services.

Therefore, we can look at the competitive environment [10] from two perspectives. First, as for the competition for the market, where it is assessed how the market develops over time, what conditions are set for entry into the industry, or whether barriers are set (administrative or legislative regulation by the state) for the entry of new players into the industry. Second, as the competition in the market, which replicates traditional market approaches focused on internal processes. Within this view, we can monitor the volume of total production or marginal market shares of players. In terms of the transformation process, internal as well as external factors are focused on output or are result-oriented. However, in the case of services, it is important to consider, in particular, the quality of the provision of services by individual players.

The choice of a suitable form of service provision [35, 36] is determined by many internal factors (management style, material-technical and financial possibilities of the municipality, etc.) and external (geographical location, price of services, suppliers operating in the region, competitive environment, etc.) factors. The examination of the mentioned factors is the subject of professional discussions with the aim of setting up the best possible solution for the municipality or taxpayers.

The literature is increasingly focusing on factors that could undermine savings in public–private contracting, such as high transaction costs [2], or market concentration [5]. As we saw in the introduction, a more concentrated market can cause market prices to rise. This can be justified by the fact that the provision of services to the public sector is a specific area in which there may be weak competition and high concentrations (reflected in the high HHI index), which results in higher prices. The competitive environment as a factor in the efficiency of service provision can have an impact on higher municipal expenditures or on economies of scale. According to some authors, the competitive environment is an even more significant factor than the type of ownership.

In terms of the objective of the paper, we draw attention to research [17], in which the authors use various special market concentration indexes to measure the Dutch waste collection market. The study was carried out in the period 2002–2014 and shows that the waste collection market is very concentrated, which increases the cost of private collection. In the monitored period, 25, later 16 players operated on this market. In the initial period, the largest player had a contractual relationship on the provision of waste collection services with 87 municipalities, by 2014 the share of municipalities decreased to 37. The price for providing waste collection services has increased over time, since 2006 mainly due to the introduction of the fund compensation. However, the authors point out that during the period there were also concentrations of municipalities that merged, and their number decreased from the original 496 to 403, while the area is 30–50 km. From a methodological point of view, the authors supplement the Herfindahl – Hirshman Index (HHI) with special indexes, which they compare with each other. From the results of HHI measurements, we find that if the market had an area of 50 km, the market concentration was 4,400 in 2014; if the area was 30 km, the market concentration was 6,660 in 2014. In the case of expanding the territorial area to 70 km, the concentration was 3,700 in 2014.

In terms of serviceability of the area, the authors [13] point out the high increase in concentration in the event that the monitored area shrinks. When examining the effect of market concentration on the price of the service, they found a slight increase in costs with a growing HHI index, but a decrease in costs in the case of a growing CC1 index – which examines only the largest company in the industry. Therefore, the authors hypothesize that in larger regions, where more waste is treated and competitiveness is equally higher, an oligopolistic structure could mean rising prices for the collection and disposal of municipal solid waste.

3 Materials and Methods

The degree of market concentration is an important tool that must be used by any public or private player interested in entering a particular market. There are several approaches [9] to measuring market concentration. The most well-known methods used for market analysis include statistical and econometric methods, game theory and special indexes. The literature states [6, 7, 15, 22] that the Herfindahl-Hirshman Index (abbreviation HHI). The special HHI index dates back to 1968, when it was used in the United States to assess horizontal mergers.

The HHI was followed in his work by the Hungarian economist J. Horvath, who designed a special index for measuring the complex concentration (CCI), which considers the relative size of the largest player and the variance between all players in the industry with respect to size.

Another well-known special index used in measuring concentration is the Hannaha-Kaya index [1], which aims to provide a link between concentration and inequality in the distribution of market power. Quite often, when measuring market concentration, we can also encounter the Lorenzo curve capturing the actual distribution of market shares, or the Gini index, which is used to measure the uneven distribution of market shares.

$$CR = \sum_{i=1}^{n} s_i \tag{1}$$

$$HHI = \sum_{i=1}^{n} s_i^2 \tag{2}$$

where:
s_i – market share of the market player,
i – order of the market player, where $i = 1, 2, 3, 4, \ldots n$,
n – number of market players.

In the paper, we use the HHI as a key index, which is closely related to the concentration ratio (CR index). The concentration ratio is calculated by summing the market share of the largest players in the industry. By multiplying this value by the second, we obtain an HHI, which can reach values from 1,000 to 10,000. Based on the HHI value, the market is divided (Table 1) into low to high concentration. However, it is important to note [15] that the whole percentage value is used to measure market share, not in decimal.

Table 1. Market concentration: Herfindahl – Hirshman Index (HHI) value

Concentration	Value	Market type
Low concentration	1 000–1 499	Efficient competition, part of monopolistic competition.
Moderate concentration	1 500–2 499	Part of monopolistic competition, loose oligopoly.
High concentration	2 500–10 000	Tight oligopoly, dominant player.

Current market concentration measures include the calculation of the sum of the market shares of the first four or the first eight players in relation to the total market size. The reasons for using a larger number of competitors [14] are based on the classical model of price competition (named after Bertrand). This model prescribes that at equilibrium prices, prices are equal to marginal costs. The prices do not depend on the number of competitors.

However, this result is not in line with the real-life observations known as the 'Bertrand's paradox', where we find in markets with experimental price competition that prices depend on the number of competitors. For this reason, it is not appropriate to use only two players when measuring the concentration, but four or more competitors. Similarly, larger countries use higher-class indicators to measure market concentration, where they monitor the HHI of the 50 or 100 strongest players. In smaller countries [7], the concentration rate is most often monitored on the four or eight strongest players.

The data we use in the paper are data obtained by primary research, which was carried out in the form of a questionnaire survey. For this reason, it is the object of research of 195 municipalities located in central Slovakia (Fig. 1). The subject of the investigation is market concentration as a possible factor in the cost-effectiveness of contracting public services. The aim of the paper is to analyze the market concentration as the public services contracting out efficiency factor at the local government level. We verify the set goal through two research assumptions. The first research premise (RP$_1$) is to find out whether the market of municipal solid waste collection and removal services in central Slovakia is highly concentrated. The second research premise (RP$_2$) is to verify whether higher market concentration brings with it higher prices for contracting a given service.

The price of a contracted service has an impact on the cost-effectiveness of contracting, which can normally be assessed by comparing the cost of the service in contracting and internalizing it. However, evaluating the cost-effectiveness of contracting by this comparison is not the primary goal of the work. We are interested in the cost of the contracted service, which we monitor through the cost of the service per capita and the cost

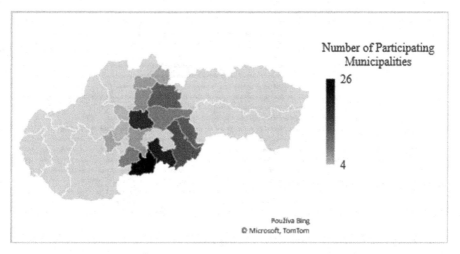

Fig. 1. Number of municipalities participating in the primary data collection by districts

of the service per performance indicator (one tonne of waste). The price in the private market of the service reflected in the service costs incurred by the municipality affects the cost-effectiveness of contracting the service. The cost of service per capita and the cost of service per performance indicator are therefore compared with the results of the first part of the analysis – HHI values in individual districts. We used causal analysis to examine the interdependencies (causes and outcomes), i.e., as the private producers that predominate in the market, they set their prices in the case of monopolies and in case the market concentration is lower. We used the comparison to compare the results relating to individual districts, taking into account the origin of private producers (purely private companies or organizations belonging to other cities). The last part of the analysis, which focused on defining the research conclusions and the validity of the assumptions, was processed using methods of synthesis and partial induction.

4   Analysis of Market Concentration in the Provision of Collection and Removal of Municipal Solid Waste in Slovakia

At the beginning, we examined the degree of contracting compared to the internal provision of the service, given that we calculate market concentration only with private players and not with technical services of the city (except in cases of technical services of one city by another municipality) or non-profit organizations.

In this paper, we used the district division to divide municipalities into groups, while the analysis was performed in the following districts of central Slovakia: Banská Bystrica, Brezno, Detva, Krupina, Lučenec, Revúca, Rimavská Sobota, Veľký Krtíš, Zvolen, Žarnovica, Žiar nad Hronom, Dolný Kubín, Liptovský Mikuláš, Martin, Ružomberok, Turčianske Teplice, Tvrdošín and Žilina. The results of the contraction rate are presented graphically in Fig. 2.

Based on the obtained data, we can see that the contracting of the service of collection and removal of municipal solid waste significantly prevails over the internal security

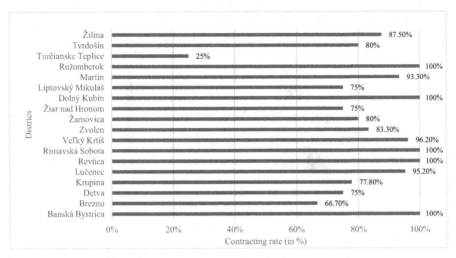

Fig. 2. Result of the contracting rate in the monitored file (in percent)

of this service. The assumption [12] is confirmed that ammunitions are not willing to provide the service internally due to the high technical complexity of the service. However, we see several exceptions, such as the district of Turčianske Teplice, but here we perceive the reason in the fact that the return from the municipalities in the district was not sufficient in comparison with other districts. The number of municipalities in this district in the basic sample was 26, in the sample only 4 answers. Therefore, we exclude this district from the observation of market concentration. The reason for this decision is also the fact that only one municipality of the district uses external security, which would be reported as an absolute monopoly in the method of evaluation. However, this result does not reflect reality.

We monitored the validity of the first research assumption using the HHI index, which expresses the absolute concentration in the industry. The index reaches values in the range <0; 10 000>. The value of 10,000 indicates a borderline situation where there is only one company on the market that provides the overall offer, and the market is highly concentrated. Conversely, HHI values approaching 0 indicate that there are many companies of similar size in the market and the market is low. Thus, the market has the character of perfect competition.

The results of the value of the CR index showed us (Fig. 3) that in several districts there is a high concentration of the market in the provision of collection and disposal of municipal solid waste. The average value of the CR index in the file is 84.28 (statistical deviation 12.88). Calculating the CR index is the first step in calculating the HHI.

When evaluating the results of the HHI index (Fig. 4), we find that we did not record a value lower than 2,500 in any of the districts. The average value of the HHI set is 7,260 (statistical deviation 2,153, 61). This excludes the existence of perfect competition in the market or the possible existence of monopolistic competition. On the contrary, the presence of a natural monopoly (HHI = 10,000) was recorded in several districts Revúca, Žiar nad Hronom, Martin, Tvrdošín and Žilina – in which municipalities use only one

Fig. 3. The result of the CR index in the monitored file

private producer of the service. For example, for Revúca and Martin, it was Brantner s.r.o. which has been operating in Slovakia since 1992. Today, it employs more than 700 workers and provides waste management services to more than 550,000 inhabitants and 2,000 corporate customers. According to annual reports, the company processes 30,000 tons of secondary raw materials per year.

For Žilina, the only private producer is T + T a.s. which was created after 1991 by the abolition of technical services of the city. Today in the Žilina, it provides waste collection for 365,000 inhabitants and annually processes 40,000 tons of municipal waste, from which alternative fuel for cement plants is created. In 2012, the company bought 90 percent of the shares of Technique services Žiar nad Hronom, which is a newly established monopoly in the district of Žiar na Hronom and provides services to more than 90,000 inhabitants. The last identified monopoly is the Technical Services of Ružomberok, which is used by municipalities in the Tvrdošín district. They were founded in 2000 and the co-founder (51% of shares) is also T + T a.s.

HHI index in the range <6,800.00; 7,654.32> reach the districts of Detva, Krupina, Veľký Kritíš, Dolný Kubín, Liptovský Mikuláš and Ružomberok. There are two or three players in these districts. The dominant company is Marius Pedersen, a. s., which has been the largest provider of waste management services in Slovakia since 2003. It currently works with more than 400 municipalities, providing its services to almost 1,000,000 inhabitants and 4,000 companies.

HHI index in the range <3,888.89; 5,987.65> reach the districts of Banská Bystrica, Brezno, Lučenec, Rimavská Sobota, Zvolen and Žarnovica. The lowest concentration of the market in the monitored group shows the district of Rimavská Sobota. The reason is that there are four organizations in the district providing collection and disposal of municipal solid waste. Companies, that serve the area in an area of 40 km^2, include Marius Pedersen, a.s., Brantner Gemer, s.r.o., Profax, MEPOS s.r.o.

Based on the values of the HHI index, we can unambiguously confirm the first research premise (RP_1). The market for the provision of municipal solid waste collection

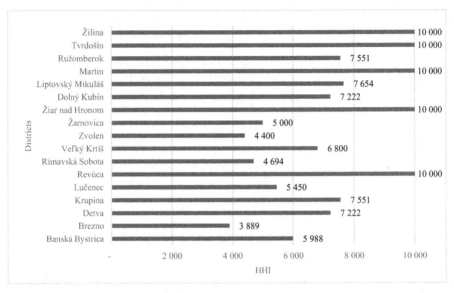

Fig. 4. The result of the HHI index in the monitored file

and removal services in central Slovakia is highly concentrated and characterized by a monopoly or oligopoly with a dominant player.

Based on the findings, we proceed to verify the second research premise (RP$_2$), which is to verify whether higher market concentration brings with it higher prices for contracting the service. As stated in economic theory, in the case of a natural monopoly, it is typical that the monopoly decides on the price with its production volume if only it remains on the market. At the same time, it may apply price discrimination to increase profits. In the first stage there are different prices for different consumers, in the second stage there are different prices for different production volumes and in the third stage there are different prices for consumer groups according to price elasticity. It is price discrimination [26] that is often present in the external provision of public services (Table 2).

When recalculating the average values, it was necessary to exclude some extreme cases, such as the municipality of Donovaly, where the first cost per capita indicator was more than 690 EUR. The reason is that the village is a well-known ski and tourist resort with high attendance and that is why it incurs high service costs with a relatively small population.

The lowest values of the first indicator were recorded in the Tvrdošín district with 14.32 EUR, which is also the district with the monopoly of Technical Services Ružomberok. It is here that we see that higher market concentration may not be reflected in higher service prices. Other low values of the first indicator were measured in the districts of Lučenec, Dolný Kubín, Ružomberok and Žiar nad Hronom, in which the monopoly of the Technical Services of Žiar nad Hronom was also recorded. In the districts of Dolný Kubín and Ružomberok, we again observed the almost monopoly position (83% and 85% market share) of the Technical Services of Cities organizations. In the

Table 2. Cost per capita and cost per tonne of waste in the monitored districts

Districts	Cost per capita (in EUR)	Cost per tonne of waste (in EUR)	HHI
Banská Bystrica	26,57	144,84	5 987,65
Brezno	23,62	119,76	3 888,89
Detva	26,07	202,12	7 222,22
Krupina	23,40	160,41	7 551,02
Lučenec	22,25	123,05	5 450
Revúca	24,41	178,81	10 000
Rimavská Sobota	24,27	161,10	4 693,88
Veľký Krtíš	23,42	148,98	6 800
Zvolen	23,89	192,89	4 400
Žarnovica	26,78	127,03	5 000
Žiar nad Hronom	22,74	130,14	10 000
Dolný Kubín	18,96	168,04	7 222,22
Liptovský Mikuláš	23,32	121,50	7 654,32
Martin	26,34	152,02	10 000
Ružomberok	22,72	102,42	7 551,02
Tvrdošín	14,32	137,27	10 000
Žilina	24,09	127,52	10 000

district of Lučenec, two companies competing among the largest in central Slovakia compete, and therefore we assume that their efforts to gain the upper hand led to lower prices for the district. The indicator reached the highest values in the districts of Banská Bystrica, Detva, Žarnovica and Martin. Only in the last district was the monopoly of Brantner s.r.o. In the remaining three districts, Brantner s.r.o. or Marius Pedersen a.s.

Based on the observed values of the indicator, we observe several phenomena – Technical services of cities, which usually operate in only one district and consider them as external suppliers, have the lowest prices for the service, despite the fact that there is no other competition at the same level. On the contrary, the highest prices were recorded in districts where the service was provided by purely private players who did not arise in connection with the city.

Looking at the second indicator, we observe the lowest value of costs per 1 ton of waste in the district of Ružomberok with the amount of 102.42 EUR. It is confirmed that the producer of Technical Services Ružomberok achieves the lowest amount. In addition, low values were recorded in the districts of Lučenec, Liptovský Mikuláš and Brezno. However, Brezno is the district with the lowest HHI value and, as in the district of Lučenec, the largest part of the market is shared by two private players – Profax and Brantner s.r.o. In the Liptovský Mikuláš district, the market was relatively evenly divided between OZO a.s., Liptovský Mikuláš public services and Liptovský Hrádok public services. We recorded the highest values of the second indicator in the district of Detva, which also had high values for the first indicator. In the district of Zvolen, the market is dominated by the private organization Marius Pedersen a.s. The monopoly of Brantner s.r.o. was recorded in Revúca. Here we also assume the same phenomenon as in the first indicator of lower prices of Technical Services of Cities.

We confirm the second research premise (RP$_2$) partially. Looking at the overall HHI values and the values for the individual indicators, we cannot confirm the assumption, but at a closer look at purely private organizations such as Brantner, a.s. or Marius Pedersen, a.s. we see the possibility of lower prices if there are at least two dominant players in the market. In the case of central Slovakia, we see a problem in that, despite the different HHI values, all the districts examined are highly concentrated and therefore it is difficult to estimate how the situation would change in less concentrated markets. Another shortcoming, despite the more than 190 participating municipalities, is the relatively low return rate and therefore the aim of future research is to supplement the observed group with other municipalities.

5 Discussion

Alternative provision of public services by contracting a service is perceived by society as an ideal way of providing services. Due to this, it is assumed that contracting services will bring cost savings together with a higher quality of secured services compared to the internal security of the organization. In recent years, however, domestic and foreign studies have moved away from the original understanding of contracting options and point to possible problems such as transaction costs or market concentration.

In the presented analysis, we focused on the degree of contracting the service of collection and removal of municipal solid waste in central Slovakia. The empirical results we find confirm the conclusions of previous studies. In verifying the research premise (RP$_1$), we find that the market for the provision of municipal solid waste collection and removal services in central Slovakia is a highly concentrated market and characterized by a monopoly or oligopoly with a dominant player. The analysis also briefly introduced the dominant players in the market for the collection and removal of municipal solid waste. We state that the result of the first research premise coincides with the results of foreign studies [2, 13, 17, 32], which often pointed to high market concentration.

To approximate the research, our research confirms the conclusions of the study [13], where the authors found that in only 4 regions out of 20 examined the value of the HHI index was lower than 2,000. The findings of 195 municipalities in 17 districts show that the HHI index is higher. The average HHI of the file is at the level of 7,260. However, we find that in the presence of several players in the market, the price decreases.

However, it is important to note that market concentration processes may also be accompanied by negative effects. Unlike vertical mergers, where a competitor integrates, which does not increase market concentration, only shifts market share [28], horizontal mergers represent a merger of players in order to increase their profits and thus often increase prices indirectly. In both cases, it is a matter of strengthening the position of the market operator to such an extent that it gains a majority share of the market. Mergers thus strengthen market power, resulting in a high level of market concentration resulting in higher prices [11, 18], and growing concerns about declining job opportunities in labor market. For this reason, the supervision of the Antitrust Authority is needed, which must monitor the situation and prevent restrictions of competition.

The influence of subjects on the price is confirmed by the findings of research [30], in which the authors examined the effect of competition on the market of collection and removal of municipal solid waste in the Czech Republic. They describe the theory of the effect of competition, which says that with a larger number of competing companies in the market, prices should theoretically fall. Given the obligation to publish the expected prices at the same time as the prices offered by the company, which follows from the Public Procurement Act, it is possible to verify this theory. In the Pilsen region, the authors recorded prices that were higher than the average prices in other regions. It is in this region that the company Západočeské komunální služby is located, with a market share of almost 50%. However, the authors point out that in order to confirm the theory of the effect of competition, in this case it would be necessary to study the contract in detail. For other larger companies in the market, the regression analysis did not show a trend of rising prices. In the context of our research, we present the example of the municipality of Donovaly, in which the indicator of costs per capita was more than 690 EUR. However, this situation is due to increased tourism in the village. The Donovaly has an officially declared population of 229 inhabitants in 2021. Thus, a possible solution [36] for reducing waste management expenditures in small municipalities with less than 1,000 inhabitants may be the application of intermunicipal cooperation.

The aim of second research premise (RP$_2$) was to verify whether a higher market concentration entails higher prices for contracting the given service, is partly confirmed. However, during its verification, we observe several significant phenomena. When a service is produced by technical services set up by municipalities, which usually operate in only one district and are considered an external supplier, they have the lowest prices for the service, even though there is no other level of competition for them in that district. On the contrary, the highest prices were recorded in districts where the service was provided by purely private companies that were not established in connection with only one municipality. For strategic planning, it is therefore necessary to recognize whether the producer is a purely private company or organization set up in cooperation with the municipality. These results are in line with foreign studies [13, 30, 33, 34], which in several cases have found that in a highly concentrated market – especially in the case of a monopoly – higher prices for service may occur. However, these studies looked at external producers as a whole and did not focus on whether it was a purely private trading company or an organization belonging to another city. However, we agree with the results of research [34] which states that competitiveness has a high impact on the prices of collection and removal of municipal solid waste. Therefore, when providing a public service by contracting, it is necessary to pay more attention to the public procurement process [23] to ensure maximum participation of competitors.

6   Conclusion

Based on the presented research results, we conclude that the contracting of municipal solid waste collection and removal services is provided externally in the monitored municipalities. The contracting of services, that means the contractual relationship between the municipality and the private player providing the service, is applied. Based on this starting point in the paper, we analyze the market concentration as the public services contracting out efficiency factor at the local government level. The main challenge is to concentrate on the market of municipal solid waste collection and removal service providers. The results of the CR and HHI indexes confirm that in the surveyed districts of central Slovakia, the market is highly concentrated, characterized by a monopoly or oligopoly with a dominant player. We point out that the consequence of such a highly concentrated market may be price discrimination in the third degree.

On the other hand, it is confirmed that if there is a monopoly player on the market, which is established with the participation of the municipality, the price of the service may not increase due to the existence of the monopoly. Examples are the municipalities of Tvrdošín, Lučenec, Dolný Kubín or Žiar nad Hronom.

However, if the contracting is provided by a private player who also has a monopoly, economic theory is confirmed. Thus, the monopoly determines the higher price of the service, an example is the ammunition of Detva. However, price developments can eliminate the entry of an additionally strong player. Therefore, when considering the possibility of providing public services by contracting, we recommend municipalities to analyze in advance not only possible economies of scale, but especially market concentration.

Acknowledgements. The paper was prepared within the project VEGA No. 1/0029/21 Management of contracting services in the public sector.

References

1. Bajo, O., Salas, R.: Inequality foundations of concentration mesasures: an application to the Hannah-Kay index. Span. Econ. Rev. **2002**(4), 311–316 (2002)
2. Bel, G., Costas, A.: Do public sector reforms get rusty? Local privatization in Spain. J. Policy Reform **9**(1), 1–24 (2006)
3. Bel, G., Fageda, X., Mur, M.: Does cooperation reduce service delivery costs? Evidence from residential solid waste services. J. Public Adm. Res. Theory **24**(1), 85–107 (2014)
4. Bel, G., Sebo, M.: Introducing and enhancing competition to improve solid waste management in Barcelona. Inst. de Recerca en Economia Aplicada Reg. i Publica **2020**(04), 1–35 (2020)
5. Bel, G., Warner, M.E.: Managing competition in city services: the case of Barcelona. J. Urban Aff. **31**(5), 521–535 (2009)
6. Brauer, J.: Market Share and Market Concentration Measures. Small Arms Survey: Working Paper, vol. 14, pp. 48–52 (2013)
7. Brezina, I., et al.: Analýza absolútnej koncentrácie vybraného odvetvia pomocou Herfindahlovho-Hirschmanovho indexu. Ekonomický časopis **57**(1), 77–94 (2009)
8. Brooks, R.C.: Privatization of government services: an overview and review of the literature. J. Pub. Budgeting Account. Financ. Manage. **16**(4), 472–480 (2004)
9. Capobianco, A.: Market Concentration. https://one.oecd.org/document/DAF/COMP/WD(2018)46/en/pdf. Accessed 02 Apr 2022
10. Common, R., Flynn, N., Mellon, E.: Managing Public Serivces: Competition and Decentralization, 1st edn. Billings & Sons, Worcester (1992)
11. De Loecker, J., Eeckhout, J., Unger, G.: The rise of market power and the macroeconomics implications. Q. J. Econ. **135**(2), 561–644 (2020)

12. Demuth, J., Friederiszick, H.W., Reinhold, S.: Reverse privatization as a reaction to the competitive environment: evidence from solid waste collection in Germany. SSRN Electron. J. (2018). https://doi.org/10.2139/ssrn.3168551
13. Di Foggia, G., Beccarello, M.: Market structure of urban waste treatment and disposal: empirical evidence from the Italian industry. Sustainability **13**(13), 7412–7424 (2021)
14. Dufwenberg, M., Gneezy, U.: Price competition and market concentration: an experimental study. Int. J. Ind. Organ. **18**(1), 7–22 (2000)
15. Evren, A., et al.: Some dominance indices to determine market concentration. J. Appl. Stat. **48**(13–15), 2755–2775 (2021)
16. Gomez-Reino, J.L., Martinez-Vazquez, J.: An international perspectives on the determinants of local government fragmentation. In: Lago-Peñas, S., MartinezVazquez, J. (eds.) The Challenge of Local Government Size. Theoretical Perspectives, International Experience and Policy Reform, pp. 8–54, 1st edn. Edward Elgar Publishing. Cheltenham (2013)
17. Gradus, R., Schoute, M., Dijkgraaf, E.: The effects of market concentration on costs of local public services: empirical evidence from Dutch waste collection. Local Gov. Stud. **44**(1), 86–104 (2018)
18. Gradus, R.H., Dijkgraaf, E.: Cost savings in unit-based pricing of household waste: the case of The Netherlands. Resour. Energy Econ. **26**(4), 353–371 (2003)
19. Grossman, G., et al.: Government fragmentation and public goods provision. J. Politics **79**(3), 823–840 (2017)
20. Halásková, M., Halásková, R., Prokop, V.: Evaluation of efficiency in selected areas of public services in European union countries. Sustainability **10**(12), 1–17 (2018)
21. Hefetz, A., Warner, M.: Privatization and its reverse: explaining the dynamics of the government contracting process. J. Pub. Adm. Res. Theory **14**(2), 171–190 (2004)
22. Heidorn, H., Weche, P.J.: Business Concentration Data for Germany, Jahrbücher für Nationalökonomie und Statistik, pp. 1–11. Pre-published (2020)
23. Horehájová, M., Křápek, M., Nemec, J.: Konkurencia vo verejnom obstarávaní v českom zdravotníctve a jej dopad na finálnu cenu. Český finanční a účetní časopis **16**(1), 23–35 (2021)
24. Jakubus, M., Stejskal, B.: Municipal solid waste management systems in Poland and the Czech Republic. Comp. Study Environ. Prot. Eng. **46**(3), 61–78 (2020)
25. Kita, P.: To certain aspects of concentration and competition in distribution in the context of globalization. J. Econ. **56**(9), 912–924 (2008)
26. Meier, J.K., Dhillon, A., Xu, X.: What sector do consumers perfer for the delivery of 'public'services? A Comparative analysis of the US and China. J. Pub. Nonprofit Aff. **8**(1), 7–28 (2022)
27. Mikušová Meričková, B.: Kontrahovanie služieb vo verejnom sektore – skúsenosti v Slovenskej a v Českej republike, 1st edn. Masarykova univerzita, Brno (2020)
28. Moresi, S., Salop, C.S.: When vertical is horizontal: how vertical mergers lead to increases in "effective concentration." Rev. Ind. Organ. **59**(1), 177–204 (2021)
29. Osborne, S.P.: Delivering public services: time for a new theory? Pub. Manage. Rev. **12**(1), 1–10 (2010)
30. Pavel, J., Slavík, J.: The relationship between competition and efficiency of waste-collection services in the Czech Republic. Local Gov. Stud. **44**(2), 275–296 (2017)
31. Savas, S.E.: Alternatives for Delivering Public Services. Toward Improved Performance, 1st edn. Routladge, New York (1997)
32. Soukopová, J., Malý, I., Ficek, V.: Má konkurenční prostředí vliv na výdaje obcí na nakládání s komunálním odpadem v ČR? Waste Forum **2013**(4), 231–239 (2013)
33. Soukopová, J., Malý, I.: Vliv konkurence na výši výdajů na nakládání s odpady obcí Jihomoravského kraje. Waste Forum **2012**(4), 173–183 (2012)

34. Soukopová, J., Vaceková, G.: Competition and municipal waste management expenditure: evidence from the Czech Republic Olomouc Region. Sci. Pap. Univ. Pr. **2015**(35), 128–138 (2015)
35. Soukopová, J., Bakoš, E.: Nekalá konkurence a její vpliv na výši výdaju obcí a nákládaní s odpady. Sci. Pap. Univ. Pr. D **39**(1), 189–199 (2017)
36. Soukopová, J., Sládeček, T.: Intermunicipal cooperation in municipal waste management and its effects on cost-effectiveness. Waste Forum **2018**(1), 17–25 (2018)

The Value Chains in Smart Regions – The Role of ICT Through the Eyes of Consumers

Lenka Veselovská[ID], Mária Pomffyová[(✉)][ID], and Mária Sirotiaková[ID]

Matej Bel University in Banská Bystrica, Institute of Managerial systems in Poprad, Francisciho 8, 05801 Poprad, Slovakia
mpomffyova@umb.sk
https://www.ef.umb.sk/index_e.asp?uid=615

Abstract. The aim of this paper is to examine the role of the use of ICT in raising own and general awareness and their impact on value chain and business transparency across the EU. An overview of the personal attitudes and preferences of 987 Slovak respondents by the statistical analyzing their answers to the questions of a questionnaire survey on the issue of dual quality of daily consumption products sold in the European Union are used. The measure of influence of socio-demographic and socio-economic determinants on the preference for the use of ICT and ways of accessing open data in the process of raising own awareness will be examined by verifying the truthfulness of the stated hypotheses. In order to verify the relationships between the dependent and independent variables we use the regression and correlation analyzes supported by SPSS program.

Raising awareness and transparency of relations can increase the pressure to increase the volume of purchases of such healthy foods or other commodities, where, in addition to quality, emphasis is placed on ensuring that fundamental human rights, health or safety are not violated at all stages of their life cycles. In addition, also participation in public dialogue related to the other adverse effects that could have a harmful impact on society or the environment should not be suppressed. Therefore, in conclusion we summarize the recommendations on how to increase the transparency of mutual dialogues, which can enhance the unique domestic production of smart regions in sustainable ways.

Keywords: Smart cities · Participation · Value chains · ICT · Consumers

1 Introduction

Current COVID-19 crisis has shown both organizations and individual consumers the need for ICT to conduct their everyday activities. Therefore, this crisis broadened the horizons of our understanding of access to information and connection to public and private institutions, acting not only in the states themselves in the EU but also abroad. ICT had provided various opportunities to use technology to make people's lives easier even before the pandemic [1–5].

An interesting and unique way to apply smart technologies is their application in value chains, as their transparency and general knowledge awareness increase and thus

O. Gervasi et al. (Eds.): ICCSA 2022 Workshops, LNCS 13382, pp. 219–234, 2022.
https://doi.org/10.1007/978-3-031-10592-0_17

the natural environment for innovation created is. The need to develop various research or testing capacities and promoting the exchange of best practices between the actors involved, cannot be done without financial support, necessary legislation changes or legalization of forms of cooperation. These processes are strongly dependent on the cooperation and participation of different consumer organizations, public and non-governmental organizations, often operating also in different EU Member States or abroad. It is also confirmed in [6], where the authors say that the application of smart technologies can increase the sustainability of business activities, but it is effective only with active support by coherent regional policies. The authors in [7] explored the challenges of process of innovation in specific regions in Europe stressing out the finding of lack of digitalization as main barrier of progress. On the other hand, authors in [8] and [9] emphasize the role of people as consumers in regional development and the consequent need for their access to digital technologies.

It is clear that the current pool of knowledge lacks the evidence of connection between role of ICT and consumer engagement in regional affairs. This paper provides an innovative perspective on ICT application in smart regions using the opinions of consumers as baseline. The main aim was to explore to perception of connection between ICT and smart regions though the opinions of consumers. Partial goals were:

– to describe the connection between ICT, consumers and smart regions;
– to examine the impact of socio-demographic and socio-economic characteristics of consumers on value perception;
– to describe the level of participation of marginal groups on regional or global problem-solving activities;
– to develop guidelines for higher participations of marginal groups and increase their trust in regional or global governments (SR or EU) using the higher digitalization as a preferred tool.

2 Literature Review

Food safety is considered a part of public wellbeing, and any form of mismanagement by its producer can cause serious harm to all those involved in the supply chain, adversely affecting public health [10]. This area is also invoked by manufacturers who argue that they comply with certain rules and regulations in the production of products, given at national or international level, so as not to violate them. This is not always the case and therefore attention needs to be paid to this issue.

2.1 The Current Views on the Issue of Dual Quality of Goods and Possibilities for Participation

In the past, several tests have been performed to confirm the existence of dual quality in several countries [11], but a uniform testing methodology was lacking. Already in 2017, at the initiative of the Minister of Agriculture of the Slovak Republic at the Council of the EU, the fight for consumer rights began, which resulted in the inclusion of the dual quality of foods in the list of Unfair Commercial Practices. The European Commission's

Joint Research Centre (JRC) developed an identical methodology for comparing product quality and composition and launched its dual-quality testing in 2018 to analyze 1380 food products in 19 EU countries (also mentioned by [12]). Subsequently, in 2019 also testing of other products, not only food, was launched. The directive on identical methodology was issued in 04/2019 by the European Commission and individual member states began to apply it to their legislation.The European Parliament responded to this situation approving the Directive (EU) 2019/2161 on better enforcement and modernization of Union consumer protection rules as a part of the "New Deal for Consumers". The aim was to ensure legal clarity in the assessment of possible cases of dual quality, to strengthen the powers of consumer protection authorities and also the possibility of imposing sanctions on producers (up to 4% of turnover) [13].

According to the European Commission, products may have different consistencies in different countries if manufacturers state this in the formulation on the product. Thus, it is not a legislative problem, but an ethical problem, because if consumers buy the same product in different places, they assume that it is the same [14]. As stated in [15], the issue of dual food quality has three planes. The first level is product safety. Although the composition of products in some countries is different in its components, it does not matter, because the products are still safe and are made from raw materials that are allowed in that country. If different raw materials are allowed in different countries, manufacturers will adapt to this regulation and choose the most advantageous option for them (often cheap, but less tasty, etc.). At the same time, manufacturers state that they provide all the information on the packaging, thus also complying with all regulations.

In the context of food safety in the EU, there is a Rapid Alert System (RAS), focusing on, for example, the presence of foreign objects in food or the concentration of food supplements. The feeling of Central and Eastern European consumers that they are a "rubbish bin" is therefore partly justified (as a 2017 survey on a sample of 1 446 samples showed, most of the contaminated food registered in the RAS system came from Eastern Europe [11]).

If we examine what legislation or measures define the transparent behaviour of companies, it can be said that in food safety measures, the basic management tool for monitoring compliance and gaining customer confidence is the introduction of a food safety management system (FSMS) according to the international standard ISO 22000: 2018, valid after 29.06.2021 [16]. This International Standard specifies the requirements for a structured food safety management system by integrating the principles of the Hazard Analysis Critical Control Points (HACCP) system and its application steps, developed by the Codex Alimentary Commission, with the system of prerequisite programs (PRPs). Adherence to it supports more effective control of processes, employees, suppliers, raw materials, as well as final products. The external benefits are gaining consumer confidence in food safety, improving the company's image in the eyes of the consumer and control authorities.

In Slovakia, the State Veterinary and Food Administration of the Slovak Republic and its regional authorities (RVPS) are responsible for food quality and safety control. They carry out supervision and inspections, about which they report regularly (monthly and random). They also have the power to receive suggestions, complaints or petitions from various bodies, as well as to provide information. Their admission is organized in the form of a web interface with the possibility of any form of submission, written, oral (documented in writing), but also through the electronic filing office - portal www.sloven sko.sk, and in the case of suggestions also in the form of an electronic form [17]. They are the basis by which the right to punish either sellers or manufacturers is enforced. The solution of these issues is also focused on the participation of citizens, who as consumers have the opportunity to address the responsible authorities. The degree of participation depends on their willingness to engage, but also on their ability to use electronic forms of communication and personal verification.

However, in addition to legislation and ethics, dual quality also has an economic dimension, which is not given the necessary attention in tests, as price comparison is usually not the primary goal of testing [11]. According to several tests, goods purchased in Western European countries not only had a healthier composition, they were still cheaper in the same package at the same weight (or were at the same price but with a higher weight) [17]. Therefore, we decided to pay attention to the issue of prices and costs. We will examine the preferences of the respondents, but they cannot be generalized. The existing pay gap in Central and Eastern Europe in comparing to Western Europe and such information create an unfair sense of their position in the EU single market.

2.2   The Ways of Supporting the Sustainable Development of Regions

Extending the participation of the widest possible range of stakeholders in solving a certain problem depends on their degree of willingness and interest to participate in solving related problems, whether on the part of a certain system or on the part of managed entities, all the more in the case of living systems, where the transparency and smart technologies have their place.

The state strives to develop wider public participation in public policy-making, with mutual interactions to be built on a platform for the strategic use of information and communication infrastructure and services. In Slovakia, the national projects Participation 1 and 2 address this issue [18]. The aim is to eliminate barriers - to explore the possibilities of open dialogue and to network experts in order to create a conceptual framework to support the creation of participatory public dialogue partnerships. Partnerships are to develop both towards state administration, towards regional territorial self-government, as well as in the field of mutual information, learning and cognition, and in the field of building mutual trust, in strengthening the perception of the role of various institutions and the public. An example of support for citizens is the portal www.slovensko.sk and their electronic identity that give possibility to connect with local, regional state or non-profit organizations with the aim to solve various things or other problems. Barriers of non-use of these tools may be related to their lower level of practical and digital skills, as well as their ignorance of forms of participation and the creation of conditions to increase comprehensive participation of stakeholders (city, region or state) [18]. This portal is also used as a tool for communication in matters such as food or goods security.

Part of the project is also to develop Knowledge Strategies - combining academic knowledge by linking national project and teaching, dedicated to participation and participatory public policy making. Creating a unified environment for KS increases the pressure to grow the need for innovation named as open innovations [19].

The Smart Cities Action Plan is a concept and its task was to follow up on the Action Plan of the Intelligent Industry of the Slovak Republic, which is covered by the Ministry of Economy of the Slovak Republic with the aim of supporting smart ecosystems as a whole with preconditions for developing the market of intelligent and innovative solutions. The primary goals are to improve the quality of life of citizens or to increase the quality and efficiency of public services provided by public administration. At the same time, it is an effort to support the emergence of Slovak innovative solutions and new companies [20, 21].

The "open innovation" concept is described as [22]:

– a distributed innovation process based on purposively managed knowledge flows across organizational boundaries, using pecuniary and non-pecuniary mechanisms in line with the organization's business model [23];
– moreover, the use of internal sources of knowledge and skills to generate new ideas.

The National Project Support for the Development of the Creative Industry in Slovakia, which is financed from the European Regional Development Fund through the Operational Program Research and Innovation, also presents an opportunity to support innovation. The focus of projects is also the issue of healthy food and the environment, population health and digitization [24]. Local, regional and national public authorities, organizations governed by public law, international organizations and private organizations, including private enterprises with legal personality, are eligible for funding.

The success rate of each concept depends largely on both the ICT skills of the individuals and the degree and willingness of stakeholder and city participation.

2.3 Strategies to Support the Expansion of Digitalization in the Slovak Republic and Sources of Their Financing

In the development of conditions for wider use of ICT, it is important to get the support of the state, which seeks to increase the quality and development of digital services and infrastructure of the new generation access network and make them accessible to a wide range of interested parties. Individual EU countries can draw support for digitization from Eurofunds.

The Digital Transformation Strategy of Slovakia 2030 is a framework supraministerial government strategy that defines the policy and specific priorities of Slovakia in the context of innovative technologies and global mega-trends of the digital age (Artificial Intelligence, IoT, 5G technology). It is formed as the vision, where the aim is to develop a functioning information society and an innovative digital economy in which businesses can innovate and create sustainable jobs that can fill a high-quality, retrained workforce with advanced digital skills. The Ministry of Investment, Regional Development and Informatization of the Slovak Republic (MIRRI), as the manager of Eurofunds in the Slovak Republic, is preparing a long-term EU budget, named the Multi-annual Financial Framework 2021–2027 [25]. These are the Partnership Agreement and the Slovakia Operational Program, where a broadly participatory approach is applied in the preparation of the new Slovakia Program (PSK). The Partnership for Cohesion

Policy 2020 + working group is working on its preparation, where a wide range of socio-economic partners is involved in the discussion in the workshops. After incorporating the comments of the European Commission in April 2022, the formal approval of the PSK is expected in the first half of 2022. The first calls from the new Slovakia Program should be announced in the second half of 2022.

As a support of global digitization, innovation and education there was also formed the Digital Europe Programme that will address complement the funding available through other EU programmes, such as the Horizon Europe programme for research and innovation and the Connecting Europe Facility for digital infrastructure, the Recovery and Resilience Facility and the Structural funds, etc. It is a part of the next long-term EU budget, the Multiannual Financial Framework 2021–2027.

The acquisition of finances from EU funds is conditioned by the declaration of an overview of the situation in the area of their development, while it is necessary to have an overview of the fulfilment of ex ante conditionality as a tool to assess the readiness of Member States to implement selected investment priorities.

The Ministry of Finance of the Slovak Republic based the elaboration of the document for monitoring the development of the digital society and economy 2014–2020 on the national Strategic Document for the growth of digital services and the infrastructure of the new generation access network (2014–2020) [26]. This document points to the need to meet the two ex ante conditionalities defined under thematic objective 2: "Improving access to information and communication technologies as well as their use and quality". The document defines the Digital Economy and Society Index (DESI), which maps the level of internet connection (broadband penetration, speed and affordability), internet skills, online activities from news tracking to shopping, as well as the degree of development of key digital technologies (electronic invoices, cloud services, e-commerce, etc.). This composite indicator is a combination of more than 30 indicators, the composition and selection of which the European Commission can change over the years. For this reason, the target values are not set for the index, as was the case, i.e., in the Digital Agenda for Europe [27].

Based on the result of the DESI index for 2018, we can assess that at least the basic level of digital skills is reached by 59% of Slovaks, which is above the EU average (57%). At the same time, however, it is necessary to create conditions for digitization. As follows from various surveys and comparisons with the situation abroad, in the Slovak Republic, the inhabitants of disadvantaged groups are at risk of digital poverty, which makes them marginalized groups. In this regard, the Slovak government is trying to minimize such segregation, for example, projects that are aimed at improving the digital skills of seniors and disadvantaged groups in public administration (worth almost 990,000 Euros). The plan for the spread of the Internet is also part of the broadband plan until 2030, where the state strives to have all Slovak households connected to ultra-fast broadband internet [25].

According to Eurostat, the percentage of the population with insufficient ICT skills for the labour market was also expected to fall from 24.7% in 2011 to 10% in the case of specific outcome indicators for eInclusion support.

The effective use of electronic support for information, business and commerce, the use of open data, cloud capabilities, as well as support, will enable them to perform intelligent analyzes in modelling systems in a virtual environment [27]. For some indicators, it will not be possible to deduct the full achievement of the target until 2023, as the eligibility of expenditure for the European Structural and Investment Funds, which are the most important instrument for financing information activities, is set at 31.12.2023 (so-called rule n + 3) [26].

Effective digitization of business and work with information increase the turnover of SMEs, and determine their interest in innovation and willingness to invest in the integration of technology and education, in research and development [29]. The strong positive correlation between competitiveness and the existence of specialized R&D departments leads to a higher willingness to invest in ICT. Nevertheless, in Slovak Republic, support for innovation is beginning to develop very slowly.

Making assumptions requires knowledge of the requirements and preferences of the population, as well as their interest in expanding their knowledge potential. The ways to increase their confidence in responsible organizations, how to stimulate their interest in participating in solving problems is the digitization with the aim to create environment for knowledge sharing and dissemination.

3   Methodology

To obtain the main aim of that article we explored the basic assumptions how the degree of digitization influences the participatory government in smart regions and also on how the government regulates the conditions of financing from EU funds in relation to SMEs and smart solutions in conditions SR.

Data was collected through survey during the period of December 2018 and April 2019 on a sample of 987 buyers (in the age range of 16 to 75 and over - with about 85 respondents over 75, by gender: female: 65.7%, male: 34.3%) of daily consumption products in Slovak republic. Sample file consisted of buyers who differed in their age, gender, household income and living locations throughout the country. The only condition was that they were the ones who purchase daily consumption goods for themselves or their household. The survey was conducted through a questionnaire method collected personally, and by e-mail. The representativeness of selected sample file was verified through the Chi-square test according to the criteria of customers' gender. The base file consisted of all people living in SR. The data concerning the base file was obtained from the Statistical Office of the Slovak republic.

We set the hypotheses with the aim to exam the extent to which selected factors affect and who opinion increases the degree of transparency of relationships and what role the general level of information and the degree of digitization play in this process. To perform both the model's variables preliminary analyzis, and to verify the validity of hypotheses we used the tools of SPSS software and Power BI tools. The multiple regression analyzes will make it possible to assess statistically significant and statistically less significant variables and the strength of the relationships between them. In this way, it is possible to determine which of these variables have the strongest relation to the dependent variable (participation or the need to clarify business transparency).

We established the following hypotheses:

H1: Individual variables (e.g. socio-demographic, socio-economic, degree of education, etc.) will be important predictors for all types of participation.
H1a: Age and education as socio-demographic factors are decisive factors that increase the level of interest in information and trust in the responsible authorities.
H1b: The amount of income as a socio-economic factor is a decisive factor that increases the level of interest in information and trust in the responsible authorities.
H1c: The amount of income is a decisive socio-economic factor that increases the level of interest in the quality of purchased products.
H2: the level of knowledge of the issue is an important predictor of participation in the solution of the issue.
H3: Confidence towards other people and between groups will be an important predictor that will influence the ways of informing each other and the level of shopping behavior and involvement in the issue.
H4: Belief in the effectiveness of citizen participation will be a significant predictor of participation.
H4a: The level of knowledge of unfair practices has a decisive influence on the perception of the importance of the dual quality problem.
H4b: Knowledge of assessing the nature of the problem decisively affects confidence in the effectiveness of participation.
H5: Trust resp. distrust in the institution will be a significant predictor of willingness to participate - willingness to inform/be informed.
H6: The region and its support for digitization is a decisive factor that increases the level of interest in information and trust in the responsible authorities.

The results of such research have fundamental implications for public dialogue, as they will make it possible to identify barriers to the use of ICT to spread awareness of the problem and also to reveal and compare the strength of the relationship of individual variables to participation in solving the problem.

4   Results and Discussion

It was discovered that more than 15% of respondents had all the necessary information, 69% of mayors had partial information, and the remaining almost 16% of respondents said they had no information at all on this agenda. The analyzes of the results were processed as a basis for further work within the national ZMOS project entitled Modernization of Local Territorial Self-Government within the Operational Program Effective Public Administration from the ESF [30].

At the same time, we were looking for certain connections in our survey on the problem of dual quality of goods of the same brand in individual EU countries. By analyzing the respondents' answers to selected questions, we tried to find out various aspects concerning the preference of methods of finding information and knowledge sharing about the given issue with regard to socio-demographic or socio-economic impacts. We examine their impact within all hypotheses.

According to the statistical evaluation of the number of answers to question 4, more than 89% of respondents heard about the problem of 2-quality food (where mean = 0.89 with st. dev. 0.31). People in productive age (from 26 to 45, that was 395 respondents) or people in older productive age (from 46–65, 278 respondents) were informed well than other (Phi = 0.212). The H1a hypothesis was partially confirmed.

We further examined how often respondents search for this information or what information they follow. There is a slight dependence between the frequency of information retrieval by reading the information on the packaging to control food quality (Phi = 0.229, but with a high degree of significance, at 0.01). The average value of information reached 1.36, which means that they find out information in a cursory rather than a thorough manner, and if they check the quality, they do so occasionally or consistently than always (mean = 2.55 with st. dev 0.301). Addiction is linear. About 12.77% of respondents do not follow this information at all. Based on the results of the regression analysis, it can be argued that if the respondents heard about the dual quality problem in the EU (mean of the awareness rate is 0.89, where 1 means yes, 0 no), they consider the dual quality problem to be moderate (with mean = 0.83).

The relationship between perceptions and the importance of the dual quality problem in the EU is moderate (Phi = 0.524), which means that if they routinely monitor quality, they attach average importance to threats to life safety. Hypothesis H2 is verified as true. We found that this information is most frequently viewed by people of working age (26 to 45) or people of advanced working age (46 to 65) (socio-demographic characteristics). From the point of view of education, this issue is of interest to more university-educated people than medium school-educated people, who either do not follow it at all or follow it occasionally. Hypothesis H1b is verified as true.

From the point of view of monitoring the type of criterion that has an impact on shopping behaviour, depending on the income categories, we found that this issue is sometimes monitored more by people with higher incomes (1001–1200) or with incomes from 801–1000. Of the available criteria, respondents will be most affected by price and quality (both with mean 0.79, where quality was a little more preferable (st. dev. 0.405 with Phi = 0.250) as in opposite to price (where st. dev. is 0.407) which a lesser extent (Phi = 0.117) influences purchasing decisions. Another criterion of interest to respondents incomes is product experience (mean is 0.6 with st. dev. 0.490, Phi = 0.172) to a lesser extent (Phi = 0.117) influences purchasing decisions. The risk to health also affects the choice when buying, although with a low degree of preference for this criterion (mean = 0.20 with st. dev. 0.404, Phi = 0.224).

If we evaluate the dependence of the criteria on each other, the highest - medium indirect dependence is between the experience with the product and the risk to health (Phi = 0.297), which can be interpreted that the higher the experience with the product, the less fears the risk of endangering the health or unavailability of the store (Phi = −0.225) or the product (Phi = −0.197). On the other hand, the less experience the consumer has, the greater the emphasis on the risk to health. There is also a significant indirect dependence between the quality and availability of the store (Phi = −0.200) or product (Phi = −0.194). The H1c hypothesis was confirmed.

About the problem of dual quality of goods, respondents learned mostly from the media (mean = 0.72, st. dev. = 0.014). The evaluation of the dependencies using the correlation table of relations shows that if they have personal experience, they search less for the media (Phi $= -0.113$), but rather rely on the experience of a friend (0.123). Personal experiences (Phi $= 0.213$), as friend's experiences (Phi $= 0.143$), or media knowledge (Phi $= 0.078$) have a higher weight in assessing the importance of health risks. The H3 hypothesis was confirmed.

Next we examined the respondents' opinion on whether they were hindered by unfair practices of manufacturers, we found a slight direct dependence between the salary groups of the respondents (0.158, at $p = 0.003 < 0.005$). Such practices hinder the third salary group the most - from € 1200–1600, (mean 1.52, st. dev. 0.772). In the group from € 800–1200, where (mean $= 1.71$ with st. dev $= 0.762$) such practices are not decisive. It means the socio-economical criterion has a positive impact on the interest in solving quality issues. Participation efficiency is influenced by income as a socio-economic factor, which is also confirms the H1 hypothesis.

About 81.1% of respondents are very obstructing (45.8%) or obstructing (37.7%) by such practices of manufacturers (mean $= 1.54$ with st. dev. 0.663) and attach much more importance to this problem than to who do not attach importance to (mean $= 1.96$ with st. dev. 0.998). There is a medium dependence (Phi $= 0.442$), which was also confirmed by the Independent Samples T tests (Levene's Test for Equality of Variances). Hypothesis H4a is verified as true.

Of the practices, they are most hampered by different component ratios (mean $= 0.84$ with st. dev. 0.368), different substitute quality (mean $= 0.64$ with st. dev. 0.480), or different raw material ratio (mean $= 0.32$ with st. dev. 0.468). The strongest indirect slight dependence of dissatisfaction was manifested by the different ratio of raw materials and poor quality of ingredients (Phi $= -0.229$), or product quality and substitute quality (Phi $= -0.216$). Dissatisfaction with the proportion of raw materials is directly caused by both factors (quality of substitution or ratio of raw materials).

According to the age or income, statistically significant is the obstacle ratio of components depending on age, where by $p = 0.023 < 0.05$ is Phi $= 0.068$), where this criterion is most observed by people of working age (from 26–65). If the manufacturer uses a better replacement, they are less bothered by the poor quality of processing (where for $p = 0.027 < 0.05$ with st. dev. 0.096). That confirm the Hypothesis H1 and H2.

People over 75-aged are most bothered by the quality of the replacement, the ratio of ingredients and the weight of the products. Preference for monitoring the composition of goods in working age and in older age categories may be related to a healthy lifestyle, where if the goods have a different composition, it may contain more allergens that can endanger human health. These criteria are crucial and need to be addressed.

Next, only in the case of the quality of compensation we found a statistically significant relationship with a weak dependency (Phi $= 0.106$) to income groups (where $p = 0.011 < 0.05$). The most significant differences in preferences were in groups with income from € 800–1200 and over € 1600 and more, and subsequently in € 1200–1600. Other criteria (where $p > 0.05$) do not statistically significantly affect respondents' dissatisfaction depending on income groups. The quality of compensation for age groups shows a higher dependence (Phi $= 0.068$).

To summarize the overall validity of hypothesis H1, people of working age are more active, interested in quality (especially in the age range of 25–45). In the case of the criterion relating to producers' practices, H1 was only partially confirmed, with signs of age dependence being significant in particular for the ratio of ingredients (Phi = 0.068) or the quality of the ingredients (Phi = 0.096). Depending on the income, the H2 hypothesis was only confirmed in the case of the quality of the replacement (Phi = 0.106).

They consider the problem of dual quality (question 12) to be a significant ethical-legislative problem (46.15%) (depending on the income categories the perception is weakly statistically significant, p = 0.011 with Phi = 0.022). If it is an economic problem (19.13%), then it is only an ethical problem (14.05%). About 9.79% cannot distinguish what the problem is, where we found a statistically significant relationship between age and ignorance to assess the form of the problem (25–45 with p = 0.04 with Phi = 0.09). If we evaluate the relationship between the nature of the problem, we found a moderate indirect dependence between ethical-legislative and ethical nature (Phi = −0.412). It follows that if such cases occur, the less they are dealt with legislatively, the more they perceive them as a breach of ethics, and customers perceive this as a frivolous supplier, who should be subject to legislative sanctions. There is less indirect dependence on the economic nature (Phi = −0.286) and on the purely legislative nature of the problem (Phi = −0.241). The economic problem related to the occurrence of cases where they perceive the efforts of producers to reduce their costs at the expense of the quality of goods, especially in the eastern EU countries [28]. Hypothesis H4b has been confirmed.

In answer to question 13, who should solve the problem of dual quality of goods on behalf of consumers, respondents do not prefer the solution by government measures. The difference in opinion of age categories is weakly significant (especially at 26–45 years, where p = 0.0499 < 0.05 with Phi = 0.115). Thus, national institutions (e.g. the Slovak Trade Inspection Authority, the National Testing Institutions, and universities) should solve the problem rather, where in total up to 43.56% of respondents prefer these options. In contrast, 37.2% of respondents think that the European Commission should address this issue (age: p = 0.026 < 0.05, with Phi = 0.097). Customers themselves (by boycotting brands, reporting them to SOI, etc.) are not very willing to take on their responsibilities (only 9.02% prefer it). We did not notice the effect of income differences. Hypotheses 3 and 5 have been confirmed, where the predominant socio-demographic impact prevails.

We further examined the degree of need for interest in the problem of dual quality goods. In this case, all respondents said they wanted to be informed (mean = 0.9, st. dev. 0.295). In this case, age shows a weak dependence on the expression of interest, where again for people of working age information is the most preferred (24–45 with Phi = 0.029). People who make purchases want to be more informed (p < 0.01 with Phi = 0.132). As a source of information, they would prefer the following options: media coverage in dailies or weeklies (mean = 0.47 with st. dev. 0.499), a transnational internet portal (page) (mean = 0.20 with st. dev. 0.399), together with Phi = −0.279, and 14.83% would prefer current information of the Slovak Trade Inspection Authority, 14.08% would like information on these cases to be provided in the form of a regular report by the Prime Minister and also the Ministry of Agriculture and Rural Development of the Slovak Republic (Phi = 0,304). Only 10.73% of respondents would welcome a regular report from the European Commission.H2 and H4 were confirmed.

The respondents surveyed consider their own experience to be the most credible sources of information (mean $= 0.78$, st. dev. 0.413), and it is verified both in the family (Phi $= 0.169$) or in acquaintances (Phi $= 0.078$). This choice being most often preferred by up to 32.68% of respondents with incomes from € $801–1000$, as well as from € $1001–1200$, which do not prefer acquaintances knowledge ($p = 0.048 < 0.05$ with Phi $= 0.089$). By age category (from $26–45$ years old) more trust their own experience (Phi $= 0.132$). Media preference is also age-dependent ($p = 0.011 < 0.05$, with Phi $= 0.107$). The environment will affect those who make purchases ($p = 0.045 < 0.05$ with Phi $= 0.064$).

Young people prefer more information from acquaintances (48.85%) than the results of scientific research (45.37% in total). As the results of our research show, the media and results of scientific research are most believed by people with a medium school education, followed by high university-educated respondents and university students in their bachelor studies (Phi $= 0.107$). These results are moderately less affected than information from acquaintances or family (Phi $= -0.330$). AlsoH3 and H4 were confirmed.

If the respondents were to inform themselves about the problem of dual quality of goods, 82.37% would be willing to inform (mean $= 0.83$, st. dev. 0.38), especially medium schools and university-educated people and those who make purchases. Other would not be willing to inform at all. Women (mean $= 0.91$, st. dev 0.72) are more willing to inform than men (mean $= 0.82$, st. dev 0.77). From the point of view of the size of the seat, the inhabitants of smaller settlements in the Prešov Region (seat up to $5,000$ or up to $10,000$ inhabitants) are willing to inform, and then from larger settlements (seat from $20,000$ to $50,000$ inhabitants in the BB Region).

As a tool with which they would like to inform, respondents most often chose a specialized website (after registration the possibility to directly insert information, photos, etc.), (mean $= 0.34$, st. dev. 0.475), sharing via social networks - on a specialized profile (mean $= 0.22$, st. dev. 0.41), and information via the mobile application (mean $= 0.14$, st. dev. 0.345). They also trust the Slovak Trade Inspection Authority (mean $= 0.17$, st. dev.0.377). As a result, they are open to the digitization and use of ICT and the tools they support and they consider the available means of transmitting information to be credible and easily accessible. Hypothesis 6 was partially confirmed.

The specialized site is most preferred by residents of up to $10,000$ inhabitants, and then by up to $5,000$ inhabitants, followed by respondents from larger settlements. In small settlements, the situation is almost the same, which means that the size of the settlement does not significantly affect the willingness to use different forms of electronic communication. The lowest income groups prefer social networks (Phi $= 0.062$), a specialized portal or state control institution, followed by mobile applications. Their use has a significant impact on dual quality control at the time of purchase (Phi $= 0.092$). This confirmed hypothesis H5, but hypothesis H6 in the section on the impact of differences in digitization of regions was not confirmed.

We further examined the preferences of respondents in the area of measures proposed by them, where respondents propose to distinguish goods with different quality by different packaging and different price (mean $= 0.77$, st. dev. 0.422), or to provide information on the packaging and differentiate by price (Phi $= -0.354$), or differentiate different packaging, while the price may remain the same (Phi $= -0.328$). Only 1.32% of respondents prefer to search information only on the Internet.

The number of respondents whose dual quality problems have affected is dependent on income categories ($p = 0.04 < 0.05$, Phi $= 0.117$) where more well informed are people in (€ 800–1200 or in € 1400 and more). The impact of age categories was not significant. The impact of education manifested itself, both among medium school and university-educated respondents. If the respondents were influenced by the information, they are also willing to provide this information (Phi $= 0.334$) and they attach importance to the problem (Phi $= 0.289$) and they want to be informed (Phi $= 0.339$). This confirmed the validity of hypothesis H5.

5 Conclusion

Despite the helplessness within the situation around double quality of foods in 2017–2018, the assumption that the increase in information leads to an increase in the respondents' interest in dealing with this issue, has been confirmed. It was reflected in the need to address the issue at both national and EU level. We found that the difference in the quality of goods in the EU greatly hinder or hinder to customers (81.1%), and they consider this problem to be both ethical, legislative (46.15%) and economic (19.13%). An example is our own and global awareness of double quality in the field of food quality control, where based on customer suggestions, authorities at national levels, as well as the EC, which were trusted by respondents in our survey (25.56% in total), encouraged steps to address this issue. Media coverage has led to an increase in information awareness, which has led to a solution to the problem both by countries and by EU, which has manifested itself in the creation of sets of measures and changes of directives. As we can see in [13], the JRC created he unified testing methodology and extend the testing not only foodstuffs but also other categories of goods [31].

In 2022 the permanent monitoring centre was formed. The evaluation of the means of regular collection of comparative information, whether at global or regional level, is carried out. In Slovakia, the State Veterinary and Food Administration of the Slovak Republic and its regional authorities (RVPS) are responsible for food quality and safety control. To strengthen the participation there are formed the branches of organizations in the regions, such as the departments of food hygiene, food safety and cosmetics, while they work within the advisory centre for health protection and support at the RÚVZ (RIPH) based in the cities of regions. They also carry out surveillance and inspections and regularly publish reports (monthly and random).

Such institutions also have the power to receive suggestions, complaints or petitions from various subjects, as well as to provide information. In this example, we see how participation in problem solving is developed. Submission of complaints is organized in the form of a web interface with the possibility of any form of submission, written, oral (also documented in writing), but also through an electronic filing system - portal www.slovensko.sk, and in the case of complaints also in the form of an electronic form [17]. However, the degree of participation depends on their willingness to engage, but also on their ability to use electronic forms of communication and personal verification. As we further deduced that if people do not follow the information on the packaging, they will obtain information from other sources. This is also confirmed by the degree of preferences of the media (mean = 0.72, st. dev. 0.014), social networks or websites as sources of our own and shared information.

Based on the personal experience of the respondents, we state that even though a citizen is the owner of an eID Card, if he does not need to communicate with the public administration often, his digital soft skills are weak, which weakens his communication opportunity. Another problem is its connectivity to the Internet, where user verification sometimes takes a long time or does not work correctly. The solution here is broadband internet as part of a digitization policy, especially for marginalized groups. Since young people and older categories observe the behaviour of family, surroundings and acquaintances, they often follow them on social media; it is assumed that they are interested in this issue and that they will address it.

In our opinion, the values of digital society indicators related to skills as well as the level of Internet use will be exceeded (countdown in 2023). It is due to the situation with the measures of the Government of the Slovak Republic in connection with the COVID 19 pandemic, where purchases and provision of services as well as other communication activities are increasingly moving into the field of e-space, forcing the population to learn to use e-connectivity, which is confirmed by the perception of the low impact of the digital divide by region or settlement size.

Reports and other activities of control institutions are the basis to strengthen the powers of consumer protection authorities and the possibility of imposing sanctions on producers. Media coverage contributes to the detection of unfair practices and to the resolution of cases in public [32], thus creating an opportunity for the transparency of chains and raising awareness of unfair practices. Targeted teaching or labelling of goods and advertising can also help. We want to address these issues in our further research, as it is a way of preconditions for developing the sustainable development of the regions, by raising awareness of the possibilities of exploiting the potential of the regions.

The EC has also proposed measures to strengthen and improve the existing system of production and sale [24]:

- greater sustainability by enabling manufacturers to assess their social, environmental and economic sustainability measures in product specifications;
- increased protection of IPOs on the Internet, in particular as regards sales through online platforms,
- strengthening the role of producer groups so that they can manage, promote and develop their PPPs by having access to anti-counterfeiting and customs authorities in all EU countries;

The shortened and simplified registration procedure combines both different technical and procedural rules, leading to a uniform GI registration procedure for EU or non-EU applicants. The Commission proposal is the result of an extensive consultation process. We can see that successful implementation is heavily dependent on a mutual public dialogue with the all of stakeholders.

- Voluntary certification schemes at national level or run by private operators can also help consumers to be sure of the quality of the products they buy.

– In addition to EU schemes, there are a large number of private and national food quality schemes or logos that cover a range of initiatives and are used between businesses or between businesses and consumers.

These measures also help to reduce the pressure of control authorities due to raising the quality and safety standard, supports the easier introduction and promotion of new products on the market, as well as easier and more effective company's marketing position in the segment.

Acknowledgement. This contribution was supported by the project No. 1/0134/22, "Changes in consumer behaviour due to the COVID-19 pandemic with intent to predict its development".

References

1. Naghizadeh, R., Allahy, S., Ranga, M.: A model for NTBF creation in less developed regions based on the Smart Specialisation concept: the case of regions in Iran. Reg. Stud. **55**(3), 441–452 (2021)
2. Markkula, M., Kune, H.: Making smart regions smarter: smart specialization and the role of universities in regional innovation ecosystems. Technol. Innov. Manag. Rev. **5**(10), 7–15 (2015)
3. Tsonkov, N., Petrov, K., Berberova-Valcheva, T.: Adoption of information technologies for black sea region municipalities' smart development. Int. J. Inf. Technol. Secur. **14**(1), 87–96 (2022)
4. Slavin, B., Yamalov, I.: Creating smart-region's infrastructure through the development of information technology and e-learning. BiznesInformatika - Bus. Inform. **25**(3), 72–76 (2013)
5. Rigby, D.L., et al.: Do EU regions benefit from Smart Specialisation principles? Reg. Stud. Early Access (2022)
6. Wolfslehner, B., Huber, P., Lexer, M.J.: Smart use of small-diameter hardwood - a forestry-wood chain sustainability impact assessment in Austria. Scand. J. For. Res. **28**(2), 184–192 (2013)
7. Morgan, K., Marques, P.: The public animateur: mission-led innovation and the "smart state" in Europe. Cambridge J. Reg. Econ. Soc. **12**(2), 179–193 (2019)
8. Bal-Domanska, B., Sobczak, E., Stanczyk, E.: A multivariate approach to the identification of initial smart specialisations of Polish voivodeships. Equilibr. Q. J. Econ. Econ. Policy **15**(4), 785–810 (2020)
9. Minbashrazgah, M.M., Maleki, F., Torabi, M.: Green chicken purchase behavior: the moderating role of price transparency. Manage. Environ. Qual. **28**(6), 902–916 (2017)
10. Dual food quality: The Commission advises Member States on how to tackle unfair practices more effectively. https://ec.europa.eu/commission. Accessed 26 Sept 2021
11. The results of the tests confirmed the dual quality of food in the countries of the European Union. https://vedanadosah.cvtisr.sk. Accessed 11 Jan 2021
12. Bartková, L., Veselovská, L., Zimermanová, K.: Possible solutions to dual quality of products in the European Union. Sci. Pap. Univ. Pardubice **26**(44), 5–16 (2018)
13. Double quality of foods: https://ec.europa.eu/info/live-work-travel-eu/consumer-rights-and-complaints. Accessed 17 May 2022
14. Mokrišová, V.: Ekoinovácie ako determinant efektívneho podnikateľského rozvoja. Zarzadzanie. Theory Pract. Manage. **17**(3), 35–40 (2016)

15. Bartková, L.: The dual quality of daily needs in the EU and its impact on cosumer behavior. Belianum. Matej Bel University, Banská Bystrica (2020)
16. ISO 22000: https://www.qscert.sk/sluzby/certifikacia-manazerskych-systemov. Accessed 12 Jan 2022
17. News and current information: https://www.svps.sk/podania21/. Accessed 17 May 2022
18. National project Support for partnership and dialogue in the field of participatory public policy making. https://www.minv.sk/?ros_np_participacia. Accessed 21 Mar 2022
19. Lament, M., Wolak-Tuzimek, A., Maráková, V., Krištofik, P.: Innovation in selected sectors of the economy. PH KP UTH, Radom (2020)
20. Magoni, M., Adami, R., Radaelli, R.: Governance for Sustainable Development. Partnerships for the Goals. Encyclopaedia of the UN Sustainable Development Goals. Springer, Cham, (2021)
21. The first FinTech Hub in Slovakia: https://www.finreport.sk/fintech. Accessed 20 Dec 2021
22. Marzouki, R., Belkahla, W.: Innov. Manage. Rev. **17**(1), 86–111 (2020)
23. West, J., Salter, A., Vanhaverbeke, W., Chesbrough, H.: Open innovation: the next decade. Res. Policy **43**(5), 805–811 (2014)
24. CKO/Eurofunds: https://www.mirri.gov.sk/sekcie/cko/strategia-vyskumu-a-inovacii-pre-int eligentnu-specializaciu-sr. Accessed 28 Apr 2021
25. Strategy-of-digital-transformation-of Slovakia-2030. https://www.mirri.gov.sk. Accessed 20 Mar 2022
26. Indicators for monitoring the development of the digital society 2014–2020. http://www.inf ormatizacia.sk. Accessed 22 Jan 2022
27. Tens of thousands of Slovaks are threatened by digital poverty. https://www.mirri.gov.sk/akt uality/digitalna-agenda. Accessed 20 Mar 2022
28. Theorin, A., et al.: An event-driven manufacturing information system architecture for Industry 4.0. Int. J. Prod. Res. **55**(5), 1297–1311 (2017)
29. Piccarozzi, M., Aquilani, B., Gatti, C.: Industry 4.0 in management studies: a systematic literature review. Sustainability 10(10), 3821 (2018)
30. Smart Digital Ports of the Future Agenda: https://sdp.ptievents.com/agenda. Accessed 19 Dec 2021
31. Sedliačiková, M., et al.: Quality cost monitoring models in practice of wood working company in Slovakia. In: Procedia Economics and Finance: 4th World Conference on Business. Economics and Management, vol. 26, pp. 77–81. Elsevier, Amsterdam (2015)
32. Compensation squeezed out the sugar. Two sugar factories remained in Slovakia (Nestlé, Kičina). https://ekonomika.pravda.sk/. Accessed 12 May 2022

International Workshop on Theoretical and Computational Chemistry and Its Applications (TCCMA 2022)

A Theoretical Study on *trans*-Resveratrol - Cu(I) Complex

Concetta Caglioti[1,2] ⓘ, Antonella De Luca[2], Chiara Pennetta[2], Lorenzo Monarca[1,2], Francesco Ragonese[2], Paola Sabbatini[2], Maria Noelia Faginas Lago[2,3] ⓘ, Andrea Lombardi[2,3] ⓘ, Federico Palazzetti[2(✉)] ⓘ, and Bernard Fioretti[2]

[1] Dipartimento di Medicina e Chirurgia, Università degli Studi di Perugia, piazzale Gambuli 1, 06129 Perugia, Italy
[2] Dipartimento di Chimica, Biologia e Biotecnologie, Università degli Studi di Perugia, via Elce di Sotto 8, 06123 Perugia, Italy
federicopalazzetti@yahoo.it
[3] UdR INSTM di Perugia, via Elce di Sotto 8, 06123 Perugia, Italy

Abstract. Resveratrol is a natural occurring phenol, found in peanuts, cocoa, and fruits like for example grapes, blueberries, and strawberries. It has become popular in the last decades for the possible correlation of wine, especially red wine, and cardioprotective properties. It is widely employed in nutraceutics production. It presents stilbenoid structure; in nature there are two isomers, *cis* and *trans*, this latter is the most stable. Here, we present a preliminary investigation on the most stable complex that *trans*-resveratrol forms with Cu(I), an essential trace element in living organisms, that takes part to redox processes, where resveratrol plays an antioxidative role. The structure of *trans*-resveratrol - Cu(I) is optimized in vacuum and in solvents like water and ethanol, by Density Functional Theory methods. Dissociation and solvation energies of the complex are calculated. Infrared spectra are calculated and compared with experimental data, available in literature.

Keywords: Density functional theory · Nutraceutics · IR spectra

1 Introduction

Resveratrol (3,5,4′-trihydroxy-trans-stilbene) is a stilbenoid, a class of natural phenols. It is formed by a phenol and a resorcinol group connected by an ethylene radical (Fig. 1). It is present in *cis* and *trans* isomers, although this latter is the most stable and common. In nature, it is found essentially in *Polygonum cuspidatum* [1], a flowering plant already employed in the traditional Chinese medicine. It became very popular for the reduced incidence of coronary heart disease in countries with high consumptions of saturated fats and red wine [2], this latter suggested a correlation between resveratrol and cardio-protective properties. Grape is in fact one of the main sources of resveratrol. Other plants containing this natural phenol are blueberries, strawberries, ribes, peanuts, cocoa, and *itadori* tea.

Resveratrol has antioxidant, chemopreventive and anticancer properties [3]. It has been proved to regulate proteins and enzyme activity [4]. Preclinical studies reported a

O. Gervasi et al. (Eds.): ICCSA 2022 Workshops, LNCS 13382, pp. 237–248, 2022.
https://doi.org/10.1007/978-3-031-10592-0_18

positive effect in anti-glioblastoma therapy [5]. Its effects have been studied on mito-chondrial biogenesis of granulosa cells, suggesting beneficial effects on the physiology of female reproductive system, with possible therapeutic implications [6]. Solid for-mulations have been produced to overcome the low solubility in water and improve bioavailability (see for example [7]).

Computational chemistry has been largely employed both to support experimental studies or to predict chemical properties of this molecule, mostly for the *trans* isomer. Iuga *et al.* [8] applied quantum chemistry to investigate the antioxidant activity of *trans*-resveratrol toward hydroxyl and hydroperoxyl radicals. Density Functional Theory, DFT, was employed by Mazzone *et al.* [9] and by Benayahoum *et al.* [10] to study antioxidant mechanisms of resveratrol and its analogues. Other computational and theoretical studies were devoted to study homolytic and heterolytic bond cleavage in the hydroxyl radical [11] and its interactions with hemoglobin [12]. Frau *et al.* studied the chemical reactivity of the *cis* and *trans* isomers by Molecular Electron DFT [13, 14]. The isomerization process was accurately described by Feng and Chatterjee [15]. Kores *et al.* applied inverse molecular docking to investigate new potential human targets for this molecules [16]. Very recently, Nakajima *et al.* reported a computation-guided asymmetric synthesis of resveratrol dimers [17].

Interaction of resveratrol with metal ions have been studied both to investigate antiox-idant activity and in view of biological studies on the interaction of this molecule with essential trace elements in living organisms [18–20]. Copper has the capability of switch-ing the two oxidation forms Cu(II) and Cu(I). This feature plays an important role in biochemical processes related to the electron transfer processes in proteins and enzymes, and in redox reactions producing free radicals. Resveratrol acts as prooxidant in pres-ence of Cu(II), producing reactive oxygen species. The oxidation process leads to the formation of a phenoxide radical and reduction of Cu(II) to Cu(I).

In this paper, we report a preliminary study of the complex *trans*-Resveratrol - Cu(I), here denoted as [Resv]Cu$^+$. DFT has been used to calculate the dissociation energy of the complex, *i.e.* the difference in energy between the stable complex and resveratrol - Cu(I) isolated. Solvation energy was also calculated for water and ethanol solvents. This latter has been studied in view of possible applications in analytical chemistry. Vibrational spectra of [Resv] Cu$^+$ in vacuum, in water and in ethanol have been calculated and discussed in relations to the experimental data obtained by infrared multiple-photon dissociation (IRMPD) spectroscopy [19].

2 Background

Calculations have been performed by the Gaussian 09 package software [21]. Struc-ture optimizations, as well as single point energies and vibrational spectra, have been calculated by means of Density Functional Theory (DFT) methods, by employing the hybrid functional B3LYP with the Pople basis set 6-31G(d,p), already used by Beneya-houm [10] to optimize the structure of *trans*-resveratrol and the Electron Core Potential LanL2DZ, Los Alamos National Laboratory 2 double ζ, largely employed for metal transition complexes [22].

Dissociation energies of the copper complex were determined by calculating the difference in energy between the complex in its equilibrium geometry and the energies

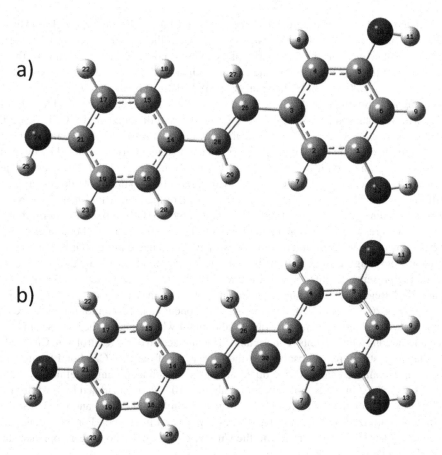

Fig. 1. Structures of *trans*-Resveratrol (a) and *trans*-Resveratrol - Cu (I) complex (b) optimized by B3LYP/6-31G(d,p). In orange the Cu atom, in grey the carbons, in white the hydrogens and in red the oxygens. The atoms are labelled by numbers from 1 to 29, the copper is labelled by 30. (Color figure online)

of resveratrol and Cu$^+$ at infinite distance. The solvation energy, for complex dissolved in water and in ethanol was determined by the difference between the energy of the complex in the solvent and in vacuum. The solvent interaction was calculated by applying the IEFPCM model (see for example [23]).

3 Results and Discussion

The structure of [Resv]Cu$^+$ was optimized by B3LYP with 6-31(d,p) and LanL2DZ basis sets. Here, we report a comparison of the structures in the neighboring of the Cu$^+$ ion obtained by these two basis sets (Fig. 1). We also compare these geometrical features with those of the *trans*-resveratrol molecule in vacuum to evaluate the effect of the copper ion to the molecule. The atoms we considered are C28, C26, C3, and C2, for which we calculated the mutual interatomic distances and bond angles, the dihedral angle and their distances from Cu^+. Additionally, we calculated the dihedral angle among C16, C28, C26, and C4, to evaluate the coplanarity of the phenol and resorcinol fragments. In Table 1, we report the distances among the four carbon atoms closest to the Cu atom in the complex, C28, C26, C3, and C2, the dihedral angle defined by these four atoms, and the dihedral angle among C16, C28, C26, and C4. In Table 2, we report the bond lengths of Cu^+ with four carbon atoms C28, C26, C3, and C2, and the bond angles C27-Cu-C26, C26-Cu-C3, and C3 - Cu - C2. This calculations aim at comparing the structure changes related to the coordination with the copper ion and the geometries predicted by the two basis sets both in vacuum and in the cases when a solvent is considered. The geometrical features of resveratrol calculated by the two basis sets are similar, while remarkable differences are observed in the copper complex. Comparison between the two basis sets in vacuum shows that the structure optimized by 6-31G(d,p) presents shorter bond lengths with respect to that calculated by LanL2DZ, with less ample bond angles. For what concerns the solvent interaction, the structure calculated by 6-31G(d,p) basis sets does not show significant changes about distances and bonds involving the copper ion, while the presence in ethanol and water lead to changes in the structure optimized by LanL2DZ. Regarding the geometrical features related to the carbon atoms coordinate by Cu^+, C28, C26, C3 and C2, and the atoms of the phenol and resorcinol fragments, C16 and C4, no substantial changes are observed both for what concerns the basis set and for the interactions with solvents or in vacuum. The interaction of resveratrol with Cu^+ leads to change in structure, as observed by the increasing of the C28-C26 bond length and especially from the change of the dihedral angles. The dihedral angle defined by C28, C26, C3, and C2 in the complex becomes about $-10°$ when calculated by 6-31G(d,p), while is $-25°$ for the structure optimized in vacuum by LanL2DZ, and *ca.* 2° for the structure optimized by this latter basis set, in water and in ethanol. For what concerns the phenol and resorcinol groups, in the Cu-complex they are no longer coplanar, the dihedral angle is about 160°.

Table 1. Geometrical features of trans-resveratrol. We report the distances C28-C26, C26-C3, and C3-C2, in Å, and the dihedral angles for C28-C26-C3-C2, and for C16-C28-C26-C4, in degrees. The structures have been optimized by B3LYP/6-31G(d,p) and B3LYP/LanL2DZ for the molecule in vacuum.

		C28-C26 (Å)	C26-C3 (Å)	C3-C2 (Å)	C28-C26-C3-C2 (degrees)	C16-C28-C26-C4 (degrees)
In vacuum	6-31G(d,p)	1.35	1.47	1.41	0	180
	LanL2DZ	1.35	1.46	1.41	0	180

Dissociation energies of the [Resv]Cu^+ complex in vacuum have been calculated by using the 6-31G(d,p) and LanL2DZ basis sets (Table 3). For both basis sets the energy is negative, corresponding to a more stable complex, if compared with the energy of resveratrol - Cu^+ system separated by infinite distance. The 6-31G(d,p) overestimates the

Table 2. Geometrical features of the [Resv]Cu$^+$ complex. We report the distance between Cu and the four adjacent carbon atoms, C28, C26, C3, and C2, in Å, and the related bond angles, in degrees. We also report the distances C28-C26, C26-C3, and C3-C2, and the dihedral angles for C28-C26-C3-C2 and for C16-C28-C26-C4. The structures have been optimized by B3LYP/6-31G(d,p) and B3LYP/LanL2DZ for the molecule in vacuum, in water and in ethanol.

		Cu-C28 (Å)	Cu-C26 (Å)	Cu-C3 (Å)	Cu-C2 (Å)	C28-Cu-C26 (degrees)	C26-Cu-C3 (degrees)	C3-Cu-C2 (degrees)
In vacuum	6-31G(d,p)	2.15	2.02	2.09	2.05	38.8	42.4	41.0
	LanL2DZ	2.70	2.24	2.26	2.29	30.9	38.8	37.0
In water	6-31G(d,p)	2.15	2.01	2.10	2.12	38.8	42.3	39.8
	LanL2DZ	2.20	2.14	2.92	3.61	37.6	29.2	22.0
In ethanol	6-31G(d,p)	2.15	2.01	2.10	2.11	38.7	42.3	39.9
	LanL2DZ	2.20	2.14	2.92	3.60	37.6	29.2	22.0
		C28-C26 (Å)	C26-C3 (Å)	C3-C2 (Å)		C28-C26-C3-C2 (degrees)		C16-C28-C26-C4 (degrees)
In vacuum	6-31G(d,p)	1.39	1.49	1.45		-12.6		-163.6
	LanL2DZ	1.39	1.50	1.44		-25.9		-152.5
In water	6-31G(d,p)	1.39	1.49	1.44		-10.3		-162.8
	LanL2DZ	1.40	1.47	1.42		2.1		-166.2
In ethanol	6-31G(d,p)	1.38	1.49	1.44		-10.3		-163.6
	LanL2DZ	1.40	1.47	1.42		2.3		-166.1

dissociation energy if compared with LanL2DZ by a factor 2 (Fig. 2). In this preliminary work, possible errors due to basis set superposition were not considered.

Table 3. Dissociation energy, in kJ/mol, of the [Resv]Cu$^+$ complex in vacuum, calculated by B3LYP/6-31G(d,p) and B3LYP/LanL2DZ.

	Dissociation energy (kJ/mol)
6-31G(d,p)	−522.4
LanL2DZ	−269.7

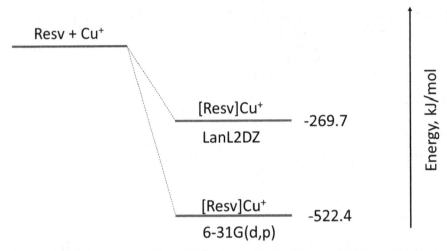

Fig. 2. Dissociation energies of Resv[Cu]$^+$ calculated by LanL2DZ and 6-31G(d,p) basis sets.

The solvation energy was calculated both for the complex in water and in ethanol, by using the two basis sets applied so far (Table 4). Solvated complexes calculated by LanL2DZ are more stable by about 50 kJ/mol with respect to the 6-31G(d,p) counterpart. For both basis sets, [Resv]Cu$^+$ in water is more stable than in ethanol by 8–9 kJ/mol (Fig. 3).

Table 4. Solvation energies of the [Resv]Cu$^+$ complex in water and in ethanol, calculated by B3LYP/6-31G(d,p) and B3LYP/LanL2DZ

		Solvation energy (kJ/mol)
In water	6-31G(d,p)	−225.5
	LanL2DZ	−263.9
In ethanol	6-31G(d,p)	−217.5
	LanL2DZ	−254.3

We report a description of the IR spectrum of [Resv]Cu$^+$ in vacuum obtained by our calculations (Fig. 4). Low intensity peaks, at wavenumbers no higher than 400 cm^{-1} are attributed to modes involving the ethylene group, especially hindered rotations, bending and stretching motions. An intense peak is found at *ca.* 450 cm^{-1}, mainly due to the motion out of the plane of the hydrogens in the resorcinol fragment: H7, H9, H11, and H13 (Fig. 5a). Motions out of the plane of the hydrogen atoms of the molecule, together with carbons in the resorcinol fragment, determine a peak of small intensity at *ca.* 850 cm^{-1}. At 1200 cm^{-1}, there are at least four intense peaks related to motions of the hydrogen atoms in the plane of the phenol and resorcinol rings (Fig. 5b). A vibrational mode related to the motion in the plane of the hydrogens of the phenol fragment correspond to a moderately intense peak at 1350 cm^{-1}. Five peaks at wave numbers between

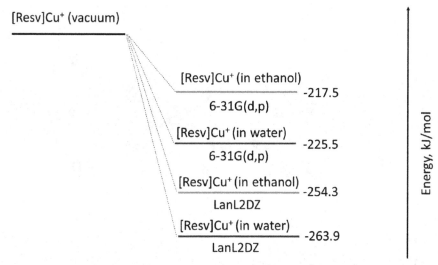

Fig. 3. Solvation energies (not in scale) of Resv[Cu]$^+$ in water and in ethanol, calculated by 6-31G(d,p) and LanL2DZ basis sets.

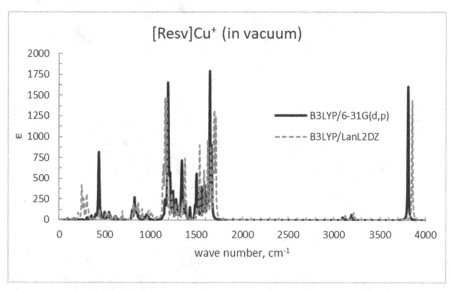

Fig. 4. IR spectra of [Resv]Cu$^+$ in vacuum calculated by B3LYP/6-31G(d,p) and B3LYP/LanL2DZ.

1500 and 1600 cm^{-1} correspond to vibrations in the plane of the two aromatics rings. At 1650 cm^{-1}, two very intense peaks correspond to bending and stretching motions in the plane involving separately the atoms of the resorcinol group and those of the phenol group. The highest in energy peaks are found at *ca.* 3800 cm^{-1} and are assigned to the

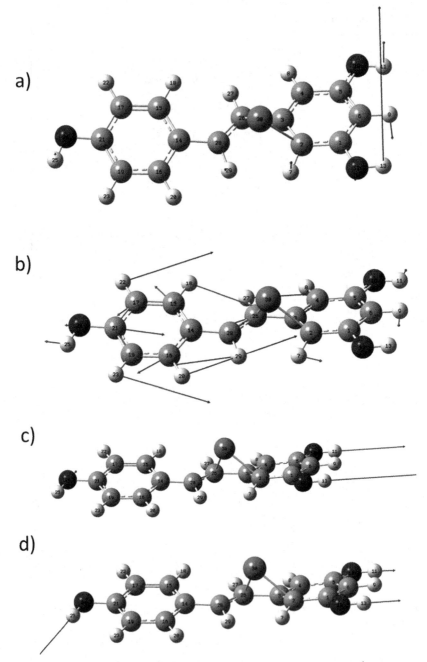

Fig. 5. Vector displacement (blue arrows) of four normal modes at a) 450 cm^{-1}, b) 1200 cm^{-1}, c) and d) 1800 cm^{-1}. (Color figure online)

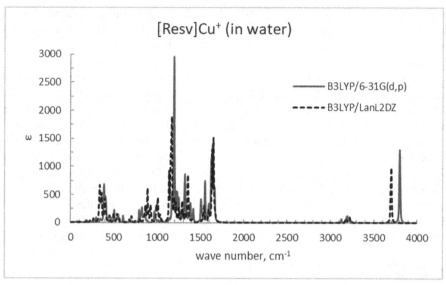

Fig. 6. IR spectra of [Resv]Cu$^+$ in water calculated by B3LYP/6-31G(d,p) and B3LYP/LanL2DZ.

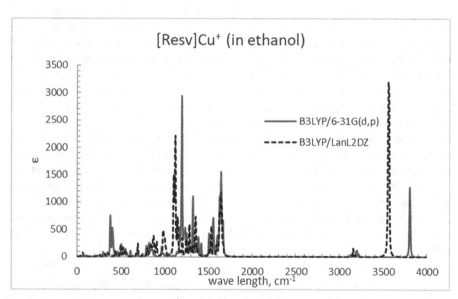

Fig. 7. IR spectra of [Resv]Cu$^+$ in ethanol calculated by B3LYP/6-31G(d,p) and B3LYP/LanL2DZ.

bond stretching involving O10-H11, O12-H13, and O24-H25 (Figs. 5c and 5d). Experimentally, IRMPD spectroscopy revealed important features of the [Resv]Cu$^+$ complex in the wave number range between 1100–1300 and 1500–1600 cm^{-1}, and a peak at 3628 cm^1 that corresponds to the OH vibrations region. Comparison of the spectra calculated by 6-31G(d,p) and LanL2DZ shows a substantial agreement between these two basis sets. The largest differences are found at low energies, in correspondence of the vibrations out of plane. Signals corresponding to the OH stretching, at *ca.* 3800 cm^{-1} are calculated with about 50 cm^{-1} of discrepancy. Effect of water as a solvent does not substantially change the spectrum, except the wave number region under 500 cm^{-1}, where the two basis sets give more similar spectra, and the intense peak found at 500 cm^{-1} by 6-31G(d,p) basis set is not found in this case (Fig. 6). Effect of ethanol does not modify the spectrum, with respect to water, while differences between the spectrum calculated by the two basis sets are more marked (Fig. 7). The most evident difference is also in this case found at high wave numbers, where the peak attributed to the OH stretching is determined at *ca.* 3600cm^{-1} by LanL2DZ and at *ca.* 3800 cm^{-1} by 6-31G(d,p).

4 Conclusions

A preliminary study has been performed on the *trans*-Resveratrol - Cu(I) complex in vacuum, in water, and in ethanol, by DFT method using the B3LYP functional combined with 6-31G(d,p) and LanL2DZ basis sets. Optimization by 6-31G(d,p) leads to structures with copper roughly equidistant to the four adjacent carbon, *ca.* 2 Å; this structure is quite similar both in vacuum, in water, and in ethanol. Structures optimized by LanL2DZ present a higher bond length between copper and the adjacent atoms. Differences are observed between the structure in vacuum and in solvents. Comparison of the structures of *trans*-resveratrol and [Resv]Cu$^+$ shows that most of differences between the two basis sets are observed in the features related to Cu$^+$, both in vacuum and when solvent interactions are considered. On the contrary, choice of the basis sets does not affect the geometry optimization of the resveratrol molecule. The effect of Cu$^+$ to resveratrol determines lose of coplanarity between phenol and resorcinol groups. It can be observed for the two basis sets, both in vacuum and in solvents.

Infrared spectra were calculated by using both the basis sets. The spectra of the complex in vacuum are compared with experimental data, showing a substantial qualitative agreement. Both calculated spectra are in agreement, with differences that concern especially the peaks at the highest wave numbers, corresponding to the OH stretching modes. Such differences increase when the complex is in water and in ethanol.

The remarkable differences in the geometrical features related to Cu$^+$ and the atoms of resveratrol closest to this metal ion, as well as the huge differences in energy, especially for the dissociation energy, suggest that future works must be addressed to the assessment of functionals and basis sets that could correctly predict energy and structural properties of this copper complex. Investigations will be extended to complexes with other trace elements.

Acknowledgements. The authors thank the Dipartimento di Ingegneria Civile ed Ambientale of Università degli Studi di Perugia for allocated computing time within the project "Dipartimenti di Eccellenza 2018–2022". N.F.-L. acknowledges the Fondo Ricerca di Base 2021

(RICBASE2021FAGINAS) of Dipartimento di Chimica, Biologia e Biotecnologie of Università degli Studi di Perugia for financial support. The authors acknowledge the Italian Ministry for Education, University and Research (MIUR) for financial support through Scientific Independence of young Researchers SIR 2014 (RBSI14U3VF) and (RBSI144EUA).

References

1. Ghanim, H., et al.: An antiinflammatory and reactive oxygen species suppressive effects of an extract of polygonum cuspidatum containing resveratrol. J. Clin. Ebdocrinol. Metab. **95**(9), E1–E8 (2010)
2. Renaud, S., de Lorgeril, M.: Wine, alcohol, platelets, and the French paradox for coronary heart disease. Lancet **339**(8808), 1523–1526 (1992)
3. Penumathsa, S., Maulik, N.: Resveratrol: a promising agent in promoting cardioprotection against coronary heart disease. Can. J. Physiol Pharmacol. **87**, 275 (2009)
4. Park, S.J., et al.: Resveratrol ameliorates aging-related metabolic phenotypes by inhibiting cAMP phosphodiesterase. Cell **148**, 421 (2012)
5. Ragonese, F., et al.: Resveratrol depolarizes the membrane potential in human granulosa cells and promotes mitochondrial biogenesis. Fertil. Steril. **115**, 1063–1073 (2021)
6. Dionigi, L., et al.: Focus on the use of resveratrol as an adjuvant in glioblastoma therapy. Curr. Pharm. Des. **26**(18), 2102–2108 (2020)
7. Iannitti, R.G., et al.: Resveratrol supported on magnesium DiHydroxide (Resv@MDH) represents an oral formulation of resveratrol with better gastric absorption and bioavailability respect to pure resveratrol. Front. Nutr. **7**, 570047 (2020)
8. Iuga, C., Alvarez-Idaboy, J.R., Russo, N.: Antioxidant activity of trans-resveratrol toward hydroxyl and hydroperoxyl radicals: a quantum chemical and computational kinetics study. J. Org. Chem. **77**(8), 3868–3877 (2012)
9. Mazzone, G., Malaj, N., Russo, N., Toscano, M.: Density functional study of the antioxidant activity of some recently synthesized resveratrol analogues. Food Chem. **141**, 2017–2024 (2013)
10. Benayahoum, A., Amira-Guebailia, H., Houache, O.: A DFT method for the study of the antioxidant action mechanism of resveratrol derivatives. J. Mol. Model. **19**, 2285–2298 (2013)
11. Benayahoum, A., Amira-Guebailia, H., Houache, O.: Homolytic and heterolytic O-H bond cleavage in trans-resveratrol and some phenantrene analogs: a theoretical study. Comp. Theor. Chem. **1037**, 1–9 (2014)
12. Tellone, E., et al.: Molecular interactions of hemoglobin with resveratrol: potential protective antioxidant role and metabolic adaptations of the erythrocyte. Biol. Chem. **395**, 347–354 (2014)
13. Frau, J., Muñoz, F., Glossman-Mitnik, D.: A molecular electron density theory study of the chemical reactivity of cis- and trans-resveratrol. Molecules **21**(12), 1650 (2016)
14. Frau, J., Muñoz, F., Glossman-Mitnik, D.: Application of DFT concepts to the study of the chemical reactivity of some resveratrol derivatives through the assessment of the validity of the "Koopmans in DFT" (KID) procedure. J. Theor. Comp. Chem. **16**, 1750006 (2017)
15. Wang, F., Chatterjee, S.: Dominant carbons in *trans*- and *cis*-resveratrol isomerization. J. Phys. Chem B **121**(18), 4745–4755 (2017)
16. Kores, K., Lešnik, S., Bren, U., Janežič, D., Konc, J.: Discovery of novel potential human targets of resveratrol by inverse molecular docking. J. Chem. Inf. Model. **59**(5), 2467–2478 (2019)
17. Nakajima, M., Adachi, Y., Nemoto, T.: Computation-guided asymmetric total syntheses of resveratrol dimers. Nature Comm. **13**, 152 (2022)

18. Tamboli, V., Defant, A., Mancini, I., Tosi, P.: A study of resveratrol-copper complexes by electrospray ionization mass spectrometry and density functional theory calculations. Rapid Commun. Mass Spectrum. **25**, 526–532 (2011)
19. Chiavarino, B., Crestoni, M.E., Fornarini, S., Taioli, S., Mancini, I., Tosi, P.: Infrared spectroscopy of copper-resveratrol complexes: a joint experimental and theoretical study. J. Chem. Phys. **137**, 024307 (2012)
20. Tamboli, V., Re, N., Coletti, C., Defant, A., Mancini, I., Tosi, P.: A joint experimental and theoretical investigation on the oxidative coupling of resveratrol induced by copper and iron ions. Int. J. Mass Spectrom. **319–320**, 55–63 (2012)
21. Frisch, M.J.: Gaussian 09, Revision A.02. Gaussian, Inc., Wallingford CT (2016)
22. Yang, Y., Weaver, M.N., Merz, K.M., Jr.: Assessment of the "6-31-G** + LANL2DZ" mixed basis set coupled with density functional theory method and the effective core potential: prediction of heats of formation and ionization potentials for first-row-transition-metal complexes. J. Phys. Chem. A **113**(36), 9843–9851 (2009)
23. Klamt, A., Moya, C., Palomar, J.: A comprehensive comparison of the IEFPCM and SS(V)PE continuum solvation methods with the COSMO approach. J. Comp. Theory Comput. **11**(9), 4220–4225 (2015)

Theoretical Study of the Reaction O(^{3}P) + 1,2-Butadiene

Gianmarco Vanuzzo$^{1(\boxtimes)}$, Andrea Giustini^1 , Marzio Rosi^2 ,
Piergiorgio Casavecchia^1 , and Nadia Balucani^1

^{1} Department of Chemistry, Biology and Biotechnology, University of Perugia,
06123 Perugia, Italy
{gianmarco.vanuzzo,andrea.giustini,piergiorgio.casavecchia,
nadia.balucani}@unipg.it
^{2} Department of Civil and Environmental Engineering, University of Perugia,
06125 Perugia, Italy
marzio.rosi@unipg.it

Abstract. The triplet and singlet potential energy surfaces of the O(^{3}P) + 1,2-butadiene reaction have been investigated by electronic structure calculations at the coupled-cluster (CCSD(T)(aug-cc-pVTZ) level. We focused our attention, in particular, on the different sites of attack of atomic oxygen to 1, 2-butadiene. The results for minima, transition states and reaction channel energetics are compared with the results of previous CCSD(T)(aug-cc-pVTZ)-CBS and CASPT2 calculations to explore the adequacy of simpler computational schemes for discussing the reaction dynamics, in particular the product branching fractions derived from crossed molecular beam experiments.

Keywords: Ab initio calculations · Reaction dynamics of oxygen atoms with dienes · Combustion chemistry

1 Introduction

The reactions between ground state atomic oxygen, O(^{3}P), and aliphatic unsaturated hydrocarbons (UHs) play a critical role in combustion chemistry [1–4], and are important in the chemistry of the terrestrial atmosphere [4, 5]. In addition, these reactions are also of some relevance in astrochemistry [6, 7]. In combustion processes, such as fuel oxidation, O(^{3}P) is generated from what is considered to be the most important reaction in combustion chemistry, namely, $O_2 + H \rightarrow O(^3P) + OH$, and generally is produced in all oxygen-rich environments [3, 4]. On the other hand, small UHs are formed during the combustion of both simple, such as methane, and complex fossil fuels, including biofuels. If both UHs and O(^{3}P) coexist in the same environment, reactions between these species can occur. Among the different molecules formed during these processes, carbon dioxide is the most important one, because it remains indefinitely in our atmosphere. For this reason, CO_2 is considered the main by-product of fossil fuel combustion [1–5]. To cut down on the overproduction of CO_2, numerous car manufacturers, utility

© The Author(s), under exclusive license to Springer Nature Switzerland AG 2022
O. Gervasi et al. (Eds.): ICCSA 2022 Workshops, LNCS 13382, pp. 249–263, 2022.
https://doi.org/10.1007/978-3-031-10592-0_19

companies, and governments have been pursuing new alternatives for energy sources. Among the leading contenders, there are new substances, the so-called *biofuels*, made from biological materials, that are considered as renewable energy sources. Among the various biofuels, the two most common that can replace gasoline are ethanol and biodiesel, where the former is mainly extracted from corn or sugarcane [1, 2, 4], while the latter is a plant/animal-based substance produced through the trans-esterification process of vegetal oil or animal fats [1]. Combustion and pyrolysis of biofuels can lead to formation of unsaturated hydrocarbons [1, 2, 4, 8]. Hence, studies of the reactions between $O(^3P)$ and UHs are useful for better understanding the kinetics and improve the modeling of combustion environments.

Since the reactions of $O(^3P)$ with UHs are particularly relevant in the global understanding of the complex mechanisms involved in combustion chemistry, the kinetics and dynamics of these processes have been investigated in depth from both experimental [5, 9–15] and theoretical [16–23] points of view. For instance, since the 1950s the global rate constants at room temperature have been determined in kinetic experiments for many of these reactions [9], and in some cases also in a range of combustion temperatures [8]. In contrast, much less is known about the identity of the primary reaction products and their relative yields (branching fractions, BFs), with the latter having often been object of uncertainty and controversy [19, 24, 25]. The difficulty in determining the product BFs is caused by the complexity of the $O(^3P)$ + UH reactions [10]. In fact, these processes are multichannel reactions, characterized by numerous thermodynamically accessible product channels. Furthermore, in these systems, nonadiabatic transitions from the entrance triplet to the underlying singlet potential energy surface (PES), namely the occurrence of *intersystem crossing* – ISC, can open other reaction channels [10, 12, 25, 27, 30]. We recall that the knowledge of both global rate constants and relative product yields are fundamental for the global understanding of these processes and for the improvement of combustion models [8], because the primary products of one elementary reaction are, basically, the reactants of the following processes in the overall combustion network, and, therefore, can determine the propagation or the termination of the chain reaction. Traditionally, only partial information on BFs has become available from kinetic studies; furthermore, not only the kinetic data available are partial, but they have been obtained mostly at room temperature, that is, far from typical combustion conditions. As a result, most combustion mechanisms describe the high temperature reactivity of $O(^3P)$ with UHs using the total rate constant partitioned in the various reaction channels based on the very limited room temperature BFs, and this can lead to substantial errors. When data are not available at all, reaction products are normally guessed by considering as most probable the most exothermic reaction channels, or by drawing analogies with similar systems, but again both approaches can be wrong [see ref. 12, 30, 31, and references therein]. In the case of multichannel reactions, such as those of $O(^3P)$ with UHs, in general the primary products are not easy to predict, because the characteristics of the underlying triplet and singlet PESs are those that govern the relative yield of the various product channels. In addition, the occurrence of ISC and its extent as a function of temperature are not easy to predict either, and only experimental determinations and/or accurate theoretical treatments can quantify it. So, there is a strong need for accurate experimental data on product BFs at the temperature (or energy) of relevance in combustion that support theoretical predictions. Importantly, the experimental results can be used to validate the reliability of the statistical predictions of product BFs, and hence of the calculated triplet and singlet PESs and their nonadiabatic couplings. Once theory is validated by experiment, it can be used with confidence to calculate channel-specific rate constants and BFs for all energetically allowed product channels as a function of temperature and pressure, which is what is needed for theoretical modelling (see, for instance, refs. 12, 26, 30, and 31).

During the past 15 years, in our laboratory the study of numerous multichannel reactions of O(^{3}P) with UHs was performed using the crossed-molecular-beam technique with mass-spectrometric detection (CMB-MS), empowered with *soft* electron ionization (EI), which allowed us to identify and quantify all primary reaction products. Using *soft* EI we were, in fact, able to mitigate or even suppress the dissociative ionization of interfering species (products, background gases, and, in particular, elastically/inelastically scattered reagents) that occurs when an electron energy of 70 eV is used in the EI source (*hard* ionization), and which usually represents the main complication in these experiments [29]. Among the various UHs, we have investigated the oxidation of molecules with different degree of unsaturation and complexity, starting from alkenes [11, 12, 21, 24–26], and moving to cumulenes [11, 14, 27], alkynes [11, 14, 15, 28, 29], and also aromatics (benzene) [30, 45] and conjugated dienes (1, 3-butadiene) [31].

It should be noted that the oxidation of dienes, such as allene (propadiene), the prototype of cumulenes, is possible through three different sites of oxygen attack, where the terminal ones are equivalent. Previous CMB studies from our laboratory on the O(^{3}P) + allene (CH$_2$ = C = CH$_2$) reaction at the collision energy, E$_c$, of 39.3 kJ/mol found that it is characterized by numerous product channels, where the dominant one is C$_2$H$_4$ + CO (BF = 0.77), followed by H$_2$CO + C$_3$H$_4$ (BF = 0.091), CH$_3$CO + CH$_2$ (BF = 0.065), HCO + C$_2$H$_3$ (BF = 0.062), and CH$_2$COCH + H (BF = 0.015) [27]. On the basis of these experimental results, it was concluded that the O(^{3}P) + allene reaction is dominated by ISC (–90%) because the main primary products, namely CO, HCO, and H$_2$CO can only originate via ISC from the entrance triplet to the lowest singlet PES. Notably, the above BFs were in line with statistical predictions of earlier *ab initio* and statistical (RRKM) calculations performed by Nguyen *et al.* [23] separately on the triplet and singlet PESs (that is, ISC was not included in the statistical calculations).

Recently, in our laboratory also the reaction O(^{3}P) + 1,2-butadiene (methylallene) was studied by a combined CMB and theoretical approach. While a preliminary report has been already published [32], more theoretical work is needed for a detailed understanding of the reaction mechanism and of the product BFs derived from the CMB experiments.

We recall that the energetically allowed reaction channels of O(^{3}P) + methylallene are the following:

$$O(^3P) + CH_2 = C = CH - CH_3 \rightarrow C_4H_5O + H \ \Delta H_0^0 = -54 \ \ kJ/mol \quad (1)$$

$$\rightarrow C_4H_4O + H_2 \ \Delta H_0^0 = -335 \ \ kJ/mol \quad (2)$$

$$\rightarrow CO + C_3H_6 \ \Delta H_0^0 = -504 \ \ kJ/mol \quad (3)$$

$$\rightarrow OH + C_4H_5 \quad \Delta H_0^0 = -59 \quad kJ/mol \tag{4}$$

$$\rightarrow C_3H_3O + CH_3 \quad \Delta H_0^0 = -95 \quad kJ/mol \tag{5}$$

$$\rightarrow H_2CO + C_3H_4 \quad \Delta H_0^0 = -326 \quad kJ/mol \tag{6}$$

$$\rightarrow HCCO + C_2H_5 \quad \Delta H_0^0 = -103 \quad kJ/mol \tag{7}$$

$$\rightarrow HCO + C_3H_5 \quad \Delta H_0^0 = -202 \quad kJ/mol \tag{8}$$

$$\rightarrow CH_3CO + C_2H_3 \quad \Delta H_0^0 = -127 \quad kJ/mol \tag{9}$$

$$\rightarrow CH_2CHO + C_2H_3 \quad \Delta H_0^0 = -98 \quad kJ/mol \tag{10}$$

$$\rightarrow CH_2CO + {}^3CHCH_3 \quad \Delta H_0^0 = -109 \quad kJ/mol \tag{11}$$

$$\rightarrow CH_2CO + {}^1CH_2CH_2 \quad \Delta H_0^0 = -444 \quad kJ/mol \tag{12}$$

where the reaction enthalpies are obtained from the standard enthalpies of formation from NIST [33] or from our previous [32] and current electronic structure calculations.

In our preliminary work [32], the C_4H_6O triplet PES was investigated in a synergistic manner combining density functional theory (DFT), coupled cluster with perturbative triple excitations (CCSD(T)) with complete basis set (CBS) extrapolation, and multireference CASPT2 calculations, while the singlet PES was not explicitly investigated; in particular, the energy barriers regarding the isomerization processes of the oxiranyl singlet intermediate to aldehydes were assumed to be the same as those calculated for propene oxide isomerization to propenal [26].

In the present paper, we have extended the theoretical investigation of the triplet and singlet PESs of the $O(^3P) + 1,2$-butadiene reaction by calculating minima, barriers, and reaction enthalpies at the coupled-cluster (CCSD(T)(aug-cc-pVTZ) level. The goal was to compare the CCSD(T) results with those from the previous CCSD(T)-CBS and CASPT2 results, to explore whether a much faster scheme of electronic structure calculations were sufficiently reliable for future statistical RRKM/ME (Rice-Ramsperger-Kassel-Marcus/Master Equation) calculations of product BFs, to be compared with experimental BFs at the E_c of the CMB experiment. We stress that the inter-conversion barriers between the singlet minima were not available previously for $O(^3P) + 1,2$-butadiene. This is expected to allow us to expand the interpretation of the experimental results and to also discuss some similarities and differences between the dynamics of the O + allene and O + methylallene (1,2-butadiene) reactions, including the relative extent of ISC.

2 Methods

2.1 Experimental

We have studied the title reaction at the collision energy, E_c, of 41.8 kJ/mol using the CMB method, as described in ref. 32. From product angular and time-of-flight (TOF) distributions at different mass-to-charge (m/z) ratios it was experimentally found that the title reaction is characterized by a large variety of sizeable competing reaction channels, of which some lead to radical products, while others to molecular products. In total, nine different product channels were characterized, specifically the channels (1), (2), (3), (5), (6), (8), (9), (10), and (11). In the previous publication [32] we focused on two main molecular channels, both involving the rupture of the carbon backbone of 1,2-butadiene; specifically on channel (3), leading to CO + propene, occurring on the singlet PES (via ISC), and on channel (11) leading to CH_2CO (ketene) + CH_3CH (ethylidene), occurring on the triplet PES. The detailed analysis and discussion of the dynamics of the nine observed channels will be reported in a future, comprehensive publication [34].

2.2 Computational Details

Quantum chemical calculations were carried out to allocate minima and first-order saddle points on both the triplet and the singlet PESs, which have been identified to characterize the reaction O(^{3}P) + 1,2-butadiene. All geometries were optimized by using the Density Functional Theory (DFT) with the wB97XD functional [35, 36] and the aug-cc-pVTZ basis set [37–39]. With respect to our previous calculations [32] this DFT method showed significant improvements in the treatment of the long-range interactions, while similarities have been obtained for bonded interactions. Intrinsic reaction coordinate (IRC) calculations were performed to verify that the transition states are connected to the corresponding reactants and products [40, 41]. In order to refine the energetics of the critical points on the corresponding PESs, the coupled cluster CCSD(T)/aug-cc-pVTZ method was thoroughly adopted afterward. Both the wB97XD and CCSD(T) energies were corrected to 0 K by adding the zero-point energy correction computed using the scaled harmonic vibrational frequencies evaluated at the wB97XD/aug-cc-pVTZ level. Since the accuracy of our best computed values should not be smaller than the "chemical accuracy" of 1 kcal/mol, we rounded all the reported energies to 1 kJ/mol. As regards the energies of the entrance channels we used the values obtained by Caracciolo et al. and reported in reference [32]. DFT calculations were performed using the Gaussian 09 software [42], while all other calculations were performed using Molpro 2021.2 [43, 44].

3 Results and Discussion

Our previous theoretical investigation on the O(^{3}P) + 1,2-butadiene reaction reported three possible sites for the attack of atomic oxygen to the $CH_2 = C = CH\text{-}CH_3$ molecule, namely the terminal carbon of the unsaturated bond (C1), the central carbon between the cumulated double bonds (C2), and the terminal carbon linked to the methyl group

(C3) [32]. A kinetic investigation, based on variational transition state theory (VTST), determined the rate constants for $O(^3P)$ addition to the C1, C2, and C3 carbon atoms, and revealed that those to C2 and C3 are the most probable sites of addition (49.0% and 36.3%, respectively), being these addition processes barrierless. In contrast, the presence of an entrance barrier of 2.2 kJ/mol for the C1 addition leads to a lower probability of attack (14.7%). In the Figs. 1, 2, and 3 are reported the schematic representations of the three partial PESs (both triplet and singlet) obtained for the different sites of attack, with the energies evaluated in the present work at the CCSD(T)/aug-cc-pVTZ level of theory, with the exception of the entrance barriers which are taken from the previous calculations at the CASPT2 level.

The addition of $O(^3P)$ to the C1 site of CH_2CCHCH_3 features a barrier in the entrance channel, located (at the CASPT2 level [32]) 2.2 kJ/mol above the energy of the reactants, and leads to the formation of the $^3W4$ intermediate, in which a new C-O bond is formed (see Fig. 1). The fission of a C-H bond in the newly formed triplet intermediate (located 112 kJ/mol below the reactant energy asymptote), allows the formation of atomic hydrogen plus the $CH_3CHCCHO$ radical (channel (1)). The global exothermicity for the process is 44 kJ/mol, and a barrier of 97 kJ/mol must be overcome from $^3W4$. The related exit transition state ($^3TS4$) (see Fig. 4) clearly shows the breaking of a C-H bond, with a bond distance increasing up to 1.758 Å (see Fig. 4). The exit barrier is then 29 kJ/mol with respect to products. In competition, a nonadiabatic transition (near $^3W4$) to the singlet PES can take place, through a triplet-to-singlet ISC (see Fig. 1) leading to the $^1W7$ cyclic intermediate, located 357 kJ/mol below the reactant asymptote. By analogy with the reaction $O(^3P)$ + allene, $^1W7$ can isomerize to $^1W8$ by ring opening and H migration via the saddle point $^1TS7$. Unfortunately, at the present level of calculations we were not able to identify the corresponding stationary point; therefore, we have reported the isomerization path from $^1W7$ to $^1W8$ in Fig. 1 with blue dashed-lines, where the energy value of the transition state $^1TS7$ is expected to be comparable to that (-139.7 kJ/mol, in square parenthesis) of the reaction $O(^3P)$ + propene [26]. Once formed, the W8 intermediate, which shows a relative energy of −487 kJ/mol, can directly dissociate to $HCO + CH_3CHCH$ (channel (8)), via a barrierless process. Competitively, two isomerization processes can take place: (*i*) The migration of a hydrogen atom from C4 to C2 leading to the formation of the $^1W9$ intermediate, located 469 kJ/mol below the reactants, overcoming a barrier of 374 kJ/mol (from $^1W8$); (*ii*) A C1-C2 hydrogen shift, together with the simultaneous formation of a new C-C σ bond, is responsible for the formation of the cyclic intermediate $^1W2$ (located at −400 kJ/mol). Also in this case, a barrier of 332 kJ/mol from $^1W8$ must be overcome during the process. The fission of two C-C σ bonds in the $^1W2$ intermediate, driven by a transition state located 250 kJ/mol below the energy of the reactants, leads to the formation of CO, together with the CH_2CHCH_3 (propene) co-product. Notably, this pathway was not determined in the previous study [32]. Alternatively, two barrierless processes can start from $^1W9$, leading to the formation of $HCO + CH_2CHCH_2$ and $CH_2CH + CH_2CHO$, respectively (Fig. 1).

The interaction of atomic oxygen with the C2 atom of 1,2-butadiene leads to the formation, on the triplet PES, of the $^3W1$ intermediate, showing a relative energy of

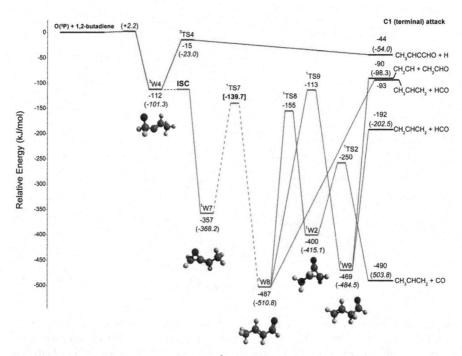

Fig. 1. Potential energy surface of the O(^{3}P) + 1,2-butadiene reaction determined at the CCSD(T)/aug-cc-pVTZ level of theory, by considering the electrophilic attack by O on the terminal carbon (C1). The H channel is formed on the triplet PES, while vinoxy and formyl radical, and CO are generated on the singlet PES via intersystem crossing (ISC). Energy values in parenthesis are for ^{3}TS4 at the CASPT2 level and for all others at the CCSD(T)/CBS/aug-cc-pVTZ level of theory (from ref. 32). The energy barrier for isomerization from ^{1}W7 to ^{1}W8 is here assumed to be the same as that calculated for propylene oxide isomerization to propenal [26] and its value is given between square parenthesis.

−287 kJ/mol (Fig. 2). This intermediate is formed through an entrance submerged barrier, located 1.5 kJ/mol below the reactant energy asymptote (at the CASPT2 level [32]), suggesting the presence of an initial long-range interacting complex, which we were not able to identify at the present level of theory. Furthermore, kinetic calculations [32] have indicated that addition to C2 is the most favoured site of attack, expectedly due to the lack of an entrance barrier and the large stability of the resonantly stabilized ^{3}W1 intermediate. This is similar to what observed in the case of the reaction O(^{3}P) + CH$_2$ = C = CH$_2$ (allene) where the O addition to C2 leads to the resonantly stabilized oxyallyl intermediate [27]. The triplet diradical ^{3}W1 intermediate can directly undergo dissociation, leading to the formation of the ketene molecule (CH$_2$CO), together with the CH$_3$CH radical (ethylidene), overcoming a barrier of 210 kJ/mol (from ^{3}W1) and featuring an exit barrier (^{3}TS1) of 23 kJ/mol with respect to products (see Figs. 2 and 4). At ^{3}TS1 the distance of the dissociating C-C bond is 2.187 Å (see Fig. 4). The global exothermicity of the process is 100 kJ/mol. Also in this case, a competitive reaction channel is represented by the nonadiabatic transition to the singlet PES, through ISC

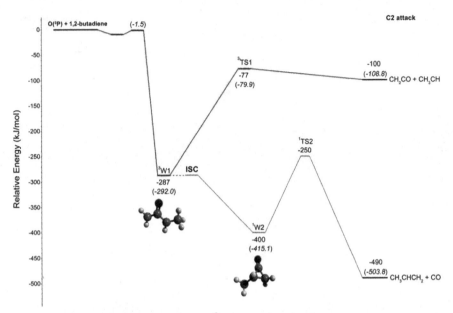

Fig. 2. Potential energy surface of the O(^{3}P) + 1,2-butadiene reaction determined at the CCSD(T)/aug-cc-pVTZ level of theory, by considering the electrophilic attack by O on the central carbon (C2). Energy values in parenthesis are for ^{3}TS1 at the CASPT2 level and for all others at the CCSD(T)/CBS/aug-cc-pVTZ level of theory (from ref. 32). The ketene formation lies on the triplet PES, while propene + CO originates from the singlet PES via ISC.

(presumably around the bottom of ^{3}W1, as in O(^{3}P) + 1,3-butadiene [31]), allowing the formation of the ^{1}W2 cyclic intermediate, located 400 kJ/mol below the reactants. The breaking of two C-C σ bond can then lead to the formation of the CO molecule, together with propene (CH$_3$CHCH$_2$), overcoming a barrier of 150 kJ/mol from ^{1}W2 and featuring a very high exit barrier of 240 kJ/mol with respect to products. Clearly, given the lower addition probability of O(^{3}P) to C1 and the high isomerization barrier between ^{1}W7 and ^{1}W8, and between ^{1}W8 and ^{1}W2, we expect that CO + propene formation (channel (3)) is dominantly arising from the C2 addition rather than from the C1 addition.

Similarly, the attack of O(^{3}P) to the C3 atom of 1,2-butadiene shows a submerged transition state, with a relative energy of −1.0 kJ/mol (at the CASPT2 level [32]), leading to the formation of the ^{3}W3 intermediate, characterized by a new C-O σ bond, located 100 kJ/mol below the energy of the reactants (see Fig. 3). The fission of a C-C σ bond leads from ^{3}W3 to the direct formation of the two radical products CH$_3$ and CH$_2$CCHO (channel (5)), via an exit barrier of 59 kJ/mol with respect to products. As mentioned for the other two cases (C1 and C2 attack), ISC near the ^{3}W3 minimum is invoked as a competitive reaction pathway (see Fig. 3). Following this approach, the formation of the singlet closed-shell cyclic ^{1}W5 intermediate, showing a relative stability of 372 kJ/mol, can be taken into account. Once formed, ^{1}W5 can isomerize to ^{1}W6, located 503 kJ/mol below the reactants, overcoming a barrier of 268 kJ/mol. The related transition state

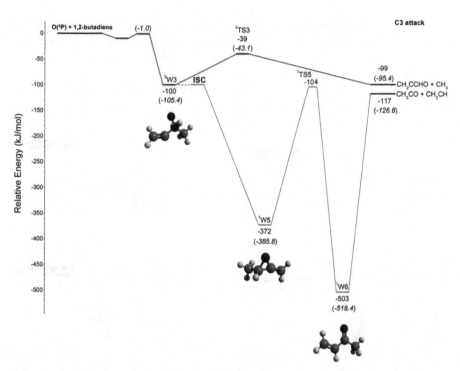

Fig. 3. Potential energy surface of the O(^{3}P) + 1,2-butadiene reaction determined at the CCSD(T)/aug-cc-pVTZ level of theory, by considering the electrophilic attack by O on the C3. Energy values in parenthesis are for ^{3}TS3 at the CASPT2 level and for all others at the CCSD(T)/CBS/aug-cc-pVTZ level of theory (from ref. 32). The CH$_3$ channel is formed on the triplet PES, while the acetyl radical + vinyl are generated on the singlet PES via ISC.

^{1}TS5 (see Fig. 4) shows the simultaneous breaking of a C-O σ bond and the migration of a hydrogen atom from C2 to C3 of the C$_4$H$_6$O intermediate. Finally, the barrierless fission of a C-C σ bond allows the formation of CH$_3$CO (acetyl) and CH$_2$CH (vinyl) radical co-products (channel (9)), showing a global exothermicity of 117 kJ/mol. The structures of the most relevant intermediates (^{3}W3, ^{1}W5, ^{1}W6) are shown in Fig. 3, while those of the transition states (^{3}TS3 and ^{1}TS5) are depicted in Fig. 4.

The comparison with the results coming from our previous investigation [32] shows some differences in the values of the energies derived for the different stationary points, the barriers, and the overall channel exothermicities. The explanation of the origin of the observed differences can be ascribed to the use of different levels of theory, especially in the cases of the stationary points that show a strong multi-reference character (such as ^{3}TS4, ^{3}TS1, and ^{3}TS3). In general, the energies of the minima at the present CCSD(T) level are about 3% higher than those obtained at the CCSD(T)-CBS level. Instead, the differences are significantly larger (in percentage) for the exit triplet barriers. Specifically, at the CASPT2 level ^{3}TS4 is at –23.0 kJ/mol, ^{3}TS1 at –79.9 kJ/mol, and ^{3}TS3 at –43.1 kJ/mol, and these values have to be compared with the present CCSD(T) values of –15 kJ/mol, –77 kJ/mol, and –39 kJ/mol, respectively.

It has been demonstrated that, together with ISC, another class of reactions shows a significant multireference character, namely the isomerization of oxyranil singlet intermediates to aldehydes [23, 26, 31]. Such a case is represented by the saddle point identified in the singlet PES related to the C3 attack, linking the [1]W5 and [1]W6 intermediates, where the calculated energy of [1]TS5 (–104 kJ/mol) is expected to be considerably higher than that at the CASPT2 level (see, for instance, ref. 31).

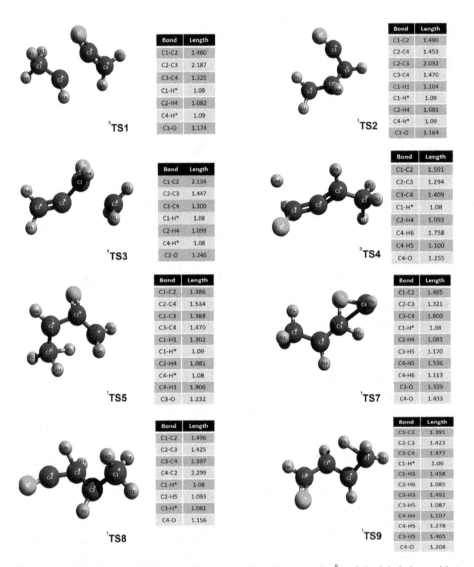

Bond	Length
C1-C2	1.460
C2-C3	2.187
C3-C4	1.325
C1-H*	1.09
C2-H4	1.082
C4-H*	1.09
C3-O	1.174

[3]TS1

Bond	Length
C1-C2	1.490
C2-C4	1.453
C2-C3	2.032
C3-C4	1.470
C1-H1	1.104
C1-H*	1.09
C2-H4	1.081
C4-H*	1.09
C3-O	1.164

[1]TS2

Bond	Length
C1-C2	2.134
C2-C3	1.447
C3-C4	1.300
C1-H*	1.08
C2-H4	1.099
C4-H*	1.08
C2-O	1.246

[3]TS3

Bond	Length
C1-C2	1.501
C2-C3	1.294
C3-C4	1.409
C1-H*	1.08
C2-H4	1.093
C4-H6	1.758
C4-H5	1.100
C4-O	1.255

[3]TS4

Bond	Length
C1-C2	1.386
C2-C4	1.534
C2-C3	1.388
C3-C4	1.470
C1-H1	1.302
C1-H*	1.09
C2-H4	1.081
C4-H*	1.08
C4-H1	1.806
C3-O	1.232

[1]TS5

Bond	Length
C1-C2	1.495
C2-C3	1.321
C3-C4	1.800
C1-H*	1.08
C2-H4	1.081
C3-H5	1.170
C4-H5	1.536
C4-H6	1.113
C3-O	1.339
C4-O	1.433

[1]TS7

Bond	Length
C1-C2	1.496
C2-C3	1.425
C3-C4	1.397
C4-C2	2.299
C1-H*	1.08
C2-H5	1.093
C3-H*	1.081
C4-O	1.156

[1]TS8

Bond	Length
C1-C2	1.391
C2-C3	1.423
C3-C4	1.477
C1-H*	1.09
C1-H3	1.458
C2-H6	1.085
C3-H3	1.492
C3-H5	1.087
C4-H4	1.107
C4-H5	1.278
C3-H5	1.465
C4-O	1.208

[1]TS9

Fig. 4. wB97XD/aug-cc-pVTZ optimized geometries (distances in Å) of the labeled transition states identified along the triplet and singlet PESs for the reaction O(^{3}P) + 1,2-butadiene.

Assuming a comparable rate of ISC following C1, C2, and C3 addition, we expect that the most favoured product channel on the singlet PES is the strongly exothermic CO + propene (channel (3)), because the pathway to this product channel is the lowest in energy, while little CH$_3$CO + C$_2$H$_3$, and also HCO + CH$_2$CHCH$_2$ (allyl) are expected. These qualitative expectations are corroborated by the preliminary estimates of the experimental BFs (0.49 for CO, 0.027 for CH$_3$CO, and 0.014 for HCO) [34]. On the triplet PES, given the higher probability of the C2 and C3 additions, we expect mainly CH$_2$CO (ketene) and CH$_3$ (methyl) formation, with the H-displacement channel being smaller. Again, these qualitative expectations are in line with our preliminary estimates [34] of the BFs (–0.13 for ketene, –0.15 for methyl, and –0.01 for H). It will be interesting and useful to perform statistical (RRKM/ME) simulations of the product BFs at the collision energy of the CMB experiment. Work in this direction is currently in progress [34].

It is also interesting to compare the dynamics of the O(^{3}P) + methylallene reaction with that of the simpler, yet closely related O(^{3}P) + allene reaction. In the oxidation of the prototype of cumulenes (allene), the co-product of carbon monoxide is ethylene [27], while in O(^{3}P) + 1,2-butadiene the co-product of CO is propene. However, in both reactions the CO main channel originates via ISC from the triplet to the singlet PES. In addition, the energy of the methyl-oxyallyl intermediate (–400 kJ/mol with respect to the energy of the reactants) and the exit barrier (250 kJ/mol for the O(^{3}P) + 1,2-butadiene reaction and 265 kJ/mol for the O(^{3}P) + allene reaction) leading to CO formation are comparable in the two reactions. The large stability of the methyl-oxyallyl radical comes from resonance effects, as in the oxyallyl intermediate of the O(^{3}P) + allene reaction [27]. The probability of the attack to the carbon atom C3 was calculated to be 36.3% by Caracciolo et al. [32] and this means that this site attack is the second most important in the title reaction. The attack to the inner carbon by O(^{3}P) leads to two different, competitive exit channels, namely methyl (CH$_3$) formation and, via ISC, acetyl (CH$_3$CO) radical formation. It is interesting to note that this attack site is not present in the reaction between O(^{3}P) and allene (see refs. 23 and 27), since the allene molecule has three attack sites, but two of these are equivalent (the two terminal carbons, namely C1 and C3). This is the first difference between the two systems, and this will lead to the experimentally observed differences regarding the BFs of the primary products and the extent of ISC (see below). Another important difference between the two systems concerns the PES that describes the attack of atomic oxygen to the terminal carbon (C1) of the unsaturated hydrocarbon. Although this mechanism is the less favoured for both reactions, in the case of the title reaction the PES is somewhat more complicated than that of O(^{3}P) + allene. In particular, the singlet PES has an exit channel that sees the formation of the vinoxy radical (CH$_2$CHO) which is not present in the equivalent singlet PES for the O(^{3}P) + allene system [23, 27] (while it is present on the C$_3$H$_4$O triplet PES). In summary, the two reactions that see the attack of O(^{3}P) on 1,2-butadiene and allene have many similarities but, at the same time, also important differences. For both reactions, the main product channel is represented by the CO molecule formation, which has an experimental BF of 49% and 81.5% for 1,2-butadiene and allene, respectively. In both cases we can assert that this primary product is formed on the singlet PES, after ISC from the entrance triplet PES. For O(^{3}P) + 1,2-butadiene, both the attack on the terminal carbon C1 and the attack on the intermediate carbon C2 can give rise to the formation of the CO molecule, but, given the greater probability of the attack to C2 (see ref. 32), we can reasonably assume that most of it is originated after the attack of atomic oxygen on C2, which leads to a resonantly stabilized triplet diradical intermediate.

As previously pointed out, the 1,2-butadiene molecule has one more attack site than the allene molecule, represented by C3, and this entails a differentiation in the global reactivity. In fact, from this attack CH_3 + CH_2CCHO can be formed on the triplet PES, as well as the acetyl (CH_3CO) radical (+ CH_2CH) after ISC to the singlet PES. Experimentally, in $O(^3P)$ + 1,2-butadiene it has been observed that the CH_3 channel has a BF = 0.14 [34], and is the second most important channel under the conditions of the CMB experiment. This essentially entails two interrelated consequences: a smaller extent of ISC in the reaction between $O(^3P)$ and 1,2-butadiene (ISC - 70–75%, [32, 34]) compared to that observed in the reaction between $O(^3P)$ and allene (ISC –85–90%) [27], and therefore a lower yield of the channel that involves the formation of CO for the title reaction (BF = 0.49 vs BF = 0.77 for $O(^3P)$ + allene).

Currently, further calculations are underway in order to perform a statistical estimate of the product BFs, separately on the triplet and singlet PES, as done by Nguyen *et al.* [23] for $O(^3P)$ + allene. The comparison between the experimental BFs and the theoretical BFs on the two distinct PESs should allow us to clarify the detailed overall reaction mechanism of $O(^3P)$ + 1,2-butadiene and to better clarify estimate the extent of ISC for the title reaction.

4   Conclusions

The study at the ab initio CCSD(T)(aug-cc-pVTZ) level of the interaction of $O(^3P)$ with 1,2-butadiene has led to a characterization of the various intermediates and transition states of the triplet and singlet C_4H_6O PESs, as well as to the determination of the energetics of the numerous, competitive product channels of this reaction. Although this level of electronic structure calculations is not fully adequate for determining accurately the energies of the entrance barriers and neither the energy of the inter-conversion and exit barriers exhibiting strong multireference character, as it has emerged from comparisons with the results of previous CCSD(T)(aug-cc-pVTZ)-CBS and CASPT2 calculations on the same system, it nevertheless provides a sufficiently reasonable description of the reactive interaction, which has been useful for a semi-quantitative description of the reaction dynamics, including ISC effects. Higher level calculations, including CBS extrapolation of some of the relevant energies, are in progress. This, together with the previous CASPT2 values of the exit barriers on the triplet PES for this system, should permit in the near future reliable statistical (RRKM/ME) calculations of product BFs, separately on the triplet and singlet PES, to be compared with experimental results of product BFs for nine different observed product channels, as obtained from CMB studies of this reaction. Because some product channels can be rationalized only invoking an important role of ISC, the comparison of experimental and theoretical BFs will shed light also on the extent of ISC in the title reaction.

Acknowledgments. We acknowledge the Italian MUR (Ministero dell'Università e della Ricerca) for "PRIN 2017" funds, project "Modeling and Analysis of carbon nanoparticles for innovative applications Generated dIrectly and Collected DUring combuSTion (MAGIC DUST)", Grant Number 2017PJ5XXX. We acknowledge support also from Italian MUR, University of Perugia within the program "Department of Excellence-2018–2022-Project AMIS", and "Dipartimento di Ingegneria Civile ed Ambientale" (DICA) of the University of Perugia for allocated computing time within the project "Dipartimenti di Eccellenza 2018–2022".

References

1. Schobert, H.: Chemistry of Fossil Fuels and Biofuels. Cambridge University Press, Cambridge, UK (2013)

2. Frenklach, M., Clary, D.W., Gardiner, W.C., Stein, S.E.: Effect of fuel structure on pathways to soot. Symp. Int. Combust. **21**, 1067–1076 (1988)

3. Gardiner, W.C.: Gas-Phase Combustion Chemistry. Springer, New York (2000). https://doi.org/10.1007/978-1-4612-1310-9

4. Kohse-Höinghaus, K., et al.: Biofuel combustion chemistry: from ethanol to biodiesel. Ang. Chem. Int. Ed. **49**, 3572–3597 (2010)

5. Wayne, R.P.: Chemistry of Atmospheres: An Introduction to the Chemistry of the Atmospheres of Earth, the Planets, and Their Satellites, 3rd edn ACS Publications, Washington, D.C. (2000)

6. Sabbah, H., Biennier, L., Sims, I.R., Georgievskii, Y., Klippenstein, S.J., Smith, I.W.M.: Understanding reactivity at very low temperatures: the reactions of oxygen atoms with alkenes. Science **317**, 102–105 (2007)

7. Occhiogrosso, A., Viti, S., Balucani, N.: An improved chemical scheme for the reactions of atomic oxygen and simple unsaturated hydrocarbons - implications for star-forming regions. MNRAS **432**, 3423–3430 (2013)

8. Simmie, J.M.: Detailed chemical kinetic models for the combustion of hydrocarbon fuels. Progr. Energy Combust. Sci. **29**, 599–634 (2003)

9. Cvetanović, R.J.: Evaluated chemical kinetic data for the reactions of atomic oxygen O(^{3}P) with unsaturated hydrocarbons. J. Phys. Chem. Ref. Data **16**, 261–326 (1987)

10. Casavecchia, P., Leonori, F., Balucani, N.: Reaction dynamics of oxygen atoms with unsaturated hydrocarbons from crossed molecular beam studies: primary products, branching ratios and role of intersystem crossing. Int. Rev. Phys. Chem. **34**, 161–204 (2015)

11. Pan, H., Liu, K., Caracciolo, A., Casavecchia, P.: Crossed beam polyatomic reaction dynamics: recent advances and new insights. Chem. Soc. Rev. **46**, 7517–7547 (2017)

12. Caracciolo, A., et al.: combined experimental and theoretical studies of the O(^{3}P) + 1-butene reaction dynamics: primary products, branching ratios and role of intersystem crossing. J. Phys. Chem. A **123**, 9934–9956 (2019)

13. Blumenberg, B., Hoyermann, K., Sievert, R.: Primary products in the reactions of oxygen atoms with simple and substituted hydrocarbons. Symp. Int. Combust. **16**, 841–852 (1977)

14. Vanuzzo, G., et al.: Isomer-specific chemistry in the propyne and allene reactions with oxygen atoms: CH_3CH + CO versus CH_2CH_2 + CO products. J. Phys. Chem. Lett. **7**, 1010–1015 (2016)

15. Vanuzzo, G., et al.: Reaction dynamics of O(^{3}P) + propyne: I. primary products, branching ratios, and role of intersystem crossing from crossed molecular beam experiments. J. Phys. Chem. A **120**, 4603–4618 (2016)

16. Nguyen, T.L., Vereecken, L., Hou, X.J., Nguyen, M.T., Peeters, J.: Potential energy surfaces, product distributions and thermal rate coefficients of the reaction of O(^{3}P) with $C_2H_4(X^1A_g)$: a comprehensive theoretical study. J. Phys. Chem. A **109**, 7489–7499 (2005)

17. Nguyen, T.L., Vereecken, L., Peeters, J.: Quantum chemical and theoretical kinetics study of the O(^{3}P) + C$_2$H$_2$ reaction: a multistate process. J. Phys. Chem. A **110**, 6696–6706 (2006)

18. Nguyen, T.L., Peeters, J., Vereecken, L.: Theoretical reinvestigation of the O(^{3}P) + C$_6$H$_6$ reaction: quantum chemical and statistical rate calculations. J. Phys. Chem. A **111**, 3836–3849 (2007)

19. Balucani, N., Leonori, F., Casavecchia, P., Fu, B., Bowman, J.M.: Crossed molecular beams and quasiclassical trajectory surface hopping studies of the multichannel nonadiabatic O(^{3}P) + ethylene reaction at high collision energy. J. Phys. Chem. A **119**, 12498–12511 (2015)

20. Rajak, K., Maiti, B.: Trajectory surface hopping study of the O(^{3}P) + C$_2$H$_2$ reaction dynamics: effect of collision energy on the extent of intersystem crossing. J. Chem. Phys. **140**, 044314 (2014)

21. Cavallotti, C., et al.: Relevance of the channel leading to formaldehyde + triplet ethylidene in the O(^{3}P) + propene reaction under combustion conditions. J. Phys. Chem. Lett. **5**, 4213–4218 (2014)

22. Li, X., Jasper, A.W., Zádor, J., Miller, J.A., Klippenstein, S.J.: Theoretical kinetics of O + C$_2$H$_4$. Proc. Combust. Inst. **36**, 219–227 (2017)

23. Nguyen, T., Peeters, J., Vereecken, L.: Quantum chemical and statistical rate study of the reaction of O(^{3}P) with allene: O-addition and H-abstraction channels. J. Phys. Chem. A **110**, 12166–12176 (2006)

24. Casavecchia, P., Capozza, G., Segoloni, E., Leonori, F., Balucani, N., Volpi, G.G.: Dynamics of the O(^{3}P) + C$_2$H$_4$ reaction: Identification of five primary product channels (vinoxy, acetyl, methyl, methylene, and ketene) and branching ratios by the crossed molecular beam technique with soft electron ionization. J. Phys. Chem. A **109**, 3527–3530 (2005)

25. Fu, B., et al.: Intersystem crossing and dynamics in O(^{3}P) + C$_2$H$_4$ multichannel reaction: experiment validates theory. In: Proceedings of the National Academy of Sciences (U.S.A.), vol. 109, pp. 9733–9738 (2012)

26. Leonori, F., et al.: Experimental and theoretical studies on the dynamics of the O(^{3}P) + propene reaction: primary products, branching ratios, and role of intersystem crossing. J. Phys. Chem. C **119**, 14632–14652 (2015)

27. Leonori, F., Occhiogrosso, A., Balucani, N., Bucci, A., Petrucci, R., Casavecchia, P.: Crossed molecular beam dynamics studies of the O(^{3}P) + allene reaction: primary products, branching ratios, and dominant role of intersystem crossing. J. Phys. Chem. Lett. **3**, 75–80 (2012)

28. Leonori, F., Balucani, N., Capozza, G., Segoloni, E., Volpi, G.G., Casavecchia, P.: Dynamics of the O(^{3}P) + C$_2$H$_2$ reaction from crossed molecular beam experiments with soft electron ionization detection. Phys. Chem. Chem. Phys. **16**, 10008–10022 (2014)

29. Casavecchia, P., Leonori, F., Balucani, N., Petrucci, R., Capozza, G., Segoloni, E.: Probing the dynamics of polyatomic multichannel elementary reactions by crossed molecular beam experiments with soft electron-ionization mass spectrometric detection. Phys. Chem. Chem. Phys. **11**, 46–65 (2009)

30. Vanuzzo, G., et al.: Crossed-Beams and theoretical studies of the O(^{3}P, ^{1}D) + benzene reactions: primary products, branching fractions, and role of intersystem crossing. J. Phys. Chem. A **125**, 8434–8453 (2021)

31. Cavallotti, C.; Della Libera, A.; Recio, P.; Caracciolo, A.; Balucani, N.; Casavecchia, P.: Crossed-beam and theoretical studies of multichannel nonadiabatic reactions: branching fractions and role of intersystem crossing for O(^{3}P) + 1,3-butadiene. Faraday Discuss. (2022). In press. https://doi.org/10.1039/D2FD00037G

32. Caracciolo, A., et al.: Crossed molecular beams and theoretical studies of the O(^{3}P) + 1,2-butadiene reaction: dominant formation of propene + CO and ethylidene + ketene molecular channels. Chin. J. Chem. Phys. **32**, 113–122 (2019)

33. NIST Chemistry WebBook, Gaithersburg, MD: National Institute of Standards and Technology (2002)

34. Vanuzzo, G., et al.: Work in progress
35. Chai, J.D., Head-Gordon, M.: Systematic optimization of long-range corrected hybrid density functionals. J. Chem. Phys. **128**, 084106 (2008)
36. Chai, J.D., Head-Gordon, M.: Long-range corrected hybrid density functionals with damped atom–atom dispersion corrections. Phys. Chem. Chem. Phys. **10**, 6615–6620 (2008)
37. Jr Dunning, T.H.: Gaussian basis sets for use in correlated molecular calculations. I. the atoms boron through neon and hydrogen. J. Chem. Phys. **90**, 1007–1023 (1989)
38. Woon, D.E., Jr Dunning, T.H.: Gaussian basis sets for use in correlated molecular calculations. III. the atoms aluminum through argon. J. Chem. Phys. **98**, 1358–1371 (1993)
39. Kendall, R.A., Jr Dunning, T.H., Harrison, J.R.: Electron affinities of the first-row atoms revisited. systematic basis sets and wave functions. J. Chem. Phys. **96**, 6796–6806 (1992)
40. Gonzalez, C., Schlegel, H.B.: An improved algorithm for reaction path following. J. Chem. Phys. **90**, 2154–2161 (1989)
41. Gonzalez, C., Schlegel, H.B.: Reaction path following in mass- weighted internal coordinates. J. Phys. Chem. **41**, 5523–5527 (1990)
42. Frisch, M. J., et al.: Gaussian 09, Rev. A.02, Gaussian, Inc., Wallingford, CT (2009)
43. Werner, H.-J., Knowles, P.J., Knizia, G., Manby, F.R., Schütz, M.: Molpro: a general-purpose quantum chemistry program package. WIREs Comput. Mol. Sci. **2**, 242–253 (2012). https://doi.org/10.1002/wcms.82
44. Werner, H.-J., et al.: The Molpro quantum chemistry package. J. Chem. Phys. **152**, 144107 (2020). https://doi.org/10.1063/5.0005081
45. Cavallotti, C., et al.: Theoretical study of the extent of intersystem crossing in the O(^{3}P) + C_6H_6 reaction with experimental validation. J. Phys. Chem. Lett. **11**, 9621–9628 (2020)

The Assembly of a Computing Platform for Studying Protein Inhibitors Against COVID-19 Replication

Leonardo Pacifici[1]([envelope]) [iD], Ribi Akbar[1] [iD], Andrea Lombardi[1] [iD],
Giuseppe Vitillaro[2] [iD], and Maria Noelia Faginas Lago[1] [iD]

[1] Department of Chemistry, Biology and Biotechnology,
via Elce di Sotto, 8, 06123 Perugia, Italy
leonardo.pacifici@collaboratori.unipg.it
[2] CNR-SCITEC, via Elce di Sotto, 8, 06123 Perugia, Italy

Abstract. A new highly efficient GPU-equipped computing platform for studying the molecular inhibition mechanisms of the Sars-Cov-2 virus by natural compounds and aptamers has been installed and configured. Studies will be carried out by means of molecular dynamics methods and programs. For this reason, we have assembled specific hardware components into a 4U rack, together with a NVIDIA RTX 3060 GPU for speeding up molecular dynamics calculations and visualizing their outcomes. In fact, not only computational resources, in terms of computing power and execution times, are needed by molecular dynamics programs adopted by us, but also a system allowing the rendering and visualization of large biomolecules and their trajectories, such as viruses and proteins, represents a key factor for our work. Details about platform implementation and preliminary tests carried out are discussed.

Keywords: GPU · Molecular dynamics · 3D rendering · Sars-Cov-2 · Covid-19

1 Introduction

Nowadays, the two main well tested strategies designed to eradicate the Covid-19 pandemic are based either on the development of a vaccine or on the identification of proteins inhibitors involved in the replication of the Sars-Cov-2 virus, responsible for the disease. Among proteins playing a leading role in the viral replication are Sars-Cov-2 3a (or viroporin 3a), an ion channel expressed on the membranes of infected human cells and Sars-Cov-2 MPro, produced in same cells and deeply involved in the mechanism of virus replication and its maturation. More in detail, the protein Sars-Cov-2 3a is expressed on the plasma membrane of the host cell, where it forms an ion channel whose activity promotes the transport of potassium ions (K^+) across the membrane [1] and increases the pathogenicity of the virus by promoting its replication and release from the cell.

O. Gervasi et al. (Eds.): ICCSA 2022 Workshops, LNCS 13382, pp. 264–274, 2022.
https://doi.org/10.1007/978-3-031-10592-0_20

Thus, it has been supposed that inhibition of this channel could represent a potential antiviral therapy for Covid-19; among the aims of our work, in fact, there is the development of the theoretical and computational apparatus for working out molecular dynamics observables to be compared with experimental ones [2]. Moreover, it is important to point out the growing interest of scientific community on the topic of ion channels in human cells. From a biological point of view they are pores in the cell membrane that allow ions to pass through the impermeable lipid bilayer of the cells. Besides experimental works carried out in the past, previous molecular dynamics studies were not able to reproduce experimentally observed selectivities. Now, with the COVID-19 pandemic explosion, they are receiving increasing attention due to their role in the virus replication and, thus, in its circulation. Moreover, the work carried out in the last two years for identifying possible inhibitors of Sars-Cov-2 replication in human cells is also fostering computational biochemistry studies aimed at characterizing the mechanisms involved in the transfer of biomolecular species through ion channels. Therefore, this represents one of the pillars on which our work lays.

On the other hand, the viral protein Sars-Cov-2 M-Pro is one of the most studied antiviral targets, playing a key role in the processing of viral polyproteins, a family of proteins involved in the control of virus replication and maturation [3,4]. For this reason, scientific community is evaluating the effectiveness of many natural molecules for the inhibition of Sars-Cov-2 M-Pro activity in order to contrast viral replication.

The Molecular Dynamics group of the Department of Chemistry, Biology and Biotechnology of the University of Perugia within a multidisciplinary project will use classical molecular dynamics (MD) for studying Sars-Cov-2 inhibitors. MD is a theoretical chemistry method for analyzing the movement of atoms and molecules using pre-described potential functions called force fields. This method can be employed to investigate the structural rearrangement of chemical and biochemical systems, such as pure solvents, mixed solutions, gaseous separation and combustion processes [5,6]. However, a generic type of force field is often limited in its use when investigating particular systems, for instance those involving biomolecules. In this work we are facing just this problem, that is the formulation of a force field to be used in MD simulations. It represents part of a greater effort towards the development of an anti-Covid-19 therapy, by identifying molecular inhibitors for the two proteins (A) and (B), through the design of two molecular platforms similar for path but different for molecules used (natural compounds and RNA aptamers, respectively). In particular, efforts of our group are aimed at identifying both the potential sites on the Sars-Cov-2 3a channel protein and simulate the inhibitory interaction and the best potential high affinity sites of aptamers on the Sars-Cov-2 MPro protein, simulating the inhibitory interaction.

Both tasks will be carried out by means of MD simulations, making use of the well known suites of programs DLPOLY [7] and NAMD [8]. However, in order to perform the calculations mentioned above use has to be made of a suitable computing platform. As a matter of fact, dynamics simulations of large biomolecules, like viruses or proteins, are difficult to carry out due to the large number of atoms involved in the process. They request very long computing times and, in some cases, large amounts of RAM and storage memory. Another key factor in these works is concerned with the visualization of the outcomes of related simulations. When one has to visualize trajectories of hundreds of vibro-rotating molecules a standard computing platform results to be inadequate due to video rendering problems. In such cases, a GPU (Graphic Processing Unit) represents the best choice, both from a computational and cost point of view (not cheap but not too expensive either), to overcome issues related to long computing times and 3D video rendering processing. In fact, thanks to their highly parallel structure GPUs allow to speed up calculations [9,10] and make it possible the visualization of large biomolecular systems. Therefore, in order to carry out dynamics simulations outlined above a new computing platform equipped with a high performance GPU has been assembled. The paper is articulated as follows: in Sect. 2 the features of the computing platforms are discussed. In Sect. 3 preliminary results on the capabilities of the platform are illustrated. In Sect. 4 concluding remarks are given.

2   The Assembly of the Computing Platform

In order to build a suitable computing platform for our purposes we have assembled it in house. Its hostname is *axis* and it is equipped with:

- ASUS PRIME TRX40-PRO S motherboard
- AMD Ryzen Threadripper 3960X@3.8 GHz processor with 24 cores and 48 threads
- 128 GB DDR4 SDRAM
- 6 Crucial MX500 1TB SSD
- NVIDIA GeForce RTX 3060 with 3584 CUDA cores, 12 GB GDDR6 RAM and compute capability 8.6 (NVIDIA driver version 510.47.03).

We have installed on *axis* the Ubuntu 20.04 LTS server operating system (OS). In particular, we created a RAID 6 software implementation at OS level (using block-level striping with two parity blocks distributed across the six SSDs) and we installed a ZFS filesystem with a RAID-Z2 configuration at application level. This configuration guarantees high protection against data corruption, support for high storage capacities and, in general, great performances. On the pool we have also activated both compression and dedup. Finally, to the end of best compiling and running the computational packages cited above we also installed the Intel oneAPI toolkit (version 2022.1.2) and the CUDA one (version 11.6) [11].

As mentioned above, *axis* is intended for running extensive molecular dynamics calculations and for visualizing related outcomes. Taking into account the systems to be studied, for carrying out preliminary test calculations we selected NAMD, a parallel molecular dynamics code specifically designed for simulating large biomolecular systems. We adopted the 2.14 multicore release of NAMD. We built two complete NAMD binaries from source codes, a first one (standard) that makes use of C/C++ and Fortran compilers, Charm++/Converse,

TCL and FFTW libraries and a second one exploiting, in addition, the CUDA GPU acceleration. In more detail, use has been made of the g++ and gfortran compilers, while the FFTW libraries linked are those of the Intel oneAPI toolkit.

3 Preliminary Calculations on *Axis*

In order to perform tests on *axis* we ran preliminary calculations with NAMD using both binaries. The system selected is the one involving the Sars-Cov-2 3a protein, made of 11840 water molecules and 12415 residues. The total number of atoms amounts to 58352. In Fig. 1 is schematized the biomolecular system made by a lipid bilayer membrane, the Sars-Cov-2 3a protein forming the ion channel, sodium and chlorine ions. Water molecules are not shown in the figure. In order to build the initial configuration of the system and the inter- and intramolecular interactions we took advantage of:

- Orientations of Proteins in Membranes (OPM) database [12], providing spatial arrangements and orientation of the membrane protein with respect to the hydrocarbon core of the lipid bilayer;
- Protein Data Bank (PDB) [13], providing information about the shape of proteins;
- CHARMM-GUI [14], to interactively build the system and prepare its inputs, as well as for setting up the force field parametrization to obtain interaction potentials.

Once the input files are built, four steps are needed for running a full MD simulation with NAMD:

1. Minimization, to find the global energy minimum
2. Annealing, to heat the system (in the current case, from 60K to 300K)
3. Equilibration, to equilibrate the system after heating
4. Molecular Dynamics, to solve classical equations of motion.

For our simulations we adopted a NPT ensemble, a cut-off radius of 14 Å, an external electric field of 1.5 V and a timestep equal to 2 fs for a total of 10000 steps, corresponding to a simulation time of 0.02 ns. In more detail, we use a 2 fs time step because this is the most common one. Increasing the timestep might cause the system to explode because the total energy becomes very large. With respect to the whole simulation time, since this protein is a very complex system, the event normally happens in the period of nanoseconds or microseconds. Therefore for this system, we are trying to run simulations for more than 10^8 steps (200 ns), although for testing the application on our new platform we reduced the number of steps to 10000, as mentioned above. The use of an electric field is a way to force the ion to pass through the ion channel. Here we also refer

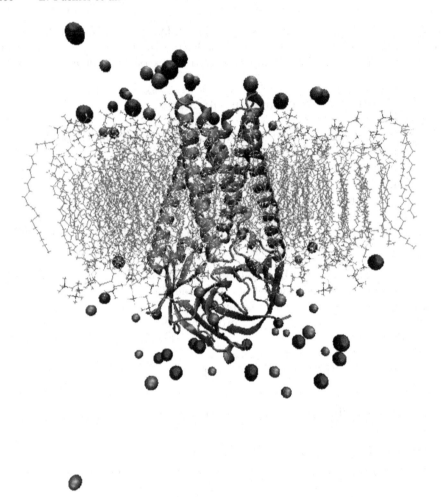

Fig. 1. Screenshot of the lipid membrane (light blue), the protein (violet) and Na$^+$ and Cl$^-$ ions (yellow and cyan, respectively) (Color figure online)

to the voltage-gated ion channel that involves the electric field for the passage of ions from extracellular to the cytosol. Regarding the composition of the systems, the ion concentration, etc. we refer to the experimental data. We measured the wall clock times for steps 1 and 4, using both the standard implementation of NAMD and the one obtained using the CUDA acceleration, running the binaries on an increasing number of cores.

Table 1. Wallclock time measurements for minimization runs using the standard implementation and the CUDA based one

Number of cores	$t_{standard}(s)$	$t_{CUDA}(s)$
1	432.72	21.93
2	221.46	14.27
4	116.43	11.81
6	81.21	10.92
8	62.78	10.72
10	53.49	10.50
12	46.10	10.32
14	40.81	10.64
16	36.77	10.55

Table 2. Wallclock time measurements for molecular dynamics runs using the standard implementation and the CUDA based one

Number of cores	$t_{standard}(s)$	$t_{CUDA}(s)$
1	2426.39	111.87
2	1224.20	61.30
4	627.76	39.91
6	434.42	35.41
8	331.80	33.81
10	274.52	32.42
12	233.98	32.16
14	205.81	32.12
16	180.64	30.68

In Table 1 and 2 the measured computing times for the minimization and MD simulations are shown, respectively. As can be seen from the Tables, in both cases the CUDA binary is drastically faster in terms of computing time. In particular, the acceleration is more pronounced when less cores are used. In fact, on a single core the time saving factor is about 20 with respect to the standard implementation, while on 16 cores it reduces to about 3.5 and 6 for the minimization simulation and for the MD one, respectively. This is likely due to the fact that the use of a larger number of cores in the calculation on one hand implies a greater number of CUDA *threads* running on the GPU (in fact, the percentage use of the GPU for MD simulations is 20% using one core and 60% using two cores), on the other hand more CPU-GPU data transfers are needed, resulting in an overall time overhead that reduces the time gain when compared to the multicore execution of the standard NAMD implementation. This is also confirmed by speedups estimates in Fig. 2, 3, 4 and 5, plotted as a function

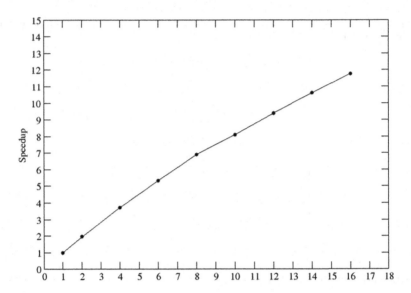

Fig. 2. Calculated speedup for the minimization runs using the standard implementation

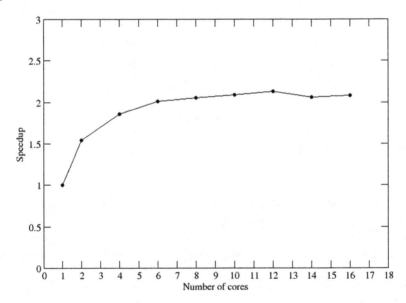

Fig. 3. Calculated speedup for the minimization runs using the CUDA based implementation

of the number of cores. From Fig. 2 and 4, where the speedups obtained using the standard compiled binary of NAMD are shown, it can be seen an almost linear speedup for the minimization runs, which improves slightly for the MD

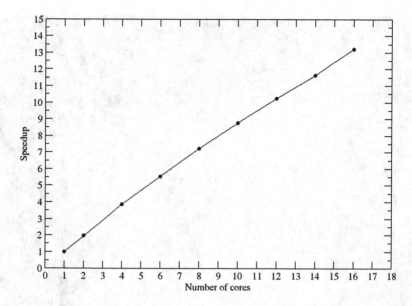

Fig. 4. Calculated speedup for the MD runs using the standard implementation

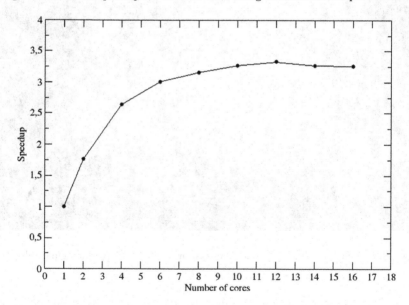

Fig. 5. Calculated speedup for the MD runs using the CUDA based implementation

ones. This means that executing NAMD on more than one core guarantees good performances and that the program scales well with the number of cores.

This is not observed in Fig. 3 and 5, where speedups obtained running the CUDA implementation of NAMD are shown. In fact, as it can be seen from the

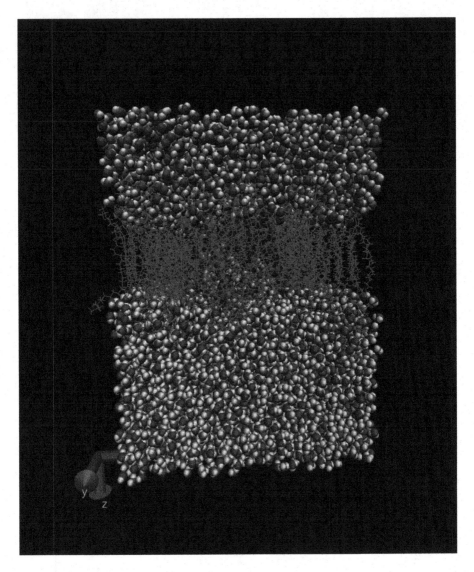

Fig. 6. Screenshot of the biomolecular system from VMD (Color figure online)

Figures, it is not linear. Speedup values increase slightly up to 8 cores for the minimization runs and to 10 for the MD ones, to become flat afterwards. The better performances shown in Fig. 5 are likely due to a heavier use of the GPU in carrying out molecular dynamics calculations whereas algorithms employed in the NAMD minimization step do not use effectively the GPU. In any case, the flattening of the curves in both simulations is probably due to CPU-GPU data transfer overhead, which masquerade the computational gain arising from a parallel multicore execution on the GPU *threads*.

As already mentioned before, the assembly of the current computing platform has been made necessary not only for the computational requirements of the programs chosen for studying the biomolecular systems described above, but also to make it possible the rendering and visualization of related outputs. In fact, a standard platform not equipped with a suitable GPU does not allow the use of any program for visualizing molecules and related trajectories, when dealing with a great number atoms, as it is the case. For our purposes use has been made of the VMD tool [15], a molecular visualization program for displaying, animating, and analyzing large biomolecular systems using 3-D graphics and built-in scripting. As an example, in Fig. 6 is depicted a typical screenshot obtained by manipulating the output of NAMD with VMD. The image is so clear that is possible to recognize the spike protein (orange), water molecules and the lipid membrane (blue), while the ions are not represented. The visualization of thousands of trajectories is also a relatively easy task when performed with the GPU acceleration.

4   Conclusions

In this work we have described the in-house assembly of a new computing platform called *axis* for the study of large biomolecular systems involved in the replication of the Sars-Cov-2 virus. *Axis* benefits from a ZFS filesystem with a RAID-Z2 configuration at application level and from a NVIDIA GPU of the RTX series with 12 GB of RAM memory. In order to test its capabilities and carry out performance tests we have compiled NAMD sources and have run preliminary molecular dynamics calculations on a system made by a human cell membrane with the ion channel represented by the Sars-Cov-2 3a protein. Related performance measurements demonstrate that calculations carried out with the CUDA acceleration are dramatically faster than those performed with the non-CUDA executable. On the other hand, the standard binary scales better with the number of cores when compared to the CUDA based one, showing an almost linear speedup up to 16 cores, whereas the CUDA one is far from linearity (the curve becomes flat starting from eight-ten cores), most likely due to the heaviness of data transfers from CPU to GPU (and vice-versa), when the number of processes involved in the calculation increases. Thanks to the rapid progress in GPU technology we will be able to run large batches of molecular dynamics calculations with NAMD within reasonable times and to visualize its outcomes. Finally, based on the results we are going to obtain by running extended MD calculations on this new computing platform we might extend them to other biological systems.

Acknowledgements. The authors thank MUR and Perugia University for financial support through the AMIS project ("Dipartimenti di Eccellenza-2018–2022"). AL and NFL also thank Fondazione Cassa di Risparmio di Perugia n.# 220.0513 to C.E.

References

1. Castaño-Rodriguez, C., et al.: Role of severe acute respiratory syndrome coronavirus viroporins E, 3a, and 8a in replication and pathogenesis. MBio **9**(3), e02325-17 (2018)
2. Kern, D., et al.: Cryo-em structure of sars-cov-2 orf3a in lipid nanodiscs. Nat. Struct. Mol. Biol. **28**(7), 573–582 (2021)
3. Zhang, X., Tan, Y., Ling, Y., et al.: Viral and host factors related to the clinical outcome of covid-19. Nature **583**, 437–440 (2020)
4. Jin, Z., Du, X., Xu, Y., et al.: Structure of mpro from sars-cov-2 and discovery of its inhibitors. Nature **582**, 289–293 (2020)
5. Faginas-Lago, N., Albertí, M., Costantini, A., Laganà, A., Lombardi, A., Pacifici, L.: An innovative synergistic grid approach to the computational study of protein aggregation mechanisms. J. Mol. Model. **20**(7), 1–9 (2014). https://doi.org/10.1007/s00894-014-2226-4
6. Lombardi, A., Faginas-Lago, N., Laganà, A.: Grid calculation tools for massive applications of collision dynamics simulations: carbon dioxide energy transfer. In: Murgante, B. (ed.) ICCSA 2014. LNCS, vol. 8579, pp. 627–639. Springer, Cham (2014). https://doi.org/10.1007/978-3-319-09144-0_43
7. Smith, W., Forester, T.R.: DL_POLY_2.0: a general-purpose parallel molecular dynamics simulation package. J. Mol. Graph. **14**(3), 136–141 (1996)
8. Phillips, J.C., et al.: Scalable molecular dynamics with namd. J. Comput. Chem. **26**(16), 1781–1802 (2005)
9. Pacifici, L., Nalli, D., Laganà, A.: Quantum reactive scattering on innovative computing platforms. Comput. Phys. Commun. **184**(5), 1372–1380 (2013)
10. Pacifici, L., Nalli, D., Skouteris, D., Laganà, A.: Time dependent quantum reactive scattering on GPU. In: Murgante, B., Gervasi, O., Iglesias, A., Taniar, D., Apduhan, B.O. (eds.) ICCSA 2011. LNCS, vol. 6784, pp. 428–441. Springer, Heidelberg (2011). https://doi.org/10.1007/978-3-642-21931-3_33
11. Cook, S.: CUDA Programming: A Developer's Guide to Parallel Computing with GPUs, 1st edn. Morgan Kaufmann Publishers Inc., San Francisco, CA, USA (2012)
12. Lomize, A.L., Pogozheva, I.D.: Orientations of proteins in membranes (OPM) database, 27 April 2022
13. Berman, H.M., et al.: The protein data bank. Nucleic Acids Res. **28**(1), 235–242 (2000)
14. Wu, E.L., et al.: Charmm-GUI membrane builder toward realistic biological membrane simulations. J. Comput. Chem. **35**(27), 1997–2004 (2014)
15. Humphrey, W., Dalke, A., Schulten, K.: VMD: visual molecular dynamics. J. Mol. Graph. **14**(1), 33–8 (1996)

Confinement of CO_2 Inside (20,0) Single-Walled Carbon Nanotubes

Noelia Faginas-Lago[1]([⊠]) , Andrea Lombardi[1] ,
Yusuf Bramastya Apriliyanto[2] , and Leonardo Pacifici[1]

[1] Dipartimento di Chimica, Biologia e Biotecnologie,
Università degli Studi di Perugia, 06123 Perugia, Italy
noelia.faginaslago@unipg.it
[2] Department of Chemistry, Indonesia Defense University,
Kampus Unhan Komplek IPSC Sentul, Bogor, Indonesia

Abstract. We present a preliminary report based on molecular dynamics (MD) simulations to study CO_2 adsorption on flexible single-walled carbon nanotubes (SWCNTs) of (20,0) size. The adsorption capacities of (20,0) SWCNT were simulated at different temperatures and the effects of its diameter and chirality were compared with a previous work of our group. The potential energy surfaces have been described by implementing the Improved Lennard Jones (ILJ) potential to specifically model the intermolecular interactions involving CO_2-CO_2 and CO_2-SWCNT pairs. The intramolecular interactions within the SWCNT were considered explicitly by employing the Morse and Harmonic potentials. These specialized potentials are well capable of defining CO_2 confinement through physisorption and guarantee a quantitative description and realistic results of molecular dynamics. Flexible (20,0) SWCNT can adsorb up to 32 wt% at 273 K, thus as sizable carbon structured materials, SWCNTs are potentially suitable for CO_2 confinement and storage to cope with CO_2 gas emission.

Keywords: SWCNT · Small gases molecules adsorption · Empirical potential energy surface · Improved Lennard-Jones

1 Introduction

Recent scientific reports have revealed that carbon dioxide emission to the atmosphere has significantly risen in the last decades [1]. Large-scale industrial activities such as manufacture materials processing (iron, steel, cement, etc.) and energy production (fossil fuel power plants), majorly contribute to this increasing trend [2]. This trend leads to many serious problems on earth, ranging from environmental pollution to a rising of global temperature along with its catastrophic climate change effects [3]. Therefore, it is urgent to implement strategies to turn the evolution trend, keeping the CO_2 at the current level or even reducing the CO_2 concentration in the atmosphere [4]. In order to achieve this goal,

O. Gervasi et al. (Eds.): ICCSA 2022 Workshops, LNCS 13382, pp. 275–289, 2022.
https://doi.org/10.1007/978-3-031-10592-0_21

capturing CO_2 molecules in sites where they are generated or known as post-combustion carbon capture is widely accepted as the most efficient, effective and energetically feasible method [5]. However, the main constraint is that typically a post-combustion flue gas is in a form of mixture composed from water, carbon dioxide, oxygen and nitrogen molecules [6]. Various methods such as those involving liquid absorbents, solid adsorbents, and a hybrid of solid-liquid based materials have been reported to selectively capture CO_2 from flue gas [7–9]. Among those methods, carbon capture using solid adsorbents attracted global attention in the last few years [10,11]. This method offers major advantages, for instance for its simplicity and the relatively cheaper implementation on existing power plants [2,5]. Moreover, solid adsorbents have minimum chemical risks that usually arise with the use of traditional amine solvents (e.g. equipment corrosion, solvent evaporation, chemical stability, and unpleasant smells) [12].

The range of options of applicable solid adsorbents for carbon capture and separation is vast, only materials with high selectivity and high gravimetric uptake is the best suited option. Permeability also plays an important role, in which it corresponds to diffusion of gas inside the materials to produce effective gas adsorption [13]. In order to attain high gravimetric value, a material should have large surface area (adsorption sites) in combination with its lightweight structure. Large surface area is normally achieved by introducing intrinsic pores on a nanometer scale, thus obtaining so-called nanoporous materials. Moreover, intrinsic pores that are available inside the nanoporous materials also enhance the permeability of materials. A range of nanoporous materials for CO_2 capture and separation have been reported, for instance, zeolitic imidazolate frameworks (ZIFs) and zeolites [14,15], porous polymer networks (PPNs) or covalent organic polymers/frameworks (COPs/COFs) [16–18], metal-organic frameworks (MOFs) [19,20], and nanoporous carbons [21–23].

In particular, carbon-based materials exhibit desirable electronic and physicochemical properties (e.g. chemically inert, relatively high hydrophobicity and thermally stable). Moreover, they are composed from lightweight carbon atoms producing low density and stable structures [24,25]. In contrast, MOFs and zeolites-based materials despite showing good gas uptake as well as good selectivity and permeability, they are made up by heavy elements in their structures. Therefore, the net of gravimetric densities reported in term of wt% are commonly quite low. Moreover, MOFs are generally known to have low structural stability at certain conditions (e.g. high temperature, acidic environment) and they are less resistant to the nucleophilic attack of water molecules [2]. Unfortunately, post-combustion flue gas commonly bear water vapour at a relatively high temperature. A class of carbon-based materials that is investigated in this work is the well-known carbon nanotubes (CNTs), in particular the single walled CNTs (SWCNTs). SWCNTs are one-dimensional carbon structures that are equipped with an intrinsic cavity inside the tubular-like structures. The large available volume within SWCNTs promises the possibility for CO_2 confinement. With their robust and light-weight structures, it is beneficial to exploit SWCNTs capacity as CO_2 capture and storage materials suitable to be used in movable/mobile platforms. The phenomenon of adsorption dynamics and the corresponding mechanism as the effect of diameter and chirality are still an important line of research [26]. Accordingly, a preliminary study using a computational modelling and running simulations is crucial to gain atomistic perception into the interactions [27–29].

Molecular dynamics (MD) simulations performed by using accurate intramolecular and intermolecular potentials are a strength tool to describe particular dynamical adsorption system and to get practical energetic details at a given temperature [30]. Although some molecular dynamics simulations have also been implemented to study the CO_2 adsorption on CNTs [31,32], in this work the emphasis is on the accuracy of the intermolecular and intramolecular potentials. These potentials have been modelled and specifically formulated for CO_2 and CNTs by adopting an improved representation of the van der Waals contribution and by applying flexibility to CNTs structures. In comparison with this work, three charge-site of CO_2 models, rigid CNTs and the conventional Lennard-Jones potential were used in reported literatures [31,32]. This work is a continuation of a previous work of our group in which different types of SWCNTs have succesfully been exploited [33].

2   Computational Methods

The total potential energy function, V_{total}, adopted to calculate the total interaction energy for CO_2 molecules and the SWCNT is formulated as a sum of two separable terms. Of these, one, denoted as V_{SWCNT}, accounts for the SWCNT intramolecular potential energy, and the other one, denoted as $V_{intermol}$, accounts for the intermolecular potential energy of the SWCNT–CO_2 and CO_2–CO_2 interacting pairs:

$$V_{total} = V_{SWCNT} + V_{intermol} \qquad (1)$$

where

$$V_{intermol} = \sum_{i=1}^{l} \sum_{j=1}^{n} V_{C_i-(CO_2)_j} + \sum_{j=1}^{n-1} \sum_{k>j}^{n} V_{(CO_2)_j-(CO_2)_k} \qquad (2)$$

In the above equation n is the amount of CO_2 molecules, while l represents the number of carbon atoms in the SWCNT.

2.1   Bonding Interactions in SWCNT

In the course of MD simulations, the carbon nanostructures were allowed to vibrate to reproduce the consequent out-of-plane movements of SWCNT surfaces by adopting intramolecular potential reported in Ref [34]. The corresponding intramolecular potential (V_{SWCNT} in Eq. 1) of flexible SWCNT is computed as a sum of potential energy terms depending on bond lengths, bending angles and dihedral angles, as follows:

$$V_{SWCNT} = \sum U(r_{ij}) + \sum U(\theta_{ijk}) + \sum U(\phi_{ijkl}) \tag{3}$$

where the r_{ij}'s are the interparticle distances, the θ_{ijk}'s are the bending angles between triples of consecutive atoms i, j, k and ϕ_{ijkl} is the dihedral angle defined by a given set of four consecutive C atoms of the SWCNT; summation, running over atom indices, is intended to avoid redundant terms. The stretching potential $U(r_{ij})$ of a C–C interatomic bond in the SWCNT is framed as a Morse potential function:

$$U(r_{ij}) = E_0[\{1 - \exp(-k_M(r_{ij} - r_0))\}^2 - 1] \tag{4}$$

where r_{ij} represents the interatomic radius between C atom i and j, E_0 is the well depth (114.4569 kcal mol^{-1} Å^{-2}), r_0 is the equilibrium distance (1.418 Å) and $k_M = 2.1867$ Å^{-1} is connected to the bond force constant.

Valence angle potential ($U(\theta_{ijk})$) terms for the bond bending of nanotubes are formulated by harmonic cosine functions:

$$U(\theta_{jik}) = \frac{k}{2}(\cos(\theta_{jik}) - (\cos(\theta_0))^2 \tag{5}$$

θ_{jik} represents the angle between C$_j$-C$_i$-C$_k$ atoms, θ_0 is the equilibrium value (120°), while k is the force constant (134.5 kcal mol^{-1}). A cosine function is used for the dihedral angle potentials ($U(\phi_{ijkl})$), describing the interaction arising from torsional forces involving atom C$_i$-C$_j$-C$_k$-C$_l$, where the parameter values A is fixed at 6.0096 kcal kcal mol^{-1}.

$$U(\phi_{ijkl}) = \frac{1}{2}A(1 - \cos(2\phi_{ijkl})) \tag{6}$$

2.2   CO$_2$-SWCNT and CO$_2$-CO$_2$ Interactions

Describing correctly the intermolecular potential ($V_{intermol}$) is essential in order to obtain accurate results in a MD simulation. In this study, the intermolecular forces of interest are those occurring between CO$_2$ molecules and between CO$_2$ and SWCNT. Electrostatic and non-electrostatic contributions are the two components that composed the intermolecular interaction energy. The electrostatic part can be simply determined by using the Coulomb law. On the other hand, the non-electrostatic contribution is evaluated by taking into consideration the pairwise induction and dispersion long range attractive interactions and short range repulsion, which add up resulting in the van der Waals forces, which are expressed for each interacting pairs using the so-called Improved Lennard-Jones (ILJ) pairwise function [35–37]:

$$V_{ILJ}(r) = \varepsilon \left[\frac{m}{n(r) - m} \left(\frac{r_0}{r}\right)^{n(r)} - \frac{n(r)}{n(r) - m} \left(\frac{r_0}{r}\right)^m \right] \tag{7}$$

In the Eq. 7, the parameters ε and r_0 correspond to the well depth and the equilibrium position of the given interacting pair, respectively. m has the value of 1 for ion-ion, 4 for ion-neutral and 6 for neutral-neutral pairs interactions.

The left term of the Eq. 7 (inside big bracket) depicts the repulsion as a function of the distance r, while the right term in the equation performs the long-range attraction. To modulate the strength of the attraction and the decline of the repulsion in Eq. 7, the $n(r)$ term is defined as follows:

$$n(r) = \beta + 4.0 \left(\frac{r}{r_0} \right)^2 \tag{8}$$

where β is a parameter for modulating the hardness of the interacting pair [38]. All of the ILJ parameters that were implemented in this study were fine-tuned and benchmarked in comparison with *ab initio* calculations as reported in Ref. [39, 40]. The ILJ function is much more accurate than the classical Lennard-Jones (LJ) potential function routinely used in Force-Fields for the prediction of static and dynamical properties of systems. In particular, ILJ systematically corrects the excessive long range attraction and short range repulsion of LJ potential, where the long and short-range deviations can impact adsorption dynamics. These advantages of using ILJ over conventional LJ potential have been reported in literatures [35–47].

3 Molecular Dynamics (MD) Simulations

The MD simulations were realized within the NVE microcanonical ensemble enforcing periodic boundary conditions with a rectangular cuboid box. In our MD simulations, starting from a given initial configuration, each system considered in the MD simulations was equilibrated for 0.3 ns. The production period was recorded for another 9.7 ns, leading to a total of 10 ns simulation time with a time step value set at 2.5×10^{-4} ps. The cutoff radius for the electrostatic and non-electrostatic ILJ terms were set to 19 Å to speed up the computation of the force field. The data collected during the equilibration period were excluded from the statistical analysis of the simulations for which the DL_POLY package [48] was used. Energy contributions, CO$_2$ distributions, gravimetric densities of CO$_2$ as a function of simulation time and the corresponding average values have been subsequently analyzed. The VMD software [49] has been used to construct the SWCNT structure. After the SWCNT structure were obtained, for each simulation systems, 100 CO$_2$ molecules were randomly added around the nanotubes surfaces at a distance of 5 to 8 Å. This corresponds to a bulk gas density value of about 89.10 g L^{-1}. A rigid type of CO$_2$ model reported in Ref. [39] was adopted with its point charge distributions corresponds to a five charge-site as shown in Fig. 1. This five charge-site model is more superior in treating quadrupole moment of CO$_2$ than the widely used three charge-site models adopted in Refs. [31, 32].

We report detailed MD simulation results for 100 CO$_2$ molecules on the (20,0) zigzag open-ended SWCNT in comparison with our previous report of different chiralities to examine their CO$_2$ confinement capabilities [33]. The (20,0) SWCNT composed by five unit cells, thus it contains 400 carbon atoms (Fig. 2). The SWCNT was modelled as a non-rigid structure during MD simulations.

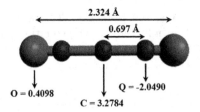

Fig. 1. Structural representation of CO_2 molecule using five charge-site model. Q is a point charge placed on the C-O bond of CO_2 molecule. The charge values are reported in a.u.

The flexibility of adsorbent materials through its molecular vibrations has been demonstrated altering its uptake capacity of adsorbing molecules such as hydrogen, nitrogen and methane [34,50]. Most importantly, treating SWCNT as a flexible structure provides more realistic representation of adsorbent and yields simulation data closer to those of the more precise results (benchmarking with respect to experimental data and higher level *ab initio* results).

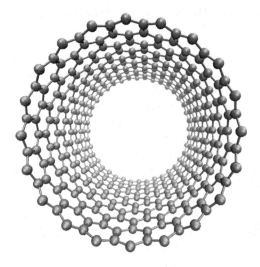

Fig. 2. (20,0) SWCNT used in the MD simulations with a diameter of 15.66 Å.

A CO_2 molecule must be within the SWCNT cavity or at a maximum distance of 7 Å from the surface of the SWCNT, in order to decide whether the CO_2 molecule is physically adsorbed. These criteria are following indications obtained in the previous works [33,40,51,52] and from the initial evaluation of radial density plots (Fig. 3). Figure 3 justifies that radius of 7 Å from CNT surface has covered the full peaks of CO_2, therefore it can be considered as adsorption region. The radial density is an analogue of z-density in which the z axis is replaced by radius from CNT surface. It can be seen from Fig. 3 that the higher the applied temperature, the lower the radial density peak. The increase of temperature makes molecules having high kinetic energy, thus adsorption events become less effective. At 353 K, the kinetic energy at certain events can overcome repulsion forces at short-range radius. As the results, there is a small peak of CO_2 density near SWCNT surface (Fig. 3).

In order to analyze the effect of various MD parameters to the distribution of CO_2 molecules, firstly, we determined the amount of adsorbed molecules at the exohedral and endohedral sites of the carbon nanotubes. The effect of temperature on this distribution was investigated by setting three initial temperatures at 273, 300 and 353 K. Meanwhile, to investigate the dependence of the CO_2 distribution on the diameter of the SWCNT, we compare these molecular simulations with a previous work of our group involving various SWCNTs [33]. The next step was analyzing the radial distribution function to determine the composition of the repulsive and attractive interactions that exists between CO_2 molecules and the SWCNT. The summary of MD parameters and simulation results of SWCNTs are presented in Table 1.

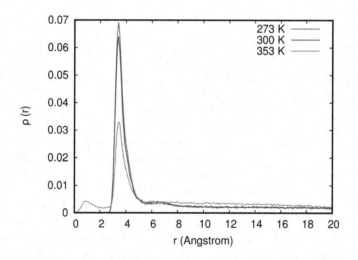

Fig. 3. Density of CO_2 inside the simulation box as function of radius from CNT surface.

Table 1 records the number of adsorbed CO_2 molecules in exohedral (N_{CO_2},out) and endohedral (N_{CO_2},in) sites simulated at NVE ensemble. The temperatures reported in Table 1 indicate the average value at the end of MD simulations. As expected, due to the adsorption phenomenon, the average temperature is lower than the initial temperature for each system. We have noticed that not all of the CO_2 molecules were physically adsorbed. Table 1 shows that the amount of CO_2 at the exohedral and endohedral sites rises with the increasing of nanotube diameter in comparison with the previous work [33]. This trend

Table 1. MD parameters and the amount of adsorbed CO_2 molecules at NVE ensemble. N_C, N_{CO_2},out and N_{CO_2}, in indicate the number of C atoms in SWCNT, the number of CO_2 molecules adsorbed outside and inside of SWCNT, respectively.

SWCNT	d (Å)	N_c	T (K)	N_{CO_2},in	N_{CO_2},out	Ref.
(5,0)	3.91	100	253.1	0 ± 0	27 ± 4	[33]
			266.8	0 ± 0	26 ± 4	
			302.8	0 ± 0	22 ± 4	
(10,0)	7.83	200	253.2	4 ± 0	43 ± 5	[33]
			277.8	4 ± 0	36 ± 7	
			305.8	4 ± 0	34 ± 4	
(15,0)	11.74	300	262.1	16 ± 1	48 ± 5	[33]
			285.6	15 ± 1	43 ± 8	
			326.8	14 ± 1	37 ± 4	
(20,0)	15.66	400	264.2	14 ± 1	53 ± 4	this work
			281.2	16 ± 1	46 ± 4	
			315.3	14 ± 1	35 ± 4	

is due to the fact that the available volume at endohedral and exohedral sites enlarges as the SWCNT diameter increases.

We also report the amount of confined CO_2 in a unit of mg g^{-1}, by considering that CO_2 molecule is confined if it is adsorbed in an endohedral site of the SWCNT. We obtained that the (20,0) structure can confine up to 146.65 mg CO_2 for 1 g of adsorbent. This value is equivalent to about 12.39 wt(%), which can fairly be considered a quite large gas uptake value. It is clear that by increasing the diameter of SWCNT, the degree of surface convexity inside the SWCNT also increases. Therefore, CO_2 confinement inside SWCNT is directly proportional with the diameter of carbon nanotubes (Table 1).

Figure 4 shows the molecular configuration after 10 ns of simulation for the (20,0) system as an illustrative example of the equilibrium. It can be seen in Fig. 4 that the endohedral site can be occupied by CO_2 to accommodate molecular confinement. In addition, the exohedral site also exhibits adsorption properties with a much higher CO_2 uptake (Table 1 and Fig. 4). Therefore, in order to provide a more quantitative ground, the total storage capacity (SC) of SWNCTs was evaluated at every step of the trajectory by calculating gravimetric density, wt(%), as the following:

$$wt\% = \frac{N_a \times M_{CO_2}}{M_{system}} \times 100 \tag{9}$$

where N_a represents the number of adsorbed CO_2, M_{CO_2} is the mass of CO_2 molecule, and M_{system} is total mass of the system including the SWCNT and the gas molecules. The adsorbed CO_2 molecules were estimated by summing CO_2 inside the cavity and those that were located at a distances of 7 Å from

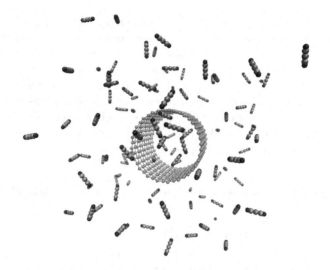

Fig. 4. Snapshot of final configuration of the (20,0) structure with 100 CO_2 molecules at 300 K.

the SWCNT surfaces [40,51,52]. SC gives us an idea regarding the amount of adsorbate that can be captured by a given amount of adsorbent at constant temperature. SC of a material is commonly expressed as a percentage by weight (wt%). At the end of each simulations, taking into account of three different temperatures; the gravimetric densities and van der Waals (vdW) energy at NVE ensemble are listed in Table 2. Note that the temperatures shown in Table 2 are the average temperatures during the MD simulations, not the initial ones.

Table 2. The vdW energy (kcal mol^{-1}) and gravimetric density (wt%) of (20,0) SWCNT at NVE ensemble.

SWCNT	d (Å)	T (K)	E_{vdW}	wt%
		264.2	-263.05 ± 11.31	32.06 ± 4.57
(20,0)	15.66	281.2	-289.19 ± 11.22	29.87 ± 2.29
		315.3	-150.64 ± 15.11	23.68 ± 4.57

We observe that the CO_2 storage capacity is inversely proportional with the temperature, the CO_2 molecules are increasingly desorbed as the temperature increases. We can try to get an idea that at high temperature the share of vdW energy, mainly responsible for adsorption, decreases (see Table 2) as well as the total potential energy. Since the total energy of system should be conserved at NVE ensemble, the decrease in the potential energy give rise to kinetic energy of the system. These factors leads to the weakening of the interaction between SWCNT and CO_2 molecules.

The manifestation of kinetic energy as well as contribution of attraction forces, leading to adsoprtion, also can be seen from Table 3 where diffusion coefficients of CO_2 molecules inside the simulation box are reported. If we compare with the previous work, in general, the maximum CO_2 storage is obtained for the SWCNT (15,0) even if it does not have the largest diameter. It seems that when the diameter increases, up to a certain limit, a competing van der Waals (vdW) attraction-repulsion contribution favour higher desorption. Nevertheless, with a relatively high CO_2 uptake, it is an early sign that this material is a good candidate for CO_2 capture and storage applications.

Table 3. The diffusion coefficients (10^{-7} m^2 s^{-1}) of four SWCNTs at NVE ensemble.

SWCNT	T (K)	D_{NVE}	Ref.
(5,0)	273	1.74	[33]
	300	1.71	
	353	1.52	
(10,0)	273	1.38	[33]
	300	1.76	
	353	2.12	
(15,0)	273	1.12	[33]
	300	1.38	
	353	2.12	
(20,0)	273	1.28	This work
	300	1.63	
	353	1.78	

The total gravimetric uptake comparison between some nanoporous materials is reported in Table 4. It shows that the (20,0) structure adsorbs CO_2 molecules up to 32.1 wt% at microcanonical NVE ensemble with an initial temperature of 273 K. This value is comparable and competitive with other materials investigated by using experimental and/or theoretical methods reported in Table 4. It can also be seen that the gravimetric values estimated from MD simulations performed using our potentials are in the same order of magnitude with the experimental results. However, all of the SWCNT gravimetric values obtained in this work are still lower than those of 3-dimensional porous carbons reported in Refs. [21] and [22], 54.3 wt% (300 K & 30 bar) and 48.1 wt% (298 K & 20 bar), respectively. This was expected to be due to the more available pores acting as adsorption sites in the 3-dimensional structure with respect to the 1-dimensional ones.

Table 4. Total gravimetric uptake comparison between various nanoporous materials.

Materials	T (K)	P (bar)	CO_2 uptake (wt%)	References
SWCNT (9,9)	298	30–60	21–23	[26]
MOFs	298	1	19.7	[53]
Graphene oxide (nanocomposite)	300	20	12.7	[54]
SWCNT	298	1.1	2.9	[55]
Nanoporous carbon	298	26	17.7	[56]
Nanosilicate	298	55	22	[57]
CNT (nanocomposite)	298	32.5	28.4	[58]
SWCNT (10,0)	253	21.7	30.6	[33]
SWCNT (10,0)	278	29.0	26.0	[33]
SWCNT (15,0)	262	17.1	34.8	[33]
SWCNT (15,0)	286	20.8	31.8	[33]
SWCNT (20,0)	264	14.9	32.1	This work
SWCNT (20,0)	281	31.6	29.9	This work

4   Conclusions

Having relatively high gas uptake and remarkable physicochemical properties of carbon-based materials, SWCNTs are equipped with a property that makes them potentially versatile materials competitive with other porous adsorbents to cope with CO_2 gas emission. Indeed, with an increase in diameter, other gas molecules can also be adsorbed by SWCNTs thus lowers the storage capacity of CO_2. However, if a material exhibits high CO_2 uptake, it is an early sign that this material is a good candidate for CO_2 capture and separation applications. Therefore, our future objective is to extensively investigate the application of SWCNTs in separating CO_2 molecules from CO_2/N_2 and CO_2/CH_4 gaseous mixtures saturated with H_2O component.

Acknowledgement. The authors thank MUR and University of Perugia for their support through the AMIS project "Dipartimenti di Eccellenza 2018–2022". NFL, AL and LP thank the Department of Chemistry, Biology and Biotechnology, University of Perugia for funding under the program "Fondo Ricerca di Base 2021" (RICBASE2021FAGINAS). NFL and AL also acknowledge support for allocation of computing time from the Oklahoma University Supercomputing Center for Education & Research (OSCER). N.F-L and A. L acknowledge also Fondazione Cassa di Risparmio di Perugia n. 220.0513 to C.E. This work is supported by a grant from Fondazione Cassa di Risparmio di Perugia n.# 220.0513 to C.E.

References

1. EPA-United States Environmental Protection Agency: Climate Change Indicators in the United States: Global Greenhouse Gas Emissions (2016)
2. Smit, B.: Carbon capture and storage: introductory lecture. Faraday Discuss. **192**, 9–25 (2016)
3. World Resources Institute: Climate Analysis Indicators Tool (CAIT) 2.0: WRI's Climate Data Explorer
4. Bui, M., et al.: Carbon capture and storage (CCS): the way forward. Energy Environ. Sci. **11**, 1062–1176 (2018)
5. Joos, L., Huck, J.M., Van Speybroeck, V., Smit, B.: Cutting the cost of carbon capture: a case for carbon capture and utilization. Faraday Discuss. **192**, 391–414 (2016)
6. Dai, N., Mitch, W.A.: Effects of flue gas compositions on nitrosamine and nitramine formation in postcombustion CO_2 capture systems. Environ. Sci. Technol. **48**(13), 7519–7526 (2014)
7. Huck, J.M., et al.: Evaluating different classes of porous materials for carbon capture. Energy Environ. Sci. **7**, 4132–4146 (2014)
8. Zhang, S., Shen, Y., Shao, P., Chen, J., Wang, L.: Kinetics, thermodynamics, and mechanism of a novel biphasic solvent for CO_2 capture from flue gas. Environ. Sci. Technol. **52**(6), 3660–3668 (2018)
9. Liu, H., et al.: A hybrid absorption-adsorption method to efficiently capture carbon. Nat. Commun. **5**, 5147 (2014)
10. Lu, A.H., Hao, G.P.: Porous materials for carbon dioxide capture. Annu. Rep. Prog. Chem. Sect. A: Inorg. Chem. **109**, 484–503 (2013)
11. Li, J.R., et al.: Porous materials with pre-designed single-molecule traps for CO_2 selective adsorption. Nat. Commun. **4**, 1538 (2014)
12. Hu, X.E., et al.: A review of n-functionalized solid adsorbents for post-combustion CO_2 capture. Appl. Energy **260**, 114244 (2020)
13. Du, H., Li, J., Zhang, J., Su, G., Li, X., Zhao, Y.: Separation of hydrogen and nitrogen gases with porous graphene membrane. J. Phys. Chem. C **115**(47), 23261–23266 (2011)
14. Kim, J., Lin, L.C., Swisher, J.A., Haranczyk, M., Smit, B.: Predicting large CO_2 adsorption in aluminosilicate zeolites for postcombustion carbon dioxide capture. J. Am. Chem. Soc. **134**(46), 18940–18943 (2012)
15. Liu, B., Smit, B.: Molecular simulation studies of separation of CO_2/N_2, CO_2/CH_4, and CH_4/N_2 by ZIFs. J. Phys. Chem. C **114**(18), 8515–8522 (2010)
16. Schrier, J.: Carbon dioxide separation with a two-dimensional polymer membrane. ACS Appl. Mater. Interfaces **4**(7), 3745–3752 (2012)
17. Zeng, Y., Zou, R., Zhao, Y.: Covalent organic frameworks for CO_2 capture. Adv. Mater. **28**(15), 2855–2873 (2016)
18. Xiang, Z., et al.: Systematic tuning and multifunctionalization of covalent organic polymers for enhanced carbon capture. J. Am. Chem. Soc. **137**(41), 13301–13307 (2015)
19. Yu, J., Xie, L.H., Li, J.R., Ma, Y., Seminario, J.M., Balbuena, P.B.: CO_2 capture and separations using MOFs: computational and experimental studies. Chem. Rev. **117**(14), 9674–9754 (2017)
20. Lin, L.C., et al.: Understanding CO_2 dynamics in metal-organic frameworks with open metal sites. Angew. Chem. Int. Ed. **52**(16), 4410–4413 (2013)

21. Srinivas, G., Krungleviciute, V., Guo, Z.X., Yildirim, T.: Exceptional CO_2 capture in a hierarchically porous carbon with simultaneous high surface area and pore volume. Energy Environ. Sci. **7**, 335–342 (2014)
22. Ganesan, A., Shaijumon, M.: Activated graphene-derived porous carbon with exceptional gas adsorption properties. Microporous Mesoporous Mater. **220**, 21–27 (2015)
23. Ghosh, S., Sevilla, M., Fuertes, A.B., Andreoli, E., Ho, J., Barron, A.R.: Defining a performance map of porous carbon sorbents for high-pressure carbon dioxide uptake and carbon dioxide-methane selectivity. J. Mater. Chem. A **4**, 14739–14751 (2016)
24. Bartolomei, M., Carmona-Novillo, E., Giorgi, G.: First principles investigation of hydrogen physical adsorption on graphynes' layers. Carbon **95**, 1076–1081 (2015)
25. Apriliyanto, Y.B., Battaglia, S., Evangelisti, S., Faginas-Lago, N., Leininger, T., Lombardi, A.: Toward a generalized hückel rule: the electronic structure of carbon nanocones. J. Phys. Chem. A **125**(45), 9819–9825 (2021)
26. Lithoxoos, G.P., Labropoulos, A., Peristeras, L.D., Kanellopoulos, N., Samios, J., Economou, I.G.: Adsorption of N_2, CH_4, CO and CO_2 gases in single walled carbon nanotubes: A combined experimental and monte carlo molecular simulation study. J. Supercrit. Fluids **55**(2), 510–523 (2010)
27. Lombardi, A., Lago, N.F., Laganà, A., Pirani, F., Falcinelli, S.: A bond-bond portable approach to intermolecular interactions: simulations for N-methylacetamide and carbon dioxide dimers. In: Murgante, B. (ed.) ICCSA 2012. LNCS, vol. 7333, pp. 387–400. Springer, Heidelberg (2012). https://doi.org/10.1007/978-3-642-31125-3_30
28. Lombardi, A., Faginas-Lago, N., Pacifici, L., Costantini, A.: Modeling of energy transfer from vibrationally excited CO_2 molecules: Cross sections and probabilities for kinetic modeling of atmospheres, flows, and plasmas. J. Phys. Chem. A **117**(45), 11430–11440 (2013)
29. Falcinelli, S., Rosi, M., Candori, P., Vecchiocattivi, F., Bartocci, A., Lombardi, A., Lago, N.F., Pirani, F.: Modeling the intermolecular interactions and characterization of the dynamics of collisional autoionization processes. In: Murgante, B. (ed.) ICCSA 2013. LNCS, vol. 7971, pp. 69–83. Springer, Heidelberg (2013). https://doi.org/10.1007/978-3-642-39637-3_6
30. DuBay, K.H., Hall, M.L., Hughes, T.F., Wu, C., Reichman, D.R., Friesner, R.A.: Accurate force field development for modeling conjugated polymers. J. Chem. Theory Comput. **8**(11), 4556–4569 (2012)
31. Rahimi, M., Singh, J.K., Babu, D.J., Schneider, J.J., Müller-Plathe, F.: Understanding carbon dioxide adsorption in carbon nanotube arrays: molecular simulation and adsorption measurements. J. Phys. Chem. C **117**(26), 13492–13501 (2013)
32. Alexiadis, A., Kassinos, S.: Molecular dynamic simulations of carbon nanotubes in CO_2 atmosphere. Chem. Phys. Lett. **460**(4–6), 512–516 (2008)
33. Faginas-Lago, N., Apriliyanto, Y.B., Lombardi, A.: Confinement of CO_2 inside carbon nanotubes. Eur. Phys. J. D **75**(5), 1–10 (2021). https://doi.org/10.1140/epjd/s10053-021-00176-7
34. Faginas-Lago, N., Yeni, D., Huarte, F., Wang, Y., Alcamí, M., Martin, F.: Adsorption of hydrogen molecules on carbon nanotubes using quantum chemistry and molecular dynamics. J. Phys. Chem. A **120**(32), 6451–6458 (2016)
35. Pirani, P., Brizi, S., Roncaratti, L., Casavecchia, P., Cappelletti, D., Vecchiocattivi, F.: Beyond the lennard-jones model: a simple and accurate potential function probed by high resolution scattering data useful for molecular dynamics simulations. Phys. Chem. Chem. Phys. **10**, 5489 (2008)

36. Lombardi, A., Laganà, A., Pirani, F., Palazzetti, F., Lago, N.F.: Carbon oxides in gas flows and earth and planetary atmospheres: state-to-state simulations of energy transfer and dissociation reactions. In: Murgante, B. (ed.) ICCSA 2013. LNCS, vol. 7972, pp. 17–31. Springer, Heidelberg (2013). https://doi.org/10.1007/978-3-642-39643-4_2

37. Albertí, M., Lago, N.F.: Ion size influence on the Ar solvation shells of $M^+C_6F_6$ clusters (M = Na, K, Rb, Cs). J. Phys. Chem. A **116**(12), 3094–3102 (2012)

38. Pirani, F., Albertí, M., Castro, A., Moix Teixidor, M., Cappelletti, D.: Atom-bond pairwise additive representation for intermolecular potential energy surfaces. Chem. Phys. Lett. **394**(1–3), 37–44 (2004)

39. Lombardi, A., Pirani, F., Laganà, A., Bartolomei, M.: Energy transfer dynamics and kinetics of elementary processes (promoted) by gas-phase CO_2-N_2 collisions: Selectivity control by the anisotropy of the interaction. J. Comput. Chem. **37**(16), 1463–1475 (2016)

40. Apriliyanto, Y.B., Faginas Lago, N., Lombardi, A., Evangelisti, S., Bartolomei, M., Leininger, T., Pirani, F.: Nanostructure selectivity for molecular adsorption and separation: the case of graphyne layers. J. Phys. Chem. C **122**(28), 16195–16208 (2018)

41. Pacifici, L., Verdicchio, M., Lago, N.F., Lombardi, A., Costantini, A.: A high-level ab initio study of the $N_2 + N_2$ reaction channel. J. Comput. Chem. **34**(31), 2668–2676 (2013)

42. Faginas Lago, N., Huarte Larrañaga, F., Albertí, M.: On the suitability of the ILJ function to match different formulations of the electrostatic potential for water-water interactions. Eur. Phys. J. D **55**(1), 75–85 (2009). https://doi.org/10.1140/epjd/e2009-00215-5

43. Albertí, M., Lago, N.F.: Competitive solvation of K^+ by C_6H_6 and H_2O in the K^+-$(C_6H_6)_n$-$(H_2O)_m$ (n=1-4; m=1-6) aggregates. Eur. Phys. J. D **67**(4), 73 (2013). https://doi.org/10.1140/epjd/e2013-30753-x

44. Faginas-Lago, N., Lombardi, A., Albertí, M., Grossi, G.: Accurate analytic inter-molecular potential for the simulation of Na^+ and K^+ ion hydration in liquid water. J. Mol. Liq. **204**, 192–197 (2015)

45. Faginas Lago, N., Albertí, M., Lombardi, A., Pirani, F.: A force field for acetone: the transition from small clusters to liquid phase investigated by molecular dynamics simulations. Theor. Chem. Acc. **135**(7), 1–9 (2016). https://doi.org/10.1007/s00214-016-1914-9

46. Lombardi, A., Faginas-Lago, N., Gaia, G., Federico, P., Aquilanti, V.: Collisional energy exchange in CO_2–N_2 gaseous mixtures. In: Gervasi, O., Murgante, B., Misra, S., Rocha, A.M.A.C., Torre, C., Taniar, D., Apduhan, B.O., Stankova, E., Wang, S. (eds.) ICCSA 2016. LNCS, vol. 9786, pp. 246–257. Springer, Cham (2016). https://doi.org/10.1007/978-3-319-42085-1_19

47. Faginas-Lago, N., Apriliyanto, Y.B., Lombardi, A.: Carbon capture and separation from $CO_2/N_2/H_2O$ gaseous mixtures in bilayer graphtriyne: a molecular dynamics study. In: Gervasi, O. (ed.) ICCSA 2020. LNCS, vol. 12255, pp. 489–501. Springer, Cham (2020). https://doi.org/10.1007/978-3-030-58820-5_36

48. Smith, W., Yong, C., Rodger, P.: DL_POLY: application to molecular simulation. Mol. Simul. **28**(5), 385–471 (2002)

49. Humphrey, W., Dalke, A., Schulten, K.: VMD: visual molecular dynamics. J. Mol. Graph. **14**(1), 33–8 (1996)

50. Vekeman, J., Sánchez-Marín, J., de Sánchez Merás, A., Garcia Cuesta, I., Faginas-Lago, N.: Flexibility in the graphene sheet: the influence on gas adsorption from molecular dynamics studies. J. Phys. Chem. C **123**(46), 28035–28047 (2019)

51. Faginas-Lago, N., Apriliyanto, Y.B., Lombardi, A.: Molecular simulations of $CO_2/N_2/H_2O$ gaseous mixture separation in graphtriyne membrane. In: Misra, S. (ed.) ICCSA 2019. LNCS, vol. 11624, pp. 374–387. Springer, Cham (2019). https://doi.org/10.1007/978-3-030-24311-1_27

52. Apriliyanto, Y.B., Darmawan, N., Faginas-Lago, N., Lombardi, A.: Two-dimensional diamine-linked covalent organic frameworks for CO_2/N_2 capture and separation: theoretical modeling and simulations. Phys. Chem. Chem. Phys. **22**, 25918–25929 (2020)

53. Spanopoulos, I., et al.: Exceptional gravimetric and volumetric CO_2 uptake in a palladated NbO-type MOF utilizing cooperative acidic and basic, metal-CO_2 interactions. Chem. Commun. **52**(69), 10559–10562 (2016)

54. Rodríguez-García, S., et al.: Role of the structure of graphene oxide sheets on the CO_2 adsorption properties of nanocomposites based on graphene oxide and polyaniline or Fe_3O_4-nanoparticles. ACS Sustain. Chem. Eng. **7**(14), 12464–12473 (2019)

55. Osler, K., Dheda, D., Ngoy, J., Wagner, N., Daramola, M.O.: Synthesis and evaluation of carbon nanotubes composite adsorbent for CO_2 capture: a comparative study of CO_2 adsorption capacity of single-walled and multi-walled carbon nanotubes. Int. J. Coal Sci. Technol. **4**(1), 41–49 (2017). https://doi.org/10.1007/s40789-017-0157-2

56. Patzsch, J., Babu, D.J., Schneider, J.J.: Hierarchically structured nanoporous carbon tubes for high pressure carbon dioxide adsorption. Beilstein J. Nanotechnol. **8**(1), 1135–1144 (2017)

57. Cavalcanti, L.P., Kalantzopoulos, G.N., Eckert, J., Knudsen, K.D., Fossum, J.O.: A nano-silicate material with exceptional capacity for CO_2 capture and storage at room temperature. Sci. Rep. **8**(1), 1–6 (2018)

58. Puthusseri, D., Babu, D.J., Okeil, S., Schneider, J.J.: Gas adsorption capacity in an all carbon nanomaterial composed of carbon nanohorns and vertically aligned carbon nanotubes. Phys. Chem. Chem. Phys. **19**(38), 26265–26271 (2017)

Structural Basis of the Biomolecular Action of Paddlewheel- and N-Heterocylic-Carbene-Based Antitumor Metallodrugs: A Computational Perspective

Iogann Tolbatov[1](✉) ⓘ and Alessandro Marrone[2] ⓘ

[1] Institut de Chimie Moléculaire de l'Université de Bourgogne (ICMUB), Université de Bourgogne Franche-Comté (UBFC), Avenue Alain Savary 9, Dijon, France
tolbatov.i@gmail.com

[2] Dipartimento di Farmacia, Università "G d'Annunzio" di Chieti-Pescara, via dei Vestini 31, Chieti, Italy

Abstract. Metallodrugs are an essential component of the contemporary medicinal chemistry since they represent a crucial inventory of therapeutic agents against a myriad of cancers as well as viral, bacterial, and parasitic infections. Their unique features based on the presence of a metal center capable of transforming the electronic and steric features of its ligands incorporate the (possible) activation mechanisms, capability to multitarget, and the specific way of attacking a target via the ligand substitution mechanism. This minireview is dedicated to a short overview of the computational studies of paddlewheel- and N-heterocylic-carbene-based antitumor metallodrugs with biomolecular targets, performed in our group. We particularly focus our attention on the structural features of the investigated systems, which present excellent examples highlighting the significance of incorporation of steric effects originating from metallodrug's ligands as well as the impact of the surrounding milieu.

1 Introduction

Development of transition-metal-based metallodrugs is a fast developing field nowadays [1, 2]. The reason of it is the wide range of properties of metal centers, the rational employment of which permits the design of the metal scaffolds with a set of desired qualities [3]. The ability to reciprocally change their electronic structure along with the structure of their ligands is the source of the transition metal center propensity to form the coordinative bonds with both electrostatic and covalent nature. This phenomenon affects greatly the flexibility of these metal centers during the ligand substitution reactions in metallodrugs [4].

Since the serendipitous finding of cisplatins's antitumor properties, metallodrugs became an essential component of a medicinal toolkit not only in the sphere of anticancer agents, but also in other domains, due to their antiviral, antibacterial, and antiparasitic qualities [5, 6]. Nevertheless, metallodrugs display severe toxic side effects, in particular nephro- and neurotoxicity, caused by the low selectivity of metal centers in targeting

O. Gervasi et al. (Eds.): ICCSA 2022 Workshops, LNCS 13382, pp. 290–304, 2022.
https://doi.org/10.1007/978-3-031-10592-0_22

various metabolic pathways simultaneously. The control of side effects motivates the ongoing efforts to fine-tune the properties of metallodrug scaffolds.

Nowadays the computational chemistry is an essential instrument in the toolkit of inorganic and bioinorganic medicinal chemistry, by providing an atomistic insight on the behavior of metal ions in physiological milieu [7, 8] as well as a support to the rational design of metallodrugs and to the exploration of their modes of action [9–11]. The central difference in the computational investigation of purely organic versus metal-based drugs is the non-applicability to the latters of the quantitative structure-activity relationships (QSAR) techniques [12, 13]. While these methods are the major workhorse in the field of prediction of biological effect of organic compounds due to the capacity to formulate connections between chemical properties and biomolecular effects, this approach is intrinsically inapt for the metal complexes due to several reasons [3]. Primarily, many metallodrugs should undergo activation before becoming capable of attacking their targets. Furthermore, the attack happens via the ligand exchange mechanism, which assumes the presence of a detachable, labile ligands at the metal center versus the carrier ligands which are strongly bound and are not expected to sustain cleavage. Finally, metallodrugs are able to coordinate to not a single but multiple biomolecular targets [14].

We describe in this minireview various computational studies performed in our group, which were focused on the reactivity of paddlewheel- and N-heterocyclic-carbene-based antitumor metallodrugs with their biological targets. These investigations shed light onto the mechanistic description of the metalation process which is the culmination of their biomolecular action.

2 Paddlewheel-Based Antitumour Metallodrugs

There is a renewed interest in the scientific community focusing on the synthesis of novel anticancer drugs in the diRh- and diRu-based paddlewheel tetraacetate complexes characterized by the formula $[M_2(O_2CR)_4L_2]^{n+}$, (M = Rh(II), Ru(II/III); R = CH_3^-, L = solvent molecule or anionic ligand) (Fig. 1) [15, 16].

The medicinal properties of diRh(II)-based complex have a broad spectrum. It is a potent agent against various types of tumours: leukemias P388 [17] and L1210 [18], sarcomas 180 [17], and the Ehrlich-Lettre ascites carcinoma [19, 20]. A plethora of various intracellular targets is suspected from amino acids [21, 22] and peptides [23, 24] to proteins [25, 26] and DNA [17]. Such an unselective behavior may explain well its heavy toxicity. However, apart from several studies on the protein and peptide metalation by these complexes, which have elucidated slightly the binding preferences of this diRh(II) complex (Asn, Asp, C-terminal, His, Lys) [25, 26], there is no consensus on its intracellular mode of action. On the contrary, the studies on the therapeutic employment of the structurally similar complex $[Ru_2(\mu\text{-}O_2CCH_3)_4Cl]$ are much more limited to date and are oriented on the usage of the Ru(II)Ru(III) core primary as a prodrug scaffold for the transport of the medicinally active ligands toward the intended target, for example, ibuprofenate, naproxenate, indomethacinate, ketoprofenate, -the deprotonated species of non-steroidal anti inflammatory drugs-, or the anti glioblastoma indolylglyoxylyl agents [27–29]. The experimental and computational analyses of the biomolecular binding preferences of the diRu(II/III) drug are very scarce [30–32].

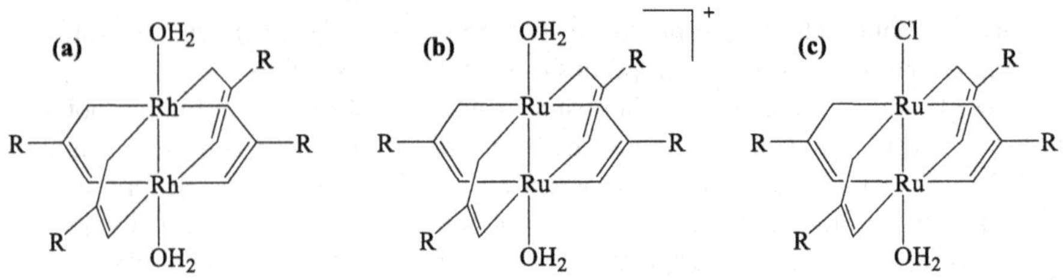

Fig. 1. Investigated dirhodium and diruthenium paddlewheel complexes: (a) [Rh$_2$(μ-O$_2$CCH$_3$)$_4$(H$_2$O)$_2$], (b) [Ru$_2$(μ-O$_2$CCH$_3$)$_4$(H$_2$O)$_2$]$^+$, (c) [Ru$_2$(μ-O$_2$CCH$_3$)$_4$(H$_2$O)Cl].

Despite of the similar structure, the Rh- and Ru-based complexes have different metallic cores Rh(II)Rh(II) and Ru(II)Ru(III), respectively. Their valences and charges dictate their structural preferences, in particular the choice of the axial ligands, as well as the metal-metal bond stability. The +4 charge of the Rh-based core is completely compensated by four anionic bridging acetates, thus, the axial ligands are weakly coordinated and are neutral. On the other hand, the Ru-based core possesses the +5 charge which after summing up with the −4 charge of four acetates, yields the uncompensated positive charge which favors the coordination of anionic ligands (such as Cl$^-$) into the axial position. Additionally, it is noteworthy to mention that the Ru-based complex has the polymeric arrangement in a solid state with a unit [ClRu$_2$(μ-O$_2$CCH$_3$)$_4$Cl] and transforms into its conventional form [Ru$_2$(μ-O$_2$CCH$_3$)$_4$Cl], only via the loss of a Cl in solution due to the replacement by a neutral solvent molecule [31].

In order to shed light onto the reactivity of both complexes, the thermodynamics of the ligand exchange reactions taking place at the axial positions of [Rh$_2$(μ-O$_2$CCH$_3$)$_4$(H$_2$O)$_2$] and [Ru$_2$(μ-O$_2$CCH$_3$)$_4$(H$_2$O)Cl] during their reactions with the protein side chains and termini was computed by means of DFT approaches (Fig. 2) [30]. A large set of possible targets was considered which included most common nucleophiles such as Arg, Asn, Asp, Asp$^-$,Cys, Cys$^-$, His, Lys, Met, Sec, Sec$^-$, as well as termini C-term, C-term$^-$, N-term, thus allowing to infer the selectivity of the studied paddlewheel complexes at different values of pH. We have found out that the reactivity patterns of both diRh and diRu complexes differ significantly. The diRh complex demonstrated a low selectivity by interacting effectively with all considered targets. Nevertheless, taking into consideration the additional parameters such as the typical pH of appearance or the usual proximity to the solvent accessible surface, the deprotonated C-term$^-$ as well as the protein side chains Asp$^-$, His, and Sec$^-$ were indicated as the most likely targets, although the latter is usually less sterically approachable. The complex [Ru$_2$(μ-O$_2$CCH$_3$)$_4$(H$_2$O)Cl] may undergo to the substitution of either water or chloride by the biomolecular nucleophiles. If the water is substituted, then the target selectivity of the diRu complex is the same as diRh complex. Nevertheless, the chloride exchange is more important at a higher pH, when the water at the axial position of diRu as well as the basic side chains are deprotonated. In these conditions, the diRu complex becomes more selective toward Arg and His via the exchange reaction with chloride. Interestingly, the reactions of both diRh and diRu complexes are highly exergonic with deprotonated Sec$^-$ and Cys$^-$. This evidence suggests the capability of these metallic scaffolds to be developed into efficacious TrxR-inhibiting anticancer agents.

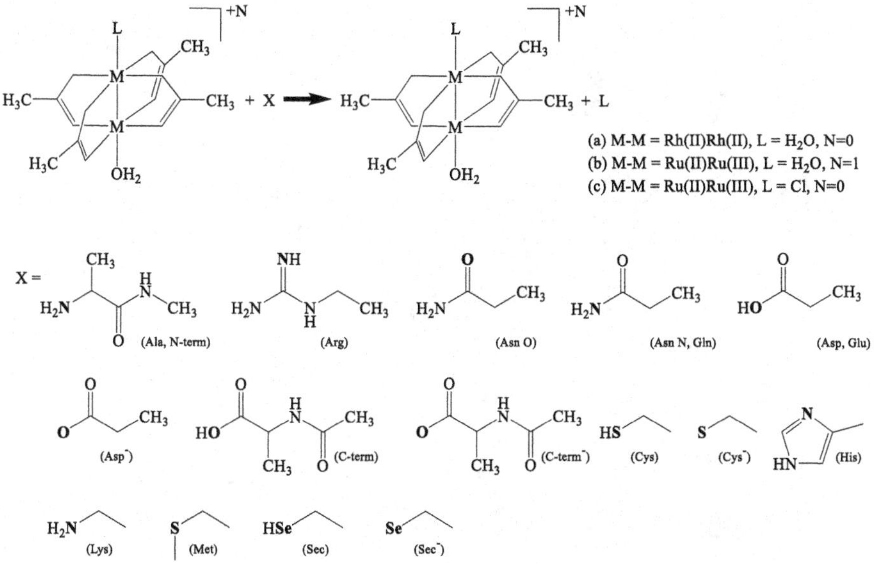

Fig. 2. The substitution reactions between the studied complexes [Rh$_2$(μ-O$_2$CCH$_3$)$_4$(H$_2$O)$_2$] (a), [Ru$_2$(μ-O$_2$CCH$_3$)$_4$(H$_2$O)$_2$]$^+$ (b), [Ru$_2$(μ-O$_2$CCH$_3$)$_4$(H$_2$O)Cl] (c) and models of targeted protein side chains (X). The atoms bound to the metal centers in the resulting reactions are represented in bold.

In principle, the dimetallic paddlewheel complexes seem to be an ideal scaffold for the development of prodrugs, as many medicinally active molecules may be utilized as the bridging ligand in place of acetate. Recently, the anti glioblastoma indolylglyoxylyl-Leu-Phe (EB106) and indolylglyoxylyl-Phe-Leu (EB776) dipeptides were used as the substitutes of acetates for the diruthenium core with the intention of developing an antitumor agent (Fig. 3) [28, 29]. Nevertheless, depending on dipeptide sequence, the medicinal properties differed greatly. The computational analysis of the most favourable geometrical configurations, provided a plausible explanation to this different activity in the location of phenyl side chain. In case of the indolylglyoxylyl-Leu-Phe dipeptide EB106, the phenyl ring is situated in alpha position to the carboxylate, thus sterically hindering the metal-bound oxygens from possible hydrolytic or nucleophilic attacks. Moreover, EB106 was shown to be lacking the hydrophilic areas close to the carboxylate oxygens. On the other hand, the indolylglyoxylyl-Phe-Leu dipeptide, EB776, is characterized by the presence of several equally favorable configurations with unshielded carboxylate oxygens and the availability of hydrophilic pockets close to them. This is an excellent example of the way how the steric effects of the ligand may modulate the stability of a metallodrug and its mode of action.

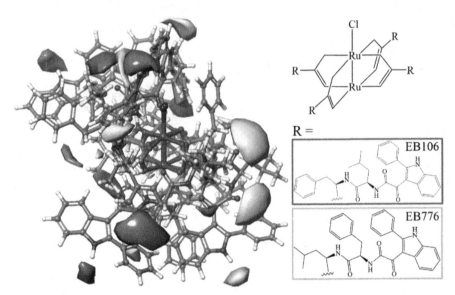

Fig. 3. (Left) Superposition of the most representative conformers of complexes [Ru$_2$(EB106)$_4$Cl] and [Ru$_2$(EB776)$_4$Cl] and their hydrophilic fragments in pink and in yellow, respectively. Color scheme: Ru (violet), Cl (dark green), O (red), C (gray), H (white). (Right top) Structure of paddle-wheel Ru$_2$(II,III) complex. (Right bottom) Its bridging ligands are either indolylglyoxylyl EB106 or EB776. Hydrophilic surface in yellow (EB776) is substantially closer to carboxylate oxygens bound to metals than the hydrophilic surface in pink (EB106). (Color figure online)

3 N-Heterocyclic-Carbene-Based Antitumor Metallodrugs

A vast exploitation of the N-heterocyclic carbenes (NHCs) in the design of antitumour metallodrugs [33, 34] can be well explained by two important features. Primarily, the increased robustness of the metal-carbene bond based on σ-donation and π-backdonation prevents its facile cleavage via the ligand substitution reactions. Secondly, it is possible to add various decorations to carbene's nitrogens, thus alternating the steric and electronic properties of the whole complex. Various transition-metal-based scaffolds have been proposed as novel anticancer agents [35, 36]. The coinage metals Au(I) and Ag(I) demonstrated peculiar cytotoxic features in vitro and in vivo [37, 38]. Although numerous modes of the apoptosis induction were proposed, including targeting of topoisomerase, DNA, and mitochondrial thioredoxin reductase (TrxR) [39, 40], the latter pathway has been shown to be of an utmost importance in NHC-based Au, Ag, Ru, Rh complexes [41–43]. These metal complexes possess a certain degree of promiscuity and are capable to multitarget various cellular biomolecules, yet they all display a special chemoselectivity toward thiols and selenols. This capability makes them excellent scaffolds for targeting the Sec-containing TrxR proteins overexpressed in several cancer types [44, 45].

The bicoordinated Au(I) complexes can be divided in two distinct groups: the neutral ones combining one monocarbene and one halide ligands, with a halide being facilely exchanged in physiological conditions, and the cationic Au(I) complexes with two attached carbenes [46].

In a recent computational study, the reactivity of the complex Au(I)(NHC)Cl (Fig. 4, complex a) with water, N-terminus, and various protein side chains was analyzed [47]. All the reactions were found to be strongly exergonic. It was clearly shown that although the aquation of the complex is characterized by a barrier of 23.0 kcal/mol, the barriers for reactions with other nucleophiles boast even lower values of less than 19 kcal/mol, thus suggesting that the complex Au(I)(NHC)Cl attacks its intracellular biomolecular targets in its administered, unhydrolyzed form. Au(I) being a soft center was found to majorly bind at Cys and Sec side chains, in their anionic thiolate and selenolate forms, with the activation energies of 17.4 and 12.8 kcal/mol, respectively, whereas neutral Cys, Sec, Arg, Lys, and N-terminus are easily targeted as well with the activation energies within the range 16.2–20.6 kcal/mol. The lack of major distinction between S^-, Se^-, and N-based binding sites implies that the accessibility of these protein targets may play a predominant role, i.e., if Cys and Sec are buried in the inner protein structure, then other nucleophile sites are attacked, nevertheless, if they are facilely approachable, they turn to represent the major targets of metallation.

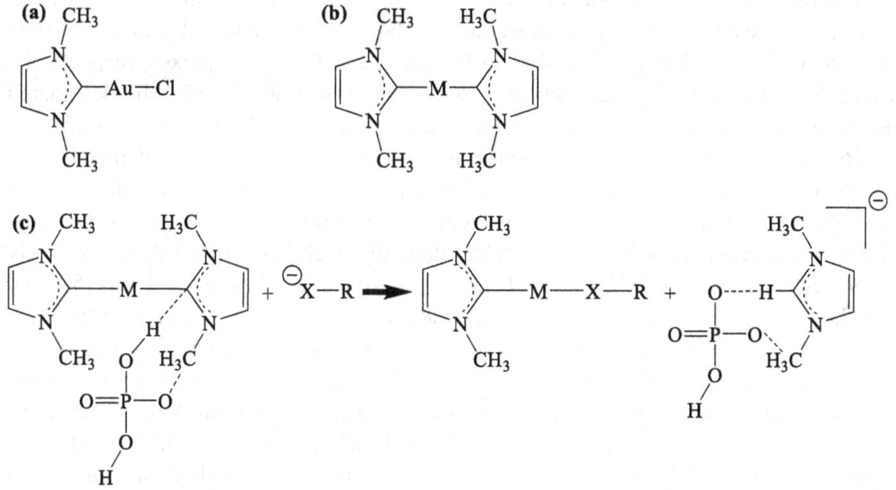

Fig. 4. Coinage metal NHC-based antitumour complexes: (a) $[Au(I)(NHC)Cl^-]$, (b) $[(Me_2Im)_2M]^+$ (M = Au, Ag, Cu), (c) Crucial reaction route incorporating aid of an outside proton donor, in which the hydrogen atom is delivered from the acidic constituent of exterior buffer to the liberated carbene (M = Cu, Ag, Au; X = S, Se; X-R = capped Cys, Sec).

Contrarily to Au(I)(NHC)Cl, which reacts with the nucleophiles via the halide sub-stitution, biscarbene complexes of the type $[Au(I)(NHC)_2]^+$ with NHC = Me_2Im, react with cysteine by releasing stepwisely both NHC moieties, and yielding the complex $[Au(Cys)_2]$ [48]. Nevertheless, the mechanism of this substitution reaction has been yet not fully elucidated. Moreover, a similar mechanism is expected to be enrolled by the analogous $[M(Me_2Im)_2]^+$ complexes with M = Ag(I) and Cu(I), indeed, both

Ag- and Cu-based biscarbene complexes were found to disclose recently a cytotoxic activity [33, 49]. Similarly, the complex bis(1-(anthracen-9-ylmethyl)-3-ethylimidazol-2-ylidene) (EIA) silver chloride, [Ag(I)(EIA)$_2$]Cl, and anthracene functionalized silver carbenes demonstrated robust cytotoxic effects incorporating TrxR inhibition [50]. Although the modus operandi of Cu(I) NHC complexes is less comprehended –likely incorporates the generation of reactive oxygen species (ROS) impairing the cytoplasm, mitochondria, and DNA [51, 52] –, the structural resemblance with the corresponding Au(I) and Ag(I) complexes advocates the targeting of TrxR as an alternative mechanism for the anticancer activity of Cu(I) NHC complexes. The metal-carbene bonds formed by gold, silver, and copper are characterized by a particular high strength and their cleavage turns to be a highly endothermic process.

Recently, computational investigations analyzed various pathways of metal-carbene dissociation through the attack of either neutral or deprotonated Cys and Sec residues and by modelling the concomitant protonation of the leaving carbene (Fig. 4) [53]. An important conclusion was made about the necessity of a simultaneous protonation of the leaving carbene that basically compensates the high energy cost for the metal-carbene dissociation, thus the availability of a proton source was demonstrated to be indispensable. Hence, the presence of a buffer in a physiological solution is crucial, and reflects the significance of the biological milieu in the thermodynamical control of these reactions. All these considerations allowed the calculation of the NHC substitution barriers of 19.8, 12.7, and 13.6 kcal/mol for Au(I), Ag(I), and Cu(I) complexes, respectively, with deprotonated Sec, which indicated Sec-containing proteins to be the designated targets of NHC coinage metal complexes, as also experimentally demonstrated [54].

Recent investigations of half-sandwich Ru-, Os-, Rh-, and Ir-based metal complexes allowed to regard them as robust leads for synthesizing new anticancer drugs [43, 55, 56]. Their hallmark is the presence of a π-bound arene, cyclopentadienyl (Cp), or its derivative, for example, η^5-pentamethylcyclopentadienyl (Cp*). Broadly employed σ-ligands are RAPTA (η^1-1,3,5-triaza-7-phosphaadamantane PTA) [57] and RAED (η^2-1,2-diaminoethane) [58] complexes. Indeed, there are many investigations focused on the cytotoxicity of Ru(II)-, Os(II)-, Rh(III)-, and Ir(III)-based half-sandwich complexes bearing a NHC ligand [43, 59, 60]. Recent studies of the cytotoxic activity against four human cancer lines involved several isostructural NHC complexes: Ru[II]-, and Os[II]-based complexes [M[II](cym)(NHC)Cl$_2$], Rh[III]- and Ir[III]-based compounds [M[III](Cp*)(NHC)Cl$_2$], NHC being either dmb = 1,3-dimethylbenzimidazol-2-ylidene or dbb = 1,3-dibenzylbenzimidazol-2-ylidene (Fig. 5, complexes 1–4) [43, 61]. Although all four complexes demonstrated an excellent cytotoxicity with the IC50 values in the low micromolar range, the complex [Rh(Cp*)(dbb)Cl$_2$] featured the most robust activity. Interestingly, several evidences indicate that all studied complexes targeted TrxR [43].

With the aim to disentangle the reaction pathways of these complexes with the selenoprotein TrxR, their reactivity toward water, Cys, Cys⁻, Sec, and Sec⁻ was analyzed via the usage of the DFT calculations of the thermodynamics and kinetics of the possibly occurring ligand exchange reactions (Fig. 5) [62].

Since the hydrolytic activation of these complexes was demonstrated to be unfavorable, it was assumed that the metal complex attack is operated via the substitution

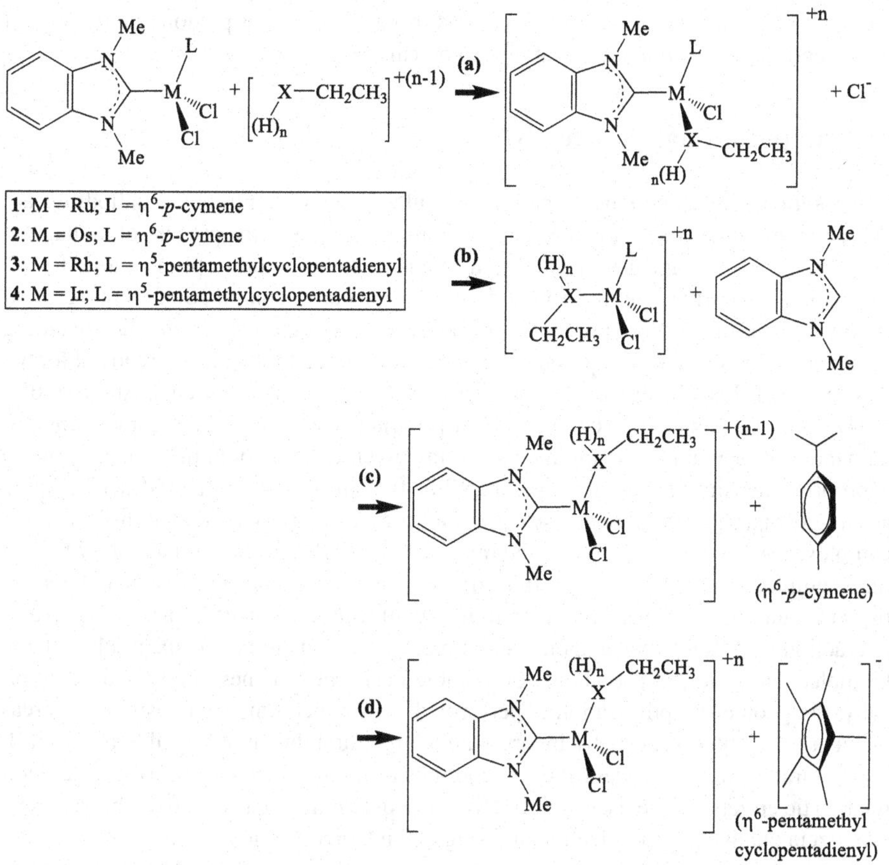

Fig. 5. Investigated NHC-complexes: (1) Ru-, (2) Os-, (3) Rh-, (4) Ir-based (top left). Studied ligand substitution reactions: (a) chloro, (b) dmb, (c) cym only for Ru- and Os-based complexes (1, 2) and (d) Cp* only for Rh- and Ir-based complexes (3, 4). X stands for S or Se in the models of side chains Cys or Sec, respectively.

of chloride, with the exception of the Ru-based complex for which the exchange of cym was shown to be feasible as well. The investigated complexes revealed a contrasting behavior in which the Ru and Os complexes displayed a higher preference toward Cys and Sec, albeit with a lesser thermodynamic favorability, whereas the Rh and Ir compounds exhibited a greater reactivity (low activation barriers), and resulted more selective to Cys$^-$ and Sec$^-$. By decomposing the activation free energy values into the sum of electronic, solvation, and thermal terms, it was shown that the higher selectivity of Ru and Os-compounds toward Cys and Sec can be explained by a solvation energy contribution more beneficial in case of these neutral moieties in comparison with their anionic forms, hence enabling these metal complexes to effectively bind to Cys and Sec in a low pH milieu. The Rh and Ir complexes majorly target the anionic forms Cys$^-$ and Sec$^-$ because of the favorable solvation contributions as well. On the basis of these findings, it was demonstrated that Cp*-bound Rh and Ir complexes are more effective binders of selenoenzymes, for instance, TrxR, because the Sec is predominantly present in its deprotonated, anionic form at physiological pH.

4 Computational Perspective

Computational investigations of the biomolecular action of antitumor metallodrugs are predominantly focused on the mechanistic comprehension of the process of metalation of the targeted biological moiety, which includes the structural optimizations for all moieties present in the reaction profile as well as the accurate computations of the reaction energy describing well the process thermodynamics and the barrier energies detailing the kinetics. This is done ubiquitously by means of DFT, a tool widely employed for the description of chemical processes in organometallic and bioinorganic chemistry [63–65].

Despite the choice of a computational program does not affect accuracy, computational cost, or memory requirements for any given computation, the selection of the appropriate density functional is crucial. While the omnipresent B3LYP describes quite accurately main-group elements' systems, the structure and reactivity of transition metal complexes are better described by the range-corrected density functional ωB97X, routinely employed in our group [3]. Indeed, the inclusion of empirical dispersion corrections accounting for dispersive interactions, i.e., the attractive part of the van der Waals interaction potential between atoms and molecules, results to be indispensable in large biomolecular systems. The choice of suitable basis set schemes is also crucial: typically, the geometry optimization is performed with a medium-sized basis set whereas the energy calculations usually incorporate a larger and thus more flexible basis set. It is a common practice to describe the core electrons of a metal atom as well as their relativistic effects via the usage of effective core potential, usually with double-zeta and triple-zeta quality for optimization and single point energy calculations [3].

The solvent (water) plays an important role in the mechanism of action of most metallodrugs which tend to undergo the hydrolytic activation prior to attacking their biomolecular targets. Based on the good accuracy/computational efficiency balance, the implicit solvation is more commonly used to predict free energies of solvation of both neutral and ionic solutes, and to model the reaction kinetics and thermodynamics in solution, as well as other bulk properties such as pKa of ionizable groups [3].

The usual biomolecular targets are DNA nucleobases or the protein side chains, among which Sec is the major target due to its overexpression in the tumor cells [44, 45]. Nevertheless, a recent discovery of the targeting of Cys in AQP3 by Aubipy resulted in a plethora of synthesized Au(III)-based drugs with the similar modes of action [46, 66].

The studies presented in this short minireview indicate that ligand decoration of active metal centers may play a pivotal role in the control of activation, approach, and final reaction with biomolecular targets. In many presented instances, the reactivity of the metal center with the intended biomolecular targets is dominated by the steric effects exerted by the metallodrug's ligands and their impact in the interaction with bulk and with the target environment [28, 29, 53]. It is worth noticing that a full elucidation of these structural aspects can be often gained only computationally by the use of multilayered approaches [3, 67].

An excellent example proving the effects of the bulky ligands on the metal center action is the sharp contrast between the reactivity of the diRu paddlewheel metallodrugs decorated with indolylglyoxylyl dipeptides, described in Sect. 2 [28, 29]. Indeed, a stark discrepancy between the stability of a scaffold with EB106 or EB776 bridging ligands means for this drug a switch between a completely uncytotoxic complex in the first case and the metallodrug with the exceptional antiprolific properties in the second case. A position of a mere phenyl ring fully determines the complex's mode of action. The conformational exploration of both EB106 and EB776 scaffolds, followed by the characterization of the corresponding solvent-accessible surfaces, resulted to be indispensable to the elucidation of their different activity, thus corroborating the importance of computational insights in the metallodrugs' molecular design.

A demonstration of the effects of the chemical environment onto the metallodrug reactivity is represented by the protonation of leaving NHC ligands upon their substitution and release into the bulk [53]. Indeed, the complexation of active metal centers like Au(I) or other coinage metals with NHC ligands has been exploited in force of the high stability of the M–C bond that, in principle, should enhance the chemoselectivity of these metal scaffolds. Indeed, without a proton transfer, the utter unfavorability of the M–C dissociation thermodynamics makes the substitution of a NHC ligand from a metal center unviable, thus evidencing the utmost importance of proton transfer processes in the metallodrugs' pharmacodynamics and pharmacokinetics. In this frame, accurate quantum chemistry methods, in particular those based on the density functional theory, are the most suitable to correctly assess the partecipation of either the bulk or the protein environment in proton transfer processes concomitant and/or assisting the exchange of NHC ligands.

A possible use of the ligand decoration is represented by the control of the solubilty or, more generally, the solvation properties of a metallodrug; such an approach is often employed to enhance the bioavaialbility of the administered metal complex [3, 67]. We envision at least two ways to control the metal complex solvation via ligand decoration: i) using ligands with highly hydrophilic pendants, or ii) using either charged or uncharged ligands to induce a non zero total charge to the metal complex. Notably, the latter approach not only enhances the metal complex solvation, but inevitably affects the reactivity of the metal center in terms of ligand exchange. As shown above, the half-sandwich metal complexes of Ru, Os, Rh, and Ir bearing either the neutral cymene or the anionic Cp* ligand show significantly different reactivity with Cys and Sec [62]. In particular, the $[M(\eta^6\text{-cym})]^{2+}$ scaffolds with M = Ru(II), Os(II) are more reactive with the neutral side chains of Cys and Sec, whereas the $[M(\eta^5\text{-Cp*})]^{3+}$ scaffolds with M = Rh(III), Ir(III) were found to be more reactive with the anionic forms of Cys and Sec. The computational analysis of the activation barriers for the binding of either $[M(\eta^6\text{-cym})]^{2+}$ or $[M(\eta^5\text{-Cp*})]^{3+}$ scaffold at nucleophilic protein sites unveiled that the above highlighted selectivity is mostly determined by solvation. Again, quantum chemistry methods can easily assess the impact of solvation on ligand exchange processes, in terms of both thermodynamics and kinetics, and thus represent indispensable components in the rational design of metallodrugs.

5   Conclusions

Modern medicinal chemistry is unimaginable without metallodrugs which form an essential supply to the treatment of a plethora of cancers, bacterial, viral, and parasitic infections.

The most advantageous feature of metallodrugs is the capacity to develop the complex scaffolds on the basis of the metal center versatile geometry. It allows to design the metallodrugs rationally via the modulation of electronic and steric features. The employment of bigger or charged ligands may modulate the membrane permeability and the ease with which the metallodrugs attack their targets. The accurate selection of ligands may allow to fine-tune their properties by alternating the bond strengths between metal centers and the ligands. Finally, the phenomenal ability of metallodrugs to bind at diverse biomolecular sites is another feature characterizing them as a source of specialized pharmaceutical agents.

In this minireview, the computational studies of reactivity paddlewheel- and N-heterocyclic-carbene-based antitumor metallodrugs with biomolecular targets, carried out in our group, were presented. A particular accent was made on the structural features of the studied systems, which form the basis of such mechanistic studies. Two main points inferred from the presented studies are noteworthy: (i) the importance of inclusion of steric effects produced by metallodrug's ligands if a complex is richly decorated and (ii) impact of the surrounding milieu.

Another important conclusion is that the computational modelling of metallodrug reactivity should be an essential step both on the stage of the metallic scaffold rational design as well as *in vitro* and *in vivo* examinations. A careful apprehension of the mechanistic processes underlying the activation of metallodrug as well as its target selectivity are essential for its structural development, whereas the computational analysis of the metal center promiscuity can be used to predict the possible toxic side effects and improve our understanding of the drug's targeted delivery.

References

1. Mjos, K.D., Orvig, C.: Metallodrugs in medicinal inorganic chemistry. Chem. Rev. **114**(8), 4540–4563 (2014). https://doi.org/10.1021/cr400460s
2. Anthony, E.J., et al.: Metallodrugs are unique: opportunities and challenges of discovery and development. Chem. Sci. **11**(48), 12888–12917 (2020). https://doi.org/10.1039/D0SC04082G
3. Tolbatov, I., Marrone, A.: Computational strategies to model the interaction and the reactivity of biologically-relevant transition metal complexes. Inorg. Chim. Acta **530**, 120686 (2022). https://doi.org/10.1016/j.ica.2021.120686
4. Yousuf, I., Bashir, M., Arjmand, F., Tabassum, S.: Advancement of metal compounds as therapeutic and diagnostic metallodrugs: current frontiers and future perspectives. Coord. Chem. Rev. **445**, 214104 (2021). https://doi.org/10.1016/j.ccr.2021.214104
5. Navarro, M., Gabbiani, C., Messori, L., Gambino, D.: Metal-based drugs for malaria, trypanosomiasis and leishmaniasis: recent achievements and perspectives. Drug Discov. Today **15**(23–24), 1070–1078 (2010). https://doi.org/10.1016/j.drudis.2010.10.005
6. Riddell, I., et al.: Metallo-Drugs: Development and Action of Anticancer Agents, vol. 18. Walter de Gruyter GmbH & Co KG, Wustermark (2018)

7. Tolbatov, I., Marrone, A.: Molecular dynamics simulation of the Pb(II) coordination in biological media via cationic dummy atom models. Theor. Chem. Acc. **140**(2), 1–12 (2021). https://doi.org/10.1007/s00214-021-02718-z

8. Paciotti, R., Tolbatov, I., Marrone, A., Storchi, L., Re, N., Coletti, C.: Computational investigations of bioinorganic complexes: the case of calcium, gold and platinum ions. In: AIP Conference on Proceedings, vol. 2186, no. 1, p. 030011:1–4. AIP Publishing LLC (2019). https://doi.org/10.1063/1.5137922

9. Tolbatov, I., Coletti, C., Marrone, A., Re, N.: Reactivity of arsenoplatin complex versus water and thiocyanate: a DFT benchmark study. Theor. Chem. Acc. **139**(12), 1–11 (2020). https://doi.org/10.1007/s00214-020-02694-w

10. Wenzel, M.N., Bonsignore, R., Thomas, S.R., Bourissou, D., Barone, G., Casini, A.: Cyclometalated AuIII complexes for cysteine arylation in zinc finger protein domains: towards controlled reductive elimination. Chem. Eur. J. **25**(32), 7628–7634 (2019). https://doi.org/10.1002/chem.201901535

11. Scoditti, S., Dabbish, E., Russo, N., Mazzone, G., Sicilia, E.: Anticancer activity, DNA binding, and photodynamic properties of a N∧ C∧ N-coordinated Pt (II) complex. Inorg. Chem. **60**(14), 10350–10360 (2021). https://doi.org/10.1021/acs.inorgchem.1c00822

12. Madhavan, T.: A review of 3D-QSAR in drug design. J. Chosun Nat. Sci. **5**(1), 1–5 (2012). https://doi.org/10.13160/ricns.2012.5.1.001

13. Verma, J., Khedkar, V.M., Coutinho, E.C.: 3D-QSAR in drug design-a review. Curr. Top. Med. Chem. **10**(1), 95–115 (2010). https://doi.org/10.2174/156802610790232260

14. Lee, R.F., Menin, L., Patiny, L., Ortiz, D., Dyson, P.J.: Versatile tool for the analysis of metal–protein interactions reveals the promiscuity of metallodrug–protein interactions. Anal. Chem. **89**(22), 11985–11989 (2017). https://doi.org/10.1021/acs.analchem.7b02211

15. Hrdina, R.: Dirhodium (II, II) paddlewheel complexes. Eur. J. Inorg. Chem. **2021**(6), 501–528 (2021). https://doi.org/10.1002/ejic.202000955

16. Rico, S.R.A., Abbasi, A.Z., Ribeiro, G., Ahmed, T., Wu, X.Y., de Oliveira Silva, D.: Diruthenium (II, III) metallodrugs of ibuprofen and naproxen encapsulated in intravenously injectable polymer–lipid nanoparticles exhibit enhanced activity against breast and prostate cancer cells. Nanoscale **9**(30), 10701–10714 (2017). https://doi.org/10.1039/C7NR01582H

17. Katsaros, N., Anagnostopoulou, A.: Rhodium and its compounds as potential agents in cancer treatment. Crit. Rev. Oncol./Hematol. **42**(3), 297–308 (2002). https://doi.org/10.1016/S1040-8428(01)00222-0

18. Howard, R.A., Kimball, A.P., Bear, J.L.: Mechanism of action of tetra-μ-carboxylatodirhodium (II) in L1210 tumor suspension culture. Cancer Res. **39**(7.1), 2568–2573 (1979)

19. Zyngier, S., Kimura, E., Najjar, R.: Antitumor effects of rhodium (II) citrate in mice bearing Ehrlich tumors. Braz. J. Med. Biol. Res. **22**(3), 397–401 (1989)

20. Nothenberg, M.S., et al.: Biological activity and crystallographic study of a rhodium propionate-metronidazole adduct. J. Braz. Chem. Soc. **5**(1), 23–29 (1994)

21. Enriquez Garcia, A., Jalilehvand, F., Niksirat, P.: Reactions of $Rh_2(CH_3COO)_4$ with thiols and thiolates: a structural study. J. Synchrotron Rad. **26**(2), 450–461 (2019). https://doi.org/10.1107/S160057751900033X

22. Enriquez Garcia, A., Jalilehvand, F., Niksirat, P., Gelfand, B.S.: Methionine binding to dirhodium (II) tetraacetate. Inorg. Chem. **57**(20), 12787–12799 (2018). https://doi.org/10.1021/acs.inorgchem.8b01979

23. Popp, B.V., Chen, Z., Ball, Z.T.: Sequence-specific inhibition of a designed metallopeptide catalyst. Chem. Comm. **48**(60), 7492–7494 (2012). https://doi.org/10.1039/C2CC33808D

24. Zaykov, A.N., Ball, Z.T.: A general synthesis of dirhodium metallopeptides as MDM2 ligands. Chem. Comm. **47**(39), 10927–10929 (2011). https://doi.org/10.1039/C1CC13169A

25. Ferraro, G., Pratesi, A., Messori, L., Merlino, A.: Protein interactions of dirhodium tetraacetate: a structural study. Dalton Trans. **49**(8), 2412–2416 (2020). https://doi.org/10.1039/C9D T04819G

26. Loreto, D., Ferraro, G., Merlino, A.: Unusual structural features in the adduct of dirhodium tetraacetate with lysozyme. Int. J. Mol. Sci. **22**(3), 1496 (2021). https://doi.org/10.3390/ijm s22031496

27. Ribeiro, G., Benadiba, M., Colquhoun, A., de Oliveira Silva, D.: Diruthenium (II, III) complexes of ibuprofen, aspirin, naproxen and indomethacin non-steroidal anti-inflammatory drugs: synthesis, characterization and their effects on tumor-cell proliferation. Polyhedron **27**(3), 1131–1137 (2008). https://doi.org/10.1016/j.poly.2007.12.011

28. Barresi, E., et al.: A mixed-valence diruthenium (II, III) complex endowed with high stability: from experimental evidence to theoretical interpretation. Dalton Trans. **49**(41), 14520–14527 (2020). https://doi.org/10.1039/D0DT02527E

29. Barresi, E., et al.: Two mixed valence diruthenium (II, III) isomeric complexes show different anticancer properties. Dalton Trans. **50**, 9643–9647 (2021). https://doi.org/10.1039/D1DT01 492G

30. Tolbatov, I., Marrone, A.: Reaction of dirhodium and diruthenium paddlewheel tetraacetate complexes with nucleophilic protein sites: a computational study. Inorg. Chim. Acta **530**, 120684 (2021). https://doi.org/10.1016/j.ica.2021.120684

31. Santos, R.L., van Eldik, R., de Oliveira Silva, D.: Thermodynamics of axial substitution and kinetics of reactions with amino acids for the paddlewheel complex tetrakis (acetato) chloridodiruthenium (II, III). Inorg. Chem. **51**(12), 6615–6625 (2012). https://doi.org/10. 1021/ic300168t

32. Messori, L., Marzo, T., Sanches, R.N.F., de Oliveira Silva, D., Merlino, A.: Unusual structural features in the lysozyme derivative of the tetrakis (acetato) chloridodiruthenium (II, III) complex. Angew. Chem. Int. Ed. **53**(24), 6172–6175 (2014). https://doi.org/10.1002/anie.201 403337

33. Teyssot, M.L., et al.: Metal-NHC complexes: a survey of anti-cancer properties. Dalton Trans. **35**, 6894–6902 (2009). https://doi.org/10.1039/B906308K

34. Patil, S.A., et al.: N-heterocyclic carbene metal complexes as bio-organometallic antimicrobial and anticancer drugs. Future Med. Chem. **7**(10), 1305–1333 (2015). https://doi.org/10.4155/ fmc.15.61

35. Patil, S.A., Hoagland, A.P., Patil, S.A., Bugarin, A.: N-heterocyclic carbene-metal complexes as bio-organometallic antimicrobial and anticancer drugs, an update (2015–2020). Future Med. Chem. **12**(24), 2239–2275 (2020). https://doi.org/10.4155/fmc-2020-0175

36. Zou, T., Lok, C.N., Wan, P.K., Zhang, Z.F., Fung, S.K., Che, C.M.: Anticancer metal-N-heterocyclic carbene complexes of gold, platinum and palladium. Curr. Opin. Chem. Biol. **43**, 30–36 (2018). https://doi.org/10.1016/j.cbpa.2017.10.014

37. Guarra, F., et al.: Cytotoxic Ag (I) and Au (I) NHC-carbenes bind DNA and show TrxR inhibition. J. Inorg. Biochem. **205**, 110998 (2020). https://doi.org/10.1016/j.jinorgbio.2020. 110998

38. Rieb, J., et al.: Influence of wing-tip substituents and reaction conditions on the structure, properties and cytotoxicity of Ag (I)–and Au (I)–bis (NHC) complexes. Dalton Trans. **46**(8), 2722–2735 (2017). https://doi.org/10.1039/C6DT04559F

39. Magherini, F., et al.: Antiproliferative effects of two gold (I)-N-heterocyclic carbene complexes in A2780 human ovarian cancer cells: a comparative proteomic study. Oncotarget **9**, 28042–28068 (2018). https://doi.org/10.18632/oncotarget.25556

40. Guarra, F., et al.: Interaction of a gold (I) dicarbene anticancer drug with human telomeric DNA G-quadruplex: Solution and computationally aided X-ray diffraction analysis. Dalton Trans. **47**, 16132–16138 (2018). https://doi.org/10.1039/C8DT03607A

41. Aher, S.B., Muskawar, P.N., Thenmozhi, K., Bhagat, P.R.: Recent developments of metal N-heterocyclic carbenes as anticancer agents. Eur. J. Med. Chem. **81**, 408–419 (2014). https://doi.org/10.1016/j.ejmech.2014.05.036

42. Oehninger, L., Rubbiani, R., Ott, I.: N-Heterocyclic carbene metal complexes in medicinal chemistry. Dalton Trans. **42**(10), 3269–3284 (2013). https://doi.org/10.1039/C2DT32617E

43. Truong, D., et al.: Potent inhibition of thioredoxin reductase by the Rh derivatives of anticancer M(arene/Cp*)(NHC)Cl$_2$ complexes. Inorg. Chem. **59**(5), 3281–3289 (2020). https://doi.org/10.1021/acs.inorgchem.9b03640

44. Berggren, M., Gallegos, A., Gasdaska, J.R., Gasdaska, P.Y., Warneke, J., Powis, G.: Thioredoxin and thioredoxin reductase gene expression in human tumors and cell lines, and the effects of serum stimulation and hypoxia. Anticancer Res. **16**, 3459–3466 (1996)

45. Nakamura, H., et al.: Expression of thioredoxin and glutaredoxin, redox-regulating proteins, in pancreatic cancer. Cancer Detect. Prev. **24**(1), 53–60 (2000)

46. Tolbatov, I., Marrone, A., Coletti, C., Re, N.: Computational studies of Au (I) and Au (III) anticancer metallodrugs: a survey. Molecules **26**(24), 7600 (2021). https://doi.org/10.3390/molecules26247600

47. Tolbatov, I., Coletti, C., Marrone, A., Re, N.: Reactivity of gold (I) monocarbene complexes with protein targets: a theoretical study. Int. J. Mol. Sci. **20**(4), 820 (2019). https://doi.org/10.3390/ijms20040820

48. Dos Santos, H.F., Vieira, M.A., Sánchez Delgado, G.Y., Paschoal, D.: Ligand exchange reaction of Au (I) RN-heterocyclic carbene complexes with cysteine. J. Phys. Chem. A **120**(14), 2250–2259 (2016). https://doi.org/10.1021/acs.jpca.6b01052

49. Touj, N., et al.: Anticancer, antimicrobial and antiparasitical activities of copper (I) complexes based on N-heterocyclic carbene (NHC) ligands bearing aryl substituents. J. Coord. Chem. **73**(20–22), 2889–2905 (2020). https://doi.org/10.1080/00958972.2020.1836359

50. Citta, A., et al.: Fluorescent silver (I) and gold (I)-N-heterocyclic carbene complexes with cytotoxic properties: mechanistic insights. Metallomics **5**(8), 1006–1015 (2013). https://doi.org/10.1039/c3mt20260g

51. Kagawa, T.F., Geierstanger, B.H., Wang, A.H.J., Ho, P.S.: Covalent modification of guanine bases in double-stranded DNA. J. Biol. Chem. **266**, 20175–20184 (1991). https://doi.org/10.1016/S0021-9258(18)54906-1

52. Shobha Devi, C., Thulasiram, B., Aerva, R.R., Nagababu, P.: Recent advances in copper intercalators as anticancer agents. J. Fluoresc. **28**(5), 1195–1205 (2018). https://doi.org/10.1007/s10895-018-2283-7

53. Tolbatov, I., Marzo, T., Coletti, C., La Mendola, D., Storchi, L., Re, N.: Reactivity of antitumor coinage metal-based N-heterocyclic carbene complexes with cysteine and selenocysteine protein sites. J. Inorg. Biochem. **223**, 111533 (2021). https://doi.org/10.1016/j.jinorgbio.2021.111533

54. Hickey, J.L., Ruhayel, R.A., Barnard, P.J., Baker, M.V., Berners-Price, S.J., Filipovska, A.: Mitochondria-targeted chemotherapeutics: the rational design of gold (I) N-heterocyclic carbene complexes that are selectively toxic to cancer cells and target protein selenols in preference to thiols. J. Am. Chem. Soc. **130**, 12570–12571 (2008). https://doi.org/10.1021/ja804027j

55. Li, J., et al.: Half-sandwich iridium and ruthenium complexes: effective tracking in cells and anticancer studies. Inorg. Chem. **57**(21), 13552–13563 (2018). https://doi.org/10.1021/acs.inorgchem.8b02161

56. Bratsos, I., et al.: New half sandwich Ru (II) coordination compounds for anticancer activity. Dalton Trans. **41**(24), 7358–7371 (2012). https://doi.org/10.1039/C2DT30654A

57. Murray, B.S., Babak, M.V., Hartinger, C.G., Dyson, P.J.: The development of RAPTA compounds for the treatment of tumors. Coord. Chem. Rev. **306**, 86–114 (2016). https://doi.org/10.1016/j.ccr.2015.06.014

58. Adhireksan, Z., et al.: Ligand substitutions between ruthenium–cymene compounds can control protein versus DNA targeting and anticancer activity. Nat. Commun. **5**, 3462 (2014). https://doi.org/10.1038/ncomms4462
59. Rodríguez-Prieto, T., et al.: Organometallic dendrimers based on ruthenium (II) N-heterocyclic carbenes and their implication as delivery systems of anticancer small interfering RNA. J. Inorg. Biochem. **223**, 111540 (2021). https://doi.org/10.1016/j.jinorgbio.2021.111540
60. Kralj, J., et al.: Half-sandwich Ir (III) and Os (II) complexes of pyridyl-mesoionic carbenes as potential anticancer agents. Organometallics **38**(21), 4082–4092 (2019). https://doi.org/10.1021/acs.organomet.9b00327
61. Sullivan, M.P., et al.: Probing the paradigm of promiscuity for N-heterocyclic carbene complexes and their protein adduct formation. Angew. Chem. Int. Ed. **60**(36), 19928–19932 (2021). https://doi.org/10.1002/anie.202106906
62. Tolbatov, I., Marrone, A.: Reactivity of N-heterocyclic carbene half-sandwich Ru-, Os-, Rh-, and Ir-based complexes with cysteine and selenocysteine: a computational study. Inorg. Chem. **61**(1), 746–754 (2021). https://doi.org/10.1021/acs.inorgchem.1c03608
63. Todisco, S., et al.: Double addition of phenylacetylene onto the mixed bridge phosphinito–phosphanido Pt (I) complex [(PHCy$_2$)Pt(μ-PCy$_2$){κ^2P, O-μ-P(O)C$_y$2}Pt(PHCy$_2$)](Pt–Pt). Dalton Trans. **49**(20), 6776–6789 (2020). https://doi.org/10.1039/D0DT00923G
64. Ritacco, I., Russo, N., Sicilia, E.: DFT investigation of the mechanism of action of organoiridium (III) complexes as anticancer agents. Inorg. Chem. **54**(22), 10801–10810 (2015). https://doi.org/10.1021/acs.inorgchem.5b01832
65. Wenzel, M.N., Meier-Menches, S.M., Williams, T.L., Rämisch, E., Barone, G., Casini, A.: Selective targeting of PARP-1 zinc finger recognition domains with Au (III) organometallics. Chem. Comm. **54**(6), 611–614 (2018). https://doi.org/10.1039/C7CC08406D
66. Wenzel, M.N., et al.: Insights into the mechanisms of aquaporin-3 inhibition by gold (III) complexes: the importance of non-coordinative adduct formation. Inorg. Chem. **58**(3), 2140–2148 (2019). https://doi.org/10.1021/acs.inorgchem.8b03233
67. Tolbatov, I., Marrone, A., Paciotti, R., Re, N., Coletti, C.: Multilayered modelling of the metallation of biological targets. In: Gervasi, O., et al. (eds.) ICCSA 2021. LNCS, vol. 12958, pp. 398–412. Springer, Cham (2021). https://doi.org/10.1007/978-3-030-87016-4_30

Quantum Confinement Effects in Materials for Daytime Radiative Cooling: An *Ab-initio* Investigation

Costanza Borghesi[1], Claudia Fabiani[2,3], Anna Laura Pisello[2,3],
and Giacomo Giorgi[1,3,4(✉)]

[1] Department of Civil and Environmental Engineering (DICA),
Università degli Studi di Perugia, Via G. Duranti 93, 06125 Perugia, Italy
[2] Department of Engineering, Università degli Studi di Perugia,
Via G. Duranti 93, 06125 Perugia, Italy
[3] CIRIAF - Interuniversity Research Centre, University of Perugia, Perugia, Italy
anna.pisello@unipg.it, giacomo.giorgi@unipg.it
[4] CNR-SCITEC, 06123 Perugia, Italy

Abstract. We have here performed a campaign of first-principles calculations comparing the effect of confinement in two ABO_3-perovskites, $SrTiO_3$ and $BaSnO_3$. The study is motivated by the quest of novel materials for daytime radiative cooling devices, a recently suggested mechanism to passively cool down the temperature of sky facing objects (mainly buildings and constructions). In particular, after assessing the computational setup for the calculation of our structures, we have similarly calculated the bandstructure of 3D, 2D, and 0D systems. We both employed standard density functional theory and meta-GGA methods to do it and discussed pros and cons of the two approaches. Finally, we discuss the possible applicability of 0D species as materials for radiative cooling as function of a large and direct bandgap.

Keywords: Daytime radiative cooling · Density functional theory · Inorganic perovskites

1 Introduction

The dependence of energy supplies from non-renewable fossil fuels is not only accompanied by dramatic effects on the environment, but is also extremely affected by geopolitical resilience factors that largely impact on the fluctuating price and availability of such resources. In addition ~10% of global CO_2 emissions are ascribed to cooling devices, i.e. air-conditioners (ACs), which exploit electricity produced mainly from non-renewable fossil fuels [1]. It should be similarly kept in mind that the technology of most ACs is still based on the emission of waste heat in air with subsequent outdoor temperature increase [2] and in some cases exploit hydrofluorocarbons (HFCs), i.e. greenhouse gases even more harmful than CO_2 itself. In addition to that, those compounds can last in the atmosphere up to many thousands of years and, once released into the air, they can partially dissolve into the oceans over few decades. This means that once in the atmosphere, greenhouse-gases will continue to affect climate for thousands of years. Thus, the reliance on fossil fuels and on traditional cooling devices is a twofold issue, i.e. it raises global warming while continuing to pollute the air. As a matter of fact, cooling seems to be one of the most detrimental factors in the climate crisis and things are unlikely to improve as the global population is constantly rising. This becomes even more serious in urban contexts, where currently 68% of the global population lives and are characterized by local overheating typically referred to Urban Heat Island (UHI) [3]. Such phenomenon is probably the best documented one as related to climate change with a clear anthropogenic responsibility imputable to vehicular traffic emissions, urban solar trapping, low solar reflectivity and evapotraspiration potential of built environment [4]. UHI may indeed reach out up to 10K air temperature increase and important relative humidity decrease [4], as registered in whole urban contexts and in microclimate granularity [5]. The community should thus proceed in two parallel directions both paying attention on optimizing efficient and renewables exploitation [6–22] as in the last few decades, but also finding strategies to manage urban overheating by means of adaptation and mitigation actions. A mitigative approach to reduce cooling energy consumption and UHI has been recently proposed and is based on the exploitation of a well-known phenomenon that is the radiative cooling [23–30]. At nighttime radiative cooling occurs naturally and takes advantage on the fact that any outdoor, sky facing, object may emit a significant fraction of thermal radiation into outer space through the so-called "atmospheric window" in the mid IR wavelength range (8–13 μm) [31]. The big challenge is to shift this nocturnal natural process to daytime when radiative conditions are clearly different. Unlike traditional AC systems, passive radiative cooling devices are energy-free and refrigerant-free cooling technologies that reflect incoming solar irradiance, while emitting thermal radiation to cool down the universe thereby achieving sub-ambient cooling. This self-cooling technique has demonstrated a tremendous potential, attracting significant interest from paint, air conditioning and building industries. Radiative passive cooling devices generally consist of two parts: a solar reflection layer and a radiative cooling layer [26,29]. While the reflective layer is mainly constituted by a metallic element, i.e. Ag and/or Al, the real core of the device is here represented by the radiative layer (responsible of both absorption in the VIS and emission in mid IR) which has been in the last decades a topic of deep investigation [25,32,33]. Recent technological developments enable the usage of metamaterials [33], of nanoparticle-doped systems [32], and of photonic structures [25] to maximise the efficiency of such component. Also halide perovskites, materials with remarkable optoelectronic features mainly investigated for photovoltaics [6], have been shown to play a relevant role in such architectures [34,35]. The first experimental sub-ambient daytime radiative cooling has been achieved based on this latter architecture by stacking layers of HfO_2 and SiO_2 with different thicknesses [25] and based on such architecture later flavours (TiO_2/SiO_2) were similarly suggested [36]. More recently, based on their optical response, photoluminescent (third generation of construction materials) [37] and/or thermochromic (next generation of construction materials) [37] materials have been predicted as optimal radiative cooling materials to replace standard materials (heat-absorbers) used in constructions. Due to their intrinsic complexity, photonic/metamaterials structures are theoretically investigated by means of Maxwell Equations [38–41] and, except for a few works that recently have appeared in literature where the metrics to define a good material as an active layer for daytime passive cooling are discussed [42], the topic remains quite overlooked from the computational modelling and atomistic points of view, despite the increasing availability of more powerful computational resources and, accordingly, the reliability/accuracy of the related simulations. In this context, our aim here is to investigate at the atomistic level the active components for the radiative part and possibly predict/suggest novel materials with improved performances. In details, high entropy alloys (HEAs) [43–45] and in particular oxides (HEOs) [46] have been recently introduced as a sort of philosopher's stone in materials science. Such compounds already play a relevant role in several technological fields ranging from catalysis [47], to photocatalysis [48], ion-batteries [49], magnetism [50], and energy storage [51], to mention just a few of them. The idea that subtends their importance is the possibility of an (almost) infinite number of combinations to form compounds which are highly stabilized because of the enhanced role played by the entropic factor (ΔS_{mix}) in the Gibbs free energy equation. Our focus is a material which embodies the optimal features that characterise the radiative cooling material in terms of absorption/emission. Accordingly, with the idea of applying HEOs to radiative cooling processes, our initial investigation is here devoted to the individuation and the analysis of candidate materials aiming to establish relationships between their structural and electronic features. Keeping in mind that the dimensionality of the radiative cooling materials is crucial for the final working principle of the device, we here provide an initial analysis about $BaSnO_3$ (hereafter also BSO) –whose applicability in the field seems quite promising and whose flexible perovskite structure can be used as network for a HEO– and its low dimensional counterparts, and compare their properties with those of another well assessed and more investigated perovskite oxide, i.e. $SrTiO_3$ (hereafter also STO).

2   Computational Details

By means of Density Functional Theory methods as implemented in the VASP code [52–55], we performed a campaign of calculations on the two previously mentioned systems, $SrTiO_3$ and $BaSnO_3$. In such simulations the electron exchange-correlation functional of Perdew, Burke, and Ernzerhof (PBE) [56] was used. The projector augmented wave (PAW) method [57,58] has been similarly adopted using a cutoff energy of 500 eV for the plane-wave basis set. For the geometry optimization the Brillouin Zone (BZ) was sampled by means of a Γ-centred $6 \times 6 \times 6$ mesh (more dense meshes are used for electronic properties calculations). Optimization of lattice parameters and ionic positions ended when residual forces were lower than 5×10^{-4} eV/Å. Due to the shortcomings associated with the DFT in predicting excited state properties, we first calculated the bandstructure at the DFT level and then to improve the agreement with the experiments we tested several other post-DFT methods with particular attention to the modified Becke-Johnson (mBJ) meta-GGA functional [59,60]. Such potential-only functional provides in principle results of electronic properties in good agreement with those typical of a GW run but at a very lower computational cost.

3   Results and Discussion

Both STO and BSO belong to the ABO_3-type perovskite crystals. Following the Goldschmidt tolerance factor, t, the empirical factor widely used over the years as a criterion for discussing the stability of perovskites [61],

$$t = \frac{R_A + R_B}{\sqrt{2}(R_B + R_O)} \tag{1}$$

where R_A, R_A, and R_A are the ionic radius for the A-site, B-site, and oxide ions [62], respectively, two values very close to the unity are predicted (1.01 and 1.02, for $SrTiO_3$ and $BaSnO_3$) assessing the ideally cubic geometry of the two systems. $SrTiO_3$ is cubic (Pm3m, space group 221) at room temperature and for ordinary pressure, undergoing phase transitions towards tetragonal ($I_{4/mcm}$, s.g. 140) and orthorhombic (Cmcm, s.g. 63) polymorphs at increasing pressure values [63]. Our optimized structure (see Fig. 1) is characterized by a lattice parameter ($a = 3.95$ Å) which is consistent with other values reported in literature (see Table 1) We then optimized the structure of BSO. Similarly to STO, bulk BSO experimentally crystallizes in the cubic perovskite structure Pm3m. The calculated lattice parameter is 4.186 Å in pretty good agreement with previously reported data (see Fig. 1). To stress that in BSO Ba atom (A-site cation) occupies the center of the cell (0.5; 0.5; 0.5), while in STO the same A-site ion, here Sr, occupies the corner (0.0; 0.0; 0.0) [64]. For the sake of comparison, in Fig. 1 we put the A-site at the corner and the B-site cation in the center of the cell, respectively.

On such optimized systems we calculated the bandstructures that are depicted in Fig. 2. As for the structural ones, the main electronic properties for both bulk STO and BSO are similarly reported in Table 1 As widely reported the bandgap of these two bulk materials is indirect (R $\rightarrow \Gamma$) and in this sense their applicability in radiative cooling devices could be potentially less efficient since they are expected to re-emit (compared to a direct-gap material) more slowly with possible heating of the material. In details, the gap calculated at the DFT level is 1.387 eV for STO and 0.218 eV for BSO. As well-known the DFT calculated value massively underestimates the experimental one. It is worth stressing that we used a reduced number of electrons in the valence of the B-site cation pseudopotentials. For both Sn and Ti indeed we used 4 electrons that we realized

Table 1. Optimized lattice parameter a and electronic bandgap at different levels of theory obtained in the present work. For the sake of comparison same data, experimental and theoretical, from previous literature are reported.

	SrTiO$_3$	BaSnO$_3$
a (Å)	3.95 (present work)	4.186 (present work)
	3.92 [63] (theo. PW91)	4.055 [65] (theo. GGA)
	3.95 [66] (theo GGA PW)	4.156 (Sn: no semicore) [67] (theo PBE)
	3.94 [66] (theo PBE PW)	4.186 (Sn semicore) [67] (theo PBE)
	3.90 [68] (exp.)	4.19903 [69] (theo FP-LAPW)
		4.115 [70] (exp.); 4.1194 [69] (exp)
E_{gap} (eV)	1.387 (R → Γ, this work, PAW/PBE)	0.218 (R → Γ, this work, PAW/PBE)
	1.722 (Γ → Γ, this work, PAW/PBE)	0.761(Γ → Γ, this work, PAW/PBE)
	2.355 (R → Γ, this work, PAW/mBJ)	3.593 (R → Γ, this work, PAW/mBJ)
	2.626 (R → Γ, this work, PAW/mBJ)	3.885 (R → Γ, this work, PAW/mBJ)
	3.25 [71] (exp)	0.4 [69] (R → Γ, (theo FP-LAPW)
		3.56 [72] (exp.); 3.4 [73](exp)

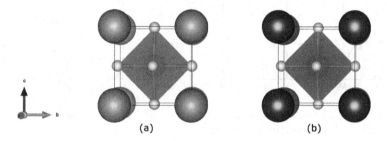

(a)   (b)

Fig. 1. Optimized structures for (a) STO and (b) BSO. [Light green, Sr; cyan: Ti; red: O; dark green: Ba; grayish: Sn atoms.] (Color figure online)

to slightly underestimate our DFT gap if compared with other previously calculated gaps at the same level of theory (using 10 electrons in the valence for Ti atoms in STO opens the gap of ∼0.3 eV) On the other hand, once we apply the mBJ potential to correct the gap we observe a two-fold behavior. Indeed, mBJ opens STO gap but not sufficiently to recover the experimental value (2.355 eV), while in the case of BSO mBJ tends to recover (3.593 eV) the experimentally reported values (∼3.5 eV) [72,73]. By means of a basic computational setup we similarly calculated the *one-shot* G_0W_0 bandgap for the two bulk systems. For STO, in particular, the *one-shot* G_0W_0 leads to a (still R → Γ) gap of 3.08 eV, not that far from the experimentally reported value of 3.25 eV [71]. In the case of BSO, the same G_0W_0 bandgap is 2.95 eV revealing at opposite the need of other iterations to reach the agreement with the experimental bandgap value [72,73].

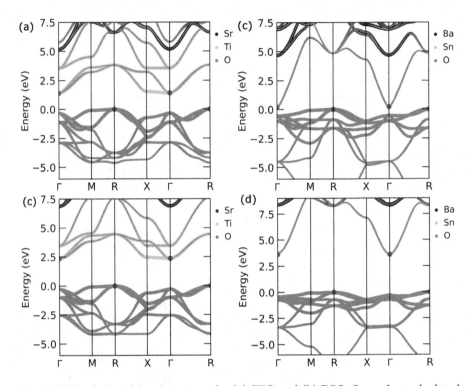

Fig. 2. DFT calculated bandstructure for (a) STO and (b) BSO. Same, but calculated at the mBJ level of theory in (c) and (d)

In view of the possible applications of $BaSO_3$ compound family in radiative cooling devices, we then focus on the structural confinement of the investigated systems by reducing their dimensionality. The most immediate and natural way to do it is the analysis of the so-called Ruddlesden-Popper (RP) phases. Recently, such mixed 2D/3D and pure 2D systems have gained particular attention because of their hybrid organic-inorganic halide counterparts which have been shown to play a main role in photoconversion processes [74–78]. In the case of STO, such RP phases – with stoichiometric relationship $Sr_{n+1}Ti_nO_{3n+1}$ – are characterized by the insertion of additional SrO planes into the perovskite lattice to form quantum wells of variable thicknesses. STO RP phases have tetragonal structure with $I_{4/mmm}$ symmetry (s.g. 139, $Z = 2$), We studied the initial members of the series $n = 1 - 3$ for both STO and BSO, i.e. the pure 2D system ($n = 1$) and the first two members of the mixed 2D/3D class. While the former compounds (STO RP phases) are well assessed and already investigated [79] with particular focus on structural, electronic and optical features [80, 81], the latter (BSO) are only hypothetical compounds that we obtained based on the STO RP structural counterparts [82]. We want to here stress that the modellization of such $n = 1 - 3$ STO (and consequently BSO) RPs stems from the structures reported in the Materials Project website [64] and that no fine tuning of atomic positions have been performed. The resulting optimized geometries of the hypothetical BSO RP phases ($n = 1 - 3$) are reported in Fig. 3.

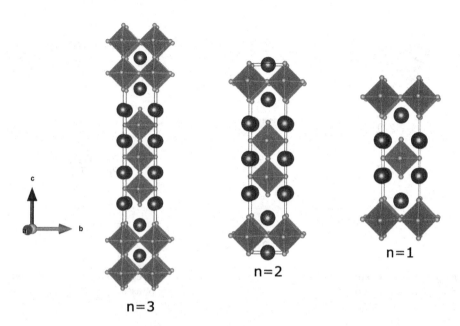

Fig. 3. DFT optimized structures for BSO RP phase ($n = 1 - 3$) [Dark green, Ba; grayish: Sn; red: O atoms]. (Color figure online)

Concerning the electronic features of such dimensionally reduced systems, in Fig. 4 we show the trend of quantum confinement effects in both STO RP and BSO RP phases and at the PBE and mBJ level of theory, respectively. As expected the reduction of the layer thickness ($n = 3 \rightarrow n = 1$) is associated with an increase of the bandgap. On the other hand, compared with PBE, the confinement effect are less marked for increasing values of n in both cases, an effect which is more noticeable in the case of BSO RP phases. Indeed, passing from $n = 2$ to $n = 1$ in BSO RP (STO RP) is associated with an increase in the gap of 34% (9%) at the PBE level of theory, from 1.640 eV to 2.488 eV (from 1.488 to 1.636 eV). The same relative bandgap increase at the mBJ level for BSO RP is halved to 15% (4.392 eV to 5.189 eV), while for STO RP the same variation is only of 6.5% (from 2.082 to 2.227 eV). All the calculations here refer to an indirect bandgap, which is the minimal one for all the investigated STO and BSO RP phases.

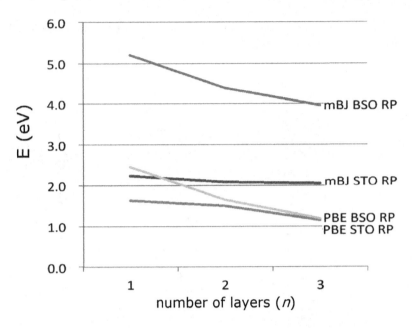

Fig. 4. Indirect (smallest) bandgap variation for the first three terms $n = 1 - 3$ of the $Sr_{n+1}Ti_nO_{3n+1}$ and $Ba_{n+1}Sn_nO_{3n+1}$ Ruddlesden-Popper phases.

The last dimensionality we want to discuss here is the 0D counterpart of both STO and BSO. Such systems are structurally characterized by the presence of isolated MO_6 octahedra (M = Ti, Sn). Now, considering the lack of literature about such systems (other 0D oxide perovskites have been investigated) [83,84] we moved from a well-assessed and investigated 0D halide perovskite (Cs_4PbBr_6) [64], replacing anion and cation positions with those of interest here, and finally fully optimized lattice parameters and ionic positions. Thus, in the 0D case both systems are theoretically engineered. As expected the value of the gap is in this case the largest one (2.809 and 2.471 eV at the PBE level, and 3.751 and 6.240 eV at the mBJ level for 0D STO and 0D BSO, respectively). The optimized structures for such systems along with bandstructures –the latter ones calculated at both level of theory– are reported in Fig. 5. Remarkably, mBJ once more shows a less marked tendency in opening the bandgap compared to the PBE level (2.809 → 3.751 eV) for the case of 0D STO, while the correction is massive (2.471 → 6.240 eV) for 0D BSO. It is worth stressing that Tong et al. [42] have predicted an enhanced efficiency as material for radiative cooling for all those that have an electronic bandgap larger than 4.13 eV, i.e. energy upper bound in solar spectrum, but smaller than that of $BaSO_4$ (another material of interest in radiative cooling oriented applications) which is 7.27 eV [42]. In this context, our 0D BSO would perfectly fit the electronic requirement, with the even more appealing feature to be a *direct* gap ($\Gamma \to \Gamma$) material which in principle should make the material able to more easily emit in the sky-window region. The other metrics the material should satisfy to be relevant for such applications is the phonon bandstructure with particular focus in the 8–13 μm region. Calculations in this sense are nowadays in progress.

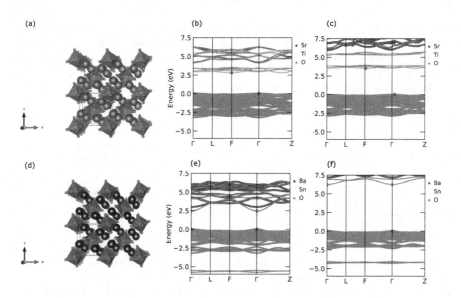

Fig. 5. 2×2 supercell of the optimized structure of (a) 0D SrTiO$_3$, (b) PBE calculated, and (c) mBJ calculated bandstructure. Same (d–f) for 0D BaSnO$_3$

4 Remarks

Aiming at investigating materials with applicability in radiative cooling devices, we here did an exploratory initial campaign of calculations from first-principles on the size reduction of two ABO$_3$-type perovskites comparing the features of the well-assessed and investigated SrTiO$_3$ and those of the tin-based BaSnO$_3$ compound. We paid attention on both bulk and on the first three terms ($n = 1 - 3$) of their related Ruddlesden-Popper phases, i.e. A$_{n+1}$B$_n$O$_{3n+1}$. Despite a very good agreement between our obtained structural parameters and previous experimental and theoretical reported ones for bulk, we note that treating the B-site cation (both Ti and Sn) with a reduced electron numbers in the valence induces a physiological contraction of their calculated bandgap, suggesting that for a very accurate prediction of the electronic and optical features the number of electrons in the valence for B-site ions must be larger than four. On the other hand we obtain a quite interesting trend: the confinement effects seem to be more noticeable in the case of BaSnO$_3$ while still interesting is the fact that the theoretically predicted zero-dimensional BaSnO$_3$ systems, i.e. Ba$_4$SnO$_6$ is the only direct (and large) bandgap material which is preferable because of a facile absorption/emission associated with possible heat reduction (purely radiative mechanism). The present is a preliminary investigation that mandatory needs further analysis, testing different pseudopotentials and calculating phonon features, and we are already working in such directions with the final aim of developing a new disruptive mitigation technique to face the urban heat island issue.

Acknowledgments. The authors thank the ERC Stg Project HELIOS (GA 101041255, PI dr. A.L. Pisello) funded by the European Union. Views and opinions expressed are however those of the author(s) only and do not necessarily reflect those of the European Union or the European Research Council. Neither the European Union nor the granting authority can be held responsible for them. G.G. and C.B. acknowledge ISCRA B, and C initiatives for awarding access to computing resources on m100 at CINECA SuperComputer Center, Italy. G.G. thanks the Dipartimento di Ingegneria Civile e Ambientale of the University of Perugia for allocated computing time within the project "Dipartimenti di Eccellenza 2018–2022". Authors are similarly grateful to Prof. L. Latterini (Dept of Chemistry, Biology and Biotechnology, Perugia University) for the very fruitful scientific discussions.

References

1. Mutschler, R., Rüdisüli, M., Heer, P., Eggimann, S.: Benchmarking cooling and heating energy demands considering climate change, population growth and cooling device uptake. Appl. Ener. **288**, 116636 (2021)
2. Calm, J.M.: Emissions and environmental impacts from air-conditioning and refrigeration systems. Int. J. Refrig. **25**(3), 293–305 (2002)
3. Fabiani, C., Pisello, A.L., Bou-Zeid, E., Yang, J., Cotana, F.: Adaptive measures for mitigating urban heat islands: the potential of thermochromic materials to control roofing energy balance. Appl. Ener. **247**, 155–170 (2019)
4. Paolini, R., et al.: The hygrothermal performance of residential buildings at urban and rural sites: Sensible and latent energy loads and indoor environmental conditions. Energ. Build. **152**, 792–803 (2017)
5. Kousis, I., Pigliautile, I., Pisello, A.L.: Intra-urban microclimate investigation in urban heat island through a novel mobile monitoring system. Sci. Rep. **11**(1), 1–17 (2021)
6. Kojima, A., Teshima, K., Shirai, Y., Miyasaka, T.: Organometal halide perovskites as visible-light sensitizers for photovoltaic cell. J. Am. Chem. Soc. **131**(17), 6050–6051 (2009)
7. Giorgi, G., Fujisawa, J.-I., Segawa, H., Yamashita, K.: Small photocarrier effective masses featuring ambipolar transport in methylammonium lead iodide perovskite: a density functional analysis. J. Phys. Chem. Lett. **4**(24), 4213–4216 (2013)
8. Giorgi, G., Fujisawa, J.-I., Segawa, H., Yamashita, K.: Cation role in structural and electronic properties of 3D organic-inorganic halide perovskites: a DFT analysis. J. Phys. Chem. C **118**(23), 12176–12183 (2014)
9. Kawai, H., Giorgi, G., Marini, A., Yamashita, K.: The mechanism of slow hot-hole cooling in lead-iodide perovskite: first-principles calculation on carrier lifetime from electron-phonon interaction. Nano Lett. **15**(5), 3103–3108 (2015)
10. Giorgi, G., Yamashita, K.: Organic-inorganic halide perovskites: an ambipolar class of materials with enhanced photovoltaic performances. J. Mater. Chem. A **3**(17), 8981–8991 (2015)

11. Giorgi, G., Fujisawa, J.-I., Segawa, H., Yamashita, K.: Organic-inorganic hybrid lead iodide perovskite featuring zero dipole moment guanidinium cations: a theoretical analysis. J. Phys. Chem. C **119**(9), 4694–4701 (2015)
12. Hata, T., Giorgi, G., Yamashita, K.: The effects of the organic-inorganic interactions on the thermal transport properties of $CH_3NH_3PbI_3$. Nano Lett. **16**(4), 2749–2753 (2016)
13. Giorgi, G., Yamashita, K.: Alternative, lead-free, hybrid organic-inorganic perovskites for solar applications: a DFT analysis. Chem. Lett. **44**(6), 826–828 (2015)
14. Giorgi, G., Yamashita, K.: Zero-dimensional hybrid organic-inorganic halide perovskite modeling: insights from first principles. J. Phys. Chem. Lett. **7**(5), 888–899 (2016)
15. Giorgi, G., Yamashita, K.: Zero-dipole molecular organic cations in mixed organic-inorganic halide perovskites: possible chemical solution for the reported anomalous hysteresis in the current-voltage curve measurements. Nanotechnology **26**(44), 442001 (2015)
16. Hata, T., Giorgi, G., Yamashita, K., Caddeo, C., Mattoni, A.: Development of a classical interatomic potential for MAPbBr₃. J. Phys. Chem. C **121**(7), 3724–3733 (2017)
17. Palummo, M., Varsano, D., Berríos, E., Yamashita, K., Giorgi, G.: Halide PB-free double-perovskites: ternary vs. quaternary stoichiometry. Energies **13**(14), 3516 (2020)
18. Giorgi, G., Yoshihara, T., Yamashita, K.: Structural and electronic features of small hybrid organic-inorganic halide perovskite clusters: a theoretical analysis. Phys. Chem. Chem. Phys. **18**(39), 27124–27132 (2016)
19. Manzhos, S., Giorgi, G., Lüder, J., Ihara, M.: Modeling of plasmonic properties of nanostructures for next generation solar cells and beyond. Adv. Phys. X **6**(1), 1908848 (2021)
20. Giorgi, G.: Structural and electronic features of $Si/CH_3NH_3PbI_3$ interfaces with optoelectronic applicability: Insights from first-principles. Nano Energy **67**, 104166 (2020)
21. Giorgi, G., Yamashita, K., Segawa, H.: First-principles investigation of the Lewis acid-base adduct formation at the methylammonium lead iodide surfaces. Phys. Chem. Chem. Phys. **20**(16), 11183–11195 (2018)
22. Manzhos, S., et al.: Materials design and optimization for next-generation solar cell and light-emitting technologies. J. Phys. Chem. Lett. **12**(19), 4638–4657 (2021)
23. Catalanotti, S., Cuomo, V., Piro, G., Ruggi, D., Silvestrini, V., Troise, G.: The radiative cooling of selective surfaces. Sol. Energy **17**(2), 83–89 (1975)
24. Granqvist, C.G., Hjortsberg, A.: Radiative cooling to low temperatures: general considerations and application to selectively emitting SiO films. J. Appl. Phys. **52**(6), 4205–4220 (1981)
25. Raman, A.P., Anoma, M.A., Zhu, L., Rephaeli, E., Fan, S.: Passive radiative cooling below ambient air temperature under direct sunlight. Nature **515**(7528), 540–544 (2014)
26. Rephaeli, E., Raman, A., Fan, S.: Ultrabroadband photonic structures to achieve high-performance daytime radiative cooling. Nano Lett. **13**(4), 1457–1461 (2013)
27. Hossain, Md.M., Gu, M.: Radiative cooling: principles, progress, and potentials. Adv. Sci. **3**(7), 1500360 (2016)
28. Kou, J.-L., Jurado, Z., Chen, Z., Fan, S., Minnich, A.J.: Daytime radiative cooling using near-black infrared emitters. ACS Photon. **4**(3), 626–630 (2017)
29. Zhao, B., Hu, M., Ao, X., Chen, N., Pei, G.: Radiative cooling: a review of fundamentals, materials, applications, and prospects. Appl. Energy **236**, 489–513 (2019)

30. Li, Z., Chen, Q., Song, Y., Zhu, B., Zhu, J.: Fundamentals, materials, and applications for daytime radiative cooling. Adv. Mater. Technol. **5**(5), 1901007 (2020)
31. Li, W., Dong, M., Fan, L., John, J.J., Chen, Z., Fan, S.: Nighttime radiative cooling for water harvesting from solar panels. ACS Photon. **8**(1), 269–275 (2020)
32. Huang, Z., Ruan, X.: Nanoparticle embedded double-layer coating for daytime radiative cooling. Int. J. Heat Mass Transfer **104**, 890–896 (2017)
33. Zhai, Y., et al.: Scalable-manufactured randomized glass-polymer hybrid metamaterial for daytime radiative cooling. Science **355**(6329), 1062–1066 (2017)
34. Jeon, S., et al.: Multifunctional daytime radiative cooling devices with simultaneous light-emitting and radiative cooling functional layers. ACS Appl. Mater. Interfaces **12**(49), 54763–54772 (2020)
35. Son, S., et al.: Colored emitters with silica-embedded perovskite nanocrystals for efficient daytime radiative cooling. Nano Energy **79**, 105461 (2021)
36. Kecebas, M.A., Menguc, M.P., Kosar, A., Sendur, K.: Passive radiative cooling design with broadband optical thin-film filters. J. Quant. Spectrosc. Radiat. Transf. **198**, 179–186 (2017)
37. Garshasbi, S., Santamouris, M.: Using advanced thermochromic technologies in the built environment: recent development and potential to decrease the energy consumption and fight urban overheating. Sol. Energy Mater. Sol. Cells **191**, 21–32 (2019)
38. Taflove, A., Hagness, S.C., Piket-May, M.: Computational electromagnetics: the finite-difference time-domain method. Electr. Eng. Handb. **3**, 629–670 (2005)
39. Taflove, A., Brodwin, M.E.: Numerical solution of steady-state electromagnetic scattering problems using the time-dependent Maxwell's equations. IEEE Trans. Microw. Theory Tech. **23**(8), 623–630 (1975)
40. Yee, K.: Numerical solution of initial boundary value problems involving Maxwell's equations in isotropic media. IEEE Trans. Antennas Propag. **14**(3), 302–307 (1966)
41. Vinattieri, A., Giorgi, G.: Halide perovskites for photonics: recent history and perspectives. In: Halide Perovskites for Photonics, vol. 1, pp. 1–28. AIP Publishing LLC, Melville (2021)
42. Tong, Z., Peoples, J., Li, X., Yang, X., Bao, H., Ruan, X.: Atomistic characteristics of ultra-efficient radiative cooling paint pigments: the case study of $BaSO_4$. Mater. Today Phys. **24**, 100658 (2022)
43. Tsai, M.-H., Yeh, J.-W.: High-entropy alloys: a critical review. Mater. Res. Lett. **2**(3), 107–123 (2014)
44. George, E.P., Raabe, D., Ritchie, R.O.: High-entropy alloys. Nat. Rev. Mater. **4**(8), 515–534 (2019)
45. Ye, Y.F., Wang, Q., Lu, J., Liu, C.T., Yang, Y.: High-entropy alloy: challenges and prospects. Mater. Today **19**(6), 349–362 (2016)
46. Rost, C.M., et al.: Entropy-stabilized oxides. Nat. Commun. **6**(1), 1–8 (2015)
47. Albedwawi, S.H., AlJaberi, A., Haidemenopoulos, G.N., Polychronopoulou, K.: High entropy oxides-exploring a paradigm of promising catalysts: a review. Mater. Des. **202**, 109534 (2021)
48. Edalati, P., Wang, Q., Razavi-Khosroshahi, H., Fuji, M., Ishihara, T., Edalati, K.: Photocatalytic hydrogen evolution on a high-entropy oxide. J. Mater. Chem. A **8**(4), 3814–3821 (2020)
49. Zhao, C., Ding, F., Lu, Y., Chen, L., Hu, Y.-S.: High-entropy layered oxide cathodes for sodium-ion batteries. Angew. Chem. Int. Ed. **59**(1), 264–269 (2020)
50. Witte, R., et al.: High-entropy oxides: an emerging prospect for magnetic rare-earth transition metal perovskites. Phys. Rev. Mater. **3**(3), 034406 (2019)

51. Sarkar, A., et al.: High entropy oxides for reversible energy storage. Nat. Commun. **9**(1), 1–9 (2018)
52. Kresse, G., Hafner, J.: Ab initio molecular dynamics for open-shell transition metals. Phys. Rev. B **48**(17), 13115–13118 (1993)
53. Kresse, G., Hafner, J.: Ab initio molecular-dynamics simulation of the liquid-metal-amorphous-semiconductor transition in germanium. Phys. Rev. B **49**(20), 14251–1426 (1994)
54. Kresse, G., Furthmüller, J.: Efficiency of ab-initio total energy calculations for metals and semiconductors using a plane-wave basis set. Comput. Mater. Sci. **6**(1), 15–50 (1996)
55. Kresse, G., Furthmüller, J.: Efficient iterative schemes for ab initio total-energy calculations using a plane-wave basis set. Phys. Rev. B **54**(16), 11169–11186 (1996)
56. Perdew, J.P., Burke, K., Ernzerhof, M.: Generalized gradient approximation made simple. Phys. Rev. Lett. **77**(18), 3865–3868 (1996)
57. Blöchl, P.E.: Projector augmented-wave method. Phys. Rev. B **50**, 17953 (1994)
58. Kresse, G., Joubert, D.: From ultrasoft pseudopotentials to the projector augmented-wave method. Phys. Rev. B **59**, 1758 (1999)
59. Becke, A.D., Johnson, E.R.: A simple effective potential for exchange. J. Chem. Phys. **124**(22), 221101 (2006)
60. Tran, F., Blaha, P.: Accurate band gaps of semiconductors and insulators with a semilocal exchange-correlation potential. Phys. Rev. Lett. **102**(22), 226401 (2009)
61. Goldschmidt, V.M.: Die gesetze der krystallochemie. Naturwissenschaften **14**(21), 477–485 (1926)
62. Shannon, R.D.: Revised effective ionic radii and systematic studies of interatomic distances in halides and chalcogenides. Acta Crystallogr. A **32**(5), 751–767 (1976)
63. Hachemi, A., Hachemi, H., Ferhat-Hamida, A., Louail, L.: Elasticity of $SrTiO_3$ perovskite under high pressure in cubic, tetragonal and orthorhombic phases. Phys. Scr. **82**(2), 025602 (2010)
64. Jain, A., et al.: Commentary: the materials project: a materials genome approach to accelerating materials innovation. APL Mater. **1**(1), 011002 (2013)
65. Moreira, E., et al.: Structural and optoelectronic properties, and infrared spectrum of cubic $BaSnO_3$ from first principles calculations. J. Appl. Phys. **112**(4), 043703 (2012)
66. Piskunov, S., Heifets, E., Eglitis, R.I., Borstel, G.: Bulk properties and electronic structure of $SrTiO_3$, $BaTiO_3$, $PbTiO_3$ perovskites: an ab initio HF/DFT study. Comput. Mater. Sci. **29**(2), 165–178 (2004)
67. Bévillon, É., Chesnaud, A., Wang, Y., Dezanneau, G., Geneste, G.: Theoretical and experimental study of the structural, dynamical and dielectric properties of perovskite $BaSnO_3$. J. Phys.: Condens. Matter **20**(14), 145217 (2008)
68. Abramov, Y.A., Tsirelson, V.G., Zavodnik, V.E., Ivanov, S.A., Brown, I.D.: The chemical bond and atomic displacements in $SrTiO_3$ from X-ray diffraction analysis. Acta Crystallogr. B **51**(6), 942–951 (1995)
69. Farfán, J.C., Rodriguez, J.A., Fajardo, F., Lopez, E.V., Tellez, D.A.L., Roa-Rojas, J.: Structural properties, electric response and electronic feature of $BaSnO_3$ perovskite. Physica B **404**(18), 2720–2722 (2009)
70. Mountstevens, E.H., Attfield, J.P., Redfern, S.A.T.: Cation-size control of structural phase transitions in tin perovskites. J. Phys.: Condens. Matter **15**(49), 8315 (2003)
71. Van Benthem, K., Elsässer, C., French, R.H.: Bulk electronic structure of $SrTiO_3$: experiment and theory. J. Appl. Phys. **90**(12), 6156–6164 (2001)

72. Shan, C., et al.: Optical and electrical properties of sol-gel derived $Ba_{1-x}La_xSnO_3$ transparent conducting films for potential optoelectronic applications. J. Phys. Chem. C **118**(13), 6994–7001 (2014)

73. Lebens-Higgins, Z., et al.: Direct observation of electrostatically driven band gap renormalization in a degenerate perovskite transparent conducting oxide. Phys. Rev. Lett. **116**(2), 027602 (2016)

74. Smith, I.C., Hoke, E.T., Solis-Ibarra, D., McGehee, M.D., Karunadasa, H.I.: A layered hybrid perovskite solar-cell absorber with enhanced moisture stability. Angew. Chem. Int. Ed. **53**(42), 11232–11235 (2014)

75. Tsai, H., et al.: High-efficiency two-dimensional Ruddlesden-Popper perovskite solar cells. Nature **536**(7616), 312–316 (2016)

76. Palummo, M., Postorino, S., Borghesi, C., Giorgi, G.: Strong out-of-plane excitons in 2D hybrid halide double perovskites. Appl. Phys. Lett. **119**(5), 051103 (2021)

77. Giorgi, G., Yamashita, K., Palummo, M.: Nature of the electronic and optical excitations of Ruddlesden-Popper hybrid organic-inorganic perovskites: the role of the many-body interactions. J. Phys. Chem. Lett. **9**(19), 5891–5896 (2018)

78. Folpini, G., et al.: Band splitting and plurality of excitons in Ruddlesden-Popper metal halides. ChemRxiv 10.26434/chemrxiv-2021-qcm36-v2 (2021)

79. Ruddlesden, S.N., Popper, P.: The compound $Sr_3Ti_2O_7$ and its structure. Acta Crystallogr. **11**(1), 54–55 (1958)

80. Reshak, A.H., Auluck, S., Kityk, I.: Electronic band structure and optical properties of $Sr_{n+1}Ti_nO_{3n+1}$ Ruddlesden-Popper homologous series. Jpn. J. Appl. Phys. **47**(7R), 5516 (2008)

81. Lee, C.-H., et al.: Effect of reduced dimensionality on the optical band. gap of $SrTiO_3$. Appl. Phys. Lett. **102**(12), 122901 (2013)

82. Li, Y., Zhang, L., Ma, Y., Singh, D.J.: Tuning optical properties of transparent conducting barium stannate by dimensional reduction. APL Mater. **3**(1), 011102 (2015)

83. Sanchez, F., Ocal, C., Fontcuberta, J.: Tailored surfaces of perovskite oxide substrates for conducted growth of thin films. Chem. Soc. Rev. **43**(7), 2272–2285 (2014)

84. Fan, D., et al.: Synergy of photocatalysis and photothermal effect in integrated 0D perovskite oxide/2D MXene heterostructures for simultaneous water purification and solar steam generation. Appl. Catal. B **295**, 120285 (2021)

Coding Cross Sections of an Electron Charge Transfer Process

Emília Valença Ferreira de Aragão[1,2(✉)] ⬩, Luca Mancini[2] ⬩, Xiao He[3],
Noelia Faginas-Lago[2] ⬩, Marzio Rosi[4] ⬩, Daniela Ascenzi[3] ⬩,
and Fernando Pirani[2,4] ⬩

[1] Master-tec srl, Via Sicilia 41, 06128 Perugia, Italy
emilia.dearagao@master-tec.it
[2] Dipartimento di Chimica, Biologia e Biotecnologie,
Università degli Studi di Perugia, 06123 Perugia, Italy
{emilia.dearagao,luca.mancini2}@studenti.unipg.it,
{noelia.faginaslago,fernando.pirani}@unipg.it
[3] Dipartimento di Fisica, Università di Trento, Trento, Italy
daniela.ascenzi@unitn.it
[4] Dipartimento di Ingegneria Civile ed Ambientale, Università degli Studi di Perugia,
06125 Perugia, Italy
marzio.rosi@unipg.it

Abstract. The paper presents the algorithm of a code written for computing the cross section for a charge transfer process involving a neutral molecule and a monatomic ion. The entrance and exit potential energy surfaces, driving the collision dynamics, are computed employing the Improved Lennard-Jones function that accounts for the role of non-electrostatic forces, due to size repulsion plus dispersion and induction attraction. In addition, electrostatic components, affecting the entrance channels, are evaluated as sum of Coulomb contributions, determined by the He^+ ion interacting with the charge distribution on the molecular frame. The cross section is estimated by employing the Landau-Zener-Stückelberg approach. The code implemented has been employed in systems involving helium cation and a small organic molecule, such as methanol, dimethyl ether and methyl formate.

Keywords: Astrochemistry · Semiempirical potential · Improved Lennard-Jones · Landau-Zener-Stückelberg · Charge exchange process

1 Introduction

In the last 70 years, more than 260 molecules have been detected in the interstellar medium [1–4]. Among them, C-bearing molecules with 6 or more atoms have been given the name of interstellar Complex Organic Molecules, or simply iCOMs [5,6]. The presence of a significant number of molecules, with increasing chemical complexity (including species that can be considered precursors

© The Author(s), under exclusive license to Springer Nature Switzerland AG 2022
O. Gervasi et al. (Eds.): ICCSA 2022 Workshops, LNCS 13382, pp. 319–333, 2022.
https://doi.org/10.1007/978-3-031-10592-0_24

of more complex and prebiotic molecules, such as formamide [7]) in different regions of the interstellar medium (ISM) is a challenge for our comprehension of interstellar chemistry, considering also the harsh conditions of some astronomical environments, which are considered prohibitive for molecular growth (where the temperature can go down to 10K and the particle density can be as low as 10^4 particles cm^{-3} [8]). Several models have been implemented with the purpose of setting a complete picture for the understanding of the chemical processes leading to the synthesis of iCOMs [9–14]. Currently, two different mechanisms can be invoked in order to explain the molecular complexity of the ISM: grain surface processes and/or gas-phase reactions. The first suggested mechanisms is related to the formation of iCOMs on the surface of the grains, through hydrogenation processes, leading to the formation of simple radicals. The subsequent warming up of the surrounding environment during the first phases of the star formation, allows the radicals to acquire mobility and diffuse on the grain surface to form several iCOMs. Grain surface chemistry cannot be invoked to reproduce the observed molecular abundances by itself. For this reason, a combined approach including gas-phase reactions is implemented in the astrochemical models. Following this approach, the formation of simple hydrogenated and oxidized species (e.g. H_2O, NH_3, CH_3OH) on the surface of the grains during the first stages of star formation is followed by the ejection of the synthesized molecules in the gas phase during the hot-corino [8] stage. At this point, subsequent gas-phase reactions are the main route of formation of iCOMs. Processes might involve ions, radicals and/or closed-shell species provided that those processes are exothermic and barrierless. Recent works [15–17] attest that the role of gas-phase chemistry appears indeed to be pivotal.

A synergistic and multidisciplinary approach is fundamental to unravel the chemistry of the ISM. Such an approach includes astronomical observations, chemical analysis (both with experiments and theoretical quantum chemistry calculations) and astrochemical/astrophysical models, allowing a comparison between theoretical predictions and astronomical observations. A peculiar example can be represented by two databases which are mostly used in astrochemical models, namely KIDA [18] and UMIST [19], in which the abundances of detected species are accounted for by considering their formation and destruction routes. Unfortunately, among all the processes included in the models, some processes might be missing while many processes are included with estimated, even just guessed, parameters considered on the basis of common sense or chemical analogies. In order to explain the abundance of a molecule, it is extremely important to properly consider, together with the formation routes, also the possible destruction reactions of iCOMs. Among the possible reaction pathways, destruction of iCOMs can happen after a collision with atomic or molecular species. A peculiar example is represented by the collision with high energetic ions. When the collision happens with an ion, for instance He^+ or H_3^+ and HCO^+, the three most abundant ions in the ISM (generated by the interaction of H, He and H_2 with cosmic rays) charge or proton exchange processes might occur, followed by the dissociation of the iCOM. The destruction of interstellar Complex Organic

Molecules appears to be indeed dominated by the reactions with He^+, H_3^+ and HCO^+. In particular, due to its high value of ionisation energy [20], helium represents a pivotal species to drive the chemistry of the ISM [21,22]. The dynamics of the charge transfer process depends on the probability of the transition between different intermolecular Potential Energy Surfaces (PESs). It is important to assess whether the collision happens with a preferential orientation, therefore a model of the cross section is proposed and their evolution is compared with experimental measurements of the cross section in order to fully understand the reaction dynamic.

In this work, we describe how the PESs have been implemented in the code written by our group, in order to calculate the cross sections for the global electron transfer process, to be compared with results measured as a function of the collision energy with the molecular beam technique, and, subsequently, to evaluate related reaction rate constants as a function of the temperature.

2   Program Implementation

The code has been developed to perform a theoretical analysis of the cross section for the charge exchange process, allowing to estimate the values of the rate constant at different temperatures. All parts of the code were written in C language, and have a common structure:

1. Inclusion of useful libraries as stdio.h, math.h, stdlib.h and string.h;
2. Definition of assorted functions;
3. Main program section, defined inside "*int main*{...}".

In the next sections, a detailed description of the contents of each piece of code is given.

2.1   Calculating Cuts of the Entrance and Exit Potential Energy Surface with *pes.c*

The program has been written in order to characterize the entrance and the exit potentials (*i.e.* before and after the charge transfer, respectively) of a reaction involving a neutral molecule (e.g. dimethyl ether, methyl formate, methanol) and a monoatomic ion (e.g. He^+). The exploration of the entrance potential energy surface serves to visualize how the reactants are approaching each other: the lower the energy at the bottom of the well, the more attractive the relative spatial orientation. Later, cuts of the entrance and exit PES are plotted to verify whether an exothermic crossing is possible. From here on, an individual relative spatial orientation between the reactants will be referred to as a "configuration".

The code requires to define the position of the reactants in space. First, the geometry of the molecule should be pre-optimized via calculations employing *ab initio* methods, so intramolecular distances and bond angles are represented correctly. Depending on the total number of atoms, it might be necessary to replace functional groups with effective atoms, for instance C_{eff} instead of CH_3.

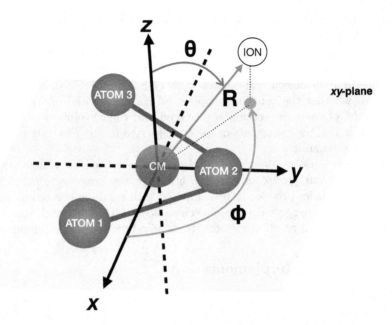

Fig. 1. Scheme representing a system in a three-dimensional space. Atoms in blue represent effective atoms in a neutral molecule. The origin of the Cartesian reference system is taken to coincide with the center of mass (CM) of the molecule. The placement of the ion is made by choosing the values of its spherical coordinates, from which the Cartesian coordinates can be obtained. Here, R is the distance between the molecule's CM and the ion, θ is the angle made by the R vector with the z-axis and ϕ is the azimuthal angle. (Color figure online)

In this case, the partial charge of the effective atom should be the sum of the partial charges of the atoms involved. For the whole molecule, the position of the center of mass (CM) is defined via the equations:

$$x_{CM} = \frac{\sum_{i=1}^{N} x_i m_i}{M}; \ y_{CM} = \frac{\sum_{i=1}^{N} y_i m_i}{M}; \ z_{CM} = \frac{\sum_{i=1}^{N} z_i m_i}{M} \qquad (1)$$

where x_i, y_i and z_i are the coordinates of each effective atom, m_i its mass, N the total number of effective atoms and M the total mass of the molecule. For an easier manipulation of the system, CM is placed at the origin of the Cartesian reference system. The new coordinates of the effective atoms are obtained by extracting the CM coordinates from the original atomic coordinates:

$$x_i' = x_i - x_{CM}; \ y_i' = y_i - y_{CM}; \ z_i' = z_i - z_{CM} \qquad (2)$$

Once the molecular frame is fixed in the 3D space, as shown in Fig. 1, a code named *"pes.c"* can be used to set the ion position in space using spherical coordinates (see Fig. 2). The Cartesian coordinates of the ion (denoted by j) can

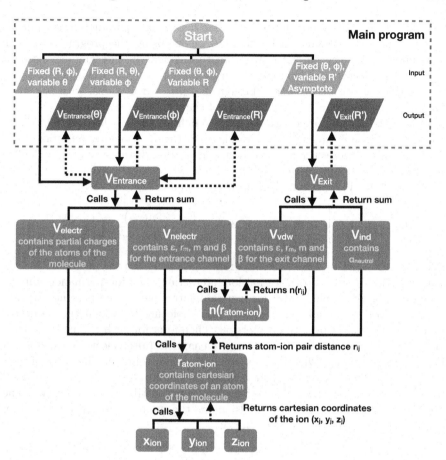

Fig. 2. An overall view of the algorithm in *pes.c* code. In green, the input information, in grey the output. Blue blocks refer to functions that have been defined outside the main section of the program. (Color figure online)

then be derived via the coordinate transformation formulae:

$$x_j = Rsin(\theta)cos(\phi) \tag{3}$$

$$y_j = Rsin(\theta)sin(\phi) \tag{4}$$

$$z_j = Rcos(\theta) \tag{5}$$

where R is the distance between the ion and CM, θ the angle in relation with the z-axis and ϕ is the azimuth angle. R values can range from 0 to infinite, θ values range from $0°$ to $180°$ and ϕ ranges from $0°$ to $360°$. Knowing the Cartesian coordinates of the ion, the distance between each atom of the molecule and the ion can be calculated considering the following relation:

$$r_{ij} = \sqrt{(x_i - x_j)^2 + (y_i - y_j)^2 + (z_i - z_j)^2} \tag{6}$$

Other than spatial position of the reactants, some parameters specific to each system are necessary to be adapted before using the program. One set of parameters are the partial charges on the neutral species that are used to estimate the electrostatic contribution for the entrance PES, $V_{electrostatic}(R)$. Atomic charges can be obtained through *ab initio* calculations, with the same level of theory used for the optimization of the molecular structure.

Other sets of parameters are adopted to define the non-electrostatic contribution V_{ij}, arising from each ij interacting pair (again, i denotes an atom of the molecule and j denotes the ion) taken at a separation distance r_{ij}. In particular, the value of the potential well ε_{ij} and of related equilibrium distance $r_{m_{ij}}$ are used to evaluate V_{ij} through the Improved Lennard-Jones model [23]:

$$V_{ij}(r_{ij}) = \varepsilon_{ij} \left[\frac{m}{n(r_{ij}) - m} \left(\frac{r_{m_{ij}}}{r_{ij}} \right)^{n(r_{ij})} - \frac{n(r_{ij})}{n(r_{ij}) - m} \left(\frac{r_{m_{ij}}}{r_{ij}} \right)^{m} \right] \quad (7)$$

As explained in [24] and [23], the m parameter depends on the nature of the system: it assumes the value of 1 for ion-ion interaction, 2 for ion-permanent dipole, 4 for ion-induced dipole, and 6 for neutral-neutral pairs. The present entrance channels involve a small ion and a neutral molecule for which the induction attraction dominates over the dispersion. Therefore, for such channels we have considered $m = 4$. Moreover, in the exit channels (after electron transfer), a molecular ion interacts with He, a low polarizabilty atom, and the value of $m = 6$ has been selected since the dispersion plays an important role and the small induction term is inserted as additive attractive contribution (see below). The modulation in the decline of the repulsion and the enhancement of the attraction in Eq. 7, $n(r_{ij})$ takes the following form:

$$n(r_{ij}) = \beta + 4 \left(\frac{r_{ij}}{r_{m_{ij}}} \right)^2 \quad (8)$$

where β is a parameter related to the nature and the hardness of the interacting particles [24–27] and the $\frac{r_{ij}}{r_{m_{ij}}}$ ratio is introduced as a reduced distance. The Improved Lennard-Jones function is then used for both entrance and exit potentials, and in each case β and m assume values according to the nature of the system. The total non-electrostatic contribution, which is the sum of all V_{ij} of a given configuration, is denoted $V_{nelectr}$ in the entrance channel and V_{vdw} in the exit channel (see Fig. 2).

In the entrance channel, the electrostatic component $V_{electr}(R)$, due to the interaction between the monocation He^+ and the anisotropic charge distribution on the molecular frame, is defined by the Coulomb's law:

$$V_{\text{electr}}(R) = \frac{1}{4\pi\varepsilon_0} \sum_{i}^{N} \frac{q_i}{r_{ij}} \quad (9)$$

where R is again the distance between the ion and CM, r_{ij} is again the distance between an atom of the molecule and the ion, obtained deconvolving R into partial components, ε_0 is the vacuum permittivity, and q_i corresponds to the partial charge on each atom of the molecule.

As indicated above, in the exit channels an induction term is inserted to represent the ion-induced dipole contribution as a pertubative approach. The induction term describes the interaction between the newly formed cation and the neutralized species. The induction term $V_{ind}(R')$ is expressed, considering the polarizability $\alpha_{neutral}$ of the neutral species, adopting the following formalism:

$$V_{ind}(R') = -7200 \frac{\alpha_{neutral}}{R'^4} \tag{10}$$

By analogy to R, R' is the distance between the neutralized species and the center-of-mass of the newly formed cation. At last, when comparing the ionization energy of the molecular orbitals of the molecule and of the ion, it is possible to estimate from which orbital(s) of the molecule the electron might be removed. The difference between the two energies must be taken into account when defining the exit PES in order to see if the cuts of the entrance and exit PESs are crossing each other at some point. This difference in energy is called the asymptote. Figure 2 shows the algorithm of the *pes.c* code. In green are represented the input information, such as the spherical coordinates of the ion. In blue are reported the functions code in the program, such as the equations previously reported. The outputs, represented in grey, contain the values of the potential for different configurations used to obtain the PESs. With this program, it is possible to have different cuts of the entrance and exit PESs, and so it is possible to visualise which part of the neutral molecule can be easily approached by the ionic species.

2.2 Finding the Point of Crossing with *pesZeri.c*

The piece of code called "*pesZeri.c*" is basically the same as "*pes.c*", with the difference that it is used to find the point of crossing between the entrance and exit PES cuts, for a specific configuration (θ and ϕ pair). As it can be seen in Fig. 3, the code enters a loop (space within the dotted blue frame) in order to find the value of R at which the crossing happens (R_0). Later, the value of the entrance (or exit) potential at the crossing point, denoted E_{R_0}, is also calculated. Finally, the difference between the slopes of the two PESs cuts is estimated through the formula:

$$\Delta_{R_0} = \left| \frac{dV_{Exit}(R_0)}{dR} - \frac{dV_{Entrance}(R_0)}{dR} \right| \tag{11}$$

When the calculation ends, the three quantities represented in grey in Fig. 3 are sent to a code called "*CS.c*", that will be presented in the next section, and the values will be used to estimate the cross section at different collisional energies.

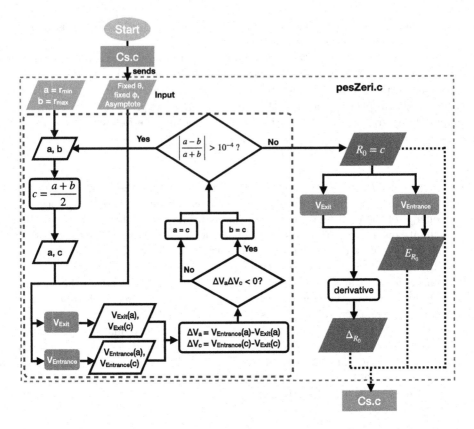

Fig. 3. Inside the *pesZeri.c* code. The region within the blue dotted frame represents a loop that works until the point of crossing between the entrance and exit PES is found.

2.3   Estimating the Transition Probability for a Configuration Using *CS.c*

The transition probability at the crossing point between the two PES cuts is treated adopting a a strategy successfully used for previous investigations [28–30]. In details, the Landau-Zener-Stückelberg approach [31–35] is used for the implementation of a one-dimensional model, that is considering specific cuts of the multidimensional PES, where R is the reaction coordinate, keeping the values of θ and ϕ fixed.

Figure 4 shows the algorithm of the program. At the start, the code reads the input file, which should contain the configuration (θ, ϕ), the value of the asymptote, the value of C (parameter used in Coriolis coupling that will be shown later), the molecular masses of the reactants and the minimum and maximum collisional energies at which the cross section is estimated. (θ, ϕ) and the asymptote values are sent to the *pesZeri.c* code, as described before, and in return the program gets the position of the crossing point, the value of the potential at

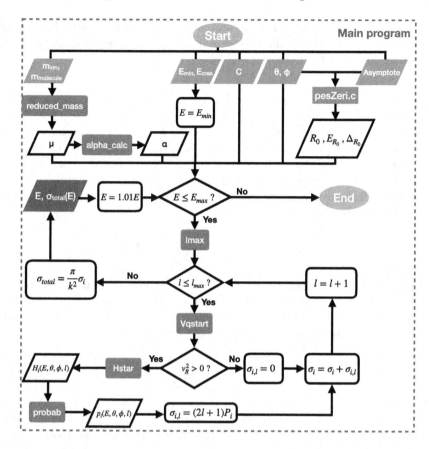

Fig. 4. Inside the $CS.c$ code.

this point and the difference between slopes (Δ_{R_0} from Eq. 11). Meanwhile, the program calls a function to compute the reduced mass μ, in kg, which is then used to calculate α. Here α is a parameter that includes conversion factors:

$$\alpha = 10^{-10} \cdot \sqrt{1.62176 \cdot 10^{-22}} \cdot \sqrt{100} \cdot \frac{\sqrt{2\mu}}{\hbar} \qquad (12)$$

where the first term is the factor of conversion from m^{-1} to $\AA^{-1}$, the second term converts $meV^{\frac{1}{2}}$ to $J^{\frac{1}{2}}$, the third term converts $\frac{meV^{\frac{1}{2}}}{100}$ to meV and $\hbar$ is the reduced Planck's constant.

The subsequent steps of the program consists in a series of loops. In the outer loop, the collisional energy E is set to E_{min}, defined by the user in units of $\frac{meV}{100}$. E will be multiplied by a factor of 1.01 at the end of every iteration, until it reaches the value of E_{max}, also defined by the user of the code. With the collisional energy E and the α parameter, the wavenumber k, not show on Fig. 4, is calculated as follows:

$$k = \alpha\sqrt{E} \qquad (13)$$

The wavenumber k is then used to compute the maximum value of the angular momentum l_{max}, for which the system is able to reach the crossing point by overcoming the centrifugal barrier is given by:

$$l_{max} = kR_0\sqrt{1 - \frac{E_{R_0}}{E}} \tag{14}$$

With this the program enters a second, inner loop where the value of l, the angular momentum quantum number of the collision complex, starts at zero and is increased by one unit until it becomes equal to l_{max}. Whenever l increases, *i.e.* in every cycle of the routine, the code estimates 3 quantities: the radial velocity v_R, the non-adiabatic coupling H_i and the probability of crossing p_i. The radial velocity v_R is defined as:

$$v_R^2(l, E) = \frac{2}{\mu}\left[E\left(1 - \frac{l(l+1)}{k^2 R_0^2}\right) - E_{R_0}\right] \tag{15}$$

All the quantities appearing in the equation have been defined before. In the systems the code was written for, the non-adiabatic coupling was treated as a Coriolis coupling, due to the fact that the electron is exchanged between orbitals of different symmetry. The Coriolis coupling expression is

$$H_i(E, \theta, \phi, l) = \frac{\hbar l}{\mu R_0^2}M \tag{16}$$

The M term has been extended to account for the dependence of the coupling on the strong stereochemistry. In systems involving helium cation and dimethyl ether or methyl formate [30, 36], the expression of M takes the form, with a dimensionless parameter C:

$$M = C\left|\frac{E}{E_{R_0}}\right|^{\frac{1}{4}} \tag{17}$$

The probability for the passage through a crossing between entrance and exit PESs is given by:

$$p_i(E, \theta, \phi, l) = exp\left(\frac{-2\pi H_i^2}{\hbar v_R \Delta_{R_0}}\right) \tag{18}$$

Finally, a conditional statement is reached: when the square radial velocity v_R^2 is smaller than or equal to zero, the total cross section $\sigma(E, \theta, \phi)$ is also zero. Otherwise, the cross section is calculated as follows:

$$\sigma_{total}(E, \theta, \phi) = \frac{\pi}{k^2}\sum_{l=0}^{l_{max}}(2l+1)P_i \tag{19}$$

where P_i, the probability of formation of the molecular ion, is expressed taking into account the previously described $p_i(E, \theta, \phi, l)$ and l_{max} is the maximum value of l for which the system is able to reach the crossing point, through the

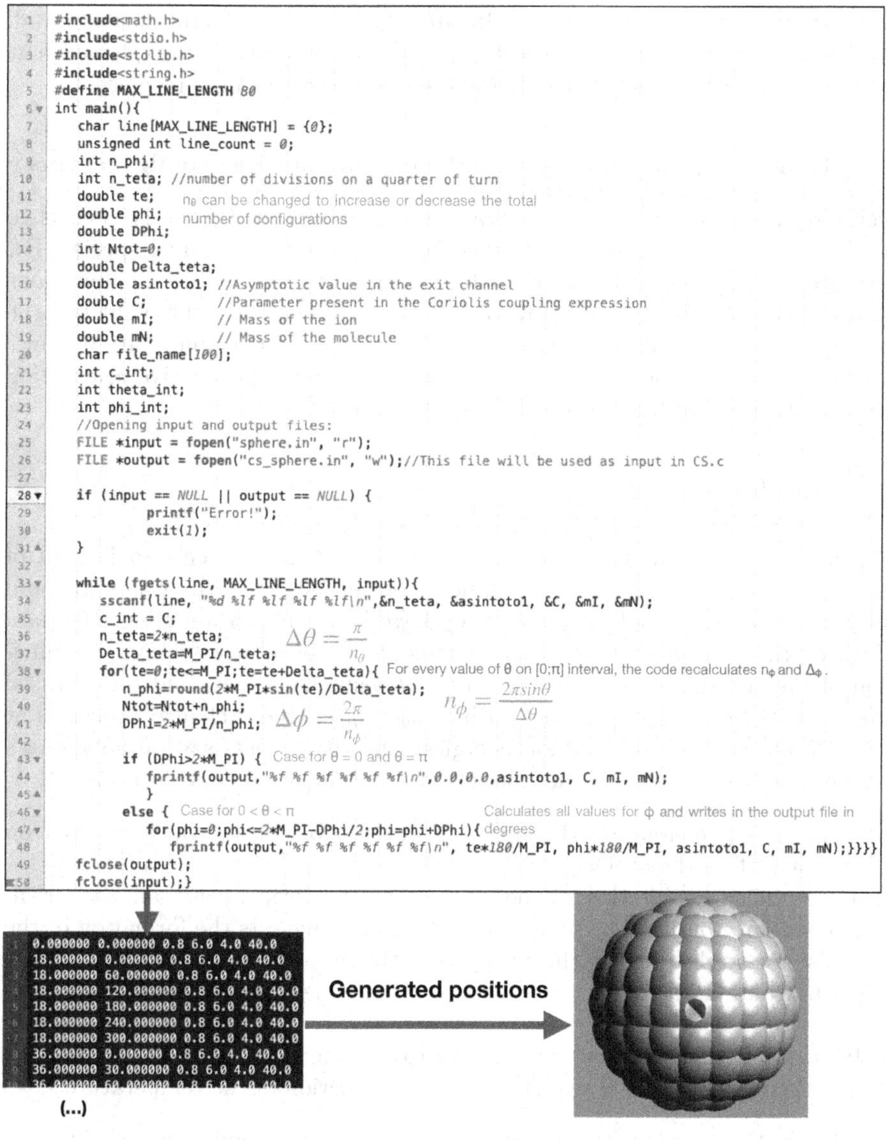

```
 1    #include<math.h>
 2    #include<stdio.h>
 3    #include<stdlib.h>
 4    #include<string.h>
 5    #define MAX_LINE_LENGTH 80
 6 ▼  int main(){
 7        char line[MAX_LINE_LENGTH] = {0};
 8        unsigned int line_count = 0;
 9        int n_phi;
10        int n_teta; //number of divisions on a quarter of turn
11        double te;      nθ can be changed to increase or decrease the total
12        double phi;     number of configurations
13        double DPhi;
14        int Ntot=0;
15        double Delta_teta;
16        double asintoto1; //Asymptotic value in the exit channel
17        double C;         //Parameter present in the Coriolis coupling expression
18        double mI;        // Mass of the ion
19        double mN;        // Mass of the molecule
20        char file_name[100];
21        int c_int;
22        int theta_int;
23        int phi_int;
24        //Opening input and output files:
25        FILE *input = fopen("sphere.in", "r");
26        FILE *output = fopen("cs_sphere.in", "w");//This file will be used as input in CS.c
27
28 ▼      if (input == NULL || output == NULL) {
29                printf("Error!");
30                exit(1);
31 ▲      }
32
33 ▼      while (fgets(line, MAX_LINE_LENGTH, input)){
34            sscanf(line, "%d %lf %lf %lf %lf\n",&n_teta, &asintoto1, &C, &mI, &mN);
35            c_int = C;
36            n_teta=2*n_teta;
37            Delta_teta=M_PI/n_teta;
38 ▼          for(te=0;te<=M_PI;te=te+Delta_teta){ For every value of θ on [0;π] interval, the code recalculates nφ and Δφ.
39                n_phi=round(2*M_PI*sin(te)/Delta_teta);
40                Ntot=Ntot+n_phi;
41                DPhi=2*M_PI/n_phi;
42
43 ▼              if (DPhi>2*M_PI) { Case for θ = 0 and θ = π
44                    fprintf(output,"%f %f %f %f %f %f\n",0.0,0.0,asintoto1, C, mI, mN);
45 ▲                  }
46 ▼              else { Case for 0 < θ < π                    Calculates all values for φ and writes in the output file in
47 ▼                  for(phi=0;phi<=2*M_PI-DPhi/2;phi=phi+DPhi){ degrees
48                        fprintf(output,"%f %f %f %f %f %f\n", te*180/M_PI, phi*180/M_PI, asintoto1, C, mI, mN);}}}}
49        fclose(output);
50        fclose(input);}
```

Within the code, the following relations appear:

$$\Delta\theta = \frac{\pi}{n_\theta}$$

$$\Delta\phi = \frac{2\pi}{n_\phi} \qquad n_\phi = \frac{2\pi\sin\theta}{\Delta\theta}$$

Generated positions

(...)

Fig. 5. Inside the *sphera.c* code

overcoming of the centrifugal barrier. In the case of a single crossing between entrance and exit channels P_i assumes the form:

$$P_i(E, \theta, \phi, l) = (1 - p_i)(1 + p_i) \tag{20}$$

Once the two loops are completed, the code returns an array containing the cross section for each collisional energy for a specific configuration. It is also possible to make the code compute the cross section for several configurations and then calculate the average cross section. In this case, the input file must contain all the configurations the user as selected. In the next section, it is explained how to make an input containing configurations equally distributed in space.

2.4   Generating an Input with *sphere.c* for multiple configurations

The purpose of *sphere.c* is to generate an input file for *CS.c*. The idea is to have several configurations evenly distributed around the neutral species. For instance, in Fig. 5, by assuming $n_\theta = 10$, the program returns 128 configurations distributed evenly in a spherical manner. The input can be used to calculate the average cross section over the three-dimensional space. This information allows to predict whether the two reactants assume a preferential relative orientation when they are close to each other.

3   Conclusions

The pieces of code described have been used in three systems so far, all of them involving He^+ colliding with dimethyl ether [30], methyl formate [36] and methanol (currently under study). They have been able to reproduce the data obtained through laboratory measurements of the total cross section as a function of the collision energy for the three systems. The code, and the physical model at its base, is of relevance in interpreting charge exchange processes at thermal and subthermal collision energies, since it presents several advantages with respect to classical capture models in the calculation cross sections:

1. It includes an estimate of the initial molecular orbital from which the electron is captured by the atom.
2. The detailed exploration of the interaction anisotropy, controlling the relative stability of different sets of configurations, suggests the formation of the collision complex, during the approach of the reagents, in preferential relative orientations, and how such orientations change their weight when the collision energy increases.
3. By using experimental values of the cross sections as benchmark data, the model can estimate the reaction rates as a function of the temperature.

Eventually, the reaction rate values can be used in astrochemical models in order to predict the chemical evolution of interstellar environments.

Acknowledgements. The authors thank Andrea Cernuto who originally developed the code. This project has received funding from the European Union's Horizon 2020 research and innovation programme under the Marie Skłodowska Curie grant agreement No 811312 for the project "Astro-Chemical Origins" (ACO). The authors thank the Herla Project (http://www.hpc.unipg.it/hosting/vherla/vherla.html) - Università degli Studi di Perugia for allocated computing time. The authors thank the Dipartimento di Ingegneria Civile ed Ambientale of the University of Perugia for allocated computing time within the project "Dipartimenti di Eccellenza 2018–2022". N. F.-L thanks MIUR and the University of Perugia for the financial support of the AMIS project through the "Dipartimenti di Eccellenza" programme. N.F.-L. also acknowledges the Fondo Ricerca di Base 2021 (RICBASE2021FAGINAS) del Dipartimento di Chimica, Biologia e Biotecnologie della Università di Perugia for financial support. D.A. and M.R. acknowledge funding from MUR PRIN 2020 project n. 2020AFB3FX.

References

1. McGuire, B.A.: 2021 census of interstellar, circumstellar, extragalactic, protoplanetary disk, and exoplanetary molecules. Astrophys. J. Suppl. Ser. **259**(2), 30 (2022). https://doi.org/10.3847/1538-4365/ac2a48
2. Müller, H.S.P., Thorwirth, S., Roth, D.A., Winnewisser, G.: The cologne database for molecular spectroscopy, CDMS. A&A **370**(3), L49–L52 (2001). https://doi.org/10.1051/0004-6361:20010367. https://cdms.astro.uni-koeln.de/classic/molecules. Accessed 13 Apr 2022
3. Müller, H.S., Schlöder, F., Stutzki, J., Winnewisser, G.: The cologne database for molecular spectroscopy, CDMS: a useful tool for astronomers and spectroscopists. J. Mol. Struct. **742**(1), 215–227 (2005). https://doi.org/10.1016/j.molstruc.2005.01.027
4. Endres, C.P., Schlemmer, S., Schilke, P., Stutzki, J., Müller, H.S.: The cologne database for molecular spectroscopy, CDMS, in the virtual atomic and molecular data centre, VAMDC. J. Mol. Spectro. **327**, 95–104 (2016). https://doi.org/10.1016/j.jms.2016.03.005. New Visions of Spectroscopic Databases, Volume II
5. Herbst, E., Van Dishoeck, E.F.: Complex organic interstellar molecules. Ann. Rev. Astron. Astrophys. **47**, 427–480 (2009)
6. Ceccarelli, C., et al.: Seeds of life in space (SOLIS): the organic composition diversity at 300–1000 au scale in solar-type star-forming regions. Astrophys. J. **850**(2), 176 (2017)
7. López-Sepulcre, A., Balucani, N., Ceccarelli, C., Codella, C., Dulieu, F., Theule, P.: Interstellar formamide (NH_2CHO), a key prebiotic precursor. ACS Earth Space Chem. **3**(10), 2122–2137 (2019). https://doi.org/10.1021/acsearthspacechem.9b00154
8. Caselli, P., Ceccarelli, C.: Our astrochemical heritage. Astron. Astrophys. Rev. **20**(1), 1–68 (2012). https://doi.org/10.1007/s00159-012-0056-x
9. Herbst, E.: The synthesis of large interstellar molecules. Int. Rev. Phys. Chem. **36**(2), 287–331 (2017)
10. Agúndez, M., Wakelam, V.: Chemistry of dark clouds: databases, networks, and models. Chem. Rev. **113**(12), 8710–8737 (2013)
11. Taquet, V., Ceccarelli, C., Kahane, C.: Multilayer modeling of porous grain surface chemistry-I. The GRAINOBLE model. Astron. Astrophys. **538**, A42 (2012)
12. Garrod, R., Herbst, E.: Formation of methyl formate and other organic species in the warm-up phase of hot molecular cores. Astron. Astrophys. **457**(3), 927–936 (2006)
13. Vasyunin, A.I., Caselli, P., Dulieu, F., Jiménez-Serra, I.: Formation of complex molecules in prestellar cores: a multilayer approach. Astrophys. J. **842**(1), 33 (2017)
14. Garrod, R.T., Weaver, S.L.W., Herbst, E.: Complex chemistry in star-forming regions: an expanded gas-grain warm-up chemical model. Astrophys. J. **682**(1), 283 (2008)

15. Balucani, N., Ceccarelli, C., Taquet, V.: Formation of complex organic molecules in cold objects: the role of gas-phase reactions. Monthly Notices R. Astron. Soc. Lett. **449**(1), L16–L20 (2015)

16. Skouteris, D., et al.: The genealogical tree of ethanol: gas-phase formation of glycolaldehyde, acetic acid, and formic acid. Astrophys. J. **854**(2), 135 (2018)

17. Rosi, M., et al.: Possible scenarios for SiS formation in the interstellar medium: electronic structure calculations of the potential energy surfaces for the reactions of the SiH radical with atomic Sulphur and S_2. Chem. Phys. Lett. **695**, 87–93 (2018). https://doi.org/10.1016/j.cplett.2018.01.053

18. Wakelam, V., et al.: A kinetic database for astrochemistry (KIDA). ApJS **199**(1), 21 (2012). https://doi.org/10.1088/0067-0049/199/1/21

19. Woodall, J., Agúndez, M., Markwick-Kemper, A.J., Millar, T.J.: The UMIST database for astrochemistry 2006*. A&A **466**(3), 1197–1204 (2007). https://doi.org/10.1051/0004-6361:20064981

20. Mallard, W., Linstrom, P.: NIST Chemistry WebBook, NIST Standard Reference Database Number 69. Gaithersburg, MD 20899 (2000). https://doi.org/10.18434/T4D303

21. Lepp, S., Stancil, P., Dalgarno, A.: Atomic and molecular processes in the early Universe. J. Phys. B: At. Mol. Opt. Phys. **35**(10), R57 (2002)

22. De Fazio, D.: The H + HeH$^+$ → He$^+$ H$_2^+$ reaction from the ultra-cold regime to the three-body breakup: exact quantum mechanical integral cross sections and rate constants. Phys. Chem. Chem. Phys. **16**(23), 11662–11672 (2014). https://doi.org/10.1039/C4CP00502C

23. Pirani, F., Brizi, S., Roncaratti, L.F., Casavecchia, P., Cappelletti, D., Vecchiocattivi, F.: Beyond the Lennard-Jones model: a simple and accurate potential function probed by high resolution scattering data useful for molecular dynamics simulations. Phys. Chem. Chem. Phys. **10**(36), 5489–5503 (2008)

24. Pirani, F., Albertí, M., Castro, A., Moix Teixidor, M., Cappelletti, D.: Atom-bond pairwise additive representation for intermolecular potential energy surfaces. Chem. Phys. Lett. **394**(1–3), 37–44 (2004). https://doi.org/10.1016/j.cplett.2004.06.100

25. Bartolomei, M., et al.: The intermolecular potential in NO-N$_2$ and (NO-N$_2$)$^+$ systems: implications for the neutralization of ionic molecular aggregates. Phys. Chem. Chem. Phys. **10**, 5993–6001 (2008). https://doi.org/10.1039/B808200F

26. Cappelletti, D., Pirani, F., Bussery-Honvault, B., Gomez, L., Bartolomei, M.: A bond-bond description of the intermolecular interaction energy: the case of weakly bound N$_2$-H$_2$ and N$_2$-N$_2$ complexes. Phys. Chem. Chem. Phys. **10**, 4281–4293 (2008). https://doi.org/10.1039/B803961E

27. Pacifici, L., Verdicchio, M., Faginas-Lago, N., Lombardi, A., Costantini, A.: A high-level ab initio study of the N$_2$ + N$_2$ reaction channel. J. Comput. Chem. **34**(31), 2668–2676 (2013). https://doi.org/10.1002/jcc.23415

28. Candori, R., et al.: Structure and charge transfer dynamics of the (Ar-N$_2$)$^+$ molecular cluster. J. Chem. Phys. **115**(19), 8888–8898 (2001). https://doi.org/10.1063/1.1413980

29. Candori, R., Pirani, F., Cappelletti, D., Tosi, P., Bassi, D.: State-to-state cross-sections for N$_2^+$ $(X, \nu' = 1,2)$ + Ar and Ar$^+(^2P_{j,mj})$ + N$_2$ $(X, \nu = 0)$ at low energies. Int. J. Mass Spectrom. **223**, 499–506 (2003). https://doi.org/10.1016/S1387-3806(02)00873-4

30. Cernuto, A., Tosi, P., Martini, L.M., Pirani, F., Ascenzi, D.: Experimental investigation of the reaction of helium ions with dimethyl ether: stereodynamics of the dissociative charge exchange process. Phys. Chem. Chem. Phys. **19**(30), 19554–19565 (2017). https://doi.org/10.1039/C7CP00827A
31. Landau, L.: On the theory of transfer of energy at collisions II. Physikalische Zeitschrift der Sowjetunion **2**, 46–51 (1932)
32. Zener, C.: Non-adiabatic crossing of energy levels. Proceedings of the Royal Society of London. Series A, Containing Papers of a Mathematical and Physical Character **137**(833), 696–702 (1932). https://doi.org/10.1098/rspa.1932.0165
33. Stückelberg, E.C.G.: Theory of inelastic collisions between atoms. Helv. Phys. Acta **5**, 369–423 (1932). https://doi.org/10.5169/seals-110177
34. Nikitin, E.E., Umanskii, S.Y.: Theory of slow atomic collisions (1984). https://doi.org/10.1007/978-3-642-82045-8
35. Nikitin, E.E.: Nonadiabatic transitions: what we learned from old masters and how much we owe them. Annu. Rev. Phys. Chem. **50**(1), 1–21 (1999). https://doi.org/10.1146/annurev.physchem.50.1.1
36. Cernuto, A., Pirani, F., Martini, L.M., Tosi, P., Ascenzi, D.: The selective role of long-range forces in the stereodynamics of ion-molecule reactions: the He$^+$ + Methyl Formate case from guided-ion-beam experiments. ChemPhysChem **19**(1), 51–59 (2018). https://doi.org/10.1002/cphc.201701096

Simulation of CO_2 Sorption from the Gas Stream by the Grain of Soda-Lime Sorbent

Vadim Lisitsa$^{(\boxtimes)}$ (iD), Tatyana Khachkova, Yaroslav Bazaikin, and Vladimir Derevschikov

Institute of Mathematics SB RAS, Koptug Avenue 4, 630090 Novosibirsk, Russia
lisitsavv@ipgg.sbras.ru

Abstract. The paper presents a numerical algorithm for conjugated reactive transport at two spatial scales, in application to $C0_2$ chemosorption. Transport at the macroporous scale (intergranular space) is supported by both the fluid flow and diffusion. At the microporous scale diffusion is assumed as the only transport mechanism. The mathematical model used in this research operates with two parameters that are unavailable from laboratory measurements, they are reaction rate and diffusion coefficient in the microporous space. We present a series of numerical experiments to calibrate these parameters to match the laboratory-measured rates of the concentration changes rates.

Keywords: Chemosorption · Reactive transport · Finite differences · Immersed boundary conditions

1 Introduction

The development of technology for carbon dioxide sorption from gas mixtures by sorbents has been an important engineering task for more than a hundred years, and interest in it is growing every year. Solid CO_2 sorbents based on soda-lime are broadly used in medical applications (inhalation anesthesia, respiratory care), hyperbaric chambers, underwater diving gear, fire safety apparatuses, and mine rescue equipment. The overall reaction of the CO2 sorption process by the soda-lime sorbent can be expressed as follows: $Ca(OH)_2 + CO_2 \rightarrow CaCO_3 \downarrow +H_2O$. Soda-lime sorption performance is mainly affected by the physical and chemical properties of the material, including the shape and the size of particles, porosity, surface area, and hydrodynamic conditions, such as gas velocity, CO_2 concentration, temperature, and humidity [2].

Computational fluid dynamics is a powerful tool for the simulation of chemical reactors. However, for gas-solid reactors such as sorption of CO_2 by solid

The research was done under the support of RSCF grant no. 21-71-20003. Numerical simulations were performed using the supercomputer facilities of Siant-Petersburg Polytechnic University.

sorbent grains in fixed beds, geometric complexity has so far prevented detailed modeling of their hydrodynamics. A special approach is needed that is general enough to be applicable for reactor design purposes, but that retains the detailed flow modeling that considers the transport of chemical species and the local concentration gradients in the sorbent grains that could influence reaction kinetics [4].

The current study aims to develop a realistic mathematical model for simulating hydrodynamics and kinetics of CO_2 sorption from the gas stream by the grain of the soda-lime sorbent and to validate the model with the experimental data.

2   Statement of the Problem

We consider two-scale porous media where we distinguish between the large- and small-scale pores. By the large scale pores, we assume those of the size of a few millimeters, whereas the small-scale pores are about several μm. Thus, we suggest that the large-scale pores may support the fluid flow. We assume both advection and diffusion of chemical species take place in the large-scale pores. On the contrary, the small-scale pores do not let the fluid flow through. Thus, the only transport mechanism at this scale is diffusion. This type of problem is also known as conjugate transport. We consider the fluid flow in macro-pores supporting the transport of chemical species. This flow satisfies the steady-state Stokes equation:

$$\begin{aligned} \nabla p - \mu \Delta \vec{u} = 0, \ \vec{x} \in D_p \\ \nabla \cdot \vec{u} = 0, \quad \vec{x} \in D_p, \\ \vec{u} = 0, \quad \vec{x} \in D_g, \end{aligned} \tag{1}$$

where p is the pressure, u is the fluid flow (averaged over the cell), μ is fluid viscosity, D_p is the macropore space, and D_g is the grain microporous space. Due to the assumption that the microporous space does not support the fluid flow we may avoid solving Stokes-Brikmann equation [6], but Stokes equation has to be solved in the macropore space with the following boundary conditions:

$$\begin{aligned} Q(x_1^{in}) = \int_{x_2, x_3} v_1(x_1^{in}, x_2, x_3) dx_2 dx_3 = Q_{in}, \\ p(x_1^{out}) = p^{out}, \\ \vec{u} = 0, \vec{x} \in \partial D_p/(x_1 = x_1^{in} \cup x_1 = x_1^{out}), \end{aligned} \tag{2}$$

where ∂D_p is the boundary of the macropore space.

The reactive transport at both pore scales satisfies the advection-diffusion-reaction equation:

$$\frac{\partial}{\partial t}(\phi C_j) + \nabla \cdot (\vec{u} C_j) - \nabla \cdot (D \nabla C_j) = g_j, \tag{3}$$

where C_j is the molar concentration of the species, ϕ is the micro-porosity, D is the effective diffusion coefficient, and g_j is the external term due to the chemical reaction. Note, that for the macroporous space; i.e., for $\vec{x} \in D_p$ the parameters are $\phi = 1$, $\vec{u} \neq 0$ is the flow velocity, and $D = D_0$ is the molecular diffusion coefficient of the species. For the microporous material; i.e., for $\vec{x} \in D_g$ we have $\phi < 1$, $\vec{u} \equiv 0$, and $D = \phi D_0/F$, where $F \in [1; 10]$ is the form factor of the micropore space [8]. Below we clarify the particular values of the considered parameters.

We consider two types of species. First is the mobile species which may be transferred by the advection-diffusion reaction 3. Let us denote them as C_m, with $m = 1, ..., M$. The second set is the immobile species which are solids forming the matrix of the sorbent, they are denoted by C_i, with $i = M + 1, ..., J$, where J is the total number of species.

In our considerations we will use the following initial conditions:

$$C_j(\vec{x}, 0) = 0, \quad \vec{x} \in D_p, i = 1, ..., J;$$
$$C_m(\vec{x}, 0) = 0, \quad \vec{x} \in D_g, m = 1, ..., M;$$
$$C_i(\vec{x}, 0) = C_i^0, \vec{x} \in D_g, i = M + 1, ..., J$$

These conditions mean that no species are present in the macroporous space at the beginning, whereas immobile solid species may form the sorbent matrix.

The boundary conditions are made to support the mobile species concentration at the inlet and free outward transport at the outlet.

$$C_m(x_1^{in}, t) = C_m^{in}, \vec{x} \in x_1^{in} \qquad m = 1, ..., M;$$
$$\frac{\partial C_m}{\partial n}(\vec{x}, t) = 0, \quad \vec{x} \in x_1^{out} \cup S_{ext}\ m = 1, ..., M;$$

where S_{ext} is the outer boundaries of the computational domain without inlet and outlet (sides of the reactor). Additionally, we need to specify, that concentrations and fluxes are about to coincide at the interfaces ∂D_p, however, we are using the heterogeneous formulation, so that Eq. (3) is valid everywhere in D but the coefficients are discontinuous.

In this research, we are focused on the particular chemical reaction:

$$Ca(OH)_2 + CO_2 \rightarrow CaCO_3 + H_2O$$

the mobile species are CO_2 and H_2O, whereas $Ca(OH)_2$ and $CaCO_3$ are immobile species. This is the first-order reaction, thus equations for the species become as follows:

$$\frac{\partial}{\partial t}(\phi C_{CO_2}) + \nabla \cdot (\vec{u} C_{CO_2}) - \nabla \cdot (D_{CO_2} \nabla C_{CO_2}) = -k\phi C_{CO_2} C_{Ca(OH)_2},$$
$$\frac{\partial}{\partial t}(\phi C_{H_2O}) + \nabla \cdot (\vec{u} C_{H_2O}) - \nabla \cdot (D_{H_2O} \nabla C_{H_2O}) = k\phi C_{CO_2} C_{Ca(OH)_2},$$
$$\frac{\partial}{\partial t}(C_{Ca(OH)_2}) = -k\phi C_{CO_2} C_{Ca(OH)_2}, \qquad (4)$$
$$\frac{\partial}{\partial t}(C_{CaCO_3}) = k\phi C_{CO_2} C_{Ca(OH)_2},$$

In these notations, k is the reaction rate, and the particular form of the right-hand side is defined by the reaction kinetics. Reaction rate may depend on numerous factors, such as temperature, specific surface of the micropores, etc. We restrict our considerations with the isothermal case with a constant reaction rate. Note, that we consider the concentrations of the gases measured in a free volume, thus they are multiplied by the porosity in Eqs. (4), whereas the concentrations of the solids are measured for the porous material (not the matrix); thus we do not need to scale them. Also, note that H_2O does not affect the reaction rate or the transport of the species, thus it can be excluded from further considerations.

The initial and boundary conditions can be rewritten as follows:

$$C_{CO_2} = C_{CO_2}^{in}, \qquad \vec{x} \in x_1^{in}$$
$$\frac{\partial C_{CO_2}}{\partial \vec{n}} = 0, \quad \vec{x} \in x_1^{out} \cup S_{ext} \tag{5}$$

$$
\begin{aligned}
C_{CO_2}(0, \vec{x}) &= 0, & \vec{x} \in D_p \cup D_g, \\
C_{Ca(OH)_2}(0, \vec{x}) &= 0, & \vec{x} \in D_p, \\
C_{Ca(OH)_2}(0, \vec{x}) &= C_{Ca(OH)_2}^0, & \vec{x} \in D_g, \\
C_{CaCO_3}(0, \vec{x}) &= 0, & \vec{x} \in D_p, \\
C_{CaCO_3}(0, \vec{x}) &= C_{CaCO_3}^0, & \vec{x} \in D_g,
\end{aligned}
\tag{6}
$$

3 Numerical Methods

3.1 Level-Set

To be able to deal with irregular boundaries of the computational domain (reactor) and the macro-pore space geometry, so that the boundaries of the pore space D_p are not aligned with the grid lines we suggest using the level-set method [5,10,13,15]. Moreover, we are dealing with two level-sets to distinguish between the exterior of the reactor where no flow no diffusion is allowed and the sorbent grains with micropores:

$$\varphi^p(\vec{x}) : \begin{cases} \varphi^p(\vec{x}) > 0, \vec{x} \in D_p, \\ \varphi^p(\vec{x}) < 0, \vec{x} \in D_g \cup D_e, \end{cases} \qquad \varphi^e(\vec{x}) : \begin{cases} \varphi^e(\vec{x}) > 0, \vec{x} \in D_p \cup D_g, \\ \varphi^e(\vec{x}) < 0, \vec{x} \in D_e, \end{cases}$$

where D_e is the exterior of the model, which is critical if a cylindrical reactor is considered. The level-sets are needed to be computed only ones at the preliminary step of the algorithm.

3.2 Solving Stokes Equation

To construct spatial approximation of the Stokes Eq. (1), we use the staggered grid scheme. The grid-functions are defined as $p_{i,j,k} = p(ih_1, jh_2, kh_3)$, $(u_1)_{i+1/2,j,k} = u_1((i+1/2)h_1, jh_2, kh_3)$, $(u_2)_{i,j+1/2,k} = u_2(ih_1, (j+1/2)h_2, kh_3)$, $(u_3)_{i,j,k+1/2} = u_3(ih_1, jh_2, (k+1/2)h_3)$ $\varphi_{i,j,k}^m = \varphi^m(ih_1, jh_2, kh_3)$, where h_1, h_2, and h_3 are the spatial steps and $m \in \{p, e\}$. The pore space D_p is defined as $\varphi^p(\vec{x}) > 0$ and the interface ∂D_p corresponds to $\varphi^p(\vec{x}) = 0$.

To approximate Stokes equation we use second order finite-difference scheme:

$$
\begin{aligned}
\mu L[u_1]_{i+1/2,j,k} - D_1^c[p]_{i+1/2,j,k} &= 0, & if \; \varphi_{i+1/2,j,k}^p > 0, \\
\mu L[u_2]_{i,j+1/2,k} - D_2^c[p]_{i,j+1/2,} &= 0, & if \; \varphi_{i,j+1/2,k}^p > 0, \\
\mu L[u_3]_{i,j,k+1/2} - D_3^c[p]_{i,j,k+1/2} &= 0, & if \; \varphi_{i,j,k+1/2}^p > 0, \\
D_1^c[u_1]_{i,j,k} + D_2^c[u_2]_{i,j,k} + D_3^c[u_3]_{i,j,k} &= 0, & if \; \varphi_{i,j,k}^p > 0,
\end{aligned}
\tag{7}
$$

where

$$L[f]_{I,J,K} = D_1^2[f]_{I,J,K} + D_2^2[f]_{I,J,K} + D_2^2[f]_{I,J,K} \tag{8}$$

is the approximation of the Laplace operator with

$$D_1^2[f]_{I,J,K} = \frac{f_{I+1,J,K} - 2f_{I,J,K} + f_{I,J,K}}{h_1^2} = \left.\frac{\partial^2 f}{\partial x_1^2}\right|_{I,J,K} + O(h_1^2), \tag{9}$$

and D_j^c is the approximation of j-th component of the divergence operator

$$D_1^c[f]_{I,J,K} = \frac{f_{I+1/1,J,K} - f_{I,J-1/2,K}}{h_1} = \left.\frac{\partial f}{\partial x_1}\right|_{I,J,K} + O(h_1^2). \tag{10}$$

Here, indices I, J, and K can be either integer or half-integer, but i, j, and k are integers only. The operators approximating derivatives with respect to the other spatial direction can be obtained by the permutations of the role of spatial indices.

Equations (1) are valid only for the internal points of the domain D_p; i.e., if all the points from a stencil belong to pore space. Otherwise we suggest applying the immersed boundary method [7,9,10,12], where the undefined solution at points from D_g and D_e is extrapolated from the neighbouring points in D_p. Details of the immersed boundary conditions implementation is presented in [10].

To resolve the discretized Stokes equation, we compute the steady-state solution of the time-dependent Navier-Stokes equation by the projection method [1]. This approach requires solving the Poisson equation for the pressure, which can be efficiently done using Krylov-type methods with appropriate preconditioner [8], based on the pseudo-spectral approximation [14].

Note that for the simulation of the chemical species transport we need to state the flow rate equal to zero inside the grains and in the exterior part of the domain which means that

$$(u_1)_{i+1/2,j,k} = 0, \; if \; \varphi_{i+1/2,j,k}^p \le 0,$$
$$(u_2)_{i,j+1/2,k} = 0, \; if \; \varphi_{i,j+1/2,k}^p \le 0,$$
$$(u_3)_{i,j,k+1/2} = 0, \; if \; \varphi_{i,j,k+1/2}^p \le 0.$$

3.3 Solution of the Advection-Diffusion-Reaction Equation

To solve advection-diffusion-reaction equations we use the splitting scheme, in particular, we solve the advection-diffusion equation using an explicit in time scheme and then solve the reactive part of the equation applying a semi-implicit scheme.

Let us state $C_{i,j,k}^n = C(ih_1, jh_2, kh_3, n\tau)$, where τ is the temporal step. After that the advection-diffusion equation is approximated by the explicit in time scheme. We use the first-order approximation in time, second-order approximation of the diffusive part and the third-order WENO scheme to approximate advective part [11,15,16]:

$$\frac{\tilde{C}_{i,j,k}^{n+1} - C_{i,j,k}^{n}}{\tau} + D_1^3[u_1 C]_{i,j,k}^n + D_2^3[u_2 C]_{i,j,k}^n + D_3^3[u_3 C]_{i,j,k}^n - [\nabla_h \cdot (D\nabla_h C)]_{i,j,k}^n = 0,$$
$$\varphi_{i,j,k}^e > 0,$$

(11)

where

$$D_1^3[u_1 C]_{i,j,k}^n = \frac{F_1[C, \vec{u}]_{i+1/2,j,k} - F_1[C, \vec{u}]_{i_1-1/2,j,k}}{h}.$$

(12)

The fluxes are defined as

$$F_1[C, \vec{u}]_{j_1 \pm 1/2, j_2 j_3} = \begin{cases} F_1^-[C]_{j_1 \pm 1/2, j_2, j_3}, \ if \ (u_1)_{j_1 \pm 1/2, j_2, j_3} < 0, \\ F_1^+[C]_{j_1 \pm 1/2, j_2, j_3}, \ if \ (u_1)_{j_1 \pm 1/2, j_2, j_3} > 0, \end{cases}$$

where

$$F_1^{\pm}[C]_{j_1+1/2, j_2, j_3} = (u_1)_{j_1+1/2, j_2, j_3} \left[(w_1)_1^{\pm} (p_1)_1^{\pm} + (w_1)_2^{\pm} (p_1)_2^{\pm} \right],$$

$$(p_1)_1^{\pm} = -\frac{(\delta_1)_{j_1-1, j_2, j_3}^{\pm}}{2} + \frac{3(\delta_1)_{j_1, j_2, j_3}^{\pm}}{2}, \ (p_1)_2^{\pm} = \frac{(\delta_1)_{j_1, j_2, j_3}^{\pm}}{2} + \frac{(\delta_1)_{j_1+1, j_2, j_3}^{\pm}}{2},$$

$$(\delta_1)_{j_1-1, j_2, j_3}^{-} = C_{j_1+2, j_2, j_3}, \ (\delta_1)_{j_1, j_2, j_3}^{-} = C_{j_1+1, j_2, j_3}, \ (\delta_1)_{j_1+1, j_2, j_3}^{-} = C_{j_1, j_2, j_3},$$
$$(\delta_1)_{j_1-1, j_2, j_3}^{+} = C_{j_1-1, j_2, j_3}, \ (\delta_1)_{j_1, j_2, j_3}^{+} = C_{j_1, j_2, j_3}, \ (\delta_1)_{j_1+1, j_2, j_3}^{+} = C_{j_1+1, j_2, j_3}.$$

The weights for the third-order WENO scheme are defined as

$$(w_1)_l^{\pm} = \frac{\gamma_l}{(\varepsilon_1^{\pm} + (S_1)_l^{\pm})^2} \frac{1}{\sum_{k=1}^2 \gamma_k (\varepsilon_1^{\pm} + (S_1)_k^{\pm})^{-2}},$$

where $l = 1, 2$. The smoothers are

$$(S_1)_1^{\pm} = \left((\delta_1)_{j_1, j_2, j_3}^{\pm} - (\delta_1)_{j_1-1, j_2, j_3}^{\pm} \right)^2, \ (S_1)_2^{\pm} = \left((\delta_1)_{j_1+1, j_2, j_3}^{\pm} - (\delta_1)_{j_1, j_2, j_3}^{\pm} \right)^2,$$

$$\gamma_1 = \frac{1}{3}, \ \gamma_2 = \frac{2}{3},$$

and

$$\varepsilon_1^{\pm} = 10^{-6} \max \left\{ ((\delta_1)_{j_1-1, j_2, j_3}^{\pm})^2, ((\delta_1)_{j_1, j_2, j_3}^{\pm})^2, ((\delta_1)_{j_1+1, j_2, j_3}^{\pm})^2 \right\} + 10^{-99}.$$

Operators, approximating the derivatives to the other spatial direction, can be obtained using the spatial indices' permutation.

For the operator $[\nabla_h \cdot (D\nabla_h C)]_{i,j,k}^n$ we consider one term; i.e., $\frac{\partial}{\partial x_1} \left(D \frac{\partial}{\partial x_1} \right)$, the other two can be constructed in the similar manner.

$$\frac{\partial}{\partial x_1} \left(D \frac{\partial}{\partial x_1} \right) \approx \frac{1}{h_1} \left[\tilde{D}_{i+1/2,j,k} \frac{C_{i+1,j,k}^n - C_{i,j,k}^n}{h_1} - \tilde{D}_{i-1/2,j,k} \frac{C_{i,j,k}^n - C_{i-1,j,k}^n}{h_1} \right],$$

where

$$D_{i+1/2,j,k} = 2 \left(D_{i+1,j,k}^{-1} + D_{i,j,k}^{-1} \right)^{-1}.$$

This operator is constructed based on the theory of conservative schemes [17]. It is second-order accurate if the coefficients are constant, however, in some cases of discontinuous coefficients it may degenerate to the first order.

The next step of the splitting scheme is the solution correction due to the reactive term. Consider the system of ordinary differential equations:

$$\begin{aligned}
\frac{\partial}{\partial t}\left(\phi C_{CO_2}\right) &= -k\phi C_{CO_2} C_{Ca(OH)_2}, \\
\frac{\partial}{\partial t}\left(C_{Ca(OH)_2}\right) &= -k\phi C_{CO_2} C_{Ca(OH)_2}, \\
\frac{\partial}{\partial t}\left(\phi C_{H_2O}\right) &= k\phi C_{CO_2} C_{Ca(OH)_2}, \\
\frac{\partial}{\partial t}\left(C_{CaCO_3}\right) &= k\phi C_{CO_2} C_{Ca(OH)_2}.
\end{aligned} \tag{13}$$

The system should be integrated at the time interval $t \in [t^n, t^{n+1}]$. We suggest using a simple semi-implicit scheme to resolve the system (13), which allows using arbitrary large time steps.

$$\begin{aligned}
\frac{C_{CO_2}^{n+1} - \tilde{C}_{CO_2}^{n+1}}{dt} &= -k C_{CO_2}^{n+1} \tilde{C}_{Ca(OH)_2}^{n+1}, \\
\frac{C_{Ca(OH)_2}^{n+1} - \tilde{C}_{Ca(OH)_2}^{n+1}}{dt} &= -k\varphi \tilde{C}_{CO_2}^{n+1} C_{Ca(OH)_2}^{n+1}, \\
\frac{C_{H_2O}^{n+1} - \tilde{C}_{H_2O}^{n+1}}{dt} &= k C_{CO_2}^{n+1} C_{Ca(OH)_2}^{n+1}, \\
\frac{C_{CaCO_3}^{n+1} - \tilde{C}_{CaCO_3}^{n+1}}{dt} &= k\varphi C_{CO_2}^{n+1} C_{Ca(OH)_2}^{n+1},
\end{aligned}$$

The obtained scheme is the first order accurate and unconditionally stable. However, the time steps $dt \le \tau$ are chosen to preserve the prescribed accuracy level.

4   Experiments

In this research, we present a series of numerical experiments to calibrate the mathematical model to match the sorbent properties measured in a lab. Soda-lime Loflosorb (Intersurgical Ltd, UK) is a commercially available CO_2 sorbent that is used in breathing systems to absorb exhaled carbon dioxide during anesthesia. Loflosorb contains an indicator that turns from white to purple upon exhaustion of the sorbent. Loflosorb contains 60 wt% of $Ca(OH)_2$, 15 wt% of water, and less than 0.1 wt% of the indicator (ethyl violet). Loflosorb sorbent pellets are spherical particles 3 mm in diameter [3]. The mass density of the granules, porosity (measured in m^3/kg), and mass fraction of H_2O, $Ca(OH)_2$ and $CaCO_3$ at the initial stage were measured in a lab. They are provided in Table 1.

Table 1. Measured properties of the sorbent at the initial stage.

Property	Notation	Loflosorb
Density (kg/m^3)	ρ	1080
Chem. porosity (m^3/kg)	v_p	$4.6 \cdot 10^{-4}$
Mass fraction of $Ca(OH)_2$	$\mu_{Ca(OH)_2}$	0.76
Mass fraction of $CaCO_3$	μ_{CaCO_3}	0.05

4.1   Lab Experiments

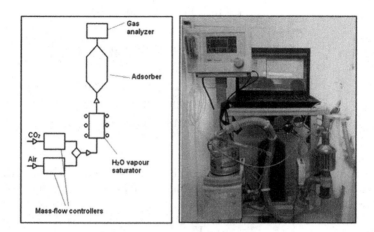

Fig. 1. Experimental setup for CO_2 chemisorption measurement: scheme - left, photo - right.

Carbon dioxide chemisorption from the gas mixtures was studied in the experimental setup shown in Fig. 1. The process of CO_2 chemisorption by samples of the soda-lime sorbent (Loflosorb, Intersurgical Ltd. and ($m_s = 3$ g) was carried out in the differential reactor mode. The granules of the sample were distributed evenly in one layer along the grid of the reactor. The gas-air mixture with a constant CO_2 content (1 vol. % or 5 vol. %) was passed through the reactor with the inlet flow rate of 100 L/h at 37°C. Each sample was kept in contact with the gas-air mixture for a specified time, after that, it was removed from the reactor and placed into the sealed container.

Elemental analysis of the sorbent samples before and after chemisorption was performed using the ARL Perform'X (Thermo Scientific) X-Ray Fluorescence Spectrometer. The chemical composition of the sorbent samples was studied by synchronous thermal analysis method (thermogravimetry (TG) coupled with differential thermal analysis (DTA)) using the STA 449 Jupiter instrument (Netzsch, Germany). The weight contents of $Ca(OH)_2$ and $CaCO_3$ were calculated from the mass loss effects around 450 and 750°, respectively. Results of laboratory measurements are provided in Table 2.

4.2   Relations Between Laboratory and Simulated Data

However, the mathematical model operates with dimensionless porosity and molar concentrations. To estimate the dimensionless porosity ϕ we need to consider the measured one v_p and the mass density of the microporous material ρ.

Table 2. Measured mass fractions of $Ca(OH)_2$ and $CaCO_3$ at different time instants

CO_2 concentration 5%				
	$t = 0$	$t = 15$	$t = 30$	$t = 60$
$\mu_{Ca(OH)_2}$	0.76	0.32	0.19	0.13
μ_{CaCO_3}	0.05	0.5	0.72	0.78
CO_2 concentration 1%				
	$t = 0$	$t = 15$	$t = 30$	$t = 60$
$\mu_{Ca(OH)_2}$	0.6948	0.4604	0.3535	0.2672
μ_{CaCO_3}	0.0522	0.2318	0.3818	0.475

If a fixed volume V of the material is given, its mass is $m_g = V\rho$, and the pore volume is $V_p = m_g v_p = V\rho v_p$. Thus, the dimensionless porosity can be found as:

$$\phi = \frac{V_p}{V} = \rho v_p.$$

The solid materials in the porous composite are defined by their mass ratio:

$$\mu_j = \frac{m_j}{m_c} = \frac{\rho_j V}{\rho V} = \frac{\rho_j}{\rho},$$

where ρ_j is the mass concentration in a unit volume of porous material (not matrix!) and ρ is the mass density of porous material. In these notations j can be either $Ca(OH)_2$ or $CaCO_3$. After that, the molar concentration can be computed as

$$C_j = \frac{\rho_j}{M_j} = \frac{\mu_j \rho}{M_j},$$

where M_j is the molar mass of the species.

The chemical reaction changes concentrations of the species which causes changes in the physical properties of the microporous material, including porosity and mass density which are important for the mass fraction estimation.

Porosity Change. Assume the initial porosity is φ^0, initial mass density of the porous material is ρ^0, mass fractions of $Ca(OH)_2$ and $CaCO_3$ are $\mu^0_{Ca(OH_2)}$, and $\mu^0_{CaCO_3}$ respectively. Thus, molar concentrations can be computed and assumed to be known at the initial stage as $C^0_{Ca(OH)_2}$ and $C^0_{CaCO_3}$. Consider a volume of the porous material V, then the masses of $Ca(OH)_2$ and $CaCO_3$ in this volume are

$$m^0_j = C^0_j M_j V,$$

where can be either $Ca(OH)_2$ or $CaCO_3$. The initial volumes of the species are

$$V^0_j = \frac{C^0_j M_j V}{r_j},$$

where r_j is the mass density of pure species, as provided in Table 3.

Table 3. Physical parameters of pure species

Property	Notation	CO_2	H_2O	$Ca(OH)_2$	$CaCO_3$
Molar mass (kg/mol)	M	0.044	0.018	0.074	0.1
Crystals density (kg/m^3)	r_j	–	1000	2240	2710
Diffusion coefficient (m^2/s)	D	$1.5 \cdot 10^{-5}$	–	–	–

Thus, we may define the unchangeable substance volume as

$$V_c = V(1 - \varphi^0) - \sum_j V_j = V(1 - \varphi^0) - \sum_j \frac{C_j^0 M_j V}{r_j}.$$

If the reaction takes place, the concentrations changes, thus, the volumes of the species change accordingly and the matrix volume is

$$V_m = V_c + \sum_j V_j$$
$$= V(1 - \varphi^0) - \sum_j \frac{C_j^0 M_j V}{r_j} + \sum_j \frac{C_j M_j V}{r_j}$$
$$= V(1 - \varphi^0) - \sum_j \frac{(C_j - C_j^0) M_j V}{r_j}.$$

Thus the porosity as a function of concentrations can be represented as

$$\varphi(C_{Ca(OH)_2}, C_{CaCO_3}) = 1 - \frac{V_m}{V} = \varphi^0 - \sum_j \frac{(C_j - C_j^0) M_j}{r_j}.$$

This equation should also be closed by the extra equation according to the reaction:

$$C_{Ca(OH)_2} + C_{CaCO_3} = const = C_{Ca(OH)_2}^0 + C_{CaCO_3}^0,$$

which allows considering porosity as a function of one independent variable.

Density Change. To estimate the changes in the density of the granules, consider a volume V. Same as above, assume the density of the porous material ρ^0, the concentrations $C_{Ca(OH)_2}^0$ and $C_{CaCO_3}^0$, and mass fractions $\mu_{Ca(OH)_2}^0$ and $\mu_{CaCO_3}^0$ are known at the initial stage. Thus, the mass of the unchanged component is

$$m_c = (1 - \sum_j \mu_j^0)\rho^0 V = (\rho^0 - \sum_j C_j^0 M_j)V$$

This mass does not change during the reaction, whereas masses of $Ca(OH)_2$ and $CaCO_3$ do. Thus, the mass of the material changes as

$$m_m = m_c + \sum_j m_j$$
$$= (\rho^0 - \sum_j C_j^0 M_j)V + \sum_j C_j M_j V = \rho^0 V + \sum_j (C_j - C_j^0) M_j V$$

and the mass density is

$$\rho(C_{Ca(OH)_2}, C_{CaCO_3}) = \rho^0(C_{Ca(OH)_2}^0, C_{CaCO_3}^0) + \sum_j (C_j - C_j^0) M_j$$

Mass Fraction. Having estimated the molar concentrations of the species one can estimate the mass fraction as

$$\mu_j(C_{Ca(OH)_2}, C_{CaCO_3}) = \frac{C_j M_j}{\rho(C_{Ca(OH)_2}, C_{CaCO_3})}.$$

4.3   Results of Simulation

In our simulations, we considered a reduced reactor model of the diameter 15 mm and length also equal to 15 mm. The granule of the diameter of 3 mm is placed in the middle of the reactor. The flow rate was $1.73 \cdot 10^{-6}\,\mathrm{m}^3/\mathrm{s}$, which ensures the same fluid flow velocity in the middle of the reactor as in the lab experiment. Note, that reduction of the reactor size does not affect the results of the experiment, because the granule is far from the reactor sides, thus the flow is not affected by the side effects. The grid step is 0.3 mm; which is 10 grid points per granule. The size of the model is 50^3 points. To simulate the conjugated reactive transport we need to define the fluid viscosity (Eq. (1)), which is $\mu = 2.8 \cdot 10^{-4}$ the dynamic viscosity of air at normal conditions; the diffusion coefficient for CO_2 in the air is $D_0 = 1.5 \cdot 10^{-5}\,\mathrm{m}^2/\mathrm{s}$. The diffusion coefficient in the microporous media, used in Eq. (3), is defined as $D = \phi D_0/F$, where ϕ is the dimensionless porosity, which is 0.49 at the initial stage for considered material. However, the parameter F is the formation factor, which characterizes the complexity of the pore space [8]. Originally it was defined as the ratio of the electric resistivity of the fluid to that of the porous material filled with this fluid. However, the same relations are valid for diffusion coefficient and thermal conductivity. Formation factor is not available from the lab measurements, but usually, it varies between 1 and 10, and it is approximately 2–4 for such high porosity. In this research, we study the effect of the formation factor on the CO_2 sorption and calibrate this parameter to match the experimental data. The other unknown parameter is the reaction rate k measured in $m^3/(mol \cdot s)$. Thus, our numerical experiments are done to calibrate two model parameters: the formation factor and the reaction rate. In particular we considered $F = 1, 2, ..., 10$ and $k \in \{10^{-4}, 10^{-3}, 10^{-2}, 10^{-1}\}$.

Following the lab experiment, we considered two cases of CO_2 concentration at the inlet. It is typically defined via volumetric fraction ξ_{CO_2}. At normal conditions, one mole of gas fills in 22.4 liters, thus molar concentration can be derived as

$$C_{CO_2} = \frac{\xi_{CO_2}}{22.4} 10^3 \quad mol/m^3.$$

We deal with volumetric concentrations of 5% and 1% which correspond to $2.2321\,\mathrm{mol/m}^2$ and $0.4464\,\mathrm{mol/m}^3$, respectively. Presented experiments illustrate that values of $k = 10^{-4}$ and $k = 10^{-3}$ are too small to match experimental data. In particular, if $k = 10^{-4}$ concentrations changes almost linearly in time up to 7200 s (2 h) (Figs. 2, 3, 4 and 5).

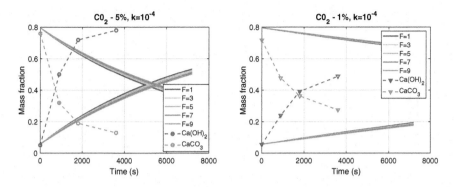

Fig. 2. Mass fraction of $Ca(OH)_2$ and $CaCO_3$ in the granule for different values of formation factor and fixed reaction rate $k = 10^{-4}$. Left plot corresponds to CO_2 volume concentration equal to 5%, right plot corresponds to 1% of CO_2.

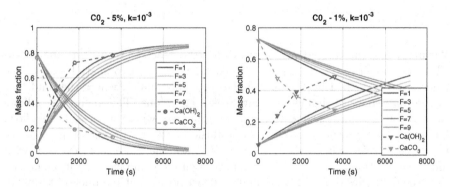

Fig. 3. Mass fraction of $Ca(OH)_2$ and $CaCO_3$ in the granule for different values of formation factor and fixed reaction rate $k = 10^{-3}$. Left plot corresponds to CO_2 volume concentration equal to 5%, right plot corresponds to 1% of CO_2.

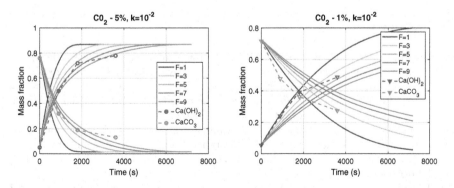

Fig. 4. Mass fraction of $Ca(OH)_2$ and $CaCO_3$ in the granule for different values of formation factor and fixed reaction rate $k = 10^{-2}$. Left plot corresponds to CO_2 volume concentration equal to 5%, right plot corresponds to 1% of CO_2.

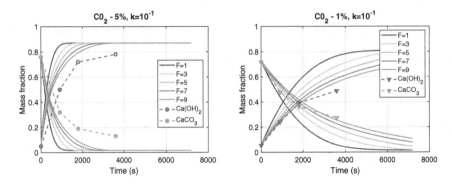

Fig. 5. Mass fraction of $Ca(OH)_2$ and $CaCO_3$ in the granule for different values of formation factor and fixed reaction rate $k = 10^{-1}$. Left plot corresponds to CO_2 volume concentration equal to 5%, right plot corresponds to 1% of CO_2.

5   Conclusions

We presented the numerical algorithm for the reactive transport simulation. The model operates with the conjugated transport at two spatial scales. The macroscale is defined by the size of the sorbent granules, where the fluid flow in the pore space is simulated using Stokes equations. The microscale follows the size of the pores inside the sorbent granules, where we assume no flow, but only the diffusion. However, the diffusion rate in the microporous space is unknown. We assumed CO_2 sorption satisfies the first-order reaction, with unknown reaction rates. In this research, we focused on model calibration, i.e., we performed a series of numerical simulations with different parameters to match the laboratory measurements of the changes in the species concentrations. We figured out that the best matching parameters are the reaction rate equals to $10^2 \, \mathrm{m}^2/(\mathrm{mol} \cdot \mathrm{s})$ with the formation factor of the microporous space less than 10.

References

1. Brown, D.L., Cortez, R., Minion, M.L.: Accurate projection methods for the incompressible Navier-Stokes equations. J. Comput. Phys. **168**(2), 464–499 (2001)
2. Derevschikov, V.S., Kazakova, E.D., Yatsenko, D.A., Veselovskaya, J.V.: Multiscale study of carbon dioxide chemisorption in the plug flow adsorber of the anesthesia machine. Sep. Sci. Technol. **56**(3), 485–497 (2021)
3. Derevshchikov, V.S., Kazakova, E.D.: Comparative analysis of the chemical composition and sorption, textural, and strength properties of commercial medical CO_2 sorbents. Catal. Ind. **12**(1), 1–6 (2020). https://doi.org/10.1134/S2070050420010043
4. Dixon, A.G., Nijemeisland, M.: CFD as a design tool for fixed-bed reactors. Ind. Eng. Chem. Res. **40**(23), 5246–5254 (2001)
5. Gibou, F., Fedkiw, R., Osher, S.: A review of level-set methods and some recent applications. J. Comput. Phys. **353**, 82–109 (2018)

6. Hwang, W.R., Advani, S.G.: Numerical simulations of stokes-brinkman equations for permeability prediction of dual scale fibrous porous media. Phys. Fluids **22**(11), 113101 (2010)

7. Johansen, H., Colella, P.: A cartesian grid embedded boundary method for Poisson's equation on irregular domains. J. Comput. Phys. **147**(1), 60–85 (1998)

8. Khachkova, T., Lisitsa, V., Reshetova, G., Tcheverda, V.: GPU-based algorithm for evaluating the electrical resistivity of digital rocks. Comput. Math. Appl. **82**, 200–211 (2021)

9. Li, X., Huang, H., Meakin, P.: Level set simulation of coupled advection-diffusion and pore structure evolution due to mineral precipitation in porous media. Water Resour. Res. **44**(12), W12407 (2008)

10. Lisitsa, V., Bazaikin, Y., Khachkova, T.: Computational topology-based characterization of pore space changes due to chemical dissolution of rocks. Appl. Math. Model. **88**, 21–37 (2020). https://doi.org/10.1016/j.apm.2020.06.037

11. Liu, X.D., Osher, S., Chan, T.: Weighted essentially non-oscillatory schemes. J. Comput. Phys. **115**(1), 200–212 (1994)

12. Luo, K., Zhuang, Z., Fan, J., Haugen, N.E.L.: A ghost-cell immersed boundary method for simulations of heat transfer in compressible flows under different boundary conditions. Int. J. Heat Mass Transf. **92**, 708–717 (2016)

13. Osher, S., Fedkiw, R.P.: Level set methods: an overview and some recent results. J. Comput. Phys. **169**(2), 463–502 (2001)

14. Pleshkevich, A., Vishnevskiy, D., Lisitsa, V.: Sixth-order accurate pseudo-spectral method for solving one-way wave equation. Appl. Math. Comput. **359**, 34–51 (2019)

15. Prokhorov, D., Lisitsa, V., Khachkova, T., Bazaikin, Y., Yang, Y.: Topology-based characterization of chemically-induced pore space changes using reduction of 3D digital images. J. Comput. Sci. **58**, 101550 (2022)

16. Qiu, J.M., Shu, C.W.: Conservative high order Semi-Lagrangian finite difference WENO methods for advection in incompressible flow. J. Comput. Phys. **230**(4), 863–889 (2011)

17. Samarskii, A.A.: The Theory of Difference Schemes. Pure and Applied Mathematics, vol. 240. CRC Press (2001)

Protein Networks by Invariant Shape Coordinates and Deformation Indexes

Lombardi Andrea[⊠], Noelia Faginas-Lago, and Leonardo Pacifici

Dipartimento di Chimica, Biologia e Biotecnologie,
Università di Perugia, Perugia & UdR INSTM di Perugia,
Via Elce di Sotto 8, 06123 Perugia, Italy
andrea.lombardi@unipg.it, noelia.faginaslago@unipg.it
http://www.chm.unipg.it/gruppi?q=node/48

Abstract. The classification of proteins according to structural similarities is an increasingly relevant issue in biochemistry in the upcoming big data era. Proper choices of parameters, containing invariant structural information, could possibly induce convenient grouping of structures depending on structural motifs or also individual amino acid properties. Here, we give a summary of the theoretical background of parameter derivation from many-body hyperspherical coordinates and continue a previous work based on the use of shape parameters and deformation indexes. Such quantities are derived from "symmetric" hyperspherical coordinates and applied to a large set of protein structures each represented as a network of nodes corresponding to the amino acid residue centers of mass.

Keywords: Protein structure classification · Hyperspherical coordinates · Invariant shape coordinates

1 Introduction

The understanding of the biological function of proteins and the relationship with the structures of these complex molecules is mainly based upon their classification in families and, as far as it concerns the arrangement of atoms and residues, domains. A proper understanding of folding is also directly related to the knowledge of such aspects. Depending on the choice of parameters and on the schematic representation that is assigned to protein geometry (e.g. networks), different classifications can be induced and patterns can be revealed through application to large set of structures. Such parameters have to be preferably invariant and uniquely associated to a given molecular geometry by a simple and clear mathematical procedure applied to the corresponding atomic coordinate set. A first obvious use of a well grounded statistics of such parameters could be as a test for the realism and accuracy of the experimental measured and theoretically predicted structures. The increasing use computational approaches based upon deep learning are expected to further enhance the potential use of new parameters for the discovery of hidden patterns and regularities [1,2].

O. Gervasi et al. (Eds.): ICCSA 2022 Workshops, LNCS 13382, pp. 348–359, 2022.
https://doi.org/10.1007/978-3-031-10592-0_26

The hyperspherical coordinates were originally adopted for quantum reactive scattering calculations, introducing convenient sets of invariant parameters. This approach can be extended to the general molecular dynamics of many-body systems, therefore directly applicable to large biomolecules. The fundamental feature of quantum hyperspherical dynamics are the hyperspherical functions which are used as wavefunction expansion basis set [3–5] for three and four-body collisions (see e.g. [6–11]). The specific form of such functions depends on the symmetry properties characterizing the set of angles adopted as coordinates, for which many choices are possible. Particularly, the Hamiltonian operator expressed in terms of the so called "symmetric" hyperspherical coordinates is a preferred choice since it is invariant with respect to all the possible product channels that characterize the given system. The clarity of the mathematical formulation and the computational efficiency is greatly improved if the same hyperspherical basis functions are combined as finite sums to represent the intermolecular and intramolecular interactions, see [12–39].

The hyperspherical coordinates are characterized by a partition of the degrees of freedom in terms of shape coordinates, ordinary rotation and kinematic rotation angles [8,40–44]. The kinetic energy associated to these different sets of degrees of freedom can be evaluated by classical mechanics as a function of hyperangular momenta. When applied to classical molecular dynamics simulations, the hyperspherical coordinates are not directly used in the integration of Hamilton's equations, since a procedure based on matrix transformations of the position vectors allows for the calculation of the energy contributions in the Hyperspherical Hamilton function as a function of time using Cartesian coordinates [8,41].

The key point for our work is that in the framework of hyperspherical coordinates the global shape of the system defined by the above mentioned shape coordinates is invariant under the action of both ordinary and kinematic rotations and so are the coordinates themselves [40,45–50]. Convenient shape parameters, to be used in classification studies of protein structures, can therefore be defined in terms of such hyperspherical degrees of freedom.

The paper is written according to the following scheme. In Sect. 2 the basic theory of hyperspherical coordinates, shape parameters and deformation indexes is outlined. Applications to a large set of protein structures is illustrated in Sect. 3. Sect. 4 draws conclusions and guesses perspectives.

2   Methodology

The $N-1$ Jacobi vectors $\mathbf{Q}_\alpha$, where $\alpha = 1, \cdots, N-1$, are the starting point to obtain the hyperspherical coordinates of a system of N particles. The Jacobi vectors are a combinations of the position vectors of the N particles in the center of mass reference frame, denoted as $\mathbf{r}_\alpha$ [40]. The recipe to construct them is as follows: take the vector which connects particles 1 and 2, then a second connecting the center of mass of the particle pair to a third one, and so on. The procedure ends with the $(N-1)$th vector, which connects the center of mass of the first

$N-1$ particles to the Nth particle. The combination coefficients depends on the mass of the individual particles, see next Sect. 2.1 for more details. Being a generalization of spherical coordinates, the hyperspherical ones, applicable to the general N particle case, have an hyperradius ρ in place of the radius, defined as simply the modulus of a vector of dimension $3N - 3$, spanning the configuration space of the system. The Cartesian components of the hyperradial vector are just the Jacobi vector components. The transformation linking the Jacobi vector components with the hyperradius and the remaining $3N - 4$ "hyperangles", mathematically defines the hyperspherical coordinates. The angular coordinates can be chosen in many alternative ways, but the one useful for us is that leading to the so called "symmetric" hyperspherical coordinates. The symmetric hyperspherical coordinates are obtained by a matrix transformation known as *singular value decomposition*, applied to the position matrix containing column-wise the Cartesian vector of the particle system. The details of such transformation are described in the following section.

2.1   Properties of the Hyperspherical Coordinates

The *singular value decomposition* [51] is a theorem for matrix decomposition that is valid for any 3 x N position matrix constructed starting from a given set of N vectors, by arranging them column-wise and is the mathematical tool for a general definition of such coordinates.

Given $N \geq 2$ particles with masses $m_1, \cdots, m_N$ and radial position vectors in the center of mass reference frame, $\mathbf{r_1}, \cdots, \mathbf{r_N}$, a corresponding set of mass *scaled* radii vectors, $\mathbf{q}_\alpha = (m_\alpha/M)^{1/2}\mathbf{r}_\alpha$ $(1 \leq \alpha \leq N)$, can be obtained, where $M = \sum_\alpha^N m_\alpha$ is the total mass of the system.

The $3 \times N$ position matrix is denoted by Z and contains, column-wise, the mass scaled vectors whose components are denoted as q_{ij}:

$$Z = \begin{pmatrix} q_{1,1} & q_{1,2} & \cdots & q_{1,N} \\ q_{2,1} & q_{2,2} & \cdots & q_{2,N} \\ q_{3,1} & q_{3,2} & \cdots & q_{3,N} \end{pmatrix} . \tag{1}$$

The orthogonal matrix R^t (transpose of a matrix $R \in O(3)$) can act on the position matrix Z by left-multiplication generating rotations in the three-dimensional physical space. Also, an orthogonal matrix $K \in O(N)$ can act on the position matrix by right-multiplication, and rotates the coordinate frame in the so called *kinematic space* [7,41], $Z' = ZK$.

Allowed K matrices have, for example, the following form:

$$K = \begin{pmatrix} k_{1,1} & k_{1,2} & \cdots & (m_1/M)^{1/2} \\ k_{2,1} & k_{2,2} & \cdots & (m_2/M)^{1/2} \\ \cdots & \cdots & \cdots & \cdots \\ k_{N,1} & k_{N,2} & \cdots & (m_N/M)^{1/2} \end{pmatrix} \tag{2}$$

such matrices applied to the Z matrix generate a subset of all the possible Cartesian frames. Note that the last column of such Z matrices are identically zero, due to the separation of center of mass motion, so the number of degrees of freedom is reduced to $3N - 3$. The matrix Z with one less column is called *reduced position matrix*.

The sets of (N-1) Jacobi and related vectors always generate reduced matrices.

Many different linear combinations of the N Cartesian particle position vectors satisfying the Jacobi vector definition can be generated as a function of the particle masses [40,52]. Some of the different resulting vector sets resemble the asymptotic (reactive) channels of the system; remarkably, properly defined kinematic rotations smoothly connect them.

The *singular value decomposition* applied to the $3 \times n$ position matrix Z (where $n = N$ or $n = N - 1$) results in a product of three matrices:

$$Z = R \Xi K^t \tag{3}$$

where $R \in O(3)$ and $K \in O(n)$ are 3×3 and $3 \times n$ orthogonal matrices, respectively. The elements of the $3 \times n$ matrix Ξ are zeroes, with the possible exception of the three diagonal entries, $\Xi_{11} = \xi_1, \Xi_{22} = \xi_2, \Xi_{33} = \xi_3$, which are subjected to the inequality $\xi_1 \geq \xi_2 \geq \xi_3 \geq 0$.

The values ξ_i, ($i = 1, 2, 3$) are called the *singular values* of the matrix Z and are uniquely determined, although the factors R and K in Eq. 3 are not. If $N \leq 3$ and Z is the full $3 \times N$ position matrix, then the smallest singular value ξ_3 is necessarily zero. The hyperradius and the ξ's are connected as follows [40,41]:

$$\xi_1^2 + \xi_2^2 + \xi_3^2 = \rho^2. \tag{4}$$

We remark that the ξ's are invariant under both ordinary rotations in the three-dimensional physical space and kinematic rotations [7,8,41,53]. This invariance makes the ξ's appropriate as parameters for molecular dynamics [40,54–57] and for the study of the minimum energy structures of N-particle systems.

It is worth to mention the special case $n = N - 1 = 3$, where the matrix Z represents four particles or four center systems and the R and K matrices cannot be chosen to be *special orthogonal* ($R \in SO(3)$ and $K \in SO(n)$), but have to be simple orthogonal matrices ($O(3)$). Accordingly if the determinant of Z is lower than zero, its sign depends on the sign of the product of the ξ's, and so one has $\xi_3 \leq 0$. This fact is directly connected to the mirror image and chirality sign of the system [45,58,59].

2.2   The Deformation Indexes

The singular values (ξ_1, ξ_2, ξ_3), are not only invariant under kinematic and ordinary rotations [60], they are also related to the moments of inertia of the system:

$$\frac{I_1}{M} = \xi_2^2 + \xi_3^2$$

$$\frac{I_2}{M} = \xi_1^2 + \xi_3^2 \qquad (5)$$

$$\frac{I_3}{M} = \xi_1^2 + \xi_2^2$$

where I_1, I_2 and I_3 are the moments of inertia in the principal axis reference frame. These three parameters therefore account for the mass distribution with respect to the principal axis frame and are consequently referred to as shape coordinates. From Eq. 4 one obtains:

$$I_1 + I_2 + I_3 = 2M\rho^2. \qquad (6)$$

The relative values of the ξ's determine whether the system is an asymmetric, symmetric or spherical rotor. Spherical top configurations are those for which $\xi_1 = \xi_2 = \xi_3$, prolate tops those for which $\xi_3 = \xi_2 < \xi_1$, while oblate tops occur when $\xi_1 = \xi_2 > \xi_3$.

The ξ's can be represented in terms of the hyperradius and two angles θ and ϕ as follows:

$$\xi_1 = \rho \sin \theta \cos \phi$$

$$\xi_2 = \rho \sin \theta \sin \phi \qquad (7)$$

$$\xi_2 = \rho \cos \theta$$

Parameters measuring the deviation from the spherical top shapes, can be conveniently introduced as *deformation indexes* [40]:

$$\xi_+ = \frac{\xi_2^2 - \xi_3^2}{\rho^2}, \quad \xi_+ \geq 0 \qquad (8)$$

which is zero for prolate top configurations, and

$$\xi_- = \frac{\xi_2^2 - \xi_1^2}{\rho^2}, \quad \xi_- \leq 0 \qquad (9)$$

which is zero for oblate top configurations. By definition, when both indexes are zero, one has a spherical rotor.

3   Invariant and Deformation Index Distribution for Protein Structures

Given a certain molecular structure, the procedure illustrated in Previous Sects. 2.1 and 2.2 gives an explicit procedure to uniquely associate to any molecular structures, expressed as a collection of atomic Cartesian coordinates, a set of values of the ξ's and of the deformation indexes.

In a previous work [61] we considered application to single protein structures for which the shape coordinates and the deformation indexes, as defined in the previous sections where calculated for three single amino acids (glycine, GLY, proline, PRO and alanine, ALA). In a another previous work a similar study was applied to Lennard-Jones clusters and chiral molecules [48, 62]. To simplify the application of the above theory, we observe that there is actually no need to perform the complete singular value decomposition, since only the singular values are needed, so one can derive the following relation from Eq. 3:

$$ZZ^t = R\Xi\Xi^t R^t \tag{10}$$

where the product $\Xi\Xi^t$ is a 3×3 square diagonal matrix, whose entries are the squares of the ξ's. The diagonal entries are just the eigenvalues of the product matrix ZZ^t, obtained from the position matrix. Once the ZZ^t matrix is built from the Cartesian components of the mass scaled atomic position vectors (see Sect. 2.1), this can be diagonalized by a numerical procedure or by the Cardano's formula for the third degree characteristic equation [40].

Here we extend the application of the hyperspherical method to a large set of structures from the Protein Data Bank [63]. For each structure the Cartesian coordinates have been extracted and used to build up the product matrix of Eq. 10 and to calculate the ξ values and the deformation indexes of Eqs. 8 and 9. We analyzed separately the ξ's and the deformation indexes for three representative amino acids, Glycine (GLY), Proline (PRO) and Alanine (ALA), considering their local structures as they occur in the protein chain (also repeatedly), for the large set of structures and also for the entire set of natural amino acids. In Fig. 1 the deformation indexes ξ_+ and ξ_- are represented in a 2-dimensional plot, accurately defining allowed index subspace for the three amino acid structures within proteins.

In Fig. 2 the values of the individual shape coordinates ξ_1, ξ_2 and ξ_3 are shown as two-dimensional plots, for the whole structure set for all natural amino acids. It is confirmed from previous figures that parameters and shape coordinates are not uniformly distributed but tend to be localized in a subset of the coordinate and parameter spaces. Being the set of structures considered here quite large (around 23000), we assume it to be potentially representative of all known proteins and the obtained plot to be an image of the "allowed" regions in the parameter space.

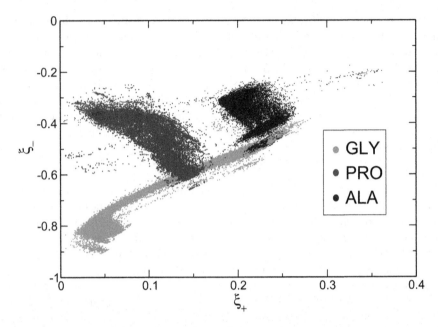

Fig. 1. Two-dimensional plot of the ξ_- and ξ_+ invariant deformation indexes, for the GLY, PRO and ALA amino acid configuration, as obtained from the large set of protein structures from the database [63]

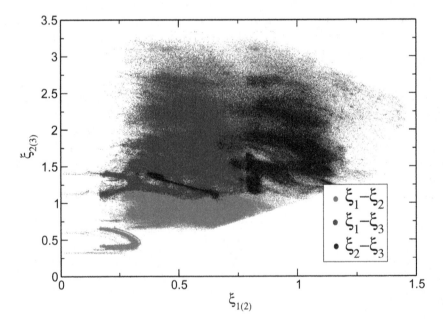

Fig. 2. Two-dimensional plots of the ξ_i, $i = 1, 2, 3$, invariant shape coordinates, for all the natural amino acids as occurring in the structure obtained from the database [63].

4   Conclusions

In this paper we analyzed a large set of protein structures using invariant structure parameters derived from hyperspherical coordinates. Using both shape coordinates and deformation indexes their distribution and the corresponding "allowed" regions in the parameter space have been obtained for three amino acids and for all the natural amino acids. This work is preluding to a systematic application of such parameters for the classification of protein molecular structures.

Acknowledgments. Thanks are due to the Dipartimento di Chimica, Biologia e Biotecnologie dell'Università di Perugia (FRB, Fondo per la Ricerca di Base 2019 and 2020) and to the MIUR and the University of Perugia for the financial support of the AMIS project through the program "Dipartimenti di Eccellenza". A.L and N.F-L. thank Fondazione Cassa di Risparmio di Perugia for funding through project n.# 220.0513 to C.E. A.L. acknowledges financial support from Fondo Ricerca di Base 2021 (RICBASE2021LOMBARDI) MIUR PRIN 2015. A.L. thanks the OU Supercomputing Center for Education & Research (OSCER) at the University of Oklahoma, for allocated computing time.

References

1. Perri, D., Simonetti, M., Lombardi, A., Faginas-Lago, N., Gervasi, O.: Binary classification of proteins by a machine learning approach. In: Gervasi, O., et al. (eds.) ICCSA 2020. LNCS, vol. 12255, pp. 549–558. Springer, Cham (2020). https://doi.org/10.1007/978-3-030-58820-5_41

2. Perri, D., Simonetti, M., Lombardi, A., Faginas-Lago, N., Gervasi, O.: A new method for binary classification of proteins with machine learning. In: Gervasi, O., et al. (eds.) ICCSA 2021. LNCS, vol. 12958, pp. 388–397. Springer, Cham (2021). https://doi.org/10.1007/978-3-030-87016-4_29

3. Zhao, B., Guo, H.: State-to-state quantum reactive scattering in four-atom systems. WIREs Comput. Mol. Sci. **7**(3), e1301 (2017)

4. Skouteris, D., Castillo, J., Manolopoulos, D.E.: Abc: a quantum reactive scattering program. Comput. Phys. Comm. **133**(1), 128–135 (2000)

5. Lepetit, B., Launay, J.M.: Quantum-mechanical study of the reaction $He+H_2^+ \rightarrow HeH^+ + H$ with hyperspherical coordinates. J. Chem. Phys. **95**(7), 5159–5168 (1991)

6. Aquilanti, V., Beddoni, A., Cavalli, S., Lombardi, A., Littlejohn, R.: Collective hyperspherical coordinates for polyatomic molecules and clusters. Mol. Phys. **98**(21), 1763–1770 (2000)

7. Aquilanti, V., Beddoni, A., Lombardi, A., Littlejohn, R.: Hyperspherical harmonics for polyatomic systems: Basis set for kinematic rotations. Int. J. Quantum Chem. **89**(4), 277–291 (2002)

8. Aquilanti, V., Lombardi, A., Littlejohn, R.G.: Hyperspherical harmonics for polyatomic systems: basis set for collective motions. Theoret. Chem. Acc. **111**(2), 400–406 (2003). https://doi.org/10.1007/s00214-003-0526-3

9. Kuppermann, A.: Quantum reaction dynamics and hyperspherical harmonics. Isr. J. Chem. **43**(3–4), 229 (2003)

10. De Fazio, D., Cavalli, S., Aquilanti, V.: Benchmark quantum mechanical calculations of vibrationally resolved cross sections and rate constants on ab initio potential energy surfaces for the F + HD reaction: comparisons with experiments. J. Phys. Chem. A **120**(27), 5288–5299 (2016)

11. Aquilanti, V., Cavalli, S.: The quantum-mechanical hamiltonian for tetraatomic systems in symmetric hyperspherical coordinates. J. Chem. Soc. Faraday Trans. **93**(5), 801–809 (1997)

12. Barreto, P.R.P., Vilela, A.F.A., Lombardi, A., Maciel, G.S., Palazzetti, F., Aquilanti, V.: The hydrogen peroxide-rare gas systems: quantum chemical calculations and hyperspherical harmonic representation of the potential energy surface for atom-floppy molecule interactions. J. Phys. Chem. A **111**(49), 12754–12762 (2007)

13. Lombardi, A., Laganà, A., Pirani, F., Palazzetti, F., Lago, N.F.: Carbon oxides in gas flows and earth and planetary atmospheres: state-to-state simulations of energy transfer and dissociation reactions. In: Murgante, B., et al. (eds.) ICCSA 2013. LNCS, vol. 7972, pp. 17–31. Springer, Heidelberg (2013). https://doi.org/10.1007/978-3-642-39643-4_2

14. Lago, N.F., Albertí, M., Laganà, A., Lombardi, A.: Water $(H_2O)_m$ or benzene $(C_6H_6)_n$ aggregates to solvate the K^+. In: Murgante, B., et al. (eds.) ICCSA 2013. LNCS, vol. 7971, pp. 1–15. Springer, Heidelberg (2013). https://doi.org/10.1007/978-3-642-39637-3_1

15. Faginas-Lago, N., Albertí, M., Costantini, A., Laganà, A., Lombardi, A., Pacifici, L.: An innovative synergistic grid approach to the computational study of protein aggregation mechanisms. J. Mol. Model. **20**(7), 1–9 (2014). https://doi.org/10.1007/s00894-014-2226-4

16. Faginas-Lago, N., Yeni, D., Huarte, F., Alcamì, M., Martin, F.: Adsorption of hydrogen molecules on carbon nanotubes using quantum chemistry and molecular dynamics. J. Phys. Chem. A **120**, 6451–6458 (2016)

17. Faginas-Lago, N., Lombardi, A., Albertí, M., Grossi, G.: Accurate analytic intermolecular potential for the simulation of Na^+ and K^+ ion hydration in liquid water. J. Mol. Liq. **204**, 192–197 (2015)

18. Albertí, M., Faginas Lago, N.: Competitive solvation of K^+ by C_6H_6 and H_2O in the K^+-$(C_6h_6)_n$-$(H_2O)_m$ (n = 1–4; m = 1–6) aggregates. Eur. Phys. J. D **67**, 73 (2013). https://doi.org/10.1140/epjd/e2013-30753-x

19. Albertí, M., Faginas Lago, N.: Ion size influence on the Ar solvation shells of M^+-C_6F_6 clusters (m = na, k, rb, cs). J. Phys. Chem. A **116**, 3094–3102 (2012)

20. Albertí, M., Faginas Lago, N., Pirani, F.: Ar solvation shells in K^+-HFBz: from cluster rearrangement to solvation dynamics. J. Phys. Chem. A **115**(40), 10871–10879 (2011)

21. Lago, N.F., Albertí, M., Laganà, A., Lombardi, A., Pacifici, L., Costantini, A.: The molecular stirrer catalytic effect in methane ice formation. In: Murgante, B., et al. (eds.) ICCSA 2014. LNCS, vol. 8579, pp. 585–600. Springer, Cham (2014). https://doi.org/10.1007/978-3-319-09144-0_40

22. Faginas-Lago, N., Huarte Larrañaga, F., Albertí, M.: On the suitability of the ILJ function to match different formulations of the electrostatic potential for water-water interactions. Eur. Phys. J. D **55**(1), 75–85 (2009). https://doi.org/10.1140/epjd/e2009-00215-5

23. Bartolomei, M., Pirani, F., Laganà, A., Lombardi, A.: A full dimensional grid empowered simulation of the CO_2+ CO_2 processes. J. Comp. Chem. **33**(22), 1806–1819 (2012)

24. Lombardi, A., Lago, N.F., Laganà, A., Pirani, F., Falcinelli, S.: A bond-bond portable approach to intermolecular interactions: simulations for N-methylacetamide and carbon dioxide dimers. In: Murgante, B., et al. (eds.) ICCSA 2012. LNCS, vol. 7333, pp. 387–400. Springer, Heidelberg (2012). https://doi.org/10.1007/978-3-642-31125-3_30

25. Albertí, M., Faginas-Lago, N., Laganà, A., Pirani, F.: A portable intermolecular potential for molecular dynamics studies of NMA-NMA and NMA-H_2O aggregates. Phys. Chem. Chem. Phys. 13(18), 8422–8432 (2011)

26. Albertí, M., Faginas-Lago, N., Pirani, F.: Benzene water interaction: from gaseous dimers to solvated aggregates. Chem. Phys. 399, 232 (2012)

27. Falcinelli, S., Rosi, M., Candori, P., Vecchiocattivi, F., Bartocci, A., Lombardi, A., Lago, N.F., Pirani, F.: Modeling the intermolecular interactions and characterization of the dynamics of collisional autoionization processes. In: Murgante, B., et al. (eds.) ICCSA 2013. LNCS, vol. 7971, pp. 69–83. Springer, Heidelberg (2013). https://doi.org/10.1007/978-3-642-39637-3_6

28. Lombardi, A., Faginas-Lago, N., Pacifici, L., Costantini, A.: Modeling of energy transfer from vibrationally excited CO_2 molecules: cross sections and probabilities for kinetic modeling of atmospheres, flows, and plasmas. J. Phys. Chem. A 117(45), 11430–11440 (2013)

29. Lombardi, A., Pirani, F., Laganà, A., Bartolomei, M.: Energy transfer dynamics and kinetics of elementary processes (promoted) by gas-phase CO_2-N_2 collisions: selectivity control by the anisotropy of the interaction. J. Comp. Chem. 37(16), 1463–1475 (2016)

30. Pacifici, L., Verdicchio, M., Faginas-Lago, N., Lombardi, A., Costantini, A.: A high-level ab initio study of the n2 + n2 reaction channel. J. Comput. Chem. 34(31), 2668–2676 (2013)

31. Lombardi, A., Faginas-Lago, N., Pacifici, L., Grossi, G.: Energy transfer upon collision of selectively excited CO_2 molecules: state-to-state cross sections and probabilities for modeling of atmospheres and gaseous flows. J. Chem. Phys. 143, 034307 (2015)

32. Celiberto, R., Armenise, I., Cacciatore, M., Capitelli, M., Esposito, F., Gamallo, P., Janev, R., Lagana, A., Laporta, V., Laricchiuta, A., et al.: Atomic and molecular data for spacecraft re-entry plasmas. Plasma Sources Sci. Technol. 25(3), 033004 (2016)

33. Faginas-Lago, N., Lombardi, A., Albertí, M.: Aqueous n-methylacetamide: new analytic potentials and a molecular dynamics study. J. Mol. Liq. 224, 792–800 (2016)

34. Palazzetti, F., Munusamy, E., Lombardi, A., Grossi, G., Aquilanti, V.: Spherical and hyperspherical representation of potential energy surfaces for intermolecular interactions. Int. J. Quantum Chem. 111(2), 318–332 (2011)

35. Lombardi, A., Palazzetti, F.: A comparison of interatomic potentials for rare gas nanoaggregates. J. Mol. Struct. (Thoechem) 852(1–3), 22–29 (2008)

36. Barreto, P.R., Albernaz, A.F., Palazzetti, F., Lombardi, A., Grossi, G., Aquilanti, V.: Hyperspherical representation of potential energy surfaces: intermolecular interactions in tetra-atomic and penta-atomic systems. Phys. Scr. 84(2), 028111 (2011)

37. Barreto, P.R., Albernaz, A.F., Capobianco, A., Palazzetti, F., Lombardi, A., Grossi, G., Aquilanti, V.: Potential energy surfaces for interactions of H_2O with H_2, N_2 and O_2: a hyperspherical harmonics representation, and a minimal model for the H_2O-rare-gas-atom systems. Comput. Theor. Chem. 990, 53–61 (2012)

38. Lombardi, A., Pirani, F., Bartolomei, M., Coletti, C., Laganà, A.: A full dimensional potential energy function and the calculation of the state-specific properties of the CO+ N_2 inelastic processes within an open molecular science cloud perspective. Front. Chem. **7**, 309 (2019)

39. Faginas Lago, N., Lombardi, A., Vekeman, J., Rosi, M., et al.: Molecular dynamics of CH_4/N_2 mixtures on a flexible graphene layer: adsorption and selectivity case study. Front. Chem. **7**, 386 (2019)

40. Aquilanti, V., Lombardi, A., Yurtsever, E.: Global view of classical clusters: the hyperspherical approach to structure and dynamics. Phys. Chem. Chem. Phys. **4**(20), 5040–5051 (2002)

41. Sevryuk, M.B., Lombardi, A., Aquilanti, V.: Hyperangular momenta and energy partitions in multidimensional many-particle classical mechanics: the invariance approach to cluster dynamics. Phys. Rev. A **72**(3), 033201 (2005)

42. Castro Palacio, J., Velazquez Abad, L., Lombardi, A., Aquilanti, V., Rubayo Soneira, J.: Normal and hyperspherical mode analysis of no-doped Kr crystals upon Rydberg excitation of the impurity. J. Chem. Phys. **126**(17), 174701 (2007)

43. Lombardi, Andrea, Palazzetti, Federico, Aquilanti, Vincenzo: Molecular dynamics of chiral molecules in hyperspherical coordinates. In: Misra, S., et al. (eds.) ICCSA 2019. LNCS, vol. 11624, pp. 413–427. Springer, Cham (2019). https://doi.org/10.1007/978-3-030-24311-1_30

44. Lombardi, A., Palazzetti, F., Sevryuk, M.B.: Hyperspherical coordinates and energy partitions for reactive processes and clusters. In: AIP Conference Proceedings, Vol. 2186, p. 030014. AIP Publishing LLC (2019)

45. Lombardi, A., Palazzetti, F.: Chirality in molecular collision dynamics. J. Phys.: Condens. Matter **30**(6), 063003 (2018)

46. Lombardi, A., Palazzetti, F., Peroncelli, L., Grossi, G., Aquilanti, V., Sevryuk, M.: Few-body quantum and many-body classical hyperspherical approaches to reactions and to cluster dynamics. Theoret. Chem. Acc. **117**(5–6), 709–721 (2007)

47. Aquilanti, V., Grossi, G., Lombardi, A., Maciel, G.S., Palazzetti, F.: Aligned molecular collisions and a stereodynamical mechanism for selective chirality. Rend. Fis. Acc. Lincei **22**, 125–135 (2011)

48. Lombardi, A., Faginas-Lago, N., Aquilanti, V.: The Invariance approach to structure and dynamics: classical hyperspherical coordinates. In: Misra, S., et al. (eds.) ICCSA 2019. LNCS, vol. 11624, pp. 428–438. Springer, Cham (2019). https://doi.org/10.1007/978-3-030-24311-1_31

49. Caglioti, C., Dos Santos, R.F., Lombardi, A., Palazzetti, F., Aquilanti, V.: Screens displaying structural properties of aminoacids in polypeptide chains: alanine as a case study. In: Misra, S., et al. (eds.) ICCSA 2019. LNCS, vol. 11624, pp. 439–449. Springer, Cham (2019). https://doi.org/10.1007/978-3-030-24311-1_32

50. Caglioti, C., Ferreira, R.d.S., Palazzetti, F., Lombardi, A., Aquilanti, V.: Screen representation of structural properties of alanine in polypeptide chains. In: AIP Conference Proceedings, Vol. 2186, p. 030015, AIP Publishing LLC (2019)

51. Horn, R.A., Johnson, C.R.: Matrix Analysis, 2nd edn. University Press, Cambridge (1990)

52. Gatti, F., Lung, C.: Vector parametrization of the n-atom problem in quantum mechanics. I. Jacobi vectors. J. Chem. Phys. **108**(21), 8804–8820 (1998)

53. Aquilanti, V., Lombardi, A., Sevryuk, M.B.: Phase-space invariants for aggregates of particles: hyperangular momenta and partitions of the classical kinetic energy. J. Chem. Phys. **121**(12), 5579–5589 (2004)

54. Aquilanti, V., Carmona Novillo, E., Garcia, E., Lombardi, A., Sevryuk, M.B., Yurtsever, E.: Invariant energy partitions in chemical reactions and cluster dynamics simulations. Comput. Mat. Sci. **35**(3), 187–191 (2006)
55. Aquilanti, V., Lombardi, A., Sevryuk, M.B., Yurtsever, E.: Phase-space invariants as indicators of the critical behavior of nanoaggregates. Phys. Rev. Lett. **93**(11), 113402 (2004)
56. Calvo, F., Gadea, X., Lombardi, A., Aquilanti, V.: Isomerization dynamics and thermodynamics of ionic argon clusters. J. Chem. Phys. **125**(11), 114307 (2006)
57. Lombardi, A., Aquilanti, V., Yurtsever, E., Sevryuk, M.B.: Specific heats of clusters near a phase transition: energy partitions among internal modes. Chem. Phys. Lett. **30**(4–6), 424–428 (2006)
58. Lombardi, A., Maciel, G.S., Palazzetti, F., Grossi, G., Aquilanti, V.: Alignment and chirality in gaseous flows. J. Vac. Soc. Jpn. **53**(11), 645–653 (2010)
59. Palazzetti, F., Tsai, P.Y., Lombardi, A., Nakamura, M., Che, D.C., Kasai, T., Lin, K.C., Aquilanti, V.: Aligned molecules: chirality discrimination in photodissociation and in molecular dynamics. Rend. Lincei **24**(3), 299–308 (2013)
60. Littlejohn, R.G., Mitchell, A., Aquilanti, V.: Quantum dynamics of kinematic invariants in tetra-and polyatomic systems. Phys. Chem. Chem. Phys. **1**, 1259–1264 (1999)
61. Lombardi, A.: Symmetry and deformations of cluster and biomolecules by invariant shape coordinates. In: AIP Conference Proceedings, Vol. 2343, p. 020004. AIP Publishing LLC (2021)
62. Lombardi, A., Palazzetti, F., Aquilanti, V.: Molecular dynamics of chiral molecules in hyperspherical coordinates. In: Misra, S., et al. (eds.) ICCSA 2019. LNCS, vol. 11624, pp. 413–427. Springer, Cham (2019). https://doi.org/10.1007/978-3-030-24311-1_30
63. Berman, H., Westbrook, J., Feng, Z., Gilliland, G., Bhat, T., Weissig, H., Shindyalov, I., Bourne, P.: The protein data bank. Nucleic Acid Res. **28**(1), 235–242 (2000)

International Workshop on Urban Form Studies (UForm 2022)

Modernist Housing Estates – Examining the Conditions of Redevelopment of Outdoor Space. The Case Study from Łódź, Bałuty

Małgorzata Hanzl[(⊠)] [ID]

Institute of Architecture and Town Planning, Lodz University of Technology,
Al. Politechniki 6A, 93-590 Lodz, Poland
mhanzl@p.lodz.pl

Abstract. The focus of the current paper is the form of outdoor space in Modernist housing estates. I examine relationships between urban health and liveability and forms of urban structures. The goal is to define the quantitative and qualitative features of the urban environment that influence the liveability of these places and evaluate their impacts. I look at forms of open spaces and their organisation. Special attention is paid to the qualities of green infrastructures (GI) and the characteristics of built structures. Modernist theoretical thinking attributed a lot of attention to assuring proper insolation thanks to the provision of ample space between buildings. However, the implementation of these ideas often lacked consistency. With time, the initial provision of green landscaped recreational space imagined by designers became replaced by congested parking lots. Once proposed as safe and cosy, actual resulting places proved windy and often isolated. In the current article, I examine the details of two housing estates located in Bałuty in Łódź. The objective of this analysis is to propose recommendations on how to improve the current situation and, at the same time, the living conditions of local residents.

Keywords: Public space · Liveability · Urban form · Morphology

1 Introduction

The current paper examines the outdoor space in the Modernist housing estates. The objective is to determine the quantitative and qualitative features of the urban environment that affect the liveability of these places and evaluate their impacts. I focus on forms of open spaces, the qualities of green infrastructures (GI) and built structures attributes.

First, the positive impact of greenery on citizens' well-being is broadly recognized; it belongs to essential exogenous factors that condition urban health. Vegetation reduces local temperatures due to evapotranspiration, provides shade and reflects solar radiation. At the same time, it absorbs air pollutants and reduces noise levels. Moreover, parks, gardens, and access to street vegetation encourage social life and physical activities. They reduce stress and help to relax, which enhances residents' mental health. Furthermore, vegetation contributes to buffering climate change risks.

© The Author(s), under exclusive license to Springer Nature Switzerland AG 2022
O. Gervasi et al. (Eds.): ICCSA 2022 Workshops, LNCS 13382, pp. 363–378, 2022.
https://doi.org/10.1007/978-3-031-10592-0_27

Second, forms of streets and open spaces affect the availability of infrastructure for various activities and mobility modes. Access to open space in the built environment has an impact on residents' lifestyles and well-being.

The current paper applies qualitative and quantitative assessment to a modernist housing estate in Bałuty, Łódź, Poland. Studying the typologies of residential structures from the 20th century, we notice the evolution of forms. The focus on residents' well-being reveals the changing roles and forms of the urban environment. The typomorphological approach proves helpful in defining the current rehabilitation strategies of modernist housing estates.

2 Research Background

2.1 Liveability and Health

Cambridge Dictionary defines liveability as *"the degree to which a place is suitable or good for living in"*. The term liveability has got multiple meanings. The concept emerged in Dutch spatial planning in the 1950s (Kaal 2011), and since it has become broadly used in various geographical and disciplinary contexts (McCann 2007, 2013; Holden and Scerri 2013; Wetzstein 2013; Teo 2014; Zhan et al. 2018; McArthur and Robin 2019; Paul and Sen 2020). Furthermore, numerous liveability indexes brought immense popularity among city governments looking to attract investments and global capital (Holden and Scerri 2013). The term is broadly used in policy documents and urban strategies (Clarke and Cheshire 2018) and has become one of the main topics of global discourse proliferating into the policy of international organisations (UN Habitat 2008, 2016; World Bank 1996, McArthur and Robin 2019). These documents present urban health and environmental resilience as essential elements of a liveable urban environment (UN Habitat 2016; WHO 2016). The importance of health as a nexus of urban design is supported by ample evidence (Saelens and Handy 2008; Jackson et al. 2013; Giles-Corti et al. 2016; Forsyth et al. 2017). Improved liveability equals residents' health and wellbeing and vice versa. Among various aspects of liveability, researchers list:

- access to public transport (Knuiman et al. 2014),
- walkability (Frank et al., 2006; Hirsch et al. 2014),
- access to multiple forms of urban greenery and recreation facilities (Sugiyama et al. 2013; Kaczynski et al. 2008; Mitchell and Popham 2008; Gascon et al. 2015).

Research provides substantial evidence that these factors affect both physical fitness and mental health (Alderton et al. 2019; Forsyth et al. 2017, Sarkar et al. 2014).

Moreover, studies (Forsyth and Musacchio 2005, pp. 3–5; Marselle et al. 2019) show that green space works the best when its various forms contribute to a system which offers a range of activities for various users. The overlap of activities also proves beneficial for specific users (Sarkar et al. 2014, p. 102). All of them should be open to all users, including those with mobility impairments and endangered by social exclusion (Harnick 2006, p. 57). The main criteria for the evaluation of green space are (Forsyth et al. 2017):

1. Access - physical access refers to the optimum distance to a park of a minimum size of 5 ha, which should be between 400 to 800 m for all the buildings. It can be enhanced thanks to the public transportation opportunities. Visual access – the later was confirmed by the study on patients' recovery (Brown et al. 2013).
2. Connections - they offer system qualities and include rows of trees in streets, boulevards or greenways and distinct paths and green trails.
3. Variety of forms - as an element which offers a range of available activities.

The forms of green spaces include (Forsyth et al. 2017): urban parks, including pocket parks, recreational facilities (e.g., playgrounds), trails, paths and greenways, tree lines, tree canopy, greenery near buildings.

A special quality which should be emphasised in the current study is safety from traffic and the availability of outdoor spaces and recreation settings and vegetation suitable for young children (0 to 7 years old). (Christian et al. 2015, pp. 30–33). When open space is limited, some benefits for residents' psychological wellbeing might be satisfied thanks to the small green yards, tree lines along streets, and even visual access to verdure from windows (Forsyth et al. 2017; Brown et al. 2013).

Moreover, green open spaces reduce summer temperatures and regulate Urban Heat Island (UHI), contribute to water retention and reduce noise and pollution levels. In the current study, I am looking to apply the results of contemporary research on liveability and urban health to assess Modernist residential development.

2.2 Modernist Concepts Versus the Organisation of Open Space

The debate on living conditions in cities started in reaction to worsening urban environments as a nexus of 19th-century industrialisation and urbanisation processes. Early hygienist movement and efforts to improve sanitary conditions led to the implementation of new building regulations at the beginning of the 20th century; for instance, in Germany, new construction codes were adopted in 1925. One focus of these debates was the integration of green spaces, which were perceived as a remedy to the artificial urban environment. These discussions continued as one of the core concepts of the Modernist movement. They were accompanied by commonly shared concerns on how to improve the housing conditions of the masses. Tony Garnier's Cité Industrielle (elaborated in 1901 and published in 1917), which introduced one of the Modernism founding concepts - functional zoning, proposed continuous and open to everyone space, which would accommodate residential structures along with all other necessary facilities (Mumford 2018, pp. 70–71). American planners at the beginning of the 20th century focused on similar issues. They looked for the introduction of greenery to the central city as a measure to address the environmental decay, along with issues of better traffic organisation and relocation of industry to the outskirts (Mumford 2018, p. 121).

In Radburn, the safe pedestrian circulation and access to green spaces materialised in residential superblocks by Clarence Stein and Henry Wright (Mumford 2018, p. 130). All the above ideas became afterwards central for Modernist planning. Le Corbusier adopted these concepts into his proposals for the ideal city. The widespread and influential series of projects started with Ville Contemporaine (The Contemporary City for Three Million Inhabitants), which in 1922 appeared in l'Esprit Nouveau - an avant-garde journal which

Le Corbusier co-edited with Amédée Ozenfan. The proposed linear forms of massive housing structures were placed in the park-like green environment. The circulation was to be provided by a system of independent roads for a variety of vehicles, covered railways and an airport (Mumford 2018, 148–149). Separate walkways were embedded in green spaces.

The Garden Cities movement and Bauhaus ideas found their continuation in workers' housing estates designed by Jacobus Oud in the Netherlands and Bruno Taut and Erns May in Germany. However, unlike Le Corbusier, these architects, who also represented Modern Movement (the name used by Eric Mendelsohn in 1931), preferred low-rise complexes with traditionally organised green spaces for recreation and social interactions over massive apartment buildings.

All the above concepts were subject to discussion by the members of Congress International d'Architecture Moderne (CIAM). They became integrated into the key document of the organisation - the Athens Charter - published after its Fourth Congress on the Functional City in 1933, which took place on the board of a ship Patrice which sailed from Marseille to Athens. This highly influential manifesto affected the development of cities globally. The role of green spaces was underlined as an element separating functional zones to reduce the negative impact of adjacent conflicting activities. Moreover, green spaces were to be embedded into urban cores to reduce the densities and satisfy the needs of citizens' recreation (Solarek 2015, p. 31).

The considerations about the right density of development and the proportions of built and open spaces were further developed by Modernist thinkers. It was reflected in Gropius'es well-known diagrams analysing the relations between buildings' insolation and available open space and their height and rhythms (published in 1929; Mumford 2018, pp. 159–160). He also verified these possibilities by proposing an 11-floor slab high-rise in Berlin district Spandau (1928, unbuilt). Another influential idea was the separation of districts with green open strips, which lowered density and formed a continuous green system; this concept was first introduced by Eliel Saarinen and Erich Gloeden in their Plan for Helsinki of 1918. It was further broadly emulated, among others, in the plan for Moscow (1935), which also proposed reduced densities (200 people per acre, 6–7 floor apartment buildings) than in other districts. The public transport development and communal facilities complimented the planning directions (Mumford 2018, p. 168).

CIAM ideas strongly influenced the organisation of European residential districts postwar. The rebuilding after war damages followed the Modernist guidance. Across Europe, numerous estates, such as London's Churchill Gardens, Westminster, and West Berlin's Hansawiertel, replaced the war-damaged districts. The typical features of this development were massive residential structures and vast open green spaces in-between. The inspiration with Le Corbusier's Unité d'Habitation de Marseille (1946) is evident. In Eastern Europe, including Poland, Modernism soon got widely adopted after the early social realism and neoclassical styles manifested in structures built directly after WW2. Projects which were built early or started yet before WW2 used the concept of "social neighbourhood" by Social Construction Company (SPB) and the Warsaw Housing Cooperative (WSM); in this group, there were, among others: Warsaw districts of Rakowiec, Żoliborz, Młynów, Muranów, Wierzbno (the 1950s). Their design (some of the concepts yet elaborated during the Nazi occupation) continued works on social housing of

PTRM started as early as 1928. In the 1960s and 1970s of the 20th century, prefabricated large scale construction systems dominated the housing industry (Chomątowska 2018). In Eastern Europe, Modernism continued until the 1990s and times of political transformation.

Throughout the whole period, some of the main features persisted. The most important was the general organisation of space which remained open and accommodated freely distributed structures. Designers planned green spaces to isolate functional zones and protect residential buildings from traffic; normative regulations determined their size (1964, 1974, after Skibniewska 1979, p. 13). As a result, in Modernist housing estates, there are a lot of open green spaces, but they often lack human scale (Solarek 2015). The critics also pointed out the lack of organisation of open spaces, which needs more specific delimitation of private, semi-private, semi-public and public zones. Besides, they referred to the lack of the context for social activities, both in terms of environmental facilities and information layer - meanings of various equipment elements (Skibniewska 1979, p. 12). Another requirement defined in norms was locating recreational facilities near residential structures. As an outcome, the greenery that accompanied housing estates connected with green spaces surrounding educational institutions and recreational facilities.

3 Methodology

The current research continues the earlier study on urban health in Modernist housing estates (Hanzl and Rembeza 2022). Similar to the previous research, the initial analysis refers to some quantitative factors, including Floor Area Ratio (FAR), Building Coverage Ratio (BCR) and Green Area Ratio (GAR). This follows the methodology proposed by Sarkar et al. (2014, pp. 84–124), who indicate the need to examine the relations between characteristics of the built environment, residents' behaviours and health outcomes. As a next step, I look at the accessibility of green spaces and recreational facilities. The focus is on the typology derived from the study by Forsyth et al. (2017), as discussed in the previous section. Accessibility also refers to public transportation opportunities and active mobility options. The latter is congruent with the pedestrian connectivity, which in the case of Modernist housing estates might be subordinated to different rules because of the segregation of traffic. In order to examine the liveability in the current study, I have complimented the earlier set of conditions by the analysis of activities. Gehl (2010) defines the following types of activities: necessary, optional and social. In order for optional and social activities to take place, the settings in which they might reveal should satisfy the need for comfort. The presence of necessary activities, which is reflected by the configuration of the sociometric layout, is the first step for other types of activities to happen. In the current research, I have been looking at three elements:

1. activities which take place in outdoor spaces,
2. arrangements of these spaces,
2. Sociometric layout.

The latter has been defined following the method proposed by Hiller and Hanson (2003), which later led o the development of the Space Syntax methodology. This method enables direct tracing of the basic layer of connectivity within the analysed housing estates. Moreover, the definition of building typology and morphological regions (Oliveira 2016) complement the conducted research.

4   Case Studies – Two Modernist Housing Estates

The spatial scope of work includes two housing estates located in Łódź, Bałuty district:

- Zgierska-Stefana estate,
- Inflancka estate.

Both estates have been designed following the Modernist principles of high-rise structures surrounded by green open spaces. They were both built using prefabricated large-scale concrete elements. The housing estate Zgierska Stefana was designed between 1971 and1972 by a team which represented Inwestprojekt included: Leszek Paperz, Ryszard Daczkowski and Andrzej Bohdanowicz. Its construction started in 1973 and lasted for over a decade. The structure used prefabricated armed concrete systems Dąbrowa 70 and W-70. The intended number of residents was approximately 9 000 (Dziennik Łódzki 1971).

The estate Inflancka was designed in 1972, and its construction started soon after. The designers' team: Krystyna Greger, Zdzisław Lipski, Jakub Wujek and Andrzej Owczarek represented Miastoprojekt. The proposed number of residents was 8000. The 11 and 5-floor slab structures were distributed among green areas and recreational facilities. Designers also proposed a system of organisation of playgrounds based on plates 10 × 10 m, each containing different facilities (Dziennik Łódzki 1972).

The contemporary Bałuty district features a number of Modernist housing estates. The post-war transformation of its territory started directly after the end of WW2 during the socio-realism period. Initially a suburb of Lodz, it housed primarily poor inhabitants in fast built, low standard houses with no water or sewage. During WW2, the Litzmannstadt Ghetto, located there by Nazi occupants, deepened local development degradation. Therefore, the socialist administration chose to rebuild the area of Bałuty and construct new neighbourhoods. The first vision was designed in the Warsaw Office of Workers Settlements[1] by a team led by Ryszard Karłowicz. The initial intervention included six estates (Ciarkowski 2018, p. 142). Its designers followed socio-realistic building methods with perimeter blocks and a regular street network.

Later interventions applied Modernist principles and prefabricated large-scale concrete building structures. The development continued until the end of the transformation period, and some elements have been added recently.

---

[1] Zakład Osiedli Robotniczych.

The history of this transformation is reflected in the forms of local structures. Specifically, due to the economic conditions, many pre-war buildings had to be left untouched, which resulted in significant fragmentation of space of both estates. In between blocks of flats, we find pieces of 19th-century development, including fragments of historical streets, some pre-war tenements, or single-family houses with private courtyards and gardens (Fig. 1).

The Zgierska-Stefana estate is surrounded by three arterial roads: Zgierska, Julianowska and Łagiewnicka. There are tramway lines in Zgierska and Łagiewnicka and numerous buses on all three streets. Inflancka Street delimits Inflancka estate on the north and Łagiewnicka on the west. The site is cut through Franciszkańska street. In these major streets, there are trams and buses. Both estates are very well connected to other parts of the town. They are also both close to nearby large parks: Julianowski Park and Szarych Szeregów Park.

5   Results and Discussion

5.1   Buildings Typology

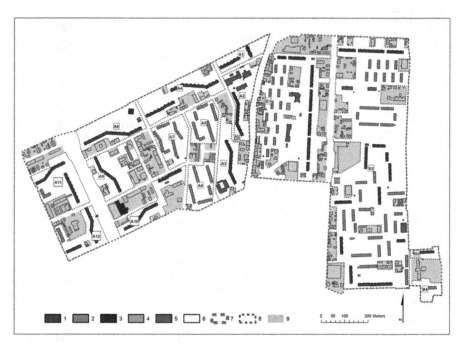

Fig. 1. Typology of built structures in Zgierska-Stefana (A) and Inflancka (B) estates, Bałuty, Łódź. Symbols: 1. 12-floors wave blocks, 2. 4–5 floors, blocks of flats, 3. tower buildings, 4.auxiliary structures, 5. services, 6. buildings in historical parts, 7. site limits, 8. historical development; A1, A2, … - units IDs.

Figure 1 depicts the locations of historical structures and Modernist residential buildings. In the Zgierska-Stefana estate, there are two main types of blocks of flats: 11–12 storey buildings in a wave-like form that isolate the development from surrounding arterial roads and lower 4–5 floors structures located inside. In the case of the Inflancka estate, there are 11-floor slabs and 5-floor, smaller blocks of flats. The distribution of both types is based on geometric rules. In both cases, the arrangement of buildings is strongly affected by the configuration of historic streets.

5.2   Quantitative Analysis

The results of the analyses based on the methodology indicated in the previous sections are shown below - in Table 1 and Fig. 3. It includes the calculations of Floor Area Ratio (FAR) and Building Coverage Ratio (BCR) parameters complemented by the analyses of Green Area Ratio (GAR).

Table 1. Results of calculations of FAR, BCR and GAR values for both estates.

Field ID	Total area [m^2]	FAR	BCR	GAR
Zgierska-Stefana estate				
Streets	77718	0	0	20
Historical development (A)	117067	0.9	32.5	10
A1	13561	1.6	13	47
A2	23710	1.5	23	26
A3	27319	1	14	33
A4	34836	1.3	12	36
A5	19557	1	20	60
A6	20049	0.9	18	54
A7	22915	0.7	15	52
A8	30258	1.4	12	55
A9	27565	1	10	41
A10	21314	1.9	16	44
A11	32028	1.4	13	36
A12	22448	1.6	18	43
Inflancka estate				
Historical development (B)	414472	0,2	10	5
B1	109270	0.8	13	34.5
B2	266759	0.8	12	48
B3	5059	2.2	20	5
B4	7623	0.4	8	19

The FAR values for Zgierska-Stefana estate are moderate (from 0.7 to 1.9), which is typical for urban areas. Inflancka estate features similar values (0.8). In Modernist estates, such values are, as a rule, accompanied by rather low BCR, ranging from 12% to 23%. Whereas FAR remains similar in the case of traditional development, the BCR values are much higher there (32.5%). The same characteristics is also followed by the share of open green spaces. In the case of Modernist estates, the GAR values range from 26 to 60%, while in the case of historical development, the share is as low as 10% or 5% for Inflancka estate (Fig. 2).

I. [ ] 8 - 10   [ ] 11 - 13   [ ] 14 - 16   [ ] 17 - 20   [ ] 21 - 23

II. [ ] 0.4   [ ] 0.5 - 0.8   [ ] 0.9 - 1.0   [ ] 1.1 - 1.6   [ ] 1.7 - 2.2

Fig. 2. The results of analysis of I. Building Coverage Ratio, II. Floor Area Ratio

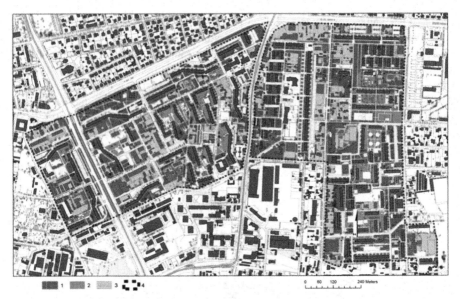

1 ▮ 2 ▮ 3 ▮ 4

0 60 120   240 Meters

Fig. 3. The general layout of Zgierska-Stefana and Inflancka housing estates with the analysis of types of open, green spaces. Symbols: 1. Greenery isolating and accompanying buildings, 2. Recreation spaces, 3. Historical parcellation, 4. Site delimitation. (Color figure online)

5.3 Forms of Open Spaces

In the housing estate Zgierska-Stefana in Łódź, there are the following types of open green spaces: recreation spaces with playgrounds, spaces of isolation which accompany parking lots and arterial roads surrounding the estate and rows of trees and lawns near buildings. The last type usually is connected with fragments of historical streets which remained from the past development. Due to the presence of these streets the segregation of traffic is not very rigorous.

Playgrounds and recreation spaces are located in the central part of the estate, surrounded by lower buildings. They are fully isolated from traffic by surrounding blocks. Green spaces located more in the outskirts due to the parking function serve more for isolation from noise and pollution of surrounding streets. People rarely sit there or stop to spend time. Contrary, the recreational sites in the middle, thanks to their scale (typical dimensions circa 50–65 m × 50 m) and safety from traffic, are popular. They invite all age groups, including children and young adults who frequently exercise there and the elderly, who meet there to chat. Tree-lined streets provide access and connectivity between other locations. Besides, greenery which accompanies both streets and urban blocks enables views from windows and thus increases the psychological well-being of inhabitants. At the same time, the presence of historical streets allows cars to penetrate the estate more freely, which reduces space available for recreation. Moreover, external locations tend to be overwhelmed by parking cars which endanger traffic safety (Table 2).

Table 2. Forms of open spaces

Type of space	Plan	Photographs
Zgierska-Stefana estate		
Recreation – playground and open space		
Isolation and parking		
Greenery near buildings		
Inflancka estate		
Recreation – playground and open space		
Isolation and parking		
Greenery near buildings		

The organisation of space in Inflancka estate is based on geometrical principles. The layout of this estate resembles the diagrammatic drawings by Walter Gropius of 1929, where the distances between buildings were adjusted to their heights. In general, rows of 11-floor slab buildings are accompanied by larger open spaces, which either accommodate parking lots or vast green spaces with some recreation facilities. In some cases, both types of activities are included. At the same time, spaces which contain these facilities are vast and their scale is not adjusted to the recreational activity which should happen there. Moreover, direct proximity of parking and playgrounds endangers safety. In the case of lower 5-floor buildings, they form comb-like rows, with small (25 m × 25 m) green yards in between. However, these green yards are not big enough to contain any kind of recreational facilities - therefore, they might be classified as greenery near buildings. In all, the scales of spaces are not adjusted to the activities happening there. What is more, the penetration of estate by numerous streets overlaps with these adverse effects, creating confusion and decreasing traffic safety.

5.4 Sociometric Layout

The analyses of the principal sociometric layout made it possible to trace how people use space based on its configuration imposed by the distribution of paths and entrances to buildings. According to Gehl (2010), spaces that integrate more activities are more active since synergy is an effect. In the case of the two analysed estates, the organisation of space in Zgierska Stefana answers these requirements better than Inflancka estate. This is partially due to the integration of historic streets, which imposed the distribution of buildings in a very clear way. Tall buildings are located outside and lower blocks inside. What is more, the organisation is to some extent concentric - turned towards the

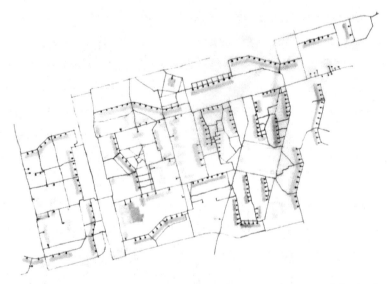

Fig. 4. The image shows a configurational analysis for the housing estate Zgierska-Stefana.

core offered by recreational spaces. This results in at least partial delimitation of zones for various activities.

In the case of Inflancka estate, the geometrical principles applied to satisfy the requirements for insulation do not take into account activities happening between blocks. Therefore, the relationships between locations of entrances and what follows - sociometric layout - and activities seem random (Figs. 4 and 5).

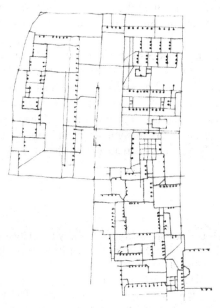

Fig. 5. The image shows the results of preminimary configurational analysis for the Inflancka housing estate.

6   Conclusions

Both analysed housing estates feature similar types of development and fulfil many of the assumptions defined by the CIAM founders. The FAR and BCR values are comparable; both estates offer good access to nearby greenery and some recreational facilities. They have good connections with other parts of the town thanks to the public transport and are close to large parks. At the same time, they both are located in the historical district, where the economic conditions imposed preservation of some of the previous structures. However, even if the dates of construction of both estates remain the same, the applied solutions differ. In the case of Zgierska-Stefana district, the organisation is more concentric, with larger units located outside and separating from arterial traffic and smaller buildings enclosing interior recreational spaces. This layout somehow relates to the traditional logic of urban perimeter blocks. Some of these principles were applied in the Inflancka estate, too; there are rows of blocks along Franciszkańska and Inflancka streets. At the same time, the overall design of this second estate is subordinated to the geometrical principles. As a result, the layout and context (scale of outdoor spaces, integration of various functions) do not consider the needs of activities in the outdoor areas. This last observation has been supported by analysing sociometric layouts of both estates.

Also, the integration of historical development differs. In the Zgierska-Stefana estate, the pieces of historical streets, on the one hand, organise space and provide greenery accompanying buildings; on the other, their presence leads to space fragmentation and decreases traffic safety-enhancing cars' presence inside the estate. In the Inflancka estate, pieces of historical development, due to their distinct forms, make understanding the logic challenging, at the same time also creating an adverse effect of more traffic inside the estate.

In all, whereas open space and greenery are abundant in both estates, their organisation could clearly be improved. The most pertinent issues are traffic safety and the better adjustment of space to the needs of activities and their synergies. The presence of open space and vegetation caters to some needs of the local residents, for instance, regulating UHI, and providing visual satisfaction. Still, however, there is a lot of space for improvements.

References

Alderton, A., et al.: What is the meaning of urban liveability for a city in a low-to-middle-income country? Contextualising liveability for Bangkok, Thailand. Glob. Health **15**(1), 51 (2019). https://doi.org/10.1186/s12992-019-0484-8

Brown, D.K., Barton, J.L., Gladwell, V.F.: Viewing nature scenes positively affects recovery of autonomic function following acute-mental stress. Environ. Sci. Technol. **47**, 5562–5569 (2013)

Chomątowska, B.: Betonia Dom dla każdego. Wołowiec, Wydawnictwo Czarne (2018)

Ciarkowski, B.: Modernizm po drugiej wojnie światowej - lata 1945–1989. In: Stefański, K., Ciarkowski, B. (eds.) Modernizm w architekturze Łodzi XX wieku, pp. 125–200. Księży Młyn Dom Wydawniczy, Łódź (2018)

Clarke, A., Cheshire, L.: The post-political state? The role of administrative reform in managing tensions between urban growth and liveability in Brisbane, Australia. Urban Stud. **55**(16), 3545–3562 (2018). https://doi.org/10.1177/0042098017753096

Dziennik Łódzki 170, 07.20, p. 6 (1971)

Dziennik Łódzki 190, 08.11, p. 4 (1972)

Forsyth, A., Salomon, E., Smead, L.: Creating Healthy Neighborhoods. Evidence-Based Planning and Design Strategies. Kindle Edition. Taylor and Francis (2017)

Forsyth, A., Musacchio, L.: Designing Small Parks: A Manual for Addressing Social and Ecological Concerns. Wiley, Hoboken (2005)

Frank, L.D., Sallis, J.F., Conway, T.L., Chapman, J.E., Saelens, B.E., Bachman, W.: Many pathways from land use to health: associations between neighborhood walkability and active transportation, body mass index, and air quality. J. Am. Plann. Assoc. **72**(1), 75–87 (2006)

Gascon, M., Triguero-Mas, M., Martínez, D., Dadvand, P., Forns, J., Plasència, A., et al.: Mental health benefits of long-term exposure to residential green and blue spaces: a systematic review. Int. J. Environ. Res. Public Health **12**(4), 4354–4379 (2015)

Gehl, J.: Cities for People. IslandPress (2010)

Giles-Corti, B., et al.: City planning and population health: a global challenge. Lancet **388**(10062), 2912–2924 (2016)

Hanzl, M., Rembeza, M.: Urban form versus health of citizens. Evaluation of modernist housing in Lodz and Gdansk. Urban Planning (2022). In Press

Hillier, B., Hanson, J.: The Social Logic of Space. Cambridge University Press, Cambridge (2003)

Hirsch, J.A., et al.: Changes in the built environment and changes in the amount of walking over time: longitudinal results from the multi-ethnic study of atherosclerosis. Am J Epidemiol. **180**(8), 799–809 (2014)

Holden, M., Scerri, A.: More than this: liveable Melbourne meets liveable Vancouver. Cities **31**, 444–453 (2013)

Jackson, R., Dannenberg, A., Frumkin, H.: Health and the built environment: 10 years after. Am. J. Public Health **103**, 1542–1544 (2013)

Kaal, H.: A conceptual history of liveability. City **15**(5), 532–547 (2011)

Kaczynski, A.T., Potwarka, L.R., Saelens, B.E.: Association of park size, distance, and features with physical activity in neighborhood parks. Am. J. Public Health **98**(8), 1451–1456 (2008)

Knuiman, M.W., et al.: A longitudinal analysis of the influence of the neighborhood built environment on walking for transportation: the RESIDE study. Am. J. Epidemiol. **180**(5), 453–461 (2014)

Marselle, M.R., Stadler, J., Korn, H., Irvine, K.N., Bonn, A. (eds.): Biodiversity and Health in the Face of Climate Change. Springer, Cham (2019). https://doi.org/10.1007/978-3-030-02318-8

McArthur, J., Robin, E.: Victims of their own (definition of) success: urban discourse and expert knowledge production in the Liveable City. Urban Stud. **56**(9), 1711–1728 (2019). https://doi.org/10.1177/0042098018804759

McCann, E.: Policy boosterism, policy mobilities, and the extrospective city. Urban Geogr. **34**(1), 5–29 (2013)

McCann, E.: Inequality and politics in the creative city-region: questions of livability and state strategy. Int. J. Urban Reg. Res. **31**(1), 188–196 (2007)

Mitchell, R., Popham, F.: Effect of exposure to natural environment on health inequalities: an observational population study. Lancet **372**(9650), 1655–1660 (2008)

Mumford, E.: Designing the Modern City: Urbanism Since 1850. Kindle Edition. Yale University Press (2018)

Oliveira, V.: Urban Morphology: An Introduction to the Study of the Physical form of Cities. Springer, Cham (2016). https://doi.org/10.1007/978-3-319-32083-0

Paul, A., Sen, J.: A critical review of liveability approaches and their dimensions. Geoforum **117**, 90–92 (2020). https://doi.org/10.1016/j.geoforum.2020.09.008

Saelens, B.E., Handy, S.L.: Built environment correlates of walking: a review. Med. Sci. Sport Exer. **40**(Suppl 7), S550–S566 (2008)

Sarkar, C., Webster, C., Gallacher, J.: Healthy Cities. Public Health through Urban Planning. Edward Elgar Publishing Inc., Northampton (2014)

Skibniewska, H., Bożekowska D., Goryński A.: Tereny otwarte w miejskim środowisku mieszkalnym. Warszawa, Arkady (1979)

Solarek, K.: Kształtowanie struktury przyrodniczej na tle koncepcji rozwoju i przekształceń współczesnego miasta. In: Szulczewska, B. (ed.) Osiedla mieszkaniowe w strukturze przyrodniczej miasta, pp. 24–45. Wydawnictwo SGGW, Warszawa (2015)

Sugiyama, T., Giles-Corti, B., Summers, J., du Toit, L., Leslie, E., Owen, N.: Initiating and maintaining recreational walking: a longitudinal study on the influence of neighborhood green space. Prev Med. **57**(3), 178–182 (2013)

Teo, S.: Political tool or quality experience? Urban livability and the Singaporean states global city aspirations. Urban Geogr. **35**(6), 916–937 (2014)

UN-Habitat: New Urban Agenda. Technical report, United Nations, New York (2016)

UN-Habitat: Broad-Based Partnerships as a Strategy for Urban Livability: An Evaluation of Best Practices. Technical report, United Nations, New York (2008)

Wetzstein, S.: Globalising economic governance, political projects, and spatial imaginaries: Insights from four Australasian cities. Geogr. Res. **51**(1), 71–84 (2013)

World Health Organization: Shanghai declaration on health promotion (2016)

World Bank: Livable cities for the 21st century. Directions in development. World Bank Group, Washington, DC (1996)

Zhan, D., Kwan, M.P., Zhang, W., Fan, J., Yu, J., Dang, Y.: Assessment and determinants of satisfaction with urban livability in China. Cities **79**, 92–101 (2018). https://doi.org/10.1016/j.cities.2018.02.025

International Workshop on Urban Regeneration: Innovative Tools and Evaluation Model (URITEM 2022)

On the Phenomenon of Depopulation of Inland Areas

Federica Russo⬤, Alessandra Marra⬤, Roberto Gerundo⬤,
and Antonio Nesticò(✉) ⬤

DICIV - Department of Civil Engineering, University of Salerno, Via Giovanni Paolo II, 132,
84084 Fisciano, SA, Italy
{frusso,almarra,r.gerundo,anestico}@unisa.it

Abstract. The demographic decline of inland areas is a phenomenon that, especially in recent decades, has reached significant dimensions in many European countries and the world. This phenomenon involves about 60% of the Italian territory, especially the South of Italy, which has been living for too many years in conditions of persistent emergency. The aim of this work is not only to highlight the importance of this phenomenon and its serious economic, social, demographic and environmental repercussions, but also to encourage reflection on the appropriate intervention strategies to be implemented. What seems to emerge from a critical analysis of the historical events and investments that have affected the Italian territory, and in particular the South of Italy, is a lack of attention to the knowledge of the places where it is called to intervene. In fact, rather than a shortage of funds or investment, as is often believed, the rapid advancement of the phenomenon is attributable to the absence of a well-structured investment program consistent and compatible with the activities and culture of the local population, as well as keeping pace with the dynamics of the global economy and the technological revolution. The critical analysis conducted is paradigmatic to address and outline actions and intervention strategies for other territorial contexts as well.

Keywords: Inland areas · Depopulation · Enhancement strategies · Decision models · Multi-criteria analysis

1 Introduction

In recent decades, depopulation and demographic decline have become significant, with serious economic, social, demographic and environmental consequences. This emergency involves many European countries and the entire world: according to the United Nations' Urbanization Prospects report, in 2050 the population that will move to cities and metropolises should reach 70%.

In Italy, migration is now increasingly substantial and involves all regions, particularly those in the South, which have a largely negative internal mobility rate. According

R. Gerundo and A. Nesticò—designed the research. All authors contributed to the definition of the methodology. Federica Russo prepared a draft manuscript. All authors enriched the manuscript. Roberto Gerundo and Antonio Nesticò revised the manuscript.

© The Author(s), under exclusive license to Springer Nature Switzerland AG 2022
O. Gervasi et al. (Eds.): ICCSA 2022 Workshops, LNCS 13382, pp. 381–391, 2022.
https://doi.org/10.1007/978-3-031-10592-0_28

to ISTAT [1], forecasts of the national demographic future are returning to a crisis situation: a demographic decline is expected from 59.6 million to 1 January 2020 to 58 million in 2030, 54.1 million in 2050 and 47.6 million in 2070.

With the aim of countering the demographic decline and promoting the development of smaller centers, in 2013 was launched in Italy a policy of National Strategy for Inner Areas (SNAI) financed by ordinary funds of the Stability Law, available regional resources and EIS funds of regional programming. In the start-up phase, this strategy has adopted a perimeter and a hierarchy of inland areas according to their degree of "peripherality" with respect to the "poles", centers of supply of essential services, such as education, health and mobility. On the basis of distance from the nearest center of supply, in average road travel time, four area categories have been identified [2]:

- Beltway Areas, 20 min drive away;
- Intermediate Areas, up to 40 min away;
- Peripheral Areas, up to 75 min away;
- Ultra-peripheral areas, more than 75 min travel time away.

Of these, the last three categories are classified as inland areas which, in Italian territory, amount to 72 for a total of around 1,060 municipalities. The incidence of these areas is comparatively higher in southern Italy and the Islands, accounting for around 80% of municipalities and 40% of the population.

The geographical location, the distance from the main centers of supply of essential services, the increasing state of abandonment and degradation of the built heritage, contribute to determine the high social and economic fragility that characterizes these territories. Moreover, the alarming phenomenon of depopulation is accompanied by a progressive process of population aging and reduction of employment [3, 4].

The abandonment of these inland areas, as well as the exploitation of local natural resources without significant spin-offs in terms of income, employment and innovation, produce negative externalities and costs for the entire country, going against increasingly frequent problems of hydrogeological instability and degradation of the cultural and landscape heritage.

Although of national importance, the theme of the fragility of inland areas shows a significant difference between the dynamics of abandonment, affecting the smaller centers of northern Italy, and those involving the southern territory. It is no coincidence that the only inland areas for which there has been a counter-exodus phenomenon in recent years are all located in northern regions such as Trentino-Alto Adige, Valle d'Aosta and Lombardy [5]. In order to understand the extent of the phenomenon treated, below: Fig. 1 shows, by breakdown, the shares of municipalities and population falling in the inland areas; Table 1 shows the demographic trends of the Italian population and of the 72 inland areas identified by SNAI.

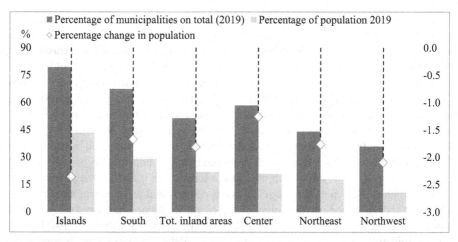

Fig. 1. Shares of municipalities and population falling in inland areas (Source: elaborations on ISTAT data-report on the territory, 2020).

Table 1. Overall demographic trends for the national territory and the 72 areas selected by SNAI (Source: Annual Report on the National Strategy for Inner Areas, 2020).

	2001	2011	2017	2020
Italy	56.995.744	59.439.792	60.589.445	59.257.566
72 areas	2.214.342	2.117.654	2.050.030	1.949.801
	Var% 2001–2011	Var% 2011–2017		Var% 2017–2020
Italy	4, 3	1, 9		−2, 2
72 areas	−4.4	−3.2		−4.9

2 Historical Evolution: Events that have Mainly Affected the Development of the Inland Areas of Southern Italy

The South has been living for too many years in conditions of persistent emergency: the expression "southern question", usually adopted, highlights the dramatic economic and social situation in the South of Italy compared to the central and northern regions. This seems to justify its history and the history of its more fragile inland areas, which, in many ways, is a history of continuous emigration in search of better living conditions [6, 7].

Already in the last decades of the 19th century, there was a significant structural differentiation of the country's productive apparatus: in the South, a purely agricultural-commercial economy contrasted with an increasingly industrialized Northern Italy. The dramatic conditions of poverty affecting the territory led to the largest mass emigration abroad in the history of Southern Italy [8].

It was only after the Second World War that there was a vigorous economic recovery that reduced the gap between South and North manifested until then. The years after the Second World War, in fact, were marked by policies aimed at bridging the infrastructure gap between the South and the rest of Italy. In particular, referred to as the "golden age", it was the period between 1951 and 1973 that marked an economic convergence between the two Italian macro-areas [9]. In 1950, in fact, under the De Gasperi VI government, the "Cassa del Mezzogiorno" was founded, a public authority that, with an extraordinary intervention, stimulated economic growth for over twenty years. Nevertheless, if until the middle of the twentieth century the Italian territory had been affected by movements from the city to the countryside, which proceeded slowly, since the Second World War such migrations grew on two different scales: a local scale, on which the population of smaller urban centers moved to larger regional centers, and an inter-regional scale, on which the industrialized urban centers of the North welcomed the population of rural southern areas, especially in the years of the so called "economic boom" [10]. In fact, the consolidation of northern urban centers was matched by a dramatic depopulation of many southern areas, with the consequent abandonment of land and the associated agricultural, pastoral and land maintenance practices. According to the records of ISTAT, the resident population in municipalities with less than 10,000 inhabitants continued to decrease, going from 45% in 1951 to 35% in 1971.

The long season of action of the Cassa del Mezzogiorno ended with D.lgs. no. 415 of 1992, converted into law no. 488 of the same year, concretely functioning only since 1996: a policy that provided for calls for projects in the sectors of industry, craftsmanship, commerce, tourism and the environment, extended not only to the South, but also to other "depressed" or disadvantaged areas of the country.The advent of this "new planning" and the lack of adequate policies for the needs of further development of the southern territories contributed to further penalizing the South, also weakening the entire country already in crisis [11].

A tragic event, moreover, further marked an already fragile territory: in 1980 a strong earthquake struck several areas between central Campania and central-northern Basilicata, with considerable damage especially in the Irpinia area. It was the most serious earthquake that struck Italy in the period following the Second World War. Although the territory did not have particular industrial characteristics before the earthquake, the reconstruction was mainly focused on the industrial revival. So, as for the earthquake of 1962 in the same areas, the State spent large sums of money with very bad results: the rain of contributions was an irrepressible temptation for many and the overestimation of investments, in relation to entrepreneurial skills, led to the failure of the initiatives. The industrialization programs were, in fact, incompatible with the activities that had been carried out for centuries in that territory and far removed from the culture of the local population.

In 1986 there was a strong demographic decline that had not occurred in Italy since 1918: migration flows, both internal and external, had been greatly attenuated, since it was no longer strictly necessary to migrate to obtain satisfactory living conditions, but there was a substantial reduction in the birth rate, which was rapidly brought to values close to or below those of mortality [12].

In that period, further unfavorable events marked the country's economy, such as the devaluation of the lira in 1992 and Italy's consequent exit from the European Monetary System (EMS), generating fluctuations and affecting levels of competitiveness with foreign countries and, consequently, exports.

A reversal in investment policies also coincided with the years of judicial investigations, known as Tangentopoli, into a widespread system of political corruption [13].

Investments in the South were rapidly reduced and the differences between regions began to widen, especially in transport infrastructures and to the advantage of the Northern regions: different infrastructural policies, less centrally coordinated, gradually took the place of those that had guided the infrastructural development of the past decades.

In 1993, the administrative instability in which almost all municipalities found themselves, especially in the South, inevitably led to a law (Law 81/1993) that introduced direct election of the mayor by the citizens. The objective, in fact, was to adopt a majority electoral system, privileging the purpose of governability to the detriment of representation.

In the 2000s, the Italian economy entered a phase of substantial stagnation: Italy was the European country that grew the less in economic terms with a decidedly more critical situation in the South, except for a slight recovery in the levels of economic activity that marked the South in the period between 2015 and 2018: the increase in the GDP growth rate was fueled by the recovery of investments and exports.

With the Great Recession that began in 2008, Italy's demographic balance has worsened: the country, having become less attractive, has seen a reduction in immigration and an increase in the emigration of young people. So for small municipalities that, while for the first decade of the 2000s have seen a slight growth of their residents, between 2011 and 2018 have been marked by an alarming demographic decline: in 2018, the South has lost 65 thousand inhabitants, more than half of whom resided in Campania and Sicily.

Moreover, with the Covid-19 pandemic, the economy and society throughout Italy were hit by an unprecedented shock in the midst of an already gradual departure from the growth rates that characterized the European average [14].

Therefore, in the last twenty years of substantial stagnation for the Italian economy, the geography of territorial differences has become even more complicated: alongside the divide between North and South, the divergence between centers and peripheries, between urban and inland areas, has increased throughout the country.

3   The Economic Structure of the Inland Areas of Southern Italy

What seems to emerge from an overview of the historical events and investments that have affected the national territory, and in particular the South, is a lack of attention to the knowledge of the places where one is called to intervene: without an adequate and thorough analysis of the territory it is difficult to enhance the identity fabric and, at the same time, preserve the historical, architectural and environmental characteristics of the place [15]. These are territories where, generally, most of the craftsmanship, excellent agri-food production and unique natural resources such as forests, woods, waterways and crops are concentrated. All factors that can develop sustainable "economies" still unexplored with high added value, able to produce well-being and protection of the territory. Places "on a human scale", with healthy air, where the ancient knowledge and traditions, preserved and handed down for generations, characterize the identity and represent a treasure of history and memory [16].

Their economic structure is characterized by a strong specialization in the primary sector: 73% of the municipalities belonging to these areas is specialized in the first sector unlike the Poles where the share drops to 43%. And yet, in the last thirty years, the share of Utilized Agricultural Area (UAA) on the total area in Italy has recorded a sharp decline, especially in inland areas.

Although the primary sector prevails, differences can still be observed on a regional basis: the areas selected in Southern Italy present a more widespread agricultural specialization compared to those in the Center-North; the inland areas of the regions of Lombardy, Piedmont, Veneto, Friuli Venezia Giulia and Liguria present above-average percentages of specialization in the secondary sector (equal to 20%); in the inland areas of the regions of Valle d'Aosta, Calabria, Campania, Lazio and Trentino-Alto Adige, above-average values can be observed in the service sector (7%) [2].

Furthermore, considering the ability to export as one of the main possibilities for the economic growth of a country, the difficulties still encountered by the South are undoubtedly one of the main factors in the gap that has, over time, distinguished it from Northern Italy. Exports from southern regions, in fact, represent only half the average of national exports and this data has been substantially stagnant for more than 10 years. In particular, the South has more marked comparative advantages in the agro-food sector, in the beverages and wine sector, and in the motor vehicle sector [17].

In addition, in the Annual Report of the Bank of Italy (2021), the available infrastructure measures point to a delay of Italy compared to the main European countries and, within the same territory, an unfavorable gap for Southern Italy. This evidence appears sharper when it is based on indicators of a physical nature, more nuanced when it is based on indicators of geographical accessibility and travel time [13]. And yet, the resources available for public works in the past decades have been modest, even if the timescales for realization have often been made long by regulations: much was accomplished in the years preceding the 2008–2009 crisis [18].

Certainly tangible progress has been made in the field of rail transport: in the last thirty years, the speed and frequency of trains on the main north-south route of the country have increased considerably, especially in the last decade thanks to high-speed rail on this axis.

Between 2009 and 2019, however, there was a reduction in public investment spending, including transfers to private entities that carry out public works or utilities, from 4.6% to 2.9% of GDP. This period has led to a consequent increase in the quantitative and qualitative gap in infrastructures, especially road infrastructures, compared with other European countries, particularly burdening those areas of the country that were already lagging behind. To date, the National Recovery and Resilience Plan (PNRR) has allocated 62 billion euros to mobility, of which more than 34 billion for the development and modernization of the rail network, particularly in the southern regions.

Another fundamental aspect concerns education and personal training in which, from a comparison with Europe, Italy lags behind, with a particularly marked disadvantage for the south of Italy, strongly marked by the phenomenon of early school leaving. The latter is linked to employment in low-skilled and low-paid jobs, less favorable career prospects, higher risks of unemployment, poverty and poor health. According to data provided by SNAI [2]: in the inland areas 83% of municipalities have an elementary school compared to the Poles where the share rises to 90%; 61% have at least a secondary school of the first degree, while in the Poles the share is about 71%; in 20% of municipalities it is possible to achieve a secondary level of education, unlike the Poles where this value is equal to 24%. In these territories, characterized for decades by a vicious circle of abandonment and demobilization of the school, in many cases schools have become a luxury, held on the edge of the last student enrolled. The situation is aggravated by the precariousness of the teaching staff, which in turn is the result of the marginal conditions in which the territory finds itself. For those who remain, these factors create the conditions for lower school performance and more intense school dropout [15]. In this regard, the PNRR has allocated almost 21 billion for the strengthening of the supply of educational services from kindergartens to universities and 13 billion for the financing of research projects.

For several years, moreover, critical issues have emerged regarding assistance in these territories, made even more evident with the Covid-19 pandemic: these are problems concerning, for example, hospitalization rates of the elderly population higher than regional averages, excessive recourse to hospitalization for conditions treatable by territorial services, long distances from the main services, long waits for emergency vehicles in cases of health emergencies. In relation to health services, the data reported by SNAI (2020), show that in the 72 selected areas the availability of hospital beds per 100,000 inhabitants is 245, compared to the Poles where the value rises to 451. In addition, considering the distances in terms of travel time from the healthcare facilities, in the inland areas the minimum distance from the nearest hospital is 18 min while the maximum is 38 min, the latter mainly for the inland areas of Southern Italy. Finally, the data relative to the quota of the elderly treated in integrated home care and the number of beds in residential structures for the elderly are very similar between the Poles and the internal areas, registering, however, significant differences between the Center-North and the South and the Islands. In this regard, the PNRR has provided funding of 19.7 billion euros for proximity networks, intermediate facilities and telemedicine for territorial health care and for innovation, research and digitalization of the National Health Service.

4 The National Strategy for Inner Areas

Attention to this sensitive issue of depopulation is not only recent. There are numerous direct and indirect actions, more or less structured, for the revitalization of these abandoned territories [19].

Mainly, the problems of public service management and cost rationalization were addressed, both with national and regional incentives: forms of inter-municipal collaboration whose outcome has been limited because they have produced significant effects mainly on the optimization of the costs of public services without directly affecting the causes of depopulation [20].

Further initiatives, increasingly frequent, are implemented by municipalities that aim to gain attractiveness, betting on the recovery of economic functions, mainly in tourism.

But the most structured intervention implemented is that provided by the National Strategy of Inner Areas (SNAI), a policy that in 2013 was promoted by the Agency for Territorial Cohesion. As anticipated, through the 2014–2020 partnership agreement, 72 pilot areas were identified in which to begin testing the strategy through the activation of public funds and the convergence of the actions of all levels of government, especially in associated form. For the following areas, the SNAI pursues different objectives: in the short term, the aim is to adjust the quantity and quality of essential services of health, school and mobility and to promote development projects for the enhancement of natural and cultural heritage, also focusing on local production chains; in the long term, the aim is to reverse the current alarming demographic trends of the inland areas of the country, both in terms of number of residents and in terms of composition by age and birth rate.

The strategy is based on the assumption that these inland areas suffer from economic and functional marginality, with a low level of access to essential services at reasonable times and costs [21–23]. Another weak point is the underutilization of the impressive territorial capital they have: artisan and agricultural know-how, tourist attractions, natural and historical-artistic capital.

What the SNAI is implementing is an approach known as "place-based" or "place-oriented development", which distances itself from traditional interventions aimed at income support, which in the past have yielded unsatisfactory results, and now focuses on promoting development. With this approach, the aim is to improve contextual conditions capable of "freeing" the potential of smaller centers, so far unused, promoting policies for contexts to the detriment of traditional policies for individual subjects, such as companies: the reasons for the failure of many investments, in fact, are not to be found within the individual company or the individual production sector, but in the conditions of the external context. In this way, public intervention does not aim to generate income and employment directly, but, by acting on the characteristics of the context, aims to improve the attractiveness of places to additional mobile resources, such as capital, labor and new population.

In this sense, SNAI focuses on services defined as preconditions for local development: health, education and vocational training, mobility [24, 25].

It is possible to continue living in inland areas if one has a job, but also access to health care, an adequate school for one's children and access to the main communication networks. In contemporary society, an insufficient quantity and quality of these essential services is a decisive obstacle for any local economic development strategy: if the territory does not offer, to an adequate extent, these essential services, any local development project will not generate the amount of effects expected due to lack of prerequisites. What is proposed, therefore, is an inseparable synergy between services and development.

A mistake often made over the years has been to aim at the regeneration of an area through a mere sum of interventions made on individual buildings and in response to critical issues concerning individual aspects, such as structural restoration, energy, etc.: the attention, directed more to the care of the built environment than to the preconditions necessary for economic development, has led to a waste of resources that, in practice, have not been able to reverse the process of marginalization of the inland areas [26].

In order to remedy the ineffectiveness of previous political seasons and past development projects, the SNAI has also provided new incentives for reflection on the interconnections between local development policies and spatial areas of reference. The need to rebalance essential services, intertwined with the local dimension of development, is linked to a broader reorganization of territories and new models of governance based on multi-level institutional cooperation (national, regional, local) and on the direct involvement of local actors in the construction of strategic and shared visions [27, 28].

Concluding Reflections

The topic of repopulation and enhancement of ancient rural villages is still a research field full of unknowns and strongly linked to a strategic management of the territory.

The critical analysis conducted for the Italian territory, with particular attention to the South, is paradigmatic to address and outline actions and strategies for intervention for other territorial contexts.

In response to a season of "institutional reforms blind to the places" [29], it is necessary to resort to appropriate strategies that have a different sensitivity to assets that represent a real cultural heritage, identity and memory.

It will be necessary to come to terms with the dynamics of the global economy, with technological revolutions, with advanced digitalization, with the speed of the changes that characterize our time and the influence that these dynamics may have on the transformations of settlements. For the recovery and the valorization of the minor centers it will be, therefore, necessary to integrate the potential of the technological innovation with the existing local resources, material and immaterial. The use of digital technologies and new cutting-edge systems could reduce the existing economic and social gap between the inland areas, the cities and the widespread territory.

In this direction, the lack of organicity of interventions, too often sporadic and isolated and almost never traceable to a well-structured investment program, requires precise criteria able to prefigure a specific protocol of technical and economic evaluation, useful for the correct selection of effective investment projects [30].

To this end, it is useful to provide stakeholders, both public and private, with models of decision support through the application of algorithms of analysis, evaluation and selection of the most effective proposals: according to multiple criteria-financial, but also environmental, social and cultural-to be chosen in the light of the fundamental principles of sustainable development, these algorithms allow to formulate judgments of convenience on options of intervention extremely relevant in the processes of allocation of resources and therefore in terms of Economic Policy [31].

In this sense, multi-criteria analysis schemes (Multiple Criteria Decision Making-MCDA) can constitute a reference methodology, since they are able to support the decision maker in solving complex problems, which pose heterogeneous and conflicting issues [32, 33].

Due to the multidimensional nature that characterizes the enhancement strategies for inland areas, even the Spatial Multicriteria Decision Making (SMDC) can be a useful tool in the decision-making process. In fact, the explicit consideration of the spatial dimension of decision-making problems, made possible by the combined analysis of spatial data and economic, social and environmental information, is the added value of the SMDC approach. The integration of MCDA and Geographic Information Systems (GIS) can support the resolution of problems such as, for example, the identification of areas with greater imbalances between economic prosperity, social equity and environmental protection, and therefore require priority interventions.

References

1. ISTAT: Report. Previsioni della popolazione residente e delle famiglie (2021). https://www.istat.it/it/files/2021/11/Report-Previsioni-Demografiche.pdf. Accessed 18 Feb 2022
2. Lezzi, B: Relazione annuale sulla strategia nazionale per le aree interne. http://territori.formez.it/content/attuazione-snai-presentata-cipe-ministra-lezzi-relazione-2018. Accessed 16 Feb 2022
3. Reynaud, C., Miccoli, S.: Depopulation and the aging population: the relationship in Italian municipalities. Sustainability 10(4), 1004 (2018)
4. Bevilacqua, P.: L'Italia dell'«osso». Uno sguardo di lungo periodo. In: Riabitare l'Italia. Le aree interne tra abbandoni e riconquiste, pp. 111–122. Donzelli Editore, Roma (2018)
5. ANCI-IFEL: Atlante dei Piccoli Comuni. https://www.anci.it/atlante-dei-piccoli-comuni/. Accessed 16 Feb 2022
6. Pescosolido, G.: La questione meridionale in breve. Centocinquant'anni di storia. Donzelli Editore, Roma (2017)
7. Barbagallo, F.: La questione italiana. Il Nord e il Sud dal 1860 a oggi. Laterza, Roma (2017)
8. Lepore, A.: Il divario Nord-Sud dalle origini a oggi. Evoluzione storica e profili economici. In: Elementi di diritto pubblico dell'economia, pp. 347–367. Cedam, Padova (2012)
9. Bianchi, L., Miotti, D., Padovani, R., Pellegrini, G., Provenzano, G.: 150 anni di crescita, 150 anni di divari: sviluppo, trasformazioni, politiche. Riv. Economica del Mezzogiorno 25(3), 449–515 (2011)
10. Celant, A., Dematteis, G., Fubini, A., Scaramellini, G.: Caratteri generali e dinamica recente del fenomeno urbano in Italia. In: Dematteis, G. (ed.), Il fenomeno urbano in Italia: interpretazioni, prospettive, politiche, pp. 13–54. Franco Angeli, Milano (1999)
11. AA.VV.: La nuova programmazione e il Mezzogiorno. Orientamenti per l'azione di governo. Donzelli Editore, Roma (1998)
12. ISTAT: L'evoluzione demografica in Italia dall'Unità a oggi (2018). www.istat.atavist.com. Accessed 06 Apr 2022
13. Di Giacinto, V., Micucci, G., Montanaro, P.: Coordinamento della spesa pubblica e spillover spaziali delle infrastrutture di trasporto: evidenze per l'Italia. In: Le infrastrutture in Italia: dotazione, programmazione, realizzazione (7), pp. 63–96. Banca d'Italia, Seminari e convegni, Roma (2011)
14. SVIMEZ: Rapporto SVIMEZ 2020 sull'Economia del Mezzogiorno. L'economia e la società del Mezzogiorno. Il Mulino, Bologna (2020)
15. De Pascale, G., Fiore, P.: Analisi e riflessioni sui centri minori in Irpinia: il caso studio di Pietrastornina. In: Fiore, P., D'Andria, E. (eds.) Small Towns from Problem to Resource. Sustainable strategies for the valorization of building, landscape and cultural heritage in inland areas, pp. 273–283. Franco Angeli, Milano (2019)
16. Coletta, T.: I centri storici minori abbandonati della Campania. Conservazione, recupero e valorizzazione. Edizioni Scientifiche Italiane, Napoli (2010)
17. Agenzia ICE: Rapporto ICE 2020–2021. L'Italia nell'economia internazionale. https://www.ice.it/it/studi-e-rapporti/rapporto-ice-2020. Accessed 28 Jan 2022
18. ISTAT: Rapporto annuale ISTAT 2021. La situazione del Paese. https://www.istat.it/storage/rapporto-annuale/2021/Rapporto_Annuale_2021.pdf. Accessed 06 Apr 2022

19. Dal Borgo, A.G., Bergaglio, M.: Sustainable places in Italian urban settings: abandonments and returnings at the time of Agenda 2030. Geogr. Notebooks 1(2), 15–30 (2018)
20. D'Amico, R., De Rubertis, S.: Istituzioni per lo sviluppo tra comune e regione. Unione Europea e prove di ente intermedio in Italia. Rubbettino Editore (2014)
21. Morazzoni, M., Zavettieri, G.G.: Tutela attiva e sistemi agroalimentari nelle aree interne italiane. Geogr. Notebooks 1(2), 45–66 (2018)
22. Prezioso, M.: Aree interne e loro potenzialità nel panorama italiano e europeo. Introduzione al tema. In: De Santis, G. (ed.) L'Umbria tra marginalità e centralità, Geotema, vol. XXI, no. 3, pp. 68–75 (2017)
23. Sommella, R.: Una strategia per le aree interne italiane. In: De Santis, G. (ed.) L'Umbria tra marginalità e centralità, Geotema, vol. XXI, no. 3, pp. 76–79 (2017)
24. Borghi, E.: Piccole Italie. Le aree interne e la questione territorial. Donzelli Editore, Roma (2017)
25. Agenzia per la Coesione Territoriale: Strategia nazionale per le Aree interne: definizione, obiettivi, strumenti e governance. Accordo di Partenariato 2014–2020, (2013)
26. Gatti, M. P., Cacciaguerra, G.: La conoscenza multidisciplinare e multiscalare per la rigenerazione dei contri storici minori. In: Fiore, P., D'Andria, E. (eds.) Small Towns from Problem to Resource. Sustainable strategies for the valorization of building, landscape and cultural heritage in inland areas, pp. 327–334. Franco Angeli, Milano (2019)
27. Gerundo, R., Marra, A.: La pianificazione urbanistica nelle aree interne: alcuni casi studio in regione Campania In: Fiore, P., D'Andria, E. (eds.) Small Towns from Problem to Resource. Sustainable strategies for the valorization of building, landscape and cultural heritage in inland areas, pp. 837–846. Franco Angeli, Milano (2019)
28. Gerundo, R., Grimaldi, M., Marra, A.: La pianificazione urbanistica a supporto della Strategia Nazionale per le Aree Interne. Il Piano strategico-strutturale del Comune di Bagnoli Irpino nell'Area Pilota Alta Irpinia. In AA. VV. (eds, Atti della XXI Conferenza Nazionale SIU. Confini, movimenti, luoghi. Politiche e progetti per città è territori in transizione, Firenze, 7–8 giugno 2018, Roma-Milano. Planum Publisher (2019)
29. Barca, F.: In conclusione: immagini, sentimenti e strumenti eterodossi per una svolta radicale. In: Riabitare l'Italia. Le aree interne tra abbandoni e riconquiste, pp. 551–566. Donzelli, Roma (2018)
30. Nesticò, A., D'Andria, E., Fiore, P.: Centri minori e strategie di valorizzazione. In: Fiore, P., D'Andria, E. (eds.) Small Towns from Problem to Resource. Sustainable strategies for the valorization of building, landscape and cultural heritage in inland areas, pp. 1397–1404. Franco Angeli, Milano (2019)
31. Nesticò, A., Morano, P., Sica, F.: A model to support the public administration decisions for the investments selection on historic buildings. J. Cult. Heritage 2018 33, 201–207 (2018). https://doi.org/10.1016/j.culher.2018.03.008
32. Della Spina, L.: Rivitalizzazione delle aree interne e marginali: un approccio di valutazione multidimensionale di supporto per l'elaborazione di strategie di sviluppo. In: Fiore, P., D'Andria, E. (eds.) Small Towns...from problem to resource. Sustainable strategies for the valorization of building, landscape and cultural heritage in inland areas, pp. 1355–1364. Franco Angeli, Milano (2019)
33. Nesticò, A., Sica, F.: The sustainability of urban renewal projects: a model for economic multi-criteria analysis. J. Property Investment Finance 35(4), 397–409 (2017)

International Workshop on Urban Space Accessibility and Mobilities (USAM 2022)

A Smart Approach for Integrated Land-Use and Transport Planning—An Application to the Naples Metro Station Areas

Carmen Guida[1], Gerardo Carpentieri[1][(✉)], and John Zacharias[2]

[1] Department of Civil, Building and Enviromental Engineering, University of Naples Federico II, P. le Tecchio 80, 80125 Naples, Italy
{carmen.guida,gerardo.carpentieri}@unina.it
[2] College of Architecture and Landscape, Peking University, Beijing, China

Abstract. In recent decades, local and metropolitan authorities worldwide have shown an increasing interest in applying new development strategies that integrate transport and land-use solutions to mitigate the negative consequences of development on the physical and social environment and the economy in urban areas. The progressive application of the smart city paradigm in different urban development sectors from mobility to urban services is influencing decision-makers' and stakeholders' choices. This research proposes a new spatial analysis method to evaluate the "smartness" of land-use and transport integration projects using an updated version of the Node-Place Butterfly model. The method was applied to the 18 stations area of Line 1 of the Naples metro. The results showed significant variation in the level of smartness from the city centre to the peripheral areas, with Node and Place components unbalanced for some stations.

Keywords: GIS · Land use · Geographical analysis · Naples (Italy)

1 Introduction

In 2021, more than 51% of the total global population was living in urban areas. Recent forecasts suggest that by 2050 this figure will exceed 66% [1].

The current 'congestion crisis' that affects most urban areas is undoubtedly a consequence of the lack of coordination of strategies, tools and measures for integrating transport and urban systems. The lack of a holistic vision has often led to the design and construction of transport infrastructure geared mainly to private transport, with inevitable negative consequences for the environment. Transport planning has been oriented towards satisfying an unconditional demand for mobility without foreseeing the impact that transport interventions may have on the urban system and city users, in terms of monetary and generalised costs. Several interesting urban models have been developed in recent decades in order to handle the challenges of today and tomorrow, among which the interactions between transport systems and urban development have received considerable critical attention [2].

O. Gervasi et al. (Eds.): ICCSA 2022 Workshops, LNCS 13382, pp. 395–409, 2022.
https://doi.org/10.1007/978-3-031-10592-0_29

Transport and land-use planning have a significant role in promoting accessibility. At the same time, accessibility is an important component of urban systems and plays a key role in guiding more sustainable and inclusive land use and transport decisions [3]. The concept of accessibility refers to the ease with which people can reach necessary/desired activities—such as goods, services and occupations—within a reasonable travel time. Ensuring high levels of accessibility and sustainable development is, therefore, one of the primary objectives of urban management in order to minimise negative impacts and improve the quality of life in the urban environment.

The transit-oriented development (TOD) approach promotes, through the implementation of eight design principles [4], the gentrification and functionalisation of transit station areas. The alignment of residential and economic densities with public transport capacity and network characteristics, encouraged by TOD principles, is key to improving urban accessibility in cities. Such an approach makes it possible to reduce the need to travel long distances (and thereby reduce greenhouse gas emissions), while promoting a more inclusive urban model.

The literature recognises the role of station areas as major determinants in the organisation of urban systems, mainly because of the strong potential generated by the interactions between the characteristics of nodes and urban places that coexist in such spaces [5, 6]. Thus, the public transport network becomes an opportunity to reorganise settlement patterns, direct growth processes, launch projects for new stations, if necessary, or conduct urban redevelopment in outlying or degraded areas.

The implementation of new technologies in urban living, such as the Internet of Things and information and communication technologies (ICTs), has led to further promising developments in the context of the smart city paradigm. The combination of hardware digital infrastructure and software elements, where city users take an active role as both "detectors" and "diffusers" of data and information, is the cornerstone of urban smartness [7].

Although several studies have recognised the main advantages of both TOD and smart city models, research has yet to systematically investigate the effect of their integration in urban planning practices. To date, there is a notable paucity of evidence-based literature describing the impact of smart and transit-oriented development.

This paper seeks to fill this gap by proposing a new methodology based in GIS (Geographical Information System) environment to assess the smartness and the transit-oriented readiness of station catchment areas. The methodology takes its cue from Bertolini's Node-Place (NP) model [3] and extends it, both in terms of the calculation procedure and the way in which the results are represented. Moreover, our paper examines a significant case study: the transit network of the city of Naples.

The manuscript begins with an overview of TOD and smart city models, with an evaluation of the main advantages and drawbacks of both. The method and materials are then presented. The third section describes the case study and its results. Finally, the concluding section summarises the potential for implementing urban development strategies that combine both approaches. In addition, some ideas for future lines of research are presented for the identification of a range of interventions to support policymakers and stakeholders.

2 Towards Smart and Transit-Oriented Cities

There are different approaches to transit-oriented development and smart cities in the literature. However, these two development paths are usually investigated as alternatives rather than as complementary. Some cross-sectional studies suggest an undeniable link between them—the common urban development objectives underlying the two urban models. The aim of our study is to propose some advances in the scientific panorama of this discussion by developing a methodology to assess the performance of transit nodes where both TOD and smart city principles have been implemented. In this section, the main traits of the two urban models are highlighted. In particular, concerning urban smartness, some of the most common gateways to the smart city model are summarised. TOD principles and some of the methodologies for analysing transit strategies are also presented.

2.1 Smart Cities

The smart city model has been widely studied but rarely deployed in real-world practices. The smart city aims to support spatial decision-making processes with the combined use of the latest scientific knowledge and ICT solutions in order to steer the development of cities towards greater economic, social and environmental sustainability [8–11].

The use of the smart approach, therefore, is proposed as a possible path to improving the efficiency, competitiveness and sustainability of urban systems in order to offer a better quality of life to citizens and more opportunities for stakeholders and entrepreneurs [12]. Smartness is also linked to the ability to foster integration and interoperability between the different components of a city. Furthermore, the concept of smartness is associated with the achievement of urban efficiency in the economic development, environmental, social, cultural and e-governance fields [13]. However, numerous researchers argue that without a real commitment to collaborating and cooperating from public institutions, the private sector and individual citizens, an adequate level of smartness cannot be achieved [14, 15].

Studying the relationships between smartness and urban development can contribute to a better understanding of those features of the smart city model that significantly contribute to improving the quality of life and well-being of citizens. Academics, practitioners, companies and public administrators, despite the commonalities in the theoretical and practical development of the smart city, have over time developed different ways of defining urban smartness.

Much of the scientific literature agrees that smart solutions in urban areas are effective only if they are developed holistically [16, 17]. The interest in improving urban smartness that has developed over the years has mainly been related to the use of new technologies to support services and infrastructure. However, substantial evidence proving that these types of interventions can provide comprehensive answers to the challenges that cities face has not yet emerged [18].

Mora et al. [19] point out that the knowledge necessary to understand the process of designing effective smart cities in the real world and the tools for supporting the actors involved in this development have not yet been produced. The innovation processes needed should be based on the interaction between different sectors and actors, in order to give rise to horizontal and vertical transformational interventions. This holistic approach to urban smartness would affect multiple components of the city system, including entrepreneurship, design, technology, public policy, urban development, social challenges and climate change adaptation.

From a marketing perspective, smartness is used to emphasise the potential of using new technological equipment to improve the well-being and safety of individuals [20, 21]. Regarding the development of new technologies, smartness refers to the capabilities of hardware and software devices to self-configure, self-repair, self-protect and self-optimise the urban system depending on the conditions that occur [22]. Within the field of urban services planning and management, smartness is associated with the use of ICTs to improve the productivity and efficiency of a city's infrastructure and resources [23, 24]. From the perspective of urban planners, the smart city model is oriented towards the development of strategies and choices that enable a quick understanding of and adaptability to the needs of urban actors and events intrinsic and extrinsic to the urban system [25].

Theoretical studies on the topic of urban smartness are numerous and constantly evolving. This phenomenon suggests that a full understanding of the concept has not yet been achieved. Moreover, until now, all the efforts made to find a synthesis capable of identifying the main elements and phenomena influencing urban smartness have not been unanimously supported by scientific evidence.

Overall, the reviewed studies suggest that ICTs are important in improving the level of urban smartness. However, it has emerged over the years that collaboration and partnerships between the different components of a city are also fundamental to achieving the desired results. In this regard, Ahvenniemi and Huovila [26] identified three different classes of urban smartness, taking into consideration the level of collaboration between the various players (public and private) involved in implementing smart projects.

2.2 Transit-Oriented Cities

TOD was formalised in 1993 by Peter Calthorpe in his book "The Next American Metropolis" [27], which expounded urban planning practices in support of travel by transit. TOD is a planning and design strategy to develop a compact, multifunctional, safe urban environment for pedestrians and cyclists, closely integrated with local public transport hubs. The idea promotes the use of soft mobility and the development of active communities. Although TOD principles were theorised for American urban environments, they found wide dissemination and application in European contexts also, across cities large and small, with great variation in outcomes. Moreover, not all station areas in the same city can support a compact urban layout with a high density of housing, employees and activities.

In order to adapt TOD strategies to different territorial and urban contexts, it is necessary to know the physical, functional and socio-anthropic characteristics of transit station areas. Starting from the planning experiences of some cities, researchers have developed a number of methodologies to study the characteristics of station areas and support public decision-makers in making transit-oriented choices for governing transformation. One of the methodologies to support the governance of urban transformations is the Bertolini

NP model [5]. It allows for an assessment of the level of integration between transport and land-use development policies.

The NP method is based on indices that numerically and synthetically define the "node" and "place" characteristics of stations and their surrounding areas. The node indexes take into account the features of transport infrastructure, while the place indexes refer to the urban characteristics of the station areas. According to this model, the stronger the integration between the node and place value, the better the transit node performance is [28, 29].

The main purpose of the NP model is to assess the functionality of a transit node by analysing the relationship between the properties of the node and the quality of its location. The NP model is based on the reasoning of the land-use feedback loop [30]: Improving the transport supply (or node value) of a place through improved accessibility creates favourable conditions for further development of the place. In turn, the development of an area (or its place value) will create favourable conditions for the further development of the transport system due to increasing demand for transport. The NP model cannot predict developments, but it can help identify where actions can be taken to improve certain aspects.

The NP model helps determine where improvements are needed; therefore, this model lends itself well to identifying which aspects that characterise transit nodes require intervention to increase their accessibility. The model, as developed by Bertolini, is not uniquely applicable to different territorial contexts; it needs to be adapted according to the type of application to take into consideration differing physical-functional characteristics and the varying availability of data useful for calculating the indicators. Although this dynamism and adaptability of the model can be considered a strength, the consistency and quality of the results depends on the type and number of indicators that can be selected.

Hence, a large body of scientific literature has developed enhanced NP models to best suit ad hoc case studies and development objectives. Balz et al. [31] proposed one called the NP Butterfly. It resembles the shape of a butterfly as its final diagram is composed of two wings: a left wing that includes all indicators related to the 'ode' and a right wing that includes 'place' indicators. Each wing is divided into different dimensions: The node wing includes the accessibility of the station to people walking, cycling, using public transport or driving cars, while the place wing includes the proximity of the station to the city centre, the intensity of use by city users (inhabitants, employees and visitors) and the degree of functional diversity.

Another development of the original NP model includes indicators that assess the design of the environment [32–34]. This extension of the model makes it possible to assess not only aspects of land use ('place') and transport ('node') but also the ways in which the design of the built environment stimulates pedestrian and cycling conditions to support access to and from the station.

The quality of a transit node is relative, which means that the quality is determined by the other transit nodes in a network or a selection of them. By normalising the scores for each criterion, the relative score of a specific transit node can be calculated in relation to the others [29].

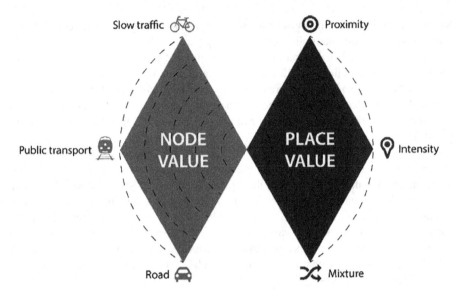

Slow traffic   Proximity

Public transport   **NODE VALUE**   **PLACE VALUE**   Intensity

Road   Mixture

Fig. 1. Application of the vereniging deltametropool node-place method.

3   Materials and Methods: The Smart Spatial Indices of the Node-Place Model

This section describes the phases of the GIS-based spatial analysis methodology to support the evaluation and definition of priority transformation projects in station areas from a smart perspective. It is an integrated approach capable of relating the level of smartness of a station node to the level of smartness of the station surrounding the urban context. This methodology can be applied to any rail transport network by using open data to overcome the difficulties related to low availability of data necessary to define the synthetic indexes of "node" and "place".

Before selecting NP indicators, we identified the five smart dimensions that best contribute to defining integrated transport-territory development policies for station areas. These smart dimensions, obtained from previous studies, are described below.

Smart Economy refers mainly to the ability of a station area to create the best possible environment to encourage the development of businesses. The presence of commercial activities, public and private companies and an adequate functional mix represents the economic dynamism of a station area.

Smart Mobility has as its starting point the problems related to traffic congestion, which increasingly pose the question of how to move people and goods in the urban environment and ensure more efficient levels of service, while reducing the negative externalities that burden citizens. Therefore, the goal is not only to optimise transport infrastructures but also to improve the mobility of people and, in particular, the development of new ecological and sustainable mobility solutions in a station area.

Smart Environment focuses on environmental protection, which mainly involves good management of natural resources (including soil resources), and on the quality of the station environment. These aspects are essential to create the conditions for an urban environment that is oriented to improving citizens' quality of life.

Smart Living and People concerns the ability of a station area to favour a "user-friendly" transport system, which is necessary to encourage people to use the railway system while also guaranteeing greater accessibility for the elderly and people with reduced mobility. This dimension also refers to the potential of a station environment to advance urban liveability by improving the services offered to citizens. Therefore, we can refer to enhancing cultural heritage and using it more intelligently through services supporting tourism, culture and free time.

Smart Technology refers to the enormous potential of technology to facilitate a station's operation and help improve the urban environment around it. Interactive terminals are an important source of information for passengers arriving at an unknown station, and digitisation makes it possible to increase the reliability of the information provided to users.

To enable the application of the methodology in different urban contexts, we selected a set of 32 indicators (19 for the Place component and 13 for the Node component). The indicators were defined to assess the degree of smart development of a station environment and its surrounding urban environment. Table 1 shows the list of indicators for each smart component.

Specifically, the indicators were chosen based on their ability to effectively describe an aspect consistent with the dimension to which they belong, the availability of data for the Italian context, the level of detail of the data acquired, and the availability of data for the two reference areas, namely the Node and the Place.

The main phases to apply this GIS-based methodology for the smart spatial analysis of railway station areas are:

Phase I—Data collection. For the data sources, we refer to the open databases provided by national statistical agencies and national and regional official portals.

Phase II—Creation of the GIS geodatabase. This involves the development of a relational data database (geodatabase) that is usable in the GIS environment and contains all the alphanumeric and spatial data necessary to calculate the selected indicators.

Phase III—Calculation of smart indicators. This entails evaluating the numerical value of each indicator and normalising from 0 to 1.

Phase IV—Graphic representation of the results. A quantitative analysis graphic model was developed based on the NP method proposed by Vereniging Deltametropool [35] as a fundamental support for defining priority interventions in station areas. This method proposes an innovative representation of transit nodes assessment which resembles the shape of a butterfly. It presents two wings: a left wing that includes all node indicators, and a right wing that presents 'place' features.

Table 1. The set of node-place indicators for each smart category.

Smart category	Component	ID	Indicators
Smart economy	Place	01	Number of private entrepreneurships
		02	Number of public education buildings
		03	Employment rate
		04	Population density
		05	Employment territorial distribution
	Node	06	Number of commercial activities
		07	Number of tourist attractors
		08	Number of smart economic activities
Smart mobility	Place	09	Bike lanes
		10	Parking spaces for electric mobility
		11	Surface of walking areas
		12	Density of road intersections
		13	Parking spaces for bikes
	Node	14	Number of park and ride spaces
		15	Number of tourist bus parks
		16	Infomobility services
		17	Level of intermodality
Smart environment	Place	18	Green areas
		19	Built areas
		20	Urban design
	Node	21	Safety of the station environment
		22	Station average attendance rate
Smart living and people	Place	23	Hotel facilities
		24	Cultural activities and entertainment
		25	Housing
		26	Public services
	Node	27	Level of disabled accessibility
		28	Station facilities
Smart technology	Place	29	Wi-Fi connectivity
		30	Smart roads
	Node	31	Transport information systems
		32	Video surveillance cameras

4 The Case Study

To apply the methodology, we selected the case study of the urban metropolitan railway (Line 1) in the city of Naples. Line 1 was preferred due to the fact that the municipality of Naples owns it, which could represent a strength in choosing and applying integrated interventions on both the Place and Node. Moreover, since the beginning of service, even partial, of the line, the city of Naples has experienced, in various forms, the strong influence of the station nodes, both in the central areas, since the stations themselves became touristic poles, and in outlying areas, finally reconnected to the entire urban structure (Fig. 2).

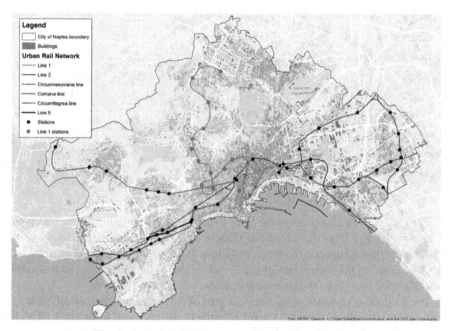

Fig. 2. The urban railway network in the city of Naples.

Line 1 is managed by Azienda Napoletana Mobilità and it includes 18 stations: Piscinola, Chiaiano, Frullone, Colli Aminei, Policlinico, Rione Alto, Montedonzelli, Medaglie d'Oro, Vanvitelli, Quattro Giornate, Salvator Rosa, Materdei, Museo, Dante, Toledo, Municipio, Università and Garibaldi.

The current operational section, which goes from the Piscinola district to Piazza Garibaldi, has an average frequency of one run every nine minutes. The line is 18 km long with a travel time of 33 min. The first two sections, from Vanvitelli to Colli Aminei, and from Colli Aminei to Piscinola, were activated in 1993 and 1995 respectively, while the remaining part was completed from 2001 to 2013. Of the 18 stations that make up the line today, 11 of them have been called "Art Stations" in which particular attention was paid to making the environments beautiful, comfortable and efficient to redevelop large areas of the urban fabric. The Art Stations are: Garibaldi, Università, Municipio,

Toledo, Dante, Museo, Materdei, Salvator Rosa, Quattro Giornate, Vanvitelli and Rione Alto.

In Table 2, we provide a list of alphanumeric and spatial open data selected for the application of the GIS-based methodology to Line 1 in the city of Naples.

Table 2. Data source for the calculation of selected node-place indicators.

Data	Source	Year
Population	ISTAT	2011
Census track	ISTAT	2011
Walking network	Open street map	2021
Transport stops	Open street map	2021
Railway urban network	Open street map	2021
Buildings	Geoportale Nazionale	2011
Companies	ISTAT	2011
Public offices	ISTAT	2011
Urban services	Open street map	2021
Urban green areas	Municipality of Naples	2021
Hotspot Wi-Fi	Google Maps	2021

The results show that most of the Line 1 stations are localised in the balanced part of the NP diagram. This distribution of stations reveals an optimum condition, with a substantial balance between the Node and Place indices for the analysed stations. The stations located in the central part of the diagram close to the middle line have a higher level of accessibility than the outermost stations.

The 14 stations included in the balanced part of the diagram have very different values for their NP indices, from 0.25 to 0.54 for the Node index and from 0.29 to 0.63 for the Place index. In these balanced stations, we identify two main subgroups: subgroup 1 includes Colli Aminei, Policlinico, Rione Alto, Montedonzelli, Quattro Giornate, Salvator Rosa, Materdei and Museo; and subgroup 2 includes Medaglie d'Oro, Vanvitelli, Dante, Toledo and Municipio. The stations with low NP indices values are in subgroup 1, while subgroup 2 contains the stations with higher values.

Table 3. Data source for the calculation of selected node-place indicators.

	Node					Place					Node	Place
	Economy	Mobility	Environment	People and living	Technology	Economy	Mobility	Environment	People and living	Technology		
Piscinola	0.079	0.243	0.333	0.300	0.012	0.035	0.047	0.305	0.157	0.210	**0.193**	**0.151**
Chiaiano	0.023	0.186	0.000	0.200	0.000	0.113	0.018	0.736	0.263	0.065	**0.082**	**0.239**
Frullone	0.023	0.222	0.455	0.373	0.000	0.150	0.001	0.324	0.267	0.000	**0.215**	**0.148**
Colli Aminei	0.015	0.080	0.560	0.456	0.181	0.591	0.029	0.337	0.321	0.195	**0.258**	**0.295**
Policlinico	0.142	0.124	0.495	0.517	0.177	0.572	0.026	0.360	0.307	0.290	**0.291**	**0.311**
Rione Alto	0.087	0.054	0.636	0.542	0.163	0.550	0.036	0.476	0.328	0.194	**0.296**	**0.317**
Montedonzelli	0.087	0.083	0.617	0.570	0.238	0.563	0.024	0.472	0.333	0.161	**0.319**	**0.311**
Medaglie d'Oro	0.578	0.125	0.929	0.717	0.358	0.410	0.119	0.389	0.466	0.568	**0.541**	**0.390**
Vanvitelli	0.404	0.198	0.936	0.682	0.349	0.409	0.163	0.653	0.529	0.635	**0.514**	**0.478**
Quattro Giornate	0.182	0.250	0.508	0.565	0.247	0.422	0.087	0.321	0.445	0.700	**0.350**	**0.395**
Salvator Rosa	0.175	0.125	0.495	0.517	0.330	0.343	0.132	0.443	0.408	0.468	**0.328**	**0.359**
Materdei	0.293	0.125	0.553	0.552	0.346	0.231	0.045	0.419	0.403	0.244	**0.374**	**0.268**
Museo	0.309	0.202	0.728	0.557	0.212	0.289	0.486	0.279	0.727	0.358	**0.402**	**0.428**
Dante	0.420	0.317	0.598	0.499	0.254	0.359	0.813	0.247	0.769	0.710	**0.418**	**0.580**
Toledo	0.277	0.365	0.670	0.662	0.278	0.591	0.769	0.340	0.632	0.839	**0.451**	**0.634**
Municipio	0.499	0.405	0.618	0.631	0.398	0.601	0.668	0.421	0.527	0.934	**0.510**	**0.630**
Università	0.143	0.500	0.540	0.384	0.092	0.848	0.758	0.307	0.740	0.819	**0.332**	**0.694**
Garibaldi	0.968	0.846	0.910	0.846	0.997	0.323	0.250	0.482	0.268	0.490	**0.914**	**0.363**

The Università station is out of the balanced area, and it is unbalanced for the Node index (Smart Economy and Smart Technology). The Università station deserves separate consideration as it is located outside the central spindle, as visible from the NP diagram in Fig. 3. Its decentralised position towards the right part of the graph reveals notable development regarding the Place indicators and lower values for the Node indicators.

In addition, Garibaldi station is located in the "unsustained" part of the diagram, where values for the Place indicators are too low compared with those for the Node indicators. This station obtained the highest Node indicator values of all the stations of Line 1 but low Place indicator values. The stations of Piscinola, Frullone and Chiaiano are located in the lower part of the NP diagram. These stations show a substantial equilibrium between the Node and Place components. However, they have a low degree of development of transport infrastructure and the urban and social characteristics of the station areas. Therefore, it would be advisable to intervene in these stations to reduce the marked differences between them and the remaining stations and improve the average values of Line 1 overall. A possible positive consequence of these interventions would be greater balance, which could trigger greater flows of displacement by railway and increase the attractiveness of the station areas.

Figure 5 shows the Smart Butterfly NP diagrams, as final stages of the methodology, for the four stations previously discussed, comparing the values of their indicators with the average values of the indicators for all the stations. This comparison could be useful to identify in detail the aspects that need to be improved in each station.

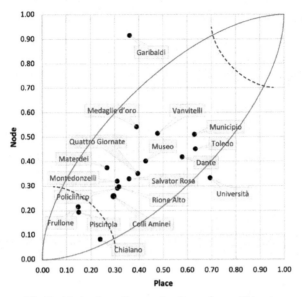

Fig. 3. Node-place diagram for the stations of Line 1.

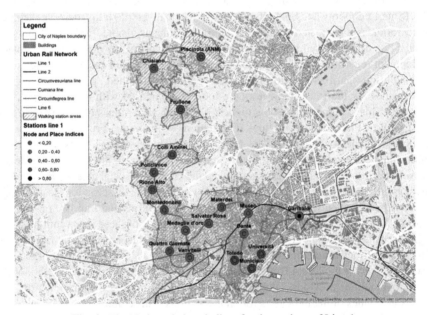

Fig. 4. The Node and place indices for the stations of Line 1.

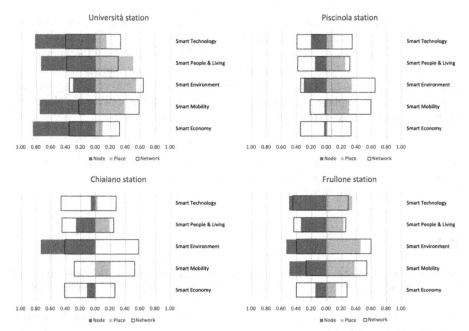

Fig. 5. The Smart butterfly node-place diagram for the stations of Università, Frullone, Piscinola and Chiaiano (in blue, the average value of indicators for Line 1 and in yellow, the value of indicators for the single station). (Color figure online)

5   Conclusion

This first application of the Smart Butterfly NP model to Line 1 of Naples as a preliminary step of our research attempts to define integrated land-use and transport methodologies and guidelines to improve the transit orientation strategy of station areas. In line with the scientific literature on smart cities, for this study, we considered five different categories of smartness (Smart Economy, Smart Mobility, Smart Environment, Smart Living and People and Smart Technology) to collect the indicators for the Node and Place components. The selected set of indicators (13 components for Node and 19 for Place) was obtained through an in-depth study of the scientific literature on the interaction between land use and transport and smart cities, but also through expert knowledge and the availability of open data.

The results showed that the stations of Line 1 are generally balanced, with the exceptions being some peripheral stations (Frullone, Chiaiano and Piscinola) and the station of Università (in the central area of the city). These unbalanced stations have deficiencies in all smart categories for the Node and Place components, and policymakers and technicians will need to implement specific solutions to improve them. Garibaldi station is an interesting case: its values for the Node component are very high because of its spatial proximity to the transport services of Naples railway central station.

A further result of this research concerns the methodological advancement of the Node-Place model and its integration with smart-city dynamics, in order to assess the performance of transit nodes as urban and, potentially, smart places. The integration of transit-oriented development and smart city principles may be a solution for more sustainable and inclusive urban planning practices.

In our opinion, further developments should focus on increasing the number of indicators selected, applying a correlation analysis to choose the final set of indicators, defining a set of planning strategies for each group of stations and proposing specific transport and land-use planning solutions to increase the balance between the Node and Place components of the stations in each group.

Acknowledgments. The work, of which this paper is a product, although the result of a common reflection, was divided as follows. Carmen Guida: Introduction (1) and Towards smart and transit-oriented cities (2). Gerardo Carpentieri: Materials and methods: the smart spatial indices of the Node-Place model (3), The case study (4), Conclusion (5). John Zacharias: supervision.

References

1. World Bank: Global Economic Prospects, January 2022. Washington, DC: World Bank. © World Bank. https://openknowledge.worldbank.org/handle/10986/36519 License: CC BY 3.0 IGO (2022)
2. Meyer, M.D., Miller, E.: Urban Transportation Planning. McGrall-Hill Series in Transportation, New York (2001)
3. Bertolini, L., Le Clercq, F., Kapoen, L.: Sustainable accessibility: a conceptual framework to integrate transport and land use plan-making. Two test-applications in the Netherlands and a reflection on the way forward. Transp. Policy **12**(3), 207–220 (2005)
4. Newman, P.: Planning for transit oriented development: strategic principles. In: Transit Oriented Development, pp. 33–42. Routledge (2016)
5. Bertolini, L.: Spatial development patterns and public transport: the application of an analytical model in the Netherlands. Plan. Pract. Res. **14**(2), 199–210 (1999)
6. Chorus, P., Bertolini, L.: An application of the node place model to explore the spatial development dynamics of station areas in Tokyo. J. Transp. Land Use **4**(1), 45–58 (2011)
7. Papa, R., Gargiulo, C., Cristiano, M., Di Francesco, I., Tulisi, A.: Less smart more city. TeMA – J. Land Use Mobility Environ. **8**(2), 159–182 (2015)
8. Hollands, R.G.: Will the real smart city please stand up? intelligent, progressive or entrepreneurial? City **12**(3), 303–320 (2008)
9. Albino, V., Berardi, U., Dangelico, R.M.: Smart cities: definitions, dimensions, performance, and initiatives. J. Urban Technol. **22**(1), 3–21 (2015)
10. Battarra, R., Gargiulo, C., Pappalardo, G., Boiano, D.A., Oliva, J.S.: Planning in the era of information and communication technologies. Discussing the "label: Smart" in South-European cities with environmental and socio-economic challenges. Cities **59**, 1–7 (2016)
11. Girardi, P., Temporelli, A.: Smartainability: a methodology for assessing the sustainability of the smart city. Energ. Procedia **111**, 810–816 (2017)
12. Ooms, W., Caniëls, M.C., Roijakkers, N., Cobben, D.: Ecosystems for smart cities: tracing the evolution of governance structures in a Dutch smart city initiative. Int. Entrepreneurship Manag. J. **16**(4), 1225–1258 (2020). https://doi.org/10.1007/s11365-020-00640-7
13. Carli, R., Dotoli, M., Pellegrino, R., Ranieri, L.: Measuring and managing the smartness of cities: a framework for classifying performance indicators. In: 2013 IEEE international conference on systems, man, and cybernetics, pp. 1288–1293. IEEE (2013)
14. Battarra, R., Zucaro, F., Tremiterra, M.: Smart mobility and elderly people. can ICT make the city more accessible for everybody? TeMA – J. Land Use Mobility Environ. 23–42 (2018)

15. Aldegheishem, A.: Success factors of smart cities: a systematic review of literature from 2000–2018. TeMA – J. Land Use, Mobility Environ. **12**(1), 53–64 (2019)
16. Papa, R., Galderisi, A., Vigo Majello, M.C., Saretta, E.: Smart and resilient cities. a systemic approach for developing cross-sectoral strategies in the face of climate change. TeMA – J. Land Use Mobility Environ. **8**(1), 19–49 (2015)
17. Leach, J.M., Lee, S.E., Hunt, D.V., Rogers, C.D.: Improving city-scale measures of livable sustainability: a study of urban measurement and assessment through application to the city of Birmingham UK. Cities **71**, 80–87 (2017)
18. Yigitcanlar, T., Kamruzzaman, M., Foth, M., Sabatini-Marques, J., da Costa, E., Ioppolo, G.: Can cities become smart without being sustainable? a systematic review of the literature. Sustain. Cities Soc. **45**, 348–365 (2019)
19. Mora, L., Bolici, R., Deakin, M.: The first two decades of smart-city research: a bibliometric analysis. J. Urban Technol. **24**(1), 3–27 (2017)
20. Lee, S.M., Trimi, S.: Innovation for creating a smart future. J. Innov. Knowl. **3**(1), 1–8 (2018)
21. Trencher, G., Karvonen, A.: Stretching "smart": advancing health and well-being through the smart city agenda. Local Environ. **24**(7), 610–627 (2019)
22. Soyata, T., Habibzadeh, H., Ekenna, C., Nussbaum, B., Lozano, J.: Smart city in crisis: technology and policy concerns. Sustain. Cities Soc. **50**, 101566 (2019)
23. Gil-Garcia, J.R., Pardo, T.A., Nam, T.: What makes a city smart? identifying core components and proposing an integrative and comprehensive conceptualization. Inf. Polity **20**(1), 61–87 (2015)
24. Dameri, R.P., Ricciardi, F.: Leveraging smart city projects for benefitting citizens: the role of ICTs. In: Rassia, S.T., Pardalos, P.M. (eds.) Smart city networks. SOIA, vol. 125, pp. 111–128. Springer, Cham (2017). https://doi.org/10.1007/978-3-319-61313-0_7
25. Moustaka, V., Maitis, A., Vakali, A., Anthopoulos, L.G.: Urban data dynamics: a systematic benchmarking framework to integrate crowdsourcing and smart cities' standardization. Sustainability **13**(15), 8553 (2021)
26. Ahvenniemi, H., Huovila, A.: How do cities promote urban sustainability and smartness? an evaluation of the city strategies of six largest Finnish cities. Environ. Dev. Sustain. **23**(3), 4174–4200 (2020). https://doi.org/10.1007/s10668-020-00765-3
27. Calthorpe, P.: The Next American Metropolis: Ecology, Community, and the American Dream. Princeton architectural press, NY (1993)
28. Mamdoohi, A., Janjany, A.: Modeling metro users' travel behavior in Tehran: frequency of use. TeMA – J. Land Use Mobility Environ. 47–58 (2016)
29. Groenendijk, L., Rezaei, J., Correia, G.: Incorporating the travellers' experience value in assessing the quality of transit nodes: a Rotterdam case study. Case Stud. Transp. Policy **6**(4), 564–576 (2018)
30. Wegener, M., Fuerst, F.: Land-Use Transport Interaction: State of the Art. Elsevier, London (2004)
31. Balz, V., Schrijnen, J.: From concept to projects: stedenbaan, the Netherlands. In: Transit Oriented Development, pp. 95–110. Routledge (2016)
32. Zhang, Y., Marshall, S., Manley, E.: Network criticality and the node-place-design model: classifying metro station areas in greater London. J. Transp. Geogr. **79**, 102485 (2019)
33. Zacharias, J.: The contribution of a tramway to pedestrian vitality. TeMA – J. Land Use Mobility Environ. **13**(3), 445–457 (2020)
34. Liao, C., Scheuer, B.: Evaluating the performance of transit-oriented development in Beijing metro station areas: integrating morphology and demand into the node-place model. J. Transp. Geogr. **100**, 103333 (2022)
35. Vereniging Deltametropool. https://deltametropool.nl/publicaties/maak-plaats-nieuwe-visie-op-ruimtegebruik-in-noord-holland/

Developing Cities for Citizens: Supporting Gender Equity for Successful and Sustainable Urban Mobility

Tiziana Campisi[1]([⊠]) [iD], Georgios Georgiadis[2] [iD], and Socrates Basbas[3] [iD]

[1] Faculty of Engineering and Architecture, University of Enna Kore, 94100 Enna, Italy
tiziana.campisi@unikore.it

[2] Department of Transportation and Project Management, School of Civil Engineering, Aristotle University of Thessaloniki, 54124 Thessaloniki, Greece

[3] Department of Transportation and Hydraulic Engineering, School of Rural and Surveying Engineering, Aristotle University of Thessaloniki, 54124 Thessaloniki, Greece

Abstract. Cities today face unprecedented challenges generated, among others, by climate change, demographic change, economic crisis and technological innovation. The Agenda 2030 sustainable goals aim to create more equitable and sustainable cities which account for all citizens' needs and break down gender stereotypes. The mobility sector is still characterised by an uneven choice of travel modes due to multiple economic, social and cultural reasons. The COVID-19 crisis imposed harsh travel restrictions that had differentiated impacts on the mobility of various user groups, including the gender-defined ones. In this paper, the main social and economic trends, which affect gender demand, are identified along with their main characteristics. An overview of successful pre-pandemic European experiences in the gender planning field is discussed, with the aim of increasing the level of knowledge on the issue, adapting mobility services to meet the needs of all people, rethinking urban mobility and public space planning by incorporating more criteria of accessibility and sustainability, and improving the quality and safety of cycling, walking and public transport routes. For the recent pandemic circumstances, we indicate the facts that led women to experience a differentiated mobility landscape than men. Our research findings highlight the main factors that have led to gender inequality and discuss the gender gaps which emerged. Finally, we provide suggestions for the mitigation of this problem, laying the foundations for defining best practices useful for transport managers and authorities, which also increase both the quality of life and economic and employment opportunities.

Keywords: Gender equity · Urban accessibility · Mobility disparities · Sustainable cities · Sustainable urban mobility

1 Introduction

The recent COVID-19 pandemic and the emerging energy crisis have destabilized the globe economically and socially as well as in terms of health. The transport and mobility system has been among the most affected, both because of possible contagions and because of rising fuel prices. Therefore, the outbreak of the pandemic at the beginning of 2020 had a number of negative effects on all the social and economic sectors, changing behavior at various levels and particularly affecting mobility in general and the transport and logistics sectors in both the short and long term.

All modes of transport had an increase in their respective performances in 2021, compared to 2020. In general, a variety of trends emerged compared to the last 'normal' year, with road and rail passenger traffic still declining, while heavy vehicle traffic, on the other hand, exceeded pre-pandemic levels. For example, the measures to curb and stop traffic have had an impact on private mobility and, on the other hand, the need to avoid crowding on public transport has reduced the use of local public transport, encouraging people to use their own vehicles when the long-awaited reopening takes place.

Cities attract people from all walks of life and they are configured not only as an attractor but also as a container of services and a transformer of them [1]. These aspects allow people to exchange values, concepts and practices, allowing cities to become spaces of involvement, regardless of size, density or complexity. Indeed, citizens often create, negotiate and test ideas and solutions in this context, collectively contributing to shape the future urban condition [2]. At times of increasingly uncertainty (due to the pandemic but also to the fear of war), the actions of citizens become fundamental for the planning of urban spaces. The 15-min city concept allows greater involvement of citizens in activities initiated by public authorities and citizen participation regularly offers paths not considered or followed by other actors [3, 4]. In addition, cities try to create a walking friendly environment for their citizens in order to promote sustainable urban mobility [5]. It must be mentioned at this point that Well-Being plays a crucial role in mode choice and in travelers' psychology towards the direction of sustainable urban mobility [6]. The cooperation between citizens, service managers and local administrations allows to put into practice some of the new developments sanctioned by the objectives of the New Urban Agenda [7] which requires more inclusive, responsible and participatory urbanization and planning of sustainable settlements.

The evolution and greater diffusion and availability of new technologies is opening up a particularly wide range of possibilities for citizen participation in addressing complex issues. In particular, technological evolution has allowed citizens to more easily participate in the processes which concern:

- Governing the city
- Investing in the city
- Planning the city
- Making the city

The recent pandemic and the emerging energy crisis have hampered these activities, increasing numerous economic and social criticalities and a growing gender gap in some sectors such as mobility. The contribution of citizens is therefore fundamental for the growth of the city as well as greater attention to the needs of all citizens regardless of social class and psycho-physical conditions. Furthermore, the study of the criticalities and factors that do not guarantee gender equity for sustainable and successful urban mobility is fundamental for the improvement of the actions and strategies to be undertaken in the short, medium and long term.

This paper performs an extensive literature review aiming to analyze the main factors, which, in terms of mobility, have contributed to an increase in the gender gap and in general the social gap in the last three (3) years. This was a period when the COVID-19 crisis affected personal mobility in various ways among the user groups and vulnerable individuals in particular. The gender gap needs to be narrowed or eliminated as it increases inequality in several areas and has repercussions in daily life (i.e. in social relationships and psychological aspects) but also in the employment and economic sector. This gap must be narrowed even further in the light of strategies that can lead to a recovery from the pandemic phase and the recent energy crisis. This research paper highlights how the gender inequality in transport was recorded in several states before and after the pandemic and attempts to provide in the concluding part some useful findings to better define planning strategies for future mobility in accordance with the sustainable development goals of Agenda 2030.

In the next Sections of this paper, we discuss and synthesize past research findings that pertain to the (a) fundamental differences regarding women's and men's mobility needs, preferences and perceptions (Sect. 2), (b) pre-pandemic initiatives and attempts to narrow the gender inequality gap based on women's transport behaviour findings (Sect. 3), and (c) influence of COVID-19 travel restrictions measures in women's mobility patterns. Our conclusions along with the future research steps are summarized in the last Sect. 5.

2 Background

The concept of gender equity has been considerably researched in the recent decades, paying particular attention to the imbalance in the mobility sector. Numerous surveys have been released to understand the change in modal choices and daily habits before and after the pandemic. A study conducted by [7] points out that women in the European Union prefer to use urban public transport and extra-urban trains (31%, men are 24%), or to travel on foot, while men are more willing to choose private means of transport. In addition, more men (59%) than women (49%) own a private car, although in the last decade the number of women using cars daily has increased.

Gender differences are also highlighted with regard to the reasons for the displacements. Men travel more often for personal purposes, including leisure, while women travel mainly for care and assistance activities. Mobility patterns of women are more complex than those of men. This stems from the fact that women are primarily responsible for care within families (mobility of care). Added to this is that women use public transport more because they are less likely to have a driving license and even more rarely have a car available (one of the aspects that defines the concept of transport poverty) [8, 10]. Because of the more frequent use of public transport, women are more interested in the quality of the service.

Women are also more attentive to environmental issues related to transport and more interested in sustainable mobility (61% against 55% of men), even if they show less enthusiasm than men towards innovative technologies, such as electromobility and automated vehicles. This aversion seems to be linked above all to security issues [11, 12].

There are many reasons that make the transport sector unattractive for women. First, it is perceived as a typically male sector, where women fear of being discriminated against and where there is little attention to the need for reconciliation between private life and work. Furthermore, being a highly male-dominated sector, the equipment and services are not women-friendly. Additionally, there is no particular attention to safety, including violence: it is indeed a sector where sexual harassment is particularly widespread. Another criticality is connected to the problem of skills: the scarcity of women with degrees and diplomas in STEM subjects (science, technology, engineering and mathematics) constitutes a further obstacle for a more substantial presence of experts, given that the technological and engineering skills are of particular importance for transport [13].

Therefore, concrete policies to encourage the entry of women in the sector must be undertaken with more energy, while it is also necessary to promote a cultural and organizational change that contrasts gender stereotypes and promotes the careers of women [14]. At the same time, initiatives are also required to combat harassment and discrimination, even in its most subtle and hidden forms. The greater involvement of women in the sector could lead to greater sensitivity to women's needs and more attention to safety issues.

Several European studies show that there is a shortage of data disaggregated by gender, both in terms of transport use and working conditions. The data referred to are mostly the result of various unsystematic research and pertain to a few countries or allow an analysis only at European level, without being able to go into the specific situations of individual countries. Therefore, greater commitment is needed, particularly in the collection of data and information to explore more in depth a topic that is of interest to everyone.

The reasons behind the differences found in the mobility of the female population compared to the male one, are mostly attributed to demographic factors (aging of the population) and to the division of roles within the labour market and family. These values have undergone enormous growth, due to the restrictions provided by the pandemic and the implementation of teleworking and online teaching. Finally, the presence of elderly people in the family and the need to look after them has also increased the gender gap in travel [15].

Before the pandemic, the female employment rate in Europe, although growing, was still lower than that of men (58% against 70%) [16–18]. Today, women account for the largest share of workers in part-time jobs in Europe and in many other countries around the world. These structural differences are consequently reflected in differences between male and female mobility patterns, which can be summarized in three aspects:

- Mode of transport used,
- Travel purpose, and
- Distances travelled.

2.1 Women and Men Move Differently in the City

Women move more because they are more likely to have part-time jobs and their daily commuting involves numerous places related to housework and childcare [19]. This involves movement needs within complex cities compared to the traditional home-work journeys. Urban planning has often been the prerogative of male decision makers, who do not always take into account the need to design mobility that recognizes the different needs of the female population, but also of the disabled, migrants or those who do not own a car.

With regard to modal choices, various studies show that men use private vehicles more than women, who, on the other hand, represent the largest share of public transport users and those who travel on foot or by bicycle: the reason of this lies in the lower average economic availability of women to support the comparatively higher costs of a private vehicle.

Women are more inclined to choose sustainable travel modes, from an environmental point of view, and they are generally more inclined to support values related to environmental protection. They consequently have a more positive perception of men regarding regulatory (physical or restrictive) measures implemented in order to achieve sustainable mobility (speed limits, restricted traffic areas or charging schemes) [20].

As regards the travel purposes, women travel less than men for professional reasons but make a greater number of trips to make purchases, to accompany family members or relatives and to carry out activities and functions inherent to family management. Their trips are characterized by a greater dispersion of origins and destinations and they are being carried out mainly outside the conventional peak hours.

Finally, regarding the average distances travelled, it has been found that men cover greater distances than women in almost all age groups. The most consistent differences are found in relation to the trips made for the purpose of work, where the distances travelled by men are greater. The result is an urban system built on car travel and the interests of motorists [21, 22].

2.2 Men Cause More Emissions Related to Transport than Women

Not only does urban mobility often ignore the gender issue, but according to a Swedish research, men's spending causes 16% more emissions harmful to the environment than that of women, despite the fact that the amount spent is practically the same. The explanation is simple: men, moving more by car, spend more money on fuel than women, whose spending is directed towards other sectors [23, 24].

Gender differences in emissions are still poorly understood by scholars, but it would be useful to keep them in mind for the decision-making process to combat climate change. It is therefore crucial to take gender differences into account when aiming to develop solutions that work for everyone. This is a reasoning that is well applicable to the relationship between urban mobility and the gender issue.

2.3 Welcoming Diversity in the Planning of the Urban Fabric

Gender equity and, more generally, inclusiveness in urban mobility assumes a central role in the public debate of many European cities, which are already working for sustainable mobility, discouraging car traffic and offering an efficient public transport system capable of responding to the needs of all citizens.

For some time now, Paris has been aiming to build an urban system capable of enabling residents to reach basic services within fifteen minutes on foot, by bike or by public transport. Important examples of inclusive mobility can be found in the city of Offenbach am Main in Hesse. Here, the residential areas have been connected with a network of cycle paths to the commercial areas and schools in order to promote the sustainable mobility of pedestrians, made up mainly of mothers and children [25, 26]. In Munich, green politicians and social democrats called for a city council hearing on gender planning with the aim of addressing issues, such as the safety of underpasses, the barriers encountered by people with strollers and the duration of traffic lights for pedestrian crossing [26]. Urban mobility will need to be rethought to accommodate diversity in planning processes as happened in Oslo, Norway, where bike sharing docking stations, initially located near downtown offices, were mostly used by men. The spread among women remained limited until stations were also added in peripheral areas and near homes. Inclusive urban mobility, which also directly affects the fundamental principle of equity and accessibility, presents itself as a useful element to rethink urban routes and create cities which are increasingly sustainable and within everyone's reach.

The most "friendly to women" European city is Vienna, Austria, with the creation of the Frauenbüro and a coordination office for planning and building on the needs and requirements of everyday life for women [27, 28]. The Austrian capital has been practicing gender mainstreaming for thirty years, defined by the European Institute for Gender Equality as the (re) organization, improvement, development and evaluation of political processes on gender equality at all levels and phases of decision-making processes. Vienna is classified as the easiest and safest European city for women, since a series of actions on sustainable mobility have been implemented. These concern the expansion of bus stops and sidewalks, thinking about the passage of prams with children, all the public transport network is wheelchair accessible, crossings have been made safer and the lighting of the city has been improved.

3   Sustainable Mobility Choices in Europe Before Pandemic

Since 2015, several research studies have been focusing on gender equality and mobility. In accordance with [29], the EU policy defined as "Gender Mainstreaming" should analyse in depth:

- The obstacles to effective gender mainstreaming,
- The mechanisms of resistance to gender mainstreaming, and
- The steps towards positive change, which gender mainstreaming can produce, even when the results stop before the "transformation".

A 2015 study by [30] focused on gender equity and on what extent both genders cooperate to expand access to paid work and control over material resources, while sharing reproductive care and responsibilities. Building on complexity theory, this paper proposes a theoretical framework for identifying cooperative behaviours within the family and workplace, as well as within broader socioeconomic, political and institutional domains.

In the same year, the UN member states unanimously adopted 17 Sustainable Development Goals (SDGs), as part of the Sustainable Development Agenda, with a planned completion date of 2030. Considering Agenda 2030, the objectives SDG 9, 12, 13, and 15 are related to innovation and infrastructures, to responsible production and consumption, and to climate change, while they all have direct links with transport. The SDG 5, i.e. "gender equality", has particularly powerful connections and an impact on transport.

The main differences in mobility patterns between women and men lie in modal choice and travel distance. Women's practices tend to be related to more sustainable means of transport, while men's practices are tied to more unsustainable transport. A study conducted by [31] analysed the relationship between mobility and gender equity by analysing the relationship between sustainability, gender equity and air transport and making recommendations for a future of transport that is economically, socially, financially and environmentally more sustainable. A study conducted in Portugal in 2015–2016 explored knowledge about women's and men's mobility and time use by considering real-time monitoring of a working day in order to examine commuting patterns. Through the acquisition of data provided by smartphones and/or devices with integrated GPS (trackers), the results highlighted gender disparities in mobility and time use [32]. Similarly, research conducted in Chile, utilising mobile phone data, showed that women visit fewer unique places than men and distribute their time less equally between these places. Mapping this mobility gap onto administrative divisions, the researchers observed a wider gap often associated with lower income and lack of public and private transport options [33].

In 2018, a study conducted by [34] highlighted the health benefits associated with cycling as a means of daily travel. This study investigated the relationship between gender equality and a range of factors using the Gender Equality Index composite indicator and its six main domains (work, money, knowledge, time, power and health), including factors related to violence and women's participation in cycling in the 28 EU member states. The results showed that the main domains of health and work were not related to women's participation in cycling. Women's participation in bicycle transport was associated with the following domains: time, power and violence. The effect of gender equality varied across indicators, with the strongest effect found for time.

As the role of women in the social structure has changed in recent decades, the question arises whether the 'gender' factor still plays a decisive role in the differences in mobility within the working population. Therefore, a Rhône-Alpes regional survey on family travel (2012–2015) and the research conducted by [35] showed that even if gender differences in working conditions and access to private cars are eliminated, differences in travel patterns between men and women would however be observed because the two genders do not have sensitivity to identical factors.

Research on shared mobility conducted in 2018 [36], through a literature review, revealed that most research is focused on assessing its impact on circulation, congestion, environmental factors, car ownership and modal shift. Very little attention is paid to how it impacts access, safety, ease or comfort of mobility for women, whose travel needs are strikingly different from those of men. The information analysed showed that shared mobility is mainly used by men [37], which implies that they are only widening the gender gap in our cities.

A study conducted in 2019 through the creation of interviews and a workshop in Sweden, analysed and correlated the concepts of gender equality, contemporary planning and sustainable "smart" mobility. In particular, it was investigated how the knowledge of gender equality is elaborated in the practice of regional planning. The results revealed that both gender equality and diversity were perceived as difficult in regional transport planning and that more knowledge and experience was needed [38].

A study conducted in Sicily, Italy on a sample of more than 1,000 adult women showed that the presence of children and income characteristics are factors that can influence women's mobility choices, such as the use of public transport, micro-owned/shared mobility or electric bicycles. The critical issues that emerged from this study are related to a different perception of safety on board public and/or shared transport or gender equality considering both the passenger and the driver's point of view [39].

Finally, a study conducted by [40] starts with an examination of gender equality goals in Sweden and suggests exploring the model in an international context through gender impact assessment (GIA) by analysing 10 years of research in transport planning. This GIA model provides insight into how transport planners would be able to assess the achievement of the 2030 Agenda goals or national gender equality targets and could establish evaluation criteria to be used to test the gender equality effects of strategic actions in transport plans sometimes generating potential conflicts of objectives [40].

4   Sustainable Mobility Choices in Europe After Pandemic

Various initiatives for the collection of data disaggregated by gender in transport have been implemented and concluded. The project Diamond provided a European reference tool for obtaining knowledge, recommendations and support on gender inclusion in current and future transport systems. It promoted the analysis of data and strategies to move towards a more inclusive and efficient transport system from a gender perspective. In particular, this project has identified and evaluated specific measures to meet the needs and expectations of women as users of different modes of transport and as workers in the sector [41].

Gender issues are of fundamental importance for the evolution of mobility and transport planning; this issue was analysed by a European project called TInnGO, that developed a network of 10 national HUBs to build capacity to generate and apply evidence on gender equality and transport issues at the European level [42]. The main factors analysed were women's mobility experience, namely safety, accessibility and reliability of transport. After March 2020, there is a large amount of research literature focusing on changing modal choices and mobility habits of users before and after the different pandemic phases [42–44]. A series of studies have generally analysed the impact of the recent pandemic on mobility. It has created enormous inconvenience by causing a sudden decrease in the number of journeys and changes in the choice and use of modes of transport. Furthermore, the effects of this health crisis on the social and economic spheres have exacerbated inequalities between population groups, with women among the most affected groups; a fact that could accentuate the already known gender gap in mobility. A study conducted by [45] defined a strategic assessment of urban mobility from the point of view of sustainability and gender equity in the context of the pandemic through a SWOT-type analysis, identifying a series of effective strategies to address the mobility scenario urban post-COVID-19. A study conducted in the Barcelona metropolitan area before and after the COVID-19 outbreak focused on gender and equality using data from smartphones. The results showed that gender plays an important role when analysing mobility patterns, as already highlighted in other studies, but, after the outbreak of the pandemic, certain population groups were more likely to change their mobility patterns, for example, highly educated population groups and those with higher incomes [46].

In the post-pandemic phase, several studies have been conducted on micro-mobility and on the use of electric scooters. Empirical findings from Italy showed that there is no heterogeneity in gender and age groups in the sub-categories that represented the people who use, do not use and reject fully the use of scooters in urban areas. While employment status was considered an important parameter in transport planning, these results are partly in contrast with the data of other Italian regions. It was also shown that there was an inconsistency between local and national results. The results suggested that socio-demographic characteristics and public opinion should be investigated in further studies. In addition, a participatory planning process should be carried out to monitor reliable evaluation in urban transport planning [47]. Another study conducted in Sicily showed, through the dissemination of an online survey that age, employment and perceived safety level of micro-mobility modes play the most important role [48]. The literature review found prior to COVID-19, placed much of its emphasis on transport policy, demand management, 'smart' technological interventions and sustainable mobility, while in the post-pandemic phase the focus had to be on the public health aspect of the crisis, rethinking transport and its contribution to post-COVID-19 economic recovery. Recognising the importance of individual behaviour and collective responsibility in protecting personal and public health during the crisis, recent research proposes a new concept of Responsible Transport to help inform and shape transport policy and practical responses to COVID-19. What is new about this proposal is that it incorporates not only environmental considerations with respect to sustainability, but also includes considerations of individual and community health and well-being. It also emphasises the role of the individual as an autonomous and responsible actor in achieving socially desired transport outcomes [49].

A study conducted on 13 different European countries considering both a pre-COVID-19 and a post-COVID-19 scenario focused on the use of the mode of transport defined as Smart Mobility. The results of that survey revealed a greater number of people walking their daily commutes, while a significant decrease in the use of public transport is observed. Although these changes affect women the most, the main reason behind this, is the need for greater security in terms of low risk of contagion, regardless of gender. Furthermore, a specific focus on the use of sustainable transport modes such as shared modes, public transport, walking and cycling with the evolution of smart cities reveals differences that arise when comparing the responses of men and women and the various groups of age [50]. Finally, the new circumstances created by the pandemic have influenced the interdependencies between the objectives of Agenda 2030. In particular, a study conducted by [51] highlighted the additional spillover effects with negative results for the achievement of SDG 5 (Gender equity) but also for SDG 9 (Infrastructure and innovation) and SDG 10 (Reduce inequalities), SDG 17 (partnerships for the objectives), and SDG 11 (sustainable cities).

5 Conclusion

Women still experience inequality issues when travelling and seeking employment in the transport sector. Due to their lifestyles and daily commitments, women's mobility patterns have significant differences on transport mode choice, travel purposes and distances travelled, when compared to the men ones. However, these differences lead women to develop more sustainable travel behaviours, which pertain to the comparatively greater use of public transport, cycling, walking and micromobility transport services. Promotion of such habits is also associated with the fulfilment of the globally recognized SDGs.

In this paper, we performed an extensive literature review to highlight the spectrum of gender inequality in transport before and after the COVID-19 crisis. In the pre-pandemic phase, our research findings highlight a widespread gender gap in all areas of shared and public mobility across Europe. During the COVID-19 pandemic, gender inequalities in transport sector have been deteriorated in some cases, due to the reduction of public transport services and the general (comparatively higher) fear of women to travel and move on their own amid serious threat of contagion.

Modern societies have realized the requirements to enhance the accessibility of women to transport sector and services. The improvement of soft modes of transport along with public transport services, as well as the employment of ITS (for getting relevant info, alerting for potential security threats etc.) lies in the core of these endeavours. These initiatives, however, are mainly observed in the comparatively wealthier and more developed countries in Europe and worldwide so far. The implementation of a gender perspective at all stages of decision-making, planning and execution is necessary especially in light of the sustainability goals introduced through the United Nations 2030 Agenda for Sustainable Development.

Future research should particularly highlight the differentiated transport needs of women, taking into account the new conditions after the pandemic. Our research has shown that in many cases the perceptions and needs of women are not investigated separately from those of men, and thus there is not enough knowledge about the conditions and potential weaknesses when using transport modes and services. A comprehensive consideration of all these differentiated needs will inevitably lead to the organization of a more resilient and inclusive transport system, which will also meet the sustainable development criteria that have been set in intergovernmental level .

Acknowledgments. The authors acknowledge the financial support from the MIUR (Ministry of Education, Universities and Research [Italy]) through a project entitled WEAKI TRANSIT: WEAK-demand areas Innovative TRANsport Shared services for Italian Towns (Project code: 20174ARRHT /CUP Code: J74I19000320008), financed with the PRIN 2017 (Research Projects of National Relevance) program. We authorize the MIUR to reproduce and distribute reprints for Governmental purposes, not-withstanding any copyright notations thereon. Any opinions, findings, and conclusions or recommendations expressed in this material are those of the authors and do not necessarily reflect the views of the MIUR.

Funding. This research work was partially funded by the MIUR (Ministry of Education, Universities and Research [Italy]) through a project entitled WEAKI TRANSIT.

References

1. Mumford, L.: The city in history: its origins, its transformations, and its prospects, Vol. 67. Houghton Mifflin Harcourt (1961)
2. Sassen, S.: Cities are at the center of our environmental future. Rev. de Ing. **31**, 72–83 (2010)
3. Moreno, C., Allam, Z., Chabaud, D., Gall, C., Pratlong, F.: Introducing the "15-Minute City": sustainability, resilience and place identity in future post-pandemic cities. Smart Cities **4**(1), 93–111 (2021)
4. Allam, Z., Nieuwenhuijsen, M., Chabaud, D., Moreno, C.: The 15-minute city offers a new framework for sustainability, liveability, and health. Lancet Planet. Health **6**(3), e181–e183 (2022)
5. Campisi, T., Basbas, S., Tesoriere, G., Trouva, M., Papas, T., Mrak, I.: how to create walking friendly cities. A multi-criteria analysis of the central open market area of Rijeka. Sustainability **12**, 9470 (2020). https://doi.org/10.3390/su12229470
6. Vaitsis, P., Basbas, S., Nikiforiadis, A.: How Eudaimonic aspect of subjective well-being affect transport mode choice? the case of thessaloniki Greece. Soc. Sci. **8**, 9 (2019). https://doi.org/10.3390/socsci8010009
7. Las Casas, G., Scorza, F., Murgante, B.: New urban agenda and open challenges for urban and regional planning. In: Calabrò, F., Della Spina, L., Bevilacqua, Carmelina (eds.) ISHT 2018. SIST, vol. 100, pp. 282–288. Springer, Cham (2019). https://doi.org/10.1007/978-3-319-92099-3_33
8. Ortega Hortelano, A., et al.: Women in European transport with a focus on research and innovation, Publications Office of the European Union (2019)
9. Beirão, G., Cabral, J.S.: Understanding attitudes towards public transport and private car: a qualitative study. Transp. Policy **14**(6), 478–489 (2007)
10. Tiikkaja, H., Liimatainen, H.: Car access and travel behaviour among men and women in car deficient households with children. Transp. Res. Interdisc. Perspect. **10**, 100367 (2021)
11. Eurobarometer 'Quality of Transport', Special Eurobarometer Report, no (422a) (2014)
12. Eurobarometer 'Mobility and Transport', Special Eurobarometer Report, No (495) (2020)
13. Makarova, E., Aeschlimann, B., Herzog, W.: The gender gap in STEM fields: the impact of the gender stereotype of math and science on secondary students' career aspirations. Front. Educ. **4**, 60 (2019)
14. Rudman, L.A., Phelan, J.E.: Backlash effects for disconfirming gender stereotypes in organizations. Res. Organ. Behav. **28**, 61–79 (2008)
15. Zanier, M.L., Crespi, I.: Facing the gender gap in aging: Italian women's pension in the European context. Soc. Sci. **4**(4), 1185–1206 (2015)
16. Sovacool, B.K., Kester, J., Noel, L., de Rubens, G.Z.: The demographics of decarbonizing transport: the influence of gender, education, occupation, age, and household size on electric mobility preferences in the Nordic region'. Glob. Environ. Chang. **52**, 86–100 (2018)
17. Berliner, R.M., Hardman, S., Tal, G.: Uncovering early adopter's perceptions and purchase intentions of automated vehicles: insights from early adopters of electric vehicles in California. Traffic Psychol. Behav. **60**, 712–722 (2019)
18. Pillinger, J.: Violence against women at work in transport, European Transport Workers Federation, ETF (2017)
19. Stein, M., Nitschke, L., Trost, L., Dirschauer, A., Deffner, J.: Impacts of commuting practices on social sustainability and sustainable mobility. Sustainability **14**(8), 4469 (2022)

20. Scorrano, M., Danielis, R.: Active mobility in an Italian city: Mode choice determinants and attitudes before and during the Covid-19 emergency. Res. Transp. Econ. **86**, 101031 (2021)
21. Olivieri, C., Fageda, X.: Urban mobility with a focus on gender: the case of a middle-income Latin American city. J. Transp. Geogr. **91**, 102996 (2021)
22. Macedo, M., Lotero, L., Cardillo, A., Menezes, R., Barbosa, H.: Differences in the spatial landscape of urban mobility: gender and socioeconomic perspectives. PLoS One **17**(3), e0260874 (2022)
23. Polk, M.: Are women potentially more accommodating than men to a sustainable transportation system in Sweden? Transp. Res. Part D: Transp. Environ. **8**(2), 75–95 (2003)
24. Räty, R., Carlsson-Kanyama, A.: Comparing energy use by gender, age and income in some European countries. Stockholm, Sweden: Research Support and Administration, Swedish Defence Research Agency (FOI) (2009)
25. Busch-Geertsema, A., Lanzendorf, M., Klinner, N.: Making public transport irresistible? the introduction of a free public transport ticket for state employees and its effects on mode use. Transp. Policy **106**, 249–261 (2021)
26. Heinelt, H., Egner, B., Hlepas, N.K. The Politics of Local Innovation
27. Will, L.: Wie die männlich geprägten Strukturen der Universität zu wanken begannen: Frauenbüro und Gleichstellungsbeauftragte (2021)
28. Herbut, I., Herbut, N.: THE IMAGE OF "WOMEN FRIENDLY CITY". Друкується за рішенням Головної Вченої Ради Київського національного університету культури і мистецтв (Протокол № 09 від 02 березня 2021 року) Редколегія, 39 (2021)
29. Cavaghan, R.: Making gender equality happen: Knowledge, change and resistance in EU gender mainstreaming. Routledge (2017)
30. Marra, M.: Cooperating for a more egalitarian society: complexity theory to evaluate gender equity. Evaluation **21**(1), 32–46 (2015)
31. Leuenberger, D.Z., Lutte, R.: Sustainability, Gender Equity, and Air Transport: Planning a Stronger Future. Public Works Management & Policy, 1087724X221075044 (2022)
32. Queirós, M., et al.: Gender equality and the city: a methodological approach to mobility in space-time. TRIA Territorio della Ricerca su Insediamenti e Ambiente **2**(9), 143–157 (2016)
33. Gauvin, L., et al.: Gender gaps in urban mobility. Humanit. Soc. Sci. Commun. **7**(1), 1–13 (2020)
34. Prati, G.: Gender equality and women's participation in transport cycling. J. Transp. Geogr. **66**, 369–375 (2018)
35. Havet, N., Bayart, C., Bonnel, P.: Why do gender differences in daily mobility behaviours persist among workers? Transp. Res. Part A: Policy Pract. **145**, 34–48 (2021)
36. Singh, Y.J.: Is smart mobility also gender-smart? J. Gend. Stud. **29**(7), 832–846 (2020)
37. Campisi, T., Tesoriere, G., Ignaccolo, M., Inturri, G., Torrisi, V.: A Behavioral and Explanatory Statistical Analysis Applied with the Advent of Sharing Mobility in Urban Contexts: Outcomes from an Under Thirty-Age Group Perspective. In: La Rosa, D., Privitera, R. (eds.) INPUT 2021. LNCE, vol. 146, pp. 633–641. Springer, Cham (2021). https://doi.org/10.1007/978-3-030-68824-0_67
38. Levin, L.: How to Integrate Gender Equality in the Future of "Smart" Mobility: A Matter for a Changing Planning Practice. In: Krömker, H. (ed.) HCII 2019. LNCS, vol. 11596, pp. 393–412. Springer, Cham (2019). https://doi.org/10.1007/978-3-030-22666-4_29
39. Campisi, T., Nahiduzzaman, K.M., Akgün, N., Ticali, D., Tesoriere, G.: Gender equality on developing transport system in Sicily: a consideration on regional scale. In: AIP Conference Proceedings, Vol. 2343(1), p. 090003. AIP Publishing LLC (2021)
40. Levin, L., Faith-Ell, C.: How to apply gender equality goals in transport and infrastructure planning. In: Integrating Gender into Transport Planning, pp. 89–118. Palgrave Macmillan, Cham (2019)

41. Gorrini, A., et al.: Unveiling women's needs and expectations as users of bike sharing services: the H2020 DIAMOND project. Sustainability **13**(9), 5241 (2021)
42. Pirra, M., Kalakou, S., Carboni, A., Costa, M., Diana, M., Lynce, A.R.: A preliminary analysis on gender aspects in transport systems and mobility services: presentation of a survey design. Sustainability **13**(5), 2676 (2021)
43. Torrisi, V., Campisi, T., Inturri, G., Ignaccolo, M., Tesoriere, G.: Continue to share? an overview on Italian travel behavior before and after the COVID-19 lockdown. In: International Conference of Computational Methods in Sciences and Engineering ICCMSE 2020 (2021). https://doi.org/10.1063/5.0048512
44. Torrisi, V., Inturri, G., Ignaccolo, M.: Introducing a mobility on demand system beyond COVID-19: evidences from users' perspective. In: International Conference of Computational Methods in Sciences and Engineering ICCMSE 2020 (2021). https://doi.org/10.1063/5.0047889
45. González-Sánchez, G., Olmo-Sánchez, M.I., Maeso-González, E.: Challenges and strategies for post-COVID-19 gender equity and sustainable mobility. Sustainability **13**(5), 2510 (2021)
46. Mejía-Dorantes, L., Montero, L., Barceló, J.: Mobility trends before and after the pandemic outbreak: analyzing the metropolitan area of Barcelona through the lens of equality and sustainability. Sustainability **13**(14), 7908 (2021)
47. Campisi, T., Akgün, N., Ticali, D., Tesoriere, G.: Exploring public opinion on personal mobility vehicle use: a case study in Palermo. Italy. Sustainability **12**(13), 5460 (2020)
48. Campisi, T., Skoufas, A., Kaltsidis, A., Basbas, S.: Gender equality and e-scooters: mind the gap! a statistical analysis of the Sicily region Italy. Soc. Sci. **10**(10), 403 (2021)
49. Budd, L., Ison, S.: Responsible transport: a post-COVID agenda for transport policy and practice. Transp. Res. Interdisc. Perspect. **6**, 100151 (2020)
50. Carboni, A., Costa, M., Kalakou, S., Pirra, M.: Gender, Smart Mobility and COVID-19. In: Krömker, H. (ed.) HCII 2021. LNCS, vol. 12791, pp. 469–486. Springer, Cham (2021). https://doi.org/10.1007/978-3-030-78358-7_33
51. Shulla, K., et al.: Effects of COVID-19 on the sustainable development goals (SDGs). Discover Sustain. **2**(1), 1–19 (2021)

Sustainable Mobility and Accessibility to Essential Services. An Assessment of the San Benedetto Neighbourhood in Cagliari (Italy)

Gloria Pellicelli[1] , Barbara Caselli[1] , Chiara Garau[2] , Vincenza Torrisi[3] , and Silvia Rossetti[1(✉)]

[1] Department of Engineering and Architecture, University of Parma, Parco Area delle Scienze, 181/A, 43124 Parma, Italy
silvia.rossetti@unipr.it
[2] Department of Civil and Environmental Engineering and Architecture, University of Cagliari, 09129 Cagliari, Italy
[3] Department of Civil Engineering and Architecture, University of Catania, Viale Andrea Doria, 6, 95125 Catania, Italy

Abstract. In line with the leading European directives, i.e. the Sustainable Goals of the 2030 Agenda, concerning urban development and emissions reduction, the authors find in the *15-min city* a model that prioritises active mobility as the main way to reach services within a neighbourhood. The paper is based on the concept of the Smart City (SC), which is defined as a city capable of serving and integrating the demands of individual citizens while concentrating on sustainability and hence on environmentally friendly lifestyles. In this context, the paper highlights pedestrian and bicycle accessibility in relation to essential services, by considering the San Benedetto neighbourhood in the city of Cagliari as a case study. The pedestrian accessibility to essential services is measured in a range of influences based on home-service travel times between 5 and 15 min, using a GIS tool. The contribution aims at identifying action plans for implementing local mobility strategies.

Keywords: GIS · Sustainable mobility · Accessibility · Smart city · Historic centre · Cagliari (Italy)

1 Introduction

According to the European report *Mapping Smart Cities in EU* [1], 248 out of 468 European cities with more than 100,000 inhabitants are considered Smart. Although there is no single definition of a Smart City (SC) [2], some key characteristics can help distinguish it from a simple sustainable city, e.g. the use of new technologies applied to urban and mobility management, to governance and urban transformation [3–8].

This paper is the result of the joint work of the authors. 'Abstract', and 'Discussion and Conclusions' were written jointly by the authors. GP wrote the 'Materials and Methods', 'Case study' and 'Results' sections, BC wrote the 'Introduction', SR wrote the 'Introduction' and the 'Materials and Methods' sections. SR, CG and VT coordinated and supervised the paper.

© The Author(s), under exclusive license to Springer Nature Switzerland AG 2022
O. Gervasi et al. (Eds.): ICCSA 2022 Workshops, LNCS 13382, pp. 423–438, 2022.
https://doi.org/10.1007/978-3-031-10592-0_31

The European policy framework on SC (Europe 2020 Strategy, adopted in 2010 by the European Commission), provides a clear plan to deal with the economic crisis by increasing European competitiveness through a smart, sustainable, and inclusive growth.

Numerous studies on the SC have been conducted in the field of urban studies, not only for metropolitan cities [9, 10] but also for medium-sized cities. A first classification of medium-sized Smart Cities can be found in the work conducted by the University of Vienna [11], which considers the SC dependent on 6 key axes (mobility, governance, living, people, economy and environment) and proposes a European ranking based on the different degrees of performance in these 6 axes. The report considers 77 medium-sized cities, of which 7 are Italian (section updated in 2014), and 90 larger cities, of which 7 are Italian (section updated in 2015) [12]. In Italy, in recent years, medium-sized cities have adopted increasingly innovative and competitive policies to reach the top positions within the Italian ranking ICity Rank 2019.

According to Garau and Pavan [13] the SC is a city that integrates different ecological, social and technological models using available resources to improve the quality of life of its inhabitants, improve efficiency in the use of environmental resources, build a green and innovation-driven economy, and promote democracy through citizen participation. Indeed, the SC concept, as a technologically advanced urban environment, meets the issue of environmental sustainability. In the last decade, the major Smart Cities in Europe and Italy have voluntary signed the Covenant of Mayors [14] (starting 2008), with the aim of reducing polluting emissions through the drafting of the Sustainable Energy Action Plan (SEAP) and, starting 2015, the Sustainable Energy and Climate Action Plan (SECAP). Indeed, in the main domain of Smart and Sustainable Cities, sustainability and urban resilience need to be prioritised as a central theme, in order to improve the liveability of cities and provide them with the essential tools to adapt to climate change [15–17].

Another relevant issue is undoubtedly sustainable mobility, which is one of the main topics addressed by Goal 11 'Sustainable Cities and Communities' of the 2030 Agenda [18]. Considering that the transportation sector accounts for approximately a quarter of Europe's greenhouse gas emissions [19], planning for a sustainable urban mobility is indispensable to pursue the objectives of CO_2 emission reduction. For this purpose, many Italian cities have implemented Sustainable Urban Mobility Plans (SUMPs), drawn up according to the European guidelines [20, 21].

Within this context, the paper focuses on the issue of sustainable and active mobility (i.e. walking and cycling), analysing and identifying critical aspects related to pedestrian and bicycle accessibility to essential public services, within the conceptual framework of the 15-min city. In particular, the study focuses on the city of Cagliari, which is not included in the European ranking, but which, according to the Italian ICity Rank 2021, it is in 9th place as the smartest city in southern Italy.

The SUMP of Cagliari [22] has been drafted both at the municipal level (from 2018) and in the Metropolitan City (starting in 2019). The main objectives concern the improvement of active mobility, the introduction of road safety measures (e.g. traffic calming solutions), the reduction of road congestion, inclusiveness towards different means of transport and, of course, the reduction of GHG emissions and pollutants. Active mobility, according to the metropolitan SUMP guidelines, will be promoted by reconnecting and extending existing routes, providing safe home/school/work routes, improving dedicated infrastructure, and encouraging cycling and walking at the social level.

The relationship between the aim of improving sustainability and meeting citizens' needs is expressed through a reconversion of urban spaces and a careful organisation and planning of the neighbourhood unit, rethinking services on the proximity dimension [23, 24]. This vision, rediscovered following the advent of the health emergency, has been embodied in the 15-min city concept centred on the 'walkable distance' from home to nearby amenities and urban spaces [25–29].

Therefore, the study is conducted at the neighbourhood scale, choosing the San Benedetto neighbourhood in Cagliari as a case study, demonstrating which public facilities and green areas, citizens can easily reach by walking or cycling, also thanks to the careful location of bike-sharing stations. Among the analysed public assets, the authors mainly see green areas as crucial, not only as meeting and socialising areas, but also as elements of the ecological-environmental infrastructure functional to climate change adaptation goals.

The remainder of the paper is organised as follows: Sect. 2 presents the analysed case study of the San Benedetto neighbourhood, a central area in the city of Cagliari; Sect. 3 illustrates the applied GIS methodology to map isochrones for assessing pedestrian accessibility levels of essential services; Sect. 4 presents the results of the methodology application in the case study. The section also analyses intermodal opportunities for the district, considering alternative means of transport, such as bike-sharing, cycle paths, and local public transport. Finally, through discussion and concluding remarks, Sect. 5 outlines some possible sustainable mobility strategies that can encourage active mobility within the neighbourhood, also thanks to specific urban policies already undertaken by the municipal administration.

2   Case Study

The chosen research area is located in the San Benedetto neighbourhood, a central district in the municipality of Cagliari, the capital of Sardinia, located in the South of the island (Fig. 1).

The district is affluent in activities and commercial services, and it is characterised by a heterogeneous road system. Via Dante Alighieri is the main street that crosses the neighbourhood from north to south. Piazza San Benedetto is the main square that serves as a roundabout rather than a gathering area. The main streets of S. Benedetto radiate out from that square.

San Benedetto is one of the most densely populated neighbourhoods in the municipality with approximately 8,000 inhabitants (in 2019) and an area of app. 1.15 km^2 (Fig. 2). The study area considered in this paper corresponds to the central part of the district, covering an area of 0.4 km^2.

Fig. 1. Location of the Municipality of Cagliari in relation to the South of Sardinia. Source: Google earth.

Fig. 2. Aerial view of the San Benedetto district in Cagliari. Source: elaboration from Google earth.

Within the neighbourhood, pedestrian spaces have been mapped and, starting from the street graph, cycle paths have been identified. Furthermore, the neighbourhood contains also traffic calming areas such as Restricted Traffic Areas (ZTL) or 30 km/h zones, as further discussed in Sect. 5: these solutions are used in historic city centres and areas close to public services and facilities to encourage slow mobility where there are no adequate spaces or road sections large enough to create new cycle paths. Those areas, properly equipped with traffic calming measures, are meant to reduce pollution in certain areas of the city and give priority to pedestrians and cyclists without diversifying roadway functions.

Another element that supports slow mobility in the neighbourhood is the presence of bike-sharing stations, as planned in the SUMP of Cagliari. Figure 3 shows the location of these elements, as well as the presence of many local public transport nodes within the neighbourhood.

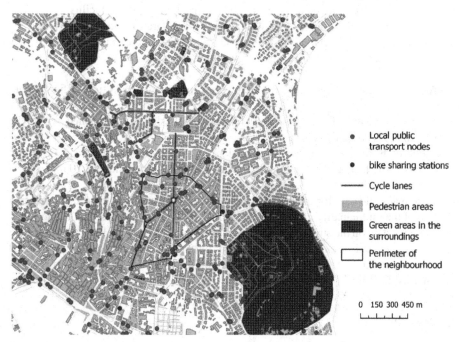

Fig. 3. Slow mobility infrastructures in the studied area: public transport nodes, bike-sharing stations, cycle lanes, pedestrian and green areas. (Color figure online)

3   Materials and Methods

In the proposed study, the accessibility assessment to essential services in the San Benedetto neighbourhood of Cagliari is based on a GIS methodology to map spatial and temporal isochrones for a specific urban area and its road network.

In this sense, isochrones represent an accessibility measure aimed at identifying the area that is within a certain distance or time from a given origin or destination. Starting from a precise spatial point, which corresponds to the location of a public facility, isochrones are created to map the service area, i.e. the area accessible in a given time from each analysed service.

There are many GIS-based methodologies and tools that can be used for this kind of analysis (some of them are described in [30]). Within the context of this paper, an online tool called ISO4app, which determines a specific pedestrian network to reach a service by means of a certain setting, was used.

To map the pedestrian isochrones, it was necessary to set in the online tool some specific key elements such as speed and time factor: an average pedestrian speed of 4 km/h was considered for all the analyses, while the time factor for the service area was modified in relation to each type of analysed service, looking at the travel time that a possible target user may be disposed to walk to reach that specific facility.

In particular, as also highlighted by the Universal Declaration of Human Rights ([31] art. 25–26), despite the fact that wellbeing today has increased their number, the essential services considered in the analysis and their optimal access times are:

- grocery shops, which should be reached within an optimal access time of 5 min from home;
- personal services (pharmacies, polyclinics), which should be reached within an optimal access time of 10 min;
- schools of the first cycle of education (kindergartens, nurseries, primary and secondary schools), which should be optimally reached within an access time of 10 min.

Base maps and data for the analysis were collected from the Territorial Information System of the municipality of Cagliari and from the Geoportal of Sardinia Region (e.g. cartographic data on the street network and on buildings, but also the location of existing public services and of public transport stops). Furthermore, some data were collected also from open data websites, like Open Street Map for the location of certain types of commercial facilities.

4   Results

4.1   Access Time to Grocery Shops, Personal Facilities and Schools

A first step of the analysis focused on the service area of essential services of daily or frequent access for the users: grocery shops, personal care and basic health facilities (pharmacies, medical doctors and polyclinics), and schools (nursery schools; kindergartens; primary and secondary schools).

Starting from the location of each essential service typology in the San Benedetto analysed area and its immediate surroundings (Fig. 4), the pedestrian isochrones for each service were calculated. As it emerges for the analysis, these services are available in the district, and they are easily accessible by foot from almost all the residential buildings located in the district.

Specifically, as shown in Table 1, the 96% of the buildings in S. Benedetto are located within a 5-min isochrone from a grocery shop (Fig. 5). The only two areas of the analysed area in the North-West and South-West that are not contained within the 5-min isochrone, have however a pedestrian access time to grocery shops of less than 15 min.

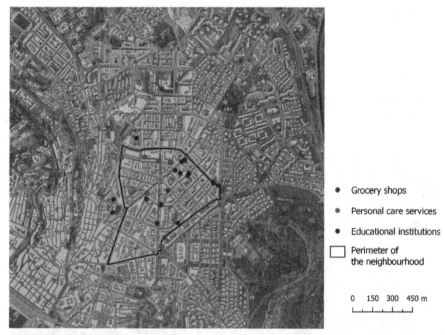

Fig. 4. Essential services (Grocery shops, personal care, education) within the neighbourhood and in the immediate proximity.

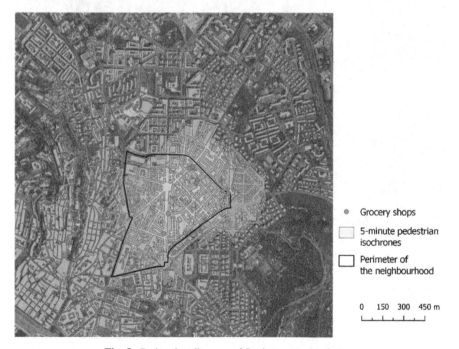

Fig. 5. Pedestrian distance of 5 min to grocery shops

Table 1. Percentage of buildings in the analysed area of S. Benedetto within the 5-min pedestrian isochrone from a grocery shop.

Total number of buildings in the analysed area	Buildings included in the 5-min isochrone from a grocery shop	% of analysed buildings located within 5 min walking from a shop
114	110	96%

Looking at personal care and basic health services, the whole analysed area is well served and included in a 10-min isochrone (Fig. 6a), with the exception of two medical clinics that serve the analysed neighbourhood, but they are not within walking distance (Fig. 6b). Similarly, school services can be reached by each residential building in the neighbourhood and in the close surroundings outside the perimeter (Fig. 7).

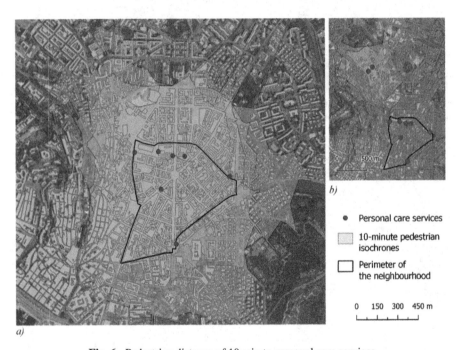

• Personal care services

☐ 10-minute pedestrian isochrones

☐ Perimeter of the neighbourhood

0   150   300   450 m

Fig. 6. Pedestrian distance of 10 min to personal care services

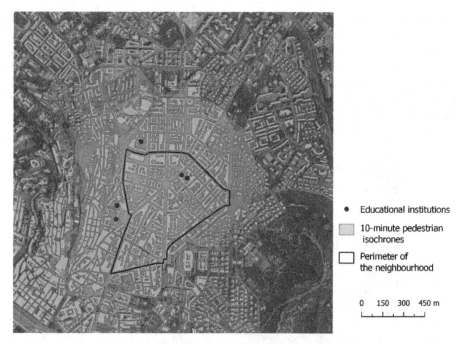

Fig. 7. Pedestrian distance of 10 min to first cycle schools

4.2 Accessibility to Public Green Areas

The second step of the analysis focused on accessibility to public green areas, which are probably the only type of public facility which is lacking within San Benedetto district. However, as it emerges from Fig. 8, there are some green areas in the surrounding, and the performed analysis focused on assessing their accessibility levels from the analysed area, checking if they are reachable by foot and by bike, also considering the availability of urban bike lanes and bike-sharing stations.

The most significant public green areas in the surrounding of the San Benedetto neighbourhood are:

- to the north, *Giardino della fermata di Genneruxi* (a green area of app. 1,000 m^2); *Giardini di via Castiglione* (a green area of app. 2,000 m^2); *Parco Giovanni Paolo II* and the adjacent *Parco Lions*, which cover an area of over 20,000 m^2 and include also a restaurant; *Giardino Biasi* of about 2,200 m^2; and *Parco Siro Vannelli* of almost 5,000 m^2. To the north, we also consider the largest urban park, *Parco di Monte Claro*;
- to the South, two adjacent parks: *Parco Martiri delle Foibe* and *Parco delle Rimembranze* of app. 4,000 m^2.
- to the East, a large open space *Parco di Monte Urpinu*.
- to the West, *Giardini pubblici*, an area of app. 16.000 m^2 which also host artworks.

The optimal access time considered to reach a public green facility should be of app. 10 min by foot. San Benedetto neighbourhood is well equipped with pedestrian facilities and infrastructures and has very good connections with surrounding districts of Cagliari thanks to evenly distributed local public transport stops (Fig. 3). On the contrary, bicycle lanes are scarcely present (Table 2) and cover only 15% of the length of the streets in the district. Outside the district, there are bicycle lanes on the extension of *via Dante Alighieri* and further north on *via dei Giudicati*. With reference to green areas, the cycle path that goes around the *Parco di Monte Urpinu* to the east is of considerable importance.

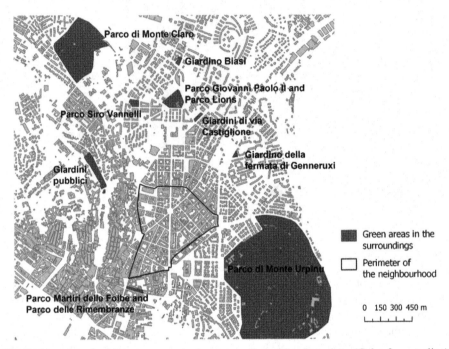

Fig. 8. Location of public green areas in the surrounding of San Benedetto (Color figure online)

Table 2. Presence of cycle lanes along the streets of the analysed San Benedetto area

Total linear meters of streets in the analysed area	Linear meters of cycle lanes	%
9,678 m	1,477 m	15%

The implementation of bike-sharing stations, planned in the ongoing SUMP of Cagliari (2021), provides a good modal choice to move in the area quickly and sustainably. The pedestrian accessibility of the bike-sharing stations shown in Table 3 is easy for about half of the buildings, and less for the rest, although the distances are not too wide (Fig. 9).

Table 3. Accessibility of bike sharing stations by buildings in the neighbourhood

Total number of buildings	Buildings included in the 5-min isochrone from a bike sharing station	% of buildings
114	56	49%

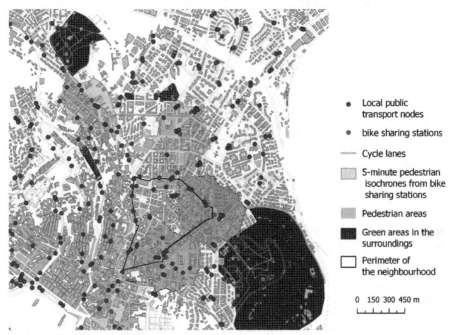

Fig. 9. 5-min pedestrian isochrones from bike sharing facilities in San Benedetto and its surroundings (Color figure online)

Nevertheless, by calculating through the ISO4app tool the isolines starting from the main public green areas in the surroundings of San Benedetto neighbourhood, it was possible to identify the areas covered within 10 min of walking time (Fig. 10). Just from over half of the buildings in the analysed areas, it is possible to reach a green area within a 10-min walk (Table 4).

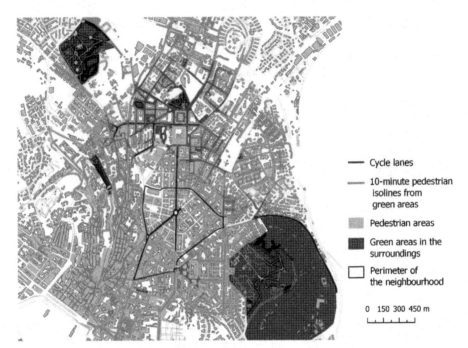

Fig. 10. 10-min pedestrian isolines from the public green areas surrounding the neighbour-hood. (Color figure online)

Table 4. Buildings in the neighbourhood from which it is possible to reach a public green area within 10 min.

Total number of buildings in the analysed area	Buildings included in the 10-min isochrone from a green area	% of buildings
114	61	53%

5 Discussion and Conclusions

Today, sustainable mobility should play a leading role of daily movements in the city, both from the energy transition and SC perspective, and cities should aim at enhancing and rediscovering the values of proximity, socialisation, and physical health.

An important element of smart planning is therefore to return to a human-centred vision to focus on citizens in designing urban environments and services able to meet citizens' needs, including the most vulnerable ones [32–35].

Within this framework, the contribution proposed an accessibility study to proximity services for a central district in the city of Cagliari, with the aim of verifying if all residents have the possibility to easily reach essential amenities by foot.

From the data collected and the analysis performed, it emerged that the neighbour-hood is very well served and provides high accessibility levels. However, even if the neighbourhood is well equipped in terms of footpaths and pedestrian infrastructures, high traffic flows are still resulting in a greater potential risk for pedestrians and cyclists. Many areas of the neighbourhood are not included yet in the 30 km/h zones, nor in the Restricted Traffic Zones. Furthermore, bike lanes are only present along the main street and not all buildings have high accessibility (less than 5 min on foot) to the bike sharing facilities.

In accordance with the SUMPs that are being developed in Italy, active mobility could be encouraged and made safer by limiting vehicle traffic and introducing Traffic Calming areas such as the extension of Restricted Traffic Areas (ZTL) or 30 km/h zones in the historic centre [36], as it has already been proposed even in Cagliari at municipal level (Fig. 11).

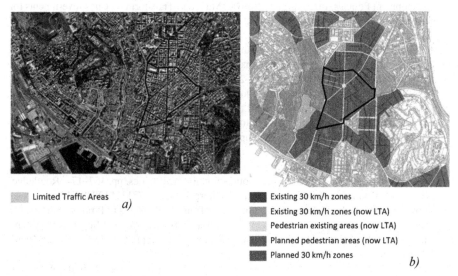

Limited Traffic Areas

a)

Existing 30 km/h zones
Existing 30 km/h zones (now LTA)
Pedestrian existing areas (now LTA)
Planned pedestrian areas (now LTA)
Planned 30 km/h zones

b)

Fig. 11. a) Limited Traffic Areas and b) existing and planned 30 km/h zones. Sources: Municipality of Cagliari Geoportal.

In conclusion, as it emerged from the analysis, the neighbourhood is very rich in services and facilities, and therefore accessibility levels are very high, with the partial exception of pedestrian accessibility to public green areas, whose accessibility is guaranteed in times of more than 10 min walking. An accessibility study like the one proposed may be certainly more effective and highlight more possible accessibility weaknesses in more critical areas that need urban regeneration interventions or that are more peripheral.

A possible development of this work is to link bike-sharing data with the distance to green areas to combine pedestrian mobility with cycling, also taking into consideration the usage patterns and adoption barriers [37]. Further developments of the work may also include a more detailed definition of the isochrones (e.g. by including in the service area the waiting time at road intersection), and a detailed mapping of population distribution within the neighbourhood to assess the exact percentages of inhabitants served within the service areas (as proposed in [25]) .

Acknowledgements. This work started and developed as a result of a project proposal within the doctoral course "Smart and Sustainable Cities (2nd edition)" held at the University of Cagliari (https://dottorati.unica.it/dotticar/smart-and-sustainable-cities-2-Edizione/).

References

1. Manville, C., et al.: Mapping smart city in the EU (2014). https://www.europarl.europa.eu/RegData/etudes/etudes/join/2014/507480/IPOL-ITRE_ET%282014%29507480_EN.pdf
2. Hollands, R.G.: Will the real smart city please stand up? intelligent, progressive or entrepreneurial? City **12**, 303–320 (2008). https://doi.org/10.1080/13604810802479126
3. Lombardi, P., Vanolo, A.: Smart City as a Mobile Technology: Critical Perspectives on Urban Development Policies. In: Rodríguez-Bolívar, M.P. (ed.) Transforming City Governments for Successful Smart Cities. PAIT, vol. 8, pp. 147–161. Springer, Cham (2015). https://doi.org/10.1007/978-3-319-03167-5_8
4. Nam, T., Pardo, T.A.: Smart city as urban innovation: focusing on management, policy, and context. In: Proceedings of the 5th International Conference on Theory and Practice of Electronic Governance (ICEGOV 2011, 26–28 September 2011, Tallin, Estonia). ACM Press, New York, pp. 185–194 (2011). https://doi.org/10.1145/2072069.2072100
5. Garau, C., Nesi, P., Paoli, I., Paolucci, M., Zamperlin, P.: A Big Data Platform for Smart and Sustainable Cities: Environmental Monitoring Case Studies in Europe. In: Gervasi, O., et al. (eds.) ICCSA 2020. LNCS, vol. 12255, pp. 393–406. Springer, Cham (2020). https://doi.org/10.1007/978-3-030-58820-5_30
6. Garau, C., Desogus, G., Zamperlin, P.: Governing technology-based urbanism. In: Willis, K.S., Aurigi, A. (eds.) The Routledge Companion to Smart Cities, pp. 157–174. Routledge, New York : Routledge, 2020. (2020). https://doi.org/10.4324/9781315178387-12
7. Torrisi, V., Ignaccolo, M., Inturri, G.: Innovative Transport Systems to Promote Sustainable Mobility: Developing the Model Architecture of a Traffic Control and Supervisor System. In: Gervasi, O., et al. (eds.) ICCSA 2018. LNCS, vol. 10962, pp. 622–638. Springer, Cham (2018). https://doi.org/10.1007/978-3-319-95168-3_42
8. Campisi, T., et al.: A New Vision on Smart and Resilient Urban Mobility in the Aftermath of the Pandemic: Key Factors on European Transport Policies. In: Gervasi, O., et al. (eds.) ICCSA 2021. LNCS, vol. 12958, pp. 603–618. Springer, Cham (2021). https://doi.org/10.1007/978-3-030-87016-4_43
9. Battarra, R., Gargiulo, C., Tremiterra, M.R., Zucaro, F.: Smart mobility in Italian metropolitan cities: a comparative analysis through indicators and actions. Sustain. Cities Soc. **41**, 556–567 (2018). https://doi.org/10.1016/j.scs.2018.06.006
10. Zamperlin, P., Garau, C.: Smart region': analisi e rappresentazione della smartness delle città metropolitane Italiane. Bollettino dell'Associazione Italiana di Cartografia, 59–71 (2017). https://doi.org/10.13137/2282-572X/21828
11. Giffinger, R., Fertner, C., Kramar, H., Kalasek, R., Pichler-Milanovic, N., Meijers, E.: Smart Cities: Ranking of European Medium-Sized Cities. Centre of Regional Science (SRF), Vienna, Austria, January (2007). http://www.smartcities.eu/download/smart_cities_final_report.pdf
12. European Smart Cities ranking (2019). http://www.smart-cities.eu/index.php?cid=-1&ver=Icity%20Rank
13. Garau, C., Pavan, V.: Evaluating urban quality: indicators and assessment tools for smart sustainable cities. Sustainability **10**, 575 (2018). https://doi.org/10.3390/su10030575
14. Covenant of Mayor. https://www.pattodeisindaci.eu/about-it/l-iniziativa/obiettivi-e-finalita.html

15. Strategia Nazionale di Adattamento ai Cambiamenti Climatici (2015). https://www.mite.gov.it/sites/default/files/archivio/allegati/clima/documento_SNAC.pdf
16. EU Adaptation Strategy. https://climate-adapt.eea.europa.eu/eu-adaptation-policy/strategy
17. Intergovernmental Panel on Climate Change. Sixth Assessment Report (2022). https://www.ipcc.ch/report/ar6/wg2/
18. United Nation's Sustainable Development Goals of Agenda 2030. https://www.un.org/sustainabledevelopment/
19. European Environmental Agency (2021), Greenhouse gas emissions from transport in Europe. https://www.eea.europa.eu/ims/greenhouse-gas-emissions-from-transport
20. Torrisi, V., Garau, C., Ignaccolo, M., Inturri, G.: "Sustainable Urban Mobility Plans": Key Concepts and a Critical Revision on SUMPs Guidelines. In: Gervasi, O., et al. (eds.) ICCSA 2020. LNCS, vol. 12255, pp. 613–628. Springer, Cham (2020). https://doi.org/10.1007/978-3-030-58820-5_45
21. Torrisi, V., Garau, C., Inturri, G., Ignaccolo, M.: Strategies and actions towards sustainability: encouraging good ITS practices in the SUMP vision. In: AIP Conference Proceedings, Vol. 2343(1), p. 090008. AIP Publishing LLC (2021).https://doi.org/10.1063/5.0047897
22. Città metropolitana di Cagliari, SUMP–Plan objectives (2021). https://www.cittametropolitanacagliari.it/documents/36143/0/Relazione_del_primo_rapporto_PUMS+%281%29.pdf/e55c9ddb-92d4-0b0f-32c3-b3068397469e.   https://www.cittametropolitanacagliari.it/web/cmdca/documenti-scaricabili
23. Campisi, T., Caselli, B., Rossetti, S., Torrisi, V.: The evolution of sustainable mobility and urban space planning: exploring the factors contributing to the regeneration of car parking in living spaces. Transp. Res. Procedia 60, 76–83 (2022). https://doi.org/10.1016/j.trpro.2021.12.011
24. Ignaccolo, M., Inturri, G., Calabrò, G., Torrisi, V., Giuffrida, N., Le Pira, M.: Auditing streets' pedestrian compatibility: A study of school sites' requalification. In: Tira, M., Pezzagno, M., Richiedei, A. (eds.) Pedestrians, Urban Spaces and Health, pp. 30–34. CRC Press (2020). https://doi.org/10.1201/9781003027379-6
25. Caselli, B., Carra, M., Rossetti, S., Zazzi, M.: From urban planning techniques to15-minute neighbourhoods. A theoretical framework and GIS-based analysis of pedestrian accessibility to public services. Eur. Transp. 60, 1–15 (2022). https://doi.org/10.48295/ET.2021.85.10
26. Moreno, C., Allam, Z., Chabaud, D., Gall, C., Pratlong, F.: Introducing the '15-Minute City': sustainability, resilience and place identity in future post-pandemic cities. Smart Cities 4, 93–111 (2021). https://doi.org/10.3390/smartcities4010006
27. Pozoukidou, G., Chatziyiannaki, Z.: 15-minute city: decomposing the new urban planning eutopia. Sustainability 13, 1–25 (2021). https://doi.org/10.3390/su13020928
28. Weng, M., et al.: The 15-minute walkable neighbourhoods: measurement, social inequalities and implications for building healthy communities in urban China. J. Transp. Health 13, 259–273 (2019). https://doi.org/10.1016/j.jth.2019.05.005
29. Carra, M., Rossetti, S., Tiboni, M., Vetturi, D.: Urban regeneration effects on walkability scenarios. An application of space-time assessment for the people-and-climate oriented perspective. Tema J. Land Use Mobility Environ. 15, 101–114 (2022). https://doi.org/10.6092/1970-9870/864
30. Rossetti S., Tiboni M., Vetturi D., Zazzi M., Caselli B.: Measuring pedestrian accessibility to public transport in urban areas: a GIS-based discretisation approach. Eur. Transp. (76), 1–12 (2020). ISSN 1825-3997. (Paper n° 2)
31. United nation's universal declaration of human rights (1948)
32. Tira, M., Tiboni, M., Rossetti, S., De Robertis, M.: "Smart" Planning to Enhance Nonmotorised and Safe Mobility in Today's Cities. In: Papa, R., Fistola, R., Gargiulo, C. (eds.) Smart Planning: Sustainability and Mobility in the Age of Change. GET, pp. 201–213. Springer, Cham (2018). https://doi.org/10.1007/978-3-319-77682-8_12

33. Tiboni, M., Rossetti, S., Vetturi, D., Torrisi, V., Botticini, F., Schaefer, M.D.: Urban policies and planning approaches for a safer and climate friendlier mobility in cities: strategies initiatives and some analysis. Sustainability **13**, 1778 (2021). https://doi.org/10.3390/su13041778

34. Carra, M., Rossetti, S., Tiboni, M., Vetturi, D.: Can urban regeneration improve walkability? a space-time assessment for the Tintoretto area in Brescia. Transp. Res. Procedia **60**, 394–401 (2022). https://doi.org/10.1016/j.trpro.2021.12.051

35. Guida, C., Carpentieri, G.: Quality of life in the urban environment and primary health services for the elderly during the Covid-19 pandemic: an application to the city of Milan (Italy). Cities **110**, 103038 (2021). https://doi.org/10.1016/j.cities.2020.103038

36. Pellicelli, G., Rossetti, S., Caselli, B., Zazzi, M.: Urban regeneration as an opportunity to redesign sustainable mobility. experiences from the Emilia-Romagna regional call. Transp. Res. Procedia **60**, 576–583 (2022). https://doi.org/10.1016/j.trpro.2021.12.074

37. Torrisi, V., Ignaccolo, M., Inturri, G., Tesoriere, G., Campisi, T.: Exploring the factors affecting bike-sharing demand: evidence from student perceptions, usage patterns and adoption barriers. Transp. Res. Procedia **52**, 573–580 (2021). https://doi.org/10.1016/j.trpro.2021.01.068

Health and Mobility in the Post-pandemic Scenario. An Analysis of the Adaptation of Sustainable Urban Mobility Plans in Key Contexts of Italy

Alfonso Annunziata[1] , Giulia Desogus[1] , Francesca Mighela[2],
and Chiara Garau[1(✉)]

[1] Department of Civil and Environmental Engineering and Architecture, University of Cagliari,
09129 Cagliari, Italy
cgarau@unica.it
[2] Space S.p.A, 09134 Cagliari, Italy

Abstract. The combination of concerns about the Covid-19 pandemic and structural problems relating to social injustice, climate change, and public health requires a radical reorganisation of transport structures, urban services, and the built fabric of metropolitan regions. This need is central to the pandemic era's public debate: more significantly, it is reflected in the stimuli to metropolitan and urban policies aimed at adapting regional and mobility plans in order to realise a model of a smart, inclusive, sustainable, competitive and resilient city. The paper proposes a comparative content analysis to investigate the SUMPs adopted by the Italian metropolitan cities of Milan and Bologna, as well as their modification via the adoption of emergency plans and adaptation strategies for the post-pandemic scenario. The study's purpose is to deduce a set of transferable guidelines. Based on earlier research, this study selects the Metropolitan City of Cagliari as a case study for implementing the set of guidelines derived from the comparative content analysis. The study significantly contributes to urban studies by investigating the transformation of concepts and criteria that underpin transport and mobility policies in the Italian context.

Keywords: Sustainable Urban Mobility Plans · Health · Pandemic · Urban policies

1 Introduction

The increasing social, economic and environmental impacts of mobility dependency on private motorised transport have determined the need for a radical transformation

---

This paper is the result of the joint work of the authors. 'Abstract' 'Methodology', and 'Selection of the Case Study' were written jointly by the authors. Alfonso Annunziata wrote the 'Literature review'. Giulia Desogus wrote the 'Results'. Francesca Mighela wrote the 'Introduction' and Chiara Garau wrote the 'Discussion and Conclusions'. Chiara Garau and Francesca Mighela coordinated and supervised the paper.

O. Gervasi et al. (Eds.): ICCSA 2022 Workshops, LNCS 13382, pp. 439–456, 2022.
https://doi.org/10.1007/978-3-031-10592-0_32

of transport policies in recent years. According to the European Strategy and Policy Analysis System [1], the transport and mobility sectors influence cities' climate change, energy consumption, and pollution levels. The European Union (EU) has promoted legislation to foster the integration of sustainable mobility projects and new modes of transportation in order to mitigate mobility and its associated consequences in large cities. Since 2013, the need for more sustainable and integrated planning protocols has been recognised [2, 3].

The EU has identified the Sustainable Urban Mobility Plan (SUMP) as a paradigm shift in urban transport planning. The SUMP is defined as a strategic plan to boost people's quality of life by assuring universal access to services and urban amenities and by strengthening the social, economic, and environmental sustainability of urban mobility systems [4, 5].

Moreover, the need for social distancing, the consequent reduction of the number of public transit users, and the modification of social and individual practices that underpin pandemic and post-pandemic scenarios requires a radical re-organisation and re-structuration of the city and, in particular, of the mobility system [6]. Consequently, municipalities and metropolitan cities are faced with the challenge of revising and adapting SUMPs, that have been implemented or are already being prepared to meet the requirements arising from the pandemic emergency's demands.

The present study is concerned with the Italian situation. It includes a comparative content analysis of the SUMPs and of the adaptation strategies formulated by the Metropolitan Cities of Milan (MCMI) and Bologna (MCBO). The aim is twofold: 1) to examine how the conceptual premises and policies included in the SUMPs have evolved or can change in response to the post-pandemic scenario needs and 2) to define a set of guidelines transferable to other metropolitan areas, and in particular to the Metropolitan City of Cagliari (MCCA). The relevance of this study is based on two aspects: firstly, it frames the discourse on smart and sustainable mobility within the general discourse on the re-organisation of urbanised areas, underlining the need for integrating transport and urban strategic plans at the metropolitan scale. Secondly, it highlights the centrality of interdependencies among transport infrastructures, land uses and metropolitan scale amenities, and built-up areas as a central aspect of strategies for adapting metropolitan areas to the post-pandemic scenario.

The article is divided into five sections. Following the introduction, Sect. 2 discusses the structure and aims of the SUMP and strategies for cities' adaptation to the post-pandemic scenario. Section 3 illustrates and describes the technique and case study. Section 4 summarises the relevant findings of the comparative content analysis of the SUMPs and the adaptation strategies adopted by the MCMI and the MCBO. Finally, Sect. 5 discusses the significance of the findings for developing a set of transferrable guidelines.

2   Literature Review

The European Strategy and Policy Analysis System [1] underlines the transport sector's impact on climate alteration, soil and energy consumption and pollution levels in cities. These problems have led to a deterioration in citizens' quality of life. For this reason, mobility and transport [7] have become central concepts in the scientific literature on urban development and social and environmental sustainability and in public debates on the main European and international initiatives concerning smart cities and sustainable mobility. Coni et al. [8] provide an example of a smart, sustainable, and green mobility transition. The authors outline the strategic plan adopted by the Metropolitan City of Cagliari. This plan includes implementing Intelligent Transportation Systems (ITSs) technologies, improving routes and fleet buses, limiting vehicular traffic in the historic centre, extending pedestrian areas, developing a network of cycle paths, promoting car-sharing, car-pooling, bike-sharing, electric mobility, and completing and integrating the tramway network.

Citizens' lifestyles have altered as a result of these actions: they began walking, running, cycling, and taking public transportation, discovering a new way to explore their city. As a result, public transportation services play a crucial part in the sustainability of cities, and regardless of how appealing they are, citizens might consider them as a real and practical instrument for getting around a city and fostering sustainable mobility [9]. For a public transport system to be attractive, it must meet users' needs. Several authors have focused on the aspects that are essential for them, analysing the quality of these services through a survey campaign conducted among passengers [10–15]. Therefore, a good public transport system is a key aspect of a smart city for ensuring mobility opportunities for all citizens, containing the environmental impacts generated by traffic, and improving road safety.

Besides, in terms of healthy cities, air pollution, noise, congestion, and accidents, sustainable mobility has become the primary goal of EU initiatives and current research on the subject of smart city 3.0 [16–20]. Indeed, the EU has increasingly encouraged policies focused on sustainable mobility projects and integrating new forms of mobility to significantly reduce pollution in large cities. Within this perspective, the EU introduces a new paradigm for urban transportation planning by adopting the Sustainable Urban Mobility Plan (SUMP) [21, 22]. The "SUMP" is defined as a strategic plan that aims to deliver a higher quality of life, while also meeting the mobility needs of people and businesses in cities and their environs. SUMPs are based on current planning methodologies and consider the notions of integration, participation, and evaluation [23]. Thus, the SUMPs are based on principles designed to guarantee that the EU's goals for a competitive and resource-efficient European transportation system are achieved [8].

According to Troisi et al. [23], SUMPs are no longer exclusively concerned with the concept of mobility, but rather with sustainability, embracing a human-centred focus [24]. Sampaio et al. state that "SUMPs were established and implemented to reduce externalities associated with transportation by outlining various methods to improve the efficiency and sustainability of urban mobility" [25, p. 1].

Italian Institutions acknowledged in 2017 the importance of SUMPs as the fundamental tool for establishing a balanced, sustainable, and effective system of mobility and access. Indeed, the Italian Ministry of Infrastructure and Transport (IMIT) adopted the rules for SUMPs in 2017, dubbed "Piano Urbano della Mobilità Sostenibile – PUMS" in Italian. The national regulations are based on the publication "Guidelines. Developing and Putting in Place a Long-Term Urban Mobility Plan" [26, p. 9] and define the structure of the drafting and adoption process of the SUMPs, the reference strategies, the general and specific objectives, and the indicators to be used in determining if the SUMPs' goals are met.

More precisely, the European and national legislation - particularly the instructions provided by the European Commission's Directorate-General for Mobility and Transport and the Italian Ministry of Infrastructure and Transport's decree of 4 August 2017 – identify the eight stages of the drafting of the SUMP: i) Definition of the interdisciplinary/inter-institutional group of work; ii) Preparation of the baseline scenario that describes the current situation; iii) Start of the participatory process; iv) Definition of objectives; v) Participatory construction of the Plan scenario; vi) Strategic Environmental Assessment (SEA); vii) Adoption of the Plan and subsequent approval; viii) Monitoring. In particular, the participated construction of the plan scenario is articulated in three stages: i) the development of a reference scenario that describes the transformation of the metropolitan area as a result of the evolution of socio-economic trends and the completion of planned interventions in urban form and infrastructures; ii) the development of alternative scenarios, comprising alternative sets of measures; iii) the evaluation and comparison of sets of alternative measures and the development of the Plan Scenario. Thus, the formulation of the project scenario derives from an iterative process of perfecting the measures comprised in the alternative scenarios: these alternative measures are evaluated in terms of economic, financial, and managerial sustainability, and of expected benefits resulting from the reduction of congestion, consumption, and emissions, and from the improvement of safety, and of the quality of life of citizens. The alternative measures, considered to meet the requirements and quantitative targets defined in the preliminary stages, are then combined and integrated into the Plan scenario. Consequently, the Plan Scenario formalises the strategies and the related actions that structure the Sustainable Urban Mobility Plan. Lastly, the Plan's specific objectives must refer to four general purposes, including i) the development of access and the functionality of the transportation system, ii) environmental sustainability; iii) socioeconomic sustainability, iv) road safety; v) Improved integration of mobility system development and territorial organisation and development (residential areas and urban planning for economic, cultural, and tourism poles);

The mobility and urban structure organisations are made particularly urgent by reducing available resources and the permanent, radical modification of social practices determined by the Pandemic. Consequently, the post-pandemic scenario poses the need for public actions that combine the goal of the economic restart, the purpose of contrasting climate alteration, and the intent of re-structuring spaces, infrastructures, and urban functions/ services to meet sanitary precautions and to accommodate the modified lifestyles [27].

The Italian National Institute for Urban Studies (INU) states that the need to ensure substantial consistency among relevant and diverse objectives postulates the relevance of future visions and strategic plans as instruments for facilitating the transition to a new development model [28]. Hence, strategic plans and future visions emerge as a central aspect of implementing the European strategy of the Green Deal. This strategy intends to mitigate the adverse outcomes of climate alteration and the construction of fairer and more sustainable urban environments via the decarbonisation of the productive system, the promotion of circular economy and sustainable tourism, and urban regeneration [29–31].

Within this perspective strategic plans must include specific lines of actions related to the re-organization of mobility structures, the built-up areas, urban equipment and facilities and the public space, including: i) the promotion of sustainable mobility by expanding the system of pedestrian and cycle routes, the regeneration and valorisation of open spaces contiguous to pedestrian and cycling surfaces; ii) the increase in the service offer of metropolitan rail systems and local transport system; A peculiar problem regards the increase of motorized private transport travels to replace public transport trips, as a consequence of concerns related to inter-personal distancing and the reduction of contacts; iii) the modification of public transportation nodes, including the adaptation of platforms, to accommodate longer trains, configured to increase the capacity of public transport and ensure physical distancing; iv) the modernization of secondary roads, particularly in the marginal suburban areas; v) the regeneration of public spaces and of road spaces, aimed at improving and creating public spaces for social and recreational activities, including green areas, parks, gardens, natural and semi-natural areas, and urban vegetable gardens [32, 33]. The subsequent section describes the methodology with the case study. It investigates the actions proposed by the SUMPs and the Emergency Plans of the Metropolitan Cities of Milan and Bologna to meet the objectives of climate resilience, salubrity, and social and economic sustainability.

3 Methodology

The analysis focuses on the Sustainable Urban Mobility Plans of the Metropolitan cities of Bologna and Milan. It investigates the mobility systems' adaptation strategies to the pandemic and post-pandemic scenarios.

The analysis is articulated in four stages: i) a content analysis of the documents describing the SUMP; ii) a content analysis of the documents presenting the adaptation strategies adopted for the post-pandemic scenarios; iii) comparison and identification of the most significant modifications in the conceptualisation of the urban environment, public spaces and mobility structures; iv) identification of most significant actions proposed to combine the objectives of the SUMP and the need for improving the sustainability, inclusion, resilience, and salubrity of the built environment, determined by the COVID-19 pandemic [37].

The comparative content analysis investigates and compares the contents of the selected SUMPs and of the adaptation strategies related to specific dimensions of metropolitan mobility.

These dimensions include road infrastructure, pedestrian and cycling infrastructure, public transportation, circulation, parking, urban form, and mobility culture.

Moreover, the specific dimensions of the actions proposed by the SUMPs and by the Adaptation strategies are articulated in several sub-categories related to distinct aspects of the components of the urban environment. More precisely, the category road infrastructures include the sub-categories Configuration, Maintenance, Composition, Intersections, and Coexistence. These sub-categories refer to the configuration of the system of roads and open spaces, the functional conditions of the road infrastructure equipment, the composition of the road space, the design of intersections, and the co-existence or competition among road functions. Public transport is described in terms of configuration and arrangement of infrastructure, service offer, configuration, design, and functional diversity of stations and nodes. The configuration of land plots and buildings, land use pattern, the location of large-scale facilities, such as industrial regions and functional poles, and the configuration of metropolitan ecological infrastructure are the considered aspects of urban form. Lastly, parking infrastructure is described as availability, determined by its size and density, distribution in relation to arterial infrastructure, and location concerning road space. The findings from the comparative content analysis are then utilised to define a set of guidelines for drafting the SUMP for the Metropolitan City of Cagliari. A description of the case study is presented in the subsequent section.

3.1 Selection of the Case Study

The study focuses on SUMPs adopted by the metropolitan cities of Milan and Bologna. These SUMPs are selected based on four criteria: i) participation in the Italian SUMPs Observatory initiative; ii) state of advancement of the SUMP; the analysis focused on approved SUMPs; iii) scope of the SUMP. The study identifies as the unit of analysis the metropolitan area to understand the entire field of socio-economic interdependencies that engenders the demand for mobility involving urbanised areas; iv) Publication of guidelines for the adaptation of mobility and urban policies to the post-pandemic scenario. The preliminary analysis of the SUMPs underlines the criticalities of the present scenarios and the general objectives identified by the Local government of the Metropolitan Cities of Milan and Bologna. The main criticalities concern the configuration of the road infrastructure, the configuration and organisation of the public transport system, the anisotropic distribution of services and amenities, and the quality of the public space. Important concerns are related to the misalignment of the configuration of the public transport system in relation to the transformation of the urbanised area: The radial structure of the main routes of the Public transport system is no more adequate to serve the transport demand engendered by tendencies of Dispersed urbanisation and by the emergence of new centralities in suburban areas, constituted by residential areas, service poles, industrial and logistic facilities, transportation infrastructures, places of consumption, and recreation.

Another issue is the lack of coordination between different modes of public transportation, the misalignment of the distribution of transportation demand with the structure of the public transportation service offer, and the existence of sparsely populated areas that are not served by public transportation. In terms of active mobility, the SUMPs underline the cycling route discontinuity and the concentration of high-quality pedestrian areas, such as pedestrian areas, Privileged pedestrian Transit areas, and limited transit zones, in the central districts of compact urbanised areas. These conditions result in the unbalanced modal split and the dominance of private motorised transport. The latter, in turn, emerges as a primary determinant of emissions of pollutants, including Nox, CO_2, $PM10$, $PM2.5$, COV, energy consumption, and road accidents.

On the other hand, the Metropolitan City of Cagliari is selected based on four criteria: firstly, the initiatives of local authorities in terms of policies aiming to foster sustainable modes of transport. In particular, the procedure for adopting a metropolitan and for an urban SUMP started, respectively, in 2019 and 2018. Moreover, the program document for the Strategic Plan of the Metropolitan City was approved in 2021;

Secondly, the unbalanced distribution of services and amenities, among central, vibrant, compact districts and suburban areas and the emergence of specialised poles of function along main road infrastructures inadequately served by public transport. A relevant aspect concerns the unbalanced modal split: the reliance of mobility in the metropolitan area on private car-based travel determines an intense pressure on arterial distributors and on the system of urban primary and secondary distributors. In particular, recent surveys conducted in 2017 measured 175,639 vehicles per day entering the urban area of Cagliari in May and 162,272 vehicles per day in August.

The last considerations refer to the inadequate usability of pedestrian spaces outside the pedestrian areas located in the compact central districts and the discontinuity of cycle itineraries. The findings from the comparative content analysis are presented and discussed in the subsequent section.

4   Results

The SUMPs of the Metropolitan Cities of Milan and Bologna identify the balancing of the modal split, the improvement of conditions of access to transportation, services, and employment, the usability of public open spaces and transportation infrastructures, the reduction of road accident casualties to zero by 2050, the reduction of CO_2, NO_2, and PM_{10} emissions, and the reduction of soil consumption as fundamental targets.

These objectives, related to the general aim of improving the sustainability, inclusivity, safety, resilience and salubrity of the metropolitan areas, are pursued via the Avoid, Shift, Improve (ASI) paradigm. The ASI paradigm refers to the adoption of strategies aimed at reducing long-distance trip demand (Avoid), promoting the transition to more sustainable modes of transportation (Shift), and minimising the outcomes of private transportation by encouraging a transition to low-emission vehicles (Improve).

The avoid dimension, for instance, is actualised via measures of land-use and built-environment re-configuration and of mobility management in private companies and public institutions, aimed at decreasing the need for long-distance travel.

The Metropolitan City of Milan's SUMPs proposes that the development of planned communities be subordinated to the verification of the resultant prospective mobility demand. Finally, the SUMP of Bologna Metropolitan City presents a set of criteria for urban regeneration and densification interventions, as well as interventions in urban development. These criteria include i) dimensioning these interventions based on the transport system's capacity; ii) increasing building density and diversity of Land Uses in areas adjacent to MRS nodes and intermodal centres; iii) limiting dispersed urbanisation by locating urban development interventions along the edge of densely urbanised areas with a significant density and diversity of services, and iv) relocating the building capacity of rural areas.

The modal transition, vice versa, is realised via the re-organization of the public transport system: a relevant aspect is the introduction of transversal public transport routes to serve the transportation demand originating in suburban areas and attracted by emerging centralities located in dispersed urbanisation areas.

The integration of distinct public transport modes into a multi-level, pluri-modal metropolitan transport system and the re-configuration of transport nodes as intermodal hubs are central actions identified by the studied SUMPs to improve public transport. The SUMPs adopted by the Metropolitan Cities of Milan and Bologna define a public transportation system articulated on four sub-systems: the arterial system, which is made up of the radial structure of the metropolitan rail system; the primary system, which is constituted by the reticular structure of the Metropolitan Rapid Transit system; the complementary system, which is formed by secondary and tertiary bus lines; and the integrative system, constituted by local, low frequency or "targeted" and/or flexible services. The improvement of the public transport system is recognised as a central aspect of sustainable urban mobility also with the adaptation strategies. Yet, the need for social distancing requires to combine the re-organization of public transport with actions aimed at the reduction and temporal redistribution of the transport demand; The adaptation strategies elaborated by the City of Milan and the City of Bologna, thus underline the need for the Reorganization of services and logistics, to reduce travel during critical hours and reduce the impact on public transportation and the road system.

The SUMPs also pursue the modal transition via the improvement of active mobility infrastructures: redesigning pedestrian and cycling routes to increase the usability of public space and assure vulnerable users' access to services, public transportation, and jobs is a central component of the SUMPs adopted by the MCMI and the MCBO.

The regeneration of the road space as a multi-functional environment is a final point to consider. Distinct conceptualisations of the road and pedestrian spaces are revealed in the selected SUMPs. The Metropolitan City of Milan's SUMP focuses primarily on creating a system of safe pedestrian itineraries to ease access to the Public Transportation System's nodes. As a result, pedestrian spaces are conceived as mobility infrastructure, set within policies to improve public transportation accessibility and attractiveness. Vice versa, The SUMP of the Metropolitan City of Bologna embodies the concept of road space as a multi-functional, vibrant public space that integrates economic, transportation, social, and ecological functions.

Considering the measures contained in the SUMPs and in Metropolitan and urban strategic plans, the Municipalities of Milan and Bologna elaborate a set of adaptation strategies for re-organising public spaces and mobility based on the need for social distancing and of the radical modification of social and individual practices related to the coronavirus. The aim is to define rapid solutions for social through reconfiguration of areas and modes of transportation, with the goal of achieving long-term benefits, such as improved local mobility and relations, increased quality and quantity of distributed public spaces and pollution reduction.

In particular, the emergency plan for cycle mobility formulated by the Municipality of Bologna focuses on two types of actions: Interventions that can be realised rapidly and at a modest cost; and the anticipated completion of interventions related to the creation of segments of the leading cycling routes system. As a result, the actions proposed to focus on three aspects: i) construction of a strategic system of itineraries along important roads coinciding with the lines of the desire of users and integrated into the metropolitan system; ii) the construction of recognisable, continuous, safe, attractive itineraries; iii) the creation of an integrative cycling system, environmental islands and moderate traffic areas to ensure equal conditions of safety, and to integrate local routes into the strategic system. Moreover, the plan for pedestrian mobility aims to improve pedestrian usability in all districts of the urban area via a system of micro-interventions that actualise a polycentric and sustainable urban model. The plan identifies three actions: i) creation of Pedestrian spaces near educational facilities via agile interventions of Ground painting, the transformation of lanes or parking lots into pedestrian zones, an extension of pavements, and insertion of seats and vegetation; ii) Design of playgrounds in pedestrianised paved areas; iii) Actions of urban regeneration based on interventions aiming at acquiring new spaces for socialisation, recreational activities, and trading in poorly managed road areas. The aim is, thus, to reduce the environmental impact of the built environment and improve the functional and architectural quality of the urban space. The Adaptation Strategies proposed by the City of Milan reveal a similar perspective and focus on specific criticalities of the SUMP, particularly on the absence of measures aimed at coordinating urban and transport planning and on the conceptualisation of pedestrian spaces as mere mobility infrastructures. As a result, the Adaptation strategies propose strategies to reduce the demand for long-distance trips. These strategies include: i) increasing the availability of local public services to ensure the availability of fundamental services by a 15-min trip on foot; the aim is to balance the inequalities among districts and reduce inter-district travels; ii) creating local clinics, starting from low-income, densely-populated areas and areas with a higher number of elderly citizens; iii) promoting an increasingly widespread cultural structure, versus a condensed and centralised cultural model: a widespread culture not only in terms of genres and target audience but, above all, in terms of availability and distribution (Table 1).

Table 1. Results of the comparative content analysis for the SUMP of Milan and Bologna

Category	Milan		Bologna	
	SUMP	Adaptation strategies	SUMP	emergency plan
Road infrastructure	Amelioration of existing infrastructures; Construction of Local Variants; Redesign of intersections to reduce conflict among road uses		Re-design of road edges as ecological buffer zones	

(continued)

Table 1. (*continued*)

Category	Milan		Bologna	
	SUMP	Adaptation strategies	SUMP	emergency plan
Pedestrian cycling infrastructure	Completion of a metropolitan system of direct, safe, continuous, legible, recognisable cycle routes integrated into regional and national systems; Safe pedestrian routes;	Project "Strade Aperte" + developing tactical urban planning projects and extended cycle network; Adapting the sidewalks to physical distancing requirements; Creating temporary pedestrian areas in districts lacking green spaces; Encouraging local bars and restaurants to create outdoor seating areas	Completion of a metropolitan system of direct, safe, continuous, legible, recognisable cycle routes integrated into regional and national systems; Construction of a continuous, trans-scalar structure of pedestrian areas, temporary pedestrian areas, Privileged pedestrian Transit areas, dedicated routes, and improvement of conditions of pedestrian fruition across the entire system of roads	Rapid and economic Interventions and anticipated completion of interventions for; i) construction of a strategic system of cycling itineraries along important roads; ii) the construction of recognisable, continuous, safe itineraries; iii) the creation of an integrative cycling system; Identification of potential district centralities to be qualified as areas with a predominant pedestrian vocation; Interventions for creating distributed pedestrian areas, including i) Pedestrian spaces near educational facilities; ii) Ground games on previously pedestrianised paved areas; iii) Urban regeneration

(*continued*)

Table 1. (*continued*)

Category	Milan		Bologna	
	SUMP	Adaptation strategies	SUMP	emergency plan
Public transport	From the radial configuration of public transport to a reticular structure; Integration of distinct modes of public transport into a multi-level system; Design the nodes of the Metropolitan public transport system as centralities of the metropolitan area;	Improving and diversifying mobility services; Limiting the number of people using PT;	From the radial configuration of public transport to a reticular structure; Integration of distinct modes of public transport into a multi-level system; Design the nodes of the Metropolitan public transport system as centralities of the metropolitan area	
Circulation	Valorisation of actions of mobility management; Promotion of free flow and station-based shared mobility and micro-mobility	Adapting Time Plan of public services; Promote remote learning + smart and remote work models; Mobility as a Service model; Promoting shared mobility solutions Reorganising delivery logistics by encouraging them to "buy local."	Valorisation of actions of mobility management; Promotion of free flow and station-based shared mobility and micro-mobility	Reorganise offices, enterprises, public services, and logistics to restrict travel during peak hours;

(*continued*)

Table 1. (*continued*)

Category	Milan		Bologna	
	SUMP	Adaptation strategies	SUMP	emergency plan
Urban form	Verification of impacts of planned settlements on demand for mobility;	Increasing the availability of public services in the district, implementing the 15-min city model; Creating local clinics; Promoting a widespread cultural system	Verification of impacts of planned settlements on demand for mobility; Increase in building density and of the diversity of Land Uses in areas adjacent to MRS nodes and intermodal centres; Limiting dispersed urbanisation; Re-locating the building capacity of rural areas in urban areas presents a good provision of services and public transport infrastructures	

Moreover, the adaptation strategies incorporate a conceptualisation of roads and pedestrian surfaces as places for socialisation that integrates the measures to promote active mobility. More precisely, besides actions aimed at reducing car spaces, implementing 30 km/h zones, and realising a continuous system of pedestrian and cycle routes along the main routes - such as San Babila Square, Buenos Aires Boulevard, Monza Boulevard and Sesto Marelli Boulevard - the adaptation strategies include a set of actions of re-configuration and re-organization of road spaces. These actions have five forms of interventions: i) the realisation of the Project "Strade Aperte" and the development of residential roads; ii) the adaptation of pedestrian surfaces to social distancing requirements and the identification of "protected" routes for vulnerable individuals; iii) the extension of public spaces creating temporary pedestrian areas in districts lacking green areas, to promote children's independent outdoor activities (Play Streets); iv) the realisation of open squares in every district: Developing large-scale tactical urbanism projects to promote pedestrianisation, particularly around educational facilities, amenities and in districts with fewer green areas, to provide spaces for children to exercise and play; v) the creation of outdoor spaces for the service industry, extension of seating space for bars and restaurants on pavements, or as replacement of parking spaces.

Thus, the measures adopted by the City of Milan and by the City of Bologna for the post-pandemic scenario can delineate a set of transferable strategies to provide long-term benefits and a radical re-organization of the urban environment for the post-pandemic scenario. Building on the results of the comparative analysis, a set of guidelines for the Metropolitan City of Cagliari is presented in the subsequent section.

5   Discussion and Conclusions

A set of general considerations related to the impact of Covid-19 on urban policies emerges from the results of the comparative content analysis: the first consideration concerns the effects of the pandemic on urban governance and policies in terms of the need to adopt strategic plans for the post-pandemic scenario. The second aspect regards the emerging need to coordinate urban and mobility planning related dimensions. The last consideration concerns the radical re-conceptualization of specific components of the built environment due to the modification of individual and social practices determined by the pandemic. This aspect is particularly evident in the distinct conceptualisation of pedestrian spaces in the SUMP and in the adaptation strategies of the City of Milan: from an understanding of pedestrian spaces as infrastructures of active mobility to multifunctional places for sociality and recreational activities. The results of the analysis of the SUMPs and of related adaptation strategies are a valid starting point for the definition of a set of guidelines for the drafting of the SUMP of the Metropolitan City of Cagliari. A first aspect concerns the centrality of strategies aimed at reducing the demand for long-distance trips, including i) re-organization of the infrastructure of services and urban functions based on the 15-min city; ii) limiting dispersed urbanisation by locating interventions of urban development along the edge of densely urbanised areas and presenting a significant density and diversity of services. A central aspect of policies for sustainable mobility in the metropolitan city of Cagliari regards the radical reorganisation of public transport to favour a modal transition and realise a more balanced modal split. The fundamental strategies include:

i) developing a reticular strategic system of interurban and metropolitan itineraries for rapid mobility services - train, Light Rail System (LRS), Bus Rapid Transit (BRT); ii) developing a distribution system consisting of local bus lines; the strategic system, in particular, includes the radial itineraries aimed at serving the transport demand convergent on the urban area of Cagliari and transversal and tangential itineraries aimed at serving inter-municipal trips in suburban areas and trips converging on the centralities emerging in the areas of dispersed urbanisation, along with the main road infrastructures; iii) creating an integrative system, based on shared mobility services local, low frequency or "targeted" and/or flexible services and Demand responsive transport services (DRT). In particular, DRT services are central to serve the demand for mobility originating in marginal areas and in areas of dispersed urbanisation.

A second aspect regards the need to coordinate actions aimed at improving the level of service of public transport and actions of mobility management aimed at re-organizing the temporal distribution of the transport demand as a fundamental requirement for favouring the modal transition from private transport to sustainable forms of mobility; as a consequence, the organisation of a multi-modal, multi-level transport system, based on a grid configuration, is to be supported by the re-organization of timetables of public services – particularly social and educational services - and productive activities to avoid overlaps in entry and exit times, regulate the demand for mobility and facilitate social distancing. The redevelopment of train and MetroCagliari stations as intermodal centres and as multifunctional spaces, including services and amenities, constitutes a central aspect of actions aimed at the improvement of public transport and at connecting public transport and the urban landscape [34]. Moreover, a relevant consideration concerns the development of a continuous, pervasive metropolitan-scale infrastructure of pedestrian and cycling routes and its integration with the infrastructure of public transport: A central requirement for the project and integration of these infrastructural systems is to connect the emerging centralities located in the suburban areas, along with main transport infrastructures, and the dense and compact urbanised districts.

The last consideration concerns the qualification of road spaces as multifunctional spaces, integrating the transport and social and ecological functions. As a consequence, large-scale tactical urbanism interventions, focusing on the development of usable public spaces, in particular in areas presenting scarcity of green areas, is a fundamental aspect of policies aimed at promoting sociality, inclusion and independent activities of the vulnerable users, in every district of the metropolitan city [34–36]. These strategies are to be complemented by measures to reduce on-street parking spaces, and the incidence of private motorised transport along local roads, by implementing car-free districts and Local Environmental Areas. Consequently, a model of the organisation of the mobility system emerges based on the pre-eminent function of public transport and active mobility in serving the transport demand, and on the complementary role of motorised private transport. This organisation of mobility can result in a radical re-organization of the metropolitan city, based on the abstract grid, the supervillains and on the 15-min city models; these models can be summarised in a four principles structure; the qualification of districts as urban units, presenting significant density and diversity of services and functions; the requalification of local roads as spaces for active mobility and for optional-recreational and social activities; the concentration of residual motorised transport on distribution roads tangential to urban districts, and the development of protected Public transport itineraries, that intersect pedestrian and cycle routes, and that constitute the infrastructure for inter-districts and inter-municipal movements. The implementation of the proposed strategies, and the definition of a set of specific, measurable, realistic and time-bound objectives, to monitor the impact of adopted actions are thus central to facilitate the transition to a development model that realises the objectives of resilience, environmental sustainability, social inclusion, economic development and protection, of urbanised areas, from environmental and health concerns. In this regard, the research underlines that the sustainable mobility model is not resolved by the mere decarbonisation of the transport sector. Nonetheless, it mainly results from the integration of participative practices [38–41] with actions aimed at reorganising the distribution of services and amenities, and of building density, and at re-configuring transport infrastructures. In particular, preventing dispersed urbanisation, promoting the regeneration of suburbs, increasing the density and diversity of functions, developing public transport strategic and distribution itineraries to serve inter-municipal travels, improving the usability of public spaces and creating a continuous and pervasive infrastructure for active mobility emerge as the central strategies to meet the requirements of salubrity, sustainability, resilience, universal access, and to accommodate the new lifestyles resulting from the pandemic.

Acknowledgements. This study was supported by the MIUR through two projects: 1) "WEAKI TRANSIT: WEAK-demand areas Innovative TRANsport Shared services for Italian Towns (Project protocol: 20174ARRHT_004; CUP Code: F74I19001290001), financed with the PRIN 2017 (Research Projects of National Relevance) programme; 2) "CAGLIARI2020" (Project code: PON04a2_00381). We authorise the MIUR to reproduce and distribute reprints for Governmental purposes, notwithstanding any copyright notations thereon. Any opinions, findings and conclusions or recommendations expressed in this material are those of the authors, and do not necessarily reflect the views of the MIUR. This paper is also supported by Cagliari Accessibility Lab, an interdepartmental centre at the University of Cagliari (Rector's Decree of 4 March 2020. https://www.unica.it/unica/it/cagliari_accessibility_lab.page).

References

1. ESPAS (2019). http://www.espas.eu/. Accessed 04 Apr 2022
2. Urban Mobility Package. European Commission, Mobility and Transport (2013). https://ec.europa.eu/commission/presscorner/detail/en/MEMO_13_1160. Accessed 04 Apr 2022
3. Sustainable Urban Mobility Plans. European Commission Clean transport, Urban transport, Mobility and Transport (2021). https://ec.europa.eu/transport/themes/urban/urban-mobility/urban-mobility-actions/sustainable-urban_en. Accessed 04 Apr 2022
4. Pinna, F., Masala, F., Garau, C.: Urban policies and mobility trends in italian smart cities. Sustainability **9**, 494 (2017). https://doi.org/10.3390/su9040494
5. Garau, C., Masala, F., Pinna, F.: Cagliari and smart urban mobility: analysis and comparison. Cities **56**, 35–46 (2016). https://doi.org/10.1016/j.cities.2016.02.012
6. Pinna, F., Garau, C., Annunziata, A.: A literature review on urban usability and accessibility to investigate the related criteria for equality in the city. In: Gervasi, O., et al. (eds.) ICCSA

2021. LNCS, vol. 12958, pp. 525–541. Springer, Cham (2021). https://doi.org/10.1007/978-3-030-87016-4_38

7. Horizon 2020 Work Programme. Smart, Green and Integrated Transport Revised, 10 December 2013 (2015). http://ec.europa.eu/research/participants/data/ref/h2020/wp/2014_2 015/main/h2020-wp1415-transport_en.pdf. Accessed 04 Apr 2022

8. Coni, M., Garau, C., Pinna, F.: How has cagliari changed its citizens in smart citizens? exploring the influence of ITS technology on urban social interactions. In: Gervasi, O., et al. (eds.) ICCSA 2018. LNCS, vol. 10962, pp. 573–588. Springer, Cham (2018). https://doi.org/10.1007/978-3-319-95168-3_39

9. Campisi, T., Basbas, S., Tanbay, N.A., Georgiadis, G.: Some considerations on the key factors determining the reduction of public transport demand in Sicily during COVID-19 pandemic. Int. J. Transp. Dev. Integr. 6(1), 81–94 (2022)

10. Barabino, B., Deiana, E., Mozzoni, S.: The quality of public transport service: the 13816 Standard and a methodological approach to an Italian case, Ingegneria Ferroviaria 68(5), 475–499 (2013). ISSN: 0020–0956

11. Barabino B., Deiana, E., Tilocca, P.: Urban transport management and customer per- ceived quality: a case study in the metropolitan area of Cagliari, Italy. Theor. Empir. Res. Urban Manag. 6(1), 19–32 (2011). ISSN: 2065–3913

12. Maltinti, F., et al.: Vulnerable users and public transport service: analysis on expected and perceived quality data. In: Gervasi, O., et al. (eds.) ICCSA 2020. LNCS, vol. 12255, pp. 673–689. Springer, Cham (2020). https://doi.org/10.1007/978-3-030-58820-5_49

13. Barabino, B.: Automatic recognition of "low-quality" vehicles and bus stops in bus services. Public Transp. 10(2), 257–289 (2018). https://doi.org/10.1007/s12469-018-0180-8

14. Barabino, B., Coni, M., Olivo, A., Pungillo, G., Rassu, N.: standingp assenger comfort: a new scale for evaluating the real-time driving style of bus transit services. IEEE Trans. Intell. Transp. Syst. 20(12), 4665–4678 (2019). https://doi.org/10.1109/TITS.2019.2921807

15. Coni, M., et al.: On-board comfort of different age passengers and bus-lane characteristics. In: Gervasi, O., et al. (eds.) ICCSA 2020. LNCS, vol. 12255, pp. 658–672. Springer, Cham (2020). https://doi.org/10.1007/978-3-030-58820-5_48

16. Campisi, T., Garau, C., Ignaccolo, M., Coni, M., Canale, A., Inturri, G., Torrisi, V.: A new vision on smart and resilient urban mobility in the aftermath of the pandemic: key factors on european transport policies. In: Gervasi, O., et al. (eds.) ICCSA 2021. LNCS, vol. 12958, pp. 603–618. Springer, Cham (2021). https://doi.org/10.1007/978-3-030-87016-4_43

17. Garau, C., Desogus, G., Zamperlin, P.: Governing technology-based urbanism: degeneration to technocracy or development to progressive planning? In: Aurigi, A., Willis, K.S. (eds.) The Routledge Companion to Smart Cities Routledge pp. 157–173 (2020). https://doi.org/10.4324/9781315178387

18. Garau, C., Nesi, P., Paoli, I., Paolucci, M., Zamperlin, P.: A big data platform for smart and sustainable cities: environmental monitoring case studies in Europe. In: Gervasi, O., et al. (eds.) ICCSA 2020. LNCS, vol. 12255, pp. 393–406. Springer, Cham (2020). https://doi.org/10.1007/978-3-030-58820-5_30

19. Garau, C., Desogus, G., Maltinti, F., Olivo, A., Peretti, L., Coni, M.: Practices for an inte- grated planning between urban planning and green infrastructures for the development of the municipal urban plan (MUP) of Cagliari (Italy). In: Gervasi, O., et al. (eds.) ICCSA 2021. LNCS, vol. 12958, pp. 3–18. Springer, Cham (2021). https://doi.org/10.1007/978-3-030-870 16-4_1

20. Garau, C., Pavan, V.: Evaluating urban quality: indicators and assessment tools for smart sustainable cities. Sustainability 10(3), 575 (2018)

21. Torrisi, V., Garau, C., Inturri, G., Ignaccolo, M.: Strategies and actions towards sustainability: Encouraging good ITS practices in the SUMP vision. In: International Conference of Computational Methods in Sciences and Engineering ICCMSE 2020 (2021). https://doi.org/10. 1063/5.0047897

22. Torrisi, V., Garau, C., Ignaccolo, M., Inturri, G.: "Sustainable Urban Mobility Plans": key concepts and a critical revision on SUMPs guidelines. In: Gervasi, O., et al. (eds.) ICCSA 2020. LNCS, vol. 12255, pp. 613–628. Springer, Cham (2020). https://doi.org/10.1007/978-3-030-58820-5_45

23. SUMP. The Urban Mobility Observatory, Eltis (2019). https://www.eltis.org/mobility-plans/ sump-concept. Accessed 04 Apr 2022

24. Garau, C., Desogus, G., Torrisi, V.: (being published). From Smart Urbanism to Sustainable Urban Mobility Plan: A Critical Evaluation on Objectives and Strategies of Metropolitan City of Cagliari 's SUMP. Wiley, Hoboken, New Jersey, United States

25. Sampaio, C., Macedoa, E., Coelhoa, M.C., Bandeira, M.J.: Economic and environmental analysis of measures from a sustainability urban mobility plan – application to a small sized city. Transp. Res. Procedia **48**, 2580–2588 (2020). https://doi.org/10.1016/j.trpro.2020.08.253

26. Rupprecht, S., Brand, L., Baedeker, S.B., et al.: Guidelines for developing and implementing a sustainable urban mobility plan second edition (2019). https://www.eltis.org/sites/default/ files/sump_guidelines_2019_interactive_document_1.pdf. Accessed 04 Apr 2022

27. Cerasoli, M., Amato, C., Ravagnan, C.: An antifragile strategy for Rome post-Covid mobility. Transp. Res. Procedia **60**, 338–345 (2022)

28. INU. Le proposte dell'Istituto Nazionale di Urbanistica per il superamento dell'emergenza e il rilancio del Paese (2020). https://www.inu.it/news/post-covid-le-proposte-dell-inu-per-il-rilancio-del-paese/. Accessed 04 Apr 2022

29. Haas, T., Sander, H.: Decarbonizing transport in the European union: emission performance standards and the perspectives for a European green deal. Sustainability **12**, 8381 (2020). https://doi.org/10.3390/su12208381

30. Montanarella, L., Panos, P.: The relevance of sustainable soil management within the European Green Deal. Land Use Policy **100**, 104950 (2021)

31. Kumar, V., Vuilliomenet, A.: Urban nature: does green infrastructure relate to the cultural and creative vitality of European Cities? Sustainability **13**, 8052 (2021). https://doi.org/10.3390/ su13148052

32. OECD. Respacing our cities for resilience (2020). https://www.itf-oecd.org/sites/default/files/ respacing-cities-resilience-covid19.pdf. Accessed 04 Apr 2022

33. OECD. City policies responses, in Tackling Coronavirus. Contributing to a Global effort (2020). https://www.oecd.org/coronavirus/policy-responses/cities-policy-responses-fd1053ff/#part-d1e2443

34. Garau, C., Annunziata, A.:. A method for assessing the vitality potential of urban areas: the case study of the metropolitan City of Cagliari, Italy. City Territory Arch. **9**(7) (2022). https:// doi.org/10.1186/s40410-022-00153-6

35. Garau, C., Annunziata, A., Yamu, C.: A walkability assessment tool coupling multi-criteria analysis and space syntax: the case study of Iglesias, Italy. Eur. Plan. Stud., 1–23 (2020). https://doi.org/10.1080/09654313.2020.1761947

36. Garau, C., Annunziata, A.: Public Open Spaces: connecting people, squares and streets by measuring the usability through the Villanova district in Cagliari, Italy. Transp. Res. Procedia **60**, 314–321 (2022). https://doi.org/10.1016/j.trpro.2021.12.041, ISSN 2352–1465

37. Campisi, T., et al.: Anxiety, fear and stress feelings of road users during daily walking in COVID-19 pandemic: Sicilian cities. Transp. Res. procedia **62**, 107–114 (2022)

38. Garau, C.: Focus on citizens: public engagement with online and face-to-face participation—a case study. Fut. Internet **4**(2), 592–606 (2012)

39. Garau, C.: Citizen participation in public planning: a literature review. Int. J. Sci. 1(12), 21–44 (2012)
40. Garau, C.: Processi di piano e partecipazione. Gangemi Editore Spa, Rome (2013)
41. Garau, C.: Optimizing public participation through ICT and social networks: questions and challenges. In: Proceedings: REAL CORP 2013, Rome, Italy, 20–23 May 2013 (2013)

International Workshop on Virtual Reality and Augmented Reality and Applications (VRA 2022)

A Multi-agent Body Tracking Application Framework Applied to Physical and Neurofunctional Rehabilitation

Felipe Reis Valente[1]([⊠]) [ID], Marcelo de Paiva Guimarães[2,3] [ID],
Elder José Reioli Cirilo[1] [ID], and Diego Roberto Colombo Dias[1] [ID]

[1] Universidade Federal de São João del-Rei, São João del-Rei, Minas Gerais, Brazil
felipevalente@ufsj.edu.br
[2] Universidade Federal de São Paulo, São Paulo, Brazil
[3] Centro Universitário Campo Limpo Paulista, Campo Limpo Paulista, Brazil

Abstract. Stroke is one of the most disabling diseases today, so investigating methods for rehabilitation of post-stroke patients is of utmost importance. Thus, significant benefits can be achieved by using body tracking systems and virtual environments. However, the development of such applications involves a large set of requirements, such as the construction of virtual environments, the interaction devices, and the storage and processing of data collected during rehabilitation sessions. This paper presents a multi-agent framework that abstracts the difficulties involved in developing applications using body tracking devices and virtual environments in neuromotor and neurofunctional rehabilitation.

Keywords: Body tracking · Framework · Multi-agent and rehabilitation

1 Introduction

Events such as stroke and degenerative diseases limit mobility, as does advancing age or accidents that a person may have suffered [36]. Consequently, people who have suffered a stroke need rehabilitation, which is a process of therapy that aims to partially or entirely recover a patient's motor abilities. However, traditional rehabilitation with traditional aids (e.g., walkers and crutches) do not allow an objective analysis of the evolution of the patient's condition [8].

Among the difficulties that physical therapists encounter in the process of rehabilitation of patients, there are those related to the metrics because they are not easy to be observed visually, often being subjective to evaluate the patient's progress [31]. Accurate metrics require rehabilitation equipment with sensors that monitor movements more accurately, providing more detailed feedback to the physical therapist. The physical therapy process can also be enhanced with the use of games allied to motion sensors or depth cameras, as they can facilitate

Supported by organization UFSJ.

the execution of new functional motor and or cognitive tasks [20]. Thus, it is possible to combine technology with health care using serious games, which are games designed to achieve a relevant goal, i.e., that go beyond the idea of entertainment, offering learning and training possibilities [3].

The use of depth cameras plays a central role in capturing human body movements for body tracking applications. Through infrared sensors, joint data is captured and can be stored for later playback [23]. There are also inertial sensors (e.g., accelerometers, magnetometers, and gyroscopes). They can infer the position and orientation of tracked objects [32]. Based on the data collected from the patient, the physical therapist can verify that movements are being performed appropriately [9].

This paper presents a framework that facilitates the employment of motion sensors by encapsulating the functionality of different interfaces, either wired or wireless. The developed framework allows developers to quickly develop new applications, increase productivity, reduce error-prone code, improve maintenance, and standardize the project. A case study is also presented in which a new application is developed.

The rest of the paper is organized as follows: Sect. 2 presents the theoretical framework used to build the framework, such as design patterns and motion sensors; Sect. 3 presents our framework, describing its classes and methods. Finally, Sect. 4 presents the conclusions of the work.

2 Theoretical Referential

2.1 Framework

According to Gamma [16], a framework is defined as a set of classes that cooperate, providing a reusable design for a specific domain of system classes. Their use by software engineering provides the developer with a context-specific modular structure, allowing the reuse of components and the coupling of new technologies, creating a new application [4].

The literature shows several frameworks focused on the context of motion capture. Amiri [2] presents a framework for assistive technology-based mobility capture and tracking in individuals with spinal cord injury. Some authors explore the use of Kinect as a body-tracking device [7,26,27,33,34]. [6] aims to create a framework for coupling serious games into a robot that provides corrective feedback during user interaction. [22] shows a framework for monitoring and improving the quality of physical therapy exercises. An Android smartphone application connects to the wristband, transmits the data in real-time for storage in the database, and shows the movement's evolution.

The work of [11] created a framework using Unity to analyze the effectiveness of using a 3D camera to stabilize the reading of data from inertial sensors in the context of rehabilitation. The work of [28] is focused on human activity recognition, for example, identifying whether a person is sitting, walking, or standing, among others. [18] presented a framework that integrates an omnidirectional treadmill with virtual reality to provide a unique rehabilitation experience.

The objective of most of the works is to create a framework for motor rehabilitation using Kinect. Some works have different proposals, such as: creating a framework for noise reduction to improve the accuracy of captured movements, comparing performance in physical activities, using virtual and augmented reality with Kinect, and creating a framework for wearable clothing.

2.2 Neurorehabilitation

Neurorehabilitation is a form of non-invasive intervention to treat cognitive impairment without surgical or pharmacological intervention. It is also valid for patients with memory problems due to Alzheimer's disease. Stroke is one of the most significant causes of neuromotor debilitation. Approximately 80% of the patients who survive the most severe phase are left with sequels afterward. Most can regain the ability to walk; however, 30% to 66% cannot use their upper limbs after suffering a stroke.

Neurorehabilitation treatments are possible because the Central Nervous System is a flexible structure in which its cells can be regenerated, and through specific physiotherapy, the patient can recover lost movements. The Central Nervous System has great adaptability even in adult brains [29];

The application of body-tracking games in rehabilitation centers to aid patient therapy is a growing trend because, with the cheapening of the technology, it is even easier to bring the equipment to the patient's home. In this way, it is possible for the patient to have physiotherapy at home while the data is captured and sent to the physiotherapist remotely to be analyzed later. That makes it easy to use in remote and hard-to-reach places, such as rural areas, requiring only the internet to send the data.

2.3 Body Tracking

The human body is composed of the skeletal system and the articular system. The bones are connected through joints, with the joints acting as axes and the bones as levers, thus favoring the mobility of the human body [21];

The body tracking is responsible for capturing each joint's X, Y, and Z positions. In our framework, 20 joints are monitored at a frequency 30 Hz.

The human body can be divided into three planes: Coronal, Transverse, and Sagittal. The coronal plane passes over the coronal suture of the skull, dividing the body into posterior and anterior; the transverse plane divides the body into two parts, one closer to the ground as inferior and one farther away as superior; and the sagittal plane defines as the plane that passes over the sagittal suture of the skull, dividing the body into left and right [10].

Optical Tracking. Computer vision is an area of research that aims to simulate human vision. The machine receives as input an image, making the extraction, characterization, and interpretation of information from the real world through the captured image [19]. The machine can do body tracking due to it being able to process and interpret the images captured from the physiotherapy sessions [14].

Optical Tracking allows the user to be tracked without the need for any device attached to the body, i.e., without any wires or transmitters, using only a video camera, which offers good freedom to the user. It also allows the capture of multiple users. The capture areas can be larger than other tracking systems. Although there are several advantages to using Optical Tracking, there are also some disadvantages, such as pre-processing, which requires more computing power, occlusion problems, and the ambient lighting that needs to be controlled.

Inertial Tracking. Inertial Tracking uses measurement sensors attached to the user's body, such as accelerometers, magnetometers, and gyroscopes. With the data captured by these sensors, the angular velocity and linear acceleration are obtained, allowing the position and orientation of the tracked objects to be calculated.

Due to the advancement in technology, inertial devices have become smaller and cheaper, which has made it possible to use these devices for body tracking. However, miniaturization also brought problems such as decreased accuracy. Unlike Optical Tracking, it does not suffer from occlusion problems but can suffer from electromagnetic interference.

2.4 Biomechanics Sensor Node

The Biomechanics Sensor Node (BSN) device was created to miniaturize the body tracking device based on inertial sensors, as it is a device that can be attached to various parts of the user's body. In addition, it has a battery and good ergonomics for use. The communication of the device is performed by using Bluetooth Low Energy (BLE). The BSN has several sensors, such as a gyroscope, accelerometer, and compass, which in combination allow for body tracking of the user [5].

2.5 MediaPipe

MediaPipe is an open-source framework developed by Google, meant to be used on mobile devices and desktops with the purpose of facilitating development when working with user gesture detection.

It is also possible to use MediaPipe combined with machine learning techniques to detect and track objects, faces, and even strands of hair from a person [1]. Machine learning techniques achieve good real-time results even on more limited devices, such as mobile devices. MediaPipe uses two approaches: first, it delimits a box around the object in a complete image, identifying the object to be tracked, and once the object is found, the second approach works only on the delimited region to identify specific key points.

2.6   Kinect

Kinect is a body-tracking device developed and maintained by Microsoft. It is capable of capturing all of the user's joints, as well as their voice. The great thing about this device is that it allows optical tracking through structured light (infrared). Through the sensor, it is possible to reconstruct the three-dimensional space with millimeter precision, capturing the user's depth between 0.8 m and 3.5 m.

Initially, Kinect was developed to be used in electronic games on the Xbox360 console, but with the popularization of the device, today it is being used in Medicine, Robotics, Physiotherapy, Physical Education, among others [12,24,25,35]. Kinect has good documentation and a highly regarded Software Development Kit (SDK) that facilitates the development of the most diverse applications.

3   Our Framework

In the framework developed in this work, we used the following design patterns: (1) the Abstract Factory, which provides an interface for creating families of related or dependent objects without specifying their concrete classes [17]; (2) the Repository, which is a way to encapsulate details of the data access infrastructure, mediating between the data mapping layers and the domain layers [15]; (3) and the Strategy which defines a family of algorithms and arranges the algorithms into separate classes, making them interchangeable [13]. We employed the multi-agent concept in the framework to abstract the difficulties in developing solutions that involve body tracking devices on different platforms. We developed the framework as a Unity asset.

The main class of our framework is the **Core**, whose purpose is to synchronize all the others, which are the following: (1) **Input**; (2) **DataManager**; (3) **Analysis**; and (4) **Utilities**. It is necessary to import its package into Unity to use the developed framework. Thus, it is possible to use the classes already defined with their respective methods, allowing the developer to focus exclusively on the application, not worrying about the particularities of the body tracking devices, database, authentication, data import, and machine learning approaches.

3.1   Input Module

The project pattern used in the **Input** module was the **Abstract Factory**, which is of the creative type since it allows you to create families of related objects without having to specify their concrete classes. It provides some advantages like knowing that the products from a factory are compatible, easy to maintain, and avoid coupling between concrete products and client code. As a disadvantage, it can make the code more complex at first because of the larger number of classes and interfaces [30]. The class diagram shown in Fig. 1 represents the module **Input**.

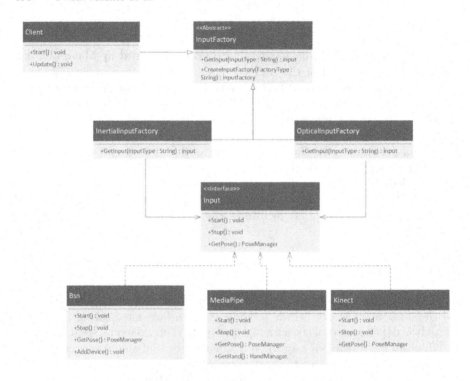

Fig. 1. Class diagram of the **Input** module

In the **framework** the **AbstractFactory** declares an interface for operations that will create **AbstractProduct** objects. In the **framework** these are input devices. This class contains two methods. The **GetInput** method, which is an abstract method that will be implemented by the child factory classes; and the **CreateInputFactory** method, which receives an input parameter (factory type) and then creates and returns the appropriate factory object to the caller.

The concrete class implements the abstract class **AbstractFactory (InputFactory)**. In our work, this class implements the **GetInput** method of the **InputFactory** class. There are two concrete types of factories in our example: **InertialInputFactory**, for inertial devices; and **OpticalInputFactory**, for optical devices.

The method **GetInput** creates and returns the appropriate inertial object based on the input parameter, that is, the received **InputType**. Analogously, the same is true for the optical devices of the concrete class **OpticalInputFactory**.

An interface is used to declare the methods of the Product. In our framework, these are the **start**, **stop** and **getPose** methods of the **Input** object.

The **start** method is responsible for starting the device; the **stop** for stopping the started device; and the **getPose** for returning the registered joints. The concrete product class implements the **AbstractFactory (InputFactory)** interface to create concrete products. In our example, the product classes are:

MediaPipe, BSN and Kinect. The BSN product class has one more method, **AddDevice**(), responsible for pairing new Bluetooth wristbands, thus increasing the number of tracking points.

3.2   DataManager Module

The **DataManager** module is responsible for handling the data captured via the devices, from an external file to the application, or simply using the captured data directly in the application and persisting it to disk. The class diagram shown in Fig. 2 represents the **DataManager** module.

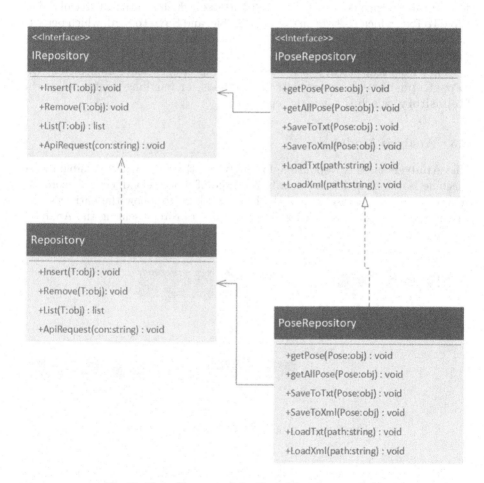

Fig. 2. Class diagram of the **DataManager** module

We employed the **Repository** design pattern to create an abstraction layer between the data access layer and the business layer of an application. Advantages of using this pattern are easier testing, simpler application management with the data store, and easy switching between multiple data stores without changing the application programming interface (API).

The **IRepository** interface is a generic interface that defines some methods, such as **Insert**, responsible for inserting into the DBMS; **Remove**, for deleting; **List**, for searching; and **ApiRequest**, for working with the API.

The **Repository** is a generic class that implements the **IRepository** interface. Note that the generic repository does not have specific functions to work with the joints.

The **IPoseRepository** interface is a specific interface that defines some specific methods to work with the articulations, such as **getPose**, responsible for returning a specific articulation; **getAllPose**, which returns all articulations; **SaveToTxt**, which persists on disk in a txt file; and **SaveToXml**, which persists on disk in an XML file. The **LoadTxt** and **LoadXml** load joints from a text and XML file, respectively.

The **PoseRepository** is a specific repository that implements the **IPoseRepository** interface, with its methods for handling joints, unlike the **Repository**, which is a generic repository.

3.3   Analysis Module

The **Analysis** class is responsible for analyzing the data; being possible to use machine learning models to identify the type of movement done and score the movement by comparing it with the historical base to follow the patient's evolution, among other possibilities. The class diagram representing the Analysys module is shown in Fig. 3.

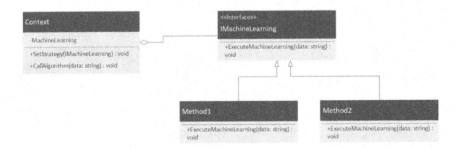

Fig. 3. Class diagram of the **Analysis** module

We employed the behavioral design pattern **Strategy** in the development of this module because several related classes differ only in their behaviors, and variants of the machine learning algorithms [13] are required.

The **IMachineLearning** class declares an interface that is common to all machine learning algorithms. That declares a method that the application context uses to execute some approach.

Each concrete class must implement the **ExecuteMachineLearning** method of the **IMachineLearning** interface. If the need for more algorithms arises, the developer needs to add new concrete classes that implement the interface mentioned above. The **ExecuteMachineLearning** method receives a string with data to be processed. Thus, the concrete class implements different variations of an algorithm that the application context requires.

The **Context** class contains a property that is used to contain the reference of a **strategy** object. The client sets this property according to the required machine learning algorithm.

The **Client** class creates a specific **strategy** object and passes it to the context. The context defines a setter that allows the client to change the strategy associated with the context during execution.

3.4 Utils Module

The **Utils** class is a supporting class to facilitate the developer to work with the data obtained from body tracking, as per Fig. 4.

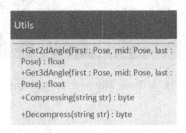

Fig. 4. Utils class structure

We implemented the **Get2dAngle** method to get the angle when working in two dimensions. Three positions must be entered: start, middle, and end. The **Get3dAngle** method works analogously, however, in three dimensions. The **Compressing** and **Decompress** methods compress and decompress data, making it easier to manipulate data when working with databases.

The four defined modules: **Input**; **DataManager**; **Analysis** and **Utilities** define the structure of the framework. The synchronism of the **Core** class with the **Input** and **DataManager** modules allows the framework to be compatible with devices from different platforms, for example, allowing Kinect data, which only works on Windows operating system, to be used on Android operating system.

4 Using Our Framework

We created a simple example as a Unity project with an avatar moving with the data captured by MediaPipe and Kinect. With a new project created, the avatar in the scene, and the framework imported, we used the Pose Manager component to deal with 20 avatar articulations. We placed this component script in the avatar (Fig. 5).

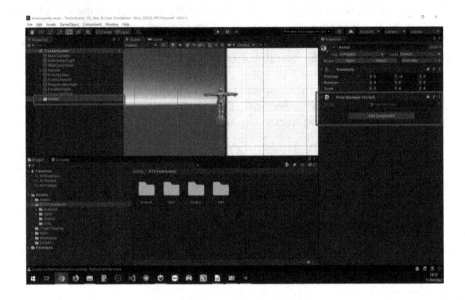

Fig. 5. Pose Manager component

All the libraries needed to work with Kinect and MediaPipe are already included in the framework, so all the compilation and configuration were unnecessary for the devices to work.

The code responsible for working with the Input must be included in the project in the start method. The Client uses the *AbstractFactory* and *AbstractProduct* interfaces to create a family of related objects. We will use MediaPipe capture (Code 1.1).

```
using System.Collections;
using System.Collections.Generic;
using UnityEngine;
using System;

namespace AbstractFactoryDesignPattern
{
    class Client: MonoBehaviour
    {
        // Start is called before the first frame update
        void Start()
        {
            Input input = null;
            InputFactory inputFactory = null;
```

```
// Create the OpticalInput factory object by
    passing the factory type as Optical
inputFactory =
    InputFactory.CreateInputFactory("Optical");

// Get MediaPipe Input object by passing the
    input type as MediaPipe
input = inputFactory.GetInput("MediaPipe");
    }

}
```

Listing 1.1. Client

If the developer wants to use a Kinect, it is effortless if they are using our framework. They just need to change **GetInput("MediaPipe")** to **GetInput("Kinect")**. Pose Manager works with any device without any need to map the joints for each device.

It is necessary to add the code **input.Start()** to start the device and start capturing the joints. If the developer wants to stop the device, they must use **input.Stop()**. With these steps, it is now possible to move the avatar with the data captured by the device (Fig. 6).

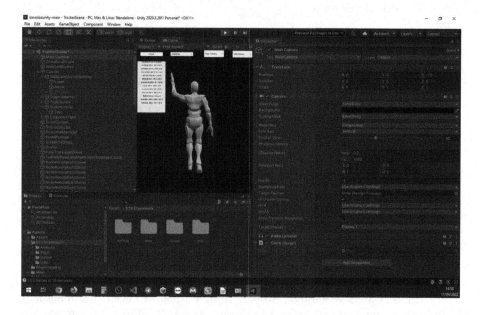

Fig. 6. Example with avatar

5   Conclusion

In this paper, we describe the creation of a framework capable of facilitating the creation of body tracking applications aimed at neuromotor rehabilitation.

We compared two development approaches in our tests: without the framework and with the framework. We could observe that it took much more time to achieve the same result. Besides that, several other factors made the development of a quality application difficult, highlighting: the high coupling of the code without the framework, the lack of construction of a project following the concepts of software engineering, poor documentation, and difficulty of reuse.

The framework is currently only available on the private GitHub of our research group. Later, the framework will be made available on GitHub for everyone so that more people can contribute to the work.

Health professionals are already testing some works of our research group. We hope that with the adoption of the framework, more works can be developed with better code quality, greater reuse, better maintenance, and increased productivity so that more software systems can reach patients, thus having a more significant social impact and at the same time collecting more data that can help in future treatments.

The captured data can help bring important information on how patients behave to specific treatments. The data can help develop better treatments and help evolve the systems developed. In the future, machine learning algorithms will be applied to this data.

References

1. On-device, real-time hand tracking with mediapipe (2019). https://ai.googleblog.com/2019/08/on-device-real-time-hand-tracking-with.html
2. Amiri, A.M., Shoaib, N., Hiremath, S.V.: A framework to enhance assistive technology based mobility tracking in individuals with spinal cord injury. In: 2017 IEEE Global Conference on Signal and Information Processing (GlobalSIP), pp. 467–471. IEEE (2017)
3. Barnes, T., Encarnação, L.M., Shaw, C.D.: Serious games. IEEE Comput. Graph. Appl. **29**(2), 18–19 (2009)
4. Braga, R.T.V.: Um processo para construção e instanciação de frameworks baseados em uma linguagem de padrões para um domínio específico. Ph.D. thesis, Universidade de São Paulo (2002)
5. Brandão, A.F.: Biomechanics sensor node for virtual reality: a wearable device applied to gait recovery for neurofunctional rehabilitation. In: Gervasi, O., et al. (eds.) ICCSA 2020. LNCS, vol. 12255, pp. 757–770. Springer, Cham (2020). https://doi.org/10.1007/978-3-030-58820-5_54
6. Brown, L., García-Vergara, S., Howard, A.M.: Evaluating the effect of robot feedback on motor skill performance in therapy games. In: 2015 IEEE International Conference on Systems, Man, and Cybernetics, pp. 1060–1065. IEEE (2015)
7. Chang, R., Lau, S., Sim, K., Too, M.: Kinect-based framework for motor rehabilitation. In: 2016 International Conference on Robotics, Automation and Sciences (ICORAS), pp. 1–4. IEEE (2016)

8. Cifuentes, C.A., Rodriguez, C., Frizera-Neto, A., Bastos-Filho, T.F., Carelli, R.: Multimodal human-robot interaction for walker-assisted gait. IEEE Syst. J. **10**(3), 933–943 (2014)
9. Da Gama, A., Chaves, T., Figueiredo, L., Teichrieb, V.: Poster: improving motor rehabilitation process through a natural interaction based system using kinect sensor. In: 2012 IEEE Symposium on 3D User Interfaces (3DUI), pp. 145–146. IEEE (2012)
10. Dhawan, A.P., Huang, B.H., Kim, D.S.: Principles and Advanced Methods in Medical Imaging and Image Analysis. World Scientific, Singapore (2008)
11. Drobnjakovic, F., et al.: Fusing data from inertial measurement units and a 3D camera for body tracking. In: 2018 IEEE International Instrumentation and Measurement Technology Conference (I2MTC), pp. 1–6. IEEE (2018)
12. Duarte, N., Postolache, O., Scharcanski, J.: KSGphysio-kinect serious game for physiotherapy. In: 2014 International Conference and Exposition on Electrical and Power Engineering (EPE), pp. 606–611. IEEE (2014)
13. Ferreira, I.A., de Resende, A.M.P., Costa, H.A.X.: Análise do impacto da aplicação de padrões de projeto na manutenibilidade de um sistema orientado a objetos. Monografia de Graduação do Departamento de Ciência da Computação da Universidade Federal de Lavras, 78p (2012)
14. Forsyth, D.A., Ponce, J.: Computer Vision: A Modern Approach. Pearson, London (2012)
15. Fowler, M.: Padrões de arquitetura de aplicações corporativas. Bookman (2009)
16. Gamma, E.: Design Patterns. Pearson Education India (1995)
17. Gamma, E.: Padrões de projetos: soluções reutilizáveis. Bookman editora (2009)
18. Gauthier, S., Cretu, A.M.: Human movement quantification using Kinect for in-home physical exercise monitoring. In: 2014 IEEE International Conference on Computational Intelligence and Virtual Environments for Measurement Systems and Applications (CIVEMSA), pp. 6–11. IEEE (2014)
19. Gavrila, D.M.: The visual analysis of human movement: a survey. Comput. Vis. Image Underst. **73**(1), 82–98 (1999)
20. Gordon, C., Roopchand-Martin, S., Gregg, A.: Potential of the nintendo wii^{TM} as a rehabilitation tool for children with cerebral palsy in a developing country: a pilot study. Physiotherapy **98**(3), 238–242 (2012)
21. Van de Graaff, K.M.: Anatomia humana. In: Anatomia Humana, p. 840 (2003)
22. Gwak, M., et al.: EXTRA: exercise tracking and analysis platform for remote-monitoring of knee rehabilitation. In: 2019 IEEE 16th International Conference on Wearable and Implantable Body Sensor Networks (BSN), pp. 1–4. IEEE (2019)
23. Kitsunezaki, N., Adachi, E., Masuda, T., Mizusawa, J.I.: Kinect applications for the physical rehabilitation. In: 2013 IEEE International Symposium on Medical Measurements and Applications (MeMeA), pp. 294–299. IEEE (2013)
24. Kurillo, G., Han, J.J., Nicorici, A., Bajcsy, R.: Tele-MFAsT: kinect-based tele-medicine tool for remote motion and function assessment. In: MMVR, pp. 215–221 (2014)
25. Macknojia, R., Chávez-Aragón, A., Payeur, P., Laganière, R.: Calibration of a network of kinect sensors for robotic inspection over a large workspace. In: 2013 IEEE Workshop on Robot Vision (WORV), pp. 184–190. IEEE (2013)
26. Maggiorini, D., Ripamonti, L., Scambia, A.: Videogame technology to support seniors. In: Proceedings of the 5th International ICST Conference on Simulation Tools and Techniques, pp. 270–277 (2012)

27. Maggiorini, D., Ripamonti, L.A., Zanon, E.: Supporting seniors rehabilitation through videogame technology: a distributed approach. In: 2012 Second International Workshop on Games and Software Engineering: Realizing User Engagement with Game Engineering Techniques (GAS), pp. 16–22. IEEE (2012)

28. Myagmarbayar, N., Yuki, Y., Imamoglu, N., Gonzalez, J., Otake, M., Yu, W.: Human body contour data based activity recognition. In: 2013 35th Annual International Conference of the IEEE Engineering in Medicine and Biology Society (EMBC), pp. 5634–5637. IEEE (2013)

29. de Oliveira, C.E.N., Salina, M.E., Annunciato, N.F.: Fatores ambientais que influenciam a plasticidade do snc. Acta Fisiátrica 8(1), 6–13 (2001)

30. Patterns, D.: Erich gamma, richard helm, ralph johnson, john vlissides. 2003 (1994)

31. Postolache, O.: Physical rehabilitation assessment based on smart training equipment and mobile apps. In: 2015 E-Health and Bioengineering Conference (EHB), pp. 1–6. IEEE (2015)

32. Rodriguez-Martin, D., Sama, A., Perez-Lopez, C., Catala, A., Cabestany, J., Rodriguez-Molinero, A.: SVM-based posture identification with a single waist-located triaxial accelerometer. Expert Syst. Appl. 40(18), 7203–7211 (2013)

33. Sinha, S., Bhowmick, B., Sinha, A., Das, A.: Accurate estimation of joint motion trajectories for rehabilitation using Kinect. In: 2017 39th Annual International Conference of the IEEE Engineering in Medicine and Biology Society (EMBC), pp. 3864–3867. IEEE (2017)

34. Stütz, T., et al.: An interactive 3D health app with multimodal information representation for frozen shoulder. In: Proceedings of the 19th International Conference on Human-Computer Interaction with Mobile Devices and Services, pp. 1–11 (2017)

35. Vaghetti, C.A., Duarte, M.A., Ribeiro, P.O., Botelho, S.S.: Using exergames as social networks: testing the flow theory in the teaching of physical education. In: Brazilian Symposium on Computers in Education (Simpósio Brasileiro de Informática na Educação-SBIE), vol. 23 (2012)

36. Whitall, J., Waller, S.M., Silver, K.H., Macko, R.F.: Repetitive bilateral arm training with rhythmic auditory cueing improves motor function in chronic hemiparetic stroke. Stroke 31(10), 2390–2395 (2000)

A Mobile App to Help People Affected by Visual Snow

Damiano Perri[1,2]([✉]) [iD], Marco Simonetti[1,2] [iD], Osvaldo Gervasi[2] [iD],
and Natale Amato[3] [iD]

[1] Department of Mathematics and Computer Science, University of Florence,
Florence, Italy
[2] Department of Mathematics and Computer Science, University of Perugia,
Perugia, Italy
damiano.perri@unifi.it
[3] University of Bari, Bari, Italy

Abstract. Visual Snow Syndrome is a neurological disease that causes flashing dots to appear throughout the visual field. Patients claim to see an endless stream of flashing dots throughout their visual area. Although patients frequently experience concurrent migraine, visual snow appears to be a distinct phenomenon from prolonged migraine aura. VSS has been linked to eye illness, thalamic dysfunctions, pure cortical phenomena, and disturbing connections between optical networks and nervous system networks. Any process may interact with or be causative of various symptoms and clinical aspects associated with VSS. The pathophysiology of Visual Snow Syndrome (VSS) and its likely location are currently being debated. In this work, the goal we have set as a team is to create an Android software application capable of representing what people with Visual Snow Syndrome perceive. The aim is to help patients to describe (and even show) the symptomatology of their problem to their doctor. That may be a non-trivial problem since sharing with somebody the shapes, the colours, and the movement of artefacts due to VS-related pathology(s) is a highly complex and, in some cases, frustrating task since this pathology is still little known.

Keywords: Augmented reality · Eyes disease · Visual Snow Syndrome · Unity

1 Introduction

Visual Snow Syndrome is a chronic condition that has only been described and studied in recent years. Its sufferers have a visual impairment in which tiny dots of light are superimposed on the perceived image, which is difficult to describe and explain. Generally, the image perceived by these patients is described as that obtained with an incorrectly tuned television setting. In addition to the ether's information content, we get a partial snow effect.

© The Author(s) 2022
O. Gervasi et al. (Eds.): ICCSA 2022 Workshops, LNCS 13382, pp. 473–485, 2022.
https://doi.org/10.1007/978-3-031-10592-0_34

In this article, we propose an application realised through modern Virtual Reality and Augmented Reality technologies that allow simulating the vision of people affected by Visual Snow. The advantages of this application are twofold. The first is from the patients' point of view: it gives people the possibility to show doctors or family members what their eye sees, overcoming the language barrier that makes it difficult to explain the problem. Consequently, misunderstandings can be avoided. The second is from the doctors' point of view: thanks to a mobile app, they can ask the patient to confirm if the image they perceive is similar or the same as the one shown by the software. The development of this project is carried out using the Unity[1] software, and the target environment is the Android operating system. In the Sect. 2 the most recent literature addressing the Visual Snow problem is discussed. In the Sect. 3 the steps and techniques used for the realisation of the Mobile Android application are illustrated. In the Sect. 4 the first evaluations and opinions expressed by the users of the application are reported. In the Sect. 5 outlines the main objectives obtained after the development of the mobile app and anticipates the future developments.

To try to provide help to people who have this type of condition, we have outlined the following research methodology. First of all we will make an Android application so that we can reach a large percentage of users in a very short time. After the release of the application we want to collect as much feedback as possible from people. After a subsequent phase of the improvement of the application, which will come as a result of the feedback received in the previous phase, we want to proceed with the creation of a series of anonymous questionnaires with which to collect opinions and specific and detailed feedback from users. What we want to outline is a development path that will not end with this article, but will have to proceed along a period of a few months in order to improve the application as much as possible.

2   Related Works

Visual snow is a neurological issue portrayed by a constant visual unsettling influence that involves the whole visual field and is depicted as tiny gleaming flecks similar to old detuned TV [1]. Notwithstanding static, or 'snow', impacted people might encounter extra visual side effects like visual pictures that continue or return after the image has disappeared, aversion to light, unique visualisations from inside the eye and hindered night vision.

The causes of visual snow in patients are still relatively obscure. The average age when the visual snow appears for the first time in the subjects seems, by all accounts, to be more premature than numerous other neurological problems [2]. This initial phase is almost always accompanied by a general lack of recognition of the pathology by specialists; this means that it is still an uncommon question.

Research suggests that visual snow is a mental problem; a preliminary examination of functional cerebrum imaging [3] and electroencephalographic tests propose this interpretation [4].

---

[1] https://unity.com/.

Visual snow is a physical condition, most often exceptionally disabling, that emerges suddenly and is highly complex to diagnose and treat [5]. That is due to the fact that it is still an open field of study: there is little much-targeted research on the phenomenon and those that do exist need to be reviewed and synthesized [6].

In 2013 the first categorization of visual snow as a new precise phenomenon was first published [7]. The authors begin with a description of a Pediatric patient who has suffered from migrainous headaches since the age of seven. The patient had an unexpected beginning of chronic visual impairment. Subsequently, data began to be collected over several years on patients complaining of a reasonably homogeneous set of symptoms suggesting a single common syndrome [8].

Most patients developed migraine, and many exhibited the classic migraine aura, indicating an overlap of illness processes [9]. However, the study highlighted that one of the significant reasons for patients' suffering was the persistent and relentless visual snow symptoms, which lack the episodic aspect characteristic of migraine [10]. Furthermore, only a minority of research participants experienced a visual aura at the outset of Visual Snow Syndrome, indicating that visual snow is distinct from chronic migraine aura. The connection between migraine, typical migraine aura, and Visual Snow Syndrome has been studied further. It was discovered that individuals with Visual Snow Syndrome and simultaneous migraine experienced more different symptoms [11].

Moreover, the role of visual cortical excitability in visual snow has been investigated [12,13] using visual-evoked magnetic field recording in individuals with persistent visual disturbance [14]. Some recent studies show how the VSS can appear as a result of traumatic events that affect the brain, for example explaining how a patient has manifested the disease following a cerebral infarct [15].

In conclusion, we have to admit the aetiology of visual snow is still unknown, and more research with precise criteria and control survey respondents suited for migraine and typical migraine aura is needed to better our understanding of this painful illness. Because of a lack of comprehension of the syndrome's core biology, there are no therapeutic techniques that are significantly successful.

While there is plenty of scope for research from a clinical point of view, our proposal fits into a virtually new segment in terms of applied technology. There is a great deal of work using automated solutions for disease recognition [16–18] and many others using virtual and augmented reality for diagnosis and rehabilitation [19–22]. Virtual reality is becoming an increasingly important technology in the generation of synthetic environments [23] within which therapists and patients can move easily, making everything extremely customisable. In addition, the extreme level of refinement in image definition achieved today [24,25] and the high usability of content in mobile device apps [26,27], especially in the clinical and medical fields [28,29], indeed allows for sophisticated and innovative techniques for describing a patient's symptoms.

3   The Visual Snow Simulator

This section describes the proposed application to simulate what people with Visual Snow see. The mobile app is built using the Unity software. Unity is a software for the creation of multi-platform interactive environments. It is often used to create video games, virtual reality scenarios or augmented reality scenarios [30–33]. We have set Android 11.0 (API 30) as the target environment and Android 5.0 (API 21) as the minimum supported version. That allows the application to be installed on 98.0 % of the Android devices currently in circulation, as shown in Fig. 1; the data shown in the figure are released by Google annually. The software has been developed to be compatible with the ARM64 and ARMv7 architectures, 64-bit and 32-bit, respectively.

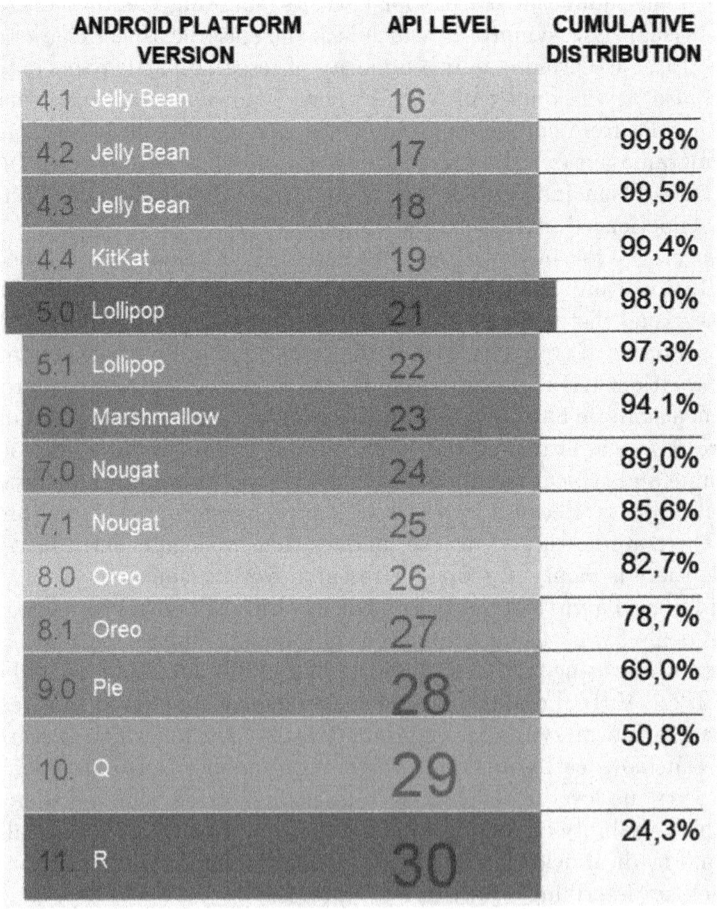

ANDROID PLATFORM VERSION	API LEVEL	CUMULATIVE DISTRIBUTION
4.1 Jelly Bean	16	
4.2 Jelly Bean	17	99,8%
4.3 Jelly Bean	18	99,5%
4.4 KitKat	19	99,4%
5.0 Lollipop	21	98,0%
5.1 Lollipop	22	97,3%
6.0 Marshmallow	23	94,1%
7.0 Nougat	24	89,0%
7.1 Nougat	25	85,6%
8.0 Oreo	26	82,7%
8.1 Oreo	27	78,7%
9.0 Pie	28	69,0%
10. Q	29	50,8%
11. R	30	24,3%

Fig. 1. Android platform distribution - November 2021

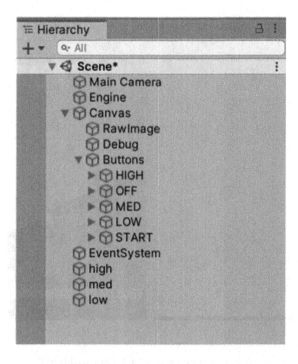

Fig. 2. Scene composition of the software

Figure 2 shows the list of Game Objects that compose the software. The first element is the *Main Camera*, its task is to capture images and show them on the user's screen. This should not be understood with the smartphone camera, but instead as a virtual camera inserted inside a Unity scene. The second Game Object is called *Engine*. Some scripts are connected to it, such as those that are executed when buttons are clicked, and it is used to manage the user interface. The third object is the *Canvas*, which represents a graphical drawing environment, on which the buttons and the whole user interface are placed. Inside the *Canvas* we can see that there is an object called *RawImage*. This is used to apply a background to the canvas. In our case the background applied to the *RawImage* (and consequently to the canvas) is the image captured by the smartphone camera. The video stream is managed by a script that periodically updates the image shown on the screen, giving the idea of a smooth view of the world captured by the camera. The buttons that make up the graphical interface are collected within a container that allows a simplified management from a programming point of view. Inside the scene we find the *EventSystem*. This is used for the recognition of user input, such as clicks on the screen. Finally, there are 3 Game Objects called *high*, *med*, and *low* that are the basis for the activation of filters that simulate the Visual Snow. These Game Objects are passed by reference to the Game Object *Engine* which will use them to activate the on-screen effects based on user input.

The initial screen, which appears on the screen, is shown in Fig. 3a.

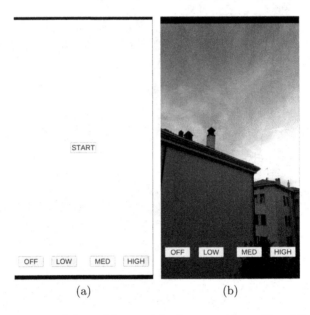

Fig. 3. Starting screen of the mobile app (**a**), Camera without Visual Snow effect (**b**)

The *START* button is in the centre of the scene, which, once pressed, will activate the user's smartphone camera. The application is programmed to ask for permission to access the API that controls the camera if necessary. If the user responds affirmatively, the captured image will be shown on the screen, as shown in Fig. 3b.

The buttons at the bottom of the user interface are needed to activate or deactivate the effect simulating Visual Snow. After careful consideration, we have programmed three different effects. The button *LOW* presents a barely perceptible Visual Snow effect and tries to simulate what a person sees when his pathology is not particularly serious. The *MED* button, when pressed, activates a much more intense effect than the previous one. The *HIGH* button sets the Visual Snow effect on screen at an extremely high intensity. The *OFF* button deactivates the Visual Snow effect (Fig. 4).

The technical realisation of these effects takes place thanks to the use of the *Post Process Volume*, which allow the insertion of graphic effects that are calculated at the end of the pipeline that manages the rendering of the scene. For each button used to activate an effect, we have programmed a specific Post Process Volume. Inside each Post Process Volume, we inserted a graphic filter of the Grain type. We found it particularly effective to simulate Visual Snow to use a filter of this type. Initially, the Grain filter is programmed to mimic what is captured by old cameras that use chemical photographic film to capture images on film and add video noise to the scene by their nature. The Grain filter

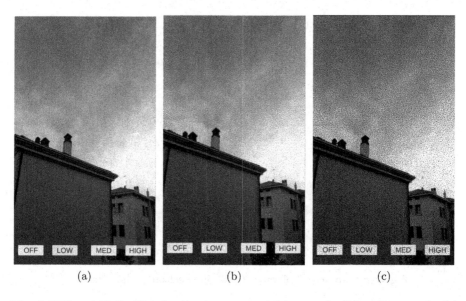

Fig. 4. Different Grain filter levels set on screen (**a**) low mode, (**b**) medium mode, (**c**) high mode

can be configured thanks to four different parameters that the developers can adjust. The first parameter is a Boolean variable called *Colored* which allows us to define whether or not the grain effect should be coloured. The second parameter is called *Intensity* and allows us to define the number of particles to be shown on the screen. The third parameter is *Size* and allows you to define the size of the particles shown on the screen. The fourth and last parameter is the *Luminance contribution* which is used by the graphics engine to modify the effect according to the brightness of the scene and to reduce its intensity in poorly lit areas. An example of how the filter has been configured for the medium intensity configuration is shown in Fig. 5. The application was developed taking into account Android's best practices. In fact, the latest versions of the operating system require to inform the user before accessing the camera or microphone. In the absence of informed consent from the user, mobile applications will not be able to use these devices. The first time the program is launched, the user is asked to authorise or not the use of the camera, and only after the user's authorisation can the program run correctly. Regarding the compilation and export phase of the application, we have used the App Bundle format instead of the old APK format as required by Google from August 2021. The final size of the app is 12 MB, which makes it possible to install the program even on devices that have minimal amounts of ROM memory. Finally, we made several measurements to estimate the minimum RAM requirements that the smartphone must have. From our tests, we found that the average RAM usage is 32.0 MB.

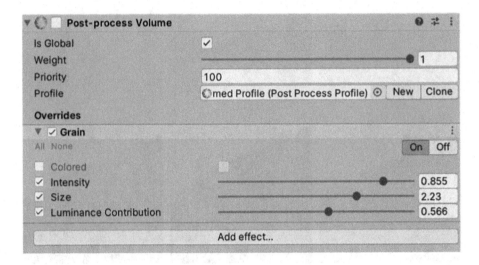

Fig. 5. Post-process Volume with Grain effect on medium settings

4   First Impressions

In this section, we report the first evaluations and opinions expressed by the users of the application. The application was made available on the Play Store on February 12, 2022. During this period of time, we detected a large flow of downloads. Many users downloaded the application from the Store.

Figure 6a shows the distribution of Android versions used by users who installed the application. As we can see, the most recent versions of Android are the most popular ones, and this parameter is in agreement with what is indicated by Google and with which we produced the graph shown in Fig. 1. Figure 6b shows the distribution of installations by geographic area, and the countries that have installed the application are shown in a pie chart. As can be seen from the figure, the greatest diffusion took place in the United States and Italy. This is probably due to the fact that the message with which we have informed people about the presence of this application in the Store has been inserted in a group composed mainly of people living in the United States.

In Fig. 7 is shown the trend of downloads from the date of publication of the application. As we can see, the growth is steady, moreover there is a peak of downloads in correspondence on March 25, the day on which we mentioned the application with a post on Facebook.

During this time period, we received many ratings that people spontaneously made within the Google Play Store and also we received several email messages from people suffering from this condition. Regarding the ratings, we got 11 reviews and all the reviews were 5 stars as shown in Fig. 8. The comments made to us are mainly of appreciation towards the work we have done. As for the suggestions, we got some very interesting ones. For example, a user asked us to implement a feature that allows us to manually set the level of Visual

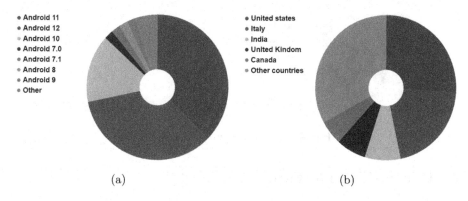

Fig. 6. Distribution of the installations across Android versions (**a**), Number of users using the application (**b**)

Snow simulated by the software, because his case did not find correspondence in the three levels we preset. The problem of this patient was characterised by an intensity lower than what we have set as "low level". This is surely a very important aspect and we will try to satisfy this request with further updates. Other suggestions concerned the possibility of making the pixels representing the Visual Snow coloured or black and white. Finally, some users have asked us to create the same application for the iOS platform as soon as possible because they are owners of iPhones and, therefore, can not install the program that, by design, is programmed to work only on Android.

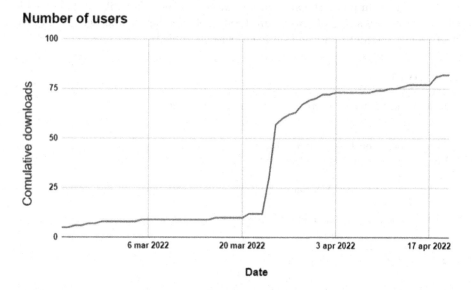

Fig. 7. Number of users using the application

Fig. 8. The mobile app in the Store

5 Conclusions and Future Work

This work aimed to create an Android software application capable of representing what people affected by Visual Snow Syndrome perceive in a simple and effective way. The application has been published on the Play Store and can be freely downloaded from any device with at least Android 7.0. The code produced during the development of the application has been made Open Source and made available to the scientific community through GitHub[2]. A short video showing the application running has been uploaded to YouTube and is publicly available[3]. We are very interested in continuing this project and analysing further developments for the application. The first goal is to make the application cross-platform, i.e., expand its compatibility with the iOS operating system and allow iPhone and iPad users to use it. A second objective is to analyse the opinions of doctors and patients suffering from Visual Snow. For this reason, we are planning to carry out a series of anonymous questionnaires to collect data that will allow us to improve the application. Moreover, hopefully, it will help people suffering from this pathology explain their problems better and better and help doctors get adequate information from patients quickly.

Acronyms

The following acronyms are used in this manuscript:

API   Application Programming Interface
APK   Android Application Package file
AR   Augmented Reality
ARM   Advanced RISC Machines
MB   MegaByte
RAM   Random Access Memory
ROM   Read Only Memory
VR   Virtual Reality
VSS   Visual Snow Syndrome

---

[2] https://github.com/DamianoP/VisualSnow.
[3] https://youtube.com/shorts/cl_SAjyGY64.

References

1. Puledda, F., Schankin, C., Goadsby, P.J.: Visual snow syndrome. Neurology, **94**(6), e564–e574, 2020. ISSN 0028–3878. https://doi.org/10.1212/WNL.0000000000008909. https://n.neurology.org/content/94/6/e564
2. Kondziella, D., Olsen, M.H., Dreier, J.P.: Prevalence of visual snow syndrome in the UK. Eur. J. Neurol. **27**(5), 764–772 (2020). https://doi.org/10.1111/ene.14150. https://onlinelibrary.wiley.com/doi/abs/10.1111/ene.14150
3. Unal, I.C., Yildiz, F.G.: Visual snow in migraine with aura: further characterization by brain imaging, electrophysiology, and treatment-case report. Headache: J.Head Face Pain, **55**(10), 1436–1441 (2015)
4. Lauschke, J.L., Plant, G.T., Fraser, C.L.: Visual snow: a thalamocortical dysrhythmia of the visual pathway? J. Clin. Neurosci.**28**, 123–127, (2016). ISSN 0967–5868. https://doi.org/10.1016/j.jocn.2015.12.001. https://www.sciencedirect.com/science/article/pii/S0967586815006530
5. White, O.B., Clough, M., McKendrick, A.M., Fielding, J.: Visual snow: visual misperception. J. Neuroophthalmol. **38**(4), 514–521 (2018)
6. Puledda, F., Schankin, C., Digre, K., Goadsby, P.J.: Visual snow syndrome: what we know so far. Curr. Opin. Neurolo **31**(1), 52–58 (2018)
7. Simpson, J.C., Goadsby, P.J., Prabhakar, P.: Positive persistent visual symptoms (visual snow) presenting as a migraine variant in a 12-year-old girl. Pediatr. Neurol. **49**(5), 361–363 (2013)
8. Klein, A., Schankin, C.J.: Visual snow syndrome, the spectrum of perceptual disorders, and migraine as a common risk factor: a narrative review. Headache J. Head Face Pain **61**(9), 1306–1313 (2021)
9. Schankin, C.J., Goadsby, P.J.: Visual snow—persistent positive visual phenomenon distinct from migraine aura. Curr. Pain Headache Rep. **19**(6), 1–6 (2015). https://doi.org/10.1007/s11916-015-0497-9
10. Schankin, C.J., Maniyar, F.H., Sprenger, T., Chou, D.E., Eller, M., Goadsby, P.J.: The relation between migraine, typical migraine aura and "visual snow". Headache J. Head Face Pain **54**(6), 957–966 (2014)
11. Schankin, C.J., Maniyar, F.H., Digre, K.B., Goadsby, P.J.: "Visual snow" - a disorder distinct from persistent migraine aura. Brain, **137**(5), 1419–1428 (2014). ISSN 0006–8950. https://doi.org/10.1093/brain/awu050
12. Bou Ghannam, A., Pelak, V.S.: Visual snow: a potential cortical hyperexcitability syndrome. Curr. Treat. Options Neuro. **19**(3), 1–12 (2017). https://doi.org/10.1007/s11940-017-0448-3
13. Eren, O., Rauschel, V., Ruscheweyh, R., Straube, A., Schankin, C.J.: Evidence of dysfunction in the visual association cortex in visual snow syndrome. Ann. Neurol. **84**(6), 946–949 (2018)
14. Chen, W.T., Lin, Y.Y., Fuh, J.L., Hämäläinen, M.S., Ko, Y.C., Wang, S.J.: Sustained visual cortex hyperexcitability in migraine with persistent visual aura. Brain **134**(8), 2387–2395 (2011)
15. Puledda, F., Villar-Martínez, M.D., Goadsby, P.J.: Case report: transformation of visual snow syndrome from episodic to chronic associated with acute cerebellar infarct. Frontiers Neurol. **13** (2022). ISSN 1664–2295. https://doi.org/10.3389/fneur.2022.811490. https://www.frontiersin.org/article/10.3389/fneur.2022.811490
16. Rajkomar, A., Dean, J., Kohane, I.: Machine learning in medicine. N. Engl. J. Med. **380**(14), 1347–1358 (2019)

17. Bhavsar, K.A., Abugabah, A., Singla, J., AlZubi, A.A., Bashir, A.K., et al.: A comprehensive review on medical diagnosis using machine learning. Comput. Mater. Continua **67**(2), 1997 (2021)

18. Benedetti, P., Perri, D., Simonetti, M., Gervasi, O., Reali, G., Femminella, M.: Skin cancer classification using inception network and transfer learning. In: Gervasi, O. (ed.) ICCSA 2020. LNCS, vol. 12249, pp. 536–545. Springer, Cham (2020). https://doi.org/10.1007/978-3-030-58799-4_39

19. O'Neil, O., et al.: Virtual reality for neurorehabilitation: insights from 3 european clinics. PM R **10**(9), S198–S206 (2018)

20. David Jack, D., et al.: Virtual reality-enhanced stroke rehabilitation. IEEE Trans. Neural Syst. Rehabil. Eng. **9**(3), 308–318 (2001)

21. Perri, D., Fortunelli, M., Simonetti, M., Magni, R., Carloni, J., Gervasi, O.: Rapid prototyping of virtual reality cognitive exercises in a tele-rehabilitation context. Electronics **10**(4), 457 (2021)

22. Mubin, O., Alnajjar, F., Jishtu, N., Alsinglawi, B., Al Mahmud, A., et al.: Exoskeletons with virtual reality, augmented reality, and gamification for stroke patients' rehabilitation: systematic review. JMIR Rehabil. Assistive Technol. **6**(2), e12010 (2019)

23. Simonetti, M., Perri, D., Amato, N., Gervasi, O.: Teaching math with the help of virtual reality. In: Gervasi, O. (ed.) ICCSA 2020. LNCS, vol. 12255, pp. 799–809. Springer, Cham (2020). https://doi.org/10.1007/978-3-030-58820-5_57

24. Putra, R.D., Purboyo, T.W., Prasasti, L.A.: A review of image enhancement methods. Int. J. Appl. Eng. Res. **12**(23), 13596–13603 (2017)

25. Greenspan, H., Anderson, C.H., Akber, S.: Image enhancement by nonlinear extrapolation in frequency space. IEEE Trans. Image Process. **9**(6), 1035–1048 (2000)

26. Briz-Ponce, L., Juanes-Méndez, J.A.: Mobile devices and apps, characteristics and current potential on learning. J. Inf. Technol. Res. (JITR) **8**(4), 26–37 (2015)

27. Mehra, A., Paul, J., Kaurav, R.P.S.: Determinants of mobile apps adoption among young adults: theoretical extension and analysis. J. Mark. Commun. **27**(5), 481–509 (2021)

28. Chandrashekar, P.: Do mental health mobile apps work: evidence and recommendations for designing high-efficacy mental health mobile apps. Mhealth **4**, 6 (2018)

29. Briz-Ponce, L., Juanes-Méndez, J.A., Garcìa-Peñalvo, F.J.: Synopsis of discussion session on defining a new quality protocol for medical apps. In: Proceedings of the 3rd International Conference on Technological Ecosystems for Enhancing Multiculturality, pp. 7–12 (2015)

30. Santucci, F., Frenguelli, F., De Angelis, A., Cuccaro, I., Perri, D., Simonetti, M.: An immersive open source environment using godot. In: Gervasi, O. (ed.) ICCSA 2020. LNCS, vol. 12255, pp. 784–798. Springer, Cham (2020). https://doi.org/10.1007/978-3-030-58820-5_56

31. Linowes, J.: Unity Virtual Reality Projects. Packt Publishing Ltd, Birmingham (2015)

32. Perri, D., Simonetti, M., Tasso, S., Gervasi, O.: Learning mathematics in an immersive way (2021)

33. Jerald, J., Giokaris, P., Woodall, D., Hartbolt, A., Chandak, A., Kuntz, S.: Developing virtual reality applications with unity. In: 2014 IEEE Virtual Reality (VR), pp. 1–3. IEEE (2014)

Strategies for the Digitalization
of Cultural Heritage

Osvaldo Gervasi[1]([📧])[ID], Damiano Perri[1,2][ID], Marco Simonetti[1,2][ID],
and Sergio Tasso[1][ID]

[1] Department of Mathematics and Computer Science, University of Perugia,
Perugia, Italy
`osvaldo.gervasi@unipg.it`
[2] Department of Mathematics and Computer Science, University of Florence,
Florence, Italy

Abstract. The COVID-19 pandemic caused despair, poverty and, above all, pain and death across the planet. Nevertheless, there is no doubt that it has also given a strong global impetus to the digital world, asserting its importance, sustainability and richness of perspectives. With our work we intend to establish a set of best practices aimed at defining methods and technologies that will enable those fascinated by digital technologies to contribute effectively to the digitisation of cultural heritage on a large scale. Various aspects that play a crucial role in the digitisation of artifacts will be discussed, with a focus on the issues involved in the manual realisation of works using Blender and Unity software. For demonstration purposes, two very popular use cases in the Umbria region of Italy are presented: "Piazza IV Novembre" in Perugia with the magnificent "Fontana Maggiore", the "Palazzo dei Priori" and the Duomo on one side and the Republic square in Foligno on the other, with the Duomo, the Bishop's house and the Diocesan Museum, the Town Hall and "Palazzo Trinci". The first realization was carried out using photogrammetry techniques, the software Blender and Unity, while the second was carried out exclusively with Blender and Unity.

The theme is highly relevant in Europe, particularly Italy, where the topic is part of the post-COVID-19 National Recovery and Resilience Plan (NRRP).

Keywords: Virtual reality · Augmented reality · Blender · Unity · Cultural heritage · Digital sustainability

1 Introduction

Virtual reality and augmented reality techniques are constantly evolving. Thanks to the development of increasingly high-performance hardware, they make it possible to achieve results and levels of realism unthinkable just a few years ago. The increase in computational power of the GPU makes it possible to create highly complex three-dimensional models rich in vertices, polygons and

O. Gervasi et al. (Eds.): ICCSA 2022 Workshops, LNCS 13382, pp. 486–502, 2022.
https://doi.org/10.1007/978-3-031-10592-0_35

very high-resolution textures. As a result, the virtual environments that can be realized allow the user to be immersed in photo-realistic worlds that can even trigger the suspension of disbelief. This sentiment is a psychological state where the user stops considering the virtual world as a fake and detached environment but rather as an alternative reality that engages him or her psychologically. In the past two years, the whole world has been affected by a pandemic whose scale and intensity have caused endless pain and problems in many sections of the population. However, there is one thing that we can ascribe to the pandemic as positive: that it has caused all segments of the world's population to make an impressive technological leap. The conjugation of this impressive technological leap of individuals, borrowed from the forced confinement for long periods in confined spaces and under travel bans, has brought the importance of digitization in cultural goods and works of art to enable their enjoyment even study remotely.

This paper aims to identify a series of methodologies that enable the creation of virtual worlds through which art treasures can be accessible to a vast population in a simple and relatively inexpensive manner in various ways. To this end, use cases are presented which were realised using two of the most successful approaches, based on the most modern virtual and augmented reality techniques. The first use case was realised through photogrammetry. The "Fontana Maggiore" in Perugia (PG, Italy), one of the main monuments in the city's historic centre, was reconstructed. Photogrammetry has made it possible, through appropriately taken photographs, to reconstruct the fountain in a highly reliable manner without manually modelling its polygonal shapes. We preferred relying solely on the results obtained by neural networks and algorithms that analyse the images produced by the three-dimensional model. Photogrammetry is a technique that allows very high-quality results that could hardly be achieved by manually producing the models and textures. As a limitation, this technology has a high number of vertices required for faithful reconstruction, limiting the virtual visualisation of the artefact with low performing hardware.

The second use case presented follows the manual modelling approach and concerns the reconstruction of the Republic square in Foligno (PG, Italy) and the surrounding areas where the buildings and architectural works were reproduced. These environments were treated using two popular 3D modelling software. The first is Blender[1], open-source software that allows the three-dimensional modelling of objects and the faithful representation of environments. The modelling tools made available to the user are of particular importance, rich in functions performed by the software that greatly facilitate the user's work.

The second software used is Unity[2], which is frequently used for the realisation of three-dimensional environments and interactive synthetic scenarios, in particular videogames and serious games.

The article is structured as follows.

---

[1] https://www.blender.org.
[2] https://unity.com.

Section 2 provides an overview of recent studies conducted by the scientific community on the digitisation of cultural heritage and the implementation of virtual environments that enable the remote visitation of sites.

Section 3 describes the state-of-the-art techniques that are used for the realisation of materials and three-dimensional polygonal models with the aim of creating synthetic, interactive and navigable worlds for the visitor.

Section 4 illustrates the use of the technologies discussed, in order to allow the replication of the approach we suggested in multiple other contexts, in order to achieve an easily realisable and low-cost methodology, describing its most relevant aspects. The discussion takes its cue from how the two use cases were realised, illustrating the salient steps and methodologies adopted.

Section 5 summarises the important aspects of our approach and provides some insights into possible future developments of this work.

2   Related Works

The reproduction of images through computer graphics and synthetic reconstruction has always been searching for a compromise between the quality of the result and processing performance [1,2]. A scene taken from a video, or an image, to be considered credible from the point of view of realism, needs a particularly advanced level of detail, which inevitably requires an underlying complex numerical processing [3]. Indeed, every image has got to be divided into numerous small adjacent polygons, the number of which is proportional to the quality and fidelity of the reproduction itself [4–6]. Certainly, the advent of more performing hardware such as GPUs has allowed a significant leap forward in the main sectors of computer graphics and virtual reality [7–9]. More recently, artificial intelligence, and more specifically convolutive networks, has made it possible to quantitatively raise the level of realism of images and video streams [10–12].

The goal becomes particularly complex when one wants to create 3D models of historical and archaeological items and monuments in their existing condition. So, a more sophisticated approach capable of capturing and digitally modelling these places' precise geometry and morphological features is required [13]. For years, close-range photogrammetry has been proposed for cultural heritage documentation and has worked very well. This conventional approach has been supplanted by digital close-range photogrammetry due to recent computer and information technology advances. This innovative technology opens up new possibilities like landscape laser scanning, automatic orientation and measurement operations, 3D vector data production, digital ortho-image generation, and digital surface model development [14]. Whereas many methodologies and sensors are now available, the correct strategy for obtaining a better and more realistic 3D model with the necessary level of detail is still a blend of multiple techniques and models. That is why a single approach is not finally capable of providing consistent results in all scenarios [15]. However, it is precisely this mix that enables a high-quality graphic reproduction and the possibility of manipulating the image to highlight and better understand its constituent details. The virtual environments present in the images can then be rotated and resized; one can enter them and explore them in their spatial depth, appreciating the aesthetic elements [16,17]. Furthermore, each environment can be enriched with a series of important information and data of different nature (*data and metadata*), such as texts and audio, useful for better describing the object under examination [18,19].

This outstanding potential to create a diverse cognitive experience in humans is precisely what makes these modern technologies an effective way of communicating ideas and culture; they already pervade numerous domains ranging from education [20] to healthcare [21,22], from recreation and entertainment [23] to tourism [24].

The growing interest in these technologies in tourism and cultural promotion is evident; by their nature, they allow the enhancement, knowledge and accessibility to the vast public of humankind's immense cultural heritage, even remotely.

3   Materials and Methods

This section describes the techniques used to create the materials and polygonal models with which the three-dimensional scenarios were realised.

3.1   Creating the Shapes with Blender

Blender is a cross-platform 3D modelling programme, i.e. it can run on various operating systems such as Linux, Windows and MacOS, offering developers the possibility of working independently of the computer being used. Blender is released under the Gnu Public Licence (GPL) and allows numerous creative functions. These include the possibility of modelling three-dimensional objects, creating animations, rendering complex scenes and exporting the result by producing PNG or JPEG images. The latest versions of this programme have considerably improved the user interface, lowering the learning curve and allowing it to be used even by people who do not have the aptitude for advanced computer software. Polygon models made with Blender can also be exported as OBJ or FBX files. These files are highly compatible and can be used by many other complementary programmes, such as Unity.

Starting Modeling from Google Maps or Other Images

Reproducing natural objects can be challenging. In particular, it is not trivial to reproduce accurately scaled shapes and dimensions within computer graphics software. Specific techniques can help the developer maintain a high fidelity of the shapes realised. The technique we recommend is the use of reference images. First of all, a photograph must be taken of the object to be modelled, acquiring the image perpendicular to the object to be reproduced. Let us suppose that we want to acquire the frontal image of a building. It is sometimes difficult to obtain images of this type when one wants to reproduce buildings built in an urban context, as there may be no suitable points for taking the images. For this reason, we recommend using a drone, on which a remote-controlled camera must be installed. After having had the drone positioned perpendicularly to the façade of a building, the shot can then be taken. Particular attention must be paid to the focal length of the camera used, as focal lengths too short, e.g. less than 50 mm, may cause perspective distortion that is difficult to correct. In this case, it could be helpful to have the drone move within an imaginary grid positioned along the façade of the building, taking photographs after moving the drone by a predefined amount of metres, an example of which is shown in Fig. 1. This operation will produce a collage of photographs, which, when joined together, will provide a faithful reproduction of the building façade without the problem of perspective distortion.

Fig. 1. Sample virtual grid applied to a building.

3.2 Procedural Textures

The realisation of realistic three-dimensional objects involves, among other things, the creation of textures, i.e., images that are applied to the object making it easily identifiable with real-world objects. A properly realised texture can simulate the materials that make up the objects in the three-dimensional scene. There are various techniques for creating realistic textures. The first involves manual creation using photo editing software (such as Gimp[3]), while the second involves the mathematical definition of the structure that the resulting texture

---

[3] https://www.gimp.org/.

should have. Textures created using the latter technique are called Procedural Textures. They are generated mathematically to simulate complex materials such as marble, wood and granite. Blender allows procedural textures to be created via a block graphics programming environment, an example of which is shown in Fig. 2.

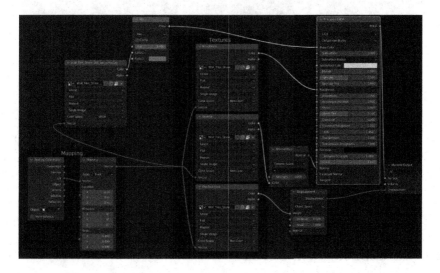

Fig. 2. Visual program related to a procedural texture of the wall.

The various blocks we can see in Fig. 2 are abstractions of mathematical algorithms that perform operations on an initially empty texture. When these blocks are interconnected, the output of the previous block is given as input to the next block. Thanks to the concatenation of these blocks, extremely complex textures can be obtained, such as the one shown in Fig. 3, which is the result of the procedural texture used to create the façade of a building in Perugia's central square next to the "Fontana Maggiore".

Another advantage of procedural textures is that they are created and managed by the software itself, eliminating the requirement for file system references to images. These textures likewise adjust to the object they're applied to and don't have any visible discontinuities. It should also be noted that if one of these textures is applied to an object, such as a building, a change in the size of the building's facade will not have an adverse effect on the texture's aesthetics because the software will handle this fully automatically and the texture will be correctly placed on the object's facade, generating the missing parts. A procedural texture has no fixed resolution and adapts to the objects to which it is applied dynamically. Finally, it should be noted that creating a procedural texture is a time-consuming process that will use the CPU for several minutes.

Fig. 3. The procedural texture output simulating the real wall.

3.3   Creating Relevant Details

The manual modelling of complex polygonal details may not be easy, and the final result may not be satisfactory. In this case, we recommend using the technique of photogrammetry, which allows a very high level of realism to be obtained by delegating the realisation of the most complex parts of 3D models to artificial intelligence techniques. To set up the photogrammetry software, one has to create an image dataset of the object to be reproduced. The dataset must consist of a sufficiently large amount of images, as all parts and facets of the object must be photographed. Most of today's cameras have an automatic mode, capable of setting photographic parameters that are most often adequate.

However, knowing how to set the correct parameters and juggle the use of manual mode will make a significant difference in terms of the quality and efficiency of the photogrammetric survey. It would be good to ensure that all photographs in the dataset are taken at the same focal length and with as similar an illumination level as possible between the various images.

In photogrammetry, similarly to human vision, if an object is captured in at least two images taken from different viewpoints, the different positions of the object in the images allow stereoscopic views to be obtained and three-dimensional information to be derived from the overlapping areas in the images. To obtain a very detailed three-dimensional model, a large amount of overlap between the different photographs is necessary; in general, it would be optimal that between one photograph and the next, approximately 70% of the details captured in the previous photograph also appear in the following photograph. Furthermore, the number of photographs required for the three-dimensional reconstruction of an object is directly proportional to its size; the larger the size of the object, the greater the number of photographs required for its reconstruction.

3.4 Creating an Interactive Environment with Unity

The creation of immersive environments is facilitated by the presence on the market of software with a large community. Thanks to constant updates, it keeps pace with the needs of developers. Unity makes it possible to realise immersive environments by inserting models and assets created with Blender into the scenes. The scenes realised in Unity can then be exported for the platforms on the market today, such as desktop computers with Windows operating system or consoles or Android or iOS smartphones.

Issues on Importing Blender Shapes and Textures

The export of models from Blender may initially present critical issues. In particular, first-time users of these programmes cannot easily export procedural textures from Blender to Unity. The correct operation involves backing the texture directly onto the UV map of the object. Through this procedure, the object will use an image that will be applied directly onto it and no longer the procedural texture. Therefore, the procedural texture must be understood as mathematical modelling used in the development phase. It must be stored in an image file applied to the object. Once this has been done, it is then possible to proceed with the export from Blender of a zip file containing the three-dimensional model and the images that will constitute its textures. Once the three-dimensional object has been imported into Unity, it will then be necessary to manually apply the various PNG or JPG textures to the various components of the object in order to obtain a faithful reproduction.

4 Digitalization of Cultural Heritage Artifacts

In this section, we describe the methodologies that can be adopted to realise virtual worlds of monuments and works of art for the remote enjoyment of the objects of interest. To this end, we will first analyse the salient phases of the work that led to the virtual representation of the areas of the two Umbrian towns considered[4].

The methodologies indicated can be reused for virtual representation and the creation of virtual journeys in other scenarios and contexts.

4.1 The Piazza IV Novembre

The "Piazza IV Novembre" is located in the centre of the city of Perugia and features several historical buildings such as the "Palazzo dei Priori" and the "Fontana Maggiore".

---

[4] Umbria is a region in central Italy untouched by the sea, rich in green areas and monuments that bear witness to the wealth and splendour experienced under the papal empire in the twelfth and thirteenth centuries.

The "Fontana Maggiore"

The "Fontana Maggiore" in Perugia has three levels, is polygonal in shape and was built in the thirteenth century using an alternating pink and white marble. The lowest level is set on a flight of steps from which rises a twenty-five-sided basin. Each face of the twenty-five sides forms a diptych, i.e. two images joined by a central link, adorned with sculpted reliefs with small, slender columns. The twenty-five sides describe the 12 months of the year, each accompanied by the zodiac symbol. Each month is associated with moments of daily life and agricultural work. Thus, each bas-relief on each side is different from the others. The photogrammetric survey of the fountain required photographs taken at different heights rotating at each iteration around the fountain to view the fountain's surroundings completely. An example is shown in Fig. 4.

Fig. 4. Images taken around the "Fontana Maggiore".

A total of 564 photographs were collected. The photographs are all taken with the same parameters: ISO sensitivity is set to 500, the focal length is 24 mm, the exposure time is 1/320 s, and the aperture is f/9. Since the scenery in which the photographs are taken is open to the public, care must be taken to avoid people appearing in the shots. Shadows of animals such as birds, dogs or cats should also be avoided as much as possible.

Palazzo dei Priori

Next, photographs were taken at the "Palazzo dei Priori", located opposite the fountain. The palace is characterised by a staircase that connects the main door with the floor of the square. There are several arches supported by columns in the lower part of the palace, while in the upper part, one can observe several windows arranged in the highest part of the façade. There are also aesthetic embellishments along the walls, signs of the wear and tear of time, and statues. The dataset, in this case, consists of 626 photographs and the parameters used are the same as those used for the fountain dataset. The point cloud of the building is shown in Fig. 5.

Fig. 5. Images taken for reproducing the "Palazzo dei Priori".

As can be seen, the photographs were taken at different heights, moving from left to right and trying to capture as much detail as possible of the building.

Photogrammetry
The dataset is then processed with the Meshroom photogrammetry software[5]. Meshroom is a software released under an open source licence, which allows the reconstruction of three-dimensional models from photographic datasets. Once the dataset has been imported into Meshroom, it is necessary to define the pipeline, i.e. the set of operations that the programme must perform to generate the object's three-dimensional model. The pipeline used is as follows: *Camera Init, Feature Extraction, Image Matching, Feature Matching, Structure from*

---

[5] https://github.com/alicevision/meshroom.

Motion, Prepare Dense Scene, Depth Map, Depth Map Filter, Meshing, Meshing filter, Texturing. The fountain model that was produced consists of approximately 2.9 million vertices and approximately 5.9 million faces. The model of the "Palazzo dei Priori" consists of approximately 2.1 million vertices and approximately 4.3 million faces. The resulting models are then imported into Blender and placed within a scenario. The square floor is then created using a procedural texture, and several adjacent buildings are modelled to give a sense of immersiveness to the scene. Figure 6 shows a view of the "Piazza IV Novembre" rendered within the virtual scenario, and the beauty of the final result can be appreciated.

Fig. 6. Final result of the virtual representation of "Piazza IV Novembre", Perugia (PG, Italy).

4.2   The Republic Square, Foligno

The Republic square in Foligno was reconstructed using the technique of manual 3D modelling with Blender. There are various buildings within the square, among them the "Palazzo Trinci", the Town Hall, the Cathedral of San Feliciano and the "Palazzo delle Canoniche". Similarly to what was done to reconstruct "Piazza IV Novembre" in Perugia, preliminary work aimed at collecting images was also crucial in this case. Images are necessary for reconstructing rooms and buildings because they provide details and proportions and are used as a trace to be followed during modelling.

The "Palazzo Trinci"
On the eastern side of the square is the "Palazzo Trinci", formerly the residence of the Foligno seigniory and now home to the City Museum. Characteristic elements

of "Palazzo Trinci" are the six large Corinthian-style columns resting on the central loggia of the palace façade, the windows are characterised by two distinct architectural forms, the 'curbs' under each row of windows, the row of small parallelepipeds positioned below the roof and the bricks decorate the lower part of the building. Figure 7 shows the virtually reconstructed "Palazzo Trinci". The picture was taken with a focal length of 35 mm.

Fig. 7. Virtual representation of "Palazzo Trinci" located in Republic square, Foligno (PG, Italy).

The Town Hall

The Town Hall is set on a medieval tower called the "Pucciarotto", which has the function of a bell tower. The elements that characterize this building are described. The façade is punctuated by six Ionic-style columns resting on a ledge from which five round arches open. The windows of four different shapes have a frame very similar to that of the "Palazzo Trinci", which is why the same model has been reused. A characteristic element of the building is undoubtedly the tower, built in the thirteenth century, which collapsed following the 1997 earthquake, and then restored in 2007. The structure of the turret ends with an umbrella-shaped dome. The virtually reconstructed Town Hall is shown in Fig. 8. The perspective distortion seen in the image is due to the focal length that was used to capture the photograph. The photo was taken with a focal length of 18 mm and this was necessary to fit the whole building into one photographic shot.

Fig. 8. Virtual representation of the Town Hall located in Piazza della Repubblica, Foligno (PG, Italy).

The Cathedral of San Feliciano

The Cathedral of San Feliciano, also called the Duomo, is the most influential building in Republic square, both from an artistic and cultural point of view. Two facades face the square, the side one and the main one, which more precisely overlooks Largo Carducci. The main facade of the cathedral, restored in 1904, has three doors in the lower part, which were completely rebuilt during the restoration work. On the axis of the side portals, there are two mullioned windows surmounted by a rhombus and a circle and a loggia articulated into eight small arches. In the second order, the facade has a central rose window. At the same time, the third level, introduced with the restoration of the sixteenth century, contains a mosaic depicting *the Redeemer enthroned, the saints Feliciano and Messalina and the Pope Leo XIII genuflected*. The minor façade of the Duomo presents, in the lower part, the multiple ring gate adorned with a series of decorative motifs. There is a large loggia in the upper order with six openings above which the two small side rosettes and the larger central one stand out. The main facade has a single rose window consisting of two rows of columns arranged radially starting from the central core and connected by small arches. The side façade, on the other hand, is characterized by three rose windows, one larger and placed centrally, and two smaller lateral ones, formed by a single row of columns. Three mullioned windows characterize the minor facade of the cathedral, created starting from the outer frame and then moving on to the modelling of the internal details. On both sides of the church, numerous bas-reliefs and sculptures present a significant level of detail, many of which were not made through modelling but simulated through procedural textures.

The Cathedral also features a bell tower and a large dome. The virtually reconstructed Cathedral of San Feliciano is shown in the Fig. 9. The picture was taken with a focal length of 35 mm.

Fig. 9. Virtual representation of the Cathedral of San Feliciano (left side) and "Palazzo delle Canoniche" (right side) located in Piazza della Repubblica, Foligno (PG, Italy).

The "Palazzo delle Canoniche"

The "Palazzo delle Canoniche" is built between the nave and the left arm of the main facade of the cathedral. Inside we can find the Capitular and Diocesan Museum of Foligno. The aesthetic aspects that characterize this building are the arches that run along the base, the windows with a very elongated shape, and the roof, with various parallelepiped-shaped elements that run along its perimeter. The "Palazzo delle Canoniche", virtually reconstructed, is shown in the Fig. 10. The picture was taken with a focal length of 30 mm.

Fig. 10. Virtual representation of "Palazzo delle Canoniche" (left side) and the Cathedral of San Feliciano (right side), Piazza della Repubblica, Foligno (PG, Italy).

5   Conclusions and Future Works

We presented some guidelines to digitally reconstruct monuments and artefacts, which enable public administrations, museums, and organizations in charge of promoting art treasures to realize virtual exhibitions and the digitization of such important cultural heritage. The theme is highly relevant in Europe, particularly Italy, where the topic is part of the National Recovery and Resilience Plan (NRRP).

Two virtual environments were created as case studies, using two different work paths in this work. In the first case, photogrammetry was used, thanks to which the Palazzo dei Priori and the Fontana Maggiore in Perugia were reconstructed. The objects obtained with photogrammetry were then arranged in an interactive Unity virtual environment. In the second case, manual three-dimensional modelling of the buildings present in the Piazza della Repubblica of Foligno was carried out. In this second case, the virtual scenario can be freely explored through virtual reality viewers or the most common desktop computers that interact with the environment via mouse and keyboard input.

The photogrammetry technology to reconstruct three-dimensional elements is able to produce very detailed models that are able to immerse a user within the scenario.

As possible future developments we will try to investigate how to use these techniques in Mataverse launched by Meta, and how to make virtual visits to museums and cultural places that can be explored through virtual reality and augmented reality techniques more and more engaging and effective. The aim is to allow even very distant people to view the works of art, the architecture of historic buildings, and appreciate the beauty of our cities from a distance.

Acronyms

The following acronyms are used in this manuscript:

AR   Augmented Reality
CPU   Central Processing Unit
GPL   General Public License
GPU   Graphic Processing Unit
UV   The u,v graphic coordinates
VR   Virtual Reality

References

1. Luebke, D., Reddy, M., Cohen, J.D., Varshney, A., Watson, B., Huebner, R.: Level of Detail for 3D Graphics. Morgan Kaufmann, Burlington (2003)
2. Akenine-Moller, T., Haines, E., Hoffman, N.: Real-Time Rendering. AK Peters/crc Press, Natick (2019)
3. Simonetti, M., Perri, D., Amato, N., Gervasi, O.: Teaching math with the help of virtual reality. In: Gervasi, O. (ed.) ICCSA 2020. LNCS, vol. 12255, pp. 799–809. Springer, Cham (2020). https://doi.org/10.1007/978-3-030-58820-5_57
4. Engel, K., Hadwiger, M., Kniss, J.M., Lefohn, A. E., Salama, C.R., Weiskopf, D.: Real-Time Volume Graphics. In: ACM Siggraph 2004 Course Notes, pp. 29–es (2004)
5. Szeliski, R.: Computer Vision: Algorithms and Applications. Springer, London (2010). https://doi.org/10.1007/978-1-84882-935-0
6. Schneider, P., Eberly, D.H.: Geometric Tools for Computer Graphics. Elsevier, Amsterdam (2002)
7. Beig, M., Kapralos, B., Collins, K., Mirza-Babaei, P.: G-spar: Gpu-based voxel graph pathfinding for spatial audio rendering in games and VR. In: 2019 IEEE Conference on Games (CoG). IEEE, pp. 1–8 (2019)
8. Lee, W.J., Hwang, S.J., Shin, Y., Yoo, J.J., Ryu, S.: Fast stereoscopic rendering on mobile ray tracing GPU for virtual reality applications. In: 2017 IEEE International Conference on Consumer Electronics (ICCE). IEEE, pp. 355–357 (2017)
9. Xie, C., Xin, F., Chen, M., Song, S.L.: OO-VR: Numa friendly object-oriented VR rendering framework for future numa-based multi-GPU systems. In: 2019 ACM/IEEE 46th Annual International Symposium on Computer Architecture (ISCA). IEEE, pp. 53–65 (2019)
10. Garbin, S.J., Kowalski, M., Johnson, M., Shotton, J., Valentin, J.: Fastnerf: High-fidelity neural rendering at 200 fps. In: Proceedings of the IEEE/CVF International Conference on Computer Vision, pp. 14346–14355 (2021)
11. Takikawa, T.: Neural geometric level of detail: real-time rendering with implicit 3d shapes. In: Proceedings of the IEEE/CVF Conference on Computer Vision and Pattern Recognition, pp. 11358–11367 (2021)
12. Milano, F., Loquercio, A., Rosinol, A., Scaramuzza, D., Carlone, L.: Primal-dual mesh convolutional neural networks. Adv. Neural. Inf. Process. Syst. **33**, 952–963 (2020)
13. Remondino, F.: Heritage recording and 3D modeling with photogrammetry and 3D scanning. Remote Sens. **3**(6), 1104–1138 (2011)

14. Yastikli, N.: Documentation of cultural heritage using digital photogrammetry and laser scanning. J. Cult. Herit. **8**(4), 423–427 (2007)
15. Guidi, G., Russo, M., Ercoli, S., Remondino, F., Rizzi, A., Menna, F.: A multi-resolution methodology for the 3D modeling of large and complex archeological areas. Int. J. Archit. Comput. **7**(1), 39–55 (2009)
16. Selmanović, E., et al.: Improving accessibility to intangible cultural heritage preservation using virtual reality. J. Comput. Cult. Heritage (JOCCH) **13**(2), 1–19 (2020)
17. Ozdemir, M.A.: Virtual reality (VR) and augmented reality (AR) technologies for accessibility and marketing in the tourism industry. In: ICT Tools and Applications for Accessible Tourism. IGI Global, pp. 277–301 (2021)
18. Garzotto, F., Matarazzo, V., Messina, N., Gelsomini, M., Riva, C.: Improving museum accessibility through storytelling in wearable immersive virtual reality. In: 2018 3rd Digital Heritage International Congress (DigitalHERITAGE) Held Jointly with 2018 24th International Conference on Virtual Systems & Multimedia (VSMM 2018). IEEE, pp. 1–8 (2018)
19. Guedes, L.S., Marques, L.A., Vitório, G.: Enhancing interaction and accessibility in museums and exhibitions with augmented reality and screen readers. In: Miesenberger, K., Manduchi, R., Covarrubias Rodriguez, M., Peňáz, P. (eds.) ICCHP 2020. LNCS, vol. 12376, pp. 157–163. Springer, Cham (2020). https://doi.org/10.1007/978-3-030-58796-3_20
20. Perry, B.: Gamifying french language learning: a case study examining a quest-based, augmented reality mobile learning-tool. Procedia Soc. Behav. Sci. **174**, 2308–2315 (2015)
21. Laverdière, C., et al.: Augmented reality in orthopaedics: a systematic review and a window on future possibilities. Bone Joint J. **101**(12), 1479–1488 (2019)
22. Marin, R., Sanz, P.J., Sánchez, J.S.: A very high level interface to teleoperate a robot via web including augmented reality". In: Proceedings 2002 IEEE International Conference on Robotics and Automation (Cat. No. 02CH37292), vol. 3, pp. 2725–2730. IEEE (2002)
23. Das, P., Zhu, M.O., McLaughlin, L., Bilgrami, Z., Milanaik, R.L., et al.: Augmented reality video games: new possibilities and implications for children and adolescents. Multimodal Technol. Interact. **1**(2), 8 (2017)
24. Jung, T.H., Han, D.I.: Augmented reality (AR) in urban heritage tourism. In: e-Review of Tourism Research, vol. 5 (2014)

International Workshop on Workshop on Advanced and Computational Methods for Earth Science Applications (WACM4ES 2022)

UAV Photogrammetry for Volume Calculations.
A Case Study of an Open Sand Quarry

Giuessppina Vacca$^{(\boxtimes)}$ (iD)

Department of Civil and Environmental Engineering and Architecture, University of Cagliari,
09123 Cagliari, Italy
vaccag@unica.it

Abstract. Traditional geomatic surveying techniques for calculating volumes of
bulk or extracted material have evolved in recent years. From the traditional GNSS
or total station survey to the current UAV photogrammetric system with the Structure from Motion (SfM) approach. The calculation of the volumes of bulk or
landfill materials is of considerable importance both from an economic point of
view and from an environmental point of view. The emergence of unmanned aerial
vehicles - UAVs made it possible to automate the entire volume detection process,
as well as reduce the time required for detection itself. This paper presents the
calculation of the volume for the heaps of material (sand) on an open sand quarry
with the use of UAV and multimages Close Range Photogrammetry. The survey
was carried out on the same sand quarry in two successive time with the DJI Phantom 4 UAV. The images processed with the Metashape software, and the volume
calculation performed with the Cloud Compare software.

Keywords: Volume · Comparison · UAV · Metashape · SfM · Cloud Compare

1 Introduction

Thanks to the technological development of recent years relating to UAV technology
both from the hardware point of view and from the software point of view in relation
to image processing, the use of UAVs in the various aspects of sustainable engineering
has increased significantly. The possibility of detecting the territory in safety, with fast
times, at low cost and with low environmental impact has facilitated its use in various
areas it has had a significant impact in mine engineering operations especially for the
survey and volume calculation of a quarry [1].

The good management of a quarry requires precise data obtained in a short time. For
quarries, its continuous survey is important to monitor its evolution. In general, these
monitoring are intensified during the periods of removal of the material, and this leads
to the need to use fast and accurate survey methods [2]. In the past, the monitoring
and calculation of volumes were performed with traditional topographic methods using
Total Stations or the Global Navigation Satellite System (GNSS) in Real Time Kinematic
mode. These systems are still used but have problems relating to access and safety of

© The Author(s), under exclusive license to Springer Nature Switzerland AG 2022
O. Gervasi et al. (Eds.): ICCSA 2022 Workshops, LNCS 13382, pp. 505–518, 2022.
https://doi.org/10.1007/978-3-031-10592-0_36

the quarry, costs and survey times which can be several days depending on the size of the quarry [3, 4].

Another method used is the Terrestrial Laser Scanner (TLS) which, however, presents greater difficulties both in the survey phase and in its processing, as well as high costs. [5–7]. UAV Photogrammetry is an alternative to TLS with the advantage of being cheaper, faster and simpler. By use of the Structure from Motion (SfM) approach, it is possible to generate dense cloud points of high accuracy that can be used for the calculation of volumes. There are many experiences that have shown its accuracy, reliability, low costs and fast times [8–10] that have made it one of the most used techniques in monitoring quarries.

The paper presents the first results obtained from research in this field. In particular, the study of the workflow for calculating the volumes of a sand quarry is presented, evaluating the best parameters to produce point clouds to be used for the calculation of the collected material. In this first phase of research, Metashape software by Agisoft was used to produce point clouds and Cloud Compare software for the calculation of volumes. The research is continuing evaluating the potential of this methodology in terms of accuracy, time and difficulty compared to the methods used in this quarry for its monitoring.

2 Materials and Method

The paper concerned the study of the potential of calculating volumes using multimages photogrammetry from UAVs with the aim of testing an economical, fast and accurate workflow that can be easily used in the frequent monitoring of quarries. The workflow studied involved two of the most popular software for processing images from UAV surveys and for processing dense point clouds: Metashape Professional 1.7.2 and the open source software Cloud Compare.

The volume was calculated between two UAV flights performed in May 2021 and February 2022 over a sand quarry. The procedure was evaluated exclusively based on processing times and on the parameters that can be used for the calculation. As for the accuracy of the UAV photogrammetry method, already widely positively evaluated by the scientific literature reported in the introduction, it will be the subject of a forthcoming publication.

In the following paragraphs the case study, the methodology followed, and the instrumentation used will be described.

2.1 Case Study

The case study is a quarry located in the municipality of Serdiana (Italy) in the locality of S'Isca Manna. It is a sand quarry of about 5.4 ha. Figure 1 shows the quarry.

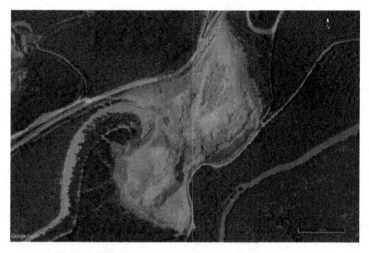

Fig. 1. S'Isca manna quarry (image from google earth)

The quarry has an average altitude of about 270 m above mean sea level. Around the quarry there is a thick vegetation with trees (Table 1).

Table 1. Geographic coordinate of the quarry

	Latitude	Longitudine
East	39°25′21.39″ N	9°10′57.37″ E
West	39°25′22.55″ N	9°10′45.24″ E
North	39°25′26.76″ N	9°10′54.30″ E
South	39°25′15.18″ N	9°10′50.81″ E

2.2 UAV Survey

The DJI Phantom 4 drone was used for May 2021 and February 2022 flights. Table 2 shows the characteristics of the UAV used (Table 3).

Table 2. DJI Phantom 4 specifications

Size	Diagonal 35 cm
Wight	1,375 kg
Max flight time	30 min
Max speed	13–89 m/s
Rotors	4
Camera	Yuneec E90
Pixel	5472 × 3080
Focal lenght	8.3 mm
Pixel size	2.41 micron
Image format	Jpeg, DNG (Raw)

Table 3. UAV survey

	May 2021	February 2022
Area covered by the images	16 ha	13 ha
Flight height	50 m	56 m
GSD	1.34 cm	1.5 cm
Longitudinal overlay	80%	80%
Transversal overlay	70%	70%
Number of strips	40	35
Number of images	1026	670

Figure 2 shows Phantom 4 and the wooden target used, during the UAV flights, to materialize the Ground Control Points (GCP).

The images were georeferenced using the Ground Control Points (GCPs) signaled with wooden circular targets with a diameter of 24 cm (Fig. 2b). The shape and size of the targets have been planning to be visible on images acquired from a height of about 50 m. The points were surveyed using a GNSS receiver in RTK mode with the ITALPOS Permanent Stations Network [11] determining their coordinates in the ETRF2000 datum with geodetic height.

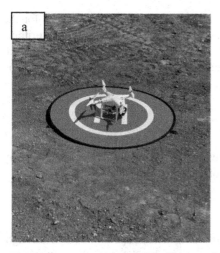
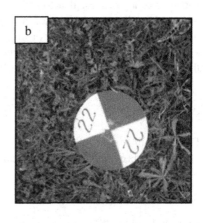

Fig. 2. Phantom 4 (a) and GCP target (b)

For the May 2021 UAV flight, 10 points were survey, of which 7 were used as Ground Control Points (GCPs) and 3 as Check Points (CP). For UAV flight February 2022, 19 points were survey, of which 10 were used as GCPs and 9 CPs.

The images from both surveys were processed using Metashaphe by Agisoft [12] software that implements the Structure from Motion (SfM) algorithm. The SfM is a low-cost photogrammetric method for high-resolution topographic reconstructions. The SfM operates under the same basic tenets of the stereoscopic photogrammetry. However, they fundamentally differ because in SfM the geometry of the scene, camera positions and orientation are solved automatically without points known. In the other method, instead, points are solved simultaneously using a highly redundant, iterative bundle adjustment procedure, based on a database of features automatically extracted from a set of multiple images with a high degree of overlap [13].

The Metashape workflows consist in the following main steps: image import, image alignment, generation of the sparse point cloud, optimization of image alignment, georeferenced, generation of the dense point cloud, generation DEM and generation orthophoto [14, 15].

The processing of the dense cloud points of the two flights was performed with different quality to evaluate the influence of this on the volume calculation and consequently also to evaluate the processing times. We then proceeded to photogrammetric process with the densities provided by Metashape: High, Medium, Low, Lowest. The processing times for the generation of clouds were various, so it is of interest to evaluate whether it is necessary to produce a dense cloud (High) or if we can reduce point cloud density. The images have processed on an HP Z420 workstation with 64 GB RAM, Intel Xeon E5–16200 3.60 GHz CPU, and NVIDIA Quadro K2000 video card.

After having generated the dense point clouds for 2021 and 2022 UAV flights, these were georeferenced in the Datum ETRF2000, we proceeded to calculate the volumes with the open source software Cloud Compare. It is a software created for the processing of point clouds and has many tools for manually editing and rendering 3D points clouds and triangular meshes. It also offers various advanced processing algorithms for the registration, distance computation, segmentation etc. Among the various algorithms implemented, the calculation of volumes 2.5 between two point clouds of different epochs or with respect to a reference plane is envisaged. This tool was used to determine the volume between the point cloud of May 2021 compared to that of February 2022.

3   Results

Below are the results obtained from the processing of the images of the flights in May 2021 and February 2022 and the calculation of the volumes.

3.1   UAV Survey May 2021

May 2021 UAV flight images were processed with Metashape software with High, Medium, Low and Lowest dense cloud quality. Figures 3 and 4 show the scattered and dense clouds produced for the High quality. The georeferencing in the ETRF2000 Datum was performed with the use of 7 GCPs. Also 3 CPs were used to check the validity of the georeferencing. Table 4 shows the RMSE of the GCPs and CPs. Figure 5 shows the arrangement of the GCPs and CPs.

Table 5 shows the number of points for each dense point cloud produced and the time taken to process the entire photogrammetric process.

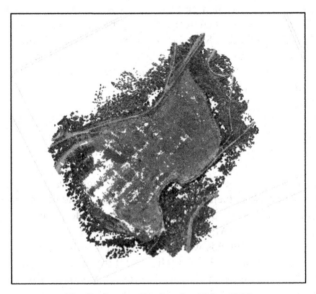

Fig. 3. Scattered point cloud May 2021

Fig. 4. Dense point cloud May 2021

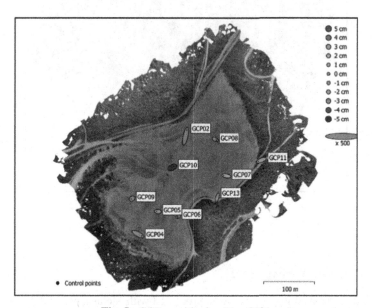

Fig. 5. GCPs positioning May 2021

Table 4. GCPs and CPs RMSE

	East (m)	North (m)	Height (m)
GCPs	0.017	0.021	0.025
CPs	0.011	0.005	0.028

Table 5. Dense point cloud and time - UAV survey May 2021

	High	Medium	Low	Lowest
N. points	274.531.436	70.769.526	17.698.572	4.241.950
Processing time (h)	32	11	5	4

Figure 6 shows orthophoto with Ground Sample Distance (GSD) of 1, 5 cm.

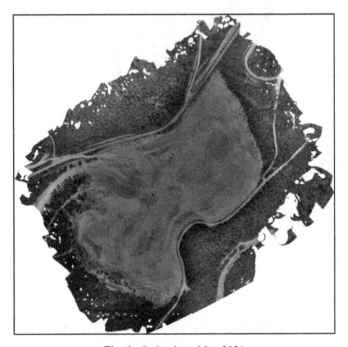

Fig. 6. Orthophoto May 2021

3.2   UAV Survey February 2022

February 2022 UAV flight images were processed with Metashape software with High, Medium, Low and Lowest dense cloud quality. Figures 7 and 8 show the scattered and dense clouds produced for the High quality. The georeferencing in the ETRF2000 Datum was performed with the use of 10 GCPs. 9 CPs were also used to check the validity of the georeferencing. Table 6 shows the RMSEs of the GCPs and CPs. Figure 9 shows the arrangement of the GCPs and CPs. Table 7 shows the number of points for each dense point cloud produced and the time taken to process the entire photogrammetric process (Fig. 10).

Fig. 7. Scattered point cloud February 2022

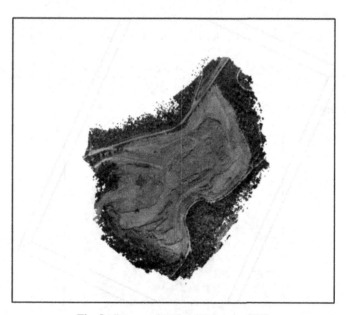

Fig. 8. Dense point cloud February 2022

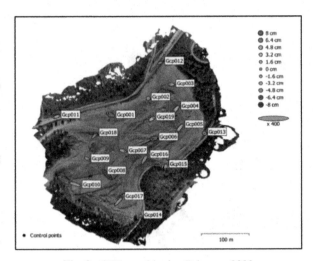

Fig. 9. GCPs positioning February 2022

Table 6. GCPs and CPs RMSE

	East (m)	North (m)	Height (m)
GCPs	0.019	0.009	0.029
CP	0.025	0.028	0.042

Table 7. Dense point cloud and time - UAV survey February 2022

	High	Medium	Low	Lowest
N. points	150.052.986	39.326.072	10.035.972	2.441.419
Processing time (h)	22	6	3	2

Fig. 10. Orthophoto February 2022 (GSD 1, 5 cm)

3.3 Volume Calculation

To calculate the volume of material removed from May 2021 to February 2022, the Cloud Compare software was used through the Compute 2.5D tool. This tool can be used to compute the volume between a 2.5D cloud and an arbitrary plane (constant height) or between two 2.5D clouds. Preliminarily to the calculation of the volume, the maps of the distances between the point clouds coming from the two UAV flights were calculated and processed at the various densities. This was done comparing the measurements of distances taken on the point clouds obtained from the two UAV survey. To perform this comparison, equal portions of point clouds were taken.

Figures 11 and 12 show the results of this comparison for the High and Lowest quality.

The volume calculation was performed on the dense point clouds 2021 and 2022, also in this case cut, respectively for High, Medium, Low and Lowest quality. The calculation was done by varying the sampling step required in the 2.5D calculation. The volumes were calculated with 1 m and 0.5 m pitch and not considering the empty cells (Fig. 13). Table 8 shows the results obtained.

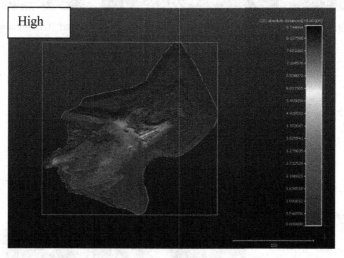

Fig. 11. Discrepancy (m) map between UAV surveys 2021 and 2022 – High

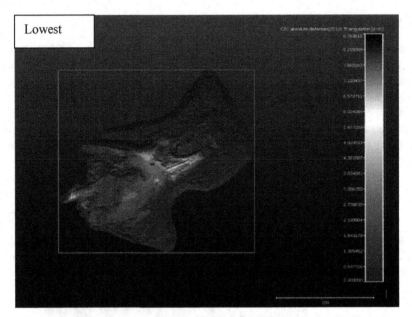

Fig. 12. Discrepancy (m) map between UAV surveys 2021 and 2022 – Lowest

Table 8. Volume calculation

		Sampling step	
		1 m	0, 5 m
Quality	High	45.342 m^3	45.185 m^3
	Medium	45.361 m^3	45.248 m^3
	Low	45.113 m^3	44.956 m^3
	Lowest	45.417 m^3	45.226 m^3

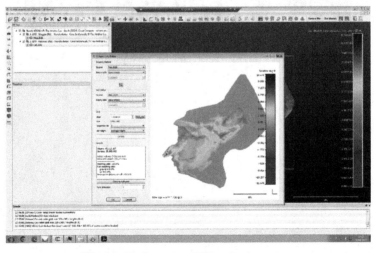

Fig. 13. Tool compute 2.5D - cloud compare

4   Discussion and Conclusions

From the first research carried out we can say that the procedure tested for calculating the volumes of the quarries certainly leads to confirm the results already obtained from other research [16]. For the calculation of volumes, images from UAVs obtained with a Low quality can be used as the variation in quality never produces volume variations greater than 1% compared to the value obtained with High quality. Even the difference in sampling step does not lead to substantial differences with respect to the sampling step of 0.5 m. Therefore, since as the quality of the dense cloud increases, there is a significant increase in processing times, it is possible to use lower point cloud qualities. The same can be said for the sampling step between 1 m and 0.5 m.

The distance map is also a good method for monitoring the most exploited areas of the quarry.

The research continues by testing the accuracy by comparing the volumes calculated with the UAV Photogrammetry with the SfM approach and the volumes calculated using point clouds from Terrestrial Laser Scanner.

Acknowledgments. This paper was supported by Fondazione di Sardegna through grant Surveying, modelling, monitoring and rehabilitation of masonry vaults and domes i.e. Rilievo, modellazione, monitoraggio e risanamento di volte e cupole in muratura (RMMR) (CUP code: F72F20000320007).

References

1. Raeva, P., Filipova, S., Filipov, D.: Volume computation of a stockpile – a study case comparing GPS and UAV measurements in an open pit quarry. ISPRS - Int. Arch. Photogram. Remote Sens. Spat. Inf. Sci. **XLI-B1**, 999–1004 (2016). https://doi.org/10.5194/isprsarchives-XLI-B1-999
2. Mazhrakov, M.: Mine Engineering. Sofia Univerisity, Sofia (2007)
3. Tucci, G., Gebbia, A., Conti, A., Fiorini, L., Lubello, C.: Monitoring and computation of the volumes of stockpiles of bulk material by means of UAV photogrammetric surveying. Remote Sens. **11**, 1471 (2019). https://doi.org/10.3390/rs11121471
4. Bai, P., Vignoli, G., Viezzoli, A., Nevalainen, J., Vacca, G.: (Quasi-)real-time inversion of airborne time-domain electromagnetic data via artificial neural network. Remote Sens. **12**, 3440 (2020). https://doi.org/10.3390/rs12203440
5. Yakar, M., Yilmaz, H.M., Mutluoglu, O.: Performance of photogrammetric and terrestrial laser scanning methods in volume computing of excavation and filling areas. Arab. J. Sci. Eng. **39**(1), 387–394 (2013). https://doi.org/10.1007/s13369-013-0853-1
6. Vacca, G., Dessì, A., Sacco, A.: The use of nadir and oblique UAV images for building knowledge. ISPRS Int. J. Geo-Inf. **6**, 393 (2017). https://doi.org/10.3390/ijgi6120393
7. Giannattasio, C., Grillo, S.M., Vacca, G.: Interdisciplinary study for knowledge and dating of the San Francesco convent in Stampace, Cagliari – Italy (XIII-XXI Century). ISPRS Ann. Photogramm. Remote Sens. Spatial Inf. Sci. **II-5/W1**, 139–144 (2013). https://doi.org/10.5194/isprsannals-II-5-W1-139-2013
8. Arango, C., Morales, C.A.: Comparison between multicopter UAV and Total Station for estimating stockpile volumes. Int. Arch. Photogramm. Remote Sens. Spat. Inf. Sci. **XL-1/W4**, 131–135 (2015)

9. Abbaszadeh, S., Rastiveisa, H.: A comparison of close-range photogrammetry using a non-professional camera with field surveying for volume estimation. Int. Arch. Photogramm. Remote Sens. Spat. Inf. Sci. **XLII-4/W4**, 1–4 (2017)

10. Wang, X., Al-Shabbani, Z., Sturgill, R., Kirk, A., Dadi, G.B.: Estimating earthwork volumes through use of unmanned aerial systems. Transp. Res. Rec. **2630**, 1–8 (2017)

11. http://it.smartnet-eu.com/. Accessed 01 Apr 2022

12. http://www.agisoft.com/. Accessed 01 Apr 2022

13. Szeliski, R.: Computer Vision: Algorithms and Applications. Springer, Heidelberg (2010). https://doi.org/10.1007/978-1-84882-935-0

14. Rossi, P., Mancini, F., Dubbini, M., Mazzone, F., Capra, A.: Combining nadir and oblique UAV imagery to reconstruct quarry topography: methodology and feasibility analysis. Eur. J. Remote Sens. **50**(1), 211–221 (2017). https://doi.org/10.1080/22797254.2017.1313097

15. Vacca, G., Furfaro, G., Dessì, A.: The use of the UAV images for the building 3D model generation. Int. Arch. Photogramm. Remote Sens. Spatial Inf. Sci. **XLII-4/W8**, 217–223 (2018). https://doi.org/10.5194/isprs-archives-XLII-4-W8-217-2018

16. Kokamagi, K., Turk, K., Liba, N.: UAV photogrammetry for volume calculations. Agron. Res. **18**(3) 2087–2102 (2020). https://doi.org/10.15159/ar.20.213

The *Pulcinella* Diagnostic Project: Introduction to the Study of the Performances of Close-Range Diagnostics Targeted to a Wooden Physical Twin of a Carnival Historical Mask

Luca Piroddi[1]([✉])(iD), Ilaria Catapano[2](iD), Emanuele Colica[3](iD),
Sebastiano D'Amico[3](iD), Luciano Galone[3](iD), Gianfranco Gargiulo[4],
and Stefano Sfarra[5](iD)

[1] Department of Civil Engineering, Environmental Engineering and Architecture,
University of Cagliari, (DICAAR-UniCA), Cagliari, Italy
lucapiroddi@yahoo.it
[2] Institute for Electromagnetic Sensing of the Environment, National Research Council of Italy,
(IREA-CNR), Napoli, Italy
catapano.i@irea.cnr.it
[3] Department of Geoscience, University of Malta, Msida, Malta
{emanuele.colica,sebastiano.damico,luciano.galone}@um.edu.mt
[4] Accademia Di Belle Arti Mario Sironi, Sassari, Italy
gargiulo@accademiasironi.it
[5] Department of Industrial and Information Engineering and Economics (DIIIE),
University of L'Aquila, L'Aquila, Italy
stefano.sfarra@univaq.it

Abstract. The *Pulcinella* diagnostic project here presented aims at testing a wide range of methodologies, technologies, and instrumentations against the imaging diagnostics of the various natural and artificial features present in the wooden physical model reproducing an archetypical historical artifact and its most common defects and in homogeneities. Due to its experimental purposes, it configures as an open diagnostic protocol – or a protocol of protocols – allowing a scalability to as many tools as wanted and, within this approach, being able to compare standard and innovative diagnostics methods related to historical wooden sculptures. The first round of diagnostic techniques includes Structure from Motion photogrammetry, Multispectral imaging, active Infrared Thermography and Terahertz imaging. The first experimental datasets and their preliminary results are analyzed against their effectiveness and failures in retrieving and characterizing standardized, specific, and known defects and features of the wooden mask investigated.

Keywords: Sculptures diagnostics · Physical twin · Wooden artworks

1 Introduction

Non-destructive or even sometimes non-invasive diagnostics are the core techniques of protocols to investigate precious and delicate goods like the ones belonging to the Cultural Heritage (CH), from artifacts to landscapes.

© The Author(s), under exclusive license to Springer Nature Switzerland AG 2022
O. Gervasi et al. (Eds.): ICCSA 2022 Workshops, LNCS 13382, pp. 519–533, 2022.
https://doi.org/10.1007/978-3-031-10592-0_37

The physical parameters of the inspected bodies are particularly indicated for being non-destructively retrieved. The societal relevance of Cultural Heritage issues has recently made possible an overcrossing of traditional disciplinary limits to new methods and technologies which of-ten start from consolidated disciplines to resolve specific issues linked to the new diagnostic targets [1].

One of the less invasive diagnostic technologies is remote sensing. Nowadays, remote sensing methods are an evolving research field taking advantage of the knowledge contamination from many specializations related to surveys and technology [2].

The most immediate demand for the documentation of historical architecture or other volumetric assets is the reconstruction of detailed and reliable 3D models of the monuments or their elements, which can be achieved by remote sensing techniques like photogrammetry or Terrestrial Laser Scanner [3–8]. Photogrammetry is a technique that allows to metrically determine the shape and position of an object, starting from at least two distinct frames (stereoscopic pair) showing the same object. This technique is often used in cartography, geomorphology, architecture, and cultural heritage [9–12]. Structure from Motion (SfM) digital photogrammetry uses computer vision algorithms derived from computer graphics to extract the corresponding points in two or more overlap-ping images, deduce the photographic parameters, cross the corresponding points on multiple photos and find the coordinates in the space of the points themselves [13].

Moving to a wider range of targets to study, thermal infrared (IR) sensing is becoming an important tool for sensing the apparent surface temperatures of valuable assets and therefore to infer, at different scales, inhomogeneities below the visible surfaces [14]. The Infrared Thermography (IRT) technique operates with active or passive measurements of the IR radiation emitted by the object under study. From the acquired data, it is possible to obtain a reliable estimation of the main physical properties of the materials; in particular, both the thermal properties (e.g. conductivity, diffusivity, effusivity, and specific heat) and spectral properties (emissivity, absorption, reflection and transmission coefficients) of the material can be assessed. IRT acquisitions allow the assessment of various issues linked to monuments and artistic studies, like detection of moisture presence, cracks, voids, and foreign materials [3, 15−22]. The application of IRT to small objects reliably identified hidden defects or invisible restoration works [15, 22−27].

For intermediate to large depths geophysical and micro-geophysical techniques can retrieve inaccessible bodies with anomalous physical properties to their surround-ing backgrounds for precious and delicate targets like for instance architectonic and archaeological sites [28–30].

One of the most recently emerging proximal sensing techniques in the field of Cultural Heritage inspection is based on the transmission and backscattering of electro-magnetic (EM) waves at the terahertz frequencies (wavelengths ranging from 30 μm to 3 mm, across air) [31]. Terahertz (THz) technology is used on various kinds of archaeo-logical or historical items allowing, under specific experimental setups, to image studies bodies at various very small depths and to produce tridimensional dataset of the recorded EM signals representing the superficial stratification of the materials of the investigated artifacts [16]. Penetration depths on small artifacts can reach the supporting structures and image their spatial in homogeneities but, thanks to its very high resolution, it is also possible to investigate and distinguish between the various pictorial layers of precious artworks [16, 31–34].

Multispectral (MS) remote and proximal sensing is a big family of techniques able to investigate precious surfaces at the widest dimensional ranges covering transnational landscapes to paintings surfaces. At the smallest depths, multispectral proximal sensing inspects the surface finishes through their interaction with the electromagnetic radiation recorded at different wavelengths, both visible and invisible to the human eye, across the EM spectrum [35, 36]. MS proximal sensing applied to CH targets includes a family of techniques that investigate the surface finishes by means of their responses to extremely high-frequency electromagnetic waves. Depending on frequency ranges used for energizing and/or sensing the artifacts, it is possible to choose transmission or re-flection experimental configurations, also depending on the thickness of investigated objects. Reflectometry, in the bands ranging from ultraviolet to near-infrared, can be used to highlight finishes defects and can enhance the readability of preparatory works, drawings, and paintings (sometimes even evidencing drawings completely invisible to eyes) by overcoming the shielding of exterior paintings layers and dirt patinas [9, 22, 34–39].

2   The *Pulcinella* Project – An Open Diagnostic Protocol

2.1   The Physical Model of the Traditional Carnival Mask

The mask under study aims to reproduce an archetype of the local sculptural tradition of small wooden artifacts. To this end, all construction techniques were guided by knowledge of the state of the ancient art for the creation and finishing of these wooden sculptures [40, 41].

Looking at the first wooden sculptures of the tradition, in ancient times, they start with coarse artifacts made from a single block of wood and arrive, in more recent times, to complex artifacts made from a set of adequately sculpted pieces. These pieces, bound with joints (Fig. 1a), will become the modeling, which in turn will be the support of the numerous finishing layers above (preparatory layers and pictorial layers), thus giving life to complex, innovative, and precious works of art created by scrupulously following the wise "Rules of Art" handed down to the master sculptors.

The mask created by a professional restorer reproduces the shapes and colors of a leather artisan scene mask with the features of *Pulcinella* (carnival mask of the Neapolitan tradition). In order to represent the most common defects or peculiar points in historical wooden sculptures, all the singular points of natural origin in the sculpture have been mapped and some simulated defects have been created (like the *pentimenti* in Fig. 1b, for instance). Their preliminary knowledge will allow validating the effectiveness of the various diagnostic approaches and tools. The wood chosen for the sculpture of the physical model of the *Pulcinella* mask is cypress. In Fig. 1c two orthogonal projections of the sculpture that is the object of the present research project are shown, with the main dimensions (before the pictorial finish).

2.2   A First Round of Proximal Sensing Diagnostics

The *Pulcinella* diagnostic project aims at testing a wide range of methodologies, technologies, and instrumentations against the imaging of the various natural and artificial

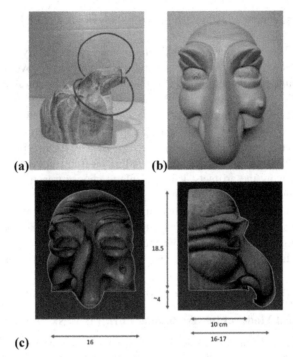

Fig. 1. Constructive phase of the *Pulcinella* physical model: roughly sculpted mask (**a**) and pre-painted mask with the second layer of *pentimenti* (**b**). Main dimensions of the mask modeled (**c**).

features present in the physical model simulating a real historical artifact and its most common defects and inhomogeneities.

The first round of diagnostic techniques is including:

- Structure from Motion (SfM) photogrammetry,
- Multispectral imaging,
- IRT,
- THz imaging.

In the followings, the authors present some of these first acquired datasets and occasionally some preliminary results.

3   Preliminary Datasets and Results

3.1   Photogrammetric Geometric Reconstruction of the Model

For the photogrammetric survey, the mask was filmed at the two main steps of realization (before spreading the pictorial plaster base and after painting) for the most complete documentation of the physical model and to crosscheck the diagnostic results with the two finishing levels.

The mask was positioned on a sheet of graph paper to correctly scale the final models. The videos were recorded by using a smartphone camera and moving that camera around the mask, recording all its solid angles (Fig. 2). This operation was repeated with the face oriented up-wards and downwards, for each finishing level. During the processing, individual frames were parametrically extracted from the videos using the 3DF Zephyr software by entering the extraction parameters, like similarity auto-discard and sharpness. The obtained pictures were im-ported in two separate projects inside the Agisoft Metashape software, one for each finishing condition. Each project contains two chunks, one with the mask facing up and one facing down. The Metashape photogrammetric software was used to orient the various frames of each chunk and to generate a sparse cloud for each one. The next step was the generation of dense point clouds and the iterative manual cleaning of the outliers. The dense clouds, in pairs, were aligned with the scale-rotate-translate (SRT) transformation software function, subject to final manual cleaning, and then the mesh and texture were generated. This procedure, which is summarized in Fig. 3, was repeated for the two datasets (raw and painted mask). The final virtual model reconstructed for the raw mask is presented in Fig. 4.

Fig. 2. Some examples of the photographic acquisitions of the raw mask (extracted from the two videos)

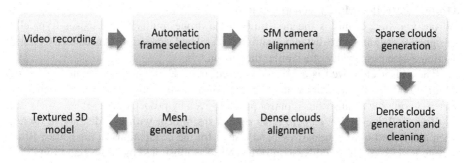

Fig. 3. Photogrammetric processing workflow for each mask model

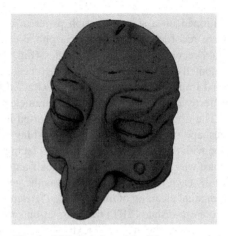

Fig. 4. SfM digital model of the raw mask

3.2 Multispectral Reflectography

To now, two different multispectral technologies have been tested on the painted mask:

- A drone-controlled multispectral camera,
- A modified Digital Single Lens Reflex (DSLR) camera.

In the following two sub-sections, the authors preliminarily present some raw data acquired.

Drone-Controlled Multispectral Camera
To our knowledge, this is the first time that a drone multispectral sensor (typically designed for a quite more distant monitoring of soil and vegetation) is used on a Cultural Heritage asset, especially of a similar dimension.

The sensor employed is a MicaSense RedEdge-MX™ camera mounted on a DJI Matrice 600 Pro drone, from which it takes power alimentation and can be controlled for triggering the acquisitions (control possible even by proper software).

The RedEdge-MX™ camera is an optical instrument with five distinctive optics, each one linked to a quite narrow band sensor for the acquisitions in the bands: Blue, Green, Red, Red Edge, and Near-Infrared (NIR) as illustrated by Table 1 and Fig. 5.

Figures 6, 7 and 8 present the raw data acquired by the MicaSense RedEdge-MX™ camera on the finished mask. Figures 6 show the acquisitions at Blue, Green and Red channels and represent the decomposition of the finished mask colors: dark tones indicate low intensity of the specific components, while bright tones indicate a high intensity (as an example, look at the blue/cyan eyes of the mask: they appear bright on Blue channel and dark on the two others, indicating a prevalence of Blue light reflection as we can also appreciate with human sight). Particularly significant are Red Edge image (Fig. 7) and NIR image (Fig. 8) which are characterized by a spectrally different behavior, especially the transparency, of the pigments used on the eyes of the *Pulcinella* mask as evidenced

Table 1. Spectral information of the MicaSense RedEdge-MX™ camera [42].

Band number	Band name	Center wavelength (nm)	Bandwidth FWNM (nm)	Range (nm)
1	Blue	475	32	459–491
2	Green	560	27	546.5–573.5
3	Red	668	16	660–676
4	Red Edge	717	12	711–723
5	NIR	842	57	813.5–868.5

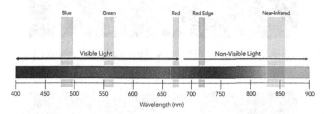

Fig. 5. RedEdge-MX™ acquisition bands [42].

by different readability of the *pentimenti* located them over the pictorial plaster base and just below the paintings.

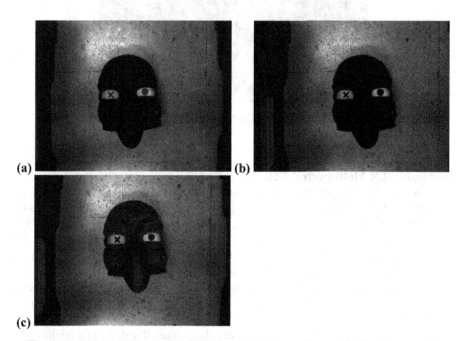

Fig. 6. RedEdge-MX™ raw data: Blue channel (**a**), Green channel (**b**), Red channel (**c**).

Fig. 7. RedEdge-MX™ raw data: Red Edge channel.

Fig. 8. RedEdge-MX™ raw data: NIR channel.

Modified DSLR Multispectral Camera

A second set of multispectral data was acquired by means of a modified Digital Single Lens Reflex (DSLR) camera by which the factory internal bandpass filter in the visible range was removed to allow the recording of the pictures across the sensitivity full-range of the internal sensor that is typically quite larger than only the visible light. The acquisitions were done applying over the optics of the camera alternated narrower bandpass filters. The external filters employed in the acquisitions and the sensitivity of the three camera RGB channels of a modified DSLR camera with characteristics similar to the Nikon D 750 used are illustrated in Fig. 9a. The acquisition instrumental setup is shown in Fig. 9b.

Figures 10, 11 and 12 show some of the raw data acquired with the Ultraviolet (UV), Fig. 10, the visible, Fig. 11, and the wider Near-Infrared (NIR1), Fig. 12, filters. It is

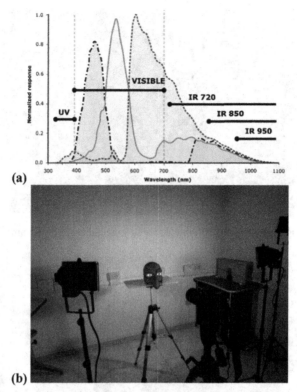

Fig. 9. Representation of multispectral bands configurations (black lines indicate the fives EM filters), plotted over the sensitivity curves of the three RGB channels of a camera, the Nikon D200, similar to the one used during MS acquisition (RGB channels sensitivity from [39] **(a).** Acquisition of the modified-Nikon-D750 multispectral dataset **(b).**

worth of noting the difference of the modified-D-750 pictures from the RedEdge-MX ones, because DSLR cameras acquire three RGB channels for each image.

3.3 Active Infrared Thermography

The active IRT was carried out via a digital thermal camera (FLIR System AB model P30 PAL, 320 × 240 pixels). The experimental setups were configured with different points of view and heat lamps positions; they were repeated in same conditions for both the two finishing stages (raw and painted) of the *Pulcinella* mask (Fig. 13). The investigated wooden mask was initially heated by one to four IR lamps for different energization time lengths that were tested in order to verify the potentialities and limits of each configuration. For each IRT experiment, the scene was recorded by the thermal camera during the heating and cooling phases for different positions of the mask to study specific defects or other peculiarities. Three samples of a raw IRT dataset are reported in Fig. 14.

Different processing approaches are being tested across the experimental datasets, such as linear regression models - aiming at detecting some of the main features in

Fig. 10. Nikon D750 raw data: UV-range filter (320–390 nm).

Fig. 11. Nikon D750 raw data: visible-range filter (390–700 nm).

Fig. 12. Nikon D750 raw data: NIR1-range filter (>720 nm).

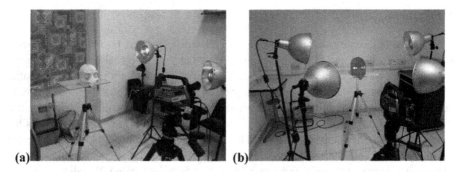

Fig. 13. Acquisition of IRT data: raw mask (**a**) and finished mask (**b**).

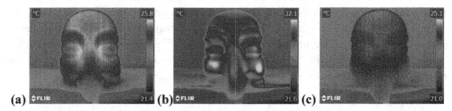

Fig. 14. IRT raw data during time-lapse acquisition (raw mask): thermogram at 5" heating (**a**), at 7′10" heating (**b**) and at 40′30" cooling (**c**).

the data by compacting the dynamic behavior into few images with approaches similar to some IR environmental monitoring [43]. Figure 15 shows the interpolated Thermal Gradient of the first ten thermograms of a cooling stage recorded at the highest sampling rate of the employed thermal camera on the raw *Pulcinella* mask: from these preliminary data, some defects are possible to be recognized within the specific experimental setup.

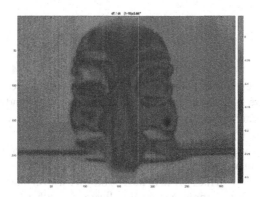

Fig. 15. Preliminary IRT processed data (raw mask): thermal gradient

3.4 THz Imaging

THz investigations are currently going on and are performed by means of a Fiber-Coupled Time-Domain (TD) - THz system equipped with a normal reflection imaging module (see Fig. 16a) which allows the scanning of planar areas with a minimum spatial offset of 0.15 mm. Such a system is designed to perform high resolution non-invasive subsurface inspections suitable to characterize the stratigraphy of the object under test and to reveal hidden details like author' signature, preparatory drawings and not visible defects. The measurements are carried in laboratory without controlling temperature and humidity values and filtering procedures, devoted to reduce the environmental noise, are exploited to improve the imaging capabilities. Specifically, beyond 2D false color THz images, time of flight imaging will be performed to achieve 3D reconstruction of the probed areas and obtain images referred to increasing constant depths starting from the surface and moving into the object. Details about the system and the data processing are given in [31] while, as an example, Fig. 16b shows a painted wood sample (left panel) and its 2D false color THz image (right panel), assessing the ability to retrieve carbon drawings covered by the black paint. THz inspected areas of the *Pulcinella* mask and related preliminary results will be presented at the conference.

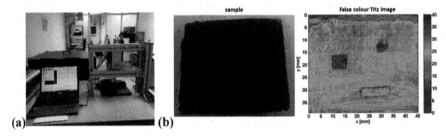

Fig. 16. The THz imaging system (**a**) and an example of the possible THz imaging results (**b**).

4 Conclusions

In this paper, an integrated experimental testing-framework is presented as a base for an expectable future standard comparability of non-destructive and non-invasive diagnostics techniques and protocols applied to the study and characterization of wooden artifacts, and, especially, precious historical sculptures.

The *Pulcinella* diagnostic project has been explained in its main features, first giving a brief description of the physical model representing the historical architype of the wooden sculptures through the shapes of a well-known carnival mask of the regional tradition. The first diagnostic approaches are also illustrated, with a description of methods, technologies and first experimental datasets.

The preliminary experimental results demonstrate effectiveness and limits of the first employed protocols, mainly, and currently, by means of the raw datasets but also by means of some processed data. The first round of diagnostic techniques has included Structure from Motion photogrammetry, Multispectral imaging, active Infrared Thermography and Terahertz imaging.

Due to its experimental purposes, the *Pulcinella* diagnostic project configures as an open diagnostic protocol – or a protocol of protocols – allowing a scalability to as many tools as wanted and, within this approach, being able to compare standard and innovative diagnostics methods related to historical wooden sculptures.

Acknowledgements. The authors thanks Antonio Trogu, Luigi Noli, Matteo Baire and Alessandro Fanti (University of Cagliari, DICAAR and DIEE) for their fundamental help in acquisitions of photogrammetric, multispectral, and thermographic datasets.

References

1. Piro, S., et al.: Geophysics and cultural heritage: a living field of research for Italian geophysicists. First Break **33**(8), 43–54 (2015)
2. Lillesand, T., Kiefer, R.W., Chipman, J.: Remote Sensing and Image Interpretation. Wiley, Hoboken (2015)
3. Costanzo, A., Minasi, M., Casula, G., Musacchio, M., Buongiorno, M.F.: Combined use of terrestrial laser scanning and IR thermography applied to a historical building. Sensors **15**(1), 194–213 (2015)
4. Fiorino, D.R., et al.: The management of the restoration site. Diagnostic techniques, problems and perspectives. In: Geores 2019 2nd International Conference on Cultural Heritage: challenges, new perspectives and technology innovation. Springer, Berlin Heidelberg (2019)
5. Salonia, P., Scolastico, S., Pozzi, A., Marcolongo, A., Messina, T.L.: Multi-scale cultural heritage survey: quick digital photogrammetric systems. J. Cult. Herit. **10**, e59–e64 (2009)
6. Shi, R., Xu, M., Zhu, L.: New techniques of remote sensing in the university of architecture and planning. In: 2009 IEEE International Geoscience and Remote Sensing Symposium, vol. 2, pp. II-642. IEEE (2009)
7. Xu, Z., Wu, L., Shen, Y., Li, F., Wang, Q., Wang, R.: Tridimensional reconstruction applied to cultural heritage with the use of camera-equipped UAV and terrestrial laser scanner. Remote Sens. **6**(11), 10413–10434 (2014)
8. Yastikli, N.: Documentation of cultural heritage using digital photogrammetry and laser scanning. J. Cult. Herit. **8**(4), 423–427 (2007)
9. Ranieri, G., Trogu, A., Loddo, F., Piroddi, L., Cogoni, M.: Digital museum from integrated 3D aerial photogrammetry, laser scanner and geophysics data. In: 24th European Meeting of Environmental and Engineering Geophysics, pp. 1–5. European Association of Geoscientists & Engineers, Houten, The Netherlands (2018)
10. Colica, E., et al.: Using unmanned aerial vehicle photogrammetry for digital geological surveys: case study of Selmun promontory, Northern of Malta. Environ. Earth Sci. **80**(17), 1–14 (2021). https://doi.org/10.1007/s12665-021-09846-6
11. D'Amico, S., et al.: Multitechnique diagnostic analysis and 3D surveying prior to the restoration of St. Michael defeating evil painting by Mattia Preti. Environ. Sci. Pollut. Res. **29**(20), 29478–29497 (2021). https://doi.org/10.1007/s11356-021-15880-5
12. D'Amico, S., et al.: Geophysical investigations, digital reconstruction and numerical modeling at the Batia Church in Tortorici (Messina, Sicily): preliminary results. In: Proceedings of the 2020 IMEKO TC-4 International Conference on Metrology for Archaeology and Cultural Heritage, pp. 22–24. Trento, Italy (2020)

13. Ma, Y., Soatto, S., Jana Košecká, S., Sastry, S.: An Invitation to 3-D Vision. Springer, New York (2004). https://doi.org/10.1007/978-0-387-21779-6
14. Maldague, X.P.: Nondestructive Evaluation of Materials by Infrared Thermography. Springer, London (2012). https://doi.org/10.1007/978-1-4471-1995-1
15. Ibarra-Castanedo, C., Sfarra, S., Ambrosini, D., Paoletti, D., Bendada, B., Maldague, X.: Subsurface defect characterization in artworks by quantitative pulsed phase thermography and holographic interferometry. Quant. InfraRed Thermography J. 5(2), 131–149 (2008)
16. Cosentino, A.: Terahertz and cultural heritage science: examination of art and archaeology. Technologies 4(1), 6 (2016)
17. Avdelidis, N.P., Moropoulou, A.: Applications of infrared thermography for the investigation of historic structures. J. Cult. Herit. 5(1), 119–127 (2004)
18. Carlomagno, G.M., Di Maio, R., Meola, C., Roberti, N.: Infrared thermography and geophysical techniques in cultural heritage conservation. Quant. InfraRed Thermography J. 2(1), 5–24 (2005)
19. Arndt, R.W.: Square pulse thermography in frequency domain as adaptation of pulsed phase thermography for qualitative and quantitative applications in cultural heritage and civil engineering. Infrared Phys. Technol. 53(4), 246–253 (2010)
20. Liu, K., Huang, K.L., Sfarra, S., Yang, J., Liu, Y., Yao, Y.: Factor analysis thermography for defect detection of panel paintings. Quant. InfraRed Thermography J. 1-13 (2021)
21. Tao, N., Wang, C., Zhang, C., Sun, J.: Quantitative measurement of cast metal relics by pulsed thermal imaging. Quant. InfraRed Thermography J. 19(1), 27–40 (2020)
22. Piroddi, L., Calcina, S., Fiorino, D., Grillo, S., Trogu, A., Vignoli, G.: Geophysical and remote sensing techniques for evaluating historical stratigraphy and assessing the conservation status of defensive structures heritage: preliminary results from the military buildings at San Filippo Bastion, Cagliari, Italy. In: Gervasi, O. (ed.) ICCSA 2020. LNCS, vol. 12255, pp. 944–959. Springer, Cham (2020). https://doi.org/10.1007/978-3-030-58820-5_68
23. Mercuri, F., Zammit, U., Orazi, N., Paoloni, S., Marinelli, M., Scudieri, F.: Active infrared thermography applied to the investigation of art and historic artefacts. J. Therm. Anal. Calorim. 104(2), 475 (2011)
24. Ibarra-Castanedo, C., Sfarra, S., Ambrosini, D., Paoletti, D., Bendada, A., Maldague, X.: Diagnostics of panel paintings using holographic interferometry and pulsed thermography. Quant. InfraRed Thermography J. 7(1), 85–114 (2010)
25. Orazi, N., et al.: Thermographic analysis of bronze sculptures. Stud. Conserv. 61(4), 236–244 (2016)
26. Di Tuccio, M.C., Ludwig, N., Gargano, M., Bernardi, A.: Thermographic inspection of cracks in the mixed materials statue: Ratto delle Sabine. Heritage Sci. 3(1), 1–8 (2015). https://doi.org/10.1186/s40494-015-0041-6
27. Peeters, J., et al.: IR Reflectography and active thermography on artworks: the added value of the 1.5–3 μm band. Appl. Sci. 8(1), 50 (2018)
28. Wiewel, A., Conyers, L., Piroddi, L., Papadopoulos, N.: An experimental use of ground-penetrating radar to identify human footprints. Revue d'archéométrie 45(1), 143–146 (2021)
29. Piroddi, L., Calcina, S.V., Trogu, A., Ranieri, G.: Automated Resistivity Profiling (ARP) to explore wide archaeological areas: the prehistoric site of Mont'e Prama, Sardinia Italy. Remote Sens. 12(3), 461 (2020)
30. Piroddi, L., Vignoli, G., Trogu, A., Deidda, G. P.: Non-destructive diagnostics of architectonic elements in San Giuseppe Calasanzio's church in cagliari: a test-case for micro-geophysical methods within the framework of holistic/integrated protocols for ARtefact knowledge. In: 2018 IEEE International Conference on Metrology for Archaeology and Cultural Heritage, pp. 17–21, New York, USA. IEEE (2018)

31. Catapano, I., Soldovieri, F.: THz imaging and data processing: State of the art and perspective. In: Persico, R., Piro, S., Linford, N. (eds.) Innovation in Near-Surface Geophysics, pp. 399–417. Elsevier, Amsterdam, Netherland (2019)

32. Seco-Martorell, C., López-Domínguez, V., Arauz-Garofalo, G., Redo-Sanchez, A., Palacios, J., Tejada, J.: Goya's artwork imaging with Terahertz waves. Opt. Express **21**(15), 17800–17805 (2013)

33. Stübling, E., Staats, N., Globisch, B., Schell, M., Portsteffen, H.D., Koch, M.: Investigating the layer structure and insect tunneling on a wooden putto using robotic-based THz tomography. IEEE Trans. Terahertz Sci. Technol. **10**(4), 343–347 (2020)

34. Catapano, I., Ludeno, G., Cucci, C., Picollo, M., Stefani, L., Fukunaga, K.: Noninvasive analytical and diagnostic technologies for studying early renaissance wall paintings. Surv. Geophys. **41**(3), 669–693 (2020). https://doi.org/10.1007/s10712-019-09545-9

35. Jones, C., Duffy, C., Gibson, A., Terras, M.: Understanding multispectral imaging of cultural heritage: determining best practice in MSI analysis of historical artefacts. J. Cult. Herit. **45**, 339–350 (2020)

36. Pelagotti, A., Del Mastio, A., De Rosa, A., Piva, A.: Multispectral imaging of paintings. IEEE Sign. Process. Mag. **25**(4), 27–36 (2008)

37. Colantonio, C., Pelosi, C., D'Alessandro, L., Sottile, S., Calabrò, G., Melis, M.: Hypercolorimetric multispectral imaging system for cultural heritage diagnostics: an innovative study for copper painting examination. Eur. Phys. J. Plus **133**(12), 1–12 (2018). https://doi.org/10.1140/epjp/i2018-12370-9

38. Piroddi, L., Ranieri, G., Cogoni, M., Trogu, A., Loddo, F.: Time and spectral multiresolution remote sensing for the study of ancient wall drawings at San Salvatore hypogeum, Italy. In: Proceedings of the 22nd European Meeting of Environmental and Engineering Geophysics, Near Surface Geoscience 2016, Houten, The Netherlands, pp. 1–5. EAGE (2016)

39. Piroddi, L., Calcina, S.V., Trogu, A., Vignoli, G.: Towards the definition of a low-cost toolbox for qualitative inspection of painted historical vaults by means of modified DSLR cameras, open source programs and signal processing techniques. In: Gervasi, O., et al. (eds.) ICCSA 2020. LNCS, vol. 12255, pp. 971–991. Springer, Cham (2020). https://doi.org/10.1007/978-3-030-58820-5_70

40. Marincola, M.D., Kargère, L.: The Conservation of Medieval Polychrome Wood Sculpture: History, Theory, Practice. Getty Publications, Los Angeles (2020)

41. Cennini, C.: Il libro dell'arte, o Trattato della pittura. F. LeMonnier, Firenze (1859)

42. Micasense: RedEdge.MX sensor documentation (Product sheet, Specifications), downloadable at. https://micasense.com/rededge-mx/. Accessed 27 Mar 2022

43. Piroddi, L.: From high temporal resolution to synthetically enhanced radiometric resolution: insights from Night Thermal Gradient results. Eur. Phys. J. Spec. Topics **230**(1), 111–132 (2021). https://doi.org/10.1140/epjst/e2020-000247-x

Joint Use of GPR Surveys, Terrestrial and Aerial Photogrammetry for the Study of the Portico of the Cathedral of S. Pietro (Isernia, Italy)

Marilena Cozzolino[1]([⊠]) [iD], Vincenzo Gentile[1] [iD], Paolo Mauriello[1] [iD], and Enza Zullo[2]

[1] Department of Agriculture, Environment and Food, University of Molise, Via De Sanctis snc, 86100 Campobasso, Italy
marilena.cozzolino@unimol.it

[2] Ministry of Culture, Regional Direction of Museums of Molise, Salita S. Bartolomeo 10b, 86100 Campobasso, Italy

Abstract. In the field of built heritage preservation, the contribution of non-destructive testing and 3D documentation represents a fundamental requirement for any project of maintenance and restoration, recording the state of conservation and enhancing irregular features. This paper presents the combined use of Ground Penetrating Radar (GPR) technique, terrestrial and unnamed aerial photogrammetry for the study of the portico of the Cathedral of S. Pietro (Isernia, Italy). It is an articulated construction, rebuilt several times over the centuries. The intent of the investigations was to offer a complete reconstruction of the architectural artefact and the morphology of the surfaces in order to guide and support strategic choices for the restoration and improvement of the building's seismic vulnerability, stopping the ongoing degradation phenomena. The results highlighted a series of critical issues such as the tilting of columns, the deformation of the morphology of the floor and the heterogeneous stratigraphy in some areas of the portico, which could affect the tolerance of the building to naturally induced flexural stresses.

Keywords: GPR · Terrestrial photogrammetry · Unnamed aerial photogrammetry · Aerial photogrammetry · Built cultural heritage · Cathedral of S. Pietro

The built cultural heritage is a trace of past human activities and an identity culture of a place. As it is very fragile, it must be preserved to avoid its irreversible loss. In dealing with these entities, one of the key requirement is the achievement of an adequate knowledge of the structures highlighting the basic building geometry, the internal composition of the materials (presence of cavities, foundations, alternation of different building materials, reinforcements) and any external irregular features such as material degradation, cracking, corrosion and tilting of vertical elements.

In recent years, scientific disciplines as geophysics and geomatics are widely applied in 3D documentation of historical building through a combination of technological systems for gathering, processing, modelling, analysing and representing all that is tangible and visible with what is hidden into the surfaces.

Geophysics, in particular in the field of structural health monitoring, was proved an efficient way to obtain high-resolution diagnosis on small-sized targets immersed also in reduced portion of soil, surfaces or volumes. Thus, methods such as infrared thermography [1, 2], sonic and ultrasonic tomography [3, 4], vibration-based methods [5] and ground-penetrating radar (GPR) [6–8] play today an important role in damage identification at a small scale of analysis regarding masonry walls, decorations and architectural elements. At a larger survey scale, methods such as seismic prospections [9, 10], electrical resistivity tomography (ERT) [11–13] and GPR surveys [10, 14, 15] are very efficient for site evaluation, mapping of soil and fill layers, foundation design, detection of cavities and underground structures, screening of floors and walls. Among these, GPR allows a faster data recording, a completely non-invasive diagnosis and high-resolution results.

On the other hand, geomatics allows the acquisition of geometric data that represent the reference basis for all the information acquired in the evaluation process of a building and gives high-resolution information about external signs of surface deterioration. In the last decade, the research on 3D survey has led to the definition of increasingly precise and realistic 3D digital models of archaeological objects and portions or entire architectural buildings through techniques such as digital (terrestrial and aerial) photogrammetry and 3D laser scanning. In any case, highly accurate point clouds are derived from the applications. Photogrammetry, compared to laser scanning, provides satisfactory results, is cheaper, is more portable and, in the case of the use of UAVs, guarantees a top view, which is very useful in the case of building surveys [16]. In literature, many cases of application of low cost image based surveys for building heritage are available [17–23].

The joint use of geophysics and geomatics is increasingly implemented in architectural heritage studies providing a complete analysis of an artifact [24–30]. Following this approach, in this paper, GPR, terrestrial and unnamed aerial photogrammetry were used for the study of the portico of the Cathedral of S. Pietro (Isernia, Italy) in the frame of a project of restoration and improvement of the building's seismic vulnerability. Being positioned on a complex archaeological stratigraphy, having had many interventions over time and showing some clear signs of decay, the investigation was carried out with the aim of a complete reconstruction of the architectural artefact and the morphology of the surfaces.

The overlay and the comparison of results led to the definition of some critical aspects to be taken into consideration in future restoration activities.

1   The Cathedral of San Pietro

The Cathedral of S. Pietro is located in Isernia (Molise, Italy) in the current Piazza A. D'Isernia where, in the basement, the ruins of the ancient city of *Aesernia* are preserved (Fig. 1 and 2). The archaeological area includes complex buildings, some of which were reused and incorporated into factories, which were rebuilt several times over the centuries. In this way, today, it represents a rich example of continuity of life characterized by structures from the Roman, early Christian and medieval periods [31–38].

In ancient times, on this area, the highest terrace of the town (432 meters a.s.l), the city forum was built. Certainly there were at least three temples concentrated here, two of which are preserved in the archaeological area while one is known only from literature, located beyond the arch of S. Pietro, where the former episcopal seminary stands today [39].

Of the two temples still partially visible today, the largest had an extension of about 31 × 21 m (blue lines in Fig. 2), and the cathedral of Isernia, named after San Pietro, was then built on its structures. While continuing to use the podium and the access stairway, in the first centuries of Christianity, in fact, the temple was transformed in its spatiality and in its deeper meaning, by adding a terminal apse (orange lines in Fig. 2). In addition, it was equipped with a baptistery, excavated in the floor of the current left nave of the church. To the side of the remains of the main temple, under the courtyard of the episcope, there is the base of the other small temple (yellow lines in Fig. 2), only partially unearthed, oriented in a convergent way with the larger structure of the temple just described [40].

A small and underground room (probably a cryptoporticus, light blue lines in Fig. 2) that had an internal coating of polychrome plaster, the destination of which still appears unknown, located between the two temples, also belongs to this first phase of frequentation of the area. Furthermore, some large capitals, the Roman paving in large blocks of limestone between the two temples (dark green lines in Fig. 2), remains of cobblestone pavement (cyan lines in Fig. 2), terracotta pipes and substantial remains of an entablature are also visible. We also know by the local historian Ciarlanti in the seventeenth century that there were two imposing sepulchral monuments of important personalities, Sesto Apuleio and Settimio Muleio [39]. They were removed during the nineteenth century [41] and today the bases are preserved in the Museum of S. Maria delle Monache.

The discovery of a fair number of early medieval burials (magenta lines in Fig. 2), in which also elements of the stripping of classical monuments appear to have been widely reused, has given the certainty that the whole area was subsequently used for sepulchral purposes. In fact, in the archaeological area there are also several sarcophagi and a circular structure, made of irregular stone drafts, in which scholars have identified a probable furnace.

Presumably, around the fifth century, the Christian church was installed on the structures of the temple and this involved, among other things, the construction of a terminal apse and the baptistery. An imposing intervention of restorations affected the factory in the 11th century when it was rotated 180°, with the entrance towards the Piazza Mercato, i.e. Piazza A. D'Isernia, the hub of city life. Thus a basilica-type church was created, with a central nave and two side ones, continuous transept and terminal apses (magenta lines in the southern part of Fig. 2).

After the earthquake of 1456, the church was probably restored following the Gothic influences and then it was rebuilt again during the 17th century. Then, a protruding presbytery flanked by chapels replaced the terminal apse, the interiors were adapted to a classicist style and a portico on arches was built on the facade. An impressive campaign of works completely changed the appearance of the church between 1776 and 1789. Thus, a new interpretation of the building was proposed according to a late Baroque orientation, partially transforming the primitive layout. Decorations, new sculptures and paintings embellished the interiors but above all the plan of the building was completely modified. So the dome at the intersection of the central nave with the transept was constructed, the wooden ceiling was replaced with a vault in the central nave, domes in the side aisles were constructed and the existing pillars were redesigned by introducing the Corinthian order. However, after a few years, on July 26, 1805, a strong earthquake seriously damaged the building and the roofs of the central nave, the dome and the portico collapsed. After various events, restoration work began in the middle of the century which gave the factory a new look according to the current neoclassical style and redeveloped the surrounding environment. In particular, the portico, built between 1847 and 1851, was designed with four large Ionic columns of about eight meters in height, enclosed by lateral walls, covered by a barrel vault and crowned by a frontispiece.

Almost a century later, further damage caused the bombing in 1943, which destroyed the entire right side of the building, its roofs and part of the portico which on that occasion was rebuilt without the lateral walls that enclosed it. From the post-war period to today, significant interventions have only affected the interior of the church. In the 1960s, marble and gilding were introduced to replace stuccos and frescoes; after the archaeological excavations of the 1980s the floor was redone, then changed again at the beginning of the 2000s according to a design that uses different types of marble, also recalling the division of the existing space in the coloring (Fig. 1).

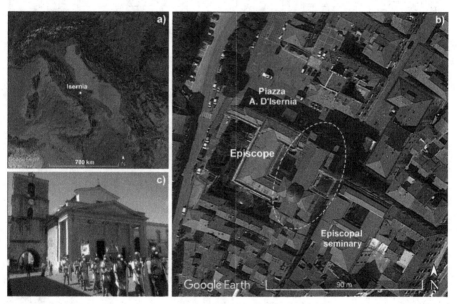

Fig. 1. Location of Isernia on a Google Earth™ satellite image of Italy (a), detail of Piazza A. D'Isernia (b) and a picture of the Cathedral of S. Pietro (c). (Color figure online)

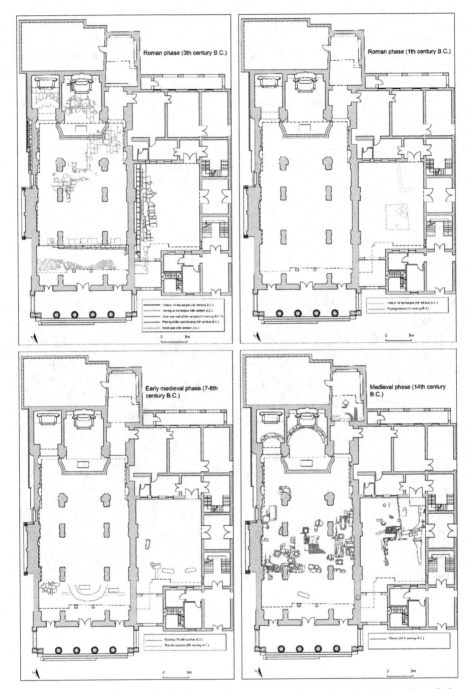

Fig. 2. Plans of the Cathedral of S. Pietro with indication of the archaeological remains relative to different construction phases. (Color figure online)

2 Methodology

2.1 Terrestrial and Unnamed Aerial Photogrammetry

In order to obtain a complete representation of the portico of the Cathedral of St. Pietro, unnamed aerial photogrammetry was integrated with terrestrial photogrammetry. Given the complexity of the building and above all of the ornaments, the choice of the two selected methods solves the need to reach high heights, in a short time, and with a good degree of accuracy. In a first phase, Ground Control Points (GCPs) consisting in chessboard-like targets were positioned on the paved surfaces according to a dense grid whose location was measured with the total station to determine their spatial coordinates. For areas that were not easily accessible because of the high altitude, geometric elements of the masonry were considered as references.

Surveying with a RPA Yuneec H20 (camera with CMOS sensor (1″), fixed focal length of 26 mm and resolution of 20 million pixels) was carried out with a manual flight control. The maximum flight duration was approximately 20 min. The images (nadiral and oblique) were acquired through a circular flight around the monument by varying the flight altitude and the distance from the cathedral. Ground photogrammetry was achieved using a Mirrorless Sony Alpha 5100, equipped of a CMOS sensor (23.5 × 15.6) with 24 million pixels and focal length 16–50 mm positioned on a telescopic pole. Frames were acquired along horizontal bands, ensuring an average overlap of 80% both horizontally and vertically. In this way, two data sets were obtained consisting of 117 frames for the drone survey and 123 frames for the survey with a digital ground camera.

Data processing of images was performed with Agisoft Metashape software (LLC, St. Petersburg, Russia) using the Structure from Motion (SfM) technique. The alignment of frames led to obtaining discrete point clouds (56.765 points for RPA survey; 125.383 for terrestrial survey) describing the object's starting geometry (Fig. 3a). In addition, the positions of the camera at the time of acquisition of frames and the internal camera calibration parameters (focal length, three radial and two tangential distortion coefficients with respect to a main point) were registered. Subsequently, the construction of the geometry was reached through the generation of dense clouds (3.378.208 points for RPA survey; 5.013.847 for terrestrial survey) (Fig. 3b). Then, the 3D model was georeferenced considering the surveyed GCPs. In this way, the alignment and the fusion of the two reliefs was achieved processing a unique and dense cloud consisting of 8.291.411 points (Fig. 3c). The average registration error was 0.009 m. Afterwards, the point cloud was transformed into a surface of triangulated points composed by 541.664 faces and 274.123 vertices (Fig. 3d). The "multi-resolution model", the "optimization method" and the "decimation filter" were applied respectively to adapt the discontinuities on the model, to smooth the nodes of the triangles and to simplify the model and generate a multi-resolution model. In the final step, the texture was constructed through the application of digital images to the model and metric and geo-referenced orthophotos were created.

Additional products derived from data processing are: the Digital Elevation Model (DEM) relating to the portico's floor (Fig. 3g), the vector representation of the facade (Fig. 3f) and sections of the columns (using CloudCompare software) (Fig. 3e) and calculation of deviations from the center of gravity (Fig. 4).

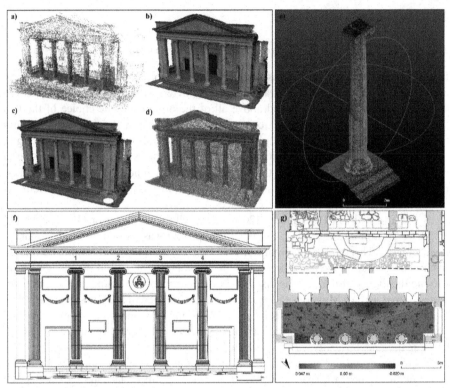

Fig. 3. Sparse point cloud (a), dense cloud (b), mesh RGB (c), solid mesh (d); 3D model of column used for extrapolation of sections using Cloud Compare (e); Front drawing of the building obtained from the photogrammetric survey (f); Digital Elevation Model of the floor with indication of the altitude (g).

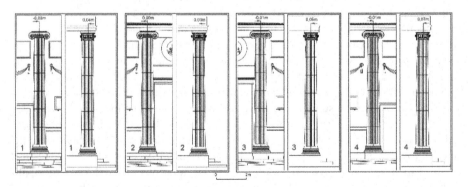

Fig. 4. Front (left) and side (right) views of columns.

2.2 Ground Penetrating Radar Survey

The GPR survey involved the flooring of the portico at the entrance to the church. The instrumentation used was the IDS RIS-K2 georadar with TRMF (200–600 MHz) multi-frequency monostatic antenna. Radar reflections on each line were recorded as 16 bit data in a time window of 90 ns, acquiring 512 samples per radar scan at 25 scan per mark (unit/marker, 1). Technically, data acquisition took place on lines where instrumental readings were performed continuously. The acquisition grid involved the creation of 20 longitudinal profiles (spaced 0.15 m apart) and 79 transversal profiles (spaced 0.3 m apart) with respect to the building entrance wall. The standard profiles representing the raw data were processed using GPR-SLICE 7.0 software through various processing techniques to emphasize the reflections coming from interfaces and buried objects: time-zero corrrenction, vertical band pass filters, background removal and automatic gain filters.

Finally, to verify the extension and size of the buried targets, the GPR profiles were inserted into a three-dimensional matrix from which sections were obtained, at a particular double time interval (measured in nanoseconds). A colour scale was assigned to the amplitude variation in the time-slices in order to show sufficient contrast and to make the anomalies easily recognizable: light green corresponds to low amplitudes, red to high amplitudes. Within the sections, low variations in amplitudes express small reflections that indicate the presence of fairly homogeneous material. High amplitudes, on the other hand, denote significant discontinuities in the investigated surface. Figure 5 shows the time-slices relating to the time intervals 14–22 ns and 29–37 ns.

3 Results and Discussion

The survey provided a precise metric and photorealistic determination of the complex structure resulting in a complete reconstruction of the architectural artefact.

From the detailed analysis of the documents, some irregularities in the arrangement of the columns emerge, resulting in slight deviations of the vertical axis from the center of gravity. In particular, in the frontal and lateral sections (Fig. 4) the following inclinations are noted: 0.03 m to the left (front) and 0.04 m towards the outside for the first column; in axis (front) and 0.03 m towards the outside for the second column; 0.01 m to the left (front) and 0.05 m to the outside for the third column; 0.01 m to the left (front) and 0.07 m to the outside for the fourth column.

Anomalies were also found in the morphology of the pavement which, according to the digital elevation model (DEM), presents an irregular slope in a spatial interval of 0.67 m (Fig. 3g). The lower points are measured between the first column and the left pillar while the highest points are located between the central entrance and the right side of the building, the latter distributed in such a way as to outline a semicircular prominence.

The GPR surveys have instead provided information on what is inside the surface of the pavement. The more superficial horizontal section (Fig. 5a) highlights the uniform presence of filling material with the exception of maximum signal amplitudes measured between the third and the fourth columns, which could be attributable to foundation

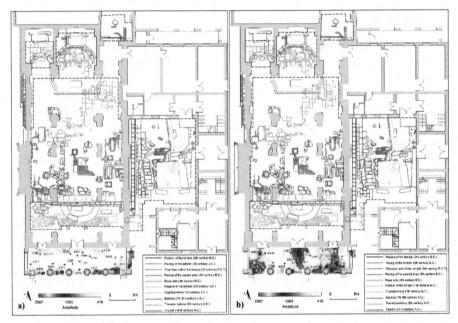

Fig. 5. Time-slice relative to the time window of 14–22 ns (a) and 29–37 ns (b) located on the plan of the Cathedral of San Pietro including the archaeological structures brought to light inside it over the years.

elements of the structure. However, this is not observed between the left pillar and the first column and between the first column and the second column.

The deeper section (Fig. 5b) highlights a semicircular anomaly, with a diameter of about 10 m, that is partially coinciding with the maximum values displayed by the DEM. Analyzing its shape, an apse, a funeral monument (like the Mausoleum of Caius Ennius Marsus in *Saepinum*, a roman town 30 km far from Isernia) but also structures of the *macellum* (a market where meat and fish were sold) or a *balneum* tank could be buried. In fact, according to Muratori, Garrucci and Mommsen [42–44], the existence in the forum, during the Augustan period, of a *macellum* with a portico and monumental entrance (*chalcidium*), a sort of covered market, built by Lucio Abullius Dexter, collapsed following the earthquake of 364 and then rebuilt at the expense of two citizens is known. Furthermore, a *balneum* and a temple with portico and kitchens, perhaps dedicated to Divus Julius, is remembered by an inscription still existing in the courtyard of the bishop's palace, adjacent to the cathedral, until 1847 [40].

To date we can certainly affirm that, if it was the foundation of an apse, it would fill that phase in the life of the building that goes from the 5th century to the 12th century approximately, integrating the knowledge that we have so far developed on the basis of the results of the previous excavation campaign. The construction of another church cannot be totally excluded, with a southern entrance as in the Christian church of the fifth century, following the strong earthquake of 847, which destroyed the city. This structure may have stood until the earthquake of 1125 after which the medieval church was built. However, there are no archaeological data to support this hypothesis.

More likely, however, the hypothesis of a funerary monument with a cylindrical drum or part of the *macellum* is more realistic. Nerveless, the position of the structures behind the larger temple and in a secluded position with respect to the main road axis are currently difficult elements to be reconciled with the description we have of it, that is a factory with a portico and monumental entrance.

Of course, at this stage there are still few elements to support any hypothesis that it may be the structures of one of the buildings mentioned or even other constructions completely unknown to date. A more advanced stage of the work in the portico of the church, following a systematic excavation and the study of materials, could give rise to a reasoned architectural reconstruction.

4   Conclusions

The joint use of ground penetrating radar (GPR) technique, terrestrial and unnamed aerial photogrammetry for the study of the portico of the Cathedral of S. Pietro (Isernia, Italy) has offered a complete reconstruction of the architectural artefact. Evaluating the results globally, the non-verticality of the columns, considered individually, could be congenital (construction defects and/or structural interventions carried out in recent times and/or deformations caused by settling of the substrate) and not compromise the stability of the building. However, the data, combined with the deformation of the morphology of the floor, the absence of foundation elements on the left side of the building below the columns and the probable presence of archaeological remains only on the right side, could affect the tolerance of the building to naturally induced flexural stresses. In addition, the anomalies found by the GPR survey provided an important starting point of reflection on possible structures or monuments still buried in the subsoil that would enrich the knowledge of the complex archaeological stratigraphy of the building. Even if at this stage it was possible to formulate only hypotheses, the data acquired opens up new research directions.

Acknowledgments. Special thanks to the Superintendence of Archeology, Arts, and Landscape of Molise for the fruitful collaboration during the research activities.

Author Contribution. Project administration: Paolo Mauriello, Enza Zullo; Writing-original draft preparation: Introduction (Marilena Cozzolino, Vincenzo Gentile, Paolo Mauriello); The Chathedral of San Pietro (Enza Zullo); Methodology (Marilena Cozzolino, Vincenzo Gentile, Paolo Mauriello); Results and Discussion (Marilena Cozzolino, Vincenzo Gentile, Paolo Mauriello, Enza Zullo); Conclusions (Paolo Mauriello, Enza Zullo).

References

1. Kylili, A., Fokaides, P.A., Christou, P., Kalogirou, S.A.: Infrared thermography (IRT) applications for building diagnostics: a review. Appl. Energy **134**, 531–549 (2014)

2. Piroddi, L., Calcina, S.V., Fiorino, D.R., Grillo, S., Trogu, A., Vignoli, G.: Geophysical and remote sensing techniques for evaluating historical stratigraphy and assessing the conservation status of defensive structures heritage: preliminary results from the military buildings at San Filippo Bastion, Cagliari, Italy. In: Gervasi, O., et al. (eds.) ICCSA 2020. LNCS, vol. 12255, pp. 944–959. Springer, Cham (2020). https://doi.org/10.1007/978-3-030-58820-5_68

3. Mesquita, E., Martini, R., Alves, A., Antunes, P., Varum, H.: Non-destructive characterization of ancient clay brick walls by indirect ultrasonic measurements. J. Build. Eng. **19**, 172–180 (2018)

4. Valluzzi, M.R., et al.: Calibration of sonic pulse velocity tests for detection of variable conditions in masonry walls. Constr. Build. Mater. **192**, 272–286 (2018)

5. Ramos, L.F., De Roeck, G., Lourenço, P.B., Campos-Costa, A.: Damage identification on arched masonry structures using ambient and random impact vibrations. Eng. Struct. **32**, 146–162 (2010)

6. Cozzolino, M., Di Meo, A., Gentile, V., Mauriello, P., Zullo, E.: Combined use of 3D metric survey and GPR for the diagnosis of the Trapezophoros with two griffins attaching a Doe of Ascoli Satriano (Foggia, Italy). Geosciences **10**(8), 307 (2020)

7. Ferrara, C., Barone, P.M.: Detecting moisture damage in archaeology and cultural heritage sites using the GPR technique: a brief introduction. Int. J. Archaeol. **3**(1–1), 57–61 (2015)

8. Piroddi, L., Vignoli, G., Trogu, A., Deidda, G.P.: Non-destructive diagnostics of architec-tonic elements in san Giuseppe Calasanzio's church in Cagliari: a test-case for micro-geophysical methods within the framework of Holistic/integrated protocols for artefact knowledge. In: 2018 IEEE International Conference on Metrology for Archaeology and Cultural Heritage, pp. 17–21, IEEE, New York (2018)

9. Lehmann. B.: Seismic traveltime tomography for engineering and exploration applications. EAGE Publications, Amsterdam, Netherlands (2007)

10. Pérez-Gracia, V., Caselles, J., Clapés, J., Martinez, G., Osorio, R.: Non-destructive analysis in cultural heritage buildings: evaluating the Mallorca cathedral supporting structures. NDT E Int. **59**, 40–47 (2013)

11. Cozzolino, M., Mauriello, P., Patella, D.: Resistivity tomography Imaging of the substratum of the Bedestan monumental complex at Nicosia. Cyprus. Archaeometry **56**(2), 331–350 (2013)

12. Cozzolino, M., Caliò, L.M., Gentile, V., Mauriello, P., Di Meo, A.: The discovery of the theater of Akragas (Valley of Temples, Agrigento, Italy): an archaeological confirmation of the supposed buried structures from a geophysical survey. Geosciences **10**, 161 (2020)

13. Piroddi, L., Calcina, S.V., Trogu, A., Ranieri, G.: Automated Resistivity Profiling (ARP) to explore wide archaeological areas: the prehistoric site of Mont'e Prama, Sardinia Italy. Remote Sens. **12**(3), 461 (2020)

14. Cozzolino, M., et al.: The contribution of geophysics to the knowledge of the hidden archaeological heritage of Montenegro. Geosciences **10**, 187 (2020)

15. Lai, W.W.-L., Dérobert, X., Annan, P.: A review of Ground Penetrating Radar application in civil engineering: a 30-year journey from locating and testing to imaging and diagnosis. NDT E Int. **96**, 58–78 (2018)

16. Altman, S., Xiao, W., Grayson, B.: Evaluation of low-cost terrestrial photogrammetry for 3D reconstruction of complex buildings. ISPRS Ann. Photogrammetry Remote Sens. Spat. Inf. Sci. IV-2/W4, 199–206 (2017)

17. Angelini, A., Portarena, D.: Advice for archaeological survey with recent technologies. Acta IMEKO **7**, 42–51 (2018)

18. Boochs, F., Heinz, G., Huxhagen, U., Müller, H.: Lowcost image based system for nontechnical experts in cultural heritage documentation and analysis. Int. Arch. Photogrammetry Remote Sens. Spat. Inf. Sci. 165–170 (2007)

19. Ellenberg, A., Kontsos, A., Bartoli, I., Pradhan, A.: Masonry crack detection application of an unmanned aerial vehicle. Comput. Civil Build. Eng. 1788–1795 (2014)

20. Ippoliti, E., Meschini, A., Sicuranza, F.: Structure from motion systems for architectural heritage. A survey of the international loggia courtyard of palazzo Dei Capitani, Ascoli Piceno, Italy. Int. Arch. Photogramm. Remote Sens. Spatial Inf. Sci. XL-5/W4, 53–60 (2015)
21. Oniga, E., Chirilă, C., Stătescu, F.: Accuracy assessment of a complex building 3D model reconstructed from images acquired with a low-cost UAS. Int. Arch. Photogramm. Remote Sens. Spatial Inf. Sci. XLII-2/W3, 551–558 (2017)
22. Remondino, F., Del Pizzo, S., Kersten, T.P., Troisi, S.: Low-Cost and open-source solutions for automated image orientation – a critical overview. In: Ioannides, M., Fritsch, D., Leissner, J., Davies, R., Remondino, F., Caffo, R. (eds.) EuroMed 2012. LNCS, vol. 7616, pp. 40–54. Springer, Heidelberg (2012). https://doi.org/10.1007/978-3-642-34234-9_5
23. Russo, M., Carnevali, L., Russo, V., Savastano, D., Taddia, Y.: Modeling and deterioration mapping of façades in historical urban context by close-range ultra-lightweight UAVs photogrammetry. Int. J. Arch. Herit. 13, 549–568 (2019)
24. Alessandri, C.: The church of the nativity in Bethlehem: an interdisciplinary approach to a knowledge-based restoration. J. Cult. Heritage 13(4) (2012)
25. Arias, P., Armesto, J., Di-Capua, D., González-Drigo, R., Lorenzo, H., Pérez-Gracia, V.: Digital photogrammetry, GPR and computational analysis of structural damages in a mediaeval bridge. Eng. Fail. Anal. 14, 1444–1457 (2007)
26. Costanzo, A., Minasi, M., Casula, G., Musacchio, M., Buongiorno, M.F.: Combined use of terrestrial laser scanning and IR thermography applied to a historical building. Sensor 15, 194–213 (2015)
27. Cozzolino, M., Gabrielli, R., Galatà, P., Gentile, V., Greco, G., Scopinaro, E.: Combined use of 3D metric surveys and non-invasive geophysical surveys for the determination of the state of conservation of the Stylite Tower (Umm ar-Rasas, Jordan). Ann. Geophys. 62(3), 339 (2019)
28. Cozzolino, M., Di Meo, A., Gentile, V.: The contribution of indirect topographic surveys (photogrammetry and the laser scanner) and GPR investigations in the study of the vulnerability of the Abbey of Santa Maria a Mare, Tremiti Islands (Italy). Ann. Geophys. 62(3), 343 (2019)
29. Lagüela, S., Solla, M., Puente, I. and F.J. Prego.: Joint use of GPR, IRT and TLS techniques for the integral damage detection in paving. Constr. Build. Mater. 174, 749–760 (2018)
30. Solla, M., et al.: Building information modeling approach to integrate geomatic data for the documentation and preservation of cultural heritage. Remote Sens. 12(24), 4028 (2020)
31. Campagnale, G.: Tesi di laurea Sulla storia di Isernia, ms (1893)
32. Coarelli, F., La Regina, A.: Abruzzo e Molise. Guida archeologica. Edizioni Laterza, Bari, Italy 185 (1984)
33. Maiuri, A.: Passeggiate Campane. Edizioni Sansoni, Firenze, Italy (1957)
34. Pagano, M.: Osservazioni Sulla storia del complesso di Santa Maria delle Monache e sulla topografia antica di Isernia. Conoscenze, Rivista semestrale della Direzione Regionale per i Beni Culturali e Paesaggistici del Molise, pp. 69–78 (2004)
35. Pasqualini, A.: Isernia. Quaderni dell'Istituto di topografia antica 2, 79–84 (1996)
36. Valente, F.: Isernia. Origine e crescita di una città. Edizioni Enne, Campobasso, Italy (1982)
37. Viti, A.: Massimi luoghi di culto in Aesernia tra l'età italico romana e l'alto medioevale 263 a.C.-943 d.C. In: Almanacco del Molise 1984. Edizioni Enne, Campobasso, Italy, pp. 257–269 (1985)
38. Zullo, E.: L'area archeologica di piazza mercato a Isernia. ArcheoMolise, I I(5), 16–22 (2010)
39. Ciarlanti, V.: Memorie historiche del Sannio. Isernia, Italy (1644)
40. Zullo, E.: La cattedrale di Isernia. Edizioni Vitmar, Venafro, Italy (1996)
41. Zullo, E.: L'antica città di Aesernia. Monumenti ed aree di interesse archeologico. Poligrafica Terenzi Editrice, Venafro, Italy (2019)

42. Garrucci, R.: La Storia di Isernia Raccolta Dagli Antichi Monumenti. Italy, Napoli (1848)
43. Mommsen, T.: CIL IX/Inscriptiones Calabriae, Apuliae, Samnii, Sabinorum, Piceni, In Corpus Inscriptionum Latinarum IX. Berlin, Germany: Berolini: Apud Georgium Reimerum (1883)
44. Muratori, L.A.: Novus thesaurus veterum inscriptionum, in praecipuis earumdem collectionibus hactenus praetermissarum, Collectore Ludovico Antonio Muratorio. Parma, Italy: Ex Aedibus Palatinis (1739)

Integrated Methodologies for the Survey and the Documentation of Two Byzantine Churches at the UNESCO Archaeological Site of Umm ar-Rasas (Jordan)

Andrea Angelini[1,2] ⓘ, Marilena Cozzolino[1](✉) ⓘ, Roberto Gabrielli[1,2] ⓘ, Pasquale Galatà[1,2], Vincenzo Gentile[1] ⓘ, and Paolo Mauriello[1] ⓘ

[1] Department of Agriculture, Environment and Food, University of Molise, Via De Sanctis snc, 86100 Campobasso, Italy
marilena.cozzolino@unimol.it
[2] National Council of Researches, Institute of Heritage Sciences (ISPC), Via Salaria Km. 29,300, Monterotondo Street, 00015 Rome, Italy

Abstract. Since 2013, a multidisciplinary research project is in progress at the UNESCO archaeological site of Umm ar-Rasas in Jordan. Among a general study of the area, a special focus is dedicated to the survey and documentation of two Byzantine churches and their mosaic floors. Different investigation techniques, such as laser scanning, photogrammetry and GPR surveys, were reciprocally integrated, in an effort to create geometric models enabling the interpretation of data related to the masonry, the mosaic floors and the buried structures as well as to the documentation of the archaeological area. The results will be the starting point to plan and develop restoration projects for the protection and valorisation of the UNESCO site.

Keywords: World heritage site · UNESCO · Jordanian cultural heritage · Applied technologies · Survey

The archaeological site of Umm ar-Rasas is located 30 km SE to the town of Madaba in Jordan, north of the Wadi Mujib and it covers approximately 10 ha on Moab's plateau (Fig. 1a). From 1986 to 2007, the archaeological researches were conducted by the Franciscan Archaeological Institute of Mount Nebo [1, 2] under the patronage of the Department of Antiquities of the Hashemite Kingdom of Jordan. In 2004, it was inscribed in UNESCO's World Heritage List. From 2013, the Institute for Technologies Applied to Cultural Heritage (now Institute of Heritage Sciences, CNR, Italy), Italian National Research Council, in collaboration with University of Molise for the geophysical research, started a research project with the aim of reconsidering previous researches, documenting the standing structures and preparing the bases for conservation, restoration and use of the site [3].

The remains consist of a huge area, fortified by a massive wall that measures 158 m × 140 m, on which numerous buildings are located and that once was a Roman Castrum (Fig. 1b). Towards the northern part of the archaeological site, housing and

© The Author(s), under exclusive license to Springer Nature Switzerland AG 2022
O. Gervasi et al. (Eds.): ICCSA 2022 Workshops, LNCS 13382, pp. 547–559, 2022.
https://doi.org/10.1007/978-3-031-10592-0_39

sacred structures have been identified, which can be dated from the Byzantine to the Early Islamic period, up to the IX century A.D. [2].

Towards north, a kilometre and a half from the residential zone, an exceptional example of Stylite Tower stands 15 m high at the centre of a courtyard protected on the northern side by a squared defensive tower nearby some water tanks dug in the rocky soil. The Stylite Tower does not have stairs; instead, it has just one room with windows in its highest portion, which is thought to be a place of meditation for a Stylite monk [4, 5].

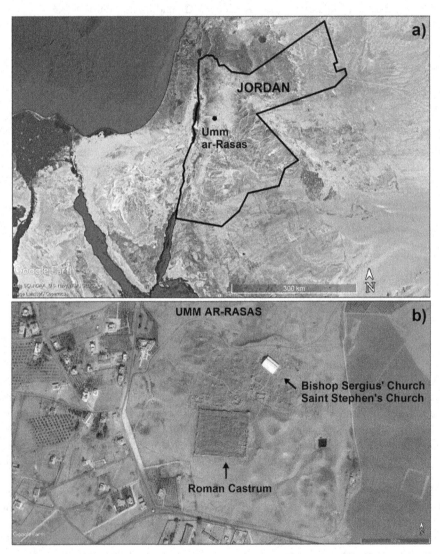

Fig. 1. Location of Umm ar-Rasas on a Google Earth™ satellite image of Jordan (a), detail of the site with indication of the roman castrum and the two Byzantine churches (b).

The most relevant religious complex is Saint Stephen's, by the name of the proto-deacon and proto-martyr to whom it was dedicated. It was developed between the VI and VIII century A.D., formed by at least four communicating buildings: the Church of the Tabernacle that is the most ancient, Bishop Sergius' Church with its baptistery and the funerary chapel to the front, Saint Stephen's Church and the Church of the Courtyard, raised between the other three churches.

This paper has focused on the rich mosaic decoration of Bishop Sergius' and Saint Stephen's Churches (Fig. 2), both with three aisles and one apse and with the chancel rose by two steps. The two churches host some mosaic floors of exceptional quality and rich with inscriptions, portraits, everyday life scenes, geometrical and plant motifs and nonetheless the representation of many towns from Palestine, Egypt and Jordan. In Bishop Sergius' Church those mosaics are dated with precision to 586 A.D. by a mosaic inscription located to the front of the altar's base, where it is mentioned the name of the commissioner, Bishop Sergius of Madaba (576–603 A.D.). Through time, they have been subject to modifications both for restoration and iconoclasm's reasons, such as in the case of many other contemporary religious complexes. The readability of the portions that represent figurative elements in fact was for the most part made uneasy to perform because of actions of censorship on the figurative images, realised taking off the *tesserae* one by one and then putting them again in position but without a precise scheme with the aim of filling the gaps in the floor. In Saint Stephen's Church also, built after Bishop Sergius' Church and dated around 717 A.D., the subjects portraying people and animals were disfigured. However, it has to be noticed that the intervention on the figures of the mosaic floor results, for its execution mode, as made by Christian workers. They cared scrupulously about the complete preservation of the floor, either for the beauty and the decorum assured to the cultic building and for its value as an offer by local community members, whose names were written together with the images in the mosaic representations.

The archaeological missions undertaken until now were mainly aimed at photogrammetric and laser scanning surveys to determine morphological anomalies of the mosaic floors. The project foresees as its ultimate goal the documentation and consecutive valorisation and accessibility of the site, though also the professional training of local technicians with the help of systems of distance learning. During the measurements' campaigns, the work proceeded in continuity with the activities realised in the previous years and the following activities are expected to be completed in the near future, representing only a small portion of actions, compared to the more general framework of issues affecting the entire archaeological site:

1. The survey of the outer walls of Saint Stephen's and Bishop Sergius' Churches, both by photogrammetric methods and by detailed and high-resolution laser scanning.
2. The documentation of the decaying state of the most relevant and at high risk structures through the use and integration of high resolution laser scanning and photogrammetric methods which will highlight the decay, even the type which is not perceivable by direct sight. These methodologies produce micro DEM of the floors useful for a correct interpretation of the structural solicitations of the building that,

if compared to the other parameters and measurements taken during the survey campaigns, will provide a punctual documentation useful to plan the following restoration and reinforcement actions on the mosaics. A further fundamental element for the documentation and conservation will be given by the high-resolution orthogonal pictures of the mosaic surface, arriving to a pixel dimension of a few tenth of square millimetres, allowing obtaining images with dimensions comparable to the real dimensions of the mosaic.

3. Non-invasive geophysical prospections of the areas of the main churches, which will allow detecting anomalies possibly indicating more ancient structures or graves.

Fig. 2. Details of the walls of two Byzantine churches (St. Stephen and Bishop Sergius).

1   Methodology

1.1   Photogrammetry

The Structure from Motion technique was utilized in order to obtain complete documentation of the floor at high resolution in terms of chromatic definition of surfaces and photographic detail. During these years, photogrammetric images were acquired from the mosaic floors, with a 21 Mpixels' resolution for every single frame, standing by 1.5 m from the floor, with the camera perpendicular to it. The images, taken in RAW format, were calibrated in the RGB map with a predisposed chromatic table. This table has also the peculiar characteristic of being recognized automatically by a specific algorithm allowing the definition of the chromatic scale. This operation was necessary to standardize the colors of the photographic takes depending on the different level of lighting to which the floor was subject to at different hours of the day and on the different spatial positions of the camera inside the church.

A test conducted on a small portion of the floor (the apse of Saint Stephen's Church) in the 2013 mission had evidenced the need to build a tool allowing the realisation of the photogrammetric images with the camera in an easy way at a fixed distance from the floor. The photogrammetric tool that was set up is made of a camera calibrated with a 20 MP Full Frame sensor and a 28 mm lens, mounted on a pole that can be put on the shoulder. The camera was constantly held to a height of 170 cm obtaining a very good compromise between the accuracy of the photogrammetric takes and a sufficient dimension of the area to be acquired ($3m^2$ for each take, GSD of 0,4 mm)[1]. The research group chose to operate using an experimental tool that allowed more freedom in movements, considering the extreme delicateness of the surface and that the main purpose of the work was documenting the decay and avoiding damage to the building. The choice has fallen on quick and light weighted tools, easy to move on the mosaic floor. Moreover, the presence of metal structures (boardwalks) *in situ* has in many cases created some difficulties on taking the pictures and has limited the action range of the group to lower heights (this brought the need to take frames at a higher frequency). In general a good quality of takes is the best guarantee of a final result in which the mapping of the model is at a good level.

For each floor approximately 2000 frames were taken, with the purpose of covering in full the surfaces of the two investigated churches (Saint Stephen: 242,26 sq.m; Bishop Sergius: 226,12 sq.m), also the use of a color-checker allowed the balancing of the color white made through the use of a raw-converter software. At every movement the operator, before taking the shot, had to assure the perfect stability of the camera, without oscillations; the movements had to allow an adequate overlapping, in order to guarantee, during the data processing phase, the assembling of the frames. It has to be noticed that, at each change of the light conditions, the color has been calibrated again with the help of the color-checker, to avoid chromatic differences between each stripe. The final point cloud is the result of the alignment of the various strips. The software application, based on the technique known as Structure from Motion [6], doesn't make the built model a metrical model; therefore it is necessary to determine a ratio based on the topographical data at hand. Hence, the photogrammetric survey was combined to the laser scanning survey [7].

1.2 Laser Scanning

To perform the survey through laser scanner on the structures subject to investigation a pneumatic pole has been used to raise the scanner up to 5 m high, allowing in this way to measure even the highest walls' crests [8] (see Fig. 3). This tool, designed and built specifically for this purpose, allowed performing 3D surveys from observation points that nowadays require the use of drones (that have sight from up above), without altering the geometric and metric accuracy which only laser instruments can offer. Another

---

[1] The processing of the photographic takes was done using the software *Agisoft Photoscan*.

advantage brought by this survey technique is that the laser scanners are tools mainly made to perform scans in the architectural and engineering field; therefore, their best application is mainly addressed at everything that stands high above the planking level (walls, ceilings and arches). It is instead less efficient to measure structures that are located on the horizontal level of the instrument (floors, mosaics, holes, depressions and digs).

The scans made were 70 in total and the survey was completed for the entire monumental structure of the two churches, Saint Stephen's and Bishop Sergius'. The scans were executed with a resolution at a half of the maximum of the instrument and acquiring the RGB component. At the moment the research group is finishing processing all the acquired scans by isolating single elements of every building (walls, apse and floor), and then we will proceed to the modelling of the structures that will help doing in the future a virtual anastylosis of the monument.

The scans were all performed through a phase-shift laser scanner Focus120 3D, produced by Faro, that gives high accuracy results, despite the scan timings. The instrument was set on the profile "Outdoor over 20 m" with a resolution to a half of the maximum and the acquisition of the RGB component. Approximately 10 to 12 scans were made each day since it took 30 min to take each scan due to the scanner configuration, considering the 8h of overall duration of the two batteries at hand and the timings of movement of the pneumatic pole and the instrument. The registration[2] of the scans was made using a double alignment process, the first based on the automatic identification of suitable 3D high reflectance white targets (spheres) provided by Faro, with a 20 cm. diameter and a magnet allowing their attachment to metal structures[3]; the second required the use of complex mathematical algorithms providing the refinement of the initial alignments (ICP) [9]. When surveying with this technique, one has to account for three factors to get a good automatic alignment: first, at least three spheres have to be visible in between two adjacent scans, secondly the scans must have a suitable spatial distribution and lastly the laser scanner has to find enough points on the scans to recognize them and then calculate precisely their center. Once it has aligned the scans through the help of the spheres, the software automatically proceeds to the identification of at least 2000 common points to refine the alignment, resulting with an average error in the range of a millimeter.

1.3 Ground Penetrating Radar Survey

During 2016, a GPR survey was conducted at the archaeological site of Umm ar-Rasas inside the Churches of Bishop Sergius and Saint Stephen. Taking into account the probable type, dimensions and depth of the submerged bodies and the surface on which the research group was working (i.e. on the mosaics), the GPR has been preferred to other methods. An IDS RIS K2 Georadar, equipped with a multi frequency antenna TRMF (600–200 MHz), has been used for data acquisition. All radar reflections were recorded digitally in the field as 16 bit data and 512 samples per radar scan. The spacing between

---

[2] The software *Faro Scene* has been used for a first alignment with spherical targets, *JRC Reconstructor* for the following processes.

[3] The research group opted to locate the instrument on mobile tripods, in order to move freely the targets.

parallel profiles at the site was 0.5 m and they were collected alternatively in opposite directions with angles of 90° in the survey grids. Radar reflections on each line were recorded at 25 scan s-1 (1 scan approximately corresponds to 0.025 m).

Standard bi-dimensional radargrams relative to single transects were processed through the GPR-SLICE 7.0 software. Band pass filters, background removal and the Gain Control were applied in order to remove high and low frequency anomalies that occurred during the data acquisition, normalize the amplification and remove reflections generated by noise due to the different signal attenuation [10].

Thus, using a sequence of parallel lines, a three-dimensional matrix of averaged square wave amplitudes of the return reflection was generated and time-slices were realized for various time windows. In the examined context, supposing a soil with a velocity v with which the wave spread into the materials equal to about 0,1 m/ns, the depth h of the reflectors could be approximately derived using the equation $h = vt/2$ (where t is the time in which the electromagnetic wave fulfils the path transmitter antenna-discontinuity-receiver antenna). Data were then gridded using a kriging routine and a radius of interpolation equal to 0.75 m.

2 Results and Discussion

The survey provided a precise metric and photorealistic determination of the complex structure resulting in a complete reconstruction of the architectural artefact. Each survey performed at Umm ar-Rasas has given us a better knowledge of the structures located on the archaeological site. It should be also noticed that all the technologies employed resulted in new issues to be solved in the future with further applications.

The work conducted until now was a useful experiment for the integration of laser scanning and photogrammetric surveys: in this way the results guarantee from one side the descriptive accuracy in the colors and in the details of the surveyed surface; from another point of view the use of the laser scanning methods allows the representation with great precision, in the range of a few millimeters, of the geometrical deformities of the mosaic floors. Figures 3 and 4 report 3D view of the two churches obtained by laser scanning procedures and an inclination map of walls (Fig. 4b). In Fig. 5, the resulting orthogonal picture of the whole Saint Stephen's mosaic floor obtained by photogrammetric techniques is shown (dimension: 1 GB, equivalent to 8000 × 60000 pixel).

By analyzing the floor of Bishop Sergius' Church it has been pointed out a lifting of the floor by 0,10 m in the central aisle towards the apse; instead it has been noted a depression in the zone near the entrance door, the presence of which is probably related to an underground water tank located on the north-western side of the building, where traces of a water channel are visible. In Saint Stephen's Church there are also liftings of the floor on the right side of the central aisle, while light slopes are visible on the rest of the floor, especially on the portion of floor that is nearer to Bishop Sergius' Church (Fig. 6). The causes of these deformities could be linked either to geological instability issues of the area and to further underground man-made structures (graves, mural structures, tanks). The following investigations are aimed at the secure interpretation of these deformities. In relation to this, the execution of high-resolution photogrammetric surveys could be used as a starting point for any conservation and restoration project to be planned for the preservation of the mosaic floors.

Fig. 3. 3D perspective view of the two churches obtained by laser scanning processing: 3D model of the two churches in their actual spatial arrangement (a); qualitative inclination map of walls where the colors indicate the direction of the surfaces (b).

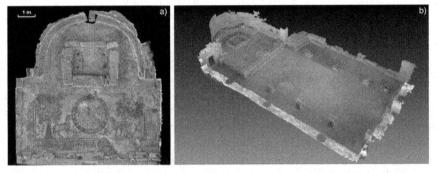

Fig. 4. Detail of the apse (a) and 3D perspective view of the model of the church of Bishop Sergius made by laser scanner (b).

Fig. 5. High-resolution orthographic view of Saint Stephen's mosaic floor obtained by integration of photogrammetric and laser scanning techniques.

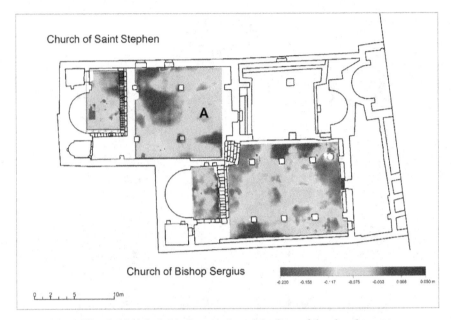

Fig. 6. Model of altitude variation of the floor of the churches.

Figure 7 reports the results of GPR investigations relative to the depth window of 0.5–0.7 m, overlapped on the map of the churches. The anomalies seen in these representations depict the spatial distribution of the amplitudes of the reflections at specific depths within the grid. Within the slice, low amplitude variations express small reflections from the subsurface and, therefore, indicate the presence of homogeneous material. High amplitudes denote significant discontinuities in the ground and evidence the presence of probable buried objects. Regarding the Church of Saint Stephen, in the most superficial map, various anomalies perpendicular to the left aisle, a longitudinal anomaly in the center of the median body of the church and an anomaly in the space in front of the apse (at the right edge) are highlighted and they are indicated with pink arrows in Fig. 7. The presence of probable structures buried under the pavement, prior to the construction phase of the church, may have caused, in a phase of settling the materials, the deformation found by the laser scanner survey in particular in the point indicated with A. In the Church of Bishop Sergius, the prospection showed, at the entrance of the structure, anomalies of regular shape probably attributable to voids and therefore to possible underground cisterns belonging to a more ancient chronological phase. Works are still ongoing and the main objective of the research is to produce a full map of hidden structures inside the walls of the city through integration of different geophysical methods such as electrical resistivity tomography, GPR and induced electromagnetic methods that generally produce a successful detection [11–14]. This application will be useful to promote archaeological excavations and project of valorization of the site.

All results are going to be stored in ad hoc geodatabase resulting from the partnership and debate between all the members of the research group made by archaeologists, art historians, geophysics and conservators [15]. The geodatabase is developing in time following some steps: beginning with the development of a GIS platform to archive the acquired interdisciplinary data, to the development of analysis models for data management (Fig. 8). Therefore, the GIS technology offers both methodological and interpretative advantages: from one point of view, it allows the realization of an interdisciplinary dialogue between different research matters through the efficient data management and registration; from another point of view, it makes easy to interpret the information acquired from the spatial queries [16]. In addition, the geodatabase can be used as a monitoring device on the state of conservation of the mosaic, becoming a valid support for the planning of future restoration actions.

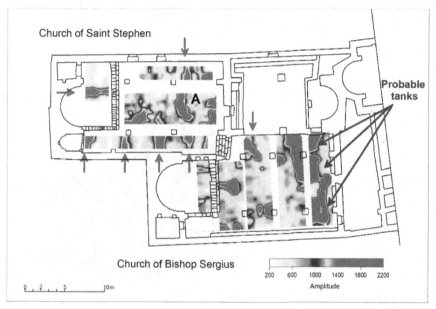

Fig. 7. Slices related to the depth window of 0.5–0.7 m overlapped on the map of the churches: the blue arrows indicate the location of probable tanks, while the pink arrows highlight probable buried archaeological structures. (Color figure online)

3   Future Outlook of the Project

The site of Umm ar-Rasas constitutes an extraordinary laboratory to study traditional masonry, either for the different use of materials in time and for the construction techniques' development. The settlement's long evolutionary history, that has its roots in the Roman castrum's implant, allows analyzing in a critical way the different typologies adopted for common houses and specialised building, such as the numerous medieval churches that have developed according to particular environmental conditions and materials' availability at the local level. The instability modes of the structures that have survived to time and earthquakes' action, typical destructive events that occur in this area, are an aspect of great interest. This issue of the research can be studied beginning from the site currently under investigation and then be extended to a wider environmental context, with effects on the western world through a comparison with other construction traditions that are affected by the same issue. Therefore, this site offers a unique opportunity to understand the construction techniques' evolution putting the accent on anti-seismic actions. In particular, there are open questions about the static and seismic behavior of the arches and more generally of the pushing structures, considered among the most vulnerable structures but also some of the few that have survived to the general framework of instability. The study of the masonry through the mechanics of the arches constitutes the interpretation key that puts Umm ar-Rasas as a key site for the analysis of these events in an environment that keeps its original construction characteristics.

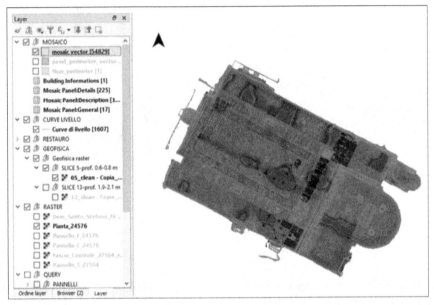

Fig. 8. Thematic map of the mosaic pavement of St. Stephen's church enriched in GIS application.

Analyses requiring superficial and underground observations of the soil and of the lithological and petrographical characteristics of the rocky subsoil have started on the area on which stands the so called Stylite Tower, this being among the most relevant structures of the archaeological complex. Moreover, the use of equipment such as georadar and geoelectric and seismic systems, both active and passive, will be implemented. Lastly, the identification of the structural mechanical characteristics and the decay, vulnerability and stability level caused by the atmospheric agents will be performed through the petrographical analysis and the direct topographical laser scanning survey. Another part will provide the realization and development of a tool for the valorisation and availability of the data by a wider range of users: the geodatabase of the mosaic floor in Saint Stephen's Church will allow the creation of a model for computerised management and interdisciplinary data analysis aimed at interpretation, conservation and valorization.

Acknowledgments. The Ministry of Foreign Affairs of Italy, in the frame of the Archaeological Missions, funded part of this research. We thank the Embassy of Italy and the Department of Antiquities of the Hashemite Kingdom of Jordan for the continuous support for the activities.

References

1. Piccirillo, M.: Umm al-Rasas, Mayfaah I. Studium Biblicum Franciscanum, Jerusalem, Israel (1994)
2. Piccirillo, M.: La Palestina cristiana I-VII secolo. Centro editoriale dehoniano (EDB), Bologna, Italy (2008)
3. Galatà, P., Zavagnini, A., Gabrielli, R., Portarena, D., Franceschinis, M.: Tecniche di documentazione dei tappeti musivi del sito archeologico di Umm Al-Rasas–Kastron Mefaa (Giordania). Archeol. Calcolatori **28**, 201–218 (2017)
4. Cozzolino, M., Gabrielli, R., Galatà, P., Gentile, V., Greco, G., Scopinaro, E.: Combined use of 3D metric surveys and non-invasive geophysical surveys for the determination of the state of conservation of the stylite tower (Umm ar-Rasas, Jordan). Ann. Geophys. **62**(3), 339 (2019)
5. Pierdicca, R., Intrigila, C., Piccinini, F., Malinverni, E.S., Giannetti, I., Caruso, G.: Multidisciplinary approach for the analysis of structural heritage at risk: the case study of stylite tower at Umm ar-Rasas (Jordan). Int. J. Archit. Herit. 1–25 (2021). https://doi.org/10.1080/15583058.2021.1966554
6. Remondino, F., Spera, M.G., Nocerino, E., Menna, F., Nex, F.: State of the art in high density image matching. Photogrammet. Rec. **29**, 144–166 (2014)
7. Cundari, C.: Il rilievo architettonico. Ragioni. Fondamenti. Applicazioni, Kappa, Rome (2012)
8. Carpiceci, M., Angelini, A.: Looking for the full scan: S. Zenone chapel. In: 2018 Metrology for Archaeology and Cultural Heritage (MetroArchaeo), pp. 345–350 (2018)
9. Remondino, F., Campana, S.: 3D Recording and Modelling in Archaeology and Cultural Heritage – Theory and best practices. BAR International Series, p. 2598. Oxford (2014)
10. Conyers, L.B., Goodman, D.: Ground Penetrating Radar. An Introduction for Archaeologists. AltaMira Press, Walnut Creek (1997)
11. Cozzolino, M., Caliò, L.M., Gentile, V., Mauriello, P., Di Meo, A.: The discovery of the theater of akragas (valley of temples, Agrigento, Italy): an archaeological confirmation of the supposed buried structures from a geophysical survey. Geosciences **10**, 161 (2020)
12. Cozzolino, M., et al.: The contribution of geophysics to the knowledge of the hidden archaeological heritage of montenegro. Geosciences **10**, 187 (2020)
13. Tsokas, G.N., et al.: ERT imaging of the interior of the huge tumulus of Kastas in Amphipolis (northern Greece). Archaeol. Prospect. **25**, 347–361 (2018)
14. Piroddi, L., Calcina, S.V., Trogu, A., Ranieri, G.: Automated resistivity profiling (ARP) to explore wide archaeological areas: the prehistoric site of Mont'e Prama, Sardinia, Italy. Remote Sens. **12**(3), 461 (2020)
15. Malinverni, E.S., Pierdicca, R., Di Stefano, F., Gabrielli, R., Albiero, A.: Virtual museum enriched by GIS data to share science and culture. Church of Saint Stephen in Umm Ar-Rasas (Jordan). Virtual Archaeol. Rev. **10**(21), 31–39 (2019)
16. Felicetti, A., et al.: Automatic mosaic digitalization: a deep learning approach to tessera segmentation. In: 2018 Metrology for Archaeology and Cultural Heritage (MetroArchaeo), pp. 132–136. IEEE (2018)

Diffraction Imaging After Diffraction Separation in Data Domain

M. Protasov[(✉)]

Institute of Petroleum Geology and Geophysics, Novosibirsk 630090, Russia
protasovmi@ipgg.sbras.ru

Abstract. Diffracted/scattered waves are used to construct diffraction images and further seismic interpretation. There are various algorithms for their extraction, which can be divided into three classes regarding the data processing steps: data do-main procedures, migration-based methods, and image processing. The paper presents the algorithm for the data domain diffraction separation. Also, it provides an investigation of the influence of the diffraction separation in the data domain, focusing on the migration procedure based on the construction of selective images. Numerical experiments are performed using synthetic data obtained for a realistic model with fractures from the field in Eastern Siberia.

Keywords: Seismic data · Diffraction imaging · Diffraction separation

1 Introduction

Currently, in the practice of seismic research, diffraction images or images in scattered waves, as well as methods for their construction, are of increasing interest. This is primarily because of the need to search and develop fractured carbonate reservoirs [1]. According to various estimates, these reservoirs contain from 35 to 48% of the world's oil reserves and from 23 to 28% of the world's gas. The scattered component of the seismic wave field carries significant information about small-scale geological objects, in particular, fracture zones. Its processing makes it possible to localize such geologically interesting objects as zones of increased fracturing, faults and surrounding crushing zones, cavernous-fractured zones [2, 3].

Diffracted/scattered waves are used as additional information for the seismic interpretation. There are various algorithms for their extraction from the seismic data, which can be divided into three classes concerning the data processing workflow: in the data domain, during the migration and image processing. One of the first is the algorithm of diffraction moveout correction and stacking [4]. The paper by Fomel, Landa, and Taner introduces the so-called plane wave destructor for separating specular reflections and scattering/diffraction in the data space [5]. In this method, they get classical images but for the scattered/diffracted component of the wavefield. Moser and Howard develop the approach of diffraction imaging in the depth domain in the context of the pre-stack migration [6]. They use the two-stage implementation of the regular migration: employment of specular reflection on the first and their suppression and weakening on the second. Analysis of seismograms in the structural angles coordinate system reveals a significant difference in the reflected and diffracted waves in these coordinates. On this basis, efficient algorithms for separating reflection and diffraction/scattering are proposed and implemented [7, 8]. In this angle domain, for many cases, the reflection is convex, whereas the diffraction corresponds to a straight line. Therefore, the effective separation procedure here is filtering in the Radon transform domain [9, 10]. Decker, Merzlikin, and Fomel further develop seismic diffraction imaging utilizing the principle of flatness of diffraction events in slope gather together with the plane wave destructor [11]. Zhang and co-authors propose a wave-equation diffraction imaging procedure based on a decomposition of the wavefields into left- and right-downgoing propagating waves [12]. The proposed method adds reasonable additional computational cost over wave-equation reflection migration and therefore provides practical wave-equation-based diffraction imaging. Wang, Liu, and Chen present one more way to separate and imagine seismic diffractions based on a localized rank-reduction method using a local plane-wave assumption [13]. The proposed method shows advantages over the plane wave destructor and general rank reduction method.

Algorithms that use diffracted/scattered waves during migration are based on suppressing the energy of reflected waves. Still, they suppress some of the energy of the diffracted/scattered waves. Image processing algorithms have the same disadvantage. Diffracted/scattered waves can be extracted when working directly in the seismic data domain not ideally, but most of their energy remains [14]. This paper proposes the new workflow for the seismic data processing of the diffracted/scattered waves, where diffraction separation in the data domain is used before application of diffraction imaging procedure. The algorithm for diffraction separation is proposed, which is based on the different kinematic behavior of the reflected and scattered waves in the common offset domain. The influence of the diffraction separation in the data domain is investigated on the results of the diffraction imaging procedure based on the construction of selective images [15]. Numerical experiments are performed using synthetic data got for a realistic fractured model of the field in Eastern Siberia.

2 Diffracted Wave Estimation

The seismic data are supposed to contain reflected waves and diffracted/scattered waves. They are considered in the mid-point offset domain:

$$d(t, x_m, h) = ref(t, x_m, h) + dif(t, x_m, h),$$ (1)

where d is the seismic data, ref are reflected waves, dif are diffracted/scattered waves, (t, x_m, h) are time, mid-point, and offset coordinates, respectively. The algorithm for separating diffracted/scattered waves dif from the seismic data d is based on the essentially different kinematic behaviour of reflected waves and diffracted/scattered waves in the common offset domain. Hodograph of the reflected wave in that domain $t_{ref}(x_m)$ «follows» the corresponding reflected interfaces, and usually, they provide locally plane events, however the hodograph of diffracted/scattered wave $t_{ref}(x_m)$ has behavior where second-order derivatives have significant influence:

$$t_{ref}(x_m) \approx t_0 + a \cdot x_m;$$ (2)

$$t_{dif}(x_m) \approx t_0 + a \cdot x_m + b \cdot x_m^2. \tag{3}$$

One can observe such behavior on a simple model example with two horizontal layers and four point scatters (Fig. 1). The reflection wave represents flat event while diffractions have significant curvature. Such a different behavior provides a wide range of algorithms [14].

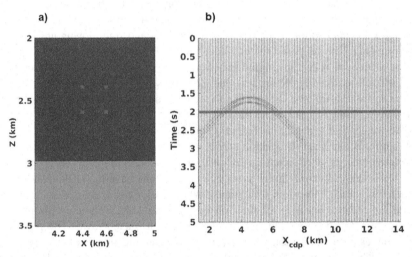

Fig. 1. a) Simple model with flat interfaces and point scatterers. b) The corresponding seismic data in the common offset domain.

The proposed here algorithm is a combination of two most effective techniques. The first part of the procedure comprises enhancing reflected waves [16] and suppressing all the other events, including diffractions followed by reflections subtraction from the initial data (it is like one algorithm from [14]). At this stage, the enhancement procedure uses kinematic of the reflected events (2) at small apertures. At the second stage, algorithm provides enhancement of the diffracted/scattered waves and suppression of the redundant reflected events. Here, the enhancement technique uses an estimation of the kinematic of the diffracted/scattered waves and their usage at rather big apertures. The last part of the procedure is like the so-called multi-focusing technique oriented on diffractions [17]. Note, for the ideal data, the first part of procedure can provide satisfactory results when the reflections are rather clear and there is no big amplitude difference in reflections and diffractions. But, for realistic cases and real data, these are rather rare circumstances, therefore second part of the procedure provides improvement of the diffractions that were extracted at the first stage.

2.1 Ideal Diffracted Wave Identification

To exclude the errors and limits of the diffraction separation algorithm, ideal extraction of diffracted waves only is provided for simple and realistic synthetic models. For simple synthetic model, such extraction is straightforward because an analytic solution can provide waves separately. For the realistic case, two synthetic models are created (Fig. 2a, 2b). Both models contain the objects of diffraction are located: one layer with fractures. The second model contains additional fracture layer that provides diffractions while first original model does not have them. In these models, synthetic data are calculated using the finite difference method (Fig. 2d, 2e). To get diffracted waves only that produced by the inhomogeneities corresponding to this bottom fractured layer of the second model (Fig. 2c), one should take the difference of the wave fields (Fig. 2d). This result provides the ideal separation of diffracted/scattered waves produced by the bottom fractured layer of the second model.

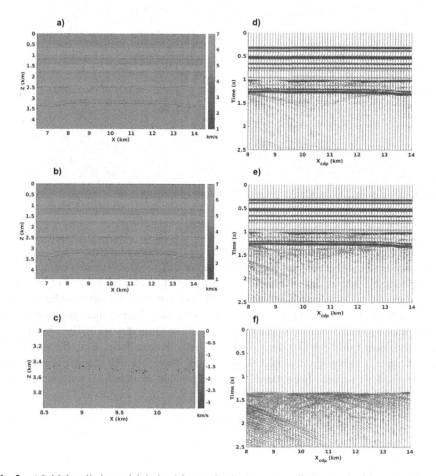

Fig. 2. a) Initial realistic model derived from seismic data. b) Realistic model with cracked layer. c) Difference of models in the region of the layer with cracks. d) Zero offset gather for the original model. e). Zero offset gather for a model with a fractured layer. f) Difference between seismograms d) and e).

2.2 Diffracted Wave Separation vs Ideal Identification

Then the described above algorithm for diffraction separation is applied to the data computed in a simple model and to the data generated in a realistic model. Results of diffraction separation for the data in the simple model show reflections are sup-pressed completely (Fig. 3b). Although the diffractions in this case do not coincide with the ideal result, the main kinematic and dynamic properties of the diffracted waves stay the same (Fig. 3).

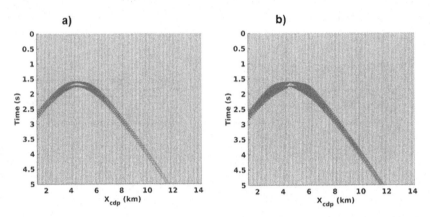

Fig. 3. Simple data: a) the ideal separation; b) results of the data domain diffraction separation.

Diffraction separation results for the data in the realistic model show reflections are removed ideally as well (Fig. 4b). One can see that the result of diffraction separation is relatively close to the ideal one (Fig. 4a) in terms of diffracted/scattered waves produced by the bottom fractured layer (Fig. 4b). There is a perfect correspondence of kinematic properties of diffracted waves and rather good match of dynamic behavior between the ideal waves and diffraction separation results. One can observe that, in this case, the diffractions produced by the top fractured layer are recovered as well. Their behavior is like the behavior of the diffractions produced by the bottom layer. Both fracture layers have identical geometric and amplitude properties. Therefore, one should expect similar properties of diffractions from these layers that provide an additional confirmation that the separation algorithm works properly.

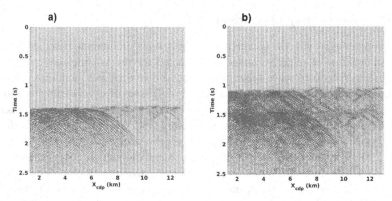

Fig. 4. Realistic data: a) the ideal separation; b) results of the data domain diffraction separation.

3   Diffraction Imaging

For diffraction image construction, the concept of selective images is used [15]:

$$SelectiveImage(\overline{x}; \alpha, \beta) = \int \frac{T_{qp}^{gbs}(x_s; \overline{x}; \alpha, \beta; \omega) \cdot T_{qp}^{gbr}(x_r; \overline{x}; \alpha, \beta; \omega)}{\cdot d(x_r; x_s; \omega)dx_r dx_s d\omega}. \qquad (4)$$

Here d is the seismic data, x_r/x_s is the source/receiver coordinate, ω is the frequency, α, β are the dip and opening angles, $T_{qp}^{gbs(r)}$ are the source(receiver) stacking weights. To calculate the stack image corresponding to the standard migration of seismic data, it is necessary to sum the selective images with respect to all available dip and opening angles.

3.1   Diffraction Imaging Resolution

A detailed examination of individual selective images and their partial sums shows that their resolution is different. Using the example of a model and data with diffractors only (Fig. 3a), one can observe that the resolution increases as the number of selective images increases, corresponding to an increase in the range of dip angles (Fig. 5). Thus, the larger the range of dip angles is available for constructing a diffraction image, the better its spatial resolution. Note that, for the construction of diffraction images, the largest range of dip angles will be available if the imaging procedure uses diffracted/scattered waves only. The presented simple example clearly shows this observation (Fig. 5).

3.2 Diffraction Imaging Comparison

Next experiments provide the comparison of the diffraction imaging based on an asymmetric summation of selective images constructed for the seismic data without and with diffracted/scattered wave separation. First, simple data and model is considered. When data contains diffractions and reflections, «full» sum of selective images provides reflections events mainly while diffractions are almost invisible (Fig. 6a). Partial sum of selective image provides diffraction events mainly (Fig. 6a, 6b). These partial images have the same resolution when partial images are constructed for the ideal diffraction data (Fig. 5a, 5b). However, when the diffraction separation algorithm provides the data that contains diffractions only then «full» sum of selective images provides diffractions only as well and the resolution of such image is higher than resolution of the diffraction images that are a partial sum of selective images (Fig. 7a, 7b, 7c). Also «full» sum of selective images provides comparable results for both cases: ideal diffractions identification (Fig. 5a) and application of diffraction separation algorithm (Fig. 7a). The conclusions from these experiments are obvious: a) one needs to separate diffractions in seismic data before diffraction imaging application; b) the proposed diffractions separation algorithm provides rather good diffraction identification so that their image is close to the image of ideal diffractions.

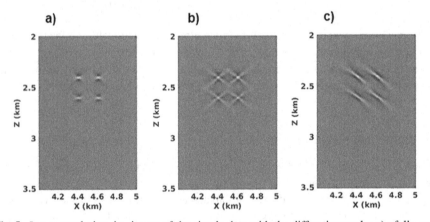

Fig. 5. Image resolution, i.e. image of the simple data with the diffractions only: a) «full» sum of selective images: a = [−40° : 1° : 40°]; b) partial sum of selective images, a = [−40° : 1° : −25°] and a = [25° : 1° : 40°]; c) partial sum of selective images, a = [−40° : 1° : −25°].

Then image results are provided for realistic synthetic model and data. Three datasets are used for diffraction imaging: the original seismic data containing all wave types, the data after ideal subtraction, where only the waves diffracted/scattered by the bottom fracture layer remain, and the data after diffraction separation. First, for the initial seismic data, a «full» image (Fig. 8b) and a diffraction image (Fig. 8c) were constructed, where selective images for the angles a = [−40° : 1° : 40°] in the first case, and for the second a = [−40° : 1° : −25°] and a = [25° : 1° : 40°]. The diffraction image shows two layers with fractures and faults, but the remnants of reflected waves are also visible. Then, to the ideal diffraction data and the data after diffraction separation, a similar imaging procedure was applied for the angles a = [−40° : 1° : 40°]. One can see a significant difference in diffraction images got from the data without preliminary separation (Fig. 8c) and from ideal data containing only scattered waves (Fig. 8d). The image is much more focused and less noisy in the second case. The last is the best achievable result in the bottom fracture layer image.

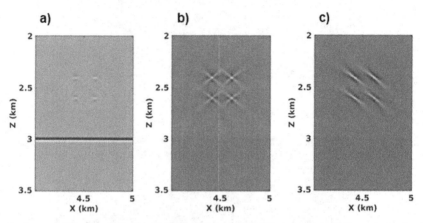

Fig. 6. Image of the simple data with the reflections and diffractions: a) «full» sum of selective images: a = [−40° : 1° : 40°]; b) partial sum of selective images, a = [−40° : 1° : −25°] and a = [25° : 1° : 40°]; c) partial sum of selective images, a = [−40° : 1° : −25°].

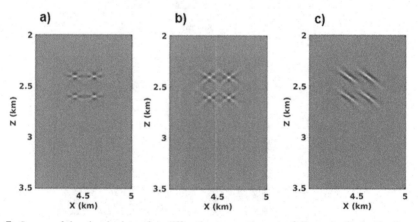

Fig. 7. Image of the simple data after diffraction separation: a) «full» sum of selective images: a = [−40° : 1° : 40°]; b) partial sum of selective images, a = [−40° : 1° : −25°] and a = [25° : 1° : 40°]; c) partial sum of selective images, a = [−40° : 1° : −25°].

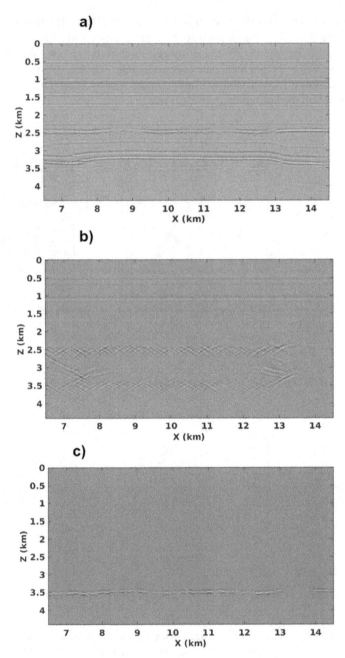

Fig. 8. a) Realistic model containing two fractures layers; b) «full» sum of selective images of the data without any processing: a = [−40° : 1° : 40°]; c) partial sum of selective images of the data without any processing, a = [−40° : 1° : −25°] and a = [25° : 1° : 40°]; d) «full» sum of selective images of the data with the «ideal» diffractions: a = [−40° : 1° : 40°].

More detailed consideration of the images near the bottom layer fractured zone illustrates the advantages of the diffraction separation in the data before diffraction imaging (Fig. 9). The image result of data after diffraction separation (Fig. 9d) is close to the ideal result (Fig. 9c). It is more focused, less noisy, and more consistent with the model (Fig. 9a) than the selective diffraction image of raw data (Fig. 9b).

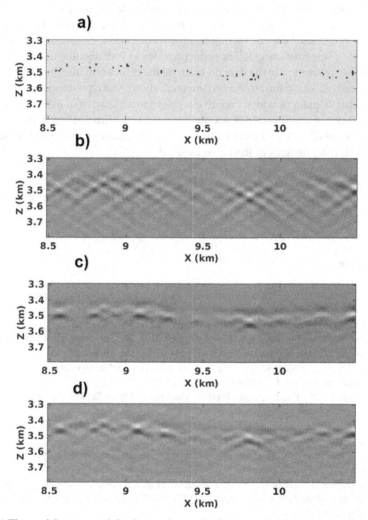

Fig. 9. a) The model area containing bottom layer with fractures. In the same area: b) partial sum of selective images of the data without any processing, a = [−40° : 1° : −25°] и a = [25° : 1° : 40°]; c) and d) are «full» sum of selective images of the data with the «ideal» and data after diffraction separation using different kinematic behavior of the reflections and diffractions: a = [−40° : 1° : 40°].

4   Conclusions

The paper presents the new workflow for the seismic data processing of the diffracted/scattered waves. It uses preliminary diffraction separation in the data domain with the following application of diffraction imaging procedure. The new algorithm for the diffraction separation in the data domain is developed and tested. The algorithm uses the different kinematic behavior of reflected and diffracted/scattered waves in common offset domain. The reflections removal and diffractions enhancement are two of the major steps in the procedure. The diffraction imaging procedure uses Gaussian beam for the construction of selective images. The paper provides an investigation of the influence of the diffraction separation in the data do-main on the diffraction imaging procedure. On the simple and realistic datasets, the investigation shows that a preliminary wave separation in the data domain provides a relatively good approximation of diffracted/scattered waves. Further construction of diffraction images of the diffracted/scattered component only makes it possible to get a more focused and less noisy image than when constructing selective diffraction images of the full wave-field.

Acknowledgments. The work is supported by RSF grant 21-71-20002. The work's numerical results were obtained using the computational resources of Peter the Great Saint-Petersburg Polytechnic University Supercomputing Center (scc.spbstu.ru).

References

1. Liu, E., et al.: Fracture characterization by integrating seismic-derived attributes including anisotropy and diffraction imaging with borehole fracture data in an offshore carbonate field. In: International Petroleum Technology Conference, IPTC-18533 (2015)
2. De Ribet, B., Yelin, G., Serfaty, Y., Chase, D., Kelvin, R., Koren, Z.: High resolution diffraction imaging for reliable interpretation of fracture systems. First Break **35**, 43–47 (2017)
3. Shtivelman, V., Keydar, S.: Imaging shallow subsurface inhomogeneities by 3D multipath diffraction summation. First Break **23**, 39–42 (2005)
4. Kanasewich, E.R., Phadke, S.M.: Imaging discontinuities on Seismic Sections. Geophysics **53**, 334–345 (1998)
5. Fomel, S., Landa, E., Taner, T.: Poststack velocity analysis by separation and imaging of seismic diffractions. Geophysics **72**, 89–94 (2007)
6. Moser, T.J., Howard, C.B.: Diffraction imaging in depth. Geophys. Prospect. **56**, 627–642 (2008)
7. Landa, E., Fomel, S., Reshef, M.: Separation, imaging, and velocity analysis of seismic diffractions using migrated dip-angle gathers. In: 72nd SEG Annual Meeting Expanded Abstracts, pp. 2176–2100 (2008)
8. Reshef, M., Landa, E.: Poststack velocity analysis in the dip-angle domain using diffractions. Geophys. Prospect. **57**, 811–821 (2009)
9. Klokov, A., Baina, R., Landa, E.: Separation and imaging of seismic diffractions in dip angle domain. 72nd EAGE Annual Meeting Expanded Abstracts (2010)
10. Klokov, A., Fomel, S.: Separation and imaging of seismic diffractions using migrated dip-angle gathers. Geophysics **77**, S131–S143 (2012)
11. Decker, L., Merzlikin, D., Fomel, S.: Diffraction imaging and time-migration velocity analysis using oriented velocity continuation. Geophysics **82**, U25–U35 (2017)

12. Zhang, D., Fei, T., Tsingas, C., Luo, Y.: Efficient wave equation based diffraction imaging. Geophysics **84**, S389–S399 (2019)
13. Wang, H., Liu, X., Chen, Y.: Separation and imaging of seismic diffractions using a localized rank-reduction method with adaptively selected ranks. Geophysics **85**, V497–V506 (2020)
14. Bansal, R., Imhof, M.: Diffraction enhancement in prestack seismic data. Geophysics **70**, 73–79 (2005)
15. Protasov, M.I., Reshetova, G.V., Tcheverda, V.A.: Fracture detection by Gaussian beam imaging of seismic data and image spectrum analysis. Geophys. Prospect. **64**, 68–82 (2016)
16. Bakulin, A., et al.: Nonlinear beamforming for enhancement of 3D prestack land seismic data. Geophysics **85**, V283–V296 (2020)
17. Berkovitch, A., Belfer, I., Hassin, Y., Landa, E.: Diffraction imaging by multifocusing. Geophysics **74**, WCA75–WCA81 (2009)

An Integrated and Cooperative Approach Between Regional and Local Public Authorities to Sustainable Development: City Logistics Projects in Calabria

Francesco Russo[1]([✉]), Giuseppe Iiritano[2], Giovanna Petrungaro[2], and Maria Rosaria Trecozzi[2]

[1] Department of Information Engineering, Infrastructure and Sustainable Energy, Reggio Calabria University, Reggio Calabria, Italy
francesco.russo@unirc.it
[2] Office of Infrastructures and Public Works, Catanzaro, Calabria, Italy

Abstract. The freight transport is essential to the functioning of cities, but impacts on sustainability and its effects negatively affecting urban development. In more cities, this problem has motivated public administrators to plan, program and executed a process to realize integrated interventions of urban logistics by CO_2 free zones. The aim is to reduce the negative effects and to improve individual and collective well-being in urban areas. Few Regions at EU level have implemented an integrated and cooperative approach to plan and program urban logistics interventions. An experimental case study is analyzed regarding a Region in Southern Italy. The collaborative process of regional and cities authorities produces the realization of city logistics projects in the cities of Calabria and in some towns with a strong tourist attraction that have traffic problems at certain times of the year. In terms of sustainable development, the results of city logistics projects are reduction of freight flows and of polluting emissions, with the increase of low-emission vehicles. The example of Calabria Region is a good practice to facilitate urban policies towards sustainability according to Agenda 2030, too.

Keywords: City logistics · Urban strategies · Sustainable development · Agenda 2030 · Public engagement · Cooperative process

1 Introduction

The urban freight transport has acquired, in the last decades, growing importance: it is an essential service for citizens because it is the main component of the supply chain and therefore of the commercial activities on one side and of the consumers on the other. The increasing number of deliveries and freight vehicles in residential areas generates heavy impacts on city sustainability and livability, also due to the Covid-19 pandemic [1, 2].

O. Gervasi et al. (Eds.): ICCSA 2022 Workshops, LNCS 13382, pp. 572–584, 2022.
https://doi.org/10.1007/978-3-031-10592-0_41

The freight transport involves air and noise pollution, congestion, energy consumption, deterioration of architecture, safety problems, etc. It contributes to non-sustainable effects on [3–6]: environment, economy, society.

Environment, economy and society are the three fundamental components of sustainable development introduced in 1987 in the Our Common Future report, better known as the Brundtland Report [7].

Sustainable development is the focus of policies and strategies adopted at international level. In 2015, UN affirmed this principle by strengthening and integrating it into a program of action for people, the planet and prosperity by Agenda 2030 [8, 9].

At European level some documents that push for sustainable transport are Action Plan on urban mobility [10], the Europe 2020 strategy [11], Transport White Paper [12] Moreover, in 2019 the European Commission has product the Country Report for Italy [13]. The goals with regard to the sustainability of transport are 2, 3 and 5.

Public authorities are primarily responsible for livable cities, where people and goods move in urban areas, and they should to work to plan movements while reducing impacts. To tend a cleaner and sustainable city they should be inspired by the Agenda 2030 also for urban freight transport and logistics.

The goal is to find a shared planning solution that satisfies the many actors involved with different perceptions and objectives [14–16]. Traditionally, public authorities promote city logistics initiatives [17]. Higher authorities also can have a role of moral suasion and can encourage the development of plans and projects at the lower authorities by and integrated approach finalized to sustainable cities [18–20]. In Italy, some example are Emilia-Romagna Region [21] and Municipality of Milano [22].

The literature shows a lack of an integrated and cooperative vertical approach between public administrations of different levels to tackle the problems deriving from urban freight transports respect to a sustainable development prospective.

Regions often have the financial resources to implement sustainable development programs, but they do not have the executive role. On the other hand, cities have the executive role, but often do not have adequate resources. The problem is how to find the correct balance between regional decision-making and cities decision-making. More generally, the problem always arises between administrations of different levels.

The paper shows how to build and realize a way towards CO2 free zones in general planning process [23, 24] through and integrated and cooperative approach. The central theme is to connect different urban centers, without obligation, within a general framework of sustainability, starting to city logistics, but also looking at the other aspects of the city linked with sustainable development.

The paper describes the technical-administrative path that leads to the realization of city logistics projects starting from the delimitation of the areas where freight traffic is regulated, named City Logistics Areas (CLA). The case study is Calabria Region, in Southern Italy. The paper reports what the results are obtained from the realization of city logistics projects by time windows, dedicated no material and material infrastructures, use of low-emission vehicles. The results are respect to estimates of the reduction of affects between actual and project scenario in terms of reduction of freight flows, emissions and economic costs.

In Calabria, it is interesting to implement an integrated approach, because there are several relatively small cities and towns, with the exception of Reggio Calabria (in the South) which about 200,000 inhabitants and the considered urban areas have similar problems. In this way, Sect. 2 reports the city logistics process and the description of all its components starting from indications given by the Regional Transport Plan. Section 3 reports public engagement activities. Section 4 describes the main characteristics of city logistics projects and their territorial impacts. Section 5 reports the conclusions.

2   City Logistics Process

Calabria Region has developed, from Regional Transport Plan (RTP), a way to promote city logistics initiatives at local level to get to zero CO_2 emissions by 2030, according to Agenda 2030, the EU and the Italian directions for sustainable development, and ready projecting itself towards the European policy objectives 2021–2027 [25].

The RTP supports regional policies for the transport and logistics system, in the medium and long term. The RTP defines a general vision that consist of 4 goals [26]: economic development; external accessibility; internal accessibility; sustainability.

According to the goals, RTP defines 10 strategic objectives and actions and 100 operational measures, 10 for each action (see Fig. 1). In particular, objective 2 Urban areas, concerns the strengthening of infrastructures and services in urban areas. Among the 10 related measures, measure 2.5 refers to City logistics [27].

The way toward CO2 free zones in urban areas is according to measure 2.5 of RTP, by a technical-administrative path integrating the responsibilities that each public actors has respect to city logistics. Other initiatives of RTP pushes to reduce CO2 emissions in a general framework to increase the livability of cities, as Green and Safety School for traffic-free, green ad equipped areas near schools [28].

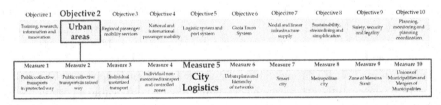

Fig. 1. RTP and city logistics

Calabria Region, as promoter and financier, has designed and realized technical and administrative process, according to indications of international authorities. The path includes the process evolution from planning, to programming, executing and Public Engagement [29, 30].

The cities and towns, as decision makers and actuators, have designed the interventions for the city logistics (see Table 1) and, after their realization with the programmed resources of the Region, they are responsible for management and monitoring.

The results of the monitoring must be returned to the Region carrying out a general monitoring. Figure 2 shows the activities of the Region with the documents accompanying each activity (on the top), and the activities of a generic local authority (on the bottom).

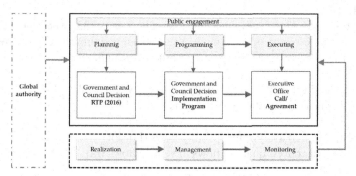

Fig. 2. City logistics activities

Table 1. City logistics interventions

Group	Interventions
Supply regulation	Time windows
	Accesses by dimensions of vehicles
	NDA*- proximity logistics areas
	UDC** - integration with long-distance intermodal transport
Infrastructures	Parking network realization (booking)
	NDA and UDC realization
	Pick-up Point realization
ICT and ITS	App or services for access control
	App or services for parking control (booking)
	Freight traffic control
Vehicles	Enhancement of zero impact fleets
	Access by environmental performance

* NDA = Nearby Delivery Area, ** UDC = Urban Distribution Center

The Region has published 2 Calls (Call 2018 and 2019) to define the rules to grant financing corresponding to: local authority that can submit a project, fund respect to the size of CLA, interventions of projects, can be (see Table 2), minimum level of project, can be (see Table 3 and Table 4), selection of projects to assign the funds on three classes of criteria.

Then, a local authority who wants to participate in the call must submit a project proposal with Type 1 or Type 2 interventions, and understand even fixed time windows in the Call 2018 or time windows and ITS in the Calls 2019 that regulate traffic flows in the CLA [31, 32].

Each project submitted is evaluated by assigning a score [33]. The score is assigned respect to ex ante estimate of variation between actual and project scenario by a set of indicators. The fund is assigned to projects in order score until the programmed resources are exhausted.

The cities and towns have been analyzed to draw a typical profile. The modelling system applied is a combination of two levels [34, 35]:

- commodity level, to analyze the quantity flows (Eq. 1);
- vehicle level, to convert quantity flows in vehicle flows (Eq. 2).

By a zoning, o is the origin zone and d is the destination zone, H is the period, $Q_{od}^H[s]$ is the average quantity flow of goods of type s generated by o; $Q_{.d}^H[s]$ is the quantity of goods s attracted by d, named attraction model; $p^H[o/ds]$ is the probability that goods s, attracted by d, arrive from o, named acquisition model.

Commodity level can be formalized:

$$Q_{od}^H[s] = Q_d^H[s] \cdot p^H[o/ds] \tag{1}$$

The average flow of commercial vehicles of type i is $VC_{o,d}^{iH}[s,m]$ related to the type of service m; p[m/ods] is the probability that the goods s, attracted by d, arrive from o and are distributed by type of service m, named service model; p[i/mods] is the whole model and calculates the probability that the goods s, attracted by d, arrive from o, are distributed by service m and vehicle i; q_{sm}^i is the quantity of goods s delivered by service m and vehicle i.

Vehicle level can be formalized

$$VC_{od}^{iH}[s, m] = \frac{Q_{od}^H[s] \cdot p[m/ods] \cdot p[i/mods]}{q_{sm}^i} \tag{2}$$

Table 2. City logistics interventions financeable

Group	Interventions	Type 1	Type 2
Supply regulation	Time windows	X	
	Accesses by dimensions of vehicles	X	
	NDA* - proximity logistics areas		X
	UDC** - integration with long-distance intermodal transport		X
Infrastructures	Parking network realization (booking)		X
	NDA and UDC realization		X
	Pick-up Point realization		X
ICT and ITS	App or services for access control	X	
	App or services for parking control (booking)	X	
	Freight traffic control		X
Vehicles	Enhancement of zero impact fleets		X
	Access by environmental performance		X

* NDA = Nearby Delivery Area,** UDC = Urban Distribution Centers

Table 3. Type 1: Time windows

Vehicle	Load	Engine	Euro	Time windows
N1, N2	Up to 12 t	Combustion	Up to 6	Max 3 h in 6 am–22 pm
N3	Over 12 t	Combustion	Up to 6	Possible in 22 pm–6 am With authorization on path and time
Lx (freight)		Combustion	Up to 6	Max 4 h in 6 am–22 pm

Table 4. Type 2: Time windows

Vehicle	Load	Engine	Euro	Time windows
All	All	Electric		Transit always open
N1, N2	Up to 12 t	Combustion	6	Max 3 h in 6 am–22 pm Max 4 h in 22 pm–6am
N1, N2	Up to 12 t	Combustion	Up to 5	Possible in 22 pm–6 am With authorization on path and time
N3	Over 12 t	Combustion	Up to 6	Possible in 22 pm–6 am With authorization on path and time
Lx (freight)		Combustion	Up to 6	Closed to transit

3 Public Engagement

Calabria Region has developed a prototypical Public Engagement process (PE) as a part of the technical and administrative path realized for city logistics to give a scientific support in addition to the financial one.

In the planning and design of transport systems, PE is usually activated at international level for big infrastructures. The process in Italy is regulated by specific norms in the national law for public works. In these cases, PE would like to search a transparent decision-making process with the involvement of the interested parties, against a DAD approach (Decide, Announce, Defend) that could have induced NIMBY-like behavior [36]. The PE is requested, in fact, only for railway and motorway belonging to TEN-T [37, 38], and any application exists for diffuse intervention as the one of city logistics.

The PE guaranteed participation and sharing of the choices, but at the same time increase knowledge and skills [39, 40]. In Calabria, it often happens that the decision-makers have little knowledge of urban logistics and its impacts, but the knowledge is important to solve the problem of the freight distribution. Calabria Region supported the decision-makers with dissemination of models and methods to analyze the current scenario and design the future one.

The PE was developed as training activities in discussion-based form, through meetings characterized by the active participation of the stakeholders involved. The parts have been chosen based on a potential profile of knowledge and skills, which had to be, from time to time, consistent with the specific aspect of the city logistics treated, to guide and maximize the effectiveness of the expected result. All the training activities have provided for by the discussion-based model have been carried out with increasing complexity from seminars, workshops, tabletops and games [30].

4 Territorial Results

The proposals project submitted at Call 2018 were 6, 3 of which funded. They are the proposal projects of some of the cities and largest towns with more than 30,000 inhabitants: Rende, Vibo and Reggio.

The proposals project submitted at Call 2019 were 7, 6 of which have been funded. They are the proposal projects of others cities with more than 30,000 inhabitants: Corigliano Rossano and Catanzaro; and of touristic towns with less 30,000 inhabitants and characterized by high flows of tourism: Paola, Fiumefreddo, Pizzo and Tropea.

After Ricadi, which is the first destination in Calabria with about 1 million of visitors per year but with a specific tourist typology linked to the high number of sea villages, Corigliano Rossano is among the main tourist destinations with more 550,000, as well as Pizzo and Tropea with almost 300,000. Moreover, Corigliano Rossano, Catanzaro, Rende, Vibo and Reggio are among the 8 largest cities in Calabria. Thus, the projects of 5 of the 8 largest cities were financed.

After the admission to financing, the Region has signed the agreements with the winning local authorities. The agreement regulates the relationships between the entities including the monitoring frequency of the project, the results of which must be transmitted to the Region for general monitoring.

The agreement also establishes that the local authority draws up an executive project, which, according to Italian law, is the most detailed project level on the basis of which it is possible to start the procedures for carrying out the interventions.

Respect to the Call 2018, Rende has closed the executive project, named Rende City port [41], and is in the realization phase. Reggio has closed the final projects, named Reggio Calabria City Log, with a lower level of detail than the executive [42]; Vibo is currently preparing the executive project.

Respect to Call 2019, executive projects have been closed and are under realization for Corigliano Rossano, named ZTL merci [43], Fiumefreddo, named Fiumefreddo Bruzio Eco-Logistic-City [44], Paola, named Paola Inblue [45], Pizzo, named Pizzo city logistic [46] e Tropea, named Tropea city log [46]. Catanzaro is currently approving the final project.

In Table 5 are reported the main characteristics of total Calabria Region and the same characteristics for the set of cities and towns for which are proposed projects of city logistics. In 2021, the people in Calabria were almost 2 million in 404 urban municipalities, of which about 618,000 in 8 largest cities. By the calls, the 23% of people and the 67% of people in largest cities is affected of city logistics projects, where the effects of the freight transport on sustainability are greater for the high concentration of the people, employees, retailers and all the other services present.

Table 6 reports the main characteristics of the cities and towns interested by the projects, the territorial intervention included in the projects: NDA, UDC and ITS. All projects have the intervention of supply regulation as the minimum time windows indicated by the calls. In Table 6 V is Vibo, R is Reggio; R is Rende; Corigliano Rossano is CR; F is Fiumefreddo; Pa is Paola; Pi is Pizzo; T is Tropea.

Except Reggio, all projects have obtained the maximum allowable amount because they have established a large CLA. Respect to interventions, all projects are Type 2 and respected the minimum level for time windows. Except Reggio, all projects include the realization of at least 1 NDA or UDC. All the projects of the Call 2018 provide for the use of ITS for the control and monitoring of flows which, on the other hand, is mandatory for the Call 2019.

Table 5. Main characteristics

	Total			Cities > 30,000 inhabitants		
	Surfaces [hectares]	Inhabitants [number]	Retailers [number]	Surfaces [hectares]	Inhabitants [number]	Retailers [number]
Calabria	1,522,200	1,947,131	45,603	117,913	618,121	14,680
Cities interested	90,041	449,696	10,962	79,993	415,543	9,937
Incidence [%]	5.92	23.10	24.04	67.84	67.23	67.69

Table 6. City logistics characteristics

Project/data	Call 2018			Call 2019					
	VV	RC	R	CZ	CR	F	Pa	Pi	T
Inhabitants [number]	33,455	180,369	35,526	89,065	77,128	2,918	15,688	9,278	6,269
Inhabitants in CLA [number]	4,923	1,200	9,961	14,198	1,481	263	2,283	892	561
Surfaces [hectares]	4,657	23,904	5,500	11,272	34,660	3,206	4,288	2,234	320
Surfaces in CLA [hectares]	124.62	24.2	198.47	175.93	20.8	8.19	36.76	15.35	12
Retailers [number]	915	3,946	1,030	2,275	1,771	73	349	277	326
Retailers in CLA [number]	612	368	426	152	53	6	31	176	168
NDA	2	–	–	2	2	1	1	2	1
UDC	–	–	1	–	–	–	–	–	–
ITS [Y/N]	Y	Y	Y	Y	Y	Y	Y	Y	Y

In Table 7 are reported, for urban areas involved in city logistics projects, the percentage of inhabitants, surfaces and retailers of CLA respect to total areas. From Table 7 emerges that the percentage of inhabitants in CLA respect to total areas varies between 0.67% for RC and 28.04% for R; VV, CZ and Pa have a value of about 15%. The percentage of surfaces varies between 0.06% for CR and 3.75% for T; R has a value of 3.61% and VV of 2.68%; the percentage of retailers varies between 2.99% for CR and 66.89% for V; Pi has a value of 63.54%, T of 51.53% and R of 41.36%.

Table 7. Percentage of inhabitants, retailers and surfaces of CLA respect to total areas

	Call 2018			Call 2019					
	VV	RC	R	CZ	CR	F	Pa	Pi	T
Inhabitants	14,72	0,67	28,04	15,94	1,92	9,01	14,55	9,61	8,95
Surfaces	2,68	0,10	3,61	1,56	0,06	0,26	0,86	0,69	3,75
Retailers	66,89	9,33	41,36	6,68	2,99	8,22	8,88	63,54	51,53

5 Conclusion

Some Regions at EU level have implemented an integrated and cooperative approach to plan and program urban logistics interventions. The case study of Calabria Region is an example of how is possible to realize city logistics projects from integration and cooperation between regional and cities authorities respecting the roles and pursuing the same goal of sustainable development.

Sustainable development and the achievement of the targets defined on an international scale, through differentiated interventions, are among the main objectives of Calabria Region. These targets also reach by intervention to reduce environmental impact of cities. The central theme is to connect different urban centers, without obligation, within a general framework of sustainability, starting city logistics interventions, but also looking at the other aspects of the city.

Calabria Region has promoted initiatives in urban areas to realize CO_2 free zones. The process for city logistics is an example of good practice to facilitate urban policies towards sustainability according to Agenda 2030, too. Another example is Green and safety school that finance the realization of traffic-free zones near schools also equipped.

Starting to RTP, the city logistics process has been implemented to contribute to reduce the negative effects of freight transport and to improve individual and collective well-being in urban areas, in a collaborative approach regional-local authorities.

The responsibilities are different: Calabria Region plans, programs and executes; local authorities realize, manages and monitors. The responsibility returns to the Region, which must receive a feedback of the monitoring data for general monitoring.

At now, 9 projects have been financed, some of which are already underway.

The projects, refers to the institution of CLA, include the time windows or the time windows and ITS mandatory, the realization of NDA or UDC and the use of new electric vehicle.

The estimated result of city logistics projects show that the sum of the interventions contributes to reduce traffic flows and CO_2 emissions.

References

1. Bhatti, A., Akram, H., Basit, H.M., Khan, A.U., Raza, S.M., Naqvi, M.B.: E-commerce trends during COVID-19 Pandemic. Int. J. Future Gener. Commun. Netw. **13**(2), 1449–1452 (2020)
2. Campisi, T., Russo, A., Tesoriere, G., Bouhouras, E., Basbas, S.: COVID-19's effects over e-commerce: a preliminary statistical assessment for some European countries. In: Gervasi, O., et al. (eds.) ICCSA 2021. LNCS, vol. 12954, pp. 370–385. Springer, Cham (2021). https://doi.org/10.1007/978-3-030-86979-3_27
3. Ducret, R.: Parcel deliveries and urban logistics: changes and challenges in the courier express and parcel sector in Europe-the French case. Res. Transp. Bus. Manag. **11**, 15–22 (2014)
4. Visser, J., Nemoto, T., Browne, M.: Home delivery and the impacts on urban freight transport: a review. In: Eighth International Conference on City Logistics, vol. 125, pp. 15–27 (2014)
5. Russo, F., Comi, A.: From city logistics theories to city logistics planning. In: Taniguchi, E., Thompson, R.G. (eds.) City Logistics 3 – Towards Sustainability and Liveable Cities, pp. 329–348. ISTE Ltd, John Wiley and sons, London (2018). ISBN 978-1-78630-207-6
6. Russo, F., Comi, A.: Investigating the effects of city logistics measures on the economy of the city. Sustainability **12**(4), 1439 (2019)

7. WCED - World Commission on Environment and Development: Report of the World Commission on Environment and Development: Our Common Future (1987)

8. United Nations: Transforming our world the 2030 Agenda for Sustainable Development (2015). https://sustainabledevelopment.un.org/content/doments/21252030%20Agenda%20for%20Sustainable%20Development%20web.pdf

9. United Nations: Global indicator framework for the Sustainable Development Goals and targets of the 2030 Agenda for Sustainable Development (2018). https://unstats.un.org/sdgs/indicators/Global%20Indicator%20Framework%20after%20refinement_Eng.pdf

10. European Commission: Action Plan on Urban Mobility. COM (2009) 490 final (2009)

11. European Commission: Communication from the Commission - Europe 2020. A strategy for smart, sustainable and inclusive growth (2010). https://ec.europa.eu/info/business-economy-euro/economic-and-fiscal-policy-coordination/eu-economic-governance-monitoring-prevention-correction/european-semester/framework/europe-2020-strategy_en

12. European Commission: White paper 2011. Roadmap to a Single European Transport Area - Towards a competitive and resource efficient transport system (2011). https://ec.europa.eu/transport/themes/strategies/2011_white_paper_en

13. European Commission: Commission Staff Working Document. Country Report Italy 2019 (2019). https://ec.europa.eu/info/sites/info/files/file_import/2019-european-semester-country-report-italy_en.pdf

14. Behrends, S., Lindholm, M., Woxenius, J.: The impact of urban freight transport: a definition of sustainability from an actor's perspective. Transp. Plan. Technol. 31(6), 693–713 (2008). https://doi.org/10.1080/03081060802493247

15. Witkowski, J., Kiba-Janiak, M.: The role of local governments in the development of city logistics. Procedia Soc. Behav. Sci. 125, 373–385 (2014). https://doi.org/10.1016/j.sbspro.2014.01.1481

16. Katsela, K., Browne, M.: Importance of the stakeholders' interaction: comparative, longitudinal study of two city logistics initiatives. Sustainability 11(20), 5844 (2019). https://doi.org/10.3390/su11205844

17. Benjelloun, A., Crainic, T.G., Bigras, Y.: Towards a taxonomy of city logistics projects. Proc. – Soc. Behav. Sci. 2(3), 6217–6228 (2010). ISSN 1877–0428. https://doi.org/10.1016/j.sbspro.2010.04.032

18. Allen, J., Browne, M., Woodburn, A., Leonardi, J.: The role of urban consolidation centres in sustainable freight transport. Transp. Rev. 32(4), 473–490 (2012). https://doi.org/10.1080/01441647.2012.688074

19. Crotti, D., Maggi, E.: Urban distribution centres and competition among logistics providers: a hotelling approach (2017). FEEM Working Paper No. 17.2017. http://dx.doi.org/10.2139/ssrn.2947584

20. European Commission: City ports project (2003). https://mobilita.regione.emilia-romagna.it/piani-programmi-progetti/progetti-europei/progetti-europei-conclusi-1/city-ports

21. Emilia Romagna Region: Bando Ecobonus veicoli commerciali (2019). https://ambiente.regione.emilia-romagna.it/it/bandi/bandi-2019/bando-ecobonus-2019/bando-ecobonus-veicoli-commerciali-2019

22. Lombardia Region: Bando per la concessione di contributi alle micro, piccole e medie imprese, ai lavoratori autonomi titolari di partita iva ed agli enti del terzo settore per l'acquisto di veicoli a minore impatto ambientale e mezzi di mobilità non alimentati con motore endotermico (2020). https://web.comune.milano.it/dseserver/webcity/garecontratti.nsf/WEBAll/04F1E41CA50FA4B7C12585B3004877C0?opendocument&fbclid=IwAR1CA7ShNpFcuWcU4wOi723jJG0u0y9OXVOwYK0mEjXkNdhhZmgehdbONho

23. Russo, F., Comi, A.: A state of the art on urban freight distribution at European scale. In: Proceedings of the European Conference on Mobility Management (2004)

24. Russo, F., Pellicanò, D.S.: Planning and sustainable development of urban logistics: from international goals to regional realization. WIT Trans. Ecol. Environ. **238**, 59–72 (2019). WIT. The Sustainable City XIII, ISSN 1743-3541. http://dx.doi.org/10.2495/SC190061

25. Calabria Region: Regional Transport Plan (2016). http://portale.regione.calabria.it/website/organizzazione/dipartimento6/subsite/pianoregionale/

26. Russo, F., Rindone, C.: Regional transport plans: from direction role denied to common rules identified. Sustainability **3**(16), 1–15 (2021). http://dx.doi.org/10.3390/su13169052

27. Russo, F., Iiritano, G., Petrungaro, G., Trecozzi M.R.: Regional transportation plan of the calabria: the mobility in urban areas. Transp. Res. Proc. **60**, 156–163(2022). ISSN 2352-1465. https://doi.org/10.1016/j.trpro.2021.12.021

28. Iiritano, G., Petrungaro, G., Trecozzi, M.R.: Limited traffic zone for walk safety around the schools. Transp. Res. Proc. **60**(2022), 204–221 (2022)

29. Trecozzi, M.R, Iiritano, G., Petrungaro G.: Liveability and freight transport in urban areas: the example of the Calabria region for city logistics. Transp. Res. Proc. **60**, 116–123 (2022). ISSN 2352–1465. https://doi.org/10.1016/j.trpro.2021.12.016

30. Russo, F., Calabrò, T., Iiritano, G., Pellicanò, D.S., Petrungaro, G., Trecozzi, M.R.: City logistics between international vision and local knowledge to sustainable development: the regional role on planning and on public engagement. Int. J. Sustain. Dev. Plan. **15**(5), 619–629 (2020). https://doi.org/10.18280/ijsdp.150504

31. Calabria Region: City Logistics (2018). portale.regione.calabria.it/website/portaltemplates/view/view_bando.cfm?2279

32. Calabria Region: City Logistics (2019). www.regione.calabria.it/website/portaltemplates/view/view_bando.cfm?2998

33. FEMA: Homeland Security Exercise and Evaluation Program (HSEEP) (2007). https://hseep.dhs.gov/pages/1001_HSEEP7.aspx

34. Russo, F., Comi, A.: A general multi-step model for urban freight movements. In: Proceedings of European Transport Conference—PTRC 2002, London, England (2002)

35. Russo, F., Comi, A.: The simulation of shopping trips at urban scale: attraction macro-model. Proc.-Soc. Behav. Sci. **39**, 387–399 (2012)

36. Cascetta, E., Pagliara, F.: Public engagement for planning and designing transportation systems. Proc. Soc. Behav. Sci. **87**, 103–116 (2013)

37. European Union: Regulation (EU) No 1315/2013 on guidelines for the development of the trans-European transport network (2013)

38. European Union: Regulation (EU) No 1316/2013 establishing the Connecting Europe Facility (2013)

39. Dablanc, L., Diziain, D., Levifve, H.: Urban freight consultations in the Paris region. Eur. Transp. Res. Rev. **3**(1), 47–57 (2011). https://doi.org/10.1007/s12544-011-0049-2

40. Rubini, L., Della Lucia, L.: Governance and the stakeholders' engagement in city logistics: the SULPiTER methodology and the Bologna application. Transp. Res. Proc. **30**, 255–264 (2018). ISSN 2352-1465. https://doi.org/10.1016/j.trpro.2018.09.028

41. Rende Municipality: City port (2020). https://archivio.comune.rende.cs.it/albo-online/archivio/?action=visatto&id=7315

42. Reggio Calabria Municipality: Reggio Calabria City Log (2021). http://albopretorio.reggiocal.it/AlboPretorio/index.jsp?ente=RDAQmwbyjKvqrtFikDsl

43. Corigliano Rossano. ZTL merci (2021). https://corigliano-rossano.halleyweb.it/c078157/mc/mc_p_dettaglio.php

44. Fiumefreddo Municipality: Fiumefreddo Bruzio Eco-Logistic-City (2021). http://albofiumefreddobruzio.asmenet.it/alle gati.php?id_doc=13110105&sez=&data1=13/01/2021&data2=28/01/2021

45. Paola Municipality: Paola Inblue (2021). http://paola-service.webgenesys.it:8080/apolfo/ArchivioController?command=visualizzaAtto&codiceAtto=2179

46. Pizzo Municipality: Pizzo city logistic (2020). http://albopizzo.asmenet.it/cercaArchivio. php?arch=ok&sez

47. Tropea Municipality: Tropea city log (2021). http://albotropea.asmenet.it/algati.php?id_doc= 29120957&sez=&data1=29/09/2021&data2=14/10/2021

Geotechnologies for Geological Mapping at the State of Tocantins/Brazil

Pedro Benedito Casagrande[1](✉) ⓘ, Diego Guilherme da Costa Gomes[2] ⓘ,
Jonas de Oliveira Laranjeira[3] ⓘ, and Ítalo Sousa de Sena[4] ⓘ

[1] Escola de Engenharia, Universidade Federal de Minas Gerais (UFMG), Av. Antônio Carlos 6627, Belo Horizonte, Brazil
pcasagrande@demin.ufmg.br

[2] Serviço Geológico Brasileiro (CPRM), Av. Brasil, 1731 - Funcionários, Belo Horizonte, Brazil
diego.gomes@cprm.gov.br

[3] Curso de Pós-Graduação em Eng. de Minas, Materiais e Metalúrgica, Escola de Engenharia, Universidade Federal de Minas Gerais (UFMG), Av. Antônio Carlos 6627, Belo Horizonte, Brazil

[4] Postdoctoral Research Virtual Geographic Environments Laboratory, Faculty of Science, Masaryk University, Brno, Czech Republic
desena@mail.muni.cz

Abstract. The study area is surrounding by a enourmos number of gold pannings in the State of Tocantins/Brazil. From this proposal, we present the analysis of the geological mapping with the use of geotechnologies to better know the area. A study and characterization of the area was made, to understand the correlation between the geological features and geophysics, and consequently, the possibility of gold and iron ore occurrence. In addition, it was possible to obtain information on the area using Also Palsar images to better understand the geomorphology and to aid during the field campaign for the geological mapping. The importance of an analysis of the elements that belong in the area of study and how they behave, in order to better know and understand the area and the correlation between field campaign and geotechnologies.

Keywords: Geotechnologies · Geophysics · Geological mapping

1 Introduction

The use of geotechnologies in mining is increasingly developed and with increasingly applications in the process of obtaining mineral occurrences. In turn, the use of geophysical data that calibrate the data obtained in field mapping enables interesting interpretations. Therefore, in a regional character study, in the region of the municipality of Natividade/TO, Brazil, it is possible to observe that the gamma spectrometry data are correlated with the data of traditional geological mapping. From the point of using the geophysical method for the production of local geological materials without the need to perform a systematic mapping, that is, enabling a mapping of targets. From this, it is possible to identify the main contacts that may have mineral occurrences and, with

O. Gervasi et al. (Eds.): ICCSA 2022 Workshops, LNCS 13382, pp. 585–594, 2022.
https://doi.org/10.1007/978-3-031-10592-0_42

this, the financial cost of a field work is extremely low. The local geomorphology, which is directly linked to geological features, are present as conditioning factors in the soil formation, consequently inthe distribution of soils and associated ores.

The work was subdivided into two stages. In the first stage, the field was defined and in the second stage corresponds to the obtaining of aerogeophysical data of gamma spectrometry, extracted from the aerogeophysical survey carried out by the Brazilian Geological Service. Then, these data underwent a processing through geoprocessing techniques aimed at the elaboration of spatialization maps of them.

The aerogeophysical data were interpolated using the minimum curvature method for gamma spectrometry data (K, eU and eTh). Finally, a digital terrain model (DEM) was elaborated, through data extracted from Alos Palsar images,to obtain relief features of interest to the work.

2   Characteristics of the Study Area

The study area is located in the northern region of Brazil, in a place with the presence of depression and local mountains (Fig. 1 & 2). The Upper Tocantins Depression is present in the northern part of the area with soft relief. In turn, the Serra de Natividade, the main geomorphological structure of the area, covers much of it, with high variation of altimetric dimension and slope of the terrain. This geomorphological feature, in its eastern part, is the main area of studies in the area for basic mineral research. This is said, it is possible to observe by the slope of the terrain, the possibility of sediments from the mountain range being driven, by gravity and other methods of detritic flows, to other areas of the area. Therefore, it is possible that the mineral occurrences are of alluvial and coluvionar origin.

The slope of the study area is possible to observe that there are two main saws in the area. One located to the north and the other across the western edge, this area of the eastern part is composed of a gold ore host rock that is leached into the study area by the drains due to the high gradient of the terrain.

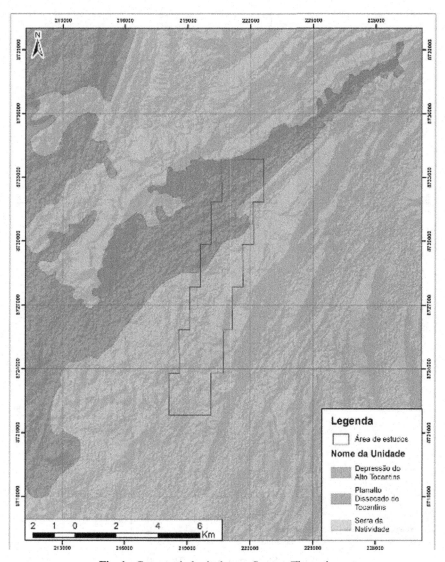

Fig. 1. Geomorphological map. Source: The authors

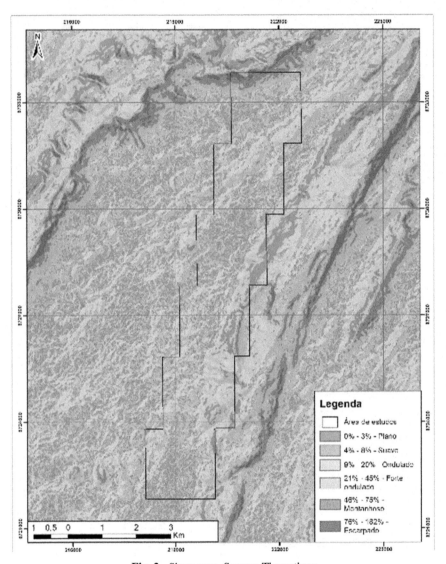

Fig. 2. Slope map. Source: The authors

3 Local Geology

The geological context of the study area is fully inserted within the rocks described in local geology as the Nativity Group. It is considered as the northern extension of the Araí Group (Dardenne, 1999) [1] and the latter, divided into the rift and post-rift phases, called Arraias and Trairas formations, respectively. The correlation with the Araí Group and consequently with the Serra da Mesa Group and Espinhaço Supergroup, inserts the Nativity Group in the processes of rifting of The Sterian Tafrogenesis between 1.8 and 1.6 Ga.

The rocks of the Nativity Group are in disagreement over the basement of granite-gnassic rocks (Almas-Cavalcante Complex and Aurumina Suite) and metavulcano-sedimentary (Riachão do Ouro and Água Suja) rocks and are covered in erosive disagreement by the Parnaíba and São Franciscan abasins.

This unit is distributed in two parts. The smaller eastern part that is not outcropin the area, located mainly north of the city of Almas, has NS structure with inflection to NNW. In images of remote sensors presents foldings clearly transposed by the extensive transcurrent shear zones.

The most expressive western portion, located in the Natividade-Pindorama region, constitutes nne steering range with inflection for NE according to regional structure and with average width of 22 km. It has bent and failed relief with regional slopes and anticline marked by the transcurrent shear zones.

In addition to the sand extension and thickness of the sedimentary package, the east and west sections show differences in relation to sedimentary facies, and in this report only the western outcrop in the area. The metamorphic degree of the sequence reached the green shale facies with formation of shales and quartzites.

From the studies carried out in regional geology, we observed that there are at least 3 geological units of the Nativity Group outcroppers within the studied area. These units were, in the field, inspected throughout the area with careful evaluations regarding their contacts, foliation, primary and secondary structures, degree of alteration, as well as sought evidence of iron ore and gold mineralization. Based on this field stage, it was possible, in addition to identifying reported geological units, subdividing them into domains and making some adjustments to their contacts in the remote sensing phase.

As a final result of this process, the 3 units of regional geology are presented here, with their nomenclature and description originally presented together with their divided domains, related to each of these units, totaling 7 local geological domains with specific characteristics (Fig. 3).

Being the domain located in the mountains to the east the most relevant, since it is place of mineralization of gold and iron.

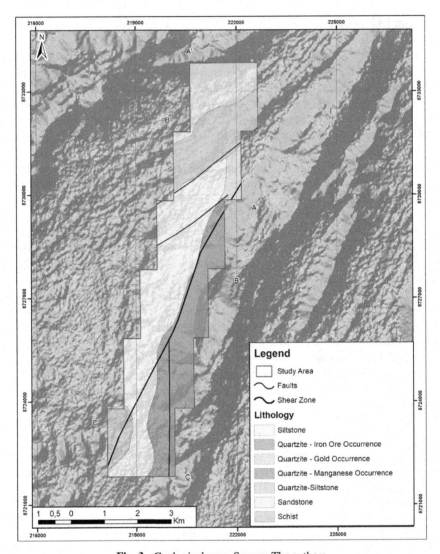

Fig. 3. Geological map. Source: The authors

The central lithology of the NNE/SSW mountain range, present in the study area, has brown soil with the presence of fine sand and drainages along the domain.

In the drains it was possible to locate quartzites, washed quartz pebbles and remnants of mining.

At some points at the foot of the mountain range, ferrous quartzites were observed, with blocks and pebbles of rock with visible presence of iron (Fig. 4 and 5), coming from the same mountain range and with research interest of the source area.

Fig. 4. Iron ore with 56% of Fe (iron). Source: The authors

The northern part of the lithology of the mountain range present in the study area has predominantly quartzite rock, with quartz granules and pebbles. It was possible to observe in drains the presence of washed quartz gravels, in addition to typical excavations of north-south direction mining. Such evidence is close to the eastern edge of the area and in some cases a few tens of meters outside the polygonal area of the study.

In some parts of the drainages located within the area in this domain it was possible to identify gold spots in concentrate, confirming some existence of gold ore that should be investigated further.

20 cm

Fig. 5. Gold spots. Source: The authors

4   Geophysical Studies - Gamma Spectometry - Secondary Data

The gamma spectrometric method detects the natural emission of gamma rays (γ) from surface rocks. This method is widely used in geological mappings due to the different radioactive signatures emitted by the different types of rocks and their minerals (Dentith and Mudge, 2014) [2].

Gamma radiation emission occurs during the process of nuclear disintegration or radioactive decay of an unstable atom whose goal is to achieve a more stable energy state. When two atoms have the same number of protons and different number of neutrons they are called isotopes. Isotopes have the same chemical characteristics, but the differences between their physical properties generate stable or instable isotopes (IAEA, 2003) [3].

In gamma spectrometric surveys the main elements used as a source of gamma radiation are potassium (40K), uranium (238U and 235U) and thorium (232Th). During their decay, these radioisotopes emit high-intensity gamma radiation, which allows the detection of the same.

By geophysical studies, the flight line Dianópolis (Empresas Nucleares Brasileiras S.A - NUCLEBRÁS, 1975) [4], with flight spacing of 2,000 m and interpolated in 500 m, it is possible to observe, in the geological contacts peaks of the U/Th ratio according to Fig. 6.

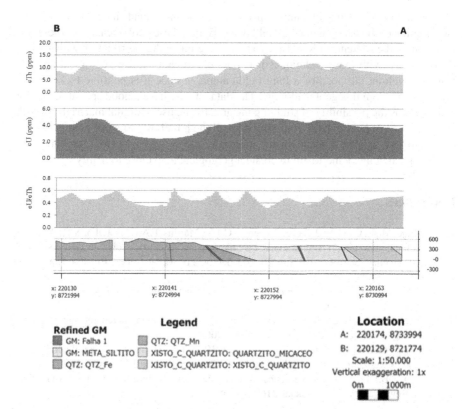

Fig. 6. The U/Tr relation with the geological contacts from the field campain. Source: The authors

This relationship demonstrates that the lithological contacts found in the area are correlated with geophysical data. In turn, the Thorium element is an excellent correlated of ultamafics rocks or even for the presence of environment with hydrothermalism. Therefore, it is possible to observe that there is a high concentration of thorium in the eastern edge and center-north part of the area, close to the occurrences of iron ore, thus validating data obtained in the field and laboratory. In turn, the accumulation of these radioelements caused by secondary variations may indicate the location of gold occurrences (Pires, 1995) [5]. Products that highlight uranium enrichment in the Northeast Region, with the corresponding values to the prospectors.

It is known that uranium anomalies present their genesis associated with shear zones and hydrothermal phenomena. In the mining region, the thorium has one of the lowest values. This high correlation between products derived from gamma spectrometric data and chemical analysis of field samples shows the potential of gamma spectrometry as a tool to indicate areas affected by hydrothermal action.

Finally, the geophysical data corroborate the various analyses performed in this paper.

5   Conclusion

The generation of the map of gamma spectrometric domains made it possible to evaluate the variation of the data obtained in field work. Within these geological units, there were variations in the contents of K, eU and eTh as a function of their correlation with geology.

Currently, with those techniques it is possible to characterize geological areas for mapping without the need of a long field campaign once it is possible to know here exactly to go from this geotechnology. The data already have a good spatial resolution, which means the possibility of studying the area by the use of digital material. Also, the Geophysical is a public data, from this, it let all the possibility to work with.

Finally, we note the demand for attention to the use of digital data to better understand de geological context and to aid to create a geological map close to reality.

References

1. Dardenne, M.A., Campos, J.E.G., Alvarenga, C.J.S., Martins, F.A.L., Botelho, N.F.: A sequên-cia sedimentar do Grupo Araí na região da Chapada dos Veadeiros, Goiás. In: SBG, Simpósio de Geologia do Centro Oeste e Simpósio de Geologia de Minas Gerais. Brasília, Atas, p. 100 (1999)
2. Dentith, M., Mudge, S.T.: Geophysics for the mineral exploration geoscientist, 438p. Cambridge University Press (2014)
3. International Atomic Energy Agency (IAEA). Guidelines for radioelement mapping using gamma ray spectrometry data. Áustria, 173 p. (2003)
4. Empresas Nucleares Brasileiras S.A – NUCLEBRÁS (1975). https://geoportal.cprm.gov.br/portal/apps/webappviewer/index.html?id=ab9142d362c24941840132959df3a179
5. Pires, A.C.B.: Identificação geofísica de áreas de alteração hidrotermal, Crixás-Guarinos, Goiás. Rev. Brasileira Geociências **21**(1), 61–68 (1995)

International Workshop on Workshop on Advanced Mathematics and Computing Methods in Complex Computational Systems (WAMCM 2022)

An Example of Use of Variational Methods in Quantum Machine Learning

Marco Simonetti[1]([✉])[iD], Damiano Perri[1][iD], and Osvaldo Gervasi[2][iD]

[1] Department of Mathematics and Computer Science, University of Florence, Florence, Italy
m.simonetti@unifi.it
[2] Department of Mathematics and Computer Science, University of Perugia, Perugia, Italy

Abstract. This paper introduces a deep learning system based on a quantum neural network for the binary classification of points of a specific geometric pattern (Two-Moons Classification problem) on a plane.

We believe that the use of hybrid deep learning systems (classical + quantum) can reasonably bring benefits, not only in terms of computational acceleration but in understanding the underlying phenomena and mechanisms; that will lead to the creation of new forms of machine learning, as well as to a strong development in the world of quantum computation.

The chosen dataset is based on a 2D binary classification generator, which helps test the effectiveness of specific algorithms; it is a set of 2D points forming two interspersed semicircles. It displays two disjointed data sets in a two-dimensional representation space: the features are, therefore, the individual points' two coordinates, x_1 and x_2.

The intention was to produce a quantum deep neural network with the minimum number of trainable parameters capable of correctly recognising and classifying points.

Keywords: Quantum computing · Variational methods · Deep learning · Quantum feed-forward neural network

1 Introduction

The stages of knowledge in the history of humankind have always alternated between amazement at the immensity of the phenomenon before us and the joyful conquest for the objectives set. The development and introduction into the science of a powerful mathematical arsenal have slowly enabled many obstacles to be overcome, confirming Galileo's intuition that mathematics is the straightforward language that enables us to dialogue with nature. At the beginning of the 20th century, our optimism in positivist determinism was strongly shaken by new phenomena that led to the birth of quantum mechanics. Nevertheless, the observation of the generation of deterministic chaos from models with a seemingly simple apparatus of differential equations and the evident need to describe

O. Gervasi et al. (Eds.): ICCSA 2022 Workshops, LNCS 13382, pp. 597–609, 2022.
https://doi.org/10.1007/978-3-031-10592-0_43

basic molecular structures by simulating them with automatic calculation tools that require ever-increasing computational capabilities are suggesting that the time has come for a profound reflection on our tools of scientific investigation. Feynman stated that describing the reality that surrounds us, which has an intrinsically quantum nature, through a type of computation based on quantum mechanics would be the key to exponentially lowering the computational complexity of the system in question and correctly managing the predictive capacity for the model. We might also add that the introduction of quantum computing machines would also solve the problems related to the imminent reaching of the construction limit of current computers (Amdahl's law), to the possibility of a drastic reduction in the energy required by today's computing machines thanks to computational reversibility, and to the development of nanotechnology.

The possibility of such opportunities has resulted in a growing international interest in such devices, with considerable funding in the relevant research areas. Quantum Computing machines can therefore respond to questions that would be unimaginable for actual old-style apparatuses [1], as they would need the whole Universe's existence time to complete the same task. That is allowed by some quantum peculiarities that show up at the littlest of scales, like Superposition, Entanglement and Interference [2]. Although the theoretical study of quantum algorithms suggests the real possibility of solving computational problems that are currently intractable [3], the current technology has not reached maturity, such as to obtain truly appreciable advantages. We are still in the so-called era of Noisy Intermediate-Scale Quantum (NISQ) [4]. NISQ-devices are noisy and have limited quantum resources; this presents various obstacles when implementing a gate-based quantum algorithm. In order to determine if an implementation of a gate-based algorithm would run effectively on a particular NISQ-device, numerous aspects of circuit implementation, such as depth, width, and noise, should be considered [5,6].

Variational Methods [7,8] are widely used in physics, and most of all in quantum mechanics [9]. Their direct successors, Variational Quantum Algorithms (VQAs), have appeared to be the most effective technique for gaining a quantum advantage on NISQ devices. VQAs are undoubtedly the quantum equivalent of very effective machine-learning techniques like neural networks. Furthermore, VQAs use the classical optimisation toolbox since they employ parametrised quantum circuits to run on the quantum computer and then outsource parameter optimisation to a classical optimiser. In contrast to quantum algorithms built for the fault-tolerant time period, this technique provides the extra benefits of keeping the quantum circuit depth small and minimising noise [10].

The aim is to find the exact, or a well-approximated, parameter values' set that minimises a given cost (loss) function, which depends on the parameters themselves and, naturally, on the input values, x; these are the non-trainable part of the schema. An output measurement apparatus and a parameter modulation circuit serve as regulators (Fig. 1). In our specific case, we are dealing with a n-qubits quantum ansatz, whose transformation is represented by the $n \times n$ unitary matrix U that depends on the vector of parameters θ, with dimensions $m \in \mathbb{N}$

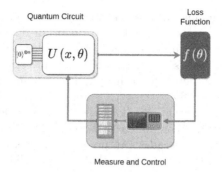

Fig. 1. Scheme

(Eq. (1)); the loss function we refer to is the *expectation value* measured on every single qubit channel (Eq. (3)); the observable is the operator O_i, where Z_i is the Z-Pauli Operator, acting on i-th qubit (Eq. (2)); the quantum state on which to operate the measurements will be the state resulting from the ansatz (ψ in Eq. (1)).

$$\left| \psi\left(\overline{\theta}\right) \right\rangle = U\left(\overline{\theta}\right) \cdot |0\rangle^{\otimes n} \tag{1}$$

$$O_i = Z_i, \quad i \in \{1..n\} \subset \mathbb{N} \tag{2}$$

$$\left\langle E_i\left(\overline{\theta}\right) \right\rangle = \left\langle \psi^\dagger\left(\overline{\theta}\right) \left| O_i \right| \psi\left(\overline{\theta}\right) \right\rangle \tag{3}$$

It is well-known that Quantum Computers can take care of specific issues quicker than traditional ones. As it may, stacking information into a quantum computer is not paltry. It should be encoded in quantum bits (qubits) to stack the information. There are multiple ways qubits can address the data, and, in this manner, various information encodings are conceivable [11]. Several methods can embed data: Basis Encoding [12,13], Amplitude Encoding [14–16], and Angle Encoding [17,18] are the most common to implant information into a firstly prepared quantum state.

Our work aims to explore aspects of the usability of quantum computation in machine learning. Specifically, we sought to compare the performance of a basic FFNN with dense layers and an analogous network composed of quantum components in learning a simple classification problem.

2   Related Works

The possibility of using machine learning techniques in quantum computing has been gaining ground since 2010 [19–21]. The incorporation of quantum algorithms into machine learning programmes is known as quantum machine learning [22–25]. The expression is most commonly used to refer to machine learning methods for evaluating classical data run on a quantum computer. While machine learning techniques are used to calculate vast quantities of data, quantum machine learning employs qubits and quantum operations or specialised quantum systems to speed up computing [26] and data storage [27]. Quantum machine learning also refers to an area of study investigating the theoretical and functional analogies between specific physical systems and learning systems, namely neural networks [28].

Unfortunately, the current technological development does not yet allow the full potential of quantum computers to be expressed, which will only reach maturity in the next few decades. At present, however, it is possible to use quantum computers in feedback circuits that mitigate the effect of various noise components [29,30]. VQAs, which utilise a conventional optimiser to train a parameterised quantum circuit, have been considered an effective technique for addressing these restrictions.

The core part of the computational stage consists of a sequence of gates applied to specified wires in variational circuits. Like the design of a neural network that merely describes the basic structure, the variational approach can optimise the types of gates and their free parameters. In time, the quantum computing community has suggested several variational circuit types that can distinguish three main base structures, depending on the shape of the ansatz: layered gate ansatz [31], alternating operator ansatz [32,33], and tensor network ansatz [34].

The first type of architecture inspired us in implementing our network, trying to keep the network simple, with a minimum number of quantum gates and trainable parameters.

3   The Architecture of the System

Our network has a general structure of this type:

- A first classical dense layer, to accept features as input
- A quantum circuit formed by a succession of rotational and entanglement gates
- A final classical dense layer for classification.

Our quantum structure differs from some other proposals, which encodes input features to transform them into quantum states [35,36]; our initial state, the "prepared state", is simply $|0\rangle^{\otimes n}$. Our architecture is based on the typical "Prepared State fixed; Ansatz parametrised" model. Several variants exist in the literature, especially the most known *Instantaneous Quantum Polynomial* (IQP) circuits [37]. The initial dense network, which we called *input-layer*, acts as an interface between the input data and the quantum layer; its output directly drives the internal rotations of the quantum state, attributing new values to the rotation angles at each epoch (Fig. 2). Almost all the simulations were conducted using quantum sub-layers consisting of a first stack of rotation gates around the Y-axis of the Bloch's sphere, a second stack of rotation gate around the Z-axis and a chain of cX gates (CNOT) to maximise the entanglement effect. Rotation

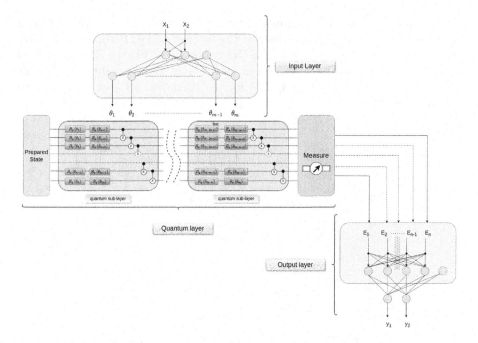

Fig. 2. Architecture of the quantum neural network

operators help primarily to ensure the *expressibility* of a parameterized quantum circuit. That is essentially the total coverage of Hilbert space by the hypothesis space of the ansatz itself [38]. In addition, the chain of CNOT operators is tasked with maximising the entanglement effect of individual qubits, as the entanglement phenomenon plays a crucial role in quantum computation. This feature is called *Entangling Capability* [39].

An authentic advantage is that the network's response remains independent of the number of qubits. The only real quantum noise that remains is due to the construction and constitution of the ansatz and the device, or simulator, used for experimentation.

3.1 Data Extraction and Processing

The database chosen for the classification problem is called *two-moons*, which generates two interleaving semicircles of 2D-points, and is characteristic for the study of clustering and classification algorithms.

The dataset was generated thanks to the dedicated function from the Python Scikit-Learn library[1].

The input domain is $[-2.0, 3.0] \times [-2.0, 2.5] \subset \mathbb{R}^2$. One thousand samples were randomly generated, equally distributed over the two classes. The classes

---

[1] https://scikit-learn.org/stable/index.html.

were initially chosen with a Gaussian Error Coefficient of 0.05: this coefficient quantifies the capacity of separation of the two categories: the higher its value, the greater the degree of overlap of the two classes (Fig. 3). The number of samples in the dataset was divided in such a way as to ensure the following quotas: 70% for the training set, 20% for the validation set and the remaining 10% for the test set.

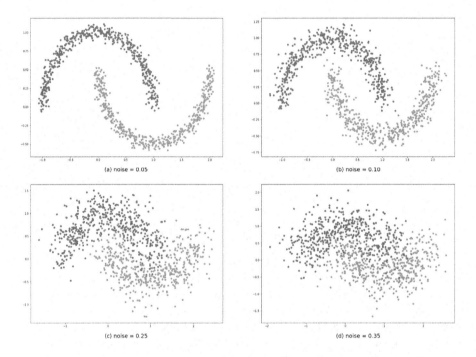

Fig. 3. Distribution of pattern points on the plane in relation to Gaussian Noise

3.2   Model Construction and Validation

Two twin models have been realised in parallel, using for one of them the Python library for quantum simulation Cirq[2] with TensorFlowQuantum[3], by Google, and for the other an open-source Python library, PennyLane[4], by Xanadu, which can be perfectly interfaced with the most famous Deep Learning frameworks, such as Keras, and of course TensorFlow, and PyTorch.

All tests and simulations were performed using the specialised open-source library for Deep Learning, Keras[5].

---

[2] https://quantumai.google/cirq.
[3] https://www.tensorflow.org/quantum.
[4] https://pennylane.ai/.
[5] https://keras.io/.

The TFQ (TensorFlowQuantum) model is composed as follows (Fig. 4a):

- A layer for data input, called *input_layer*.
- A Dense layer, which adapts the input to the number of parameters, in our specific case 16, called *FFNN*.
- A layer for the ansatz input in the form of a tensor, called *qc_layer*.
- A control layer (called *TOTAL*), which receives the two inputs, modulates the values of the parameters and returns, for each wire in the circuit, the expected value.
- A final Dense layer (called *output_layer*), with a number of outputs equal to the number of classes in the dataset, which returns the probability of belonging to them (*softmax* activation).

The PQML (PennyLane Quantum Machine Learning) model is composed as follows (Fig. 4b):

- A layer for data input, called *DATA*.
- A Dense layer, which adapts the input to the number of parameters, in our specific case 16, called *layer1*.
- A custom layer, called *quantum_layer*, designed as a subclass of the Layer class from the Keras library, which receives in input the values of the parameters of the ansatz and returns, for each wire of the circuit, the expected value.
- A final Dense layer (called *output_layer*), with a number of outputs equal to the number of classes in the dataset, which returns the probability of belonging to them (*softmax* activation).

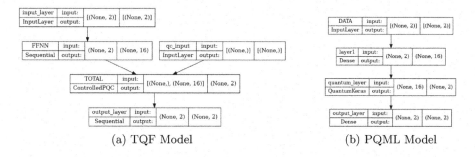

(a) TQF Model   (b) PQML Model

Fig. 4. Quantum neural network models utilised

The number of ansatz parameters is given by the product of the number of qubits, the number of rotation operators acting on each line of the circuit within each sublayer, and the number of sublayers. For our tests and simulations, we have opted to use an ansatz consisting of 4 sublayers to avoid creating an excessive computational load on the quantum layer. By initially constraining the number of qubits to 2 and not introducing any form of noise, we can say that both models proved to be extremely light in terms of the number of trainable parameters: 54 against the 354 of a similar FFNN Fully-Connected, with three layers. The disadvantage is that the simulation run times are about one order of magnitude longer than the latter. In fact, to simulate an ansatz is necessary to operate many matrix products against only one matrix product for a standard dense layer.

The entire model was compiled using a classical optimiser, *SGD* (Stochastic Gradient Descent), with *Mean Absolute Error* as the Loss Function and *Accuracy* as the metric.

3.3   Analysis of Results

The results obtained are excellent. Figure 5 shows the metrics (LOSS: loss function on training set, ACCURACY: accuracy on training set, VAL_LOSS: loss function on validation set, VAL_ACCURACY: accuracy on validation set,) for the TFQ model, trained for 20 epochs, with different values of Gaussian Noise on the dataset generation (legend).

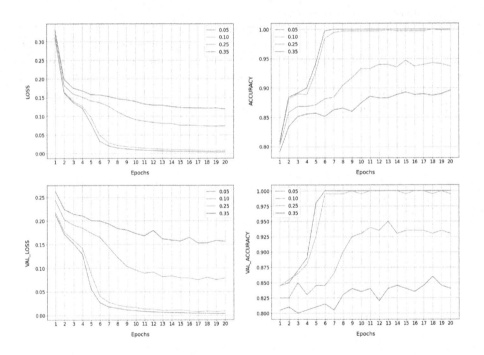

Fig. 5. Metrics for TFQ model

The model achieves 100% accuracy for low-noise datasets and more than 80% accuracy for high-noise datasets.

Table 1. Percentage of correct evaluations on the test set for TFQ model.

| | Samples: 20 / 200 | | | Samples: 100 / 1,000 | | | Samples: 500 / 5,000 | | |
| | n qubits | | | n qubits | | | n qubits | | |
NOISE	2	3	4	2	3	4	2	3	4
0.05	100.0%	95.0%	95.0%	100.0%	100.0%	100.0%	100.0%	100.0%	100.0%
0.10	100.0%	95.0%	95.0%	100.0%	100.0%	100.0%	100.0%	100.0%	100.0%
0.25	95.0%	80.0%	90.0%	93.0%	94.0%	94.0%	93.8%	93.8%	90.0%
0.35	80.0%	75.0%	85.0%	88.0%	86.0%	89.0%	88.4%	88.6%	88.4%

Table 1 shows the percentages of correct evaluations on the test set as a function of the Gaussian Noise on the dataset, the number of qubits used, datasets with different cardinalities (the header of the table shows the number of samples of the test set on the number of total samples). It is referred to TFQ model.

Figure 6 shows the usual metrics for the PQML model, trained for 20 epochs, with different values of Gaussian Noise on the dataset generation (legend).

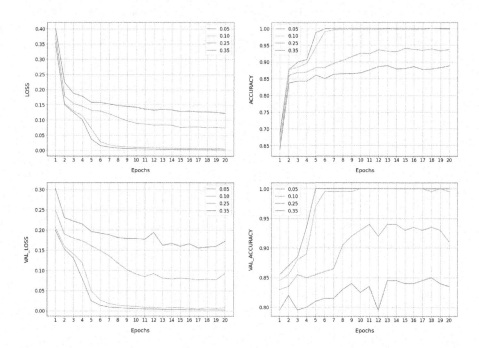

Fig. 6. Metrics for PQML model

The model achieves 100% accuracy for low-noise datasets and beyond 80% accuracy for high-noise datasets.

Table 2. Percentage of correct evaluations on the test set for PQML model.

NOISE	Samples: 20 / 200 n qubits			Samples: 100 / 1,000 n qubits			Samples: 500 / 5,000 n qubits		
	2	3	4	2	3	4	2	3	4
0.05	100.0%	100.0%	95.0%	100.0%	100.0%	100.0%	100.0%	100.0%	100.0%
0.10	95.0%	100.0%	95.0%	100.0%	100.0%	100.0%	100.0%	100.0%	100.0%
0.25	95.0%	100.0%	80.0%	94.0%	93.0%	94.0%	94.8%	94.0%	93.8%
0.35	75.0%	90.0%	75.0%	87.0%	88.0%	86.0%	88.2%	88.4%	87.2%

Table 2 shows the percentages of correct evaluations on the test set as a function of the Gaussian Noise on the dataset, the number of qubits used, datasets with different cardinalities (the header of the table shows the number of samples of the test set on the number of total samples). It is referred to PQML model.

Figure 7 shows the usual metrics for a simple FFNN Fully-Connected, three dense layers, with the same inputs and output as quantum networks, trained for 20 epochs and with 354 trainable weights. Without the use of regularisers or drop-out layers, an early overfitting of the model can be observed.

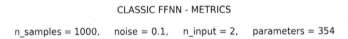

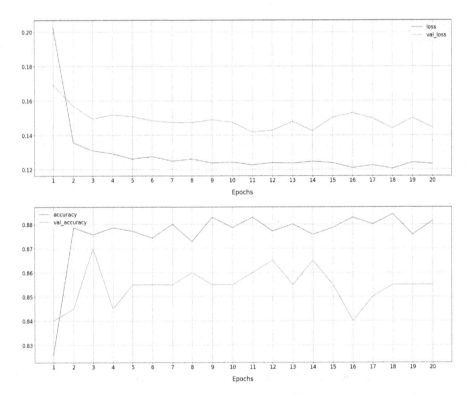

Fig. 7. Metrics for an analogue FFNN

4   Conclusions and Future Works

The two models exhibit remarkably similar tendencies, demonstrating their quality and validity.

Interestingly, unlike an analogous FFNN, a quantum network, since it contains only unitary transformations, can reduce the overfitting phenomenon without the necessity of introducing any particular regularizers or drop-out layers (at least for certain values of ansatz depth).

In our future works, we intend to continue our investigations into quantum neural networks, working on various fronts: new datasets, different ansatz topologies, optimisers and loss functions. Since we focused our attention on some implementation aspects in this paper, ending up working on quantum simulators, we intend to conduct further tests on real machines (e.g. IBM Quantum Experience or Google's Sycamore). We would like to understand better the real effects of quantum noise on circuits.

References

1. Deutsch, D., Jozsa, R.: Rapid solution of problems by quantum computation. Proc. Roy. Soc. London. Ser. A: Math. Phys. Sci. **439**(1907), 553–558 (1992)
2. Grover, L.K.: Quantum mechanics helps in searching for a needle in a haystack. Phys. Rev. Lett. **79**(2), 325 (1997)
3. Shor, P.W.: Polynomial-time algorithms for prime factorization and discrete logarithms on a quantum computer. SIAM Rev. **41**(2), 303–332 (1999)
4. Preskill, J.: Quantum computing in the NISQ era and beyond. Quantum **2**, 79 (2018)
5. Leymann, F., Barzen, J.: The bitter truth about gate-based quantum algorithms in the NISQ era. Quantum Sci. Technol. **5**(4), 044007 (2020)
6. Salm, M., Barzen, J., Leymann, F., Weder, B.: About a criterion of successfully executing a circuit in the NISQ era: what wd $\ll 1/\epsilon$ eff really means. In: Proceedings of the 1st ACM SIGSOFT International Workshop on Architectures and Paradigms for Engineering Quantum Software, pp. 10–13 (2020)
7. Zeidler, E.: Nonlinear Functional Analysis and Its Applications: III: Variational Methods and Optimization. Springer, Cham (2013)
8. Smith, D.R.: Variational methods in optimization. Courier Corporation (1998)
9. Borghi, R.: The variational method in quantum mechanics: an elementary introduction. Eur. J. Phys. **39**(3), 035410 (2018)
10. Cerezo, M., et al.: Variational quantum algorithms. Nat. Rev. Phys. **3**(9), 625–644 (2021)
11. Weigold, M., Barzen, J., Leymann, F., Salm, M.: Data encoding patterns for quantum computing. In: Proceedings of the 27th Conference on Pattern Languages of Programs, pp. 1–11 (2020)
12. Vedral, V., Barenco, A., Ekert, A.: Quantum networks for elementary arithmetic operations. Phys. Rev. A **54**(1), 147 (1996)
13. Cortese, J.A., Braje, T.M.: Loading classical data into a quantum computer. arXiv preprint arXiv:1803.01958 (2018)
14. LaRose, R., Coyle, B.: Robust data encodings for quantum classifiers. Phys. Rev. A **102**(3), 032420 (2020)

15. Harrow, A.W., Hassidim, A., Lloyd, S.: Quantum algorithm for linear systems of equations. Phys. Rev. Lett. **103**(15), 150502 (2009)
16. Schuld, M., Fingerhuth, M., Petruccione, F.: Implementing a distance-based classifier with a quantum interference circuit. EPL (Europhys. Lett.) **119**(6), 60002 (2017)
17. Weigold, M., Barzen, J., Leymann, F., Salm, M.: Expanding data encoding patterns for quantum algorithms. In: 2021 IEEE 18th International Conference on Software Architecture Companion (ICSA-C), pp. 95–101. IEEE (2021)
18. Grant, E., et al.: Hierarchical quantum classifiers. NPJ Quant. In. **4**(1), 1–8 (2018)
19. Lloyd, S., Mohseni, M., Rebentrost, P.: Quantum algorithms for supervised and unsupervised machine learning. arXiv preprint arXiv:1307.0411 (2013)
20. Wiebe, N., Kapoor, A., Svore, K.: Quantum algorithms for nearest-neighbor methods for supervised and unsupervised learning. arXiv preprint arXiv:1401.2142 (2014)
21. Lloyd, S., Mohseni, M., Rebentrost, P.: Quantum principal component analysis. Nat. Phys. **10**(9), 631–633 (2014)
22. Perri, D., Simonetti, M., Lombardi, A., Faginas-Lago, N., Gervasi, O.: Binary classification of proteins by a machine learning approach. In: Gervasi, O., et al. (eds.) ICCSA 2020. LNCS, vol. 12255, pp. 549–558. Springer, Cham (2020). https://doi.org/10.1007/978-3-030-58820-5_41
23. Benedetti, P., Perri, D., Simonetti, M., Gervasi, O., Reali, G., Femminella, M.: Skin cancer classification using inception network and transfer learning. In: Gervasi, O., et al. (eds.) ICCSA 2020. LNCS, vol. 12249, pp. 536–545. Springer, Cham (2020). https://doi.org/10.1007/978-3-030-58799-4_39
24. Perri, D., Simonetti, M., Lombardi, A., Faginas-Lago, N., Gervasi, O.: A new method for binary classification of proteins with machine learning. In: Gervasi, O., et al. (eds.) ICCSA 2021. LNCS, vol. 12958, pp. 388–397. Springer, Cham (2021). https://doi.org/10.1007/978-3-030-87016-4_29
25. Perri, D., Simonetti, M., Gervasi, O.: Synthetic data generation to speed-up the object recognition pipeline. Electronics **11**(1), 2 (2021)
26. Yoo, S., Bang, J., Lee, C., Lee, J.: A quantum speedup in machine learning: finding an N-bit Boolean function for a classification. New J. Phys. **16**(10), 103014 (2014)
27. Ouyang, Y.: Quantum storage in quantum ferromagnets. Phys. Rev. B **103**(14), 144417 (2021)
28. Wan, K.H., Dahlsten, O., Kristjánsson, H., Gardner, R., Kim, M.S.: Quantum generalisation of feedforward neural networks. NPJ Quant. Inf. **3**(1), 1–8 (2017)
29. Bharti, K., et al.: Noisy intermediate-scale quantum algorithms. Rev. Mod. Phys. **94**(1), 015004 (2022)
30. Endo, S., Cai, Z., Benjamin, S.C., Yuan, X.: Hybrid quantum-classical algorithms and quantum error mitigation. J. Phys. Soc. Jpn. **90**(3), 032001 (2021)
31. Schuld, M., Killoran, N.: Quantum machine learning in feature Hilbert spaces. Phys. Rev. Lett. **122**(4), 040504 (2019)
32. Farhi, E., Goldstone, J., Gutmann, S.: A quantum approximate optimization algorithm. arXiv preprint arXiv:1411.4028 (2014)
33. Verdon, G., Broughton, M., Biamonte, J.: A quantum algorithm to train neural networks using low-depth circuits. arXiv preprint arXiv:1712.05304 (2017)
34. Huggins, W., Patil, P., Mitchell, B., Whaley, K.B., Stoudenmire, E.M.: Towards quantum machine learning with tensor networks. Quant. Sci. Technol. **4**(2), 024001 (2019)
35. Romero, J., Olson, J.P., Aspuru-Guzik, A.: Quantum autoencoders for efficient compression of quantum data. Quant. Sci. Technol. **2**(4), 045001 (2017)

36. Schuld, M., Bocharov, A., Svore, K.M., Wiebe, N.: Circuit-centric quantum classifiers. Phys. Rev. A **101**(3), 032308 (2020)
37. Shepherd, D., Bremner, M.J.: Instantaneous quantum computation. arXiv preprint arXiv:0809.0847 (2008)
38. Sim, S., Johnson, P.D., Aspuru-Guzik, A.: Expressibility and entangling capability of parameterized quantum circuits for hybrid quantum-classical algorithms. Adv. Quant. Technol. **2**(12), 1900070 (2019)
39. Hubregtsen, T., Pichlmeier, J., Stecher, P., Bertels, K.: Evaluation of parameterized quantum circuits: on the relation between classification accuracy, expressibility, and entangling capability. Quant. Mach. Intell. **3**(1), 1–19 (2021). https://doi.org/10.1007/s42484-021-00038-w

International Workshop on Transport Infrastructures for Smart Cities (TISC 2022)

Sardinia Granite Scraps Application in Road Pavement Layers

J. Rombi⑩, F. Maltinti$^{(\boxtimes)}$ ⑩, and M. Coni⑩

Department of Civil Environmental Engineering and Architecture,
University of Cagliari, 09042 Cagliari, Italy
maltinti@unica.it

Abstract. Sardinia is the second-largest island of Italy after Sicily, in this region, large volumes of granite scraps deriving mainly from the ornamental quarry industry, lie abandoned in stockpiles. The ornamental query industry, very active in the region since the late 1900s, has produced large volumes of granite scraps causing several environmental and landscape issues. Therefore, there is a need to find potential applications for such materials, previously extracted, for which energy has already been consumed and CO_2 emitted. This research focuses on the possibility of introducing granite scraps for road construction processes. Achieving several benefits, ecological by restoring landscape integrity and reducing CO_2 emissions, economical by decreasing road construction costs. For this reason, three types of granite scraps, obtained from the same granitic body using two types of excavation methods and treatment, were studied. In the first phase of the research the evaluation of the environmental compatibility of the scraps, based on Italian regulations, was investigated. Also, chemical, and mineralogical analyses were performed to establish the correct granite family. Mechanical properties were evaluated to assess the possibility of using them to their fullest extent in booth unbound and hydraulically bound pavement layers. From the test conducted useful information were obtained showing how granite scraps, can achieve good physical and mechanical performances if compared with those of natural aggregates normally used in road pavement layers. The test conducted demonstrated how granite scraps can be used with high performances in road pavement structures, contributing to the reduction of quarrying new materials, and introducing a circle economy approach with several benefits for the Sardinian Island.

Keywords: Granite scraps · Recycle · Pavement layers · Circular economy · Quarry waste

1 Introduction

Large volumes of scraps are produced each year during manning and quarrying activities, generating high environmental impacts. The possibility of using quarrying waste materials to create a new product or as admixtures so that natural sources can be preserved or used more efficiently is becoming a challenging field [1, 2]. Many of these

© The Author(s), under exclusive license to Springer Nature Switzerland AG 2022
O. Gervasi et al. (Eds.): ICCSA 2022 Workshops, LNCS 13382, pp. 613–623, 2022.
https://doi.org/10.1007/978-3-031-10592-0_44

materials are considered waste and are not used to the fullest extent for construction purposes, limiting their potential use.

In Sardinia, one of the largest islands of Italy, quarrying activity of marble and granite, used as ornamental and building stones, has been very active in the region for decades [3].

There are 11 types of commercialized granite [4], that differ not only in colour but in some cases for physical and mechanical properties.

Commercial ornamental granite is subjected to many processes like excavation, cutting, polishing and grinding. The yield wastage ratio during processing varies between 65% and 50% depending on the type of granite. It is very important to understand and evaluate what must be considered a waste or what can be considered a by-product evaluating their possible application. Analyzing the data of Sardinia granite quarrying production for ornamental use (see Fig. 1), obtained from the Italian National Institute of Statistics (ISTAT), the estimated average annual production between 2015 and 2019 [5] has been 361000 m^3.

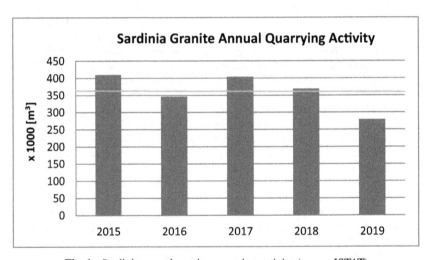

Fig. 1. Sardinia annual granite quarrying activity (source ISTAT)

Assuming that in the next 10 years Sardinian production will remain at the actual average, assuming a yield wastage ratio during the processing of 50%, there will be approximately 1,5 million m^3 of suitable granite scraps. Also, there are over 40 million m^3 of large and medium size shapeless granite by-products already stockpiled, belonging to the past granite query activity. All this stockpiled material, an example can be seen in Fig. 2, is subtracting and will continue to consume land if a solution isn't found. There is a need of possible strategies for limiting the consumption of natural aggregates, as well as the use of recycled aggregates [6]. Possible correlation of the main planning tools regarding extractive activities for geo-resources planning sector, and the urban master plan, to identify environmental indicators, useful for monitoring and for decision support systems [7].

Fig. 2. Granite scraps in the district of Calangianus

Since the commercialization of Sardinia granite has become an organized trade in 1870, there are four leading ornamental quarrying districts: Arzachena-Luogosanto, Tempio-Calangianus, Buddusò-Ala dei Sardi, and Ovodda, such districts are located for the majority on the northeast of Sardinia as shown in Fig. 3.

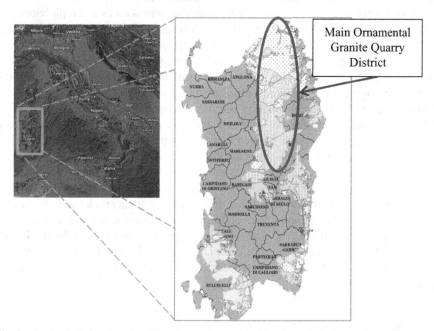

Fig. 3. Geological sketch map of late-hercynian granitoids of Sardinia, in which is highlighted the ornamental quarry district (source Secchi and Lorrai, 2001)

Almost more than 89% of the international quarrying activity is concentrated in nine Countries, each of them producing more than 2 million tons of natural ornamental stones per annum: China, Italy, India, Iran, Spain, Turkey, Brazil, Greece, and Portugal [8].

In this scenario Italy is one of the leading countries for the commercialization of granite, making Sardinian granite account for 75% of Italy's total granite output, although this tendency is drastically decreasing. Some of the major producing countries are researching the possible use of what remains from the many processes to which granite and other ornamental stones are subjected before reaching commercialization.

Mainly the attention is being focused on the use of the fine particles that due to their dimensions can become threatening to human and animal health. The use of such material is being studied to be used as filler in the construction industry.

In Brazil, the possibility of using granite and marble dust deriving from the cutting of the larger blocks has been evaluated. The main objective of the research evaluated the incorporation of these fines as a mineral aggregate in asphalt formation and analyze the performance and compare it with that of basalt rocks [9]. In Turkey studies on how to be able to recycle granite and marble wastes deriving from ornamental quarrying activities are being developed considering both coarse and fine aggregates. The durability of concrete using granite and marble wastes with a maximum nominal size of 19 mm was studied. The results of this study showed that ornamental quarrying wastes deriving from marble and granite can be used to improve the mechanical properties, workability, and chemical resistance of conventional concrete mixtures [10].

The potential use of marble and granite quarrying scraps rocks as a replacement for natural aggregates in civil engineering projects is being studied in many fields [11–13].

There is a high scientific interest to evaluate the possible applications of this type of scrap in many parts of the world because it would be capable of solving many environmental issues resulting from the exhaustion of the natural resources of aggregates.

In this context, the paper focuses the attention on verifying potential applications of granite scraps for road construction purposes and evaluating if different excavation techniques could modify the physical and mechanical behaviour when used in road pavement layers. The research focused its attention on a construction site located on the southeast coast of Sardinia (Sarrabus-Gerrei) in which five natural tunnels were being excavated, in compacted and homogenous granite rocks. The project consisted in the realization of the new road S.S.125 involving three main tunnels plus two service tunnels. The excavated granite was derived from the same mother rock but was subjected to different excavation methodologies and treatment processes, leading to three types of materials to be analyzed. The tunnels were being excavated using a Tunnel Boring Machine (TBM) for the service tunnels while Drilling and Blasting (D&B) technique was adopted for the realization of the three main tunnels. The estimated excavated material resulted in 800000 m^3.

2   Case Study

Three types of granite scraps were tested, in Table 1 are reported the three different types of material. Granite aggregate named by code AG-1 derived from the excavation of the two service tunnels using an open shield TBM machine. The AG-2 material came from the excavation of the main tunnels using D&B technique, such material was subjected to screening and passing a 60 mm sieve.

Also, AG-3 came from the D&B excavation technique, in this case, the larger blocks were reduced in size using a mobile jaw crusher with a feed size ranging from 600–900 mm obtaining a material passing a 50 mm sieve.

Table 1. Granite aggregate scrap samples

Code	Tunnel type	Excavation method	Treatments
AG-1	Service tunnels	TBM	No further treatment
AG-2	Main tunnels	D&B	Screening
AG-3	Main tunnels	D&B	Crushing screening

The samples were collected according to UNI EN 932-1 [14] (Italian national standards institute) specifications for stockpiles. Once in the laboratory, they were reduced according to UNI EN 932-2 [15] specifications to perform further tests. Preliminary tests were conducted to evaluate if the scraps could be environmentally suitable. For this reason, leaching tests were performed to evaluate the permissible concentrations of elemental species according to Italian legislation. To evaluate the uniformity of the geological body, chemical and mineralogical composition was analyzed. A petrographic examination can give general indications of the potential performance of the aggregates. After this preliminary characterization, specific tests were performed to analyze the use of such materials in road pavement layers. Unbound granular layers were analyzed first, gradation of the aggregates was analyzed as one of the factors that most companies use in the selection of the aggregates. Also, Atterberg limits tests were performed to classify the aggregates. To measure aggregates toughness Los Angeles abrasion test was performed. Moisture and density relationship was obtained by performing laboratory compaction using the modified proctor method. Finally, Cement Bound Granular Material (CBGM) layers were studied, and tests conducted to evaluate the performance following the specifications imposed by the Italian National Center of Research (CNR) 29/72 [16]. Specimens were molded using five different percentages of Portland cement contents ranging from 0.5%, 1.5%, 2%, 3% and 3.5%. According to the specifications, it is possible to use cement content of up to 5%. The potential use of coarse granite and marble scraps as replacement soil under foundations has been investigated with good results in Egypt [17]. In this paper granite scraps will be characterized to evaluate potential applications not only in unbound granular layers but also in CBGM layers and the entire mix will be composed of granite scraps. Also, alternative hydraulic binders are being studied in order to partially replace ordinary Portland cement in CBGM layers. The main materials are Fly Ash (FA) and Silica Fume (SF) but also Anhydrous Calcium Solfate (ACS) [18] is being studied. In this research ordinary Portland cement type CEM IV/B 32.5 R was used.

3 Experimental Results

The results obtained from the leaching tests, to evaluate the environmental compatibility of the scraps, were conducted following the Italian legislation and regulation LG.D. n.152/2006 [19] and the D.M. n. 161/2012 [20]. Such regulations give the guidelines on which procedure to use to perform the tests and the list of elements that must be tested with the maximum permissible concentration. The range values of pH, must be between 5.5–12. In Table 2 are reported the obtained average values for pH and conductivity, pH values are inside the imposed range.

Table 2. pH and conductivity values

Code	pH	Cond. (μS/cm)
AG-1	9.95	119.22
AG-2	11.85	755.5
AG-3	9.65	138.00
Blanck	8.95	29.65

Of all the twenty tested elements only Fluoride (F) was over the maximum concentration limit. This value was obtained for samples AG-2 and AG-3. Such values can be attributed to the type and amount of explosives used during the D&B excavation method. Samples collected from AG-1 stockpiles, in which the TBM was used, didn't show any contamination from Fluoride and the other remaining tested elements.

From the geological maps of the region, the granite had to be a Granodiorite. Chemical and mineralogical composition tests were conducted, on the material deriving from the main and the service tunnels to evaluate the uniformity of the geological body. To perform the measurements the granite aggregates were reduced to a granular size of 0.063 mm. In Table 3 is reported the average chemical composition of granite aggregate samples collected from stockpiles.

After this preliminary characterization, physical tests were performed. Particle size distribution was conducted according to UNI-EN 933-1 [21] specification. In Fig. 4 are reported the average particle size distribution of the three materials obtained from the samples collected from different stockpiles. If compared with the grading imposed by the Italian Ministry of infrastructure and transport for unbound granular layers in foundation and base layers, these materials must need further screening to have the correct percentage of aggregate fractions.

Other conducted tests were: density according to UNI EN 1097-6 [22] specification, Atterberg limit according to CNR UNI 10014 [23], abrasion and sand equivalent value according to UNI EN 1097-2 [24].

Table 4 reports the obtained average results from all the collected samples on freshly excavated material and crushed granite scraps.

The values reported in Table 4 show for sample AG-1 values slightly over the limit for Los Angeles Abrasion test that must be 30% or lower. While sample AG-2 and AG-3 didn't reach the minimum value of 40% for the sand equivalent test. To determine

Table 3. Chemical composition of granite

Component	AG-1 (%)	AG-2 (%)
SiO_2	69.69	66.64
TiO_2	0.39	0.52
Al_2O_3	14.43	14.58
Fe_2O_3	3.53	4.46
MnO	0.07	0.08
MgO	1.20	2.07
CaO	2.84	5.09
Na_2O	3.00	2.82
K_2O	3.75	3.50
P_2O_5	0.12	0.15
LOI	1.55	1.09
Total	100.59	101.04

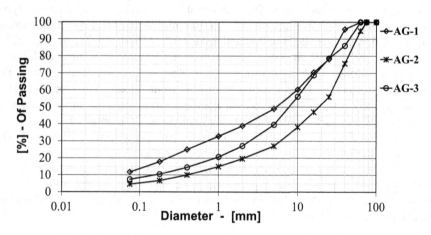

Fig. 4. Particle size distribution of the three types of granite scraps

Table 4. Physical and mechanical properties of granite aggregates

Sample	Particle density (g/cm^3)	Los angeles abrasion (%)	Sand equivalent (%)	Atteberg limit
AG-1	2.65	31.01	40.81	Non-plastic
AG-2	2.66	25.79	39.92	Non-plastic
AG-3	2.66	28.02	37.02	Non-plastic

the bearing capacity of the three granite aggregates tests were performed on unbound granular samples. The preliminary moisture and density relationship was measured by performing a modified Proctor test using specifications UNI-EN 13286-2 [25]. In the tests conducted samples were prepared using each of the three granite scraps and mixing each of the aggregates with six selected water content values: 2%, 4%, 5%, 6%, 8%, and 10%. The average optimum water content and corresponding dry density are reported in Table 5.

Table 5. Optimum water content and dry density mean values

Sample	Dry density (kN/m^3)	Optimum water content (%)
AG-1	21.55	6.50
AG-2	21.30	5.40
AG-3	21.65	6.00

In the next phase, mechanical characteristics were measured on CBGM mix design. A total of n°60 samples were prepared to evaluate the performance following the specifications imposed by the C.N.R. 29/72 protocol. Tests were performed on two types of materials AG-1 n°30 samples and AG-2 n°30 samples. The specimens were molded using five different percentages of Portland cement (CEM IV/B 32.5 R) contents ranging from 0.5%, 1.5%, 2%, 3% and 3.5%. For each chosen percentage of cement, preliminary tests were performed to obtain optimum moisture content and maximum density. The initial water content used was the one obtained from the modified proctor tests. Then the water content was gradually increased when increasing the percentage of cement in the mixtures. Before performing the tests the right grading was obtained.

After seven days of curing time, compressive strength tests were performed. The obtained results are shown in Table 6, in which is reported the compressive strength resistance value and the amount of cement, and water that has been used for each mix. The C.N.R. 29/72 specification imposes that the compressive strength value must be between 2.50 and 4.50 MPa. These values are reached for booth aggregates with a low percentage of cement 2.0%.

4 Data Analysis

Evaluating the environmental compatibility of such aggregates, the tests have shown that in some cases the processes to which these materials are subjected can contaminate them. The results obtained from the leaching tests have proven that aggregates AG-2 and AG-3 have a concentration of Fluoride (F) over the concentration limit (1.5 mg/l). This can be attributed to the type and amount of explosive that was used during the D&B excavation phase, which it has contaminated the aggregates during the explosion. For this reason, the washing of the aggregates could be considered in order to reduce such contamination inside the imposed limits. The pH values that were measured showed that all the three materials were always in the imposed limit range. Values of pH like the one

Table 6. Compressive strength tests mean values

Sample	Cement content (%)	Water content (%)	Compressive strength (MPa)
AG-1	0.50	6.60	1.05
	1.50	6.70	1.62
	2.00	6.80	3.28
	3.00	7.10	4.19
	3.50	7.30	5.16
AG-2	0.50	5.60	1.03
	1.50	5.70	2.46
	2.00	5.90	2.79
	3.00	6.30	3.73
	3.50	6.50	5.34

obtained for AG-2 aggregate have been measured when performing leaching tests on granite fines deriving from gang saw [26]. Test conducted on the three types of granite by-products to evaluate the possible application for unbound layers has shown that first of all the process to which they are subjected can influence the grading but also the shape. Following the results from the particle size distribution, it is possible to establish that aggregates deriving from TBM have a content in fines that is in the range of 10% more if compared with the other two types of aggregates. Analyzing the values obtained from the modified Proctor test it is possible to see that these values can be related to the particle size distribution of the three aggregates. In AG-1, the optimum water content values has an average value of 6.5% while dry density is 21.55 kN/m^3. This can be related to the presence of more fines, which not only absorb more water they tend to fill the voids in the coarse aggregate acting as workability agents and improving dry density values. Also, the slightly higher values obtained performing the Los Angeles abrasion tests on AG-1 aggregates can be explained by the shape. They have a flat and elongated form, that tends to disaggregate more easily. Following the results from the Atterberg limit test, the three types of aggregates resulted non plastic. The sand equivalent value for AG-2 and AG-3 didn't achieve the minimum value of 40% for foundation layers.

The tests conducted on CBGM specimen have shown, according to the specifications, that the two types of granite scrap tested, AG-1 and AG-2, achieved excellent compressive strength values with low cement content only 2%.

5   Conclusions

It is possible to state that granite scraps can be considered a valid alternative to natural aggregates currently used in Sardinia for road construction purposes. More specifically, the potential use in both unbound and hydraulically bound pavement layers has high-lighted in some cases issues that can be easily solved. First of all, despite the pavement layer we want to introduce the scraps, washing the aggregates must be performed to reduce Fluoride contamination when it appears. Following the results from the tests conducted, it is possible to establish that the three granite scraps if they are to be used in foundation and base layers they need to be crushed and screened in order to have the correct fractions to achieve the specified blend. Also, the crushing will be useful especially for aggregate AG-1 in order to modify the shape of the aggregates to achieve better values when performing the Los Angeles abrasion test. In CBGM layers the results obtained showed how this type of aggregate can achieve good values of compressive strength with low percentages of Portland cement only 2%. Usually, the minimal amount introduced in the mix using natural aggregates is 3%. Overall, there are no specific limitations to not use such materials, there is a need to encourage their use towards a circular economy model.

Author Contributions. Concept and methodology, J.R., M.C., and F.M.; experimental campaign and validation, J.R.; analysis, J.R., M.C., and F.M.; writing, review and editing, J.R. and F.M.; project administration, M.C.. All authors have read and agreed to the published version of the manuscript.

References

1. Karasahin, M., Terzi, S.: Evaluation of marble waste dust mixture of asphaltic concrete construct. Constr. Build. Mater. **21**(3), 616–620 (2007)
2. Contu, A., et al.: Applications of super compaction technique using granite by-products. sustainability, eco-efficiency and conservation in transportation infrastructure asset management. In: 2014 Proceedings of the 3rd International Conference on Tranportation Infrastructure, Pisa, Italy, pp. 255–261 (2014)
3. Rombi, J.: The use of Sardinian granite by-products from the Sarrabus-Gerrei region to be used in road pavement layers. Ph.D. thesis University of Cagliari, Sardinia, Italy (2014)
4. Natural Stone from Sardinia, Technical Handbook, 229 p. (2002)
5. ISTAT Homepage. http://dati.istat.it/Index.aspx?QueryId=8909
6. Balletto, G., Mei, G., Garau, C.: Relationship between quarry activity and municipal spatial planning: a possible mediation for the case of Sardinia, Italy. Sustainability **7**(12), 16148–16163 (2015)
7. Balletto, G., Garau, C.: Smart city governance in the geo-resources planning paradigm in the metropolitan city of Cagliari (Italy). In: Gervasi, O., et al. (eds.) ICCSA 2017. LNCS, vol. 10406, pp. 368–379. Springer, Cham (2017). https://doi.org/10.1007/978-3-319-62398-6_26
8. Founti, A.M., et al.: Environmental management aspects for energy saving in natural stone quarries. In: Proceedings Global Stone Congress 2010, Alicante, Spain (2010)
9. Ribeiro, R.C.C., et al.: Uses of aggregates produced from marble and granite quarry waste in asphalt pavements: a form of clean technology. In: Proceedings of the 2008 Global Symposium on Recycling, Waste Treatment and Clean Technology, Cancun, Mexico (2008)
10. Binici, H., et al.: Durability of concrete made with granite and marble as recycle aggregates. J. Mater. Process. Technol. **208**(1–3), 299–308 (2008)
11. Aliabdo, A., et al.: Re-use of waste marble dust in the production of cement and concrete. Constr. Build. Mater. **50**, 28–41 (2014)
12. Tunc, E.T.: Recycling of marble waste: a review based on strength of concrete containing marble waste. J. Environ. Manag. **231**, 86–97 (2019)
13. Hebhoub, H., et al.: Use of waste marble aggregates in concrete. Constr. Build. Mater. **25**(3), 1167–1171 (2011)

14. UNI EN 932-1. Tests for general properties of aggregates - Methods for sampling. Italian Organization for Standardization (U.N.I.)
15. UNI EN 932-2. Tests for general properties of aggregates - Methods for reducing laboratory samples. Italian Organization for Standardization (U.N.I.)
16. CNR 29/72, Italian National research council, specification for Cement Bound Granular Material
17. Ahmed, H. M., Abdelhaffez, G. S., Ahmed, A. A.: Potential use of marble and granite solid wastes as environmentally friendly coarse particulate in civil constructions. Int. J. Environ. Sci. Technol. **19**(2), 889–896 (2020). https://doi.org/10.1007/s13762-020-03014-2
18. Rombi, J., Coni, M., Olianas, M., Salis, M., Portas, S., Scanu, A.: Application of anhydrous calcium sulphate in cement bound granular pavement layers: towards a circular economy approach. In: Gervasi, O., et al. (eds.) ICCSA 2021. LNCS, vol. 12958, pp. 91–99. Springer, Cham (2021). https://doi.org/10.1007/978-3-030-87016-4_7
19. Legislative Decree No. 152/2006 Italian Legal Framework, approving the Code on the Environment, which sets out the legislative framework applicable to all matters concerning environmental protection
20. D.M. n. 161/2012: regulates terms and conditions at which excavated materials may be reused as by-products and thus managed as non-waste
21. UNI EN 933-1. Tests for geometrical properties of aggregates - Determination of particle size distribution - Sieving method. Italian Organization for Standardization (U.N.I.)
22. UNI EN 1097-6. Tests for mechanical and physical properties of aggregates, determination of particle density and water absorption
23. CNR-UNI 10014. Determination of the Consistency (Atterberg) of a Soil. Italian National Research Council (C.N.R.) and Italian Organization for Standardization (U.N.I.)
24. UNI EN 1097 2, 2010. Tests for mechanical and physical properties of aggregates. Methods for the determination of resistance to fragmentation
25. UNI EN 13286-2. Unbound and hydraulically bound mixtures – Test methods for laboratory dry density and water content – Proctor compaction. Italian Organization for Standardization (U.N.I.)
26. Delgado, J., et al.: Geochemical assessment of the contaminant potential of granite fines produced during sawing and related processes associated to the dimension stone industry. J. Geochem. Explor. **8**, 24–27 (2005)

Sidewalk Cafe: Analysis of Safe Solutions for Customers

Francesca Maltinti[1]([✉]) [iD], Nicoletta Rassu[1]([✉]) [iD], Alessandro Plaisant[2] [iD],
and Francesco Pinna[1] [iD]

[1] Department of Civil and Environmental Engineering and Architecture, University of Cagliari,
09129 Cagliari, Italy
{maltinti,nicoletta.rassu}@unica.it
[2] Dipartimento di Architettura, Design e Urbanistica, University of Sassari, 07041 Alghero, Italy

Abstract. Faced with the global epidemiological situation during the last two years, which has inevitably limited and affected the daily routines, this paper focused on how urban spaces can adapt to shifting demands. Specifically, it is important to consider the catering activities that, after a series of closures during the imposed lockdowns, are unable to fulfil the demands of the shifting requirements during the reopening phases, owing to a lack of open available spaces. This criticality is amplified in an urban environment, where converting public properties into "commercial" uses is difficult, if not impossible, owing to the lack of available spaces. However, in many Italian scenarios, local administrations have created concession spaces on carriageways, turning in some instances parking stalls into refreshment areas, in order to address the demand of restaurateurs penalised by these circumstances. Despite this solution has solved the problem of those activities, it raises two concerns: the first is about safety, because the solutions adopted are exposed to vehicular traffic, and the second is regarding pedestrian passages' flow. This is the circumstance that motivated the authors to conduct an assessment of the contingent reality in the Sardinian capital city, Cagliari, evaluating alternative and definitive solutions for urban space regeneration.

Keywords: Urban spaces · Sidewalk café · Curbside café · Parklet cafe · Safety · Pedestrian passages

1 Introduction

The paradigm of the "*Smart city*" foresees a city that mobilises and uses its resources to improve the quality of life of its inhabitants [1, 2], promoting an anthropocentric, social and economic development but at the same time sustainable [3]. In this context, public space assumes a fundamental role: it is a place of aggregation, of which everyone has the right to enjoy without any kind of restriction that can be both physical and temporal [4]. As Indovina says *"The public space is a space of connection, of social interaction, of collective expression, it is the whole place of the urban and the civitas. It is the space of all, therefore it deserves opportune attention in the planning, it cannot be of "turns out"; moreover, it must be managed, taken care of, guaranteed and defended. It is not a space of anyone, but the space of all"* [5]. Also, Jacobs reports *"The streets and sidewalks constitute the most important public places of a city and its most vital organs. When you think of a city, the first thing that comes to mind is its streets: according to whether they seem interesting or insignificant, the city also appears as such"* [6].

According to Lefebvre [7], *"the right to the city"* is identified with the social links, functions, and services that develop in the urban public space but also with its practicability and vocation to meet the individual needs of all users of the city. Public space is a privileged place for exposure to diversity, for the production of new experiences and for the expression of individual identity [8].

Garau et al. [9] develop a methodology to evaluate the practicability of urban spaces starting from the analyses of the existing literature on creating audit tools for evaluating the quality of the urban space related to both its accessibility and walkability.

According to Moura et al. [10], walkability can be identified as the extent to which the urban environment is usable by pedestrians, while Jun and Hur point out that the recognition of walking is a key factor in promoting a sustainable, active and inclusive [11] community. Garau et al. [12] deepen the topics of walkability and develop an analytical tool to evaluate the walkability of public spaces and apply it to a case study. Analytical tools have great importance in the planning process and in supporting the decision-making process, since they help to orient the project of public space in such a way that it really becomes a place of social participation, inclusion, and sustainable ways of life.

The current times, with the increasingly frequent manifestation of critical environmental events and, especially with the pandemic from Covid 19, have seen the need for a profound review of urban public spaces [13, 14]. In this context, the usability of public space has become the priority condition for ensuring health, control over the environment and relations between people but at the same time relaunching the mobility of people and utilitarian, recreational and social activities [15].

As a result of the epidemiological situation of the last two years, the authors have focused their attention in this research on the response that urban spaces may provide to changing requirements. In particular, the authors focused on the criticalities experienced by operators in the catering sector, forced to respect prolonged cycles of business closures. In addition, during the opening phases, since these were governed by the preference for open spaces that not everyone had, a disparity was created between the operators. Added to this is the widespread "psychosis" among customers who, feeling safer in outdoor convivial spaces, choose precisely those activities that have this option to offer. It is evident that the situation has created disparities between the various activities, a problem that has not taken a back seat even with respect to local administrations which, in order to deal with this problem, have had to review plans and regulatory tools to allocate, where possible, spaces public roads, sidewalks, parts of carriageways, etc., to operators in difficulty. This aspect does not concern the concessions regularly ceded in the pre-pandemic periods, but the study addresses precisely those emergency situations implemented in the coexistence of the epidemiological emergency.

For this reason, in the face of municipal regulations and the changes that have been implemented, the authors wanted to analyse the situation in order to propose solutions that did not have a temporal character, but that looked at the long term, in order to make definitive, which can be standardised and adapted to the context, taking into account the plurality of factors. Specifically, in the analysis of the solutions, two important aspects were taken into account:

- The safety of the customers of public services and pedestrian and vehicular currents;
- Any protection and separation schemes between the two user segments: commercial establishments and mobility.

The backdrop for the analysis is Cagliari, a municipal reality in Southern Sardinia which, also favoured by a mild climate, allows you to use and enjoy the outdoors throughout the year.

The remaining paper is organised as follows. Section 2 presents an overview of its regulations adopted both internationally and nationally, with particular reference to the municipality of Cagliari. Section 3 illustrates a comparison between the solution put in place by the municipality of Cagliari and that proposed by the authors. Finally, Sect. 4 draws conclusions.

2   Analysis of the International and National Context

The Règlement de l'installation des étalages et ter- rasses sur la voie publique ainsi que des contre-étalages et contreterrasses, des commerces accessoires aux terrasses et des dépôts de matériel ou objets divers devant les commerces et des terrasses estivales [16] was published in the Bulletin Officiel De La Ville De Paris on June 18, 2021. For the whole of the public road sector situated in the territory of the City of Paris, the Regulation lays down the rules applicable specifically to installations (whether they are enclosed terraces, open terraces, exhibitions, etc.) on car parks. Article P.4.3.3 lays down the conditions for the authorisation and operation of the Dehors on parking: limits the length of the installations to the linear of the facade and, in the case where a road sign does not border the parking, the maximum length of the space is 5 m. The structure must leave in sight the markings on the ground representing the length and width of the parking lot. The regulation also allows the use of parking stalls on parking lots located on the other side of the roadway, even in the streets open at any time to traffic, but whose maximum authorized speed is less than 50 km.

The occupation must allow the passage of the cleaning trucks and must not prevent the outflow of water. The perimeter of the terraces on the parking lot shall be equipped with uniform barriers or protection screens fixed in such a way as to guarantee their solidity and stability in order to ensure the safety of customers against traffic and to prevent any fall towards the roadway. The height of these protections is limited to 1.30 m, including the height of the floor. In no case should protective barriers be covered and their appearance masked. The regulation lays down special rules for specific sectors such as the Avenue des Champs-Élysées, the Place de la République, the Avenue de l'Opéra, etc.

The authors also analysed Chapter 742 "Sidewalk cafés, parklets and marketing displays" [17] of the Toronto Municipal Code which is particularly detailed with the prescriptions of the Dehor. First of all, it calls the dehor, generically called sidewalk café, depending on the area they occupy, and, specifically: a Curbside café is a sidewalk café that is located curbside; a Frontage Café is a sidewalk café that is located immediately adjacent to the frontage wall of the associated establishment and, a Parklet café is a type of sidewalk café that is a temporary lateral projection into the curb lane or parking lane of a street.

L'art. 7.1 establishes minimum width between permitted encroachments and adjacent pedestrian clearway depending on the type of road: 1.8m on a local road; 2.1 m on a collector or arterial road; or 2.5 m, or a different minimum approved by the General Manager, on streets where the sidewalk is at least 5 m. Further detailed requirements are established for each type of coffee sidewalk and, expressly, for parklet caffe, it is stated that the concession can be granted if the parklet café is located on roads where the limit of 40 km/h is imposed or even where it is possible to exceed 40 km/h once elements such as the number and width of lanes, traffic flows, speeds and other safety consideration have been assessed. Further precise provisions are established related to distances with intersections or pedestrian crossings. About the protections, the same article states that there must be a barrier 0.9 m high from the road surface and from 1.2 m from the coffee limit an anti-slip curb to protect the installation from traffic.

The installation will have a height equal to that of the sidewalk, must be designed so that it can withstand the expected loads, must not prevent the outflow of water, there must be no barriers in New Jersey.

In the national context, the Regulations of the city of Cagliari, Sassari, Milan, the Guidelines of the city of Paullo and the Technical Standards of the city of Turin were examined.

The Regulation of the city of Cagliari has been analyzed in more depth since it is the place where the case study was addressed.

Cagliari

The *"Regolamento per la concessione del suolo pubblico per l'esercizio dell'attività di ristoro all'aperto, a servizio di attività commerciali e artigianali e per attività occasionali"* [18] was issued by the Municipality of Cagliari, approved by the City Council with deed n°72 of 22/05/2018 and subsequently amended with deed n°152 of 2/10/2018 [19], n°12 of 9/05/2019 [20] and finally with n°79 of 14/05/2021 [21].

In its first version (2018) the Regulation did not allow any type of occupation of the roadway and/or parking spaces. This prohibition was lifted with Resolution n° 79/2021 with which the original title was modified with the addition: *"Revisione del divieto di occupazione degli stalli di sosta"*. The update of the Regulations was done precisely to respond to the contingent epidemiological circumstance.

The regulation as a whole has 25 articles and *"governs the procedure for issuing temporary concessions of public land and the methods of use of the related spaces"* [18]. It is aimed at public operators for the administration of food and beverages, for artisanal and commercial businesses for the purposes indicated in Article 1 c.ii b) and c) [18].

The general principle of granting concessions is part of the general criteria *"for the requalification of the urban environment, for economic development and for tourism promotion"* (Article 2 – [18]). Concessions, the maximum allowable areas of which are regulated by art. 12 [18], may however be subject to limitations on release for the most varied reasons of public interest including: "*safety reasons, with particular reference to road or pedestrian traffic*" [18].

For the purposes of the study, Article 13 [18] deserves a more in-depth reading, which contains information on the regulation of concession spaces. In its updated version it has been integrated with 4 paragraphs (4 clauses (8 ÷ 11) [21] which refer precisely to the management of the spaces on the roadway.

The conditions that land occupations must comply with are listed in paragraph 1, without prejudice to the provisions of art. 20 of the C.d.S. [22] which governs occupations of the roadway, underlining, in the event of physical occupation of the sidewalks, the respect and guarantee of mobility for pedestrians and users with reduced mobility. According to the aforementioned article of the Regulation, the areas of public land that can be granted are:

a. Those in front of the production activity and adjacent to it;
b. Those in front but separated by the carriageway only in conditions in which 1) the carriageway hosts only one lane and is one-way, 2) the travel speed is limited to 30 km/h and 3) the pedestrian crossing is within a radius of 20 m.

At clause 2, in the concession space, when it "*falls within the historic center or in all cases in which the proposed positioning insists on the carriageway or parking stalls*" [21], the installation of fixed structures such as "*[..] gazebos, dehors or other fixed structures such as to configure closed spaces functional to the exercise able to close, even partially, the required space [..]*" [21]. Probably this prohibition could be due to the temporary nature of the concession.

By submitting the integration [21] in clauses 8 ÷ 10, the specific indications for the occupation of the parts of the carriageway are transcribed.

• Clause 8 [21]: "*The occupation of parking stalls is permitted exclusively in favor of public establishments for the non-occasional carrying out of the activity of outdoor administration of food and drinks and in the presence of the following conditions which mst all be simultaneously exist:*

  – *Local roads interests, as defined in the functional hierarchy of city traffic [...];*
  – *It is possible to subtract the space without prejudice to road and pedestrian traffic, which must always be guaranteed in safe conditions;*
  – *The business does not have or may have other public or private outdoor space, unless it has assumed a formal obligation to renounce its use by means of a declaration of responsibility;*
  – *The roads on which the parking stalls are located are included in zone 30;*
  – *The installations necessary for the safety of the spaces are not such as to require the construction of masonry, closing or grounding works of any kind*".

• Clause 10 [21]: "*Removal from road traffic occurs through the positioning, at the expense of the applicant, of suitable systems to ensure the protection of the installation [..]*".

In the light of the analysis of the contents of the Resolution [18] and its updates [21], in favour of public establishments that carry out the non-occasional activity of outdoor administration of food and drinks, which do not have o may have other public or private outdoor space, the spaces that fall within the parking stalls are allowed under concession, provided that these concern local roads included in the 30 zones provided that the space taken away does not create any prejudice for road and pedestrian traffic. If the occupation concerns parking areas assigned to the concessionary companies of the paid parking service, the interested party must pay the concessionary company an amount equal to the loss of earnings suffered by the latter due to the occupation of the parking spaces (clause 11. [21]).

The relevant aspect also concerns the protection of spaces that must be made safe through systems *"designed to guarantee the protection of the installation [..] in terms of the impact resistance of the systems themselves, their visibility at night and compliance with the regulations. on road traffic safety"* [21]. However, still, with regard to protection, these must not be carried out through masonry, closing or grounding works of any kind.

This last criterion, namely the protection of the roadway granted under concession, is the most controversial and main topic, the subject of this study, and will be discussed in the following sections.

Comparative Regulations

In the *"Regolamento per l'occupazione del suolo pubblico con dehors e altre attrezzature temporanee e amovibili"* of the municipality of Sassari [23] it is reported that the concessions can be temporary or permanent but valid for three years and then renewable. The structure must be removable and without foundations. Regarding the size, the dehors must have an extension not exceeding the width of the facade of the public establishment, and in any case a total area not exceeding 20 m^2 extending up to 35 m^2 exclusively in the squares and villages and fractions. The occupation on the road is allowed on areas where the parking of vehicles is allowed but only in *limited traffic areas* (ZTL) and pedestrian areas. Roadway installations shall ensure protection with elements on three sides. The concessionaire is directly and personally responsible, civilly and criminally, for any damage to persons or things of third parties also resulting from the lack of vigilance and bad conservation of the artefact with which the public soil is occupied.

The city of Milan [24] also provides temporary concessions and removable structures. Employment may not be granted on carriageways (except in pedonability areas) and in rest areas. The occupation must take place in front of the exercise and, if on board sidewalk, must start at a minimum distance of 1.20 m from the curb. In this case, the sidewalk must have a minimum section of 5.00 m.

Any damage caused to citizens, to public land or to private property by the elements exposed, shall be borne by the concessionaire.

The *"Linee guida comunali per dehor e arredo urbano per attività' stagionali e continuative"* [25] established by the municipality of Paullo, provide detailed information, also through images, on the requirements of the dehors. The structures are temporary and easily removable. The concession may be granted on areas designated for public parking provided that they respect the modularity of the parking stall and do not flood the transit and manoeuvring lanes. In this case, the concession area may extend to the internal delimitation line of the parking area, maintaining a vehicle safety franc of at least 30 cm. The encumbrance of the dehor must allow the transit of emergency vehicles, and public waste collection services, providing a free lane of not less than 3.50 m.

The City of Turin attaches the technical standards "*Guida alla progettazione di spazi e strutture all'aperto, su suolo pubblico o privato ad uso pubblico, attrezzati per il consumo di alimenti e bevande annessi a locali di pubblico esercizio di somministrazione*" to the Regulation No 388 [26]. The municipality of Turin provides temporary concessions and removable structures, the closing hours are established after which the furniture must be collected. The dehor can be placed in public parking spaces but cannot extend beyond the front of the building. In pedestrian spaces or in pedestrian areas it is allowed to occupy additional spaces, within the limit of 30%, compared to those placed on the front projection but the maximum linear extension cannot exceed 15.00 m. Any damage caused to citizens, public or private property by the elements constituting the dehors shall be borne by the concessionaire.

From a comparison between the different regulations, in a nutshell, it emerges that:

a. Concessions are generally temporary;
b. The structures adopted are removable;
c. Some Administrations establish the opening/closing time in the concession;
d. Not all administrations (see Milan) allow the occupation of parking spaces, others (Sassari) grant employment on the roadway where parking is normally allowed only in limited traffic areas and pedestrian areas;
e. The municipality of Paullo specifies that the occupation of public land can be released on the areas intended for public parking provided that the area subject to the concession extends up to the internal delimitation line of the parking area and that one franc is maintained vehicle safety of at least 30 cm;
f. As far as safety is concerned, only the Regulations of the Municipality of Sassari establish that occupations on the carriageway must guarantee protection with elements placed on three sides. However, these elements, as they are described, seem more of a delimitation of the space allowed than of safety for the customers of the commercial establishment or road users;
g. With the exception of the Municipality of Paullo, the other Regulations establish that any liability for damage to property and people is borne by the operator.

3   The Case Study in Cagliari, Italy

The current analysis took into account the Cagliari scenario, in which the municipal rule governing concessions on public property was analysed in the preceding section. To summarise the major steps, the municipality of the Sardinian capital, in response to the epidemiological emergency from Covid 19, integrated its own regulation [21] by granting concessions on carriageway spaces intended for stalls to managers of public establishments engaged in the sale of food stop. However, following its approval which dates back to May 2021, in the following July (12/07/2021), the concessions of public land were temporarily suspended due to an accident involving two vehicles passing through the intersection between *via Istria* and *via Molise*, in an area temporarily granted to a public establishment in order to use it as a refreshment area. Although the accident was of a modest entity, the barriers erected to defend the occupation failed to withstand the impact, to the point that one of the vehicles invaded the area and the equipment present, fortunately without causing any harm to humans, as there are currently no neither customers nor passers-by (Figs. 1 and 2).

Fig. 1. Cagliari - intersection Via Istria - Via Molise

Fig. 2. Cagliari - accident

This incident highlighted critical concerns regarding the safety of concessions located in carriageway spaces. This is why the municipal administration was forced to suspend the concessions in order to assess their applicability in terms of safety.

Before moving on to the proposed solution, the following paragraph will describe and examine the solution adopted by the Municipality of Cagliari.

3.1 Solution Adopted by the Municipality of Cagliari

With regards to the solution adopted already by the Municipality of Cagliari, it is necessary to preliminarily highlight that it represents the most used solution in many Italian and international cities, as determined by an analysis of the previous rules. In the past, the municipal administration has chosen to adopt this type of accommodation, furthermore identifying, in the *"Linee guida per l'arredo e le attrezzature per le attività di ristoro all'aperto nelle occupazioni di suolo pubblico negli stalli dei parcheggi e nelle altre aree pubbliche, non disciplinate da specifico regolamento di pianificazione, richieste provvisoriamente per far fronte all'emergenza COVID-19"* [27], including the type of furniture that can be used. This situation was called into question following the accident described above and which highlighted some critical issues in terms of traffic safety, especially towards customers of commercial activities.

In the solution proposed by the Regulation [21] and adopted by the Municipality, a series of critical issues were observed, which can be summarized as follows:

a. The accident showed the lack of protection of the concession space, especially towards customers and staff. In fact, the use of the roadway to position the set-ups of commercial activities and obviously host the customers, not providing for any invasive protection that acts as a real divider between the two spaces, poses safety problems, especially for the former. However, there have been individual and unco-ordinated initiatives, such as the affixing of removable New Jersey barriers, flower boxes, pylons etc. which had, in the intention, the sole purpose of delimiting the space under concession without any claim in terms of cushioning and dissipation of the impact energy and therefore of protection in the event of a vehicle diversion;
b. The proximity to the spaces travelled by vehicles, in addition to the aforementioned safety problems, exposes customers and staff to exhaust gases, with all that this entails in terms of public health and in the workplace;
c. The current layout of the platforms, in fact, interrupts the continuity of the pedestrian paths. In this configuration, the sidewalk becomes an internal transit area for the staff and customers who make the move - activities - refreshment area - activities, as well as a waiting area for customers waiting to sit at the table or pay the bill. These elements could create an interruption in the pedestrian flow, a circumstance that would become a real nuisance if not a real criticality, for users with reduced mobility both for disabilities (visually impaired and blind, people in wheelchairs, etc.) and for contingent and / or temporary situations (pregnant women, people with strollers, the elderly, etc.);
d. According to the regulation [21], the concessions are required to be issued in the streets in zone 30, one-way and with a low volume of traffic.

Regarding this last point it is necessary to make an observation to clarify what is commonly defined as zone 30. According to the CdS [22] a 30 Zone is an area of the urban road network where the speed limit is set equal to 30 km/h. In logic, the containment of speed would have the purpose of promoting coexistence between the various components of traffic: cars, bicycles and pedestrians. It follows that according to this definition it is sufficient to limit the travel speed to 30 km/h and to affix the vertical signpost (Fig. 3) to delimit a 30 area.

Actually, the question is a bit more complex. In order for a 30 zone to be such it must be in shape and must possess a series of regulation characteristics. In detail, in the 30 zones, the design of the road and all related spaces has been corrected and integrated

Fig. 3. Vertical signs delimiting 30 Zone

through the environmental requalification of the mobility spaces. In particular, through the adoption of traffic moderation and fluidization measures, we want to ensure that the permitted vehicle components transit at a speed of 30 km/h as this is what the average user perceives as the maximum feasible. In other words, it is the geometry of the platform that induces the travel speed and not the simple regulation through the imposition of the limit.

Other regulatory aspects that characterize the 30 zones are:

- At the intersections, the right of way is valid;
- Signs and relative "stop" or "give way" manoeuvres are not contemplated;
- Pedestrian crossings are not demarcated, except in exceptional cases.

It follows that in order for the elements described above to coexist, it is necessary to systematically adopt traffic moderation measures, in order to:

a. Prevent these areas from being affected by crossing traffic;
b. Create a continuous system of safe and comfortable pedestrian and cycle paths;
c. Induce in driver that virtuous driving behaviour, which guarantees maximum safety and favours the development of forms of use of road space other than motorized mobility and connected to the social life of urban space.

From this it follows that, in reality, many of the existing 30 Zones are not able to ensure minimum acceptable safety conditions, due to the type and extent of vehicular traffic, the real speeds of travel, the size of the carriageway, the spaces for pedestrian and bicycle mobility, visibility of intersections, etc.

3.2 Proposed Solution

Based on these premises, the authors examined and proposed a solution capable of overcoming the problems encountered. This project can be counted among the interventions of traffic moderation and protection of weak users. Its peculiarity is that it reverses the scale of priorities by placing the needs of pedestrians in the foreground and following those of the exhibitors. The reversal of priorities is accompanied by the inversion of the destination of the spaces. In this way, the space acquired on the roadway is not intended for customers but is converted into an extension of the sidewalk [28] The same [22] contemplates a solution of this type, as in art. 20, the occupation of pavements by kiosks, newsstands or other installations may be allowed up to a maximum of half of their width, provided that adjacent to the buildings and provided that an area for the movement of pedestrians remains free, no less than 2 m.

The issues addressed in the two references above have been reworked in order to respond to the two fundamental needs:

• Maintaining the continuity of pedestrian paths by removing external interference that can make transit difficult, especially for users with reduced mobility;
• The space intended for public concession must be adjacent to the buildings and not on the opposite side of the pavement.

From this perspective, the intention was to reverse the intended use of the spaces, using the extension in the carriageway as a continuity of the sidewalk and placing the merchants' supplies adjacent to the building, as depicted in the following Fig. 4.

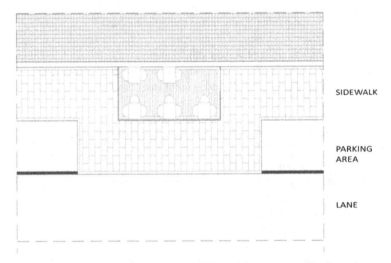

Fig. 4. Solution's Schema Widening of the pavement/Platform

This solution satisfies at the same time the safety needs for the circulation and usability of pedestrian spaces for weak users without neglecting the right requests of the operators.

The positive elements of this intervention are:

a. The continuity of the pedestrian flow is ensured without any interference. In fact, the mere fact that the concession space is adjacent to the building means that both customers and staff gravitate around the granted area, effectively eliminating the flow crossing the sidewalk, a circumstance that occurs with the displacement of the space. "Commercial" on the roadway;

b. The safety of traffic and patrons is guaranteed. In fact, according to this configuration, the vehicular current is separated from the concession area by a space that is in fact a sidewalk and, as such, does not require protection. It should be remembered, in fact, that the sidewalk is an area of the road intended for pedestrians that must be raised or in the absence of a rise, delimited and protected. This protection, in the case of roads with a design speed of less than 70 km/h, can be obtained simply by creating a shaped edge. This edge must be characterized by the so-called "non-surmountable profile" as represented in the image below (Fig. 5);

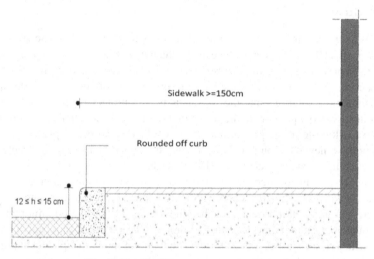

Fig. 5. Detail of the non-surmountable curb

c. The extension of the sidewalk guarantees the overcoming of architectural barriers;
d. The choice of a single typological solution guarantees the improvement of the urban decor, in fact, whatever the material used, the homogeneity makes the public space recognizable and more orderly;
e. The continuity of the rainwater flow lines on the edges that can be easily obtained with simple technical measures that do not prevent the regular flow of the same;
f. The possibility of seizing the opportunity with these interventions to rethink the dimensions of the vehicle lanes, bringing them to values that allow better speed control;
g. The improvement of traffic conditions on internal roads within 30 Zone as the extension of the sidewalks is useful for delimiting the perceptual space for the driver, making him think he is crossing a bottleneck, with the result of a reduction in real travel speeds.

It is clear that, to obtain the advantages described, the concession area must be physically limited, through parapets, flower boxes, etc., even if adjacent to the building.

Firstly, since the concession is expensive, its cost depends on the area requested and obtainable and, as such, it must be delimited to prevent unauthorized use. Secondly, the delimitation of the concession identifies the pedestrian area and therefore the distance from vehicular traffic.

Finally, we want to highlight an aspect that is certainly not secondary. The solution adopted up to now by the Municipality is applicable only to the roads included in the 30 one-way traffic zones. That proposal, due to its characteristics and the resulting advantages, potentially has a greater scope. In fact, it is achievable not only in 30 Zone but also in all the local and residential roads characterized by two-way traffic and with two total lanes as long as they are not affected by important flows. In fact, much of the Cagliari road network can be considered as falling into this category.

4 Conclusions

How does the urban space respond to the changing situations? This is the question that the authors asked themselves in the face of the change of scenery offered by the Covid 19 pandemic. In particular, the authors observed the critical issues encountered by operators in the catering sector who were forced to redesign spaces for customers. Subsequently, they examined the solutions that the various administrations have proposed to support the growing needs of operators in the sector in order to find functional and valid answers especially in a long-term perspective and not only subject to the period pandemic. Finally, they proposed a new solution which meets both the new urban space requirements and the safety requirements for vehicles and pedestrians.

The direct examination concerned the reality of the Sardinian capital, Cagliari, a city of about 154,000 inhabitants and with a high concentration of bars and restaurants in historic and non-historic districts. The study revealed that the commitments made by the municipal administration and the solutions proposed in this regard were not without critical issues, especially in terms of safety and fluidity of pedestrian mobility. It has been observed that allocating the spaces on the roadway to catering activities has brought out two kinds of problems. In the first place, the safety of customers and staff, who are adjacent to the vehicular current, are exposed to the risk of investment in the event of accidental diversion of a vehicle. Secondly, according to this configuration, the sidewalk becomes a crossing and rest area for customers and staff, effectively creating an interruption of ordinary mobility and creating inconvenience, especially for that part of weak users.

Based on the analysis conducted by the authors, the critical issues just exposed can be removed in full, maintaining the acquisition of the spaces on the road but completely reversing the intended use of the spaces. According to this configuration, the concession space would be adjacent to the commercial activity building and the space on the roadway would be intended for the sidewalk. In this way, the safety of traffic and customers is guaranteed, as the vehicular current is separated from the concession area by a space that is in fact a sidewalk and, as such, does not require protection. Furthermore, the continuity of the pedestrian flow is guaranteed. In fact, the mere fact that the concession space is adjacent to the building means that customers and staff gravitate around the granted area, effectively eliminating the flow crossing the sidewalk, a circumstance that occurs with the displacement of the space "commercial" on the roadway.

Acknowledgements. This study is supported by the MIUR (Ministry of Education, Universities and Research [Italy]) through project entitled: the SMART CITY framework (project: PON04a2_00381 "CAGLIARI2020") and the project "WEAKI TRANSIT: WEAK-demand areas Innovative TRANsport Shared services for Italian Towns (Project protocol: 20174ARRHT_004; CUP Code: F74I19001290001), financed with the PRIN 2017 (Research Projects of National Relevance) programme. We authorize the MIUR to reproduce and distribute reprints for Governmental purposes, notwithstanding any copyright notations thereon. Any opinions, findings and conclusions or recommendations expressed in this material are those of the authors, and do not necessarily reflect the views of the MIUR.

Author Contributions. Conceptualization, all; methodology and formal analysis, Francesco Pinna, Nicoletta Rassu, Francesca Maltinti; introduction and literature review Francesca Maltinti, Alessandro Plaisant; writing-original draft preparation Nicoletta Rassu, Francesca Maltinti; writing review and editing, Nicoletta Rassu and Francesca Maltinti; visualization, all. All authors have read and agreed to the published version of the manuscript.

References

1. Hajek, P., Youssef, A., Hajkova, V.: Recent developments in smart city assessment: a bibliometric and content analysis-based literature review. Cities 103709 (2022)
2. Garau, C., Pavan, V.M.: Evaluating urban quality: Indicators and assessment tools for smart sustainable cities. Sustainability **10**(3), 575 (2018)
3. Annunziata, A., Garau, C.: Understanding kid-friendly urban space for a more inclusive smart city: the case study of Cagliari (Italy). In: Gervasi, O., et al. (eds.) ICCSA 2018. LNCS, vol. 10962, pp. 589–605. Springer, Cham (2018). https://doi.org/10.1007/978-3-319-95168-3_40
4. "Città e necessità. Il rapporto tra pubblico e privato nell'organizzazione e gestione dello spazio pubblico della città contemporanea", Fabiana Frisanco Thesis's, Supervisor: prof. ing. Alessandro Plaisant, AA 2012–2013, Università Degli Studi Di Sassari Dipartimento di Architettura, Urbanistica e Design - Corso di Laurea in Pianificazione Territoriale Urbanistica ed Ambientale
5. Indovina, F.: Governare la città con l'urbanistica, 43 (2005)
6. Jacobs, J.: Vita e morte delle grandi città, Edizioni di comunità, 2 (2000)
7. Lefebvre, H., Kofman, E., Lebas, E.: The right to the city. In: Writings on Cities, Cambridge, MA, USA, pp. 63–184 (1995). ISBN 978-0631191889
8. Pavia, R.: Il Passo della Città, 1st edn., pp. 15–30. Donzelli Editore, Roma (2015). ISBN 9788868431693
9. Garau C., Annunziata A., Coni M.: A methodological framework for assessing practicability of the urban space: the survey on conditions of practicable environments (SCOPE) procedure applied in the case study of Cagliari (Italy). Sustainability **10**(11), 4189 (2018). https://doi.org/10.3390/su10114189
10. Moura, F., Cambra, P., Gonçalves, A.B.: Measuring walkability for distinct pedestrian groups with a participatory assessment method: A case study in Lisbon. Landsc. Urban Plan. **157**, 282–296 (2017)
11. Jun, H.J., Hur, M.: The relationship between walkability and neighborhood social environment: the importance of physical and perceived walkability. Appl. Geogr. **62**, 115–124 (2015)
12. Garau C., Annunziata A., Yamu C.: A walkability assessment tool coupling multi-criteria analysis and space syntax: the case study of Iglesias, Italy. Eur. Plann. Stud. (2020). https://doi.org/10.1080/09654313.2020.1761947

13. Campisi, T., Garau, C., Acampa, G., Maltinti, F., Canale, A., Coni, M.: Developing flexible mobility on-demand in the era of mobility as a service: an overview of the Italian context before and after pandemic. In: Gervasi, O., et al. (eds.) ICCSA 2021. LNCS, vol. 12954, pp. 323–338. Springer, Cham (2021). https://doi.org/10.1007/978-3-030-86979-3_24

14. Campisi, T., et al.: A new vision on smart and resilient urban mobility in the aftermath of the pandemic: key factors on european transport policies. In: Gervasi, O., et al. (eds.) ICCSA 2021. LNCS, vol. 12958, pp. 603–618. Springer, Cham (2021). https://doi.org/10.1007/978-3-030-87016-4_43

15. Garau, C., et al.: Public Open Spaces: connecting people, squares and streets by measuring the usability through the Villanova district in Cagliari. Transp. Res. Proc. **60**, 314–321 (2022)

16. Règlement de l'installation des étalages et ter- rasses sur la voie publique ainsi que des contre-étalages et contreterrasses, des commerces accessoires aux terrasses et des dépôts de matériel ou objets divers devant les commerces et des terrasses estivales. Bulletin Officiel De La Ville De Paris, 18 June 2021

17. Chapter 742, "Sidewalk cafés, parklets and marketing displays" - Toronto Municipal Code, 5 February 2021

18. Deliberazione n. 72/2018: Regolamento per la concessione del suolo pubblico per l'esercizio dell'attività di ristoro all'aperto, a servizio di attività commerciali e artigianali e per attività occasionali. Consiglio Comunale, Comune di Cagliari, May 2018

19. Deliberazione n. 152/2018: Revisione regolamento per la concessione del suolo pubblico per l'esercizio dell'attività di ristoro all'aperto, a servizio di attività commerciali e artigianali e per attività occasionali, approvato con deliberazione del Consiglio comunale n. 72 del 22 maggio 2018. Consiglio Comunale, Comune di Cagliari, October 2018

20. Deliberazione n. 12/2019: Revisione dell'articolo 18, comma 26, del regolamento per la concessione di suolo pubblico per l'esercizio delle attività di ristoro all'aperto, a servizio di attività commerciali e artigianali e per attività occasionali, approvato con deliberazione del Consiglio comunale n. 72 del 22 maggio 2018 come modificato dalla deliberazione deli Consiglio comunale n. 152 del 02 ottobre 2018. Commissario straordinario, Comune di Cagliari, May 2019

21. Deliberazione n. 79/2021: Regolamento per la concessione del suolo pubblico per l'esercizio dell'attività di ristoro all'aperto, a servizio di attività commerciali e artigianali e per attività occasionali. Revisione del divieto di occupazione degli stalli di sosta. Consiglio Comunale, Comune di Cagliari, May 2021

22. D.lgs. n. 285 del 1992, Codice della strada, 30 April 1992

23. Deliberazione n. 49/2021: Regolamento per l'occupazione del suolo pubblico con dehors e altre attrezzature temporanee e amovibili. Consiglio Comunale, Comune di Sassari, n.31 del May 2018

24. Deliberazione n.132/2020: "Disciplina del diritto ad occupare il suolo, lo spazio pubblico o aree private soggette a servitu' di pubblico passo mediante elementi di arredo quali: tavoli, sedie, fioriere, ombrelloni, tende solari, tende ombrasole, pergolati, faretti, pedane mobili, gazebi, dehors stagionali e altri elementi similari", Consiglio Comunale, Comune di Milano, December 2000

25. Comune di Paullo: Linee guida comunali per dehor e arredo urbano per attività' stagionali e continuative

26. Deliberazione n. 388/2019 Mod. il 20 aprile 2020: "Disciplina dell'allestimento di spazi e strutture all'aperto su suolo pubblico, o privato ad uso pubblico, attrezzati per il consumo di alimenti e bevande annessi a locali dl pubblico esercizio di somministrazione" - Allegato A: Guida alla progettazione di spazi e strutture all'aperto, su suolo pubblico o privato ad uso pubblico, attrezzati per il consumo di alimenti e bevande annessi a locali di pubblico esercizio di somministrazione, 20 April 2020

27. Deliberazione n. 88/2020: Linee guida per l'arredo e le attrezzature per le attività di ristoro all'aperto nelle occupazioni di suolo pubblico negli stalli dei parcheggi e nelle altre aree pubbliche, non disciplinate da specifico regolamento di pianificazione, richieste provvisoriamente per far fronte all'emergenza COVID-19. Giunta Comunale, Comune di Cagliari, July 2020

28. Turner, S., Sandt, L., Toole, J., Benz, R., Patten, R.: Federal highway administration university course on bicycle and pedestrian transportation. Publication No. FHWA-HRT-05-133. US Department of Transportation, July 2006

Performance Evaluation of in Situ Application of Anhydrous Calcium Sulphate in Pavement Layers

J. Rombi$^{(\boxtimes)}$ ⓘ, M. Olianas ⓘ, M. Salis ⓘ, A. Serpi ⓘ, and M. Coni ⓘ

Department of Civil Environmental Engineering and Architecture, University of Cagliari, 09042 Cagliari, Italy
james.rombi@unica.it

Abstract. The following paper concerns the in situ application of Anhydrous Calcium Sulphate (ACS) in Cement Bound Granular Material (CBGM) pavement layers. The ACS used in this research derives from an industrial process. If no applications are found for this industrial by-product, ACS is discharged into landfills. The research aims to evaluate the mechanical performances in real working conditions in which ACS partially replaces Portland Cement (PC). In the last years, the annual cement production worldwide is increasing rapidly reaching approximately 4.0 billion tons, responsible for around 8% of the total CO_2 emitted into the atmosphere. A trial four layers pavement, divided into two sections, was constructed and subjected to heavy traffic. Each section had the same type of layers except for the CBGM one. The first section was constructed using ACS in partial replacement of PC, while for comparison a reference section incorporated only PC was created. Each section was subjected to the same traffic flow and loads. To evaluate the performances of the two sections, tests were performed during the construction of the single layers. Also, after that the sections were completed, periodic tests were conducted. To perform the test a Falling Weight Deflectometer (FWD) was used, capable of measuring the pavement layers moduli. The results are encouraging, after six months from construction, the section incorporating ACS showed higher values of layer moduli if compared with the reference section. If the results are confirmed, the potential use of ACS in partial replacement of PC could decrease not only CO_2 emissions but also construction costs, with higher mechanical performance.

Keywords: Anhydrous Calcium Sulphate · Cement Bound Granular Material · Portland Cement · Industrial by-product · Circular economy

1 Introduction

The most common materials used in civil engineering are cement, steel, and sand. Each year, these three materials, are produced globally to supply the continuous demand to construct buildings and human-built environments [1]. Analyzing global 2020 annual productions of these materials, data from U.S. Geological Survey [2], cement production

O. Gervasi et al. (Eds.): ICCSA 2022 Workshops, LNCS 13382, pp. 640–649, 2022.
https://doi.org/10.1007/978-3-031-10592-0_46

reached 4.1 billion tonnes, which accounted for 8% of global CO_2 emissions [3, 4]. Steel is the most commonly used metal, its production reached 1.8 billion tonnes, emitting around two tonnes of CO_2 for every tonne of steel produced. Sand and gravel production reached 265 million tonnes. As the world tries to reduce carbon emissions, by adopting various mythologies, it is important to study and evaluate new materials that can reduce the consumption of these essential materials. Cement is widely used in the road construction industry for many purposes like the construction of bridges, tunnels, and concrete roads. Also, it can be used for the treatment of aggregates as a hydraulic binder, and in the stabilization of soils, cement binding mixtures have a relevant contribution to upgrading the bearing capacity of the subgrade. In many parts of the world, researchers are studying alternative hydraulic binders to partially replace Portland Cement (PC). Normally such materials are by-products like fly ash [5], silica fume, and artificial gypsum [6–8].

The research investigates the potential application of Anhydrous Calcium Sulphate (ACS) in the partial replacement of PC as a binder in cement-treated base layers. Laboratory tests have already been conducted on the mechanical and physical behavior of ACS in partial replacement of PC in Cement Bound Granular Material (CBGM) layers with good results [5]. In this research, a mixed design incorporating 2% of PC and 5% of ACS in the CBGM layer is studied to evaluate mechanical performances, in real working conditions, while constructing a real scale trial road section.

ACS is a by-product obtained with lower temperatures than the calcination of PC that must reach 1400 °C [9, 10]. It is known that in the production of cement half of the CO_2 produced derives from the calcination of limestone [11] and the other half is produced using fossil fuels to heat the kilns. For this reason, all the potential applications of using ACS, that being by-product energy and CO_2 emissions for its production have already been spent, which could decrease the exploitation of natural resources, and limit energy consumption and CO_2 emissions.

2   Materials and Methods

The ACS used in this research is a by-product deriving from the industrial process to obtain Aluminum Fluoride and Cryolite that is used in the Aluminium industry. ACS has the chemical formula $CaSO_4$ and is also called milled anhydrite. It is obtained from the reaction of dried acid grade Fluorspar (CaF_2 97%) and Sulphuric Acid (H_2SO_4) during the production of Hydrogen Fluoride (HF) and consequent neutralization with lime [5], as shown in Eq. 1:

$$CaF_2 + H_2SO_4 \rightarrow 2HF + CaSO_4 \tag{1}$$

In Fig. 1 it can be seen an illustration of the industrial production process from which ACS derives.

The industrial plant that has supplied the ACS, is located on the island of Sardinia, Italy. The plant has an average annual production of 240000 t/year.

In this research CBGM layers, in which PC, type CEM IV/B 32.5 R, was partially replaced with ACS, are being studied to evaluate mechanical performances in real working conditions. In the summer of 2021, a trail embankment was constructed inside the

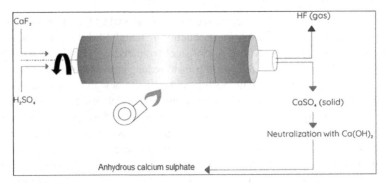

Fig. 1. Industrial production process of CaSO₄

industrial plant that supplied the ACS (see Fig. 2). It consists of two semi-rigid pavements with the same layers of thickness. The embankment was in total 90 m long and 6 m wide, formed of two sections that differ only on the composition of the CBGM layers. In Fig. 3 are shown the two test sections and the pavement layer thickness.

Fig. 2. Trial embankment inside the industrial plant

The section containing the innovative mix design, CBGM layer in green, has 5% ACS and 2% PC, while the section with traditional CBGM has only 3% PC used as a reference mix. Figure 4 is shown a typical layout of semi-rigid pavement, with materials normally used to prepare a CBGM mix, that is PC, water, and granular material. The trial section

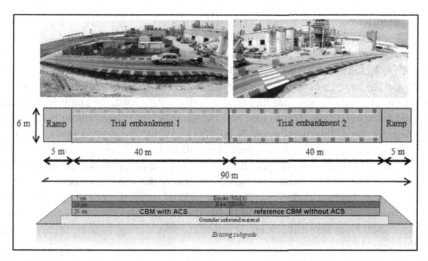

Fig. 3. The two trial pavements sections: in green pavement with ACS and in blue without.

was constructed on the pre-existing unbounded road, on top of that 20 cm of unbound granular material were laid to construct the foundation. On top of the foundation, the CBGM layer was constructed, with a thickness of 20 cm. The paving was then completed with two bituminous layers of Hot Mix Asphalt (HMA), respectively 10 and 7 cm thick, in total, the embankment was 57 cm high. Upgrading the bearing capacity of the hydraulically bound layers has a relevant contribution to the lower layers, this provides

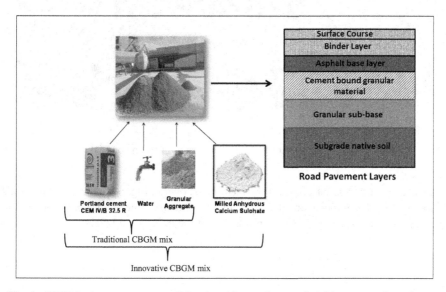

Fig. 4. CBGM mix components traditional and innovative; semi-rigid pavement layer layout.

the possibility to construct road surfaces (HMA) of lesser thickness with the result of decreasing road construction costs [12].

To evaluate the mechanical performances of the trial section a dynamic Falling Weight Deflectometer (FWD) was used (see Fig. 5). The FWD is a non-destructive testing device used to perform in situ tests on pavements. It is capable of measuring deflections obtained by applying an impulse with a falling load, the aim is to reproduce the vehicle wheel loads. The weight and the drop height of the falling mass can be modified: the weighting mass range is 50–350 kg, while the drop height is from 50–390 mm, so the impulse load can range from 40 to 120 kN acting on mass and drop height. Once the load stress is applied by control-shape dropping weight on a circular load plate, a line of 12 sensors (geophones) registers the vertical velocity at different distances from the load plate [13]. The main field of application of the FWD is in the monitoring of pavements: flexible (asphalt), rigid (concrete), and semi-rigid (asphalt and concrete). New applications are being tested like the application in rapid bridge conditioning [13–15].

Fig. 5. FWD on trailer towed by vehicle ready for testing on trial section

The amplitude and the shape of the basin, as shown in Fig. 6, contain information's about the stiffness of the layers of the pavement. While the time history of the deflection is useful to understand the dynamic properties of the underlying layers.

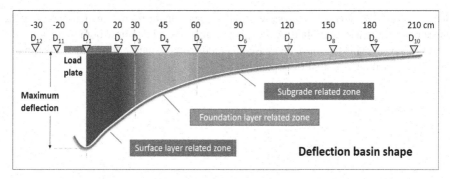

Fig. 6. Basin shape profile

3 Experimental Result

The testing campaign started in June 2021 and was repeated after 3 months, to evaluate the stiffness of the layers. Figure 7 reports the position of the testing points during the two testing campaigns (in June and September 2021).

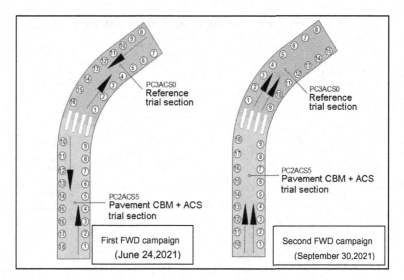

Fig. 7. Survey testing campaign layout

The grid to perform the tests used two alignments with a 4.0 m distance, while each station was 5.0 m distant from the next. On each tested point, the loading was repeated three times, each time increasing the load level 1000, 1300, and 1500 kPa. The impulse and that for deflections measured by the geophones were normalized in respect to the initial load and arranged on graphs showing the shape of the deflection basin. Figure 8, Fig. 9, and Fig. 10 are reported the mean deflection values of the two testing campaigns for each section, and for each applied contact pressure. It can be seen that the innovative CBGM mix has always lower deflections than the reference mix for each of the three contact pressures applied. Also, it is possible to evaluate how both innovative and traditional CBGM layers have decreased the deflection values, comparing the campaign conducted in June with that of September.

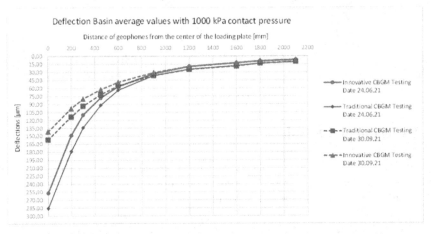

Fig. 8. Average deflection values with 1000 kPa contact pressure

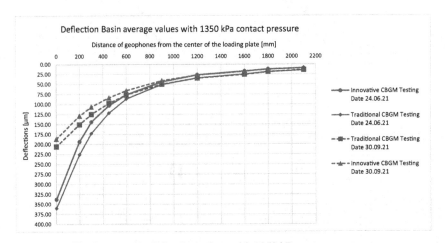

Fig. 9. Average deflection values with 1350 kPa contact pressure

To be able to obtain elastic moduli of the layers, from the data collected during the FWD campaign, back-calculation was performed using Elmod 6 software. In Fig. 11 are reported the mean elastic moduli values obtain performing back-calculation, for each of the layers of the campaign performed in June, and Fig. 12 the results for the tests performed in September. In particular, in the testing campaign performed in June 2021, the traditional mix had a value of elastic modulus 1398 MPa, while the innovative had

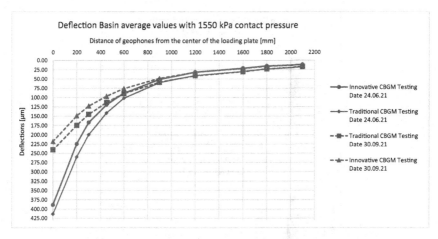

Fig. 10. Average deflection values with 1550 kPa contact pressure

a value of 1797 MPa. In the campaign conducted in September, the traditional mix had a value of 2818 MPa while the innovative mix had a value of 4082 MPa.

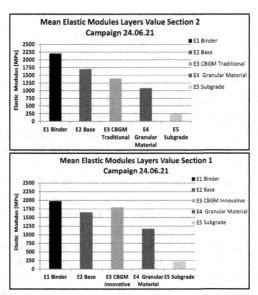

Fig. 11. Comparison of mean elastic moduli values of innovative and traditional CBGM Layers (Campaign 24.04.2021)

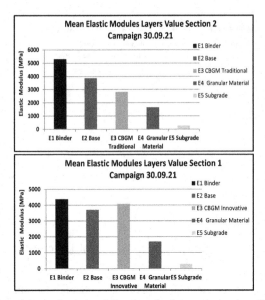

Fig. 12. Comparison of mean elastic moduli values for innovative and traditional CBGM layers (Campaign 30.09.2021)

4 Conclusions

The experimental campaign performed to evaluate the mechanical properties in real working conditions of CBGM layers incorporating ACS in partial replacement of PC, has demonstrated good mechanical performances. The in situ tests conducted using the FWD have highlighted an increase in stiffness for both the traditional and innovative cemented mix, as the curing times increase, with greater increases in stiffness of the section with the innovative mix design. The construction of the trial section has underlined some minor issues that can be simply solved, especially in the mixing and laying phases. Optimum water content in the mix must be strictly respected and the laying and compacting procedures must be done in a short period of time, in order to achieve good mechanical performances. ACS has a tendency to absorb more water than PC, making workability and compaction procedures difficult to perform.

The possibility of reducing the amount of PC in the mix, and introducing ACS, can be considered one way to decrease CO_2 emissions, but also construction costs.

The trial section will be periodically monitored, while it has been over a year since it has been constructed and subjected to heavy traffic. On the bases of the results obtained, new mixes will be tested, aiming for a further reduction of PC content, maintaining good mechanical performances, and also workability.

Acknowledgements. Authors would like to thank Fluorsid S.p.a and in particular Dr. Luca Pala, R&D Director at Fluorsid S.p.a., for promoting and funding the project R.I.U.S.A. (Road Infrastructures by Using Synthetic Anhydrite).

Author Contributions. Concept and methodology, Rombi, J., and Coni, C.; experimental campaign and validation, Rombi, J., Olianas, M., Salis, M., and Coni, M.; analysis, Rombi, J., Salis, M., and Coni, M.; writing, review and editing, Rombi, J., Salis, M., Serpi, A., and Coni, M.; project administration, Coni, M.. All authors have read and agreed to the published version of the manuscript.

References

1. https://elements.visualcapitalist.com/sand-steel-and-cement-the-annual-production-of-the-worlds-building-blocks/
2. https://www.usgs.gov/centers/national-minerals-information-center
3. Lehne, J., Preston, F.: Making Concrete Change, Innovation in Low-Carbon Cement and Concrete. Chatham House, London (2018)
4. Andrew, R.M.: Global CO_2 emissions from cement production. Earth Syst. Sci. Data **10**, 195–217 (2018). https://doi.org/10.5194/essd-10-195-2018
5. Li, J., et al.: Investigation on the preparation and performance of clinker-fly ash-gypsum road base course binder. Constr. Build. Mater. **212**, 39–48 (2019). https://doi.org/10.1016/j.conbuildmat.2019.03.253
6. Rombi, J., Coni, M., Olianas, M., Salis, M., Portas, S., Scanu, A.: Application of anhydrous calcium sulphate in cement bound granular pavement layers: towards a circular economy approach. In: Gervasi, O., et al. (eds.) ICCSA 2021. LNCS, vol. 12958, pp. 91–99. Springer, Cham (2021). https://doi.org/10.1007/978-3-030-87016-4_7
7. Usmen, M.A., Lyle, K.M.: Construction and Performance of Experimental Base Course Test Sections Built with Waste Calcium Sulfate, Lime, and Fly Ash, Transportation Research Record No. 998, Washington, DC (1984)
8. Taha, R., Roger, K.S., Willis, T., James T.H.: The use of by-product phosphogypsum in road construction. Presented at the 71st Annual Meeting of the Transportation Research Board, Washington, DC, January 1992
9. O'Rourke, B., et al.: Development of calcium sulfate–GGBS–Portland cement binders. Constr. Build. Mater. **23**, 340–346 (2009). https://doi.org/10.1016/j.conbuildmat.2007.11.016
10. Gartner, E.: Industrially interesting approaches to "low-CO_2" cements. Cem. Concr. Res. **34**, 1489–1498 (2004). https://doi.org/10.1016/j.cemconres
11. Chen, I.A., Juenger, M.C.G.: Incorporation of waste materials into Portland cement clinker synthesized from natural raw materials. J. Mater. Sci. **44**(10), 2617–2627 (2009). https://doi.org/10.1007/s10853-009-3342-x
12. Contu, A., et al.: Applications of super compaction technique using granite by-products. Sustainability, eco-efficiency and conservation in transportation infrastructure asset management. In: Proceedings of the 3rd International Conference on Transportation Infrastructure, Pisa, Italy, pp. 255–261 (2014)
13. Coni, M., et al.: Fast falling weight deflectometer method for condition assessment of RC bridges. Appl. Sci. **11**, 1743 (2021). https://doi.org/10.3390/app11041743
14. Grimmelsman, K.A., Eric, V., Carreiro, J.L., Rawn, J.D.: Rapid Bridge Condition Screening by Falling Weight Deflectometer Submitted by MBTC 3015 October 2014, Mack-Blackwell Rural Transportation Center University of Arkansas, Fayetteville (2014)
15. Rawn, J.D.: Rapid Condition Assessment of Bridges by Falling Weight Deflectometer. Graduate Theses, University of Arkansas, Fayetteville (2014)

Safety Oriented Road Asset Management Methodology for Urban Areas

Mauro D'Apuzzo[1]([✉]) [iD], Azzurra Evangelisti[1] [iD], Giuseppe Cappelli[1,2],
and Vittorio Nicolosi[3] [iD]

[1] University of Cassino and Southern Lazio, Via G. Di Biasio 43, 03043 Cassino, Italy
{dapuzzo,giuseppe.cappelli1}@unicas.it
[2] University School for Advanced Studies, IUSS, Piazza della Vittoria n.15, 27100 Pavia, Italy
giuseppe.cappelli@iusspavia.it
[3] University of Rome "Tor Vergata", Via del Politecnico 1, 00133 Rome, Italy
nicolosi@uniroma2.it

Abstract. Modern cities require new engineered approaches to tackle the challenges related to smart, sustainable and safe urban mobility. In this connection, preserving the functional condition of road infrastructures is of paramount importance. Following the recent European Directive on Road Safety Management, in this paper a new safety-oriented methodology for road asset management system in urban areas has been developed and presented.

The proposed methodology is based on the results obtained from the accident analysis and the current road assets conditions gained by means of road safety inspections.

All the collected data are combined into an urban road management system model that is able to convert qualitative judgements into quantitative values in order to evaluate budget allocation and prioritization of road maintenance interventions basing on a global performance safety function.

In order to validate the proposed method, a 30 km long Italian urban road network has been examined and safety inspections have been carried out to gain information on asset conditions together with related traffic and accident data. Finally, according to a hypothesized triennial investment plan, the best three-years maintenance program has been identified accomplishing the principle of maximum reduction of accident rate.

Results obtained so far highlight that the proposed method may be a useful tool for municipal road agencies.

Keywords: Urban road asset management · Road safety · Budget allocation

1 Introduction

Transportation organizations have the responsibility and the challenging task to maintain, preserve and improve infrastructure assets for current and future generations since transport infrastructures play a critical role in the development of the modern communities' economic and social aspects.

However, due to both economic (as funds deficiency) and environmental (as territory revaluation) aspects, in recent years, the main aim of transportation systems administrations has been the *"existing infrastructures' heritage maintenance"*, implying the use of renewed approaches for resources optimization.

Therefore, engineering-economic procedures have been developed and implemented into proprietary tools with various purposes as: more efficient management of ordinary and extraordinary maintenance operations; rational support decision-making and road asset risk evaluation.

These tools are known as Asset Management Systems, AMS [1] which are usually composed by a GIS (Geographical Information System) architecture with database and, eventually, a decision support system. The new paradigm introduced by Asset Management represents a recent evolution of traditional maintenance approaches that are no longer be suitable to meet future business and political challenges.

The new framework already adopted in several countries has proved to provide a reliable response to various stakeholders' needs since it addresses *"demands of a nation's citizens and industry for greater accountability and transparency, more efficient use of funds, greater focus on customer expectations and more sustainable solutions"* [2].

In smart urban environment where most or individual mobility is still occurring, the recent instances related to sustainable development goals require a higher attention on transportation infrastructure preservation because of higher complexity of the transportation network systems and of multiple users (drivers as well pedestrian) and of the relationship between infrastructure assets.

On the other hand, it has to be reminded that every year 1.25 million people are killed and around 50 million are injured in road traffic crashes, providing the clear evidence that road safety is one of the most demanding health emergencies of our time [3].

In European Union, recent crash reports still highlight nearly one million of crashes resulting in injuries or death for 2019 year (pre Covid-19 pandemic period), with crashes involving vulnerable users (pedestrian and bicycles) that are almost three times higher in urban area with respect to rural one [4]. In the European area, as regards only the number of victims of road accidents, there was a significant reduction of -13% in 2020 and +5% respect 2020, in 2021 [5]. Unfortunately, it is mainly due to the strong mobility restriction caused by the Covid-19 pandemic and its effects.

In this connection, European Union, whose vision is to reduce to zero the crash related deaths by 2050, has helped the authorities, road managers and road safety professionals in making Europe's road infrastructure and management safer, by promulgating new regulations, and by promoting the adoption of guidelines concerning road safety impact assessments, road safety audits and inspections, safety rankings, management of the road network in operation [6].

Basing on these aforementioned premises, several authors proposed new methodological approaches for pavement maintenance in small municipalities [7] whereas other ones focused on infrastructure degradation modelling [8] or investigated on embedding risk into pavement management procedures [9] or resilience into asset management systems [10] but there is still a need to develop tailored urban transport infrastructures asset management procedures that may provide feasible tools for optimal budget allocation and intervention planning, as far as the impact to road safety of each maintenance action (undertaken for the specific asset element) is concerned, in order to provide clear and transparent evidence of the management policy to the various stakeholders.

In this connection, ad innovative methodological approach that is able to combine a holistic urban transport asset management vision with the new approaches to be undertaken by safety inspections according to recent European Regulations on Road Safety Managements, is presented.

The framework of the methodology and a case study, where the original methodology has been applied, are conveniently reviewed in the followings.

2   Methodology - Model Framework

The framework of the model initially consists of two analyses of the network: the accident analysis and the current road asset condition analysis. Both of them are based on the detailed knowledge of the network, in terms of network geometry, operating speeds and traffic volumes (expressed as Average Daily Traffic, ADT).

In order to perform the analyses, the identification of homogeneous sections (specific nodes as intersections, roundabouts, etc. are not included), in terms of road layout features and percentage of occurred accidents is required and, according to the Italian guidelines [11], 100 m long road section (suggested for urban areas), has been chosen.

The core of the proposed model consists into the prioritization process which combines the previous analyses results by means of several matrixes and vectors in a series combination and obtaining a synthetic index able to identify critical assets of critical segments worthy of interventions and investments.

The output of the proposed simplified road asset management model, mainly aim to improve road safety and designed to act at network level, is the multi-year scheduling for ordinary maintenance interventions as [12, 13]:

– road pavement resurfacing;
– road markings painting;
– vertical signs substitution;
– drainages and side vegetation cleaning;
– safety barriers retrofit or substitution;
– streetlight devices improvement or substitution.

In Fig. 1, the framework of the simplified proposed model has been represented and in the following paragraphs a more detailed description of the model has been provided.

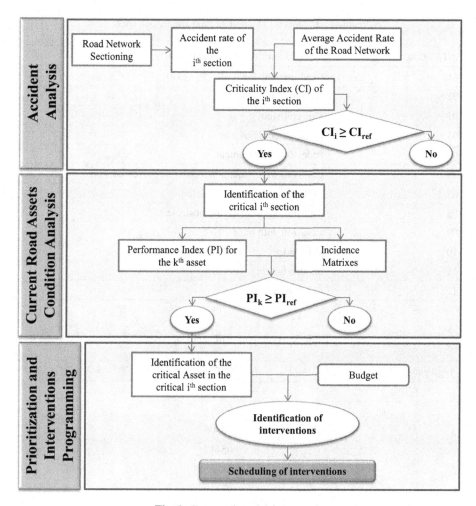

Fig. 1. Proposed model framework

2.1 Accident Analysis

The input data for the accident analysis consist on the accidents data occurred on the study road network. For each accident, the minimum requirement is the knowledge of the location, the type of accident, the day and hour, the severity of the accident (deaths, injuries, damage), the weather conditions and the pavement conditions.

These data are easily available for all the local agencies or municipalities which developed a customized accident database. On the same time, the National opensource database ISTAT [14] supplies these information with an acceptable level of precision.

The ISTAT database provides for the use of 12 different categories of accident types (see Table 1), and in the proposed model, an aggregation to 7 is performed (see Table 2).

Table 1. Categories of accident type and ISTAT code

ISTAT code	ISTAT definition of accident type
01	Head-on collision
02	Front-side collision
03	Side collision
04	Rear-end collision
05	Pedestrian involvement
06	Collision with vehicle in momentary arrest or stop
07	Collision with parked vehicle
08	Collision with accidental obstacle
09	Collision with train
10	Off-road
11	Sudden braking
12	Fall from vehicle

Table 2. Aggregation of accident types

Aggregation	ISTAT code
1	01–03
2	02
3	04–06
4	05–12
5	08
6	07–10
7	09–11

According to [15], for each road section and consequently for the overall road network, different Accident Rates (AR), depending on the daily period (night/day) and aggregation of accident type, could be evaluated. Thus 14 Average Network Accident-Type Rates that acts as reference values, have been calculated.

The accident analysis provides for the comparison of the accident rate, evaluated for each specific road section, with corresponding reference value, with the aim to identify accident-prone sections (with a Critical Index, CI, higher than the reference one) requiring a further investigation on road asset conditions.

2.2 Current Road Assets Condition Analysis

The analysis of the current conditions of the network is based on the evidences collected during the road network safety inspections which have the main aims to:

- identify road infrastructure problems that may constitute potentially dangerous situations;
- define a prioritization of corrective interventions in order to reduce number and severity of accidents;
- monitor in a continuous and systematic manner the safety conditions of the road network.

In particular the road network safety inspections, according to [6, 16, 17], consist into visual safety inspections of the roads in operation, by a team of experts, in different daily periods (day and night), during which fills technical sheets to describe the real conditions of the main road assets as: vertical road signs (replacement in case of aging or damage) and horizontal road signs (replacement in case of aging), streetlights (replacement of lamp or pole in case of damage), pavements (milling and remaking), hydraulics (lateral drainage gutter: cleaning or refurbishment/replacement in case of damage), roadside conditions (roadside greenery care) and safety barriers (replacement of road restraint systems in case of damage).

Following the inspections, for each asset and sub-asset, the qualitative judgments, are converted into quantitative values, which are appropriately weighted and combined in order to evaluate, for each road section and daily period (night/ day), the corresponding Performance Indexes (PI) related to the main road assets summarized in Table 3.

Table 3. Main assets identified for describing the current conditions

Asset		PI
Horizontal road signs	HS	PI_{HS}
Vertical road signs	VS	PI_{VS}
Hydraulics conditions	HC	PI_{HC}
Safety barriers	SB	PI_{SB}
Streetlights	SL	PI_{LS}
Pavements conditions	PC	PI_{PC}
Roadside conditions	RC	PI_{RC}

2.3 Prioritization and Interventions Programming

As previously mentioned, the core of the proposed method consists into the combination, by means of several matrices and vectors in series, of the results of the preceding analyses.

In particular, can be defined:

- the *Condition State Vector* which, for each segment and for each asset, contains the judgments of the safety inspectors;
- the *Accident-Type Risk Matrix*, one for each Accident-type aggregation, and conceived according to technical-scientific literature with the aim to identify which assets may affect occurrence and effects of a specific accident type;
- the *Risk Matrix*, one for each road segment, which is the combination of the latest two and provides the identification of the critical road segments.

Then, for each critical road segment, the Synthetic Index, defined in the Eq. 1 as function of traffic exposition, CI, AR and PI, can be calculated and their ascending order guarantees the evaluation of the maintenance interventions prioritization.

$$SI_{k,i} = \frac{ADT_i}{ADT_{max}} \left(W_d \sum_{AT} \frac{AR_{an,d,AT}}{AR_{an,d,AT_{Tot}}} PI_{d,AT} CI_{d,AT} \right.$$
$$\left. + W_n \sum_{AT} \frac{AR_{an,n,AT}}{AR_{an,n,AT_{Tot}}} PI_{n,AT} CI_{n,AT} \right) \tag{1}$$

Where:

$SI_{k,I}$ = Synthetic Index for the kth asset and the ith critical road segment;
ADT_i = Average Daily Traffic of the ith critical road segment;
ADT_{max} = Maximum Average Daily Traffic of the network;
$AR_{an,d/n,AT}$ = Diurnal/Nocturnal Average Network Accident Rate for the specific Accident Type (AT) aggregation;
$AR_{an,d/n,AT_{Tot}}$ = Total Diurnal/Nocturnal Average Network Accident Rate for the specific AT aggregation;
$PI_{d/n,AT}$ = Diurnal/Nocturnal Performance Index for the specific AT aggregation, of the ith critical road segment;
$CI_{d/n,AT}$ = Diurnal/Nocturnal Critical Value for the specific AT aggregation, of the ith critical road segment;
$AR_{an,n,AT}$ = Nocturnal Average Network Accident Rate for the specific AT f aggregation;
$AR_{an,n,AT_{Tot}}$ = Total Nocturnal Average Network Accident Rate for the specific AT aggregation;
$PI_{n,AT}$ = Nocturnal Performance Index for the specific AT aggregation, of the ith critical road segment;
$CI_{n,AT}$ = Nocturnal Critical Value for the specific AT aggregation, of the ith critical road segment;
$W_{d/n}$ = Diurnal/Nocturnal Accident Weight, evaluated by means of the Eq. 2 and Eq. 3 respectively;

$$W_d = \frac{\sum_d AR_{an,d,AT}}{\sum_{d+n} AR_{an,AT}} \tag{2}$$

$$W_n = \frac{\sum_n \text{AR}_{\text{an},n,\text{AT}}}{\sum_{d+n} \text{AR}_{\text{an},\text{AT}}} \tag{3}$$

Finally, in order to improve the safety conditions of the critical road sections, by means of a prioritization of maintenance interventions, an effective budget allocation has to be performed.

The proposed budget allocation strategy, follows the principle of maximum reduction of accident rate produced by different assets [18] and it is based on the Global Safety Performance Index (I_{GSP}) evaluation, for the entire road network, which can be defined as follows:

$$I_{GSP} = \frac{1}{M} \sum_{i=1}^{M} \text{GAR}_n \left(1 - \sum_{k=1}^{J_i} RF_{k,i} \right) \tag{4}$$

Where:

I_{GSP} = Global Safety Performance Index of the road network;
M = Total number of road sections;
GAR_n = Global Average Network Accident Rate of the ith critical road segment, before the maintenance interventions;
J_i = number of maintained assets within the ith critical road segment;
RF_{ki} = Accident Reduction factor due to the maintenance action on the kth asset, of the ith critical road segment.

Through this synthetic index, the local agencies and municipalities, on one hand can set the performance target to be achieved and the related needed budget and on the other hand, evaluate the performance level that can be reached with a fixed budget.

3 Case Study

A sample of over 30 km (15 bidirectional km), belonging to 4 urban areas located in the central Italy has been selected for the application of the method previously presented. In Fig. 2, the location of the study areas can be seen.

As specified in the previous paragraph, the nodes of the network have been excluded from analysis and 312 homogeneous sections have been identified.

According to the accident analysis, for the overall road network and for each specific road section, the accident rates have been evaluated. By way of example, the 14 Average Network Accident-Type Rates obtained have been summarized in Table 4.

At the same time, safety inspections have been carried out and the current conditions of each asset and sub-asset have been collected. A three member crew employing video-camera has been involved in the inspection task that has been carried out at normal travel speed and at reduced speed with help of law enforcement assistance. According to the current road assets condition analysis, for each road section, the relative Performance Indices (PI), one for each asset (see Table 3), have been assessed.

For example, the results, in terms of Performance Indices, obtained for the "Horizontal Signage" asset have been represented in Fig. 3. As it is possible to see, according to the

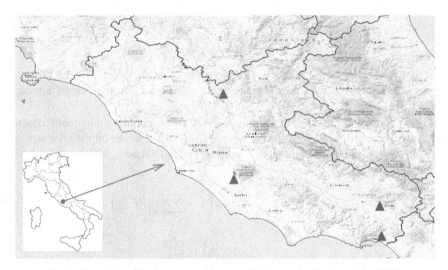

Fig. 2. Road network study areas (Source: Esri topographic base-map, [19]).

Table 4. Percentage of the Accident Type Incidence for each aggregation (columns 2 and 3) and Average Network Accident-Type Rates (columns 4 and 5) for the overall urban areas.

Accident Aggreg.	ISTAT code	% Incidence ISTAT cat.	Daily Period	
			Day	Night
Aggr. 1	01–03	32,5–67,5	0,00529	0,00878
Aggr. 2	02	100	0,02032	0,01421
Aggr. 3	04–06	89,6–10,4	0,00901	0
Aggr. 4	05–12	66,7–33,3	0,00068	0,00128
Aggr. 5	08	100	0,00109	0,0027
Aggr. 6	07–10	0–100	0,02189	0,00892
Aggr. 7	09–11	50–50	0	0
TOT			0,05827	0,04562

inspectors' evaluation, the conditions of the horizontal markings were on average compromised and severely compromised, within nocturnal and diurnal safety inspections respectively.

The application of the two analyses, allowed to identify the critical segments, in terms of both accident rate and current asset performance index and, for each for each asset of each critical segment, according to the assets performance levels detected within the safety inspections, the best maintenance strategy has to be identified, with the aim to improve safety aspects.

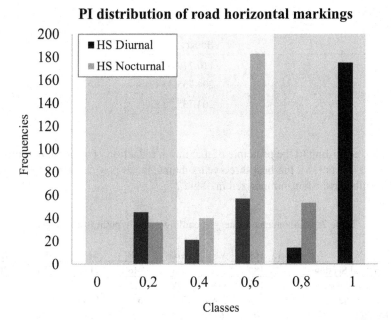

Fig. 3. PI distribution of the current condition of the asset HS.

For this reason, for each asset, three maintenance interventions with increasing cost have been proposed and, by way of example, the types of intervention suggested for the pavement maintenance strategy, have been reported in Table 5.

Table 5. Type of interventions for the asset PC.

Level of intervention	Type of intervention
Light	Milling and remaking of wear layer
Medium	Milling and remaking of wear and binder layers
Heavy	Milling and remaking of overall layers

It is worth to be highlighted that, in order to obtain the best multi-year ordinary maintenance strategy, the ordinary life cycle of each asset intervention has been taken into account (i.e. cleaning drainages and gutters and cleaning side vegetation two times for year or painting road markings one time every two years).

A plausible triennial investment plan has been hypothesized and summarized in Table 6.

Table 6. Hypothesis of triennial investment plan.

Year	Budget
1	110.779,67 €
2	204.735,33 €
3	204.735,33 €

Finally, according to the principle of maximum reduction of accident rate produced by different assets [18], the best three-years maintenance program has been identified and its results have been summarized in Table 7.

Table 7. Maintenance strategy according to the hypothesized budget

	Asset	HS	VS	HC	SB	SL	PC	RC
	Total Critical Sections	180	180	186	46	218	218	204
Year 1	Maintained sections	180	148	104	25	35	3	99
	Used Budjet [€]	3.324	11.994	13.663	36.530	14.908	10.733	14.785
	Rest [€]	0	62	23	951	372	3.392	44
Year 2	Maintained sections	mc	32	186	21	137	15	204
	Used Budjet [€]	0	2.633	24.687	29.532	57.273	56.525	30.740
	Rest[€]	0	0	0	0	251	3.095	0
Year 3	Maintained sections	180	mc	186	mc	46	14	204
	Used Budjet [€]	3.324	0	24.687	0	19.712	125.920	30.740
	Rest [€]	0	0	0	0	0	353	0
	Total Maintained sections	180	180	186	46	218	32	204

mc = maintenance completed.

4   Conclusions

In this paper a simplified road asset management system for Local Agencies and Municipalities has been proposed. The main aim of this method is to improve road safety combining traffic and accident data with current performance conditions of the network. The output of the method is the multi-year scheduling for ordinary maintenance interventions on the main road assets.

The method has been applied on 312 homogeneous sections, corresponding to more than 30 km of urban road network, in central Italy. In order to fulfill the principle of maximum reduction of accident rate, based on a plausible hypothesized triennial investment plan, the most effective multi-year ordinary maintenance strategy has been evaluated.

Relevant points in favor of the proposed method are resumed the followings: the input data of the model can be easily collected from public database and from safety inspections, furthermore, the methodology itself can be simply implemented in a conventional spreadsheet. Given the great flexibility of the method, it can also be applied to suburban or rural areas, without losing validity. The results obtained by the application of the simplified road asset management system, seem to provide evidence that the method can be considered an effective tool for Local Road managers.

Acknowledgements. Authors wish to thanks Lazio Highway Agency (ASTRAL) for their support in this research.

References

1. ISO 55000. Asset management - Management systems - Requirements. Standard for Asset Management. International Standards Organization. Geneva (2014)
2. World Road Association (PIARC). "Asset Management Manual". https://road-asset.piarc.org/en. Accessed Mar 2022
3. World Health Organization. Global status report on road safety 2015. Geneva, Switzerland (2015). World Health Organization. https://www.afro.who.int/sites/default/files/2017-06/9789241565066_eng.pdf. ISBN 9789241565066. Accessed Mar 2022
4. European Commission: "European Road Safety Observatory, Annual statistical report on road safety in the EU 2020" Road safety thematic report – Fatigue. European Road Safety Observatory. Brussels, European Commission, Directorate General for Transport (2021)
5. European Commission: Directorate-General for Mobility and Transport. "Road safety in the EU: fatalities in 2021 remain well below pre-pandemic level" (2022). https://transport.ec.europa.eu/news/preliminary-2021-eu-road-safety-statistics-2022-03-28_en. Accessed May 2022
6. EU Directive 2008/96/EC of the European Parliament and of the Council of 19 November 2008 on road infrastructure safety management
7. D'Apuzzo, M., Evangelisti, A., Nicolosi, V., Di Silvestro, A.: Pavement maintenance of small municipalities: evaluation of the quality evolution for different budget scenarios. In: Pavement and Asset Management: Proceedings of the World Conference on Pavement and Asset Management (WCPAM 2017), Baveno, Italy, 12–16 June 2017, vol. 1, pp. 293–300 (2019). https://doi.org/10.1201/9780429264702. ISBN 9780429264702
8. Nicolosi, V., D'Apuzzo, M., Evangelisti, A.: Cumulated frictional dissipated energy and pavement skid deterioration: evaluation and correlation. Constr. Build. Mater. **263**, 120020–120029 (2020). https://doi.org/10.1016/j.conbuildmat.2020.120020. ISSN 0950-0618
9. Nicolosi, V., Augeri, M., D'Apuzzo, M., Santos, L.P., Evangelisti, A., Santilli, D.: Economic risk evaluation in road pavement management. In: Gervasi, O., et al. (eds.) ICCSA 2021. LNCS, vol. 12950, pp. 394–410. Springer, Cham (2021). https://doi.org/10.1007/978-3-030-86960-1_28. ISBN 978-3-030-86959-5. ISSN 0302-9743
10. Nicolosi, V., Augeri, M., D'Apuzzo, M., Evangelisti, A., Santilli, D.: A probabilistic approach to the evaluation of seismic resilience in road asset management. Int. J. Disaster Risk Sci. **13**, 114–124 (2022). https://doi.org/10.1007/s13753-022-00395-5
11. Italian Ministerial Decree of May 2nd, 2012, according to Legislative Decree n° 35 of March 15th 2011
12. Italian Legislative Decree n°163/2006 – for implementation of European directives 2004/17/CE and 2004/18/CE
13. Italian Legislative Decree n° 50 of April 18th, 2016 - for implementation of European directives 2014/23/UE, 2014/24/UE and 2014/25/UE

14. Italian National Institute of Statistics. http://dati.istat.it/. Accessed Mar 2022
15. Italian Ministerial Circular n° 3699 of Jun 8th, 2001. Ministry of public works and transport
16. Italian Legislative Decree n° 35 of March 15th, 2011 - for implementation of European directive 2008/96/CE
17. Publication No. FHWA-SA-06-06. Road Safety Audit Guidelines. Synectics Transportation Consultants Inc. Center for Transportation Research and Education (CTRE), Iowa State University Pennsylvania State University. Kittelson & Associates, Inc. Science Applications International Corporation (SAIC) (2006)
18. Elvik, R., Vaa, T., Hoye, A.: The Handbook of Road Safety Measures (2009)
19. QGIS.org. QGIS Geographic Information System. QGIS Association (2022). http://www.qgis.org

Deflection and Friction Performance
of Waste-Wooden Block Pavements

Mauro Coni[1]([✉]) [ID], Giovanna Concu[1], Carla Carcangiu[2], and Francesca Maltinti[1] [ID]

[1] Department of Civil and Environmental Engineering and Architecture (DICAAR), University of Cagliari, via Marengo 2, 09123 Cagliari, Italy
mconi@unica.it
[2] E-Distribuzione, Italian Authority for Electric Energy Distribution, Rome, Italy

Abstract. The use of waste wood for road light pavements is essential for environmental and economic sustainability.

The paper investigates the mechanical performance of pavements built with waste wood elements discarded from Sardinia manufacture (Italy). Without structural value, mainly Sardinian wood is used for combustion and heating due to the characteristics of dimensional irregularity, non-homogeneity, and the presence of defects. Even small urban and forest furniture comes from foreign markets. Landscape reasons, emissions reduction, and environmental integration with the local context could encourage its use if reliable techniques are available.

The study first analyzed the structural response of a portion of pavement made with waste wood bricks (pine and Eucalyptus). Subsequently, a Finite Element simulation of the pavement has been validated with the tests' results. The experimental pavement was created with Interlocked Block Pavement (IBP) technique, using brick elements $13 \times 6 \times 10$ cm. The behavior of the pavement was analyzed in situ with dynamic deflection tests using the Falling Weight Deflectometer test (FWD). Further tests performed in the laboratory investigated the friction of the wood pavement surface. The simulation results show that the wooden pavement elements do not differ substantially from the classic concrete IBP and HMA cracked pavement. The mean deflections are greater than 19%, while the vertical stress on the foundation layer is equivalent. As with the classic concrete IBP, the results largely depend on the bearing capacity of the substrate and the degree of interlocking.

Friction tests show good values with mean values of $53 \div 64$ BPN. The most significant values were observed in the elements eucalyptus. The direction of the wood fibers also influences the results: about 3 points in the case of pine and over 7 points in the case of Eucalyptus. The study shows how the use of wood for the pavement with elements is sustainable and practicable due to the minor and low-traffic roads while also guaranteeing permeability and low-cost maintenance.

Keywords: Wood pavement · Forest road · Reuse of waste wood · FWD alternative application · Wood element pavement

---

C. Carcangiu—Independent Researcher.

© The Author(s), under exclusive license to Springer Nature Switzerland AG 2022
O. Gervasi et al. (Eds.): ICCSA 2022 Workshops, LNCS 13382, pp. 663–677, 2022.
https://doi.org/10.1007/978-3-031-10592-0_48

1 Introduction

The construction of road pavements has a significant impact on the environment: the removal of aggregates from nature, the energy conduction for the production of materials, and the alteration of the superficial and deep flow of water. Furthermore, road construction must follow rational criteria to gain mechanical performances, costs, and traffic [1]. In the mid-19th century, Samuel Nicolson invented the wooden block pavement, but over the centuries, the use of wood has been limited due to its mechanical characteristics and durability. Many applications remain confined to pedestrian and cycle paths and forest roads (Fig. 1).

Fig. 1. South Camac street (Philadelphia, USA) was paved in wood in 1917 and restored in 2017. It is an example of "Nicolson pavement" still exists in several Countries

Many previous studies of forest roads point out how the bearing capacity of the road subgrade affects the regularity and quality of the road surface [2–5]. Since waste-wood element is a by-product, almost the energy and CO_2 emissions for its manufacture have already been spent, and all the possible use in the road construction can decrease the exploitation of natural resources and limit energy consumption and CO_2 emissions. In addition, wood accumulates carbon captured by trees as CO2 from the atmosphere [6].

Many studies underline as the road subgrade bearing capacity [2–5] and the wood's resistance to biotic factors and fungi [7, 8] affect the durability. These investigations are not exhaustive why the complexity of the mechanical response of the elements pavement and the interpretation of the results are not comparable in many different approaches. For this reason, a typical approach adopted by road pavement engineers has been implemented in two-phase. First, a FE model of segmented pavement, assembled with waste wood elements, was validated with dynamic deflectometer test results. Subsequently, the model was subjected to mechanical stresses from the heavy axles.

The Falling Weight Deflectometer (FWD) is an impulsive test developed for road and airfield pavement to reproduce the wheel loads transit. The vertical applied stress has a control-shaped dropping weight on a circular load plate. At the same time, 12 geophones inline register the vertical velocity in different positions every 0.05 ms. The stress can be modified, varying the drop height (50 ÷ 390 mm) and the weight (50 ÷

350 kg) of the falling mass so that the impulse load can range from 40 to 120 Kn in the period of $25 \div 30$ ms [9]. The load and measures the time history for each drop is stored for 60 ms. An instrumented vehicle tows the FWD, and the operator can control the test with a laptop computer (Fig. 2).

Fig. 2. FWD equipment

From the shape and the amplitude of the deflection basin (Fig. 3), it is possible to estimate the value of the stiffness of each pavement layer throughout *"backcalculation"* post-processing, implemented by ELMOD6[(c)].

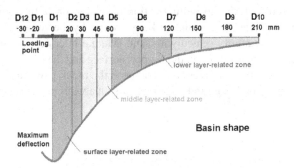

Fig. 3. Basin shape profile

In addition, from the raw FWD data acquired, it is possible to obtain particular indices, called Basin Index, which are well correlated with the stiffness of the layers. Those considered relevant for the trials were:

- Base Layer Index BLI = D_0–D_{300}
- Middle Layer Index MLI = D300–D600
- Lower Layer Index LLI = D600–D900.

The FWD is developed to monitor flexible (asphalt), rigid (concrete), and semi-rigid pavements (asphalt and concrete). Some recent applications concern unconventional investigations such as bridges [10–12] and paving stones [13]. Some Authors use the FWD for research purposes in testing and simulating pavement structures [14–16]. The

FWD became a standard to assess the performance of pavements and roads, and airport National and International authorities have integrated FWD equipment and related analysis into the regulations and technical specifications.

Brick pavements have increased considerably in Europe in the last 30 years, using stone and concrete materials for the elements. Thanks to their aesthetic characteristics and high permeability, they have been used for paving squares, parks, and residential areas. Furthermore, in Northern Europe, they have also been widely used to construct urban roads, ports, and airports.

Another practical aspect in the urban context is their ability to mitigate the thermal field, mitigating the UHI (Urban Heat Islands), and further reduction could result from the use of wood.

The pavements capable of decreasing thermal field are known as "cool pavements". The reduction can be achieved with highly reflective materials and porous layers [17]. The "cool pavements", include conventional asphalt and concrete pavements, stone pavement [13], and nonconventional surfaces (white-colored course, resin-bonded pavements, micro-surfacing, and porous layer) [18].

Brick-pavement, under the action of traffic, tends to self-lock due to mutual action on lateral or vertical contact surfaces. The pavement is characterized by interlocking, created by the system of elements, dry-laid on a bed of sand and dry sealed with sand. Mutual interlocking ensures adequate distribution of surface loads through the support surface and the friction generated in the joints. Brick-pavement, under the action of traffic, tends to self-lock due to mutual action on lateral or vertical contact surfaces. The pavement is characterized by interlocking, created by the system of elements, dry-laid on a bed of sand and dry sealed with sand. Mutual interlocking ensures adequate distribution of surface loads through the support surface and the friction generated in the joints. Figure 4 shows typical layers that compose the block pavement: a layer of self-locking blocks, one in bedding sand, a base layer (not always present), and a foundation layer.

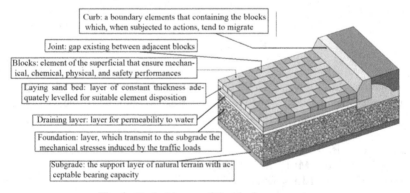

Fig. 4. Typical layers of the block pavements

The presence of the joints considerably influences the regularity of block pavements. The sealing of the joints is essential for the efficiency of the structure. The interlocking effect, which is the ability to distribute the load from a block to the adjacent contact blocks, is ensured by the sand friction in the joints. The filling of the joints guarantees the mechanical function of joint-element connection and the mutual collaboration between the elements. When laying block paving, it is good practice to pre-clog the joints as soon as the installation of the elements is finished. The sand is spread and distributed over the entire surface, then vibro-compacted. Subsequently, a final clogging of the joints with further application of sand completes the pavement. A good laying is achieved mainly through the sealing of the joints. The use of unsuitable sand, incorrect clogging, or sand removal before complete clogging under load can compromise its overall stability. For block pavement, the boundary containment, suitably dimensioned, can oppose the horizontal tensions due to trafficking. The retain can be determined by the presence of fixed structures or, more frequently, by installing prefabricated containment curbs in concrete or stone, laid in place before laying the elements.

2   Data and Methodology

To find a way to use wood waste, friction tests were carried out in the laboratory, while a portion of pilot waste-wood block pavement was made in situ and subjected to bearing capacity and deflectometric tests. The wood species used were wood and Eucalyptus combined in different configurations. Subsequently, a finite element model was developed, validated by in situ tests, which allows for analyze in detail the mechanical response of the block pavement and optimize it in terms of materials, configuration and thickness.

Starting from the wooden waste planks of Eucalyptus and Maritime Pine 13.0 × 6.0 cm, through the use of a band saw, wooden bricks were obtained, each with a height of 10.0 cm.

Friction Tests in the Laboratory
According to Standard Test [19], the surface adhesion of the pavement was investigated using the British Pendulum equipment. The test simulated the grip of the tires, in good condition, of a vehicle at a speed of 50 km/h when braking on a wet road, at a temperature of 15 °C. The British pendulum tester is a dynamic pendulum impact tester based on the mechanical energy loss when a rubber slider edge is propelled over the pavement surface.

The equipment consists of a pendulum with a movable arm, adjustable in height, at the end, a slide is applied, covered with a special rubber with known characteristics, preloaded with a system of springs (Fig. 5).

The test is performed by manually lifting the pendulum arm and letting it fall sparsely against the surface. The ascent is detected on the appropriate scale, equipped with a maximum index.

The measured values are expressed in "BPN" units by "British Portable Tester Number." For the results to be comparable and repeatable, it was necessary to determine the value of the test temperature, as the values need adjustment factor and referred to the standard temperature of 15 °C.

To evaluate the adherence results, the results were compared with the typical road pavement values in Table 1.

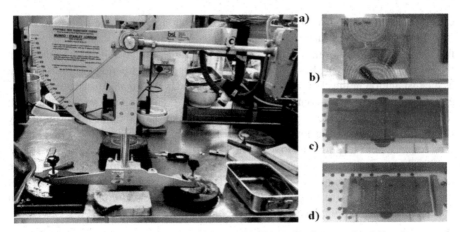

Fig. 5. Laboratory adherence tests: a) British Portable Tester, b) pine sample, c) Eucalypt sample in orthogonal, and d) parallel direction.

Table 1. Typical BPN road pavement values

Type	BPN value	Quality
A	>65	Excellent
B	55 ÷ 65	Good
C	45 ÷ 55	Acceptable
D	<45	Slippery pavement

Seven specimens of Maritime Pine were tested, on which the test was followed on both sides, and one specimen of Eucalyptus, obtained from 6 side-by-side and locked bricks, which were arranged to perform the test in two directions. The identification of the specimens was performed for the Maritime Pine by assigning a different letter starting from A and the two faces with the numbers 1 and 2. For the Eucalyptus, the test was carried out on the faces indicated as A1 and A2, in a direction perpendicular, A3 and A4, in a direction parallel.

Deflection Tests In Situ

A prototype of the waste-wood block pavement with dimensions of 6.0 × 4.0 m was built on site. Before laying the wooden bricks, the substrate was adequately prepared, leveled, and rolled. A layer of sand was placed on this to ensure the drainage of the water. Subsequently, Maritime Pine planks have been placed on the boundaries of the pavement to retain it in place. Then have been laid the wooden bricks placed them side by side, creating a collaborative pavement structure. The joints between the brick have been filled with sand, guaranteeing mutual interaction between the wooden elements (Figs. 6 and 7).

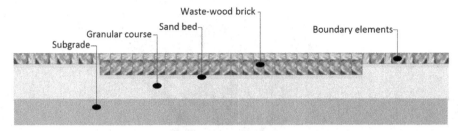

Fig. 6. The layers of pavement trial section

Fig. 7. Performing FWD tests on the pavement trial section

Finite Element Simulaiton

Structural analysis has been implemented in ANSYS, which allows to solve complex structural engineering problems and make better and faster decisions during the the design process. In addiction, it is possible to customize and automate solutions for mechanical structural problems and parameterize them in order to analyze different design scenarios. The finite element model of the developed woodblock pavement has dimensions of 1.39 × 1.39 m and is 2.0 m high. The first 10 cm of the model represents the waste-wooden blocks. The 5 cm below the blocks is the layer of bed sand. Below is the foundation layer of 20 cm and the subgrade of 1.65 m. Each element representing the wooden brick of the pavement has dimensions in plan equal to 6.0 × 13.0 cm and is 10 cm high (Fig. 8).

The model was set on a square grid of points by arranging the rows of points alternately spaced 6 cm to identify the wooden bricks and 0.2 cm to identify the sand joints. The properties of the materials were then associated with the various elements identified by the grid. In particular, the wood material properties have been associated with bricks, while the properties of a fictitious material with a low modulus of elasticity have been associated with sand joints. This procedure has been developed in such a way as to be

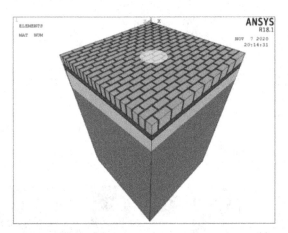

Fig. 8. The finite element model implemented with ANSYS[(c)] software

able to make it automatic and generate the mesh of the FEM model for all possible configurations of the arrangement of the blocks.

The load was applied to the center of the model, as shown in Fig. 8. The maximum load applied is equal to 1000 kPa, equivalent to the maximum load applied with the third stress level in the FWD test.

3   Results

Friction Tests in the Laboratory
Table 2 shows the friction test performed with British Pendulum. By comparing the results obtained in Table 2 with the values shown in the Table 1, it can be seen that most of the Maritime Pine specimens belong to category C. Only one specimen belongs to class D. The results obtained from the tests on Eucalyptus show that 50% of the specimens can be classified in category A, while the remaining 50% in category B.

Deflection Tests In Situ
First, the identification and analysis of the deflection basins were carried out. The 16 tests were performed in different positions, repeating the tests with increasing load levels equal to 600, 800, and 1000 kPa.

The FWD tests were performed both on the substrate without pavement, on the layer of sand, and the waste-wood block pavement. The tests on the sand layer were carried out twice on six points. Four stations have been on the wooden pavement. In Table 3, it is possible to observe the value of the displacements for each station for the maximum load value.

Table 2. BPN tests data.

Wood	Fibber direction	Samples	Data 1	Data 2	Data 3	Data 4	Data 5	Mean (3,4,5)	Temp °C	Temp. adjustment	Adjusted values
Pine	Orthogonal	A1	56	53	55	50	51	52	20	1	53
Pine	Orthogonal	A2	57	54	52	49	50	50	20	1	51
Pine	Orthogonal	B1	50	49	48	54	46	49	20	1	50
Pine	Orthogonal	B2	55	53	51	50	50	50	20	1	51
Pine	Orthogonal	C1	61	55	55	55	50	53	20	1	54
Pine	Orthogonal	C2	56	52	51	50	50	50	20	1	51
Pine	Orthogonal	D1	60	55	55	54	52	54	20	1	55
Pine	Orthogonal	D2	55	50	50	50	50	50	20	1	51
Pine	Orthogonal	E1	60	55	54	51	50	52	20	1	53
Pine	Orthogonal	E2	56	55	52	51	52	52	20	1	53
Pine	Orthogonal	F1	60	55	54	53	51	53	20	1	54
Pine	Orthogonal	F2	60	55	54	54	51	53	20	1	54
Pine	Orthogonal	G1	60	55	54	54	50	53	20	1	54
Pine	Orthogonal	G2	60	50	50	50	48	49	20	1	50
Eucalypt	Orthogonal	A1	66	66	66	65	65	65	20	1	66
Eucalypt	Parallel	A2	69	69	69	68	68	68	20	1	69
Eucalypt	Orthogonal	A3	62	60	59	58	57	58	20	1	59
Eucalypt	Parallel	A4	63	61	60	60	60	60	20	1	61

Table 3. Deflection data

					Sand								Pavement			
Distance [mm]	Station 1 [µm]	Station 2 [µm]	Station 3 [µm]	Station 4 [µm]	Station 5 [µm]	Station 6 [µm]	Station 7 [µm]	Station 8 [µm]	Station 9 [µm]	Station 10 [µm]	Station 11 [µm]	Station 12 [µm]	Station 1 [µm]	Station 2 [µm]	Station 3 [µm]	Station 4 [µm]
-450	-551	-914	-505	-614	-340	-556	-505	-500	-380	-374	-73	-75	-3	-75	-207	-213
-300	-904	-679	-478	-360	-309	-462	-422	-414	-397	-431	-47	-53	0	-172	-187	-240
0	-1390	-1425	-1350	-1398	-1558	-1537	-1175	-1309	-1600	-1592	-1616	-1652	-2106	1794	-1857	1643
200	-320	-281	-312	-415	-282	-298	-287	-241	-256	-259	-301	-457	-277	-218		
300	-855	-610	-746	-792	-570	-283	-675	-592	-803	-244	-596	-446	-84	-181	-279	-324
450	-413	-510	-345	-358	-375	-332	-359	-351	-505	-576	-391	-380	-198	-257	-225	-243
600	-213	-215	-297	-295	-252	-439	-230	-230	-244	-284	-231	-261	-131	-155	-172	-178
900	-133	-307	-161	-322	-151	-236	-167	-352	-152	-123	-233	-228	-67	-81	-73	-85
1200	-145	-159	-92	-91	-94	-102	-97	-185	-71	-74	-160	-147	-39	-53	-53	-59
1500	-55	-60	-59	-67	-58	-61	-146	-75	-50	-53	-118	-104	-37	-43	-45	-45
1800	-43	-55	-47	-57	-50	-40	-43	-43	-47	-51	-45	-43	-38	-38	-37	-38
2100	-33	-35	-45	-41	-49	-30	-71	-55	-42	-49	-30	-26	-30	-31	-40	-32

(Drop 3)

In the graph (Fig. 9) of the deflection basins, it is possible to observe how these have an irregular trend, typical in pavements made up of elements. The wood elements exhibit anomalous behaviors, with a rigid rotation of the wooden elements due to the action of the load. The geophones farthest from the load axis are affected by the deformation of the subgrade, with low and graduated values.

The stress-strain relationship obtained also considering the layer of the wooden pavement also has a nonlinear trend.

An analysis was then conducted on the deflection data, through which the stiffness index of the surface layers and the stiffness index of the intermediate layers were

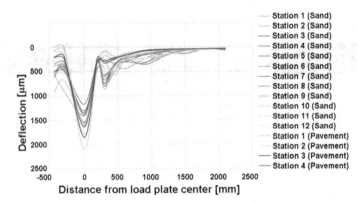

Fig. 9. The deflection basin measured applying FWD drop weight with 1000 kPa pressure

obtained. The indexes which referred to each load level and for each station, were determined (Fig. 4).

Table 4. Basin index

	sand												pavement			
	Station 1	Station 2	Station 3	Station 4	Station 5	Station 6	Station 7	Station 8	Station 9	Station 10	Station 11	Station 12	Station 1	Station 2	Station 3	Station 4
BLI1	535	815	604	606	988	1254	500	717	797	1348	1020	1206	1932	1613	1578	1319
MLI	642	395	449	497	318	-156	445	362	559	-40	365	185	-47	26	107	146
DLI	80	-92	136	-27	101	203	63	-122	92	161	-2	33	64	74	99	93

The value of the BLI, indicative of the surface stiffness, eexhibits an average value referred to the wooden pavement lower than that obtained on the sand. This denotes how the pavement is more deformable than the sand layer. The anomalousbehavior is that the wooden blocks are moving under load. However, the positive effect of the presence of wood is found in the deeper layers, distributing the load. The deep stiffness indices (DLI) are much lower than those obtained with the sand layer.

Finite Element Simulation

For the validation of the FEM model, the deflection basin obtained from the FEM simulation was compared with that obtained from the trial section. In particular, mean stiffness values obtained by back-calculation of the deflectometric data have been adjusted to consider a joint efficiency factor. Therefore, these values express an "effective" value averaged over the entire pavement rather than the stiffness modulus of the single wooden element.

Figure 10 shows the two curves representing the deflection basins, the experimental one obtained using the data from the on-site test with FWD (in red) and through the FEM simulation (in blue).

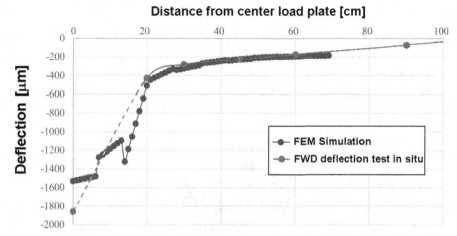

Fig. 10. The deflection basin was simulated (blue line) and measured in situ (red). (Color figure online)

In the first 20 cm, it is possible to observe the polyline profile of block pavement simulated and the red dashed line inferred by deflection measures at the first and second geophone. Overall, the red dots corresponding to the geophones position correlate well with FEM simulation, excluding the first one (D0). This is clearly explained because the woodblock dimension of 6 × 13 cm is less than the load plate diameter (30 cm) and less than the second geophone distance (20 cm from load plate center).

Structural analysis of the validated FEM model how to better understand the mechanical behavior of the block pavement. In the FEM simulation, it is possible to observe how the elements tend to rotate towards the center of application of the load, and the material associated with the joints does not contribute and does not allow the pavement to work uniformly. This causes no mutual collaboration between the blocks as there is no transmission of stresses between them. Figure 11 shows the results of the FEM simulation in terms of displacements, stresses, and deformations.

In addition, the simulations were developed considering four types of block arrangements, two load configurations, and three block thicknesses. For each analysis, the distributions of 25 stress-strain parameters were considered:

- displacements in x, y, and z-direction (δ_x, δ_y, δ_z)
- normal, tangential, and equivalent stresses (σ_x, σ_y, σ_z, τ_{xy}, τ_{xz}, τ_{yz}, σ_1, σ_2, σ_3, σ_{int}, σ_{eqv})
- normal, tangential, and equivalent deformation (ε_x, ε_y, ε_z, ε_{xy}, ε_{xz}, ε_{yz}, ε_1, ε_2, ε_3, ε_{int}, ε_{eqv}).

The study is still ongoing, but it is possible to illustrate some results. In general, it is observed that the lateral retain and the joints efficiency allow the pavement to work uniformly and therefore represent one of the crucial aspects in pavement construction.

Achieving this result means that the blocks in which the loads are applied undergo a failure and the adjacent ones collaborate, transmitting the stresses.

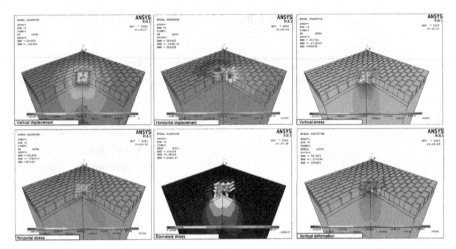

Fig. 11. Stresses and strains distributions in the FEM simulation

As the thickness of the block increases, the stress distribution is uniform, and the maximum deflection decreases, thanks to the greater frictional force generated between the blocks. When there are only vertical loads, more significant differences occur between the four distributions of the blocks studied. The presence of horizontal components also determines a uniform behavior making for thicknesses more significant than 10 cm, the tension level of the four configurations almost coincident.

The maximum deflections are almost independent of the arrangement of the elements but significantly depend on the thickness. They increase by 78% for thicknesses of 8 cm and by 274% for thicknesses of 6 cm.

4   Conclusions and Remarks

The investigation allowed to highlight some critical aspects of the use of waste Sardinian wood to create block pavement for light-load roads. This use would have several benefits compared to cementitious and bituminous materials: high architectural and landscape qualities, better integration with local contexts, reduced emissions, lower energy consumption, more excellent permeability, reduced thermal field, and recovery of waste materials. For this purpose, it is necessary to ensure the pavement's adequate and reliable mechanical design. The research suggests reducing waste wood into small elements ($13 \times 6 \times 10$ cm.), thus removing the effect of geometric imperfections, irregularities, and inhomogeneity.

Two main aspects are investigated: adherence and mechanical stability. The adhesion characteristics were first analyzed in the laboratory. The BPN tests have shown that the elements in Maritime Pine offer an acceptable performance while the elements in Eucalyptus exhibit high performance. Therefore, the pavement construction mixing the two species would result in suitable for transit safety. The structural response was investigated both in situ, through the construction of a trial section, and numerical simulation with the FEM model of a portion of block pavement made with waste wood bricks.

The experimental pavement was investigated with dynamic deflection using the Falling Weight Deflector. The data measurements show that:

- the deflections of wood pavement are comparable to those of similar road HMA pavements cracked. The mean deflections are greater than 19%. Improving the characteristics and compaction of the subgrade would further reduce deflections. The tests also show a nonlinear response due to the lack of joints load transfer efficiency.
- The mechanical response is complex and nonlinear.
- The BLI, surface stiffness index, exhibits an average value greater on the sand surface than pavement surface. The pavement is more deformable than the sand layer, and this anomalous behavior is related to wooden block's movement under load.
- The woodblock pavement has a positive effect in the deeper layers due to its ability to distribute the load. The deep stiffness indices (DLI) are much lower than those obtained with the sand layer.

Some valuable findings can be deduced from these results:

- the coupling and the interlocking between the wooden elements is a critical issue
- The loads transmitted by the FWD assume typical road values and for DROP3 equal to 1000 kPa they correspond to an axle of a heavy vehicle of 14 tons.
- The FWD imposes excessive stresses and, by its nature of a dynamic type. Therefore, it will be necessary for future research to adapt the equipment and the stress profile to the typical ones that may affect wooden floors, in general, less than 5 tons and with low speed (<30 km/h).
- The position of geophones is typically set for a road application, but in element block, pavement investigation needs to be modified to measure deflection every 5 ÷ 10 cm to follow block movements.

Finally, a different block configuration, thickness, and subgrade were simulated. The woodblock thickness is the main parameter that affect the pavement response, while the block configuration exhibit a low influence.

The maximum deflections are almost independent of the arrangement of the elements but significantly depend on the thickness. They increase by 78% for thicknesses of 8 cm and by 274% for thicknesses of 6 cm.

Acknowledgments. This study was supported by the MIUR (Ministry of Education, Universities and Research [Italy]) through a project entitled WEAKI TRANSIT: WEAK-demand areas Innovative TRANsport Shared services for Italian Towns (Project protocol: 20174ARRHT_004; CUP Code: F74I19001290001), financed with the PRIN 2017 (Research Projects of National Relevance) program. We authorize the MIUR to reproduce and distribute reprints for Governmental purposes, notwithstanding any copyright notations thereon. Any conclusions, opinions, findings, or recommendations expressed in this paper are those of the authors and do not necessarily reflect the visions of the MIUR.

The research is also supported by Sardinia Regional Administration (Italy) under SRACC (Regional Adaptation Strategy to Climate Change).

Author Contributions. Concept and methodology, M.C., G.C., C.C., and F.M.; experimental campaign and validation, M.C., and C.C.; analysis, M.C., G.C., and F.M.; writing, review and editing, M M.C., C.C., and F.M.; project administration, M.C. and F.M. All authors have read and agreed to the published version of the manuscript.

References

1. Demi, M.: Impacts, management and functional planning criterion of forest road network system in Turkey. Transp. Res. Part A Policy Pract. **41**, 56–68 (2007)
2. Miler, A.T., Czerniak, A., Grajewski, S., Kaminski, B., Okonski, B.: Marshlands of "LasyRychtalskie" forest promotion complex—present state and perspective of changes. Infrastruct. Ecol. Rural. Areas **3**, 21–36 (2007)
3. O'Mahony, M.J., Ueberschaer, A., Owende, P.M.O., Ward, S.M.: Bearing capacity of forest access roads builton peat soils. J. Terramech. **37**, 127–138 (2000)
4. Martin, A.M., Owende, P.M.O., O'Mahony, M.J., Ward, S.M.: Estimation of the serviceability of forest access roads. J. For. Eng. **10**, 55–61 (1999)
5. Trzcinski, G., Kozakiewicz, P., Selwakowski, R.: The technical aspects of using timber in the construction of forest roads. J. Water Land Dev. **34**, 241–247 (2017)
6. Kozakiewicz, P., Trzciński, G.: Wood in the construction of forest roads on poor-bearing road subgrades. Forests **11**, 138 (2020). https://doi.org/10.3390/f11020138
7. Jensen, P., Gregory, D.J.: Selected physical parameters to characterize the state of preservation of waterlogged archaeological wood: a practical guide for their determination. J. Archaeol. Sci. **33**, 551–559 (2006)
8. Kim, Y.S., Singh, A.P.: Micromorphological characteristics of wood biodegradation in wet environments: a review. IAWA J. **21**, 135–155 (2000)
9. Federal Highway Administration Research and Technology, "Using Falling Weight Deflectometer Data With Mechanistic-Empirical Design and Analysis, Volume III: Guidelines for Deflection Testing, Analysis, and Interpretation. FHWA-HRT-16-011, December 2017
10. Coni, M., et al.: Fast falling weight deflectometer method for condition assessment of RC bridges. Appl. Sci. **11**, 1743 (2021). https://doi.org/10.3390/app11041743
11. Coni, M., Knapton, J., Senes, R., Annunziata, F.: FEM simulation and experimental analysis of block pavements in airfield apron. In: Proceedings IX Conference S.I.I.V. Italian Society of Transport Infrastructures, Cagliari (1999)
12. Rawn, J.D.: Rapid condition assessment of bridges by falling weight deflectometer. University of Arkansas (2014)
13. Coni, M., Portas, S., Maltinti, F., Pinna, F.: Sealing of paving stone joints. IJPRT – Int. J. Pavement Res. Technol. Elsevier Chin. Soc. Pavement Eng. (2018). https://doi.org/10.1016/j.ijprt.2018.07.002
14. Pigozzi, F., Coni, M., Portas, S., Maltinti, F.: Implementation of deflection bowl measurements for structural evaluations at network level of airport pavement management system. In: FAA - Worldwide Airport Technology Transfer Conference (2014)
15. Al-Qadi, I.L., Portas, S., Coni, M., Lahouar, S.: Runway pavement stress and strain experimental measurements. J. Transp. Res. Board **1**(2153), 162–169 (2010). Scopus Code: 2-s2.0-78651268142, ISI: Pavement Management 2010
16. Wang, H., Al-Qadi, I.L., Portas, S., Coni, M.: Three-dimensional finite element modeling of instrumented airport runway pavement responses. In: TRB Transportation Research Board, 92th Annual Meeting, Washington, 12–17 January 2013
17. U.S. EPA, Cool Pavements. In: Reducing Urban Heat Islands: Compendium of Strategies, U.S. Environmental Protection Agency (EPA) (2012). https://www.epa.gov/sites/production/files/2017-05/documents/reducing_urban_heat_islands_ch_5.pdf

18. Coni, M.: Ultrathin multi-functional overlay. In: ASCE Airfield and Highway Pavements Conference 2013, Los Angeles, 9–12 June 2013
19. ASTM E303-93: Standard Test Method for Measuring Surface Fric-tional Properties Using the British Pendulum Tester (2018)

Author Index

Akbar, Ribi 264
Amato, Natale 473
Anatriello, Giuseppina 3
Andrea, Lombardi 348
Angelini, Andrea 547
Annunziata, Alfonso 439
Apriliyanto, Yusuf Bramastya 275
Arman, Ala 173
Ascenzi, Daniela 319

Balucani, Nadia 249
Basbas, Socrates 410
Bazaikin, Yaroslav 334
Bellati, Riccardo 109
Bellini, Pierfrancesco 173
Borghesi, Costanza 305
Borseková, Kamila 191

Caglioti, Concetta 237
Campisi, Tiziana 410
Cappelli, Giuseppe 650
Carcangiu, Carla 663
Carpentieri, Gerardo 93, 395
Casagrande, Pedro Benedito 585
Casavecchia, Piergiorgio 249
Caselli, Barbara 423
Catapano, Ilaria 519
Chiordi, Simone 67
Cicchiello, Elisabetta 3
Cirilo, Elder José Reioli 459
Colica, Emanuele 519
Concu, Giovanna 663
Coni, Mauro 613, 640, 663
Cozzolino, Marilena 534, 547

D'Amico, Sebastiano 519
D'Apuzzo, Mauro 650
da Costa Gomes, Diego Guilherme 585
de Aragão, Emília Valença Ferreira 319
De Lotto, Roberto 109
De Luca, Antonella 237
de Oliveira Laranjeira, Jonas 585
de Paiva Guimarães, Marcelo 459
de Sena, Ítalo Sousa 585

Derevschikov, Vladimir 334
Desogus, Giulia 67, 439
Di Carlo, Ferdinando 54
Dias, Diego Roberto Colombo 459
Dolak, Radim 125

Evangelisti, Azzurra 650

Fabiani, Claudia 305
Faginas-Lago, Noelia 275, 319, 348
Fioretti, Bernard 237
Floris, Maddalena 19

Gabrielli, Roberto 547
Galatà, Pasquale 547
Galone, Luciano 519
Garau, Chiara 67, 423, 439
Gargiulo, Carmela 93
Gargiulo, Gianfranco 519
Gatto, Rachele 40, 48
Gentile, Vincenzo 534, 547
Georgiadis, Georgios 410
Gerundo, Roberto 381
Gervasi, Osvaldo 473, 486, 597
Giorgi, Giacomo 305
Giustini, Andrea 249
Guida, Carmen 395

Hanzl, Małgorzata 363
He, Xiao 319

Iiritano, Giuseppe 572

Khachkova, Tatyana 334

Laco, Peter 191
Lago, Maria Noelia Faginas 237, 264
Lazzeroni, Michela 85
Leccis, Francesca 19
Lisitsa, Vadim 334
Lombardi, Andrea 237, 264, 275
Lucchese, Manuela 54

Majerova, Ingrid 125
Mališová, Daniela 204

Maltinti, Francesca 613, 624, 663
Mancini, Luca 319
Marra, Alessandra 381
Marrone, Alessandro 290
Mauriello, Paolo 534, 547
Mighela, Francesca 439
Mikušová Meričková, Beáta 204
Monarca, Lorenzo 237
Monastra, Melissa 109
Montesano, Nicola 3
Moretti, Marilisa 109
Murgante, Beniamino 54
Murínová, Kristína 204
Murys, Martin 125
Muthová, Nikoleta Jakuš 141

Nesi, Paolo 67, 173
Nesticò, Antonio 381
Nicolosi, Vittorio 650

Olianas, M. 640

Pacifici, Leonardo 264, 275, 348
Pagliara, Francesca 3
Palazzetti, Federico 237
Pellegrino, Sabrina Francesca 157
Pellicelli, Gloria 423
Pennetta, Chiara 237
Perri, Damiano 473, 486, 597
Petrungaro, Giovanna 572
Pinna, Francesco 624
Pirani, Fernando 319
Piroddi, Luca 519
Pisello, Anna Laura 305
Plaisant, Alessandro 624
Pomffyová, Mária 219
Protasov, M. 560

Ragonese, Francesco 237
Rassu, Nicoletta 624
Rojíková, Darina 191
Rombi, J. 613, 640
Rosi, Marzio 249, 319
Rossetti, Silvia 423
Russo, Federica 381
Russo, Francesco 572

Sabbatini, Paola 237
Salis, M. 640
Santopietro, Luigi 31, 40, 48, 54
Scorza, Francesco 31, 40, 48, 54
Serpi, A. 640
Sfarra, Stefano 519
Sgambati, Sabrina 93
Simonetti, Marco 473, 486, 597
Sirotiaková, Mária 219
Solimene, Silvia 54
Svidroňová, Mária Murray 141

Tasso, Sergio 486
Tolbatov, Iogann 290
Torrisi, Vincenza 423
Trecozzi, Maria Rosaria 572

Vacca, Giuessppina 505
Valente, Felipe Reis 459
Vaňová, Anna 191
Vanuzzo, Gianmarco 249
Venco, Elisabetta M. 109
Veselovská, Lenka 219
Vitálišová, Katarína 141, 191
Vitillaro, Giuseppe 264

Zacharias, John 395
Zamperlin, Paola 67, 85
Zullo, Enza 534